RACE AWARENESS

RACE

The Nightmare and the Vision

Edited by

and

STATE UNIVERSITY OF NEW YORK

New York   OXFORD UNIVERSITY

AWARENESS

RUTH MILLER

PAUL J. DOLAN

AT STONY BROOK

PRESS   London Toronto   1971

Peter Abrahams: from *Holiday Magazine,* April 1959. Copyright © 1959 by Curtis
 Publishing Co. Reprinted by permission of the publisher.
Nnamdi Azikiwe: from *My Plan for Africa,* Anno Press, n.d. Reprinted by permission
 of Prentice-Hall, Inc.
James Baldwin: from *The Fire Next Time.* Copyright © 1963, 1962 by James Baldwin.
 Reprinted by permission of The Dial Press. From *Notes of a Native Son.* Copy-
 right © 1955 by James Baldwin. Reprinted by permission of the Beacon Press.

CONTENTS

3 THE VISION

INTRODUCTION

This collection of readings in race awareness has been arranged in
three parts. The first section consists of personal narratives of the
experience of race consciousness, and ranges from the discomforts
and indignities of oppression to the suffering and martyrdom of the
victims. The second section offers a series of speculations on the origin
of race consciousness, justifying, rationalizing, defending, or explaining why race awareness mutates to oppression. The third section
presents various solutions for eradicating the conflict generated by
racial antagonism, some bleak in outlook, some hopeful, some maudlin,
threatening, pragmatic.

Since race awareness and its attendant quarrels are not products
of America only, nor is race conflict limited to black and white, at
sudden odds with each other in this second half of the twentieth
century, readings are included that explore the experience of men of
color in diverse parts of the world—Japan, Ghana, Algeria, South
Africa, and England—although the emphasis does fall on the United
States, on Texas, on California, Ohio, Mississippi, and New York. And
they reach back into the eighteenth century and proceed past repre-
sentations from the nineteenth century to the properly well-represented
post World War II era, the time of explosion and fury, of retrenchment,
of slippage and bumbling, the time too of visions. Nightmares, yes,
but visions.

Stony Brook   R. M.
January 1971   P. J. D.

RACE AWARENESS

1 THE NIGHTMARE

Every experience of race is finally a personal experience. But the assumption of any community is that personal experiences may be articulated and thereby shared. Sharing leads to understanding. This is not simply the vicarious understanding of the other, but it involves a better understanding of the self. Honesty in race awareness begins here.

The selections in this section are representative, not comprehensive. They are representative not only in the sense that they were chosen from among many, but in the more significant sense that the articulate must stand for the inarticulate. To know Fanon and Holman, Orwell and Kriegel is to know more about those whom they represent.

It is our hope that at the end of this section the reader can be more honest about his own feelings and their complexity and recognize that his responses and attitudes when confronted by the fact of race are a peculiar combination of the particular and the general—they are uniquely his, but they are very like the human responses of others. A sense of community may, therefore, come from real experiences shared in honest statement.

Burk Uzzle—Magnum

Bruce Davidson—Magnum

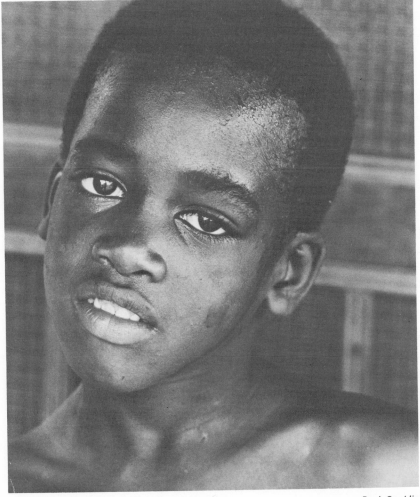

Paul Conklin

Jim Kappes

Blessings on thee, little man, barefoot b[...]
with cheeks full of *Kellogg's* CORN FL[...]

Don Mitchell—Magnum

Burk Uzzle—Magnum

FRANTZ FANON

The Fact of Blackness

Fanon is the most famous contemporary spokesman for the sense of
race in what is called "the third world." A doctor from Martinique,
he experienced the fact of race consciousness in the native struggle
for independence in Algeria. Despite a dense and difficult prose
style, his ideas have provided a basis for the revolutionary sense of
race identity based on the physical fact of blackness. In the chapter
reprinted here, Fanon explores the psychological results of the biological
fact of his race.

"**D**IRTY NIGGER!" Or simply, "Look, a Negro!"
I came into the world imbued with the will to find a meaning
in things, my spirit filled with the desire to attain to the source of
the world, and then I found that I was an object in the midst of
other objects.

Sealed into that crushing objecthood, I turned beseechingly to others.
Their attention was a liberation, running over my body suddenly abraded
into nonbeing, endowing me once more with an agility that I had thought
lost, and by taking me out of the world, restoring me to it. But just as I
reached the other side, I stumbled, and the movements, the attitudes, the
glances of the other fixed me there, in the sense in which a chemical solution is fixed by a dye. I was indignant; I demanded an explanation. Nothing happened. I burst apart. Now the fragments have been put together
again by another self.

As long as the black man is among his own, he will have no occasion,
except in minor internal conflicts, to experience his being through others.
There is of course the moment of "being for others," of which Hegel
speaks, but every ontology is made unattainable in a colonized and civilized society. It would seem that this fact has not been given sufficient attention by those who have discussed the question. In the *Weltanschauung*
of a colonized people there is an impurity, a flaw that outlaws any ontological explanation. Someone may object that this is the case with every individual, but such an objection merely conceals a basic problem. Ontology
—once it is finally admitted as leaving existence by the wayside—does not
permit us to understand the being of the black man. For not only must the
black man be black; he must be black in relation to the white man. Some
critics will take it on themselves to remind us that this proposition has a

converse. I say that this is false. The black man has no ontological resistance in the eyes of the white man. Overnight the Negro has been given two frames of reference within which he has had to place himself. His metaphysics, or, less pretentiously, his customs and the sources on which they were based, were wiped out because they were in conflict with a civilization that he did not know and that imposed itself on him.

The black man among his own in the twentieth century does not know at what moment his inferiority comes into being through the other. Of course I have talked about the black problem with friends, or, more rarely, with American Negroes. Together we protested, we asserted the equality of all men in the world. In the Antilles there was also that little gulf that exists among the almost-white, the mulatto, and the nigger. But I was satisfied with an intellectual understanding of these differences. It was not really dramatic. And then. . . .

And then the occasion arose when I had to meet the white man's eyes. An unfamiliar weight burdened me. The real world challenged my claims. In the white world the man of color encounters difficulties in the development of his bodily schema. Consciousness of the body is solely a negating activity. It is a third-person consciousness. The body is surrounded by an atmosphere of certain uncertainty. I know that if I want to smoke, I shall have to reach out my right arm and take the pack of cigarettes lying at the other end of the table. The matches, however, are in the drawer on the left, and I shall have to lean back slightly. And all these movements are made not out of habit but out of implicit knowledge. A slow composition of my *self* as a body in the middle of a spatial and temporal world—such seems to be the schema. It does not impose itself on me; it is, rather, a definitive structuring of the self and of the world—definitive because it creates a real dialectic between my body and the world.

For several years certain laboratories have been trying to produce a serum for "denegrification"; with all the earnestness in the world, laboratories have sterilized their test tubes, checked their scales, and embarked on researches that might make it possible for the miserable Negro to whiten himself and thus to throw off the burden of that corporeal malediction. Below the corporeal schema I had sketched a historico-racial schema. The elements that I used had been provided for me not by "residual sensations and perceptions primarily of a tactile, vestibular, kinesthetic, and visual character," [1] but by the other, the white man, who had woven me out of a thousand details, anecdotes, stories. I thought that what I had in hand was to construct a physiological self, to balance space, to localize sensations, and here I was called on for more.

"Look, a Negro!" It was an external stimulus that flicked over me as I passed by. I made a tight smile.

1. Jean Lhermitte, *L'Image de notre corps* (Paris, Nouvelle Revue critique, 1939), p. 17.

"Look, a Negro!" It was true. It amused me.

"Look, a Negro!" The circle was drawing a bit tighter. I made no secret of my amusement.

"Mama, see the Negro! I'm frightened!" Frightened! Frightened! Now they were beginning to be afraid of me. I made up my mind to laugh myself to tears, but laughter had become impossible.

I could no longer laugh, because I already knew that there were legends, stories, history, and above all *historicity,* which I had learned about from Jaspers. Then, assailed at various points, the corporeal schema crumbled, its place taken by a racial epidermal schema. In the train it was no longer a question of being aware of my body in the third person but in a triple person. In the train I was given not one but two, three places. I had already stopped being amused. It was not that I was finding febrile coordinates in the world. I existed triply: I occupied space. I moved toward the other . . . and the evanescent other, hostile but not opaque, transparent, not there, disappeared. Nausea. . . .

I was responsible at the same time for my body, for my race, for my ancestors. I subjected myself to an objective examination, I discovered my blackness, my ethnic characteristics; and I was battered down by tom-toms, cannibalism, intellectual deficiency, fetishism, racial defects, slave-ships, and above all else, above all: "Sho' good eatin'."

On that day, completely dislocated, unable to be abroad with the other, the white man, who unmercifully imprisoned me, I took myself far off from my own presence, far indeed, and made myself an object. What else could it be for me but an amputation, an excision, a hemorrhage that spattered my whole body with black blood? But I did not want this revision, this thematization. All I wanted was to be a man among other men. I wanted to come lithe and young into a world that was ours and to help to build it together.

But I rejected all immunization of the emotions. I wanted to be a man, nothing but a man. Some identified me with ancestors of mine who had been enslaved or lynched: I decided to accept this. It was on the universal level of the intellect that I understood this inner kinship—I was the grandson of slaves in exactly the same way in which President Lebrun was the grandson of tax-paying, hard-working peasants. In the main, the panic soon vanished.

In America, Negroes are segregated. In South America, Negroes are whipped in the streets, and Negro strikers are cut down by machine-guns. In West Africa, the Negro is an animal. And there beside me, my neighbor in the university, who was born in Algeria, told me: "As long as the Arab is treated like a man, no solution is possible."

"Understand, my dear boy, color prejudice is something I find utterly foreign. . . . But of course, come in, sir, there is no color prejudice among us. . . . Quite, the Negro is a man like ourselves. . . . It is not because he is black that he is less intelligent than we are. . . . I had a Senegalese buddy in the army who was really clever. . . ."

Where am I to be classified? Or, if you prefer, tucked away?

"A Martinican, a native of 'our' old colonies."

Where shall I hide?

"Look at the nigger! . . . Mama, a Negro! . . . Hell, he's getting mad. . . . Take no notice, sir, he does not know that you are as civilized as we. . . ."

My body was given back to me sprawled out, distorted, recolored, clad in mourning in that white winter day. The Negro is an animal, the Negro is bad, the Negro is mean, the Negro is ugly; look, a nigger, it's cold, the nigger is shivering, the nigger is shivering because he is cold, the little boy is trembling because he is afraid of the nigger, the nigger is shivering with cold, that cold that goes through your bones, the handsome little boy is trembling because he thinks that the nigger is quivering with rage, the little white boy throws himself into his mother's arms: Mama, the nigger's going to eat me up.

All round me the white man, above the sky tears at its navel, the earth rasps under my feet, and there is a white song, a white song. All this whiteness that burns me. . . .

I sit down at the fire and I become aware of my uniform. I had not seen it. It is indeed ugly. I stop there, for who can tell me what beauty is?

Where shall I find shelter from now on? I felt an easily identifiable flood mounting out of the countless facets of my being. I was about to be angry. The fire was long since out, and once more the nigger was trembling.

"Look how handsome that Negro is! . . ."

"Kiss the handsome Negro's ass, madame!"

Shame flooded her face. At last I was set free from my rumination. At the same time I accomplished two things: I identified my enemies and I made a scene. A grand slam. Now one would be able to laugh.

The field of battle having been marked out, I entered the lists.

What? While I was forgetting, forgiving, and wanting only to love, my message was flung back in my face like a slap. The white world, the only honorable one, barred me from all participation. A man was expected to behave like a man. I was expected to behave like a black man—or at least like a nigger. I shouted a greeting to the world and the world slashed away my joy. I was told to stay within bounds, to go back where I belonged.

They would see, then! I had warned them, anyway. Slavery? It was no longer even mentioned, that unpleasant memory. My supposed inferiority? A hoax that it was better to laugh at. I forgot it all, but only on condition that the world not protect itself against me any longer. I had incisors to test. I was sure they were strong. And besides. . . .

What! When it was I who had every reason to hate, to despise, I was rejected? When I should have been begged, implored, I was denied the slightest recognition? I resolved, since it was impossible for me to get away from an *inborn complex,* to assert myself as a BLACK MAN. Since the other hesitated to recognize me, there remained only one solution: to make myself known.

In *Anti-Semite and Jew* (p. 95), Sartre says: "They [the Jews] have allowed themselves to be poisoned by the stereotype that others have of them, and they live in fear that their acts will correspond to this stereotype. . . . We may say that their conduct is perpetually overdetermined from the inside."

All the same, the Jew can be unknown in his Jewishness. He is not wholly what he is. One hopes, one waits. His actions, his behavior are the final determinant. He is a white man, and, apart from some rather debatable characteristics, he can sometimes go unnoticed. He belongs to the race of those who since the beginning of time have never known cannibalism. What an idea, to eat one's father! Simple enough, one has only not to be a nigger. Granted, the Jews are harassed—what am I thinking of? They are hunted down, exterminated, cremated. But these are little family quarrels. The Jew is disliked from the moment he is tracked down. But in my case everything takes on a *new* guise. I am given no chance. I am overdetermined from without. I am the slave not of the "idea" that others have of me but of my own appearance.

I move slowly in the world, accustomed now to seek no longer for upheaval. I progress by crawling. And already I am being dissected under white eyes, the only real eyes. I am *fixed.* Having adjusted their microtomes, they objectively cut away slices of my reality. I am laid bare. I feel, I see in those white faces that it is not a new man who has come in, but a new kind of man, a new genus. Why, it's a Negro!

I slip into corners, and my long antennae pick up the catch-phrases strewn over the surface of things—nigger underwear smells of nigger—nigger teeth are white—nigger feet are big—the nigger's barrel chest—I slip into corners, I remain silent, I strive for anonymity, for invisibility. Look, I will accept the lot, as long as no one notices me!

"Oh, I want you to meet my black friend. . . . Aimé Césaire, a black man and a university graduate. . . . Marian Anderson, the finest of Negro singers. . . . Dr. Cobb, who invented white blood, is a Negro. . . . Here, say hello to my friend from Martinique (be careful, he's extremely sensitive). . . ."

Shame. Shame and self-contempt. Nausea. When people like me, they tell me it is in spite of my color. When they dislike me, they point out that it is not because of my color. Either way, I am locked into the infernal circle.

I turn away from these inspectors of the Ark before the Flood and I attach myself to my brothers, Negroes like myself. To my horror, they too reject me. They are almost white. And besides they are about to marry white women. They will have children faintly tinged with brown. Who knows, perhaps little by little. . . .

I had been dreaming.

"I want you to understand, sir, I am one of the best friends the Negro has in Lyon."

The evidence was there, unalterable. My blackness was there, dark and unarguable. And it tormented me, pursued me, disturbed me, angered me.

Negroes are savages, brutes, illiterates. But in my own case I knew that these statements were false. There was a myth of the Negro that had to be destroyed at all costs. The time had long since passed when a Negro priest was an occasion for wonder. We had physicians, professors, statesmen. Yes, but something out of the ordinary still clung to such cases. "We have a Senegalese history teacher. He is quite bright. . . . Our doctor is colored. He is very gentle."

It was always the Negro teacher, the Negro doctor; brittle as I was becoming, I shivered at the slightest pretext. I knew, for instance, that if the physician made a mistake it would be the end of him and of all those who came after him. What could one expect, after all, from a Negro physician? As long as everything went well, he was praised to the skies, but look out, no nonsense, under any conditions! The black physician can never be sure how close he is to disgrace. I tell you, I was walled in: No exception was made for my refined manners, or my knowledge of literature, or my understanding of the quantum theory.

I requested, I demanded explanations. Gently, in the tone that one uses with a child, they introduced me to the existence of a certain view that was held by certain people, but, I was always told, "We must hope that it will very soon disappear." What was it? Color prejudice.

> It [colour prejudice] is nothing more than the unreasoning hatred of one race for another, the contempt of the stronger and richer peoples for those whom they consider inferior to themselves, and the bitter resentment of those who are kept in subjection and are so frequently insulted. As colour is the most obvious outward manifestation of race it has been made the criterion by which men are judged, irrespective of their social or educational attainments. The light-skinned races have come to despise all those of a darker colour, and the dark-skinned peoples will no longer accept without protest the inferior position to which they have been relegated.[2]

I had read it rightly. It was hate; I was hated, despised, detested, not by the neighbor across the street or my cousin on my mother's side, but by an

2. Sir Alan Burns, *Colour Prejudice* (London, Allen and Unwin, 1948), p. 16.

entire race. I was up against something unreasoned. The psychoanalysts say that nothing is more traumatizing for the young child than his encounters with what is rational. I would personally say that for a man whose only weapon is reason there is nothing more neurotic than contact with unreason.

I felt knife blades open within me. I resolve to defend myself. As a good tactician, I intended to rationalize the world and to show the white man that he was mistaken.

In the Jew, Jean-Paul Sartre says, there is

> a sort of impassioned imperialism of reason: for he wishes not only to convince others that he is right; his goal is to persuade them that there is an absolute and unconditioned value to rationalism. He feels himself to be a missionary of the universal; against the universality of the Catholic religion, from which he is excluded, he asserts the "catholicity" of the rational, an instrument by which to attain to the truth and establish a spiritual bond among men.[3]

And, the author adds, though there may be Jews who have made intuition the basic category of their philosophy, their intuition

> has no resemblance to the Pascalian subtlety of spirit, and it is this latter —based on a thousand imperceptible perceptions—which to the Jew seems his worst enemy. As for Bergson, his philosophy offers the curious appearance of an anti-intellectualist doctrine constructed entirely by the most rational and most critical of intelligences. It is through argument that he establishes the existence of pure duration, of philosophic intuition; and that very intuition which discovers duration or life, is itself universal, since anyone may practice it, and it leads toward the universal, since its objects can be named and conceived.[4]

With enthusiasm I set to cataloguing and probing my surroundings. As times changed, one had seen the Catholic religion at first justify and then condemn slavery and prejudices. But by referring everything to the idea of the dignity of man, one had ripped prejudice to shreds. After much reluctance, the scientists had conceded that the Negro was a human being; *in vivo* and *in vitro* the Negro had been proved analogous to the white man: the same morphology, the same histology. Reason was confident of victory on every level. I put all the parts back together. But I had to change my tune.

That victory played cat and mouse; it made a fool of me. As the other put it, when I was present, it was not; when it was there, I was no longer. In the abstract there was agreement: The Negro is a human being. That is to say, amended the less firmly convinced, that like us he has his heart on

3. *Anti-Semite and Jew* (New York, Grove Press, 1960), pp. 112–113.
4. *Ibid.,* p. 115.

the left side. But on certain points the white man remained intractable. Under no conditions did he wish any intimacy between the races, for it is a truism that "crossings between widely different races can lower the physical and mental level. . . . Until we have a more definite knowledge of the effect of race-crossings we shall certainly do best to avoid crossings between widely different races." [5]

For my own part, I would certainly know how to react. And in one sense, if I were asked for a definition of myself, I would say that I am one who waits; I investigate my surroundings, I interpret everything in terms of what I discover, I become sensitive.

In the first chapter of the history that the others have compiled for me, the foundation of cannibalism has been made eminently plain in order that I may not lose sight of it. My chromosomes were supposed to have a few thicker or thinner genes representing cannibalism. In addition to the *sex-linked*, the scholars had now discovered the *racial-linked*. [6] What a shameful science!

But I understand this "psychological mechanism." For it is a matter of common knowledge that the mechanism is only psychological. Two centuries ago I was lost to humanity, I was a slave forever. And then came men who said that it all had gone on far too long. My tenaciousness did the rest; I was saved from the civilizing deluge. I have gone forward.

Too late. Everything is anticipated, thought out, demonstrated, made the most of. My trembling hands take hold of nothing; the vein has been mined out. Too late! But once again I want to understand.

Since the time when someone first mourned the fact that he had arrived too late and everything had been said, a nostalgia for the past has seemed to persist. Is this that lost original paradise of which Otto Rank speaks? How many such men, apparently rooted to the womb of the world, have devoted their lives to studying the Delphic oracles or exhausted themselves in attempts to plot the wanderings of Ulysses! The pan-spiritualists seek to prove the existence of a soul in animals by using this argument: A dog lies down on the grave of his master and starves to death there. We had to wait for Janet to demonstrate that the aforesaid dog, in contrast to man, simply lacked the capacity to liquidate the past. We speak of the glory of Greece, Artaud says; but, he adds, if modern man can no longer understand the *Choephoroi* of Aeschylus, it is Aeschylus who is to blame. It is tradition to which the anti-Semites turn in order to ground the validity of their "point of view." It is tradition, it is that long historical past, it is that blood relation between Pascal and Descartes, that is invoked when the Jew

5. Jon Alfred Mjoen, "Harmonic and Disharmonic Race-crossings," The Second International Congress of Eugenics (1921), *Eugenics in Race and State*, vol. II, p. 60, quoted in Sir Alan Burns, *op. cit.*, p. 120.
6. In English in the original. (Translator's note.)

is told, "There is no possibility of your finding a place in society." Not long ago, one of those good Frenchmen said in a train where I was sitting: "Just let the real French virtues keep going and the race is safe. Now more than ever, national union must be made a reality. Let's have an end of internal strife! Let's face up to the foreigners (here he turned toward my corner) no matter who they are."

It must be said in his defense that he stank of cheap wine; if he had been capable of it, he would have told me that my emancipated-slave blood could not possibly be stirred by the name of Villon or Taine.

An outrage!

The Jew and I: Since I was not satisfied to be racialized, by a lucky turn of fate I was humanized. I joined the Jew, my brother in misery.

An outrage!

At first thought it may seem strange that the anti-Semite's outlook should be related to that of the Negrophobe. It was my philosophy professor, a native of the Antilles, who recalled the fact to me one day: "Whenever you hear anyone abuse the Jews, pay attention, because he is talking about you." And I found that he was universally right—by which I meant that I was answerable in my body and in my heart for what was done to my brother. Later I realized that he meant, quite simply, an anti-Semite is inevitably anti-Negro.

You come too late, much too late. There will always be a world—a white world—between you and us. . . . The other's total inability to liquidate the past once and for all. In the face of this affective ankylosis of the white man, it is understandable that I could have made up my mind to utter my Negro cry. Little by little, putting out pseudopodia here and there, I secreted a race. And that race staggered under the burden of a basic element. What was it? *Rhythm!* Listen to our singer, Léopold Senghor:

> It is the thing that is most perceptible and least material. It is the archetype of the vital element. It is the first condition and the hallmark of Art, as breath is of life: breath, which accelerates or slows, which becomes even or agitated according to the tension in the individual, the degree and the nature of his emotion. This is rhythm in its primordial purity, this is rhythm in the masterpieces of Negro art, especially sculpture. It is composed of a theme—sculptural form—which is set in opposition to a sister theme, as inhalation is to exhalation, and that is repeated. It is not the kind of symmetry that gives rise to monotony; rhythm is alive, it is free. . . . This is how rhythm affects what is least intellectual in us, tyrannically, to make us penetrate to the spirituality of the object; and that character of abandon which is ours is itself rhythmic.[7]

7. "Ce que l'homme noir apporte," in Claude Nordey, *L'Homme de couleur* (Paris, Plon, 1939), pp. 309–310.

Had I read that right? I read it again with redoubled attention. From the opposite end of the white world a magical Negro culture was hailing me. Negro sculpture! I began to flush with pride. Was this our salvation?

I had rationalized the world and the world had rejected me on the basis of color prejudice. Since no agreement was possible on the level of reason, I threw myself back toward unreason. It was up to the white man to be more irrational than I. Out of the necessities of my struggle I had chosen the method of regression, but the fact remained that it was an unfamiliar weapon; here I am at home; I am made of the irrational; I wade in the irrational. Up to the neck in the irrational. And now how my voice vibrates!

> Those who invented neither gunpowder nor the compass
> Those who never learned to conquer steam or electricity
> Those who never explored the seas or the skies
> But they know the farthest corners of the land of anguish
> Those who never knew any journey save that of abduction
> Those who learned to kneel in docility
> Those who were domesticated and Christianized
> Those who were injected with bastardy. . . .

Yes, all those are my brothers—a "bitter brotherhood" imprisons all of us alike. Having stated the minor thesis, I went overboard after something else.

> . . . But those without whom the earth would not be the earth
> Tumescence all the more fruitful
> than
> the empty land
> still more the land
> Storehouse to guard and ripen all
> on earch that is most earth
> My blackness is no stone, its deafness
> hurled against the clamor of the day
> My blackness is no drop of lifeless water
> on the dead eye of the world
> My blackness is neither a tower nor a cathedral
> It thrusts into the red flesh of the sun
> It thrusts into the burning flesh of the sky
> It hollows through the dense dismay of its own pillar of patience.[8]

Eyah! the tom-tom chatters out the cosmic message. Only the Negro has the capacity to convey it, to decipher its meaning, its import. Astride the world, my strong heels spurring into the flanks of the world, I stare into the shoulders of the world as the celebrant stares at the midpoint between the eyes of the sacrificial victim.

8. Aimé Césaire, *Cahier d'un retour au pays natal* (Paris, Présence Africaine, 1956), pp. 77–78.

But they abandon themselves, possessed, to the essence of all things,
knowing nothing of externals but possessed by the movement of all things

uncaring to subdue but playing the play of the world
truly the eldest sons of the world
open to all the breaths of the world
meeting-place of all the winds of the world
undrained bed of all the waters of the world
spark of the sacred fire of the World
flesh of the flesh of the world, throbbing with the very movement of the
world! [9]

Blood! Blood! . . . Birth! Ecstasy of becoming! Three-quarters engulfed
in the confusions of the day, I feel myself redden with blood. The arteries
of all the world, convulsed, torn away, uprooted, have turned toward me
and fed me.

"Blood! Blood! All our blood stirred by the male heart of the sun." [10]

Sacrifice was a middle point between the creation and myself—now I
went back no longer to sources but to The Source. Nevertheless, one had
to distrust rhythm, earth-mother love, this mystic, carnal marriage of the
group and the cosmos.

In *La vie sexuelle en Afrique noire,* a work rich in perceptions, De
Pédrals implies that always in Africa, no matter what field is studied, it
will have a certain magico-social structure. He adds:

All these are the elements that one finds again on a still greater scale in
the domain of secret societies. To the extent, moreover, to which persons
of either sex, subjected to circumcision during adolescence, are bound
under penalty of death not to reveal to the uninitiated what they have experienced, and to the extent to which initiation into a secret society always excites to acts of *sacred love,* there is good ground to conclude by
viewing both male and female circumcision and the rites that they embel-
lish as constitutive of minor secret societies. [11]

I walk on white nails. Sheets of water threaten my soul on fire. Face to
face with these rites, I am doubly alert. Black magic! Orgies, witches' sab-
baths, heathen ceremonies, amulets. Coitus is an occasion to call on the
gods of the clan. It is a sacred act, pure, absolute, bringing invisible forces
into action. What is one to think of all these manifestations, all these ini-
tiations, all these acts? From every direction I am assaulted by the obscen-
ity of dances and of words. Almost at my ear there is a song:

First our hearts burned hot
Now they are cold
All we think of now is Love

9. *Ibid.,* p. 78.
10. *Ibid.,* p. 79.
11. De Pédrals, *La vie sexuelle en Afrique noire* (Paris, Payot), p. 83.

> When we return to the village
> When we see the great phallus
> Ah how then we will make Love
> For our parts will be dry and clean. [12]

The soil, which only a moment ago was still a tamed steed, begins to revel. Are these virgins, these nymphomaniacs? Black Magic, primitive mentality, animism, animal eroticism, it all floods over me. All of it is typical of peoples that have not kept pace with the evolution of the human race. Or, if one prefers, this is humanity at its lowest. Having reached this point, I was long reluctant to commit myself. Aggression was in the stars. I had to choose. What do I mean? I had no choice. . . .

Yes, we are—we Negroes—backward, simple, free in our behavior. That is because for us the body is not something opposed to what you call the mind. We are in the world. And long live the couple, Man and Earth! Besides, our men of letters helped me to convince you; your white civilization overlooks subtle riches and sensitivity. Listen:

> Emotive sensitivity. *Emotion is completely Negro as reason is Greek*.[13] Water rippled by every breeze? Unsheltered soul blown by every wind, whose fruit often drops before it is ripe? Yes, in one way, the Negro today is richer *in gifts than in works*.[14] But the tree thrusts its roots into the earth. The river runs deep, carrying precious seeds. And the Afro-American poet, Langston Hughes, says:

> I have known rivers
> ancient dark rivers
> my soul has grown deep
> like the deep rivers.

> The very nature of the Negro's emotion, of his sensitivity, furthermore, explains his attitude toward the object perceived with such basic intensity. It is an abandon that becomes need, an active state of communion, indeed of identification, however negligible the action—I almost said the personality—of the object. A rhythmic attitude: The adjective should be kept in mind.[15]

So here we have the Negro rehabilitated, "standing before the bar," ruling the world with his intuition, the Negro recognized, set on his feet again, sought after, taken up, and he is a Negro—no, he is not a Negro but the Negro, exciting the fecund antennae of the world, placed in the foreground of the world, raining his poetic power on the world, "open to

12. A. M. Vergiat, *Les rites secrets des primitifs de l'Oubangui* (Paris, Payot, 1951), p. 113.
13. My italics—F.F.
14. My italics—F.F.
15. Léopold Senghor, "Ce que l'homme noir apporte," in Nordey, *op. cit.*, p. 205.

all the breaths of the world." I embrace the world! I am the world! The white man has never understood this magic substitution. The white man wants the world; he wants it for himself alone. He finds himself predestined master of this world. He enslaves it. An acquisitive relation is established between the world and him. But there exist other values that fit only my forms. Like a magician, I robbed the white man of "a certain world," forever after lost to him and his. When that happened, the white man must have been rocked backward by a force that he could not identify, so little used as he is to such reactions. Somewhere beyond the objective world of farms and banana trees and rubber trees, I had subtly brought the real world into being. The essence of the world was my fortune. Between the world and me a relation of coexistence was established. I had discovered the primeval One. My "speaking hands" tore at the hysterical throat of the world. The white man had the anguished feeling that I was escaping from him and that I was taking something with me. He went through my pockets. He thrust probes into the least circumvolution of my brain. Everywhere he found only the obvious. So it was obvious that I had a secret. I was interrogated; turning away with an air of mystery, I murmured:

> Tokowaly, uncle, do you remember the nights gone by
> When my head weighed heavy on the back of your patience or
> Holding my hand your hand led me by shadows and signs
> The fields are flowers of glowworms, stars hang on the bushes, on the trees
> Silence is everywhere
> Only the scents of the jungle hum, swarms of reddish bees that overwhelm the crickets' shrill sounds,
> And covered tom-tom, breathing in the distance of the night.
> You, Tokowaly, you listen to what cannot be heard, and you explain to me what the ancestors are saying in the liquid calm of the constellations,
> The bull, the scorpion, the leopard, the elephant, and the fish we know,
> And the white pomp of the Spirits in the heavenly shell that has no end,
> But now comes the radiance of the goddess Moon and the veils of the shadows fall.
> Night of Africa, my black night, mystical and bright, black and shining.[16]

I made myself the poet of the world. The white man had found a poetry in which there was nothing poetic. The soul of the white man was corrupted, and, as I was told by a friend who was a teacher in the United States, "The presence of the Negroes beside the whites is in a way an insurance policy on humanness. When the whites feel that they have become too mechanized, they turn to the men of color and ask them for a little human sustenance." At last I had been recognized, I was no longer a zero.

16. Léopold Senghor, *Chants d'ombre* (Paris, Editions du Seuil, 1945).

I had soon to change my tune. Only momentarily at a loss, the white man explained to me that, genetically, I represented a stage of development: "Your properties have been exhausted by us. We have had earth mystics such as you will never approach. Study our history and you will see how far this fusion has gone." Then I had the feeling that I was repeating a cycle. My originality had been torn out of me. I wept a long time, and then I began to live again. But I was haunted by a galaxy of erosive stereotypes: the Negro's *sui generis* odor . . . the Negro's *sui generis* good nature . . . the Negro's *sui generis* gullibility. . . .

I had tried to flee myself through my kind, but the whites had thrown themselves on me and hamstrung me. I tested the limits of my essence; beyond all doubt there was not much of it left. It was here that I made my most remarkable discovery. Properly speaking, this discovery was a rediscovery.

I rummaged frenetically through all the antiquity of the black man. What I found there took away my breath. In his book *L'abolition de l'esclavage* Schoelcher presented us with compelling arguments. Since then, Frobenius, Westermann, Delafosse—all of them white—had joined the chorus: Ségou, Djenné, cities of more than a hundred thousand people; accounts of learned blacks (doctors of theology who went to Mecca to interpret the Koran). All of that, exhumed from the past, spread with its insides out, made it possible for me to find a valid historic place. The white man was wrong, I was not a primitive, not even a half-man, I belonged to a race that had already been working in gold and silver two thousand years ago. And too there was something else, something else that the white man could not understand. Listen:

> What sort of men were these, then, who had been torn away from their families, their countries, their religions, with a savagery unparalleled in history?
>
> Gentle men, polite, considerate, unquestionably superior to those who tortured them—that collection of adventurers who slashed and violated and spat on Africa to make the stripping of her the easier.
>
> The men they took away knew how to build houses, govern empires, erect cities, cultivate fields, mine for metals, weave cotton, forge steel.
>
> Their religion had its own beauty, based on mystical connections with the founder of the city. Their customs were pleasing, built on unity, kindness, respect for age.
>
> No coercion, only mutual assistance, the joy of living, a free acceptance of discipline.
>
> Order—Earnestness—Poetry and Freedom.
>
> From the untroubled private citizen to the almost fabulous leader there was an unbroken chain of understanding and trust. No science? Indeed yes; but also, to protect them from fear, they possessed great myths in which the most subtle observation and the most daring imagination were

balanced and blended. No art? They had their magnificent sculpture, in which human feeling erupted so unrestrained yet always followed the obsessive laws of rhythm in its organization of the major elements of a material called upon to capture, in order to redistribute, the most secret forces of the universe. . . .[17]

Monuments in the very heart of Africa? Schools? Hospitals? Not a single good burgher of the twentieth century, no Durand, no Smith, no Brown even suspects that such things existed in Africa before the Europeans came. . . .

But Schoelcher reminds us of their presence, discovered by Caillé, Mollien, the Cander brothers. And, though he nowhere reminds us that when the Portuguese landed on the banks of the Congo in 1498, they found a rich and flourishing state there and that the courtiers of Ambas were dressed in robes of silk and brocade, at least he knows that Africa had brought itself up to a juridical concept of the state, and he is aware, living in the very flood of imperialism, that European civilization, after all, is only one more civilization among many—and not the most merciful.[18]

I put the white man back into his place; growing bolder, I jostled him and told him point-blank, "Get used to me, I am not getting used to anyone." I shouted my laughter to the stars. The white man, I could see, was resentful. His reaction time lagged interminably. . . . I had won. I was jubilant.

"Lay aside your history, your investigations of the past, and try to feel yourself into our rhythm. In a society such as ours, industrialized to the highest degree, dominated by scientism, there is no longer room for your sensitivity. One must be tough if one is to be allowed to live. What matters now is no longer playing the game of the world but subjugating it with integers and atoms. Oh, certainly, I will be told, now and then when we are worn out by our lives in big buildings, we will turn to you as we do to our children—to the innocent, the ingenuous, the spontaneous. We will turn to you as to the childhood of the world. You are so real in your life—so funny, that is. Let us run away for a little while from our ritualized, polite civilization and let us relax, bend to those heads, those adorably expressive faces. In a way, you reconcile us with ourselves."

Thus my unreason was countered with reason, my reason with "real reason." Every hand was a losing hand for me. I analyzed my heredity. I made a complete audit of my ailment. I wanted to be typically Negro—it was no longer possible. I wanted to be white—that was a joke. And, when I tried, on the level of ideas and intellectual activity, to reclaim my negri-

17. Aimé Césaire, Introduction to Victor Schoelcher, *Esclavage et colonisation* (Paris, Presses Universitaires de France, 1948), p. 7.
18. *Ibid.*, p. 8.

tude, it was snatched away from me. Proof was presented that my effort was only a term in the dialectic:

> But there is something more important: The Negro, as we have said, creates an anti-racist racism for himself. In no sense does he wish to rule the world: He seeks the abolition of all ethnic privileges, wherever they come from; he asserts his solidarity with the oppressed of all colors. At once the subjective, existential, ethnic idea of *negritude* "passes," as Hegel puts it, into the objective, positive, exact idea of *proletariat*. "For Césaire," Senghor says, "the white man is the symbol of capital as the Negro is that of labor. . . . Beyond the black-skinned men of his race it is the battle of the world proletariat that is his song."
>
> That is easy to say, but less easy to think out. And undoubtedly it is no coincidence that the most ardent poets of negritude are at the same time militant Marxists.
>
> But that does not prevent the idea of race from mingling with that of class: The first is concrete and particular, the second is universal and abstract; the one stems from what Jaspers calls understanding and the other from intellection; the first is the result of a psychobiological syncretism and the second is a methodical construction based on experience. In fact, negritude appears as the minor term of a dialectical progression: The theoretical and practical assertion of the supremacy of the white man is its thesis; the position of negritude as an antithetical value is the moment of negativity. But this negative moment is insufficient by itself, and the Negroes who employ it know this very well; they know that it is intended to prepart the synthesis or realization of the human in a society without races. Thus negritude is the root of its own destruction, it is a transition and not a conclusion, a means and not an ultimate end.[19]

When I read that page, I felt that I had been robbed of my last chance. I said to my friends, "The generation of the younger black poets has just suffered a blow that can never be forgiven." Help had been sought from a friend of the colored peoples, and that friend had found no better response than to point out the relativity of what they were doing. For once, that born Hegelian had forgotten that consciousness has to lose itself in the night of the absolute, the only condition to attain to consciousness of self. In opposition to rationalism, he summoned up the negative side, but he forgot that this negativity draws its worth from an almost substantive absoluteness. A consciousness committed to experience is ignorant, has to be ignorant, of the essences and the determinations of its being.

Orphée Noir is a date in the intellectualization of the *experience* of being black. And Sartre's mistake was not only to seek the source of the source but in a certain sense to block that source:

19. Jean-Paul Sartre, *Orphée Noir,* preface to *Anthologie de la nouvelle poésie nègre et malgache* (Paris, Presses Universitaires de France, 1948), pp. xl ff.

> Will the source of Poetry be dried up? Or will the great black flood, in spite of everything, color the sea into which it pours itself? It does not matter: Every age has its own poetry; in every age the circumstances of history choose a nation, a race, a class to take up the torch by creating situations that can be expressed or transcended only through Poetry; sometimes the poetic impulse coincides with the revolutionary impulse, and sometimes they take different courses. Today let us hail the turn of history that will make it possible for the black men to utter "the great Negro cry with a force that will shake the pillars of the world" (Césaire).[20]

And so it is not I who make a meaning for myself, but it is the meaning that was already there, pre-existing, waiting for me. It is not out of my bad nigger's misery, my bad nigger's teeth, my bad nigger's hunger that I will shape a torch with which to burn down the world, but it is the torch that was already there, waiting for that turn of history.

In terms of consciousness, the black consciousness is held out as an absolute density, as filled with itself, a stage preceding any invasion, any abolition of the ego by desire. Jean-Paul Sartre, in this work, has destroyed black zeal. In opposition to historical becoming, there had always been the unforeseeable. I needed to lose myself completely in negritude. One day, perhaps, in the depths of that unhappy romanticism. . . .

In any case I *needed* not to know. This struggle, this new decline had to take on an aspect of completeness. Nothing is more unwelcome than the commonplace: "You'll change, my boy; I was like that too when I was young . . . you'll see, it will all pass."

The dialectic that brings necessity into the foundation of my freedom drives me out of myself. It shatters my unreflected position. Still in terms of consciousness, black consciousness is immanent in its own eyes. I am not a potentiality of something, I am wholly what I am. I do not have to look for the universal. No probability has any place inside me. My Negro consciousness does not hold itself out as a lack. It *is*. It is its own follower.

But, I will be told, your statements show a misreading of the processes of history. Listen then:

> Africa I have kept your memory Africa
> you are inside me
> Like the splinter in the wound
> like a guardian fetish in the center of the village
> make me the stone in your sling
> make my mouth the lips of your wound
> make my knees the broken pillars of your abasement
> AND YET
> I want to be of your race alone

20. *Ibid.*, p. xliv.

workers peasants of all lands . . .
. . . white worker in Detroit black peon in Alabama
uncountable nation in capitalist slavery
destiny ranges us shoulder to shoulder
repudiating the ancient maledictions of blood taboos
we roll away the ruins of our solitudes
If the flood is a frontier
we will strip the gully of its endless
covering flow
If the Sierra is a frontier
we will smash the jaws of the volcanoes
upholding the Cordilleras
and the plain will be the parade ground of the dawn
where we regroup our forces sundered
by the deceits of our masters
As the contradiction among the features
creates the harmony of the face
we proclaim the oneness of the suffering
and the revolt
of all the peoples on all the face of the earth
and we mix the mortar of the age of brotherhood
out of the dust of idols.[21]

Exactly, we will reply, Negro experience is not a whole, for there is not merely *one* Negro, there are *Negroes*. What a difference, for instance, in this other poem:

The white man killed my father
Because my father was proud
The white man raped my mother
Because my mother was beautiful
The white man wore out my brother in the hot sun of the roads
Because my brother was strong
Then the white man came to me
His hands red with blood
Spat his contempt into my black face
Out of his tyrant's voice:
"Hey boy, a basin, a towel, water." [22]

Or this other one:

My brother with teeth that glisten at the compliments of hypocrites
My brother with gold-rimmed spectacles
Over eyes that turn blue at the sound of the Master's voice
My poor brother in dinner jacket with its silk lapels

21. Jacques Roumain, "Bois-d'Ebène," Prelude, in *Anthologie de la nouvelle poésie nègre et malgache*, p. 113.
22. David Diop, "Le temps du martyre," in *ibid.*, p. 174.

Clucking and whispering and strutting through the drawing rooms of
    Condescension
How pathetic you are
The sun of your native country is nothing more now than a shadow
On your composed civilized face
And your grandmother's hut
Brings blushes into cheeks made white by years of abasement and *Mea
    culpa*
But when regurgitating the flood of lofty empty words
Like the load that presses on your shoulders
You walk again on the rough red earth of Africa
These words of anguish will state the rhythm of your uneasy gait
I feel so alone, so alone here! [23]

From time to time one would like to stop. To state reality is a wearing
task. But, when one has taken it into one's head to try to express existence,
one runs the risk of finding only the nonexistent. What is certain is that, at
the very moment when I was trying to grasp my own being, Sartre, who
remained The Other, gave me a name and thus shattered my last illusion.
While I was saying to him:

"My negritude is neither a tower nor a cathedral,
  it thrusts into the red flesh of the sun,
  it thrusts into the burning flesh of the sky,
  it hollows through the dense dismay of its own pillar of patience . . ."

while I was shouting that, in the paroxysm of my being and my fury, he
was reminding me that my blackness was only a minor term. In all truth,
in all truth I tell you, my shoulders slipped out of the framework of the
world, my feet could no longer feel the touch of the ground. Without a
Negro past, without a Negro future, it was impossible for me to live my
Negrohood. Not yet white, no longer wholly black, I was damned. Jean-
Paul Sartre had forgotten that the Negro suffers in his body quite differently from the white man.[24] Between the white man and me the connection
was irrevocably one of transcendence.[25]

But the constancy of my love had been forgotten. I defined myself as an
absolute intensity of beginning. So I took up my negritude, and with tears

23. David Diop, "Le Renégat."
24. Though Sartre's speculations on the existence of The Other may be correct (to
the extent, we must remember, to which *Being and Nothingness* describes an alienated consciousness), their application to a black consciousness proves fallacious.
That is because the white man is not only The Other but also the master,
whether real or imaginary.
25. In the sense in which the word is used by Jean Wahl in *Existence humaine et
transcendance* (Neuchâtel, La Baconnière, 1944).

in my eyes I put its machinery together again. What had been broken to pieces was rebuilt, reconstructed by the intuitive lianas of my hands.

My cry grew more violent: I am a Negro, I am a Negro, I am a Negro. . . .

And there was my poor brother—living out his neurosis to the extreme and finding himself paralyzed:

THE NEGRO I can't, ma'am.
LIZZIE Why not?
THE NEGRO I can't shoot white folks.
LIZZIE Really! That would bother them, wouldn't it?
THE NEGRO They're white folks, ma'am.
LIZZIE So what? Maybe they got a right to bleed you like a pig just because they're white?
THE NEGRO But they're white folks.

A feeling of inferiority? No, a feeling of nonexistence. Sin is Negro as virtue is white. All those white men in a group, guns in their hands, cannot be wrong. I am guilty. I do not know of what, but I know that I am no good.

THE NEGRO That's how it goes, ma'am. That's how it always goes with white folks.
LIZZIE You too? You feel guilty?
THE NEGRO Yes, ma'am.[26]

It is Bigger Thomas—he is afraid, he is terribly afraid. He is afraid, but of what is he afraid? Of himself. No one knows yet who he is, but he knows that fear will fill the world when the world finds out. And when the world knows, the world always expects something of the Negro. He is afraid lest the world know, he is afraid of the fear that the world would feel if the world knew. Like that old woman on her knees who begged me to tie her to her bed:

"I just know, Doctor: Any minute that thing will take hold of me."

"What thing?"

"The wanting to kill myself. Tie me down, I'm afraid."

In the end, Bigger Thomas acts. To put an end to his tension, he acts, he responds to the world's anticipation.[27]

So it is with the character in *If He Hollers Let Him Go* [28]—who does precisely what he did not want to do. That big blonde who was always in

26. Jean-Paul Sartre, *The Respectful Prostitute,* in *Three Plays* (New York, Knopf, 1949), pp. 189, 191. Originally, *La Putain respectueuse* (Paris, Gallimard, 1947). See also *Home of the Brave,* a film by Mark Robson.

27. Richard Wright, *Native Son* (New York, Harper, 1940).

28. By Chester Himes (Garden City, Doubleday, 1945).

his way, weak, sensual, offered, open, fearing (desiring) rape, became his mistress in the end.

The Negro is a toy in the white man's hands; so, in order to shatter the hellish cycle, he explodes. I cannot go to a film without seeing myself. I wait for me. In the interval, just before the film starts, I wait for me. The people in the theater are watching me, examining me, waiting for me. A Negro groom is going to appear. My heart makes my head swim.

The crippled veteran of the Pacific war says to my brother, "Resign yourself to your color the way I got used to my stump; we're both victims." [29]

Nevertheless with all my strength I refuse to accept that amputation. I feel in myself a soul as immense as the world, truly a soul as deep as the deepest of rivers, my chest has the power to expand without limit. I am a master and I am advised to adopt the humility of the cripple. Yesterday, awakening to the world, I saw the sky turn upon itself utterly and wholly. I wanted to rise, but the disemboweled silence fell back upon me, its wings paralyzed. Without responsibility, straddling Nothingness and Infinity, I began to weep.

29. *Home of the Brave.*

M. CARL HOLMAN

The Afternoon of a Young Poet

Race awareness is not always national or global in its significance, nor
is it always a matter of ultimate political involvement. M. Carl Holman's
experience in the span of one afternoon, in a modest literary
gathering, shows how ideas of race come to affect one's sense of self
and one's sense of achievement.

I N THE LATE WINTER of my senior year in high school I entered a
poem in an annual literary competition sponsored by the Arts Club of
St. Louis. Because I was almost pathologically shy, and because I was
not sure I actually intended to go through with it until I was picking my
way back up the icy street from the corner mailbox, I told no one what I
had done. Until that night I had submitted poems to Negro newspapers
and magazines and had won one or two small prizes, but I had never before ventured to enter a "white" contest.

I had found the announcement of the Arts Club competition in the section of one of the white dailies where I read avidly about plays, concerts
and ballets which might just as well have been taking place on the moon.
During that period of my life I was strongly influenced by three or four
university-trained teachers on our high school faculty who were still caught
up in the afterglow of the Negro Renaissance. Mr. Watts, Miss Armstrong,
Mr. Blanton and Miss Lewis taught us from the "lily-white" textbooks
prescribed by the St. Louis school system, but they also mounted on their
bulletin boards the works and pictures of Langston Hughes, James Weldon
Johnson, Claude McKay, Sterling Brown, Countee Cullen and Jean
Toomer.

Entering the contest, however secretly, represented unusual daring for
me, though it would have been as easy as breathing for Miss Armstrong, a
vibrantly energetic mahogany-skinned woman whose voice flayed our bud-
ding manhood with contempt when she read McKay's poem "If We Must
Die." (Her voice accused and disturbed me, conjuring up two confusing
memories from my childhood downtown on Carroll Street—the first, that
day in the depths of the Depression when half the fathers on the block
straggled back from their protest march on City Hall, their heads broken
and bleeding. Some of them weeping, but only one of them laughing. The
potbellied little man next door who came stumbling up the alley apart

from the others, tittering like a drunken woman, one eye puffed shut, his bloody rag of a shirt dragging in the dust. Giggling and whispering, *"Don't hit me no mo, Cap'n. You the boss. You sho God is the boss. . . ."* And less than five years later, Big Crew, standing in the middle of the yard, his lips drawn back from his blue gums in a wolfish grin, smashing his black fist like a hammer into the rent man's face, picking the man up like a sack of flour and knocking him down again. All the time talking to him as quietly as one friend to another: *"Git up and fight, you peckerwood sonuvabitch. Git up and fight for your country."*)

I yearned during those high school years to write something as defiantly bitter as McKay's "If We Must Die" or Sterling Brown's "Strong Men." My temper was capable of flaring up and consuming me so utterly that during a period of a few months I found myself in wildly hopeless fights with the older boys. Deep in hostile north St. Louis I had placed my life and those of two boys with me in jeopardy when, without thinking, I spat in the face of a young white boy seated on the stoop surrounded by at least seven members of his beefy family, because he called me a "skinny black nigger" as my friends and I were passing. My mother's long campaign to curb my temper had only taught me at last to swallow my feelings, hiding them so deep that I could not have dredged up my rages and despairs and found words for them even if I had wanted to. The long poem I finally mailed to the Arts Club was called "Nocturne on a Hill." Though it was probably honest enough in its way, it echoed more of the white writers I had been reading and told more about my reactions to the shapes and sounds of the city than it did about the people I loved and hated, or the things which delighted, hurt or confused me most.

We had moved from Carroll Street downtown three years earlier and we were living that year on Driscoll Avenue in midtown, halfway between the river on the east and that section of West End the whites had ceded to the Negro doctors, schoolteachers and postal workers. For a long time after the move to Driscoll Avenue I had continued to go back to the old neighborhood. In part this was because the customers to whom I sold Negro weekly newspapers lived there (ranging from an ancient self-ordained bishop, whose wife was never permitted to expose anything more than a slender wax-yellow hand and a black-clad sleeve as I handed the paper through the double-chained door, to the heavily powdered ladies in the big house on Seymour Street who had bought a dozen papers from me every Friday for a month before I learned how they made their living). But even on days when I had no papers to sell, Carroll Street for a long time continued to have the same love-fear magnetism for me it had exercised when I lived there; racked by sweaty nightmares on nights when the patrol wagons and ambulances pounded past our house, listening by the hour to the Italians singing from the backyards where they had strung light bulbs for the parties that left the alley littered with snail shells and the discarded bottles the winos fought over the next morning. On Carroll Street we had lived closely, though not intimately, with whites: the Italians on Bouie Avenue to the rear, the Jewish storekeepers, the Germans who worked in the bakery and the bank, the Irish truck drivers and policemen (and one saloon keeper who reconverted his storefront when Prohibition ended, returning to its old place in the window the faded, flyspecked sign whose legend we chanted up and down the street: "Coolidge Blew the Whistle, Mellon Rang the Bell, Hoover Pulled the Throttle and the Country Went to Hell").

Driscoll Avenue was a less impoverished and more self-contained world than Carroll Street. Except for the merchants and bill collectors, it was possible to walk through midtown for blocks without seeing a white face. We lived on the first floor of a three-story brick house set on a concrete terrace from which three stone steps led down to the street. My chores during that long winter included keeping the steps salted down and making sure the heavy hall door was kept tightly shut.

My mother was ill for a long time that winter, and the grown-ups came to visit her, stamped into the house wrapped like mummies with only their eyes showing, bringing pots of stew, pickled preserves and the latest tale of some drunk who had been found frozen stiff in an alley or a neighbor who had been taken to "Old Number Two" with double pneumonia. Number Two was the nearest city hospital, and the neighborhood saying was that they did more killing there than Mr. Swift did over at his packing house. Old people in the neighborhood sometimes clung stubbornly to their beds at home, hiding the seriousness of their ailments, for fear they would be sent to Number Two to die. My mother was not old, but I lay awake many nights that winter, listening to her rasping breathing and praying that she would not have to be taken to Number Two. Sometimes, after her breathing had smoothed out and she had fallen asleep, I would get out of bed and go over to the window, raising the shade enough to let in the white winter moonlight. Fumbling for a pencil and piece of paper, I would write lines and fragments which I could not see, then fold the paper and stuff it into my hiding place back of the piano which nobody in the house played.

My mother's conviction that both her children were going to finish high school and college and "amount to something" had persisted in the face of the bleakest realities her native Mississippi and a half-flat near the tracks in south St. Louis could marshal against her. Even in her illness, hollow-eyed and feverish, she wanted to know what we had done in school daily, what the teachers had said, whether our homework was done. A gifted seamstress and a careful manager of small change for most of her life, she never doubted she would one day find the proper use for the patterns, scraps of cloth, Eagle stamps, buttons and pins she scrupulously put aside, each in its proper place. She cooked huge pots of soup, with opulent aromas suggesting magnitudes of power and promise out of all proportion to the amount of meat in the pot. She felt she had ample reason to sing "He Leadeth Me," and when we had amazed ourselves and our teachers by prodigies of nerve-straining effort she only said mildly, "Didn't He promise He would make a way out of no way for those who believed in Him?"

Lacking her faith, I was so beset with premonitions and terrors during those months of her illness that I lost all recollection of the poem I had mailed to the Arts Club. The cousin I loved most had died in childbirth just two years before, at the age of nineteen, and I had been tormented ever since by the fragility of the web separating life and death. Though she met the slightest ache or pain visited on her children as if it were an outrider of the Devil's legions fully armed, my mother regarded her own illnesses as nuisances to be gotten through with as little fuss as possible. By the time the snow had melted in the gutters she was on her feet again, halfway through her spring cleaning and fretting to have the last frost gone so that she could start planting the narrow rectangle of earth out front she called her garden.

I came home from school one afternoon in early May to find a letter from the Arts Club in our mailbox. I was afraid to open it until I had first made sure it was not bulky enough to contain the rejected poem. There was only a single sheet inside, a note typed on the most elegant stationery I had ever seen, congratulating me on the selection of my poem as one of the five best works submitted in that year's contest and inviting me to meet the other winners at the club two weeks later.

The first surge of surprise and pleasure was followed almost at once by a seizure of blind panic. How could I go out there to Westmoreland Place, a street I had never seen, to meet a group of strangers, most if not all of them white—when I stammered or fell silent whenever I had to talk to one of my teachers without the supporting presence of the rest of the class? Reading the note again I saw that the meeting had been scheduled for midafternoon of a school day. For most that next week I debated whether I should accept the club's invitation or prepare to be sick on that day. Finally, just forty-eight hours before the date set in the letter, I went down to the principal and secured permission to be excused from my afternoon classes to attend the Arts Club meeting.

That same afternoon I showed my mother the letter. She knew me well enough to play down the pride she felt, complaining instead about people who would miss Heaven one day because they always waited until the last minute. She consulted with a friend who worked in the section where the club was located and wrote down the directions for me, dryly reminding me to have the conductor give me a transfer when I boarded the trolley outside the school. I had once had to walk home a distance of some six miles away because I forgot to ask for a transfer. Actually, I was less concerned about the transfer than about the possibility that on the way out to the club I might develop motion sickness. This often happened when I rode the trolleys. Usually I got off the car as soon as the first queasy stirrings began in the pit of my stomach, and walked the rest of the way. But this time I would be in a part of town that I did not know at all. I resolved to ride standing up all the way, trusting that my mother's God would not let me be sick.

I left school on a hazily bright afternoon alive with the tarry tang of smoke and the green smell of growing things which I associate still with spring in St. Louis. It was good to be a privileged truant with the whole block in front of the school to myself, the typewriters clicking behind me in the principal's office and the unheeded voices of the teachers floating out of the classroom windows overhead. The first trolley was a long time coming. When I got on I remembered to ask for the transfer, and though over half the seats were empty on both trolleys, I stood up all the way. But when I got off the second car I found that I had managed to lose the directions my mother had given me. I could not remember whether I was to go north or south from the trolley stop. My palms promptly began sweating and I took out the letter from the Arts Club, reading the address again as if that would give me a clue. In my neighborhood most of the houses were row houses, or were separated from each other by nothing more than a narrow passageway. Even houses like the one we lived in, though not flush with the pavement, were close enough so that the addresses could be easily read from the sidewalk. But out here the houses were set back from wide lawns under shade trees and there was no way of making out the addresses without going up a long walk to the front door. No small children were playing outside, there were no stores into which a stranger might go and ask directions, and the whole neighborhood was wrapped in a fragrant but forbidding stillness. Remembering that my mother had said the club was only two blocks away from the trolley stop, I started walking south, deciding that if it turned out I was going the wrong way I could always come back and go two blocks in the other direction. I walked three blocks for good measure without finding Westmoreland Place, then turned and started back.

A red-faced old man with bushy military whiskers that reminded me of pictures I had seen of the Kaiser came down one of the walks with a bulldog on a leash. I braced myself to ask him where Westmoreland Place was, but before I could speak, his china blue eyes suddenly glared at me with such venomous hatred that I had the feeling he was about to set the dog on me. I averted my eyes and walked on, trembling suddenly with an answering hatred as senseless as his. Not noticing where I was going, I was about to cross into the next block when I looked up at the street sign and found that I was on Westmoreland Place. It was a street of thick hedges and houses which, if anything, were more inaccessible than those I had already passed. I walked up the street in one direction, then crossed and reversed my course. By now the letter was wilting in my hand. The trolley ride had taken longer than I had estimated and I was sure I was already late. One of the last things my mother had said to me that morning was, "Now try to be sure not to get out there on Colored People's Time." My mind groped for a plausible lie that would let me give up the whole business and go home. I thought of saying that the meeting had been called off, that the place was closed when I got there, that I had caught the wrong car and gone too far out of the way to get back in time. At one point, I almost convinced myself that I should go back to the trolley stop and catch a car that would take me downtown to my old refuge, the main public library. I could stay there reading for an hour or two, then claim I had actually attended the tea. But my spirit quailed at the prospect of inventing answers to all the questions that would follow. And what if in the meantime someone from the club had already called my home or the school? I hated myself for entering the competition and felt sick with envy when I thought of my schoolmates who by now were idling down the halls on free period or dreaming their way through the last classes before the liberating bell.

I was plodding down the same block for the second time when around the corner of a big stone house across the street came an unmistakably colored man in work clothes, uncoiling a garden hose. We might have been the only two living souls on a desert island. Almost faint with relief I angled across the street toward him. But the handyman, his high shiny forehead furrowed in elaborate concentration, adjusted the nozzle and began playing rainbow jets of spray across the grass. I halted at the edge of the lawn and waited for him to take note of my presence. In due time he worked himself close enough so that I was able to ask him if he knew where the Arts Club was. I held out the letter as I asked him, but he merely turned his rusty deepset eyes on me with a look that plainly said, *I hope to God you ain't come out here to make trouble for the rest of us.* In later years I have seen that look in the eyes of Negro businessmen, schoolteachers, college presidents, reverend ministers—and a trio of cooks and dishwashers peering through the swinging doors of a restaurant kitchen at the dark-skinned students sitting at counters where no one of their color ever presumed to sit before.

But I was of another generation, another temperament and state of mind from those students. So when the handyman flicked one hand in the direction from which I had just come and said, "There 'tis, over there," I thanked him—rather thanked his back, which was already turned to me.

I would never have taken the two-story brick building at the end of the flagstone walk to be anything other than the residence of a comfortably well-off family. Just before I pushed the button beside the broad door it occurred to me that the handyman might be playing his notion of a joke on me. Then I looked down at the thick mat on which I was standing and saw the letters "A-C." I pressed the button, waited and was about to press it again when the door swung open. The rake-thin white maid standing there had composed for her plain freckled face a smile of deferential welcome. The smile faded and her body stiffened in the neat gray uniform. For an instant I thought she would close the door in my face, but she braked it so that it was barely ajar and said, "Yes?" I mumbled something and held out the letter. She squinted at the envelope and said, "You wait here." The door closed and I stood there with my face burning, wanting to turn and go away but unwilling to confront the expression of sour satisfaction I expected to see on the face of the handyman across the street. After what seemed fifteen full minutes a gray-haired woman in a blue uniform with starched cuffs came to the door. "All right, what is it now?" she said, sounding like a very busy woman. I held out the letter and she took it, measured me up and down with her shrewd eyes and said to the younger woman hovering behind her, "I'll be right back." The freckle-faced thin one looked miles above my head toward the street but we shared the unspoken understanding that I was not to move from where I stood and that she was to watch me.

I stood rooted there, calling myself every kind of black fool for coming in the first place, my undershirt cleaving to my damp skin. It had become clear to me that I had received the invitation by mistake. And now that I had surrendered the letter, the only proof that I had been invited, my sole excuse for being there at all was gone. I pictured them huddled inside, talking in whispers, waiting for me to have the good sense to leave. Then I heard voices coming toward the door. My keeper faded back into the gloom of the hallway and an attractive woman in her forties held the door open and smiled at me. Everything about her, her fine-textured skin, the soft-colored dress and the necklace she was wearing, her candid gaze, defined an order of relationships which did away with any need for me to deal further with the other two women. "Hello," she said. "So you're the boy who came over to tell us Mr. Holman couldn't come?"

I stared dumbly at her, wondering how I could have been fooled into thinking she was one of those white women my mother would have described approvingly as "a real lady, as nice as they come."

"Please tell him we hope he'll be feeling better soon," the woman said. "We had so hoped to meet him."

"I'm—I got the letter saying to come out here," I blurted. We stood there for a minute staring at one another and then her pink skin flushed red. "Oh, you mean you—oh, I *am* so sorry," she said. "Please do come in. I didn't know." She glanced back at the maids. "I mean, we thought—"

It was finally clear to all of us what she had thought. That the white boy who wrote the poem had been unable to come so his family thoughtfully sent their colored boy to tender his regrets.

"You come right on in," the woman said. "I'm your hostess. All the others are already here and we've been waiting for you." She drew me inside the cool, dim hallway and guided me up the stairs like an invalid. I could not remember ever walking on such thick carpets. I had a hazy impression of cut flowers in vases, and paintings hanging along the walls like those I had seen in the Art Museum in the park. As she went up she kept on talking, but I made very little of what she was saying because now I could hear the murmur of other voices and laughter coming from the floor above us. I had the feeling that an intimate and very pleasant family party was in progress which we were about to ruin and I wanted to ask my hostess if I might not be excused after all. Instead I let myself be piloted into a sunny high-ceilinged room which at one and the same time seemed as spacious as a playing field and so intimate that no one could move without touching the person beside him. A blur of white faces turned toward us, some of them young, some middle-aged, some older, but all of them clearly belonging to a different world from that of the uniformed women downstairs. A different world from mine. For a flickering moment there was a drop in energy like that sudden dimming of lights during a summer storm and then I was being introduced in a flurry of smiles, bobbing heads and a refrain seeming to consist of variations on "Delightful . . . delighted . . . so good you could come . . . a pleasure."

Whenever I have tried to recollect that afternoon since, the faces in that upstairs room elude me like objects seen through sunlit water. I remember that one of the girls was blonde and turned eagerly from one speaker to another as if anxious not to miss one word, that there was a boy there from a school out in the country who talked and moved with the casual, almost insulting assurance which for a long time afterward I automatically associated with private schools. All of the other students there who had won prizes or honorable mentions in the area-wide competition were either from private schools or from white high schools whose very names were new to me. One of the girls was from a Catholic school and one of the sisters from the faculty had come along with her. I discovered that other winners were accompanied by their teacher and I mentally kicked myself for not realizing that I might have been buttressed by the presence of Miss Armstrong or Mr. Blanton. Certainly they would have been much more at home in this company than I was. Gradually, as cookies, tea and punch were passed and the talk again swirled back and forth, I began to relax somewhat, content to be on the periphery of that closed circle. I kept stealing glances around the room, taking in the wide fireplace and the portrait above the mantel of some famous man whose identity kept eluding me, the rows of books in the recessed shelves along the wall, and the magazines scattered tantalizingly just out of reach on the long oaken table in the center of the room.

In school, except to recite, I had rarely ever talked even to my English teachers about poems, books and writers. But this group, comfortably seated or standing about the pleasant room with the haze of spring sunlight sifting through the windows, shared a community of language and interests which enabled them largely to ignore differences of age and individual preference and to move from one idea or work to another as effortlessly as fish in a pond. They talked of Shakespeare and Keats, Milton and Shelley, but there were other writers whose lines I had spoken aloud, sometimes in puzzlement, when I was alone. Now they were being argued over, attacked, defended, ridiculed: Eliot, Frost, Sandburg, Millay, Vachel Lindsay, Amy Lowell, Yeats. There were some moments when someone touched on something I had read and I was tempted to speak out in agreement or disagreement. At other times I was overcome by the gloomy conviction that I could never in the years that were left to me read all the works some of them seemed to know by heart. I felt particularly lost as the talk shifted to novels only recently written, to concerts they had attended and plays seen at the American Theatre downtown or "on our last trip to New York." I had been drunk for days on the free concert given for Negro high school students by the St. Louis Symphony the year before, shutting myself off in my room with an umbrella spoke for a baton, trying to be all the voices of the orchestra and graceful Mr. Golschmann conducting the *New World Symphony*. Later I was to go to the American as often as I could to see the road companies in performance and, during intermissions, to devour the posters advertising the plays I would not be able to see. Often my companion and I were among less than a dozen Negroes present. (Years afterward, on a trip back to St. Louis I was triumphantly informed that Negroes were no longer segregated in the second-balcony seats at the American. Second-balcony seats being all we could afford, my friend and I had never asked for anything else, a neat dovetailing of covert discrimination and economic necessity.)

Toward the end of the long afternoon, it was proposed that the young writers read their poems. Once again I was plunged into sweaty-palmed agony. My torment only increased as the first two readers read their poems like seasoned professionals, or so it seemed to me. When my turn came I tried to beg off, but the additional attention this focused upon me only increased my discomfort and I plunged in, at first reading too fast and almost inaudibly but finally recollecting some of the admonitions my teachers had dinned into my head in preparation for "recitations" before Negro school and church audiences as far back as the second grade. I had not realized how long a poem it was when I was writing it and I was squirmingly conscious of certain flaws and failures which had never before loomed so large. The applause and praise that followed when I finished, if anything, exceeded that given the others; a situation which, even then, aroused the fleeting suspicion that the dancing bear was being given higher marks than a man might get for the same performance. One of the older women murmured something about Paul Laurence Dunbar. Someone else asked me if I liked Pushkin. I could only look blank, since at that time I knew almost nothing about the great Russian's poetry and even less about his Negro lineage. Inevitably, there was a flattering and irrelevant comparison to Langston Hughes. A wavy-haired gentleman took his pipe out of his mouth to ask if I didn't think "The Negro Speaks of Rivers" was a marvelous poem. I said I certainly did. (But stopped short of trying to explain why the Mississippi always made me think not of Lincoln at New Orleans but of the playmate on Carroll Street drowned during an Easter baptism, the cold, feral grin of the garfish skeleton which two of us stumbled on as we moped along the riverfront toward the pickle factory and the high platform beyond where the city garbage trucks dumped their loads into the frothing stream, and the dimly remembered "high waters" sucking at the edge of the roadbed as the train brought my father and me back to St. Louis from our grandfather's funeral.)

Gradually, as the light faded outside the window, people began looking at their watches and saying good-by. One of the club members thanked all of us for coming and said she could not remember when the Arts Club had had such a fine and talented group. The blonde girl clapped her hands for attention, her eyes shining with the enthusiasm of the born organizer. Why, she wanted to know, did this year's group really have to scatter? It seemed to her that we should not let our companionship, our new friendships die. Some of us were going away for the summer, but there were still several weeks left yet before school would be out. Some might be going off to college in the fall, but others would not, and probably some of those who would be entering college would be going no farther away than the University of Missouri at Columbia, or St. Louis, Washington, or one of the other schools in the St. Louis area. I was silent as the others chimed in, suggesting that we meet at the various high schools or rotate meetings from one home to another before and after summer vacations. Such a point was made of including me in and I felt already so much the witch at the wedding party that I was not inclined to remind them that I would have a much harder time getting into a meeting at the schools they attended or the colleges in the area than I had had getting into the Arts Club that afternoon. To say nothing of what their parents and friends and mine would make of those meetings in the homes. I tried to picture those well-dressed and half-assured young white poets strolling past the cleaning and pressing shop to a meeting at my house. Nevertheless, my Driscoll Avenue cynicism began crumbling under the effervescent pressures of their youth and mine. We made our way down the thick-carpeted stairs, true poets and comrades, a verbal skyscraper of plans and projects rising as we descended. We would exchange our favorite original poems by phone and by mail. We would do a volume of poems together and a famous novelist who was a good friend of our hostess would get the book published for us. The Arts Club would serve as secretariat and haven, keeping track of addresses and phone numbers and providing a place where we could meet, read and write.

Good will, mutual admiration, flowering ambition united us as we parted in the gathering spring dusk. The air was scented with the watermelony smell of freshly cut grass. The lights were on in the stone house across the street, but the handyman was gone.

I did not hear from the young men and women I met that afternoon at the Arts Club the next week, the next month, or ever. But I had a great many more serious disappointments than that, along with a decent amount of good fortune, in the two remaining years I spent in my home town. Like many other young men similarly situated I was involved during those prewar years in a quiet but no less desperate scramble simply to hold on to life and not go under. By the end of that period of twenty-odd months I had run an elevator, worked as a machine operator, delivered parcels, patrolled a lake stocked with fish nobody ever tried to steal, and stood in half a hundred job lines with white and black men who showed up every morning less out of hope than the need to put off as long as possible that time of day when they must once again face their families. For me and a good many others my age it was not a question really of having something to eat and a place to sleep. The battle was, rather, to find ways of withstanding the daily erosion, through tedium, through humiliation, through various short-term pleasures, of the sense of your own possibilities. Necessary, too, was some sensitivity to possibilities outside yourself. Here I do not exclude chance, the lucky break. For me it came with the opportunity to become a part-time student at a college I might have attended full time two years earlier.

On the night before I left for college my mother gave a party for me, inviting a dozen of my friends. Some of them brought gifts. As I was walking past the Catholic church on Garth Avenue, shortly after midnight, going home to the flat I shared with my father, a squad car pulled up and two officers jumped out. Night sticks at the ready, they flashed a light in my face and wanted to know where I was coming from and where I had picked up all that stuff. They pawed through the presents I was carrying until they came across an anthology of poetry autographed for me that night by my friends. The first officer grunted and snapped off his light. The second seemed tempted to take a swipe at me anyhow for wasting their time. They got back in the car and drove off, leaving me to walk the two blocks remaining between the church and home.

The next morning, on a cold, sooty, old-style St. Louis day, I left home. I got on a bus and headed for Jefferson City, Missouri. That trip away from home has been a much longer journey than I had anticipated and a very much different one. On certain occasions, as when my poetry was published or while lecturing at Atlanta University, I have remembered that afternoon. And I have thought that perhaps when I next visited St. Louis, I would try once again to find my way to the Arts Club. I never have and it is probably just as well. It may be that I got as much as could reasonably be expected on that first visit.

KENNETH RAMCHAND

The Colour Problem at the University

Mr. Ramchand's essay illustrates very clearly that America does not
have a monopoly on racial problems. Mr. Ramchand describes his shock
upon arriving in England and discovering that he was not simply a student,
nor an immigrant, but a Black.

T HE PAPERBACK EDITION of the West Indian sees him as indulging in exotic calypso colours of red and green and yellow, riotous colours that compel attention, loud colours that are taken to indicate a coarseness of visual palate, or an eye unaware of pattern and design, and unable to discriminate between variant shades of the same colour. ("You West Indians," in despair, "you cannot appreciate Art, you only look for the bright colours.")

If this popular image is valid, we find in the West Indian an amazing double-vision. For, in the contemplation of human groups, no society has evolved a more delicate instrument of perception. The West Indian consciousness suspends, in equipoise, considerations of racial origin and considerations of degrees of blackness. In looking at the complex construct that is colonial society, it blends elements from these categories with rare flexibility.

The initial breakdown is along lines of known racial origin. Here are some children at play:

> Nigger is a nation, They stink with perspiration (African)
> Coolie, coolie, Come for roti (Indian)
> Chinee chinee never die, Flat nose and Chinky eye (Chinese)
> Whitey cock-o-roach (Not very sure)

This crude analysis is refined by a delicate perception of the variants of skin colour. At one end of the scale is "White" (roughly = English). Next come "West Indian Whites" (diverse European origin, many now carrying in their blood the secret of their fathers' dark connexions). After these come the "light-skinned" or "yellow" Chinese. Then come the black ones —Indians and Africans. Of the infinite mixtures available, all that can be said is that there is an intuitive apprehension, and a certain placing of every possible variant along the colour scale. "Black" is complex indeed. An Indian may be black, but his highest degree of blackness is indicated in that taunt, "Look at you, you just like a nigger." In West Indian society, "black" is usually reserved for "Negro," and "Negro" ranges from the "tar baby" of the West Indian Reader, to the "red nigger." It is even possible to be blacker than black: in a book by the Trinidadian Samuel Selvon, one character is called "Midnight" because he is the blackest in his group. A new figure comes along, however, and he, impossibly, is blacker still. The delicate instrument reacts sensitively; the new man is christened "Five-past-twelve."

Leaving the West Indies and coming to Britain is like entering a land where the natives suffer from a curious kind of colour blindness in the contemplation of human groups. This special form of blindness manifests itself in an insensitivity to racial discriminations and variant shades within the category "black." It registers two crude categories, black and white.

The West Indian consciousness is outraged by the crudity of the categorization. In the rarefied atmosphere of the mother country, the delicate instrument ceases to function. All West Indians are black. Under impartial pressure, the first defensive measure is the formation of West Indian groups and a kind of recognition, at last, of West Indian community.

There is another useful by-product of the coming face-to-face with the colour problem. The denial of variant shades within the category "black" in metropolitan society sharpens the vision of the West Indian. The West Indian comes to realize that if society in Britain tended to glance at the physical characteristics of groups instead of focusing upon the behaviour of the individual, the same was true of society in the West Indies. In the colonial society, the way of looking at groups was not more delicate than the distortion of the personal realities in Britain. It was only less crude. For instead of living with individuals both societies were reckoning with stereotypes.

This sketching in of the background has invited observation of the delicacy of colour perception in West Indian society, and the crudeness of colour categorization in British society, but it has indicated that the same basic fallacy—attention to the physical characteristics of groups—has marred the vision of both societies. It thus provides adequate justification for the largely personal nature of most of what follows. It is only through a series of descriptions of personal experience that the colour problem can be seen in operation. Moreover, it is felt that to set down an individual response and reflections arising out of personal involvement with people and situations in an uncensored form, would not only give the kind of insight into aspects of the colour problem which becomes crude in the analysis, but it would catch the subtle movements by which shifts of attitudes may take place. The recording consciousness may itself be a product of the apprehension of a colour problem.

As I stood on the deck of the S.S. *Antilles,* Trinidad grew smaller and smaller, and I of the big dreams reminded myself of my obligations:

"Boy, you goin' England, ah want you to eat book, don't let nobody beat you in exams nuh."

"Woman like bush up dey, partner. They like the black boys too bad."

"You better watch out, you hear, dey beatin' black fellers with all kind a bicycle chain up there dese days."

"Don't let them make you feel small man; if you look good you go see this whiteness is really a kind of skin disease all of them have."

I knew well what I wanted of "England", but long before I got to Southampton I was overwhelmed by the certainty of my inability to cope with the books, the bicycle chains and the sex-starved natives.

At Southampton, I determined to survive. The customs officer stood before me and stuck his little list in my face. I read, and turned my eyes away. Four years later, he spoke, "Have you read the list?" . . . Yes bwana, yes. . . .

Waterloo, London. A Jamaican porter approached. I ignored him and selected an English one. . . . My coolie. A big tip for you today. . . . All around, white faces closing in, and, at the last moment, going past. And then the man with the ready-made smile. The British Council man.

The West Indian's ambivalent attitude to the British Council provides a major insight into the colour problem. The British Council exists to provide organized kindness at five shillings a year. As such, it satisfies felt needs. Because the organization supplies needs which in an integrated society would have found fulfilment in human relationships, it remains, like the accommodating woman, curiously unloved, even in use.

Soon, I was on the train to Waverley, Edinburgh. In my single compartment I began to think of home, but half-way to the Scottish capital, a middle-aged man with dirty nostrils and no hair silently joined me. He seemed annoyed with himself for having intruded on my privacy, and so, all the way to Waverley he sat there looking sick (he in his corner, I in mine) in penitential silence.

Waverley at last. The man with the ready-made smile again, and in minutes I was listening to my very first landlady. I was going to be happy with her. She always preferred my kind. We were so polite. . . . "Mornin' ma'am. . . ."

I set all these things down as they strike me in retrospect, or as I might have re-lived them, after four years. At the time they were allowed to pass. My real concern at first was to avoid the bicycle chains and to watch out for the sex-starved females. As neither threatened on this first day, I wrote to Trinidad to say that I had arrived safely. I paused to look at my skin for signs of the disease, but I was as black as ever. I decided not to make that report yet. One never knew: perhaps next morning I would awake to find myself infected.

The weeks passed and the fear of the bicycle chain diminished. Violence, it seemed, occurred only in Nottingham where the workers were fighting for women and wages. In the liberal atmosphere of an ancient university one can always avoid violence by not walking too late at night.* I soon reminded myself that for four years I was to live in this land: I must not only avoid hostilities, I must invite friendships.

And so, I groomed myself (one lock of hair carefully out of place) and attended the Freshers' dance. In the huge hall, there was country dancing and shrieks of delight. Carnival, I thought. Suddenly, I felt like jumping too. I approached an approach-worthy young lady with my best smile (the lips pulled a little to the right). She was so tired. A few seconds later, she was throwing those shapely legs about in what was, presumably, a Highland fling. Her dancing partner had a fat face and straggly hair. My face was lean and youthful. My hair jet black. And my teeth were the colour of pearl. . . . But who can fathom the mind of a beautiful woman?

My next move was to join the West Indian Association.

For a year I stuck firmly to the group. For a year I had lunch with West Indians, coffee with West Indians, dates with West Indians and I attended purely West Indian parties. At the lectures I had one friend—a brave little girl whom I got to know and like well over the years. But, as in those early days I never dared disturb the universe, our relationship remained firmly platonic. Among the men, a war veteran, with memories of pre-war cricket, was my only ally.

Outside the university, matters were about to take a strange turn. I had already spent three months in the country, and having concluded that the bicycle chain did not, as it were, apply to the university student, I was about to put a similar colophon to the subject of sex-starved females. But one night, a friend arrived in a hurry.

"Want to come and meet a little thing?"

"Well . . . nothing to do."

"Come on."

He went to the telephone booth, this midnight, talked for a while, and then beckoned me.

"Come," he said, "she want to talk to you."

"But . . . she don't know me. . . ." .

"What the . . ."

I picked up the phone, searched for my best accent, and my sexiest tone, and waited:

* Last summer, a Jamaican student returning home late at night from a visit to some domino-playing friends was assaulted by a gang of youths.

"So you're coming along."

"Ye-es." (Coolly.)

"Why?"

"You never know!" (Wittily.)

"You want Scotch and Scottish hospitality?"

"Yes," (my God) I sighed, "yes."

We were on our way.

"Look nuh man, I don't want no prostitute, you know."

"Easy, clot. You young. These ain't no prostitutes."

Who were they?

For a variety of reasons, women at the university are reluctant to form relationships with coloured students. It seemed natural at first, to expect that since one spent so much time at the university, one's friends both male and female would come from the university, for it is here, we are told, that personal contacts are made, here that minds meet. It became apparent, however, that there existed a tribe of nurses, *au pair* girls, typists, shop-assistants, one or two divorcées, a few erring wives, a nymphomaniac and various rejected university girls who satisfied the emotional needs of coloured students. Many of these girls are decent girls, and the degree of promiscuity varies. Many are intelligent people. Some are victims of their own loneliness, and some are victims of the coloured men's loneliness. Many are unloved. Some are loved for a time. A few become happy wives. The overall impression, however, is that a hasty sexual connexion has taken the place of any settled human relationship between black men and white women.

The deep malaise in the man-woman relationship involving coloured men and white women is paralleled by a total absence of relationships between white men and coloured women. This is a phenomenon that needs investigation by itself. In the days of the plantation, white men satisfied organic needs on slave women. No doubt, the prevailing attitude that white men only associate with black women for possible exotic sexual thrills, is a kind of deterrent to many white students. Probably too, if there were more black women at the university, the chances of a white man-black woman relationship would be increased, at least statistically.

The relationship between white men and black men at the university seems to be, strangely, a kind of passing acquaintance. In four undergraduate years, I count three lasting male friendships, but a series of inquiries among West Indians at the university reveals my personal experience to be unusual. Here is a typical example:

"Have you any good British friends?"

"No."

"How come, man?"

"I never put myself out of the way to make friends. If nobody want to make friends with me, I don't want to make friends with them."

The attitude is powerfully defensive. Behind it is a mind which has been antagonized, or at least, thinks it has been antagonized, by the suspicion of an unspoken attitude. Friendship, in the words of C. S. Lewis, is, "in a sense not at all derogatory to it, the least natural of loves; the least instinctive, organic, biological, gregarious and necessary." Eros, the love relationship, on the other hand, is, partly a matter for the nervous system. A woman may, therefore, as many women do, have a conflict between a state of mind and a state of feeling in relation to a black man. In a fair number of cases, feeling triumphs over mental attitude. But in a relationship between man and man (homosexuality apart) it is attitude which tells. Lack of a common interest upon which friendship may be built indicates, at the university, an unhappy kind of coexistence merely. The personal contact is possible, but this is only geographical. Common interests and friendships are not allowed to develop. This refusal to make friends is to be seen as part of a mental attitude to the black man, in the case of the man-man relationship, unhampered, as it were, by emotion. It is, in other words, a studied restraint.

The attitude of the British male undergraduates, within the field of reference of this essay, carries a strong load of sexual fear and jealousy: it expresses itself in a strict slating of female offenders against an unspoken masculine code. The university woman who forms a possible love relationship with a coloured man is quietly ostracized. The male of the species considers her contaminated by a phallic performer, the West Indian. And so, sexual rivalry takes the form of contemptuous non-competition and boycott. One of the main factors behind the reluctance of the female is the intransigence of the male. The white man-black man relationship is rare, and the black man-white woman relationship is heavily censored. Thus it comes about that the macabre sexual relationship outside the university (already described) has to carry those strains that might have been borne easily within the campus, as well as the strains set up by a lack of man-man contact. The sexual connexion quickly becomes a desperate struggle in the dark to hold on to sanity. It becomes a cure for all ills. It becomes a furious masturbation.

The gradual revelation of the weakness of human relationships between white and black students at the university, and the realization that this state of affairs has created a grotesque parody of the man-woman relationship, are the major discoveries of the West Indian student. It must be emphasized that the breakdown is not complete, and that there are mature men and women in all the faculties. But it is the discoveries which are highly influencing, and they are mainly responsible for a radical shift of attitude to the colour problem. One's original conception of the colour problem was that it operated where there was little opportunity for personal contact and where the educational level was low. But after coming to Britain, one discovers that the conception was naïve, the reality was confusing. For to experience four years at the university is to progress in a kind of forbidden knowledge from dreams of rich and edifying personal contact, towards disillusionment and cynicism. Education and personal contact are not allowed to become a moving force: the follow-through is checked, defensively. One may be safe from violence, but one is exposed to a more subtle variation of the colour bar.

This new knowledge has brought a touchiness to the eater of the forbidden fruit, which, with increasing insight into the motives of his white fellow student, translates itself into a desperate kind of self-scrutiny. He, thus, becomes more and more conscious that the association of black with inferiority dies hard. As the self-scrutiny becomes more intense, he begins to be aware of a wastage of the opportunities for personal contact, by a sabotage of the West Indian personality, and its distribution into functions. The West Indian is becoming more and more aware of himself as being cast in the role of performer. The audience is physically close but the social distance is great.

The new technique of looking at the black man operates at all levels.

On the academic level a successful West Indian becomes a phenomenon to those who notice: "How *can* you be so *clever?*" The performance has a touch of the exotic in it, and somehow this has caused a lowering of the standards. Intelligence, by a mental flick of the wrist, becomes cleverness, a gimmick, and success has nothing to do with effort. (Sometimes the effort is granted, but it is turned around and seen as aggressiveness. Honest effort is impossible for the man who has to prove he is a man!) The successful West Indian is either clever (a man with a gimmick) or a performer in his own special field (a non-competitor) or at least, "an uncharacteristic West Indian," that non-defining definition.

At Edinburgh, the West Indian calypso band is the most popular student band: all, performers. Other West Indians either play cricket or sing calypsoes. Those who cannot sing are disc-jockeys. It is regrettable that these appointed roles are accepted so readily. But the temptation is great.

The West Indian, as performer, is an image borrowed from the cricket field. Shackleton is an intelligent bowler, and Wesley Hall is a magnificent specimen (potent West Indian). Close is a player of character and determination, Sobers is a *natural* stroker of the ball. Meanwhile, we hear from afar that Peter Pollick is the fastest white bowler in the world, black bowlers being non-competitors.

At a party last year, I was introduced to an obscure gentleman:

"Do you play in the band?"

"No." (With resentment.)

"Do you play cricket, then?"

"No." (Amused.)

Long silence.

"Cheerio."

He had scrutinized my personality and found it wanting.

One is either a performer or one has no personality. So far has the fragmentation proceeded.

There are no more bicycle chains. For the performers, there is applause, and after the show, social distance. The fear of physical violence is largely replaced in the individual consciousness by the fear of this new attempt to see the West Indian as performer, for this implies a kind of fragmentation, in the mind of the viewer, of the West Indian personality, a fragmentation which is a steady refusal to see the black man as a whole individual. It is, in fact, the old concept of black inferiority in a new, sophisticated form, appropriate to a centre of higher learning.

The symptoms of racial prejudice at the university are hard to discern. One finds oneself looking not for scars on one's own body, but for an attitude determining the behaviour of one's fellow students. At best, there is, after the suspicion, an unprovable certainty that there are large numbers of people at the university who constitutionally assume white superiority and its corollary. Over against this, and acting as a kind of foil to it, is another certainty—the presence of a small number who do see the black man as a full human being whom it is possible to like or dislike, because he is himself. All of this leads to a mood which is mainly despair, but one thinks of the few and clings to the hope.

The evidence of four years has not been comforting.

In the meantime, the unprovableness of his case is a source of anguish to the black man: failure of positive proof is a concomitant of increasing insight into motives and attitudes. To the accusation of being hypersensitive, the individual cannot reply convincingly. Inside, self-confidence is being destroyed. The constant necessity to ask oneself "Is it because I am black or is it because I am, in fact, inferior and objectionable?" leads to a sapping of vital creative energy, and a withdrawal into introspection.

But is there not a kind of perception which relies, for its proof, on having been perceived?

DAN JACOBSON

A White Liberal Trapped by His Prejudices

This essay, by a white South African, is an introspective anatomy of
prejudice. Jacobson admits to being racially prejudiced and offers
himself as a subject for contemplation. The essay is the personal testimony of a prejudiced man, not the victim but the afflictor.

IT IS a curious fact that we have in recent literature introspection
on practically everything that people could possibly introspect about.
We know why people become Communists, and why they cease to be
Communists, we know what it feels like to be the pilot of a jet plane
going through the sound barrier, and what it feels like to be a poet in
Bloomsbury; obliging schizophrenics have told us what an attack of schizo-
phrenia is like. But I have yet to come across any introspection on race
prejudice, though it is something that occupies our minds almost as much
as Communism, and rather more than poetry. It is the subject, certainly, of
enough reports and analyses. The reason for the gap in our knowledge
would appear to be that those who draw up the reports and analyses are
without prejudice, or believe themselves to be; and the subjects of the inquiries cannot introspect upon their prejudices—they can merely give vent
to them.

Yet the reasons may be somewhat more involved than that, and perhaps
some of them will emerge from what I am going to write. I offer myself: I
am racially prejudiced, and I don't believe in my prejudices. I would like
to get rid of them, though I do not believe that under the present circumstances I can, and I am willing to help in the fight against them within myself and others.

Having reached that stage, my evidence is perhaps suspect. I am not
really prejudiced, the argument might run, and so useless for the purposes
of introspection upon race prejudice. That may be. It may very well be.
But I sit here writing an article for a nice, enlightened magazine in America, and at the same time I know that if I go into the street and meet an
African, I will talk to him differently from the way I would talk to a white
man. I am not *really* prejudiced, perhaps: I wouldn't hit him for no reason,
as a great many of my white compatriots might if the mood was upon
them: I would shake his hand if he offered it; I would even invite him to

the house if I were sure that the police and my neighbors would not know about it. But still, as we would draw together in the darkened street, as we would meet under a lamp post, and as I would ask him for a match, say, my words would be different, my very voice would be different to what it would have been had I addressed a white man. Why? And the answer is short and unmistakable. It is because he is an African, to use the enlightened name. Because he is a Native, to use the word which comes more naturally to my lips. Because he is a Kaffir, to use the most common, insulting word of all.

But when I try to find out why I should speak like this to him, I have to admit that I am baffled. I know all the reasons, of course. I am merely responding as I was taught to respond to people with black skins, at school, at home, in the streets, in jokes, in songs, in films, at dances, in every activity that I have ever undertaken and shared with my fellow white South Africans. I know that. Yet the bafflement persists. Because when I look back, I see that there were hundreds of other things I did in common that no longer have any effect on me. We hated the other boys who went to another school and against whom we played Rugby. I no longer do. We were crazy about American swing. I now find it dull. I was in love with Ingrid Bergman. I no longer am. All the poisoned entertainments and false sentiments about England (known to thousands of people who have never been there as "Home"), all the bad Zionist propaganda, the Jewish nationalism, the enthusiasms about boxing champions, all the things that I see hundreds of thousands of people around me taking part in, leave me quite cold. They bore me. I don't believe in them. Why then do I stick at this thing—this racial prejudice?

Again, there is a large answer. Because it suits me, as a white man, as a member of the ruling group. All right, I grant that. But I am not a white man only, or a member of the ruling group only. I am also me—a reader of COMMENTARY, an admirer of George Orwell, fond of traveling, trying to write a novel, raising ten red fowls in the back yard, quite harmless. Why does this me persist with its prejudices? I don't think that there is a short answer, once the white-man-ruling-class stuff has been set aside, and I believe that, to some extent, it can be set aside.

Nor do I want to mislead myself or others about this, and I don't want to stand here as a figure of complacent race hatred. I am a "liberal" in the precise South African sense of the word, and for want of anything better to take pride in. I am proud that I am a liberal. I want houses, education, votes, and equal treatment for the Africans of this country, all the things that are so obvious one feels stale repeating them. I am prepared to work for these things, if I knew of people with whom I could work; and I am proud when I hear an African read a paper or make a good speech, or when he shakes my hand in friendliness, for then I know that I am right in what I believe, and that all the others who would treat him as a slave, and look upon him as a kind of ape, are wrong.

But the one thing doesn't cancel out the other. It is "liberalism" and myself that are condemned, but the tone of my voice, in the casual encounter, is still different from me. And why is he different? Because he is black. The argument runs in a circle; it isn't an argument, it's a statement of prejudice.

Let me approach the same thing from another angle. I say that I would like to work for votes, houses, and education for the Africans, if I knew of people with whom I could work. The answer is obvious: work with the Africans. But I don't—and it is not only because of the danger involved, the possibility of arrest and imprisonment for attempting to work with Africans in political action. There are other reasons.

The blur begins to thin out a little, and I realize that I can't work with the Africans because I don't know them. I don't know how they think or what they think. I don't know their feelings, except in a gross sort of way, without subtlety in my guesses. I don't know what they want or whether they want the same things as I do. I feel completely strange to them, alien, though they are the people among whom I grew up, the people who have nursed me, and worked for me, and with whom I spend at least as much time as I do with white men. But I don't *know* them, or feel I don't, and can never know them, because they are black.

The blur dissolves a little and returns. And returns as ignorance. I can see through it a black arm, close-packed curls of hair, a black face, unknown, impenetrable. The skin color is what I am aware of, first and last, when I think of the African people. Black, other to myself. It is extraordinarily difficult to pin the feeling down. The man, the African, is surrounded by his blackness; it moves with him wherever he goes, and whatever he does, and wherever it is, there is strangeness, the same unknown quality, until communication between us seems impossible, or possible only from a great distance, a matter of the broadest signals that cannot be misunderstood and that can say very little. For he is black and I am white, and there are differences between us, and I do not know him.

And that blur of ignorance, that failure of the imagination is at the heart of what I can only call my race prejudice. I do not know if it is only a personal failure, or whether the deliberate crippling action taken against me as a child was stronger than I thought it could be, or whether I cling to it because I believe it is in my interests to do so—but I do know that some part of my natural understanding has been extirpated and that ignorance of thought and feeling has taken its place.

But it is impossible to live in a mist, an absence of relationships. I have to place things in some sort of relationship to myself, construct some sort of hierarchy in which I and all the dark-skinned people that I meet can live, I have to give the African a place.

"Place"—the word comes appositely enough. For the first of the ten commandments in South Africa reads: every Kaffir must know his place. And what is a Kaffir's place? This image presents itself with warmth, almost with tenderness. His place is considerably below mine. It is a humble, rather poverty-stricken place, and he stands in the middle of it with his hat in his hand, waiting for me to pass, smiling, half bowing. I, then, am kind—if I too am imprisoned in my "place"; these things are double-edged—I give him the cigarette that I am smoking, and I mark that he takes it with cupped hands, for that is a sign of respect among Kaffirs who know their place. And so I pass on, warmed by my generosity, flattered by his gratitude, and soothed by the feeling that things aren't so bad after all. Later, being a liberal, I shall revile myself, but in the meantime it has been very pleasant.

And though it may go against the grain, I have to admit that that paternalism, that feudal kind of attitude, is the only one with which it is possible for me to live among the Africans that I come into contact with. For I very rarely meet the doctors, lawyers, teachers, the politicians among them. I meet only the "boys" (another interesting word—"boy") who work in the same factory as I do, and above whom I am in a position of authority. And the authority and the paternalism, the superiority, becomes automatic, unquestioned by themselves and by myself, and we have some kind of relationship. And the pattern of the relationship spreads itself, insinuates itself into every action of mine, every contact that I have with the Africans, casual or more permanent, as the case may be. I feel no sense of strain about it, as long as the African sticks to his place: my relationships are prejudiced, follow their unfree pattern without tension or hysteria or discomfort. I am prejudiced as my eyes are brown or my hair straight, my skin white, without thought.

It is a fake, though. Being prejudiced as I am may be automatic, everyday, but it works only as long as the Kaffir stays in his place. But if he doesn't—what then? Well, then—again if I am at that moment trapped in my everyday waking dream—I suppose I begin to hector, or I become effusively "liberal," or something unpleasant like that. I no longer know where I am, and I no longer know what I am. I grope insecurely, lost.

But this is a curious thing. For if I am happy only when the object of my prejudice does what the prejudice demands he should do in terms of the prejudice, what about those whose prejudices take more violent forms than my own—the Gentile who sees every Jew as a threat to his way of life, a baby killer? What about every white South African who sees every black South African as a savage, a raper, an incendiary? Are they happy only when the Jew robs them, when the African rapes their wives?

It sounds grotesque. But living in this country, one cannot escape the feeling that the whites here are not merely misguided, frightened, and vicious. One mustn't underestimate them. The will of the Nazi Gauleiter, the lyncher of Negroes, the white South African may be diseased, but it is powerful, and no one can escape from what he himself has willed into existence.

II

The two weekends before the Saturday of the riots had been troubled ones. Stones had been thrown at the police who patrol the African locations,* stones had been thrown at the buses serving the locations, notices had gone up outside the municipal beer halls in the locations calling on all Africans to boycott the beer halls.

Yet for all this, no one was expecting serious trouble. Stones are continually being thrown at the police by Africans, and the municipal ban on home-brewing of beer had been a long-standing grievance among the inhabitants of the Kimberley locations. True, there had been a new element in the preliminary troubles. The stone-throwers had shouted *"Afrika!"* when they had attacked the white man's police and the white man's buses —and *"Afrika!"* was part of the simple, effective slogan of the passive resistance campaign organized by the African and Indian Congresses in their struggle against unjust laws and *apartheid* regulations, for the sake of which 6,000 Africans and Indians had gone peacefully to jail in practically every town of importance in South Africa, including Kimberley. But if a drunkard shouts a political slogan, it is his drunkenness that is noted; if an African shouts a political slogan, memory is quick to remind that he is only a Kaffir.

We did not hear that there was a serious riot going on in No. 2 location until after we had heard the ambulance sirens down Main Road and the alarm bells of the fire brigade, that Saturday afternoon, a peaceful afternoon in our part of the town, with the summer sun shining on all the gardens kept trim by so many African servants. Then my brother came in: he had heard that the police had opened fire against rioting Africans. We heard the ambulances again, and as the warm evening drew on, and the sunlight failed, the air of the town in which I have lived all my life, and which, even now, I can think of only as a place of peace and heat and sand on the edge of the desert to the south and west, was wild with the sound of

---

* A "location" is a township outside any white town in which all Africans who work in the town have to live. One must add that they are usually the most hideous, disease-stricken slums imaginable, and that those in Kimberley are no exception.

sirens. And my sister ran into the house to tell us how lorry-loads of police had just been seen going down Central Road towards Green Point location. Central Road is the street I live in. But the police had all been
armed with rifles and Sten guns, and as they passed my sister, they had
waved and smiled and given the thumbs-up sign, and called to her, like
soldiers anywhere in the world, calling to their own people, sure of their
welcome, sure that the young girl will smile and wave back at them.

We had some sort of supper. Then it was night. The darkness was tur-
bulent. We knew that the serious rioting was in No. 2 location, which is
right at the other end of town, but why then was there so much noise in
our part of town? We heard shouts, distantly, and all the time the wailing
of the sirens. We went into the street, into Central Road, and outside it
was worse. The noises came from all sides. Our neighbors too were in the
streets, standing at the gates to their gardens, listening, standing in little
groups of whites on the pavements, talking to one another. We went back
into the house and sat around and stared at one another. I phoned up the
offices of the local newspaper, and managed to get through after some
time.

"What's going on?" I asked.

"I don't know," the voice at the other end said. "There's a bit of a do
with the Wogs at No. 2 location."

"What sort of a do?"

The man was as cheerful as anyone could be. He chirped the news over
to me. "They've burned down the beer hall and the municipal offices, and
a whole lot else. We don't know yet for certain." Then he said: "The latest
score is eighteen, I believe."

"What score? Score of what?"

"Dead Kaffirs." I could see his grin. "The police are shooting them like
hell."

"What a mess," I said.

"Well, it's a bit of excitement," the other said more warmly. "But
they're teaching them this time."

I went back and told the others what the newspaper offices had told me.
We sat on. Then we heard two bursts of fire from a Sten gun, nearer to
hand than anything that had yet happened. We had been hearing shots all
the late afternoon and evening, but from a distance. This sounded more serious. We all went into the street again, and this time we were really
frightened. For there is a police station at the bottom of the road, about
half a mile from our house. It was too dark and confused to make anything
out clearly: all we could see was a blaze of lights around the station. It was
then that I feared the most. I was sure that the Africans were storming the
police station, and how long would it be before they would be coming up

Central Road, coming for us? There were a few more volleys of shots, all with the urgent guttural sound of automatic fire. And then we heard some-one screaming, screaming, screaming, one voice over and over again, as a child screams. That was lost in a confused shouting of many voices, and then we heard a voice calling: *"Mayibuye, mayibuye!"* The word was said twice, clearer than the other shouting and the shots and the long wail of the ambulance dying away to a mutter. And *"Mayibuye!"* is the other half of the slogan in the campaign of peaceful, non-violent defiance of unjust laws. Together the words *"Mayibuye Afrika!"* mean "Come back Af-rica!" Come back Africa to the people to whom the continent belongs, the black people who work for us, and are kicked by us, and thrown into jail by us, and whom we do not allow to enter our schools and our theaters, our playgrounds, our buses, our homes. Come back Africa to your people. We who have white skins have lost you.

We knew that we were lost all that night as the sound of the fighting died down, and silence resumed. We knew that we were lost when we stood with our white neighbors, our sharp physical fear of death guttering away from us, and agreed with them that all the police could do was shoot the Kaffirs down. We knew that we were lost when we agreed with Mr. Collins from across the road that the government should give every white man a revolver. And most terribly and desolatingly of all we knew that we were lost when we wandered into the back yard of the house, and saw our two servants standing there. Ben and Betty have been with us for years, and we thought we knew them so well, and they knew us, and that there was friendship between us. But that night Betty stood at the door of her room, in the darkness, and Ben stood leaning over the wall of the back *stoep* on the other side of the yard, and I and my brother and my sister walked between them, past them, knowing that they were looking at us, all the long way to the kitchen door, and I could not say one word to them, not one word, and nor could my brother or sister, none of us could bring out a sound to the two dark people who stood unmoving in the shadow of our home, silent. They let us pass in silence to the door of our house, and we opened it and closed it behind us, to get away from their dreadful rigid silence.

And that was how the riot, one savage and hopeless rising against the authority of the white ruling race, touched me, a member of that race. Now when peace and heat have returned to Kimberley, it seems like a bad dream. And most dreamlike of all, and yet most true to our white way of life, our white way of guilt, was the immediate and overpowering fear of death by violence at the hands of a black mob. For the white police are stronger than any dark mob, and can easily stop a riot, or at least confine it to the African locations, leaving our wide, white areas quite safe. And even those shouts and shots near to hand were not, as we feared, a mob storming the police station, but only the police bringing their prisoners to Beaconsfield police station, the jail and other police stations being full. That was all it was. And we were safe that night, within our areas, as I am this night, or any other night of peace in this country. For my side have the guns. On the night of the riot those guns killed or seriously wounded over one hundred Africans.

My side. And hopelessly, I realize again that it is my side. There is a fatal logic about these things. So many whites have been oppressing so many blacks for so long that there are two sides only now, and we fall into them, willy-nilly. I am white. If the police had not been effective, and if the African mob had managed to break out of the location, I would have suffered at their hands like any other white man. I was as dependent as the most fanatical white African-hater on the Sten guns and rifles of the white police. For the Africans could not have distinguished between us; and in all humility I have to ask—why should they have distinguished? And there is no answer.

I know that it can be asked of me why I do not join the Africans in their liberatory struggle. I can plead what I believe to be the truth: that it is now too late: a skirmish in the liberatory struggle was fought recently at No. 2 location, and if I had not merely trembled at home but gone out to take part in it on the side of the Africans, with luck the police would have seen me as I approached the location and led me home as a madman who has to be protected from himself, and without luck the Africans would have got hold of me, and even though I shouted *"Afrika!"* with all the strength of my lungs they would have battered me to death or burned me to death as they have done to Europeans unfortunate enough to have been caught in African locations at the time of similar riots in the cities of Port Elizabeth and East London.

And then I can only add that I cannot join the liberatory struggle because I am an ordinary sort of person, rather feeble, prejudiced, not knowing the Africans, who wants to go on doing the sort of work that he likes and is best at. But one learns how undemanding frenzy and hatred are of their allies: it is strange to see one's desire to do the job of work that one likes and is best at, one's little prejudices, one's failures of imagination, returning, arm in arm with those who have guns in their hands and blood on their breasts.

HIROSHI WAGATSUMA

The Social Perception of Skin Color in Japan

Professor Wagatsuma is an outstanding psychologist who has worked in the United States and Japan. His essay is included in this section not only because it is a valuable work in itself, but because the material he quotes is especially relevant to the question of the individual perception of racial difference. In no other work of this length is there such a combination of historical background and personal statement on the perceptions of the white, black, and yellow races.

L ONG BEFORE any sustained contact with either Caucasoid Europeans or dark-skinned Africans or Indians, the Japanese valued "white" skin as beautiful and deprecated "black" skin as ugly. Their spontaneous responses to the white skin of Caucasoid Europeans and the black skin of Negroid people were an extension of values deeply embedded in Japanese concepts of beauty. From past to present, the Japanese have always associated skin color symbolically with other physical characteristics that signify degrees of spiritual refinement or primitiveness. Skin color has been related to a whole complex of attractive or objectionable social traits. It might strike some as curious that the Japanese have traditionally used the word *white* (*shiroi*) to describe lighter shades of their own skin color. The social perception of the West has been that the Chinese and Japanese themselves have rarely used the color yellow to describe their skin.

I

"White" skin has been considered an essential characteristic of feminine beauty in Japan since recorded time. An old Japanese proverb states that "white skin makes up for seven defects"; a woman's light skin causes one to overlook the absence of other desired physical features.

During the Nara period (710-793), court ladies made ample use of cosmetics and liberally applied white powder to the face. Cheeks were rouged. Red beauty spots were painted on between the eyebrows and at the outer corners of both the eyes and the lips. Eyelids and lips were given a red tinge. Both men and women removed their natural eyebrows and penciled in long, thick lines emulating a Chinese style. The custom of blackening teeth spread among the aristocratic ladies. In the next period (794-1185), when the court was moved to the new capital of Heian

58

(Kyoto), countless references were made in both illustration and writing to round-faced, plump women with white, smooth skin. Necessary to beauty was long, black, straight hair that draped over the back and shoulders without being tied. One can illustrate this conception of white skin as a mark of beauty from *The Tale of Genji* by Lady Murasaki, a romance of the first decade of the eleventh century:

> Her color of skin was very white and she was plump with an attractive face. Her hair grew thick but was cut so as to hang on a level with her shoulders—very beautiful.

> Her color was very white and although she was emaciated and looked noble, there still was a certain fulness in her cheek.

In her personal diary, the same author depicted portraits of several court ladies:

> Lady Dainagon is very small but as she is white and beautifully round, she has a taller appearance. Her hair is three inches longer than her height.

> Lady Senji is a small and slender person. The texture of her hair is fine, delicate and glossy and reaches a foot longer than her height.

> Lady Naiji has beauty and purity, a fragrant white skin with which no one else can compete.

Writing about the year 1002 in essays called *The Pillow Book,* the court lady Sei Shōnagon described how she despised "hair not smooth and straight" and envied "beautiful, very long hair." In *The Tale of Glory,* presumably written in 1120 by Akazome Emon, a court lady, two beautiful women of the prosperous Fujiwara family are depicted: one with "her hair seven or eight inches longer than her height," and the other with "her hair about two feet longer than her height and her skin white and beautiful." From the eighth to the twelfth century, the bearers of Japanese cultural refinement were the court nobility who idled their lives away in romantic love affairs, practicing the arts of music and poetry. The whiteness of untanned skin was the symbol of this privileged class which was spared any form of outdoor labor. From the eleventh century on, men of the aristocracy applied powder to their faces just as the court ladies did.

In 1184, the warriors took the reins of government away from the effete courtiers and abruptly ended the court's rather decadent era. To protect the *samurai* virtues of simplicity, frugality, and bravery, the warriors set up headquarters in the frontier town of Kamakura located far away from the capital. The warriors maintained Spartan standards, as is evidenced in the many portrait paintings showing rather florid or swarthy countenances. Women still continued, however, the practices of toiletry established previously in the court. In 1333 the warriors' government was moved from Kamakura back to Kyoto, where the Ashikaga Shogunate family emulated court life and re-established an atmosphere of luxury among the ruling class.

Standards of feminine beauty still emphasized corpulence of body, white skin, and black hair, which in this period was worn in a chignon. Preference was voiced for a woman with a round face, broad forehead, and eyes slightly down-turned at the corners. By this time, the old court custom of penciling eyebrows and blackening teeth had become incorporated into the puberty rites practiced for both boys and girls. Such rites were principally held by the warrior class but were later adopted by commoners. The writing of Yoshida Kenko, a celebrated poet and court official who became a Buddhist monk in 1324, exemplifies the continuing preoccupation this period had with the white skin of women. Yoshida wrote the following in his *Essays of Idleness:*

> The magician of Kume (as the legend runs) lost his magic power through looking at the white leg of a maiden washing clothes in a river. This may well have been because the white limbs and skin of a woman cleanly plump and fatty are no mere external charms but true beauty and allure.

Following a chaotic political period, the Tokugawa feudal government was established in 1603. It was to last until the modern period of Japan, more than two hundred and fifty years. Changes occurred in the ideals of feminine beauty during this period of continuing peace. Gradually, slim and fragile women with slender faces and up-turned eyes began to be preferred to the plump, pear-shaped ideal that remained dominant until the middle of the eighteenth century. White skin, however, remained an imperative characteristic of feminine beauty. Ibara Saikaku (1642-1693), a novelist who wrote celebrated books about common life during the early Tokugawa period, had the following to say about the type of female beauty to be found in Kyoto and Osaka:

> A beautiful woman with a round face, skin with a faint pink color, eyes not too narrow, eyebrows thick, the bridge of her nose not too thin, her mouth small, teeth in excellent shape and shining white.

> A woman of twenty-one, white of color, hair beautiful, attired in gentleness.

> Thanks to the pure water of Kyoto, women remain attractive from early childhood but they further improve their beauty by steaming their faces, tightening their fingers with rings and wearing leather socks in sleep. They also comb their hair with the juice of the *sanekazura* root.

Another author, depicting the beauties of the middle Tokugawa period of the 1770's, wrote: "A pair of girls wearing red-lacquered thongs on their tender feet, white as snow, sashes around their waists, with forms as slender as willow trees." Tamenaga Shunsui (1789-1843), an author of the late Tokugawa period, never forgot to mention white skin when describing the beautiful women of Edo (Tokyo):

> Her hands and arms are whiter than snow.

> You are well-featured and your color is so white that you are popular among your audience.

> This courtesan had a neck whiter than snow. Her face was shining as she always polished it with powder.

The use of good water and the practice of steaming the face were thought to make skin white and smooth. Rings and socks were worn in sleep to stunt excessive growth of limbs since small hands and feet were valued attributes of feminine charm. The juice of the *sanekazura* root was used to straighten the hair. These practices all confirm the continuous concern with white skin and straight hair. They also suggest, however, the possibility that many women were lacking in such standards of feminine beauty. The following quotation describes what was considered ugly:

> Disagreeable features for a woman are a large face, the lack of any tufts of hair under the temple, a big, flat nose, thick lips, black skin, a too plump body, excessive tallness, heavy, strong limbs, brownish wavy hair and a loud, talkative voice.

These were the comments of Yanagi Rikyō, a high-ranking warrior of the Koriyama fief, who was also a poet, artist, and noted connoisseur of womanhood in the late-eighteenth century. He contrasted these objectionable features with "the amiable features of a woman, a small and well-shaped face, white skin, gentle manner, an innocent, charming and attentive character." One might speculate that the supposed Polynesian or Melanesian strains, sometimes thought to have entered the Japanese racial mixture, would be responsible for flat noses, thick lips, or brownish, wavy hair. Such features are certainly not rare among Japanese, although they run directly counter to the Japanese image of beauty.

Because Mongoloid skin shows a very quick tendency to tan and to produce "black" skin, the Japanese can maintain lightness of skin only by total avoidance of sunlight. Not surprisingly, Tokugawa women made constant use of parasols or face hoods to hide their skin from sunlight and assiduously applied powder to face, neck, throat, and upper chest. In order to increase the whiteness and smoothness of their skin, women "polished" it in their baths with a cloth bag containing rice bran or the droppings of the Japanese nightingale. Applications of other grains such as millet, barley, Deccan grass, and beans was also considered to have some "bleaching" effect on the skin. Juices taken from various flowers were also used for the same purpose, and many medicines were sold that promised "to turn the skin as white as the snow found on the peaks of high mountains."

When a woman's constant care of her skin achieved desired results, she would enjoy such praise as "Her face is so smoothly shiny that it seems ready to reflect," and "Her face can compete with a mirror," or "Her face is so shiny as to make a well polished black lacquered dresser feel ashamed."

From the beginning of the nineteenth century, the Kabuki actors set the standards of men's beauty. A rather feminine type of male with a slender figure, well-formed face, white skin, black hair, and red lips became a favorite object of feminine desire. Men possessing these elements of attractiveness would enjoy such a flattering remark as "You should be a Kabuki actor." By the middle of the nineteenth century, these characteristics began to be considered effeminate. A man with a more dusky skin and a piquantly handsome face became the preferred type.

The word *white* repeatedly used in the quotations taken from these various sources is the same Japanese word *shiroi* that is used to describe snow or white paper. There was no intermediate word between *shiroi* ("white") and *kuroi* ("black") used to describe skin color. When distinctions were made, there would be recourse to such words as *asa guroi* ("light black").

II

Not long after the first globe-circling voyages of Magellan, Westerners appeared on the shores of Japan. Dutch, English, Portuguese, and Spanish traders came to ply their trade in Japanese ports. Both Spanish and Portuguese missionaries sought to establish Christianity in Japan. Before the Tokugawa government sealed off Japan from the West, the Japanese had ample opportunity to observe white men for the first time. In these early contacts, the Portuguese and Spaniards were called *nanban-jin* or *nanban* meaning "southern barbarians," words adopted from the Chinese who had names to designate all the "inferior savages" living to the north, south, east, and west of the Middle Kingdom. The Dutch were called *kōmō-jin* or *kōmo*, "red-haired people."

In several of the colored pictures of the day that included both Japanese and Europeans, the Japanese artists painted the faces of the Portuguese, Spanish, and Japanese men in a flesh color or light brown, but depicted the faces of Japanese women as white in hue. In a few other pictures, however, some Portuguese are given white faces like Japanese women, while other Portuguese are given darker faces. Seemingly, the Japanese artists were sensitive in some instances to some form of color differential among the foreigners. Many Portuguese and Spaniards were actually not so white-skinned as northern Europeans, and after the long sea voyage to

Japan, they undoubtedly arrived with rather well-tanned skins. The Dutch in the pictures, on the other hand, seem to be given invariably either gray or white faces. When contrasted with the Japanese women near them, the Japanese feminine face is painted a whiter hue than that of the Dutch.

The differences between the Japanese and the Europeans in these old prints are clearly depicted in hair color and facial characteristics. The Portuguese, Spaniards, and Dutch are all taller than the Japanese and are given somewhat unrealistically large noses. Their double eye folds and their bushy eyebrows and mustaches seem slightly exaggerated. The Portuguese and Spanish hair is painted brown although a few are given black hair. The Dutch hair is usually depicted as either red or reddish-brown in color. Written and pictorial descriptions indicate that the Japanese were more impressed with the height, hair color, general hairiness, big noses and eyes of the foreigners than with their lighter skin color. Some pictures include portraits of the Negro servants of the Portuguese and Dutch. The faces of Negroes are painted in a leaden- or blackish-gray, and their hair is shown as extremely frizzled. The physiognomy of the Negroes is somewhat caricatured and in some instances closely resembles the devils and demons of Buddhist mythology.

Some Japanese scholars of Dutch science seem to have had a notion that the black skin and frizzled hair of Negro servants were the result of extreme exposure to heat and sunshine in the tropical countries in which they were born. In 1787, such a scholar wrote of what he had learned from his Dutch friends about their Negro servants:

> These black ones on the Dutch boats are the natives of countries in the South. As their countries are close to the sun, they are sun-scorched and become black. By nature they are stupid.

> The black ones are found with flat noses. They love a flat nose and they tie children's noses with leather bands to prevent their growth and to keep them flat.

> Africa is directly under the equator and the heat there is extreme. Therefore, the natives are black colored. They are uncivilized and vicious in nature.

Another scholar wrote:

> Black ones are impoverished Indians employed by the Dutch. As their country is in the South and the heat is extreme, their body is sun-scorched and their color becomes black. Their hair is burned by the sun and becomes frizzled but they are humans and not monkeys as some mistakenly think.

After the closing of the country by the Tokugawa government in 1639, the only contact of Japanese with Westerners, aside from the Dutch traders, would occur when shipwrecked Japanese sailors would occasionally be picked up by Western ships and taken for a period to a Western country. The reports about the English, Russians, and Spaniards made by these Japanese sailors upon their return commented much more on the hair and eyes of the Occidentals than upon the color of skin.

In 1853 Commodore Perry of the United States Navy came to Japan with his "black ships" and forced Japan to reopen her ports to foreign vessels. When Perry visited Japan for the second time in 1854, there were two American women on board. It was reported in a Japanese document:

> On board is a woman named Shirley, 31 years old and her child Loretta, 5 years old. Their hair is red. They have high noses, white faces and the pupils of their eyes are brown. They are medium in size and very beautiful.

The portraits of Commodore Perry and five principals of his staff drawn by a Japanese artist show the Americans with noses of exaggerated size, large eyes, and brownish hair. Their faces are painted in a washed-out, whitish-ash color. In other pictures, however, both American and Japanese faces are painted with an identical whitish-gray, although the Americans are given brown hair and bushy beards. In some pictures showing the American settlements in Yokohama and Tokyo of the 1860's, the faces of both American and Japanese women are painted whiter than those of American and Japanese men. It may well be possible that the American men's faces were more sun-tanned and exposed to the elements during the voyage than the faces of the women who, observing canons of beauty much like those held by Japanese women, may have kept themselves out of the sun. Also, the artists may have simply resorted to convention by which women's faces were painted white.

In 1860 the Tokugawa government sent an envoy with an entourage of eighty-three warriors to the United States to ratify a treaty of peace and commerce between the United States and Japan originally signed in 1854. Some of the members of the entourage kept careful diaries and noted their impressions of the United States during their trip to Washington. Upon meeting the President of the United States, one *samurai* wrote: "President Buchanan, about 52 or 53 years of age, is a tall person. His color is white, his hair is white." The *samurai* leaders were surprised to attend formal receptions at which women were included and to find that American men acted toward their women as obliging servants. They were impressed with the daring exposure afforded by the décolletage of the formal evening gowns worn by women at these balls and receptions. In their diaries they noted their appreciation of American beauty, although they continued to express their preference for black hair:

The women's skin was white and they were charming in their gala dresses decorated with gold and silver but their hair was red and their eyes looked like dog eyes, which was quite disheartening.

Occasionally I saw women with black hair and black eyes. They must have been of some Asian race. Naturally they looked more attractive and beautiful.

Another man expressed his admiration for the President's niece, Harriet Lane, in true *samurai* fashion by composing a Chinese poem:

An American belle, her name is Lane,
Jewels adorn her arms, jade her ears.
Her rosy face needs no powder or rouge.
Her exposed shoulders shine as white as snow.

This American belle and her friends had asked another *samurai* at a party which women he liked better, Japanese or American. The *samurai* wrote in his diary:

I answered that the American women are better because their skin color is whiter than that of the Japanese women. Such a trifling comment of mine obviously pleased the girls. After all, women are women.

After seeing about a hundred American children aged five to nine gathered at a May festival ball, another warrior wrote of his admiration of their beauty:

The girls did not need to have the help of powder and rouge. Their skin with its natural beauty was whiter than snow and purer than jewels. I wondered if fairies in wonderland would not look something like these children.

On the way back from the United States, the boat carrying the Japanese envoy stopped at a harbor on the African coast, and the *samurai* had a chance to see the black-skinned Africans inhabiting the region. They noted with disapproval their impression of Negroid features:

The black ones look like devils depicted in pictures.

The faces are black as if painted with ink and their physiognomy reminds me of that of a monkey.

III

In the early Meiji period, the Japanese began their self-conscious imitation of the technology of the West. Less consciously, they also began to alter their perception of feminine beauty. In their writings, they referred with admiration to the white skin of Westerners, but noted with disapproval the hair color and the hairiness of Westerners. Wavy hair was not to the Japanese taste until the mid-1920's. Curly hair was considered to be an animal characteristic. Mrs. Sugimoto, the daughter of a *samurai,* writes in her autobiography that, as a child with curly hair, she had her hair dressed twice a week with a special treatment to straighten it properly. When she complained, her mother would scold her, saying, "Do you not know that curly hair is like that of animals? A *samurai's* daughter should not be willing to resemble a beast."

The body hair of Caucasian men suggested a somewhat beastly nature to Japanese women, and, probably for reasons of this kind, Japanese women of the late-nineteenth century refused or were reluctant in many instances to become mistresses to Western diplomats.

By the mid-1920's the Japanese had adopted Western customs and fashions, including the singing of American popular songs and dancing in dance halls. They watched motion pictures with delight and made great favorites of Clara Bow, Gloria Swanson, and Greta Garbo. Motion pictures seem to have had a very strong effect in finally changing habits of coiffure and attitudes toward desirable beauty. During this period many Japanese women had their hair cut and, in spite of the exhortations of proud *samurai* tradition, had it waved and curled. They took to wearing long skirts with large hats to emulate styles worn by Greta Garbo. The 1920's was a time of great imitation. Anything Western was considered "modern" and, therefore, superior. This trend lasted until the mid-1930's when, under the pressure of the ultra-nationalist, militarist regime, the ties with Western fads were systematically broken.

Already in 1924, Tanizaki Junichirō depicted a woman who represented a kind of femininity that was appealing to "modern" intellectuals of the time. She was Naomi in *The Love of an Idiot,* and her physical attractiveness had a heavy Western flavor. She was sought after by a man who "wished if ever possible to go to Europe and marry an Occidental woman." Since he could not do so, he decided to marry Naomi, who had such Occidental features. He helped her refine her beauty and educated her so that she would become "a real lady presentable even to the eyes of the Occidentals." She became, instead, a promiscuous, lust-driven woman who turned her mentor-husband into a slave chained to her by his uncontrollable passion. An important aspect of Tanizaki's depiction of this Occidental-looking girl is the whiteness of her skin:

> Against the red gown, her hands and feet stand out purely white like the core of a cabbage.

> Her skin was white to an astounding degree. . . . All the exposed parts of her voluptuous body were as white as the meat of an apple.

There is a most interesting passage in this book, however, in which Tanizaki, with a note of disappointment, compares Naomi with a real European woman, a Russian aristocrat living in exile in Japan.

> [The Russian woman's] skin color . . . was so extraordinarily white, an almost ghostly beauty of white skin under which the blood vessels of light violet color were faintly visible like the veining of marble. Compared with this skin, that of Naomi's lacked clearness and shine and was rather dull to the eye.

The subtle, not fully conscious, trend toward an idealization of Western physical features by the Japanese apparently became of increasing importance in the twenties. It remained a hidden subcurrent throughout the last war while Japan, as the "champion of the colored nations," fought against the "whites." In spite of propaganda emphasizing the racial ties between Japanese and other Asians, the "yellowness" of the Japanese was never quite made a point of pride. The rapidity with which Western standards of beauty became idealized after the war attests to the continuous drift that was occurring in spite of ten years of antagonism and military hostilities.

IV

Older Japanese who have lived overseas have been astounded upon visiting postwar Japan. The straight black hair of the past is all but gone. Even most geisha, the preservers of many feminine traditions, have permanents and wave their hair. Among ordinary women, one periodically sees extreme examples of hair that has been bleached with hydrogen peroxide or, more commonly, dyed a purplish or reddish hue. Plastic surgery, especially to alter eye folds and to build up the bridge of the nose, has become almost standardized practice among the younger movie actresses and, indeed, even among some of the male actors. There were examples of plastic surgery to be found before the war, but its wide popularity is something new.

Contemporary Japanese men interviewed in the United States and Japan all agreed in valuing the "whiteness" of skin as a component of beauty in the Japanese woman. Whiteness is very often associated in their minds with womanhood ("Whiteness is a symbol of women, distinguishing them from men"), with chastity and purity ("Whiteness suggests purity and moral virtue"), and motherhood ("One's mother-image is white"). Linked with concerns for the skin's whiteness are desires that it also be smooth with a close, firm texture, a shiny quality, and no wrinkles, furrows, spots, or flecks. Some informants mentioned the value of a soft, resilient, and subtly damp surface to the skin. This quality, called *mochi-hada* ("skin like pounded rice") in Japanese, has an implicit sexual connotation for some men.

Although many young men accept the primary preference for white skin, they also admit that sun-tanned skin in a young woman is of a "modern" healthy attractiveness. Some men contrasted such healthy charm to that of a "beautiful tuberculosis patient whose skin is pale and almost transparent," a type of helpless beauty that represented tragic charm during the 1930's. Associated with brownish, sun-tanned skin as a beauty type are large Western eyes, a relatively large mouth with bold lips, a well-developed body, and an outgoing, gay personality.

Such a creature with "Western" charm was held in direct contrast to the more traditional femininity of white skin, less conspicuous physique, gentle manner, and quiet character. One finds these contrasts and stereotypes juxtaposed in popular contemporary fiction. There is some ambivalence about light-colored skin in men. Light skin suggests excessive intellectualism, more effeteness, individuals who are impractical and concern themselves with philosophical questions of life, love, and eternity, and those who are unduly ruminative and lack the capacity to act.

Among the women interviewed, there was a general consensus that Japanese women like to be "white-skinned," but that there is a type of modern beauty in women with sun-tanned skin. The women believe that such women, however, when they marry and settle down, "stop being sporty and sun-tanned. Such a girl will take care of her skin and become white."

Several informants with working-class backgrounds said that, as children, they heard their mothers and other adult women talk about the "fragile, white-skinned women" of the wealthier class who did not have to work outside. They remembered a certain tone of both envy and contempt in their mothers' voices. There is a tendency to associate "white" skin with urban and "black" skin with rural living.

In this connection, a Japanese social psychologist who had visited Okinawa several times told us that many Okinawans become self-conscious of their "black" skin when they meet Japanese from Japan. To Okinawan eyes, the Japanese appear to have "whiter" skin and, therefore, look much more refined and urban that do the Okinawans. There used to be a general association among the Japanese of "white" skin with wealth, "black" skin with lower economic status. The younger generations, however, increasingly tend to consider sun-tanned skin as the sign of the socially privileged people who can afford summer vacations at the seaside or mountain resorts.

With only a few exceptions, the women interviewed voiced the opinion that Japanese women like light-brown-skinned men, seeing them as more masculine than pale-skinned men. Many women distinguished between "a beautiful man" and "an attractive man." A beautiful man (*bi-danshi*) is white-skinned and delicately featured like a Kabuki actor. Although he is admired and appreciated almost aesthetically, he is, at the same time, considered somewhat "too feminine" for a woman to depend upon. There is sometimes a reference to the saying, "A beautiful man lacks money and might." On the other hand, an attractive man (kō-danshi) is dusky-skinned, energetic, masculine, and dependable. Women often associate light-brown skin in a man with a dauntless spirit, a capacity for aggressive self-assertion, and a quality of manly sincerity.

A few of the women interviewed parenthetically mentioned that a woman concerned with her own "black" skin might want to marry a white-skinned man, hoping thereby to give birth to light-skinned daughters. A few younger women in favor of white skin in a man said that a white-skinned man is "more hairy" (or perhaps hair stands out better against a light background), and hairiness has a certain sexual appeal. Other women, however, expressed their dislike of body hair on a man. Some women mentioned a liking for a copper-brown skin tone. They associated this with manual outdoor labor, strong health, and masculinity, though not with intelligence. A reddish, shining face is thought to suggest lewdness in middle-aged fat men who have acquired wealth through shady activities. Such a figure stands in opposition to concepts of justice, sincerity, and spiritual cleanliness. The reddish face of a drinking man may look satisfied and peaceful to some women, though it is hardly considered attractive.

In these interviews with both men and women, the present attitudes toward Caucasian skin seem to fall into opposites of likes and dislikes depending, seemingly, upon the degree of an individual's receptivity toward or identification with Western culture. These two opposite attitudes may coexist within an individual, either appearing alternately or being expressed simultaneously. Somewhat more than half of both men and women interviewed in California and about two thirds of those interviewed in Japan considered Caucasian skin to be inferior to the Japanese from the standpoint of texture and regularity. This stereotype was among the negative attitudes expressed in the interviews.

> Caucasians' skin tends to be rough in texture, full of wrinkles, spots, and speckles.

> If you look at the neck of an old Caucasian woman with furrows and bristles, it reminds you of that of a pig.

> When I try to visualize a Caucasian woman, she is associated in my mind with skin of rough texture and unsmooth surface. Pores of her skin may be larger than ours. Young women may have smoother skin, but older women have bad skin.

> A Eurasian child will be very attractive it it takes a Japanese parent's skin and a Caucasian parent's facial structure, but the result of an opposite combination could be disastrous.

This notion concerning a Eurasian child seems to be fairly widely held among Japanese. The idea that Caucasian skin is "ugly" is also expressed in the following passage taken from the work of a contemporary Japanese novelist:

> When a kissing couple was projected on a large screen in a close-up, then the ugliness unique to Caucasian female skin was magnified. The freckles covering the woman's cheek and throat became clearly visible. . . . On the fingers of a man caressing a woman, gold hairs were seen shining like an animal's bristles.

Some informants who favored Japanese "white" skin but not Caucasian suggested that Caucasian skin is *not white* but *transparent:*

> This may be completely unscientific but I feel that when I look at the skin of a Japanese woman I see the whiteness of her skin. When I observe Caucasian skin, what I see is the whiteness of the fat underneath the skin, not the whiteness of the skin itself. Therefore, sometimes I see redness of blood under the transparent skin instead of white fat. Then it doesn't appear white but red.

> I have seen Caucasians closely only a few times but my impression is that their skin is very thin, almost transparent, while our skin is thicker and more resilient.

> The Caucasian skin is something like the surface of a pork sausage, while the white skin of a Japanese resembles the outside of *kamaboko* [a white, spongy fish cake].

Some men and women commented on the general hairiness of Caucasians. American women do not shave their faces and leave facial hair untouched. This causes the Japanese some discomfort since they are accustomed to a hairless, smooth face. (Japanese women customarily have their entire faces shaved except for the eyebrows.) Some women felt that the whiteness of Caucasian men lowered their appearance of masculinity; others disliked the hairiness of Caucasian men which they thought suggested a certain animality.

Japanese who have had little personal contact with Westerners often associate Caucasians with "strange creatures," if not with animality. Caucasian actors and actresses they constantly see on movie screens and on television may be the subject of their admiration for "manliness," "handsome or beautiful features," or "glamorous look," but "they don't seem to belong to reality." "Real" Caucasians are felt to be basically discontinuous with the Japanese. As one informant said:

When I think of actual Caucasians walking along the street, I feel that they are basically different beings from us. Certainly, they are humans but I don't feel they are the same creatures as we are. There is, in my mind, a definite discontinuity between us and the Caucasians. Somehow, they belong to a different world.

Deep in my mind, it seems, the Caucasians are somehow connected with something animal-like. Especially when I think of a middle-aged Caucasian woman, the first thing which comes up to my mind is a large chunk of boneless ham. This kind of association may not be limited to me. As I recall now, once in an English class at school, our teacher explained the meaning of the word "hog" as a big pig. A boy in our class said loudly, "Oh, I know what it is! It's like a foreign (meaning, Caucasian) woman!" We all laughed and I felt we all agreed with the boy.

For most of the Japanese without much personal contact with Westerners, skin is only one of several characteristics making up the image of a Caucasian. Other components of this image are the shape and color of eyes, hair, height, size, weight of the body, and also hairiness. Japanese feelings toward a Caucasian seem determined by all these factors. Many people interviewed in Japan talked of their difficulty in discussing their feelings toward Caucasian skin as differentiated from other Caucasian physical characteristics. An image of a Caucasian with white skin, deep-set eyes, wavy hair of a color other than black, a tall, stout, hairy body, and large hands and feet seems to evoke in many Japanese an association with "vitality," "superior energy," "strong sexuality" or "animality," and the feeling that Caucasians are basically discontinuous with Asians.

Positive attitudes toward Caucasian skin center on the idea that Caucasian skin is, in actuality, whiter than the so-called white skin of the Japanese and, therefore, more attractive. Two college students in California who had dated only Caucasian boys said Caucasian white skin meant to them purity, advanced civilization, and spiritual cleanliness. They felt that even white-skinned Japanese men were "not white enough" to attract them. Although there is no basis upon which to generalize, the following report by a student who had a sexual relationship with a white woman may deserve some note:

> Perhaps I was a little drunk. Under an electric light I saw her skin. It was so white that it was somehow incongruent with her nature. Such a pure whiteness and this girl of some questionable reputation.

He associated the whiteness of a woman's skin with purity and chastity, and felt white skin incongruent with the woman's promiscuous tendency.

A Japanese hairdresser married to a Japanese American disagreed with the notion that Caucasian skin is "ugly." She said that Caucasian women tend to have larger facial furrows; these are more visible than smaller wrinkles, but otherwise "their skin is no better or worse than ours." She added, however:

> After attending to several Caucasian customers in a row, when I turn to a Japanese lady, the change in color is very striking. She *is* yellow. It always comes to me as a kind of shock, this yellow color. Does it remind me of my own color?—I don't know. I think I know I am yellow. Do I still want to forget it?—maybe.

A sudden realization that Japanese skin color is darker when compared with the white skin of Caucasians has been the experience of several Japanese men and women in the United States:

> When I stay among Caucasian friends for some time and another Japanese joins the group, I look at him, my fellow countryman, and he looks yellow or even "black" to me. This, in turn, makes me momentarily self-conscious. I mean, I feel myself different in the group.

> My daughter is very "white" among the Japanese. Looking at her face, I often say to myself how white she is. As a mother, I feel happy. But when I see her among Caucasian children in a nursery school, alas, my daughter is *yellow* indeed.

It is interesting to note that Japanese who have spent time in the United States acquire the idea that Japanese are "yellow" rather than brown-skinned. Those we met in Japan, with only a few exceptions, hesitate or even refuse to describe their skin as "yellow." They know that the Japanese belong to the "yellow race" (*Ōshoku jinshu,* the technical term for the Mongoloid), but they cannot think of their skin as actually yellow, "unless," as some remarked, "a person comes down with jaundice."

Having few occasions to compare their skin color with that of other races, the Japanese apparently do not have any words available other than *black* and *white* to describe their skin. In modern Japan, *shakudō-iro* ("color of alloy of copper and gold") and *komugi-iro* ("color of wheat") are used to describe sun-tanned skin, but other words for brown and yellow are rarely employed. When I asked a thirty-year-old woman college graduate to describe the color of Japanese skin, she answered spontaneously, "Of course, it is *hada-iro* ['skin color']!" It is not known why the Japanese, after spending time among Caucasians, come to adopt the word *yellow* for their skin. This may be an attempt to adhere to common terminology, or it may be partially a continuation of a distinction between themselves and Southeast Asians, whom they consider to be darker-skinned.

The informant who had told us about the "yellow skin" of her daughter was asked if she felt unhappy about her daughter's "yellowness." Her answer was an emphatic no, although she admitted that the white skin of

Caucasian women is beautiful. A college graduate, married to a university professor, she suggested her solution to race problems:

> I think there should be three different standards of beauty to be applied separately to three groups of people of different colors. It is a confusion of these standards or the loss of one or two of them that leads to tragedy and frustration.

Many Japanese men, especially those in the United States, admit the beauty of white skin in Caucasian women, but also point out the sense of the inaccessibility of Caucasian women. Although the feeling of "basic discontinuity" between Japanese and Caucasians found among those without much contact with Westerners may become weakened as the Japanese spend time among the whites, it may sometimes persist in this feeling of basic remoteness and inaccessibility.

> Looking at the white skin I feel somehow that it belongs to a different world. People understand each other a great deal but there is something which people of different races cannot quite share. It sounds foolish and irrational, I know, but somehow this is the feeling I have, looking at the white skin of a Caucasian woman.

> White skin suggests a certain remoteness. When I went to Mexico, where most women are not white-skinned like the American, I felt more at home seeing them. I felt more comfortable.

> Sometimes I feel that the white skin of the Caucasians tells me that after all I am an Oriental and cannot acquire everything Western, however Westernized I might be. It is like the last border I cannot go across and it is symbolized by the white skin. Is this my inferiority feeling toward the white people—I often wonder.

An extreme expression of such inferiority feelings about the Japanese skin color compared with that of the Caucasians is found in *Up to Aden,* a short story by an award-winning, French-educated, Catholic author Endō Shūsaku. Written in 1954 when he was thirty years old, this is Endo Shūsaku's first literary work. In it he emphasizes the basic discontinuity between European tradition and Japanese culture, focusing symbolically upon the hero's somewhat exaggerated feelings about physical differences between a white French woman and himself. The hero, a Japanese student on his way home from France, shares a fourth-class cabin on a cargo boat with a very ill African woman. The story is a beautiful montage of what the student sees and feels on the boat until it reaches Aden and of his reminiscences of his painful love for a French girl while he was still in France. The following are several quotations from the story:

> "Race does not make any difference!" the [French] girl said impatiently. "The whites, the yellows or the blacks, they are all the same!" That was

what she said. Race does not make any difference. Later she fell in love with me and I did not refuse her love. Because there was this illusion that race does not make any difference. In the beginning, in love, we did not at all take into consideration that her body was white and my skin was yellow. When we kissed for the first time—it was in the evening on our way home from Mabillon where we had gone . . . dancing—I shouted almost unintentionally to the girl who was leaning against the wall with her eyes closed, "Are you sure? Are you sure you don't mind its being me?" But she simply answered, "Stop talking and hold me in your arms." If race did not make any difference, why on the earth did I have to utter such a miserable question, like a groan, at that time? If love had no frontiers and race did not matter, I should not have felt unself-confident even for a moment. In reality, however, I had to try instinctively not to envisage a certain truth hidden beneath my groan. I was afraid of it. Less than two months after that evening, the day finally came when I had to see the truth. It was in the last winter when the two of us made a trip together from Paris to Lyon. It was in the evening when for the first time we showed our skin to each other. . . . Breathlessly, we remained long in each other's arms. Golden hair had never looked to me more beautiful. Her naked body was of spotless, pure whiteness and her golden hair smoothly flowed down from her shoulders. She was facing toward a door. I was facing toward curtained windows. As the light was on, our naked bodies were visible in a mirror on an *armoire*. In the beginning I could not believe what I had seen in the mirror was really my body. My naked body had been very well proportioned for a Japanese. I was as tall as a European and I was full in chest and limbs. Speaking of the body form, I would not look inharmonious when holding a white woman in my arms. But what I saw reflected in the mirror was something else. Beside the gleaming whiteness of her shoulders and breasts in the lighted room, my body looked dull in a lifeless, dark yellow color. My chest and stomach did not look too bad, but around the neck and shoulders turbid yellow color increased its dullness. The two different colors of our bodies in embrace did not show even a bit of beauty or harmony. It was ugly. I suddenly thought of a worm of a yellow muddy color, clinging to a pure white flower. The color of my body suggested a human secretion, like bile. I wished I could cover my face and body with my hands. Cowardly, I turned off the light to lose my body in darkness. . . . "Hold me tight. We are in love and that is enough," she said to me once when we kissed at a street corner in dusk. But it was not enough that we were in love. By love only, she could not become a yellow woman and I could not become a white man. Love, logic and ideology could not erase differences in skin color. . . . White men had allowed me to enter their world as long as their pride was not hurt. They had allowed me to wear their clothes, drink their wine and love a white woman. They could not accept that a white woman loved me. They could not accept it because white people's skin is white and beautiful and because I am yellow and ugly. They could not stand a white woman falling in love with a man of such lifeless, muddy yellow color. Foolishly enough, I had not known or thought of it at all until this day [when the girl had announced her engagement to a Japanese man only to invite frightened blame and anger from her friends].

Lying down in the fourth class cabin, I watch the feverish dark brown body of a sick African woman in front of my eyes. I truly feel her skin color is ugly. Black color is ugly and yellow turbid color is even more miserable. I and this Negro woman both belong eternally to ugly races. I do not know why and how only the white people's skin became the standard of beauty. I do not know why and how the standard of human beauty in sculpture and paintings all stemmed from the white body of the Greeks and has been so maintained until today. But what I am sure of is that in regard to the body, those like myself and Negroes can never forget miserable inferiority feelings in front of people possessing white skin, however vexing it might be to admit it.

Three years ago when I came to Europe in high spirits, and when I came through this Suez canal, I had not yet given much thought to the fact that I was yellow. In my passport it was written that I was a Japanese, but at that time in my mind Japanese were the same human beings as white people, both possessing reason and concepts. I had thought, like a Marxian, of class struggle and race conflict but I had never thought of color conflict. Class conflict may be removed but color conflict will remain eternally and eternally, I am yellow and she is white.

Though it seems somewhat painful for most Japanese to be frank about it (and many of them refuse to do so), there is among Japanese intellectuals a more or less unconscious, if not conscious, ambivalence toward the world of white people. Such an attitude is understandable if one takes even a brief glance at Japan's modern history. Japan, at first overwhelmed by an apprehension of the Western world's great power, caught up with the West in an amazingly short time. Then, feeling a sense of rejection over unequal treatment, Japan appointed itself a champion of non-white Asians. In this role, it boldly tried to win a place in the company of white imperialists. Failing disastrously after all, Japan found itself receiving a "democratic education" from its American teachers toward whom it felt the greatest rivalry mixed with admiration.

The diffuse ambivalence toward Western civilization may very well be focalized in the admiration, envy, sense of being overwhelmed or threatened, fear, or disgust that are evoked in the Japanese mind by the image of a hairy giant who, with his great vigor and strong sexuality, can easily satisfy an equally energetic and glamorous creature. Consequently, actual sexual experiences with a white woman may help some Japanese to overcome such feelings of inferiority toward Caucasians.

One of the persons interviewed remarked that his uncle once told him that during Japan's control over Manchuria many Japanese men enjoyed sleeping with white Russian prostitutes:

> My uncle said, having a relationship with a white woman made these men feel different, more masculine or something. The feeling is different from that one has after having a relationship with an Asian woman.

Generally, however, Japanese men, as authors of travel books suggest, seem rather overwhelmed and discouraged by the large physique of a white woman. This is well portrayed by author Tamura Taijiō, who is known for his bold description of human sexuality. In his reminiscences on twelve women, he describes a Russian prostitute he met in Shanghai in 1934 after graduating from a university:

> Her stout body of large build also overwhelmed my feelings. . . . My arms were bigger than those of an average Japanese, but hers were much bigger than mine, almost beyond comparison. When I sat next to her, the volume and weight of her whole body made me feel inferiority and think that I was of a race physically smaller and weaker than hers. . . . "Shall we dance?" the woman talked to me perfunctorily. I put my arms around her and again I was frightened. The girth of her chest was all too broad. It did not belong to the category of chest I had known from the Japanese women. It certainly was something which wriggled in an uncanny way, something which made me wonder what she had been eating everyday. . . . "Come on!" she said. Between two heavy cylinders, like logs, covered up to thighs with black stockings, which were the only thing she wore, the central part of the woman swoll in a reddish color. It was a bizarre view. . . . It was no doubt beyond the imagination of the vegetarian Japanese how the meat-diet of these women made their sexual desire burn and blaze violently and irrepressibly.

In contrast to this complex of attitudes about Caucasoid racial traits, the Japanese attitudes toward the black skin and facial characteristics of Negro Americans encountered during the Occupation were generally negative, although a number of Japanese women married Negro men. The Japanese interviewed in California, being intellectuals and living in the United States, were all keenly aware of the recent racial issues. Most of them made such statements as:

> I know people should not feel different about Negroes and I have no negative notions about them.

> I have nothing against them. I don't think I have any prejudice against them.

These measured comments would be followed by a "but," and then would come various expressions, usually negative:

I feel resistance to coming closer to them.

It's almost a physical reaction and has nothing to do with my thinking.

It's almost like a biological repulsion.

It's the feeling of uneasiness and something uncanny.

These were the reactions of the Japanese to Negro features as a total *Gestalt* (eyes, hair, nose, and lips) but particularly to black skin.

I think it is simply a matter of custom or habit. We are not accustomed to black skin. I have a Negro friend, very black. I respect him as a scholar and we are close friends and yet I still feel I am not yet used to his black skin. It's something terribly alien to my entire life. It is much better now than it was two years ago when I first met him.

Coming to this country, I had not known that a Negro's palm was different in color from the back of his hand. I was playing cards with two Americans and one African student and I suddenly noticed the color of this African student's palm. I felt I saw something which I had never seen in my life. All that evening, playing cards, I could not help looking at his hands time after time. . . . I just could not get over it.

A year after my arrival, I was introduced to an American Negro for the first time. He was a very friendly person and immediately extended his hand toward me. At that very brief moment, I hesitated. No. I did not hesitate but my arm did. My arm resisted being extended forward. Like a light flashing through my mind, I said to myself, "there is no reason why I don't want to shake hands with this black man." I did shake hands with him and I do hope he did not sense my momentary hesitation. Since then I have never hesitated to shake hands with a Negro.

The idea that black skin is something novel to the Japanese and only for that reason difficult for them to get used to was also voiced by a Japanese woman married to a Negro American.

Frankly, I felt uneasy about it [black skin] in the beginning, but you see it every day, from morning to evening; there is nothing else you can do except to get used to it. I did get used to it. Especially since he was very nice and kind all the time. Once you get used to it, you no longer see it.

The same idea is stated in a novel by Ariyoshi Sawako, a contemporary Japanese author. Although written as a comment by the heroine, a Japanese woman married to a Negro, it most probably reflects the author's frank feminine reaction to Negroid features:

The Negro's facial features—black skin, round eyes, thick round nose, big thick lips—may very well look animal-like to the eyes of those accustomed only to a yellow or a white face. Living long enough among the Negroes, however, one comes to realize how human their faces are. . . .

> The color of the Negro skin gives one an overwhelming impression but once one gets over it, one notices how gentle their facial features are.

Incidentally, this novel, with the English subtitle *Not Because of Color,* is of special interest for us. Ariyoshi spent a few years in the United States as a Rockefeller Fellow. She then returned to Japan and wrote this novel, in which she describes the life of a Japanese woman married to a Negro in New York's Harlem. She also depicts a few other uneducated Japanese women married to Negro, Puerto Rican, and Italian Americans, as contrasted with a highly intellectual Japanese woman married to a Jewish college professor and working at the U.N. As suggested by the subtitle, Ariyoshi seemingly wanted to emphasize that—in spite of the prejudiced opinion of many white Americans and Japanese—laziness, apathy, lack of conjugal stability, and many other inferior characteristics attributed to Negro Americans are not racially inherent qualities, but the products of their degraded social status. The author accurately describes common Japanese reactions to Negro-Japanese marriages and their offspring. The heroine's mother, learning that her daughter wants to marry a Negro soldier, says:

> Our family has been honored by its warrior ancestry. Though we were not well-to-do, none of us has ever shamed the name of our family. And you, a member of our respectable family, wish to marry a man of such blackness! How shall we apologize to our ancestors? If you wish to marry an "American," that might be a different matter. But marrying that black man!
>
> Embraced by such a black one, don't you feel disgusted? I am afraid of him. Why don't you feel strange?

When the heroine takes her daughter to downtown Tokyo, people around them loudly voice their reactions to her child with Negro blood:

> Look, the child of a *kuronbo* ["black one"].
>
> Indeed, it's black, even when it is young.
>
> She looks like a rubber doll.
>
> She must have taken only after her father. So black. Poor thing.

Animal Husbandry, written by Ōe Kenzaburō when he was still a French literature student at the University of Tokyo in 1957, is the story of a Negro flier on a B-29 bomber in World War II. The flier bails out of the plane when it is shot down and lands on a mountain. Caught by Japanese villagers, he is kept in a stable like an animal. Eventually some of the villagers butcher him because they are afraid.

The story describes not only the village children's fear of an enemy soldier and their association of a Negro with an animal, but also their discovery of his "humanity" and their timid affection for him. As is already clear from the title, the Negro soldier, "with bristle-covered heavy fingers . . . thick rubber-like lips . . . springy black shining skin . . . frizzled short hair . . . and . . . suffocating body odor," was often associated with an animal. For example, "The wet skin of the naked Negro soldier shone like that of a black horse."

A third story to be mentioned here is the work of Matsumoto Seichō, a widely read author of numerous mystery and documentary stories. In this short story, two hundred and fifty Negro soldiers enroute to Korea break out of Jomo Camp in Northern Kyushu one night and attack civilian houses around the camp. Many women are raped. Two other companies of American troops are called out to subdue the disturbances; most of the soldiers are brought back to the barracks within several hours and sent to the Korean front a few days later. A Japanese man whose wife had been assaulted by a group of Negroes divorces his wife and begins working at the Army Grave Registration Service, as a carrier of corpses. One day, he finally finds what he has been looking for: the corpses of two Negro soldiers he remembered by their obscene tattoos. They were among those who raped his wife. Out of his anger, hatred, and desire for revenge, the man stabs the corpses with an autopsy knife. The Negroes in this story are frequently associated with animals and also with the primitive natives of the African jungle:

> The sound of drums at a village festival was heard from far. It reminded them [Negro soldiers] of the rapture of their ancestors, who beat cylindrical and conical drums at ceremonies and in hunting, and whose same blood was running through them. . . . The melody in the distance was following the rhythmic pulsing of the human body. Unavoidably it stimulated their dancing instinct and they began moving their shoulders up and down and waving their hands in fascination. They started breathing hard, with their heads tilted and their nostrils enlarged. . . . Thick sounds and rhythm of drums woke the hunters' blood in them.
>
> Their bodies were all dark like shadows but their eyes shone like patches of white paper. . . . His white eyes shone like the inside of a sea shell but the rest of his face was black, his nose, cheeks, jaw and all. . . . His thick lips were pink and dull in color. . . . Hair was kinky as if scorched. . . . Their bodies exhaled a strong foul smell of beasts. . . . When he took off his shirt, his upper body looked like that of a rhinoceros, with rich heaps of black flesh. The skin looked almost ready to squeak when moved, like tanned leather of black color. . . . When naked, his body was swollen, abdomen hanging low. It was cylindrical like a monkey's body.

Other Japanese interviewed considered that the Japanese attitude toward black skin is more than just a simple reaction to something novel. According to this view, black skin is associated in the Japanese mind with many undesirable traits; other Negroid features are also the opposite of what Japanese have long valued as desirable physical characteristics:

> Blackness is often combined with death, vice, despair and other kinds of negative things. "A black-bellied man" is wicked. "Black mood" is depression.

> When something becomes dirty and smeared, it gets black. White skin in our minds symbolizes purity and cleanliness. Then, by an association, black skin is the opposite of purity and cleanliness. . . . Black skin after all suggests something unclean. It is not the natural state of things.

> Speaking of a Japanese face, we do not appreciate such features as a pug nose, snub nose, squatting nose, goggle eyes, thick lips, kinky hair. They are despised and often made a laughingstock. They often suggest foolishness or crudity and backwardness among Japanese. What is preferred is all the opposites of these. But just think. Aren't they what the Negroes usually have?

The following report by a graduate student who had sexual relations with a Negro woman shows that guilt feeling over sexuality can become focused on the blackness of skin, conceived as dirty:

> I was not in love with her, nor was she with me. It was a play. To say the truth, I was curious about a Negro, after hearing so much about them. When it was over, however, I had to take a shower. The idea shocked me because it was ridiculous but I was caught by an urge. It was almost a sudden compulsion, to wash my body off, and I did.

Unlike the Japanese interviewed in California, those who were questioned in Japan expressed their feelings toward Negro Americans and Africans without reservation. They were undifferentiatedly seen by them as "black men, with inhumanly black skin, goggle eyes, thick lips, kinky hair, strong body odor, and animal-like sexuality and energy." The feelings toward such an image were invariably negative. Many said that they felt indignation toward the white American discrimination against Negroes. Some were very fond of Negro musicians. Negro baseball players were well liked. And yet, as one said, their "basic feelings are repulsion and disgust toward Negro features"; these feelings were frequently justified as a "physiological reaction, which one's reasoning cannot control."

Such strongly negative attitudes toward Negro physical characteristics certainly pose problems for the mixed-blood children of Negro American fathers and Japanese mothers, although nobody has yet made a systematic study of the lives of these children in postwar Japan. Three lower-class

Japanese with less than six years of primary education independently voiced an astonishing notion when interviewed; they believed that if a Japanese woman gave birth to the black baby of a Negro man, her next baby, and probably the third one also, of a Japanese father would show some black tinge on the body. In other words, in the mind of these men, impregnation of a Japanese woman by a Negro man was associated with "blackening" of her womb as though by ink, so that the second and even the third baby conceived in it would become "stained."

The type of Negro the Japanese think attractive or handsome, or the least objectionable, is a light-skinned individual with Caucasian features. For this reason, they all find Hindu Indians with their Caucasoid facial structure generally more acceptable, even though the Hindus' black skin still groups them with African and American Negroes. The Japanese are not ready to appreciate a very Negroid Negro as attractive; the newly emergent trend among the Negro Americans has not yet made any impression in Japan.

The Negro in the Japanese language is either *koku-jin* ("black person") or *kuronbo* ("black ones"); the former is a neutral word, but the latter has a definitely belittling, if not derogatory, tone. According to a philologist, the origin of *kuronbo* is Colombo, a city of Ceylon. In the seventeenth century, Colombo was pronounced by the Japanese as "kuronbo" or abbreviated as "kuro," probably because of the association with the word *black* (*kuro*) since the servants on the Dutch boats, identified as "people from Colombo," were actually black-skinned. The word *bo,* originally meaning a Buddhist priest's lodge and then the priest himself, came also to mean a boy or "sonny." A suffix to certain words with the meaning of "little one," such as *akan-bo* ("a little red one": "a baby") and *sakuran-bo* ("cherry"), *bo* also creates belittling or even contemptuous connotations in other words, such as *wasuren-bo* ("a forgetful one"), *namaken-bo* ("a lazy one"), or *okorin-bo* ("a quick-tempered one"). By the same token, *kuron-bo* ("a black one") carries the connotation of childishness.

Most Japanese born before 1935 first discovered Negroes by singing "Old Black Joe" and other Stephen Foster melodies in music classes at school or by reading the Japanese translation of *Uncle Tom's Cabin.* Although they might have related the lot of Negro Americans to a vague notion of injustice, such a life remained for most Japanese children a remote world. Another sort of encounter with black people, with more direct reference to their color, was evidenced in a cartoon serialized for many years in a popular magazine for children, *Adventurous Dankichi,* and in a popular song, "The Chief's Daughter," dating from the 1920's. Dankichi was a Japanese boy who put to sea one day to go fishing and, while asleep, drifted to an island somewhere in the South Pacific. On the island, Dankichi outwitted the black natives by his cleverness and ingenuity and became their king. He wore a crown on his head and rode on a white elephant near rivers inhabited by crocodiles.

This fantasy cartoon blended ideas about South Pacific islanders and primitive tribes in Africa. Originally cannibalistic and warlike, these people could become loyal though somewhat simpleminded subjects when tamed and educated. It is worth noting that this was the kind of image of "black people" to which most Japanese children of the prewar period were exposed. "The Chief's Daughter" created an image of carefree South Sea islanders with black skin who danced away their lives under the swaying palm trees.

> My lover is the Chief's daughter.
> Though her color is black
> She is a beauty in the South Seas. . . .
> Let us dance, dance under the palm trees
> Those who don't dance, no girls will care to marry. . . .

In 1958 and 1959, there was a sudden fad for a small plastic doll called *Dakko-chan* ("a caressable one"). It was a jet black and very much caricaturized Negro child of about one foot in height when inflated; its hands extended in such a way that it could cling to a person's arm or a pole. It was so widely sold that almost every house had one, and the manufacturers could not keep up with the demand. A great many teen-agers as well as younger children carried it around with them on the streets. It was, indeed, a cute little doll, but it did not help the Japanese form an image of a more dignified adult Negro.

V

Since a very early time in history, the Japanese have valued the skin color they consider "white." The Japanese "white" skin is, above all, *unsuntanned* skin, while Mongoloid skin is, in actuality, very sensitive to the tanning action of the sun. Japanese, particularly the women, tried hard to remain "white," jealously guarding their skin from exposure to the sun. An old Japanese expression observes, "In the provinces where one can see Mt. Fuji, one can hardly see beautiful women." The districts traditionally known for their white, smooth-skinned native beauties are, consequently, Izumo, Niigata, and Akita. These are all located on the Japan Sea coast where in long, snowy winter weather one rarely enjoys sunlight. Conversely, where one can see Mt. Fuji, one also enjoys a warm Pacific climate year-round and a certain continuous sunshine which can tan unguarded skin.

Mainly due to modern Japan's contact with the Western world, the Japanese became aware of the "white" skin of the Caucasians, "whiter" than the "whitest" skin of the Japanese. This could cause disappointment when they compared themselves with the Caucasians, whom they sought to emulate by guided modernization programs of industrialization, as well as in spontaneous leisure-time fads and aesthetic pursuits. During the earlier contact, the charm of the Caucasian white skin was counterbalanced by reactions to light-colored hair and eyes, and body hair—distasteful traits in terms of Japanese aesthetic standards. Under the post-World War II impact of American culture, a preference for Western facial structure and hair style brought the Japanese sense of physical aesthetics ever closer to that of Caucasians. The historical inferiority-superiority complex of this extremely Westernized Eastern nation seems today to reflect mixed attitudes toward Caucasian skin. There is the notion that Caucasian skin is "ugly" in texture and quality, thus maintaining a Japanese skin supremacy, while at the same time admitting the better appearance of the refined Caucasian facial structure.

Up to the present, the color of Negroid skin and other physical features find little favor in Japanese aesthetics. One may argue that it is simply because the Japanese are not accustomed to black skin; but one can also contend that "blackness" has been symbolically associated in the Japanese mind, as elsewhere, with things evil or negative and that the image of a Negro hitherto created in Japan has been that of a primitive, childish, simple-minded native. Relatively little note has been taken to date of the emergence of a new Africa under its modern leaders.

It remains a curious fact of Japanese identity that there is relatively little kinship expressed with any Asian countries other than China, toward which present-day Japan feels less and less cultural debt. Japanese eyes, despite cases of plastic surgery, may keep their Oriental look, but through these eyes Japanese see themselves as part of the modern Western world conceptualized in Western terms. Some Japanese wish to change their physical identity from that of a Japanese to something else, but are countered by a vague sense of resignation that such a change is not possible.

Still in search of their national identity, the Japanese are experiencing some difficulties in maintaining and protecting the standards of Japanese beauty and handsomeness from the onslaughts of standardized images produced by the Western cinema. Preoccupied with changing standards, the Japanese may be slow to note a new convergent perception of beauty entering the West, which includes traditional Japanese aesthetic standards in art, architecture, and even in Mongoloid physical beauty. Physical attractiveness is gradually losing its unitary cultural or racial basis in most societies. Art or beauty cannot be maintained in a fixed, single standard. Each changes with the diversity of experiences.

PETER ABRAHAMS

The Blacks

The theme of this essay is the conflict between tribalism and Westernism and the fact that, in tribal Africa, ". . . being black did not of itself qualify one for acceptance."

IT WAS A HOT, humid, oppressive August day in Accra, capital of the Gold Coast that was to become Ghana. The air had the stillness of death. I walked down toward the sea front. Perhaps there would be the hint of a breeze there. As I neared the sea front I was assailed by a potent stench of the sea with strong overtones of rotting fish.

The houses were drab, run-down wooden structures or made of corrugated iron, put together any way you please. The streets were wide and tarred, and each street had an open drainage system into which young boys and old men piddled when they needed to relieve themselves. I have seen women empty chamber pots into these drains in the early morning. The fierce sun takes care of the germs, but God help you if smells make you sick.

In about eight minutes of walking, some fifteen "taxis" pulled up beside me: "Hi, massa! Taxi, massa! Me go anywhere you go cheap!" They are all private taxis with no meters and driven by strapping young men with flashing teeth. The place is full of taxi drivers willing to go anywhere and do anything cheap.

The street traders here are women. "Mammy traders," they are called. They trade in everything. They sell cigarettes, one at a time; round loaves of bread and hunks of cooked meat on which the big West African flies make sport. They love bargaining and haggling. They are a powerful economic factor in the life of the country. The more prosperous ones own their own trucks, some own fleets of trucks. These "mammy trucks" are the principal carriers of the country. They carry passengers as well as produce and go hurtling across the countryside with little regard for life or limb. Each truck has its own distinctive slogan, such as: *Repent for Death is Round the Corner,* or *Enter Without Hope,* or *The Last Ride* or *If it Must it Will.* My own favorite—and I traveled in this particular truck—pleaded *Not Today O Lord Not Today.*

I passed many mammy traders, many mammy trucks, before I reached the sea front. I crossed a street, jumped over an open drain, and there was the sea. But there was no breeze, and no shade from the terrible sun. In the end I gave in to the idea of "taxi, massa, taxi" and looked about for one. But now there was no taxi in sight. Instead, I saw suddenly a long procession of many women and a few men. The procession swung round a corner and came into full view, twenty or thirty yards long. The women wore white flowing robes and white kerchiefs on their heads. Their faces were painted into grotesque masks made with thick streaks of black, red, white and yellow paints. The heavy thud of bare feet rose above the hum of the sea.

Then, all at once, the drums burst forth and there was no other sound about me. The marching women began to jig, then dance. As the tail of the procession passed me the drums reached a frenzy. A thin, pure note from a reed rose above the drums. The whole procession became a shivering, shaking mass. The reed note held longer than seemed human. And then, dramatically, there was silence. The thudding feet faded away out of sight and sound. There was silence and a slight racing of my heartbeat and the hum of the sea, and, of course, the overpowering fishy stench.

I thought of Richard Wright, with whom I had had breakfast that morning. This was his first visit to any part of Africa and he seemed to find it bewildering. Countee Cullen, the late American Negro poet, had speculated:

One three centuries removed
From the scenes his fathers loved,
Spicy grove, cinnamon tree,
What is Africa to me?

Wright was finding the answers and finding them disconcerting. He had been astounded by the casual attitude to sex. There was, he had said, too much sex, too casually given and taken; so that it worked out as no sex, with none of the emotional involvement associated with sex in the western mind. He shook his head with a slight disgust. The open drains into which young boys and old men piddled had led him to conclude that Africans piddled rather more than other people. The sight of young men dancing together, holding hands, disturbed the puritan in him. He expressed to me that morning what he later summed up in his book on the Gold Coast: "I was black and they were black but it did not help me."

What Wright did not understand, what his whole background and training had made difficult for him to understand, was that being black did not of itself qualify one for acceptance in tribal Africa. But how could he, when there are thousands of urban-bred Africans up and down the vast continent who do not themselves understand this? The more perceptive of the urban Africans are only now beginning to comprehend, but slowly.

Being black is a small matter in tribal Africa because the attitude toward color is healthy and normal. Color does not matter. Color is an act of God that neither confers privileges nor imposes handicaps on a man. A man's skin is like the day: the day is either clear or dark. There is nothing more to it until external agencies come in and invest it with special meaning and importance.

What does matter to the tribal African, what is important, is the complex pattern of his position within his own group and his relations with the other members of the group. He is no Pan-African dreaming of a greater African glory when the white man is driven into the sea. The acute race consciousness of the American Negro, or of the black South African at the receiving end of apartheid, is alien to him. The important things in his life are anything but race and color—until they are forced on him. And "Mother Africa" is much too vast to inspire big continental dreams in him. She is a land of huge mountains, dark jungles and vast deserts. In her rivers and in her jungles and in her grasslands lurk creatures that are the enemies of man: the leopard and the lion, the snake and crocodile. All this makes travel, by the old African methods, extremely difficult and makes for isolation between one group of people and another. The African who is in Britain is likely to be a deal better informed on what is happening all over the continent than would be his fellow African in any of the main centers of both tribal and nontribal Africa. In terms of communications the man in the tribe lives in the Dark Ages.

Richard Wright was surprised that even educated Africans, racially conscious literate people, had not heard of him and were skeptical of a grown man earning his living by writing. They could not understand what kind of writing brought a man enough money to support a family. Wright really wanted to understand the African, but—"I found the African an oblique, a hard-to-know man."

My sympathies were all with Wright.

The heat and salty rancid fish smell had made me desperately thirsty. Across the way a mammy trader squatted beside her pile of merchandise: cooked meats, sweet potatoes—a whole host of edibles—and some bottles of opaque white liquid that could be either coconut milk or palm juice as well as the inevitable little pile of cigarettes priced at a penny apiece. I had been warned of the risks involved in eating anything sold by the street traders. But to hell with it, I was thirsty and not exactly a stranger to African germs. I crossed the street, felt the bottles and chose the one that seemed coolest and looked the least opaque.

"How much?"

"One shilling." The carved ebony face looked at me with dead eyes.

I pulled the screwed-up newspaper stopper from the bottle, wiped its mouth and took a swig. I could not decide whether it was coconut milk or palm juice. It had been heavily watered down and sweetened. But it was wet and thirst-quenching. I drank half the bottle, firmly ignoring the little foreign bodies that floated in the liquid. Then I paid her and drank the rest. I put down the empty and began to move away.

"You African?" she asked in her harsh, cold, masculine voice.

I stopped, turned and looked at her face. It was as deadly cold and impersonal as before: not a flicker of feeling in her eyes. Like an African mask, I thought. But unlike Wright, I did not try to penetrate it; I knew the futility of trying. She would show feeling if and when she decided, not before.

"Yes," I said, and added, "from the south. Far, far south."

She paused for so long that I began to move again.

"You like here?" Nationalism had obviously touched her.

I turned back to her. "No," I said.

"Why you don't like?"

"I don't say I don't like."

"But you don't like?"

I showed her my teeth, African-wise, which is neither smile nor grimace but a blending of the two. "You like Africa?" I asked.

Now it was her turn to show me her teeth. There was a flicker of feeling in her eyes, then they went dead again. She nodded. I had established my claim. Only outsiders—white people or the Richard Wrights—liked or disliked Africa.

I left the mammy trader and carried on up the smelly and hot street. Much and little had passed between us. Out to sea some fishing boats appeared on the sky line. About me were the citizens of Accra. Some wore the cloth of the country—the men looking like pint-sized citizens of ancient Rome painted black and the women looking extraordinarily masculine—and others wore western dress.

My thoughts shifted to my forthcoming meeting with Kwame Nkrumah, Ghana's first prime minister. It was well over seven years since I had last seen him, in London. Then he was a poor struggling student; now he was the head of a state and the spokesman for the great Pan-African dream of freedom and independence.

I remembered our past friendship and wondered what changes I would find in him. Anyway, it was now 9 A.M. and my date with him was for 9:30. I would soon know.

A few minutes later I flagged a taxi and simply said, "Kwame's office."

A pale-brown West Indian miss was the prime minister's secretary. She welcomed me as though I was a V.I.P. The prime minister had not come back from a conference yet. This tribal business was taking up a lot of his attention. She told me with indignation how members of the Ashanti tribe had to crawl on their bellies for some twenty yards into the presence of their king, the Asantehene, and how tribalism had to give way or there would be no progress. If she was any indication, then Nkrumah was very worried about the opposition the tribesmen were offering his western-style Convention People's Party.

A number of officials came in. The lady stopped assailing the tribes. Then there was some bustle and the prime minister arrived. In something just over five minutes he had seen and dealt with these officials and I was ushered into his office. It was a big, pleasant, cool room.

Nkrumah came round his big official desk, took my hand and led me to a settee near the window. The now famous smile lit up his face. As we exchanged greetings, felt each other out with small talk in an attempt to bridge the gap of years, my mind went back to our London days. This poised, relaxed man, with the hint of guarded reserve about him, was a far cry from the friend I had last seen nearly eight years earlier.

For me, the most striking change of all was in his eyes. They reflected an inner tranquillity which was the one thing the Nkrumah in Europe never had.

Even his name had been subtly different then. He had been our friend Francis Nkrumah, an African student recently arrived from the United States, and he had not seen Africa for a decade and more. He had quickly become a part of our African colony in London and had joined our little group, the Pan-African Federation, in our protests against colonialism.

He was much less relaxed than most of us. His eyes mirrored a burning inner conflict and tension. He seemed consumed by a restlessness that led him to evolve some of the most fantastic schemes.

The president of our federation was an East African named Johnstone Kenyatta, the most relaxed, sophisticated and "westernized" of the lot of us. Kenyatta enjoyed the personal friendship of some of the most distinguished people in English political and intellectual society. He was subtle, subtle enough to attack one's principles bitterly and retain one's friendship. He fought the British as imperialists but was affectionate toward them as friends.

It was to this balanced and extremely cultured man that Francis Nkrumah proposed that we form a secret society called The Circle, and that each of us spill a few drops of our blood into a bowl and so take a blood oath of secrecy and dedication to the emancipation of Africa.

Johnstone Kenyatta laughed at the idea; he scoffed at it as childish juju. He conceived our struggle in modern, twentieth-century terms with no ritualistic blood nonsense. In the end Francis Nkrumah drifted away from us and started his own little West African group in London. We were too tame and slow for him. He was an angry man in a hurry.

Then he went back to his part of Africa, and Francis Nkrumah became Kwame Nkrumah. He set himself at the head of the largely tribal populace and dabbled in blood ritual. There was some violence, a spell in prison, and finally Nkrumah emerged as the first African prime minister in a self-governing British African territory.

Tribal myths grew up around him. He could make himself invisible at will. He could go without food and sleep and drink longer than ordinary mortals. He was, in fact, the reincarnation of some of the most powerful ancestral spirits. He allowed his feet to be bathed in blood.

By the time I visited the Gold Coast the uneasy alliance between Nkrumah and the tribal chiefs had begun to crack. A week or so before my arrival he had threatened that, unless they co-operated with his government in turning the Gold Coast into an efficient twentieth-century state, he would make them run so hard that they would leave their sandals behind them. This was a calculated insult to the tribal concept that a chief's bare feet must never touch the earth.

That was the beginning of the secret war. Nkrumah thought he would win it easily. He was wrong.

And the chiefs have, negatively, scored their victories too. They have pushed him to a point where his regime is, today, intolerant of opposition. The tribal society brooks no opposition. Nkrumah's government banishes its most active opponents. As a modern socialist leading a western-style government, he justifies this as a temporary expedient. But his less sophisticated ministers frankly talk the tribal language of strength, frankly express the tribal impulse to destroy those who are out of step.

There was an air of delicacy about our conversation and we were both aware of this. We touched on local politics. He let off at full blast against the tribalist. I told him I had heard that the Accra Club was still exclusively European. His eyes lit up. "You wait and see," he said. Then, in relation to nothing either of us had said, he leaned toward me and exclaimed, "This place is rich! God, man, there's so much riches here!"—as though the revelation had just been made to him.

But always, throughout our talk, I sensed a new reserve, a new caution that had not been there in the young student I had known in Europe.

As we talked in Nkrumah's cool office that hot August day in Accra, my mind kept slipping back to our mutual friend Jomo or Johnstone Kenyatta, now imprisoned in his native Kenya for leading the Mau-Mau movement. Significantly, though we mentioned many friends, both Nkrumah and I avoided Kenyatta. I had decided not to mention him first. I had hoped Nkrumah would. He did not.

A year earlier, I had flown up to Kenya from South Africa and visited Kenyatta. I felt terribly depressed as I got off the plane. Things had grown so much uglier in the Union. The barricades were up in the ugly war of color. When I had left South Africa in the dim-and-distant past, there

were isolated islands where black and white could meet in neutral territory. When I went back in 1952, the islands were submerged under the rising tide of color hatreds, and I was glad to quit that dark, unhappy land
which yet compelled my love.

It was in this mood that I got off the plane. I had not seen my friend
Jomo for years. Now there he was, just outside the airport terminal building, leaning on a heavy cane, bigger than I remembered him in Europe,
paunchy, his face looking puffy. And behind him was a huge crowd of Africans.

I began to move toward him when a lean-faced, lean-hipped white colo-
nial-administrator type suddenly appeared beside me and said: "Mr. Abrahams."

I stopped and thought, "Oh, Lord."

Kenyatta also came forward. The two men ignored each other.
Lean-face introduced himself and said the Colonial Office had alerted
them that I was coming to do some writing for the London *Observer* and
they had drawn up a provisional schedule for me. Had I done anything
about accommodations?

Before I could answer, Kenyatta said, "You are staying with me, of
course." The old detachment was back in his eyes. They seemed to say,
"You've got to choose, pal. Let's see how you choose."

Lean-face said, "We've got something set up for you for tomorrow
and—"

"I live in the bush," Kenyatta added.

It dawned on me that I had become, for the moment, the battlefield of
that horrible animal, the racial struggle. I made up my mind, resenting
both sides and yet conscious of the crowd of Africans in the background.
A question of face was involved.

"I've promised to spend this week end with Mr. Kenyatta," I said.

Lean-face was graceful about it. I promised to call the Secretariat first
thing on Monday morning. He gave me a copy of the schedule that had
been prepared for me and wondered, *sotto voce,* whether I knew what I
was letting myself in for. Kenyatta assured me that I would be perfectly
safe, that nobody was going to cut my throat. I was aware that they were
talking to each other through me. I was aware that they knew I was aware,
and that made me bad-tempered.

"Then I'll say good night, Mr. Abrahams," Lean-face said pointedly.

As soon as he was out of hearing Kenyatta began to curse.

"It's good to see you again, Johnstone," I gripped his hand.

"Jombo," he replied. The hint of ironic speculation was back in his
eyes. A slightly sardonic, slightly bitter smile played on his lips.

"Welcome to Kenya, Peter," he said. Then, abruptly: "Come meet the
leaders of my people. They've been waiting long."

We moved forward and the crowd gathered about us. Jomo made a little speech in Kikuyu, then translated it for my benefit. A little old man, ancient as the hills, with huge holes in his ears, then welcomed me on behalf of the land and its people. Again Jomo translated.

After this we all bundled into the fleet of rattling old cars and set off for the Kikuyu reserve in the heart of the African bush. Kenyatta became silent and strangely remote during the journey.

We stopped at the old chief's compound, where other members of the tribe waited to welcome me. By this time the reception committee had grown to a few hundred. About me, pervading the air, was the stench of burning flesh; a young cow was being roasted in my honor. Before I entered the house a drink was handed to me. Another was handed to the old chief and a third to Kenyatta. The old man muttered a brief incantation and spilled half his drink on the earth as a libation. Jomo and I followed suit. Then the three of us downed our drinks and entered the house.

A general feasting and drinking then commenced, both inside and outside the house. I was getting a full ceremonial tribal welcome. The important dignitaries of the tribe slipped into the room in twos and threes, spoke to me through Kenyatta for a few moments, and then went away, making room for others.

"Africa doesn't seem to change," Kenyatta murmured between dignitaries. There was a terrible undercurrent of bitterness behind the softly murmured words. I was startled by it and looked at his face. For a fleeting moment he looked like a trapped, caged animal.

He saw me looking at him and quickly composed his face into a slightly sardonic, humorous mask. "Don't look too closely," he said.

And still the dignitaries filed in, had a drink, spoke their welcome and went out.

The ceremonial welcome reached its high point about midnight. Huge chunks of the roasted cow were brought in to us, and we gnawed at the almost raw meat between swigs of liquor. Outside, there was muted drumming. Voices were growing louder and louder.

Suddenly, in the midst of a long-winded speech by an immensely dignified Masai chief from a neighboring and friendly tribe, Kenyatta jumped up, grabbed his heavy cane and half staggered through the door.

"Come, Peter," he called.

Everybody was startled. I hesitated. He raised his cane and beckoned to me with it. I knew that this would be a dreadful breach of tribal etiquette.

"Come, man!" he snapped.

I got up, aware of the sudden silence that had descended on the huge gathering. By some strange magic everybody seemed to know that something had gone wrong.

"Jomo," I said.

"I can't stand any more," he snapped. "Come!"

I followed him to the door. I knew the discourtesy we were inflicting on the tribe. I also knew that my friend was at the breaking point. We walked through the crowd of people, got into Kenyatta's car and drove off into the night. The African moon was big and yellow, bathing the land in a soft light that almost achieved the clarity of daylight.

He took me to his home. It was a big, sprawling, empty place on the brow of a hill. Inside, it had nothing to make for comfort. There were hard wooden chairs, a few tables and only the bed in the bedroom. There were no books, none of the normal amenities of western civilization. When we arrived two women emerged from somewhere in the back and hovered about in the shadows. They brought in liquor, but I never got a clear glimpse of either of them. My friend's anguish of spirit was such that I did not want to ask questions. We sat on the veranda and drank steadily and in silence until we were both miserably, depressingly drunk.

And then Kenyatta began to speak in a low, bitter voice of his frustration and of the isolated position in which he found himself. He had no friends. There was no one in the tribe who could give him the intellectual companionship that had become so important to him in his years in Europe. The things that were important to him—consequential conversation, the drink that represented a social activity rather than the intention to get drunk, the concept of individualism, the inviolability of privacy—all these were alien to the tribesmen in whose midst he lived. So Kenyatta, the western man, was driven in on himself and was forced to assert himself in tribal terms. Only thus would the tribesmen follow him and so give him his position of power and importance as a leader.

To live without roots is to live in hell, and no man chooses voluntarily to live in hell. The people who could answer his needs as a western man had erected a barrier of color against him in spite of the fact that the taproots of their culture had become the taproots of his culture too. By denying him access to those things which complete the life of western man, they had forced him back into the tribalism from which he had so painfully freed himself over the years.

None of this was stated explicitly by either Kenyatta or myself. But it was there in his brooding bitter commentary on both the tribes and the white settlers of the land. For me, Kenyatta became that night a man who in his own life personified the terrible tragedy of Africa and the terrible secret war that rages in it. He was the victim both of tribalism and of westernism gone sick. His heart and mind and body were the battlefield of the ugly violence known as the Mau Mau revolt long before it broke out in that beautiful land. The tragedy is that he was so rarely gifted, that he could have made such a magnificent contribution in other circumstances.

What then is tribal man? Perhaps his most important single characteristic is that he is not an individual in the western sense. Psychologically and emotionally he is the present living personification of a number of forces, among the most important of which are the ancestral dead. The dead have a powerful hold on the living. They control and regulate the lives and activities of the living from the grave. They hand out the rules and codes by which the living conduct their daily affairs. If there is a drought, if there is a famine, it is a sign that the ancestors are angry because someone has broken a rule of the tribe, a law laid down by the dead. There will be no peace, no order, no prosperity in the tribe until the ancestors are appeased.

So the chief calls the whole tribe to a meeting in which the guilty ones will be "smelled out." The procedure begins with the drums—a key factor in African life. Their insistent throbs call the people to the gathering on a placid, almost monotonous key at first, but working on the emotions. Everyone in the village will be present; no man, woman or child would think of not obeying the summons. They form a circle, with the witch doctor or medicine man and the drummers to the fore. When all the people are assembled the throbbing of the drums increases. They beat in tune to the heartbeats of the human circle.

The witch doctor is dressed in lion or leopard skin, sometimes in monkey skin. His face is painted in bold streaks of color: white, black, red. There are crisscrossing lines on his body too. He wanders about the center of the circle, almost idly at first. Every now and then he pauses and looks straight into someone's eyes and keeps on looking. For the person looked at, this is an encounter with fate. Few stare back. Their eyes slide past his face or go glazed. They fear but are not supposed to fear. They know the ancestors are just, that the innocent are never punished. To experience fear, therefore, is an acknowledgment of guilt. It is not necessary to know the nature of your guilt; if you were not guilty, there would be no fear in your mind.

The tempo of the drums increases. The witch doctor begins to dance, slowly at first. He begins to talk in a high-pitched nasal voice; spirits always talk through their noses. The drums and the incantations go on and on, getting faster and wilder, dominating the hearts and minds of all the circle. People begin to tremble and shiver. Some drop down in a trance and lie moaning on the ground. Everyone is possessed by the frenzy of the drums. The spirits of the ancestors are abroad.

Suddenly the drums stop. The witch doctor stands fixed for a dreadful moment that seems without end. Then he pounces. He grabs his victim and drags him or her into the center of the circle. The victim does not resist, does not protest. The ancestors are always just.

There may be one, there may be many victims. But once the victim or victims are "smelled out," the hypnotic spell of the drums is broken. People relax. Their hearts beat normally once more. Now the ancestors will be propitiated and the living freed of the evil which beset them. Now the famine or the drought or the plague or whatever had beset the land will depart from it. And so, while the victim or victims are put to death, the rest of the tribe celebrates the passing of the great evil.

Another key characteristic of tribal man is that his society is exclusive and not, like western society, inclusive. The lines are drawn very clearly, very sharply. Anybody not an "insider" is an enemy, actually or potentially—someone to distrust, someone to fear, someone to keep at bay. There is no choice, no volition about this. It is something ordained by the ancestral dead. The tribal society is therefore possibly the most exclusive society in the twentieth-century world. If you are not in the tribe, there is no way into it. If you are in it, there is no way out of it except death. Dissent is not recognized. To break the rules of the tribe is to court death.

Even the family, the foundation of the tribal in-group, is no simple affair. It is often a cluster of four generations. A man's family can be made up of his father, his father's first, second and third wives—there may be more—and the children of these. A man inherits the wives and children of his brothers who die before him. The wives then become his wives, the children of his brother become brothers and sisters to his own children by his own wife. Then there are the children's children. These and the old people, the grandparents, make up the immediate family, the heart of the in-group. Then there are the families related to one's family by blood ties —the families of uncles and cousins. These have the same complex structure of many wives and brothers and sisters, many of whom are inherited. A group of such blood-related families makes the clan. Clans have been known to be big enough to fill whole villages.

Another and most vital factor in the life of tribal man is his attitude to life and death. Neither life nor death is ever wholly accidental. Disease is never natural. These are brought about by the good and evil spirits all around us. The evil spirits are preoccupied with bringing disaster on the tribe, the good with protecting the tribe. To achieve their malign ends, evil spirits enter the bodies of ordinary human beings. To fight the evil spirits, good spirits enter the bodies of witch doctors. Life and death are thus out of the hands of mortal men.

The world of tribal man is so dominated by the spirits that some tribes will not eat birds because of the spirits that dwell in them, some will not eat fish, some are vegetarians and some eat meat only.

Tribal man is hemmed in, imprisoned by his ancestors. His horizons are only as wide as they permit. He is also protected by them. The rules are such that there are no orphans in the tribe, no misfits, no neurotics. And of course, the ancestral dead are hostile to change.

This, then, is the "oblique, the hard-to-know man" whom Richard Wright encountered on his first visit to Africa. He is the man who raised Nkrumah to power. He is the man whose pressures led Jomo Kenyatta to the Mau Mau and then to his lonely prison-exile in a barren and isolated spot. He, tribal man, will have a crucial say in the future of Africa.

The ancestral dead notwithstanding, change is being imposed on him. How he reacts to the change will have a powerful bearing on tomorrow's Africa.

If the men inaugurating the new ways have the sense and the patience to preserve the finer qualities of the old ways and fuse these with the new, then we can expect something magnificently new out of Africa.

ROBERT COLES

Whose Strengths, Whose Weaknesses

Awareness of race always involves an awareness of worlds. Robert Coles's essay deals with that difference in worlds. Coles tries to learn what he can about himself as he watches Ruth move between her two worlds. Coles, a Harvard psychiatrist, is a uniquely qualified observer of those two worlds.

THEY WOULD BE SITTING or standing there in front of the cabin, or peering at me from the inside; and I would start slowing myself down. I always needed the extra seconds that a few more steps provide. I would hold my head bowed or pretend to notice something up there in the sky, or over toward the plantation proper. That way their eyes and mine didn't connect, and I didn't have to smile and start saying hello before they could really hear me. That way I could get my mind set for the purpose of my visit, the discovery of certain things, the unearthing of information I thought I ought to possess.

In the beginning ritual masked fear on both sides. I noticed how quiet they all were. My car's noise was a signal to them. They usually heard the car before they saw it because of a sudden turn in the road that made us visible to one another only at the very end of a milelong unpaved, dusty road. By the time I was in sight they had taken up their positions. They seemed rooted. They never looked at me. Or rather, they looked at me when I would not notice. At times I thought them wooden, impassive— and, of course, frightened. When the day came that *I* was not so frightened, their eyes caught mine. I remember being close to grateful that I had someone else's nervousness to observe. Fear has power; power seeks to affirm itself by exertion. And so the edgy, responsive dark irises and white eyeballs belied the calm, the silence. I looked on feet crossed, making still circles out of many legs, and knees crossed, enabling worn, mud-caked shoes to point, but not move an inch. Hungry for the truth, I found it in movement. The eyes did, after all, move and the eyes, my mother told me, were the "windows of the soul." What is more, I thought (or had to think) I saw dilated pupils, which every doctor knows to be a telltale sign that all is not well inside, below, underneath, wherever. (And haven't we learned in this century that any worthwhile truth has to be buried, concealed, and apparent only to the well-trained, in contrast to the well-educated or the desperately or necessarily or naturally sensitive?)

I now realize that my movements and postures underwent the same careful scrutiny that theirs did. Five years later we could reminisce: "I don't believe we knew what you were after. I thought maybe you was here to spy on us, or to sell something. But my sister, she said there was nothing around here to spy, that they didn't already know, the bossman and all. And we don't have the money to buy nothing, so no one could be wasting his time every week for that, to sell. Well, we thought there was no harm just waiting to see. Before long you find out everything you ask about—that's what my daddy used to tell me, and he's right.

"Now, with you we figured you was too slow to be with the sheriff, and not sure of yourself, not enough. And my little boy, James it was, he said, 'Mama, the man doesn't always know what to say.' I think maybe that was the first time any of us, we'd seen a man in a suit be shy—I mean be shy himself and be shy with words, too. Then, when you switched to regular clothes, the summer pants, and no more of the tie and like that, well then we decided you might be from up there in Washington, and the government. You know, they're trying to be for us, on our side. I tried to tell people you are a doctor with a college, but they said doctors don't go around the country sitting and talking here and there.

"No, I can't say I ever have been to a doctor's office. They ask you to pay first, and we can't, not first or later. So, it's just as well. They'd give us medicine, if they agreed to see us, and then the next thing you knew there'd be the sheriff here, and we'd be hauled off to jail for not paying the doctor's bill."

But before we came to that kind of mutual confession—in which I replied in kind, about my thoughts about their thoughts, and finally, about my thoughts period—there had to be one long stretch of coming and going, of sly and bewildered talk, of muscles relaxed a bit, quickly tightened up, then once again allowed to slacken, now for a little more time. They began to realize that I was in fact an oddball—who belonged to no recognizable part of their world. And after much too long a period of time I began to realize—an important first step—that they were not the helpless, pitiable objects of study I have to admit I predominantly felt them to be. Oh, it was never necessary to be that blunt. Instead of calling them the wretched of the Southern earth, I could lash out at the South itself: the region's blacks are terribly poor people; they are mercilessly exploited by the individual bossmen, often "managers" or "foremen" who do the rough and tough work, the squeezing dry of lazy bodies, the extraction of ergs from machines that are running at a caloric loss. (But aren't millions of people in other countries and continents even worse off?) And finally, they are badly educated people, barely literate or for all practical purposes illiterate.

All that is true, I thought to myself in the beginning, but someone has to be hardheaded enough to document what oppression does to its victims, how degraded they actually become. Cannot relentless psychological scrutiny turn into the sharpest kind of social criticism? Romantics may speak of a "culture" that peasants have, or include them in some "agrarian tradition"; but I came to them armed with both Marx and Freud, and so in a way any desire to cover up their "condition" and my account of it with soft, understated, merely allusive or (worst of all) ambiguous language was doubly suspect. I knew to ask myself whether I was beholden to the "power structure"—perhaps one I simply don't care to recognize myself, let alone acknowledge to others. I knew to ask myself whether sharecroppers, simple sharecroppers, vulnerable sharecroppers, made me feel scared and to blame for something. And of course I knew that we are all afraid; we all feel at fault; everyone has "work" to do,. fears and guilts to understand and "resolve."

So, it is better to be blunt, I decided as I started visiting them. They are "deprived" and "disadvantaged" and all the rest. They need "higher horizons." They should go North. They need "enrichment programs." They are eligible for every "title" in every federal law; and they need more laws with more "titles." *Headstart* is only a beginning. *Leap* is a drop in the bucket. *Upward Bound* is not "relevant," not to people so badly off, so out of things, so firmly, almost intractably part of—what is it called?—the *lumpen-proletariat*. The only things that will help them, change them, make them part of America, are "massive programs," a "frontal assault" on their poverty, a "basic restructuring" of our society, a "planned attack" on—well, everything "socioeconomic" and "psychosocial" and "sociocultural" that amounts to their very bad lot.

And here are some of the things I found—in one family from the Mississippi Delta—that go to make up that bad lot. The cabin has no heat, no running water, although three miles away there is a faucet and "all the water you can tote." (Not every family in the "area" is that lucky.) And the children, the seven children: none was born in hospitals; none was delivered by doctors; none has ever seen physicians; none has taken vitamin "supplements" as infants or vitamin pills as children; none is without evidence of illness; and none has any clothes that can be called his, his alone.

"The children, they're the most trouble when they're by theirselves. Most of the time they're together, though. And then I know it's okay." They are indeed together. They sleep together: four in one bed, three in another, all in one room. The other room belongs to their parents, and also serves as the kitchen—and living room and dining room. They share not only space and time but clothes and plates and forks. There are three pairs of shoes to go around, so only certain children can fight their way into them, or fight to fill them up—and then go to church, or, yes, to school. (And, naturally, it is the absence from school that bothers us secular, twentieth-century Americans, for whom education is sacred, a way to virtually everything, at least on this earth.) As for the children in that cabin, church wins over school hands down. They fight to go with their parents on Sunday, "to walk with them" as one boy put it, and to sit there and see and hear "everyone get to talking, and have a real good time." Those who stay at home are sad, but they turn happy on Monday if spared school because they still don't have those shoes, or because they feel tired and sick, or because they have to mind the younger ones and help around the house—which means in the fields or around "the place." (It is no mansion. It has no columns, not even a magnolia tree. It is a substantial house, nondescript in style, painted white with green shutters and a green door.)

I don't know what the United States Census Bureau did with the information they obtained from the parents of those seven children. (Such families are sometimes overlooked and not counted at all.) Are they classified sharecroppers or tenant farmers or field hands or employees or retainers or servants or just plain slaves? Are they listed as educated up to this grade or that one? Are they called citizens of this country, or aliens? The questions, the questions you and I answer every decade, can be very embarrassing, although not to "us." They weren't the questions I first had in mind when I started my "study," and they may seem a bit simple-minded to serious social scientists. But they are questions that I rather think no psychoanalytic study of sharecroppers ("in depth," of course) can quite afford to ignore.

"No sir, I can't say I've ever voted," said the father one day when I got around to that issue. "Yes sir, I think I know what you mean. [He knew damn well what I meant.] They have the law now, that says we can go vote. Some are trying it, and some aren't. I'm afraid I haven't got around to it, yet. But I hope to, before I die I hope to. Right now I guess I've got some other things to do."

Well, what other things? (Those are the good moments, when the observer is practically invited to ask something.) "I don't know—things like where to live, you know. We're thinking of going North. My sister is up there, in Chicago, and she keeps telling us to leave. But we're afraid to. They don't need a lot of us here, but I hear they don't need us there, either. We don't know what to do. We work on the crops part of the time, but the machines do more and more. There's some cotton they can't get, and there's the cattle and a few vegetables we have. I've got the chores to do. And my wife helps out in The House."

His father "worked on shares." Put differently, his father produced cotton and gave it over to the present bossman's father, and in return they continued to live side by side, the sharecropper and the bossman—on the latter's land. The bossman gave the sharecropper a few hundred dollars to spend during the course of the year, and The House sent over some food and some outgrown and secondhand clothes. The man I know grew up and became a field hand. There was no point getting credit for seed and tools and living quarters and food, and then working the land and receiving a share of the crop's value, minus charges for all the credit advances, including the money required for drainage, for irrigation, for fencing: "The bossman, he came and told me that with my daddy it was one thing, but times are changing, and a lot of the sharecroppers, they're not needed, and he was switching. I could work for him and in return I could live in the house and he would make sure that I never starve to death. And even with the machines coming, we could stay, because my wife is such a good help and especially her cooking."

His wife's cooking: until then I thought I knew everything about her cooking. In the morning she makes breakfast. She fries up some grits and they are washed down with either a coke or some coffee. There is no such thing as lunch. The children have another coke, and some very cheap candy like licorice or sugarcoated gum, which they chew and chew, and chew dry, and take out of their mouths and stretch and tear into fragments and laugh over and play with and stick upon one another. The parents also have another coke and some candy, which they eat with greater reserve. Supper is the main meal. It is served early, about half past four or five, and includes without exception fried potatoes and more grits and greens; and bread with peanut butter sometimes, and fatback sometimes. Every once in a while a stew appears, made of potatoes and gravy and pork. Even more unusual is a soup, the product of boiled bones and potatoes and greens. For dessert there is another coke, and maybe more candy.

I asked about cooking and I heard this: "We have practically no money, so it's hard to get by. We grow a little, but we haven't much land to do it on, and the bossman wouldn't want us spending too much time on that. My kids grow some flowers, the zinnias. You can't eat zinnias, I know it, but you can like them—just like you can rest beside a sunflower. We get our greens from the yard, and some tomatoes, though they don't last long. We don't have the money to buy the foodstamps. We get the commodities, and that's how we live. We'd be dead right now without the lard and flour they give, the government. Yes sir, every one of us would be dead. I try to fill my kids' stomachs up as best I can. I figure if they doesn't hurt them too much, their stomachs, well then, that's good. They gets their energy from the candy and the coke. They take a drink and bite on the licorice, and I know they've got their sugar in them and can keep going."

But her husband was talking about the cooking she did for the bossman. I asked her about that and she told me: "Oh, yes. I've been helping her out for years. I go up there and do what she tells me. I don't plan anything. She always says to me: 'Ruth, I've planned today's menus out.' Then she lists what I've got to do and I go ahead and get to work there."

She gets to work in a spacious, well-equipped kitchen. The sink is stainless steel. The stove is an electric range. The refrigerator is huge, and next to it stands a freezer, and next to it stands a washing machine and then a dishwasher. ("I do the dishes and some laundry, too.") Obviously, she has a few minutes to relax, because there is a small television set on one counter—and also a waffle iron, and a toaster, and a mixer for "working up" cakes, and an electric knife sharpener, which also takes care of pencils. I never would have seen all those electrically run gadgets had I not decided to compare her place of work with her place of residence. I knew her bossman well, and, in fact, once heard him say this about Ruth: "She's a fine woman, and so is her husband a fine man. They do an honest day's work, and we'll never let them go without a roof over their heads. I'm going to build them a new place, as a matter of fact. We're letting a lot go, though a lot of them don't want to. I tell them they may as well go North. We can't use them here. One by one they slip away; but you know, we have quite a few still here, right on our land. Eventually I suppose we'll only have maybe five families left here. Imagine that! It's hard for me to believe, after all these years with about a hundred or more. But I sure hope Ruth never leaves. I told my wife I think we'd near starve to death. She's the best cook in this county, easily."

I discovered what he meant. I had lunch with him and his wife. I had a big lunch, that started with a glass of tomato juice and a neatly cut piece of lemon. Then Ruth served us hot diced chicken and rice with raisins mixed in and peas and chutney on the side. And finally we had deep-dish apple pie and ice cream and coffee. It was all tasty, all neatly and attractively presented. The rice was fluffy and warm and covered with butter and seasoned just right. The chicken was cut perfectly, not too small and not too large. The peas were not overcooked; they were fresh, not frozen or canned, and like the rice, delicately salted. The pie had a light crust, and inside were warm tart apples, neither too syrupy nor dry. I was afraid I was going to be told that the ice cream was homemade, but no, it was store-bought: "It used to be we'd make our ice cream here, when I was a child. But you know it's too easy to buy it, and I think Ruth has enough to do as it is." I had commented on how good the ice cream was, and on how good the ice cream was at a nearby (and larger) plantation, where it was a bit ostentatiously, if generously, handed over with the hostess' advice from across the table that "Mary-Jean makes it, fresh every day." Ruth's mistress had been there many times—and clearly regretted the unfavorable comparison that I suppose I had unwittingly made.

When I left the house my stomach was filled with Ruth's food, and my mind was finally brought up short, the way it should have been months before. I kept on thinking of Ruth and that kitchen and of all the Ruths in America. I was there in that county to "study" her and her family, to get to know how they *really* live and think and feel. I had spent months visiting them and being observed by them and taking stock of all sorts of things they said and did. I was really rather proud of myself; and I was ashamed, too. I had made the effort to reach Ruth's family; and in so doing found out once again how awful their kind of American experience is—in contrast, say, to mine.

But guilt masks many things, one of which is pride. The guilt I easily knew about was the kind I easily notice in both myself and in patients. We have so much; others have so little. We feel ashamed of ourselves because we know the inadequacy of whatever good deeds we have done, whatever goodwill we feel. The guilt I began to feel for the first time after that lunch was something else, though; it had to do with the recognition of a willful kind of ignorance and blindness—mine. For a long time I had known that Ruth worked for the bossman's wife—cooked and cleaned and dusted for her, looked after her clothes and her dishes and her bedroom and bathroom. I knew all that, but I never really allowed myself to go any further; in fact, to bridge the two worlds that Ruth did every day. It was all right, of course, for *me* to bridge those two worlds; but Ruth in my mind had to be a sharecropper's wife, pure and simple. (And don't thousands of them work in those big houses in one capacity or another?)

Perhaps—to be generous to myself—I was merely a pedantic, unimaginative, anxious "investigator," who was slightly overwhelmed by all he was meeting up with. The search for order and clarity can often help a case of the nerves, can help a person come to terms with his worries and fears as well as his "methodology." Somehow a confusing, ambiguous, irony-filled world becomes a little more manageable when this man is distinguished from that one; and if they both can be placed on a graph or two and made part of a few percentages and made to possess a few "attitudes" and "beliefs" and "habits" and "problems"—well then, all the better. Ruth and her mistress live worlds apart on that plantation. I was busy finding out precisely how far apart; and every liberal bone in my body, I assure you, was full of the proper mixture of outrage and pity and sadness. In my cool, farsighted, evenhanded moments I felt sorry not only for Ruth but for her mistress, a kind, soft-spoken woman who speaks ill of no one and at moments can challenge my stereotypes as significantly as Ruth eventually did: "I have a lot of respect for Ruth, and you know we have many like her in Mississippi. She is a good person, and we have never had cause to complain about her. I never made this world, but I'll admit there are times when I say to myself that there but for the grace of God go I. What I mean is that I do believe Ruth has the same intelligence we do, and if things were different—well, I think she could be, well, I think she could be just like me, more or less. She could run the house, I'm sure, and plan things and make sure everything goes according to schedule."

When I heard that, I was in danger of being a very smug listener. I felt like getting up and screaming at the polite and honorably frank speaker. I felt like telling her that Ruth already was running her house, that without Ruth the house would be messy and disorganized, and its occupants would find mealtimes a lot less pleasant. But I was really agitated because I was hearing from someone else a very familiar kind of condescension, one that I fear is all too much the property of people like me rather than of Southern white ladies who "favored" Barry Goldwater and refer to themselves as "of conservative disposition." Neither she nor I—although I have to say, she at least a little better than I—seemed able to talk about the extent of Ruth's social and cultural achievement. Yes, we know that she is a good cook; and her mistress *senses* (and perhaps does not dare let her mind become more explicit) that without such "nigra help" life would be far different; and all along I knew, prided myself on knowing, that Ruth is a fine, hardworking, reliable person who is exploited and only appreciated in ways that don't cost a cent. But in the last analysis (the commendably unsparing one) I had to conclude that Ruth lacked dignity, even as her mistress knows that Ruth is only potentially capable of being dignified. And, needless to say, I had set out to study the consequences of the indignity America has visited upon people like Ruth: what happens to a woman who is stripped of her legal rights, her rights as a citizen, and kept socially apart as well as miserably poor.

I think it was the array of electric appliances in the kitchen that first made me stop and think and realize how much had been escaping my notice. Ruth was the master of all those machines. She was a gracious hostess, who served fine meals. She knew better than I where on the table a lot of those extra forks or spoons go. She knew her spices. She knew how to take care of the finest, most expensive clothes. She knew which plants needed a lot of water, which very little. She knew how to care for flowers. I remember my mind latching on to that last fact. I remember deciding to ask Ruth about those flowers: "Well, she likes her flowers. She grows a lot of them, and there will be times when she has to send for them, from the store, you know. I fix them up. I know which vases to use for which flowers, and how she likes them. She used to say 'good'; but now she just expects it, I guess—that I'll do right. You see what I mean?"

Of course I hadn't been seeing; that is the point. I had been figuring out how Ruth lives, and how her mind deals with "reality" and what psychological "defenses" she used. I had been developing a very clear idea of the hardships she faces every day, and even the stubborn persistence she possesses. I had declared her in my mind a desperate but inventive woman who somehow, beyond all explanation, endured. I was not so sure that she would, as Faulkner predicted, prevail; but I was prepared to say it was possible. I had at least shaken off the simpleminded view that the poor and even persecuted people are *only* hurt, sad, beaten down in spirit, deracinated, and branded with the unforgettable "mark of oppression." I was not going to become a "romantic" about Ruth and her family, but I would no longer be a slobbering, so-called reformer who needs the people whose cause he espouses to be as down-and-out, wretched and shattered as possible. Life is hard and even brutal for Ruth, and to survive has cost her a lot. But she is shrewd and ingenious, I had gradually persuaded myself; in the words of contemporary psychoanalysis, her mind has learned to be "adaptive"—and so has her overworked, tired body.

For all that generosity, for all the evolution my mind had been going through before I ate Ruth's lunch in her mistress' home, I had failed miserably to realize that Ruth is a *cultured lady,* a woman who knows her cuisine and her horticulture. Her manners are impeccable; her sense of timing in polite company faultless. She knows what people want and need and deserve and she gives it all to them. She is intuitive and sensitive. Her sensibilities are refined; and she even is at ease with our reigning technology. Her hands deal with the racks of the dishwasher, the shelves of the freezer, the clocks and pointers of the stove—and that pencil sharpener. ("The mister, he taught me how, and now missus gives me the pencils every once in a while, from all over the house. She says the noise of the machine gets to her; it makes her nervous. So she has to leave the room before I start.")

I am not saying that suddenly my mind came to its senses and fought its way to a more accurate and honorable picture of Ruth and her family. But over time, starting with that lunch, I did come to see more and more of Ruth's life, and the more I saw the harder put I was to fit her into convenient categories I had brought with me when I first met her. She is still poor. She is still disenfranchised. She continues to speak ungrammatical English, and so I have to edit her remarks. To this day she needs a doctor, a lawyer, a teacher—as do her children and her husband. She has no more money now than she ever did. And *she* would like a different life—so who am I to wax ecstatic over the countryside of the lovely Delta, the trees and flowers near her cabin, the rich, productive land, the mighty and almost mythic river that she can see by taking a good long walk for herself. Yet, who am I to do something else, deny her life its achievements and its ironies and its ambiguities, refuse her mind the sense of style and the subtlety it surely demonstrates all the time?

At times I am pleased with my own ability to leave Cambridge, Massachusetts, and somehow come to a reasonably strong and valuable "relationship" with a family like Ruth's. I am not so pleased, however, when I remind myself how long it took me as an anthropologist or psychiatrist or whatever, to recognize *Ruth's* experience and competence. She, too, goes back and forth between two worlds; every day she does. She, too, watches others and tries to help them out. She, too, takes away burdens from people and makes them feel less harried, less at the mercy of this and that. Like a "trained mental health professional" (as they rather ponderously call themselves), she adjusts herself to the lives, the problems, the needs of others. She doesn't get "overinvolved," though. When she and they part company, she knows how to go back to her own life and live it. If she has any "fantasies" about life over there in The House, she controls them, buries them or, more likely, lets them quietly come and quickly go. ("Oh, every once in a while I ask myself why God did things the way he did, and made me me and her her; but pretty soon there's the next thing I have to tend to.") Ignorant and barely literate, she is sophisticated and worldly; and as the bossmen in my profession say about precious few of us, she has "very good ego-defenses." She has taught me a lot I rather expected to find out; but most of all she has taught me about the weaknesses in my way of thinking that prevented her various strengths from being immediately and properly obvious to me. The arrogant man wants to make his world the whole world. He pushes himself ahead of anyone in sight and blinds himself to all sorts of things that he might see in others. When he is safely up front he may mellow, and here or there grant a few favors; but without prodding, I fear, only a few.

GEORGE ORWELL

Shooting an Elephant

Known to a generation of students as the author of *1984* and *Animal Farm,* George Orwell is now being taken up by those concerned with sharp prose infused with a pointed moral sense. Imperialism is one of the historic forms of race politics. Orwell's essay is an insight into the relationship of imperialism and race. The sources of imperialism are economic, but the most immediate and personal manifestations are racial.

IN MOULMEIN, in lower Burma, I was hated by large numbers of people—the only time in my life that I have been important enough for this to happen to me. I was sub-divisional police officer of the town, and in an aimless, petty kind of way anti-European feeling was very bitter. No one had the guts to raise a riot, but if a European woman went through the bazaars alone somebody would probably spit betel juice over her dress. As a police officer I was an obvious target and was baited whenever it seemed safe to do so. When a nimble Burman tripped me up on the football field and the referee (another Burman) looked the other way, the crowd yelled with hideous laughter. This happened more than once. In the end the sneering yellow faces of young men that met me everywhere, the insults hooted after me when I was at a safe distance, got badly on my nerves. The young Buddhist priests were the worst of all. There were several thousands of them in the town and none of them seemed to have anything to do except stand on street corners and jeer at Europeans.

All this was perplexing and upsetting. For at that time I had already made up my mind that imperialism was an evil thing and the sooner I chucked up my job and got out of it the better. Theoretically—and secretly, of course—I was all for the Burmese and all against their oppressors, the British. As for the job I was doing, I hated it more bitterly than I can perhaps make clear. In a job like that you see the dirty work of Empire at close quarters. The wretched prisoners huddling in the stinking cages of the lock-ups, the grey, cowed faces of the long-term convicts, the scarred buttocks of the men who had been flogged with bamboos—all these oppressed me with an intolerable sense of guilt. But I could get nothing into perspective. I was young and ill-educated and I had had to think out my problems in the utter silence that is imposed on every Englishman in the East. I did not even know that the British Empire is dying, still less did I know that it is a great deal better than the younger empires that are

going to supplant it. All I knew was that I was stuck between my hatred of
the empire I served and my rage against the evil-spirited little beasts who
tried to make my job impossible. With one part of my mind I thought of
the British Raj as an unbreakable tyranny, as something clamped down, in
saecula saeculorum, upon the will of prostrate peoples; with another part I
thought that the greatest joy in the world would be to drive a bayonet into
a Buddhist priest's guts. Feelings like these are the normal by-products of
imperialism; ask any Anglo-Indian official, if you can catch him off duty.

One day something happened which in a roundabout way was enlighten-
ing. It was a tiny incident in itself, but it gave me a better glimpse than I
had had before of the real nature of imperialism—the real motives for
which despotic governments act. Early one morning the sub-inspector at a
police station the other end of the town rang me up on the 'phone and said
that an elephant was ravaging the bazaar. Would I please come and do
something about it? I did not know what I could do, but I wanted to see
what was happening and I got on to a pony and started out. I took my
rifle, an old .44 Winchester and much too small to kill an elephant, but I
thought the noise might be useful *in terrorem.* Various Burmans stopped
me on the way and told me about the elephant's doings. It was not, of
course, a wild elephant, but a tame one which had gone "must." It had
been chained up, as tame elephants always are when their attack of "must"
is due, but on the previous night it had broken its chain and escaped. Its
mahout, the only person who could manage it when it was in that state,
had set out in pursuit, but had taken the wrong direction and was now
twelve hours' journey away, and in the morning the elephant had suddenly
reappeared in the town. The Burmese population had no weapons and
were quite helpless against it. It had already destroyed somebody's bamboo
hut, killed a cow and raided some fruit-stalls and devoured the stock; also
it had met the municipal rubbish van and, when the driver jumped out and
took to his heels, and turned the van over and inflicted violences upon it.

The Burmese sub-inspector and some Indian constables were waiting for
me in the quarter where the elephant had been seen. It was a very poor
quarter, a labyrinth of squalid bamboo huts, thatched with palm-leaf,
winding all over a steep hillside. I remember that it was a cloudy, stuffy
morning at the beginning of the rains. We began questioning the people as
to where the elephant had gone and, as usual, failed to get any definite information. That is invariably the case in the East; a story always sounds
clear enough at a distance, but the nearer you get to the scene of events
the vaguer it becomes. Some of the people said that the elephant had gone
in one direction, some said that he had gone in another, some professed
not even to have heard of any elephant. I had almost made up my mind
that the whole story was a pack of lies, when we heard yells a little distance away. There was a loud, scandalized cry of "Go away, child! Go

away this instant!" and an old woman with a switch in her hand came round the corner of a hut, violently shooing away a crowd of naked children. Some more women followed, clicking their tongues and exclaiming; evidently there was something that the children ought not to have seen. I rounded the hut and saw a man's dead body sprawling in the mud. He was an Indian, a black Dravidian coolie, almost naked, and he could not have been dead many minutes. The people said that the elephant had come suddenly upon him round the corner of the hut, caught him with its trunk, put its foot on his back and ground him into the earth. This was the rainy season and the ground was soft, and his face had scored a trench a foot deep and a couple of yards long. He was lying on his belly with arms crucified and head sharply twisted to one side. His face was coated with mud, the eyes wide open, the teeth bared and grinning with an expression of unendurable agony. The friction of the great beast's foot had stripped the skin from his back as neatly as one skins a rabbit. As soon as I saw the dead man I sent an orderly to a friend's house nearby to borrow an elephant rifle. I had already sent back the pony, not wanting it to go mad with fright and throw me if it smelt the elephant.

The orderly came back in a few minutes with a rifle and five cartridges, and meanwhile some Burmans had arrived and told us that the elephant was in the paddy fields below, only a few hundred yards away. As I started forward practically the whole population of the quarter flocked out of the houses and followed me. They had seen the rifle and were all shouting excitedly that I was going to shoot the elephant. They had not shown much interest in the elephant when he was merely ravaging their homes, but it was different now that he was going to be shot. It was a bit of fun to them, as it would be to an English crowd; besides they wanted the meat. It made me vaguely uneasy. I had no intention of shooting the elephant—I had merely sent for the rifle to defend myself if necessary—and it is always unnerving to have a crowd following you. I marched down the hill, looking and feeling a fool, with the rifle over my shoulder and an evergrowing army of people jostling at my heels. At the bottom, when you got away from the huts, there was a metalled road and beyond that a miry waste of paddy fields a thousand yards across, not yet ploughed but soggy from the first rains and dotted with coarse grass. The elephant was standing eight yards from the road, his left side towards us. He took not the slightest notice of the crowd's approach. He was tearing up bunches of grass, beating them against his knees to clean them and stuffing them into his mouth.

I had halted on the road. As soon as I saw the elephant I knew with perfect certainty that I ought not to shoot him. It is a serious matter to shoot a working elephant—it is comparable to destroying a huge and costly piece of machinery—and obviously one ought not to do it if it can possibly be avoided. And at that distance, peacefully eating, the elephant looked no more dangerous than a cow. I thought then and I think now that his attack of "must" was already passing off; in which case he would merely wander harmlessly about until the mahout came back and caught him. Moreover, I did not in the least want to shoot him. I decided that I would watch him for a little while to make sure that he did not turn savage again, and then go home.

But at that moment I glanced round at the crowd that had followed me. It was an immense crowd, two thousand at the least and growing every minute. It blocked the road for a long distance on either side. I looked at the sea of yellow faces above the garish clothes—faces all happy and excited over this bit of fun, all certain that the elephant was going to be shot. They were watching me as they would watch a conjurer about to perform a trick. They did not like me, but with the magical rifle in my hands I was momentarily worth watching. And suddenly I realized that I should have to shoot the elephant after all. The people expected it of me and I had got to do it; I could feel their two thousand wills pressing me forward, irresistibly. And it was at this moment, as I stood there with the rifle in my hands, that I first grasped the hollowness, the futility of the white man's dominion in the East. Here was I, the white man with his gun, standing in front of the unarmed native crowd—seemingly the leading actor of the piece; but in reality I was only an absurd puppet pushed to and fro by the will of those yellow faces behind. I perceived in this moment that when the white man turns tyrant it is his own freedom that he destroys. He becomes a sort of hollow, posing dummy, the conventionalized figure of a sahib. For it is the condition of his rule that he shall spend his life in trying to impress the "natives," and so in every crisis he has got to do what the "natives" expect of him. He wears a mask, and his face grows to fit it. I had got to shoot the elephant. I had committed myself to doing it when I sent for the rifle. A sahib has got to act like a sahib; he has got to appear resolute, to know his own mind and do definite things. To come all that way, rifle in hand, with two thousand people marching at my heels, and then to trail feebly away, having done nothing—no, that was impossible. The crowd would laugh at me. And my whole life, every white man's life in the East, was one long struggle not to be laughed at.

But I did not want to shoot the elephant. I watched him beating his bunch of grass against his knees, with that preoccupied grandmotherly air that elephants have. It seemed to me that it would be murder to shoot him. At that age I was not squeamish about killing animals, but I had never shot an elephant and never wanted to. (Somehow it always seems worse to kill a *large* animal.) Besides, there was the beast's owner to be considered. Alive, the elephant was worth at least a hundred pounds; dead, he would only be worth the value of his tusks, five pounds, possibly. But I had got to act quickly. I turned to some experienced-looking Burmans who had been there when we arrived, and asked them how the elephant had been behaving. They all said the same thing: he took no notice of you if you left him alone, but he might charge if you went too close to him.

It was perfectly clear to me what I ought to do. I ought to walk up to within, say, twenty-five yards of the elephant and test his behavior. If he charged, I could shoot; if he took no notice of me, it would be safe to leave him until the mahout came back. But also I knew that I was going to do no such thing. I was a poor shot with a rifle and the ground was soft mud into which one would sink at every step. If the elephant charged and I missed him, I should have about as much chance as a toad under a steam roller. But even then I was not thinking particularly of my own skin, only of the watchful yellow faces behind. For at that moment, with the crowd watching me, I was not afraid in the ordinary sense, as I would have been if I had been alone. A white man mustn't be frightened in front of "natives"; and so, in general, he isn't frightened. The sole thought in my mind was that if anything went wrong those two thousand Burmans would see me pursued, caught, trampled on and reduced to a grinning corpse like that Indian up the hill. And if that happened it was quite probable that some of them would laugh. That would never do. There was only one alternative. I shoved the cartridges into the magazine and lay down on the road to get a better aim.

The crowd grew very still, and a deep, low, happy sigh, as of people who see the theatre curtain go up at last, breathed from innumerable throats. They were going to have their bit of fun after all. The rifle was a beautiful German thing with cross-hair sights. I did not then know that in shooting an elephant one would shoot to cut an imaginary bar running from ear-hole to ear-hole. I ought, therefore, as the elephant was sideways on, to have aimed straight at his ear-hole; actually I aimed several inches in front of this, thinking the brain would be further forward.

When I pulled the trigger I did not hear the bang or feel the kick—one never does when a shot goes home—but I heard the devilish roar of glee that went up from the crowd. In that instant, in too short a time, one would have thought, even for the bullet to get there, a mysterious, terrible change had come over the elephant. He neither stirred nor fell, but every line of his body had altered. He looked suddenly stricken, shrunken, immensely old, as though the frightful impact of the bullet had paralysed him without knocking him down. At last, after what seemed a long time—it might have been five seconds, I dare say—he sagged flabbily to his knees. His mouth slobbered. An enormous senility seemed to have settled upon him. One could have imagined him thousands of years old. I fired again into the same spot. At the second shot he did not collapse but climbed with desperate slowness to his feet and stood weakly upright, with legs sagging and head drooping. I fired a third time. That was the shot that did for him. You could see the agony of it jolt his whole body and knock the last remnant of strength from his legs. But in falling he seemed for a moment to rise, for as his hind legs collapsed beneath him he seemed to tower upward like a huge rock toppling, his trunk reaching skywards like a tree. He trumpeted, for the first and only time. And then down he came, his belly towards me with a crash that seemed to shake the ground even where I lay.

I got up. The Burmans were already racing past me across the mud. It was obvious that the elephant would never rise again, but he was not dead. He was breathing very rhythmically with long rattling gasps, his great mound of a side painfully rising and falling. Hs mouth was wide open—I could see far down into caverns of pale pink throat I waited a long time for him to die, but his breathing did not weaken. Finally I fired my two remaining shots into the spot where I thought his heart must be. The thick blood welled out of him like red velvet, but still he did not die. His body did not even jerk when the shots hit him, the tortured breathing continued without a pause. He was dying, very slowly and in great agony, but in some world remote from me where not even a bullet could damage him further. I felt that I had got to put an end to that dreadful noise. It seemed dreadful to see the great beast lying there, powerless to move and yet powerless to die, and not even to be able to finish him. I sent back for my small rifle and poured shot after shot into his heart and down his throat. They seemed to make no impression. The tortured gasps continued as steadily as the ticking of a clock.

In the end I could not stand it any longer and went away. I heard later that it took him half an hour to die. Burmans were bringing dahs and baskets even before I left, and I was told they had stripped his body almost to the bones by the afternoon.

Afterwards, of course, there were endless discussions about the shooting of the elephant. The owner was furious, but he was only an Indian and could do nothing. Besides, legally I had done the right thing, for a mad elephant has to be killed, like a mad dog, if its owner fails to control it. Among the Europeans opinion was divided. The older men said I was right, the younger men said it was a damn shame to shoot an elephant for killing a coolie, because an elephant was worth more than any damn Coringhee coolie. And afterwards I was very glad that the coolie had been killed; it put me legally in the right and it gave me a sufficient pretext for shooting the elephant. I often wondered whether any of the others grasped that I had done it solely to avoid looking a fool.

LOUIS LOMAX

Road to Mississippi

The nation was shocked in the summer of 1964 when three young civil
rights workers, two white and one black, were murdered and entombed in
an earthen dam in Mississippi. Our memory of that day has, of course,
been jaded by the years that have passed. For those who would remember and would learn from the horrors of the recent past, Louis Lomax's
searing essay is a reminder of both the glory and the squalor that distinguish the relations of one race with another.

A DEATHLY DARK fell over the audience in Western College's
Peabody Hall. The young students gathered together looked at
the two Negro men on the podium, men who welcomed them
to the Mississippi Summer Project and then went on to promise them that they might get killed. But Robert Moses, a serious, intent
master's degree man from Harvard, and James Foreman, a college drop-
out who has given his all for the civil rights movement, were speaking
from the depths of personal experience. And as the students talked and
questioned on the rolling green Oxford, Ohio campus, Foreman and Moses
never let them forget for one moment that death is always a possibility
for those who venture into Mississippi as civil rights missionaries.

"Don't expect them to be concerned with your constitutional rights,"
Moses said. "Everything they (the white power structure) do in Mississippi
is unconstitutional."

"Don't expect indoor plumbing," James Foreman added, "get ready to
do your business in outhouses."

The assemblage, mostly middle class white Protestants and Jews, roared
with laughter.

"Don't laugh," Moses screamed. "This is for real—like for life and
death."

"This is not funny," Foreman added, "I may be killed. You may be
killed. If you recognize that—that you may be killed—the question of
whether you will be put in jail will become very, very minute."

Andrew Goodman's lip went dry. There was no longer a sophisticated
"it can't happen to me" grin on his face. Like most of the other college
students from across the land who had volunteered to go into Mississippi,
Goodman had been motivated by a combination of conviction and adven-

ture. Now veterans of the struggle were making it plain that Mississippi was no playground for a Jewish liberal from New York who wanted to create a better world. Then R. Jess Brown, a graying and aging Negro lawyer from Jackson, Mississippi, walked to the podium to add fuel to the volunteer's mounting fear.

"I am one of the three Mississippi lawyers—all of us Negroes—" Brown said, "who will even accept a case in behalf of a civil rights worker. Now get this in your heads and remember what I am going to say. They—the white folk, the police, the county sheriff, the state police—they are all waiting for you. They are looking for you. They are ready; they are armed. They know some of your names and your descriptions even now, even before you get to Mississippi. They know you are coming and they are ready. All I can do is give you some pointers on how to stay alive."

"If you are riding down the highway, say on Highway 80 near Bolton, Mississippi, and the police stop you, and arrest you; don't get out and argue with the cops and say 'I know my rights.' You may invite that club on your head. There ain't no point in standing there trying to teach them some Constitutional Law at twelve o'clock at night. Go to jail and wait for your lawyer."

The meeting adjourned. A few of the volunteers gathered around Foreman, Moses and Attorney Brown to ask specific questions. The civil rights zealots got nothing in private that they had not been told in public: If you are going into Mississippi you must first raise—on your own—five hundred dollars bail money, list your next of kin, and then sit for a photograph with your identification number laced across your chest. These are the basic identifications the civil rights movement needs if a worker was arrested or killed.

"But if you are arrested and they start beating you," Robert Moses added, "try and protect as much of your genital organs as possible." Moses knew what he was talking about. He had been arrested scores of times; he had been beaten and each time his white tormentors aimed their booted feet at the genitals.

"Now," James Foreman asked, "do you still want to go?"

The silence shouted "yes." But behind the silent "amen" there were all the gnawing doubts and apprehensions that plague any man, or woman, who knowingly marches into the jaws of danger.

"All I can offer is an intellectual justification for going into Mississippi," one Harvard student said.

"I only want to do what I think is right . . . to help others," a Columbia University student added.

But it was Glenn Edwards, a twenty-one year old law student from the

University of Chicago, who articulated what most of those involved really felt.

"I'm scared," Edwards said, "a lot more scared than I was when I got here at Oxford for training. I am not afraid about a bomb going off in the house down there (in Mississippi) at night. But you can think about being kicked and kicked and kicked again. I know that I might be disfigured."

Then, as the private give and take continued, the civil rights volunteers raised questions that gave the Mississippi veterans fits.

"Some of us have talked about interracial dating once we get to Mississippi," one girl told Robert Moses. "Is there any specific pattern you would have us follow?"

Moses eased by the question by saying there was simply nowhere in Mississippi for an interracial couple to go. John M. Pratt, a lawyer for the National Council of Churches, one of the sponsors of the project, bluntly warned the volunteers that Mississippi was waiting for just such a thing as interracial dating.

"Mississippi is looking for morals charges," Pratt warned. "What might seem a perfectly innocent thing up North might seem a lewd and obscene act in Mississippi. I mean just putting your arm around someone's shoulder in a friendly manner."

But it was a tall, jet black veteran of the Mississippi struggle who rose and put the matter in precise perspective:

"Let's get to the point," he said (and his name must be withheld because he is one of the vital cogs in the Mississippi freedom movement). "This mixed couple stuff just doesn't go in Mississippi. In two or three months you kids will be going back home. I must live in Mississippi. You will be safe and sound, I've got to live there. Let's register people to vote *NOW;* as for interracial necking, that will come *later* . . . if indeed it comes at all."

Those who knew him say that Andrew Goodman was among the students who gathered for the private interviews. There is no record that he asked any questions or made any comments. Some of the volunteers were frightened by what they heard and they turned back, went home or took jobs as counsellors in safe summer camps in the non-south. Andrew Goodman was not among those who turned back.

A few days later the civil rights volunteers, Goodman among them, left Oxford, Ohio, for specific assignments in Mississippi. Some came into Mississippi in their own Volkswagens, some came by bus, others arrived in second hand Fords, still others stunned old line Mississippi whites and Negroes by arriving on motorcycles. All of the "invaders", as Mississippi whites called them, paid their own way. They—the "invaders", Negro and white, but mostly white—wore dirty white sneakers, sport shirts, bright shift print dresses, chinos, jeans and shorts. The natives, Negro and white, looked on in amazement. Following orders from Robert Moses and James Foreman, the civil rights volunteers fanned out over the state and began to set up shop in some twenty Mississippi cities. Andrew Goodman was assigned to Meridian, a relatively liberal Mississippi town of some fifty thousand souls located on the edge of the "black belt", some fifty miles from the Mississippi-Alabama state line. But there was nothing to distinguish Andrew Goodman from the other white, non-south liberals, who had come to Mississippi to labor in the civil rights vineyard, to work out their own sense of guilt and responsibility for what had happened in this Republic for the past four hundred years.

They—the civil rights "invaders"—were a diverse and unusual crew. Some were neat, others were beat; some were religious—deeply so— others were revolutionary—even more deeply so. Many of them were first rate scholars, others were pampered football heroes on their campuses. Most of them were bright students; all of them were argumentative; most of them were unable to contain themselves until they met some backwoods Mississippi segregationist to whom they were certain they could explain the gospel on equality and constitutionalism. In all fairness to them, it must be said that their naivete was exceeded only by their energy and their courage. They really believed that white Mississippians would listen to reason if someone were willing to expend the energy necessary to spell out the ABC's of Americanism, letter by letter, syllable by syllable, word by word, sentence by sentence. Long on energy and patience, then the civil rights missionaries set out for their assignments, the God of freedom thundering in their ears, their faith in the basic goodness of all men—including white Mississippians—gleaming in their eyes.

Like Negroes, they believed in the American Dream. It did not disturb them that once they entered the state of Mississippi, they were surrounded and followed by white policemen riding shotgun. Even as their bus curved through bayous and then raced deep into the Mississippi Delta, the civil rights volunteers amused themselves by reading dipatches from the North —particularly a column by Joseph Alsop—that warned of the "Coming Terrorism."

Said Alsop: "A great storm is gathering—and may break very soon indeed—in the State of Mississippi and some other regions of the South. The southern half of Mississippi, to be specific, has been powerfully reinvaded by the Ku Klux Klan which was banished from the state many years ago. And the Klan groups have in turn merged with, or adhered to, a new and ugly organization known as the Americans for the Preservation of the White Race."

Then Alsop loosed a blockbuster which should have made even the most committed civil rights zealot rise in his bus seat and take notice:

"Senator James O. Eastland has managed to prevent infiltration of the northern part of the state where his influence predominates. But Southern Mississippi is now known to contain no fewer than sixty-thousand armed men organized to what amounts to terrorism. Acts of terrorism against the local Negro populace are already an everyday occurrence."

Then Alsop's warning became chillingly precise:

"In Jackson, Mississippi, windows in the office of COFO (Council of Federated Organizations, under whose auspices the civil rights workers were coming to Mississippi) [are] broken almost nightly. Armed Negroes are now posted at the office each night. The same is true in other Mississippi cities."

The civil rights workers hit Mississippi. Two hundred and fifty graduates of the Oxford, Ohio, center alone cascaded upon Mississippi late in June. Hundreds came from other similar training schools. They went to "receiving centers" and then were assigned housing by some one hundred civil rights veterans of the Mississippi campaign, eighty of whom were from the battle-ridden Student Non-Violent Coordinating Committee (SNCC) and twenty of whom were from the Congress of Racial Equality, the most militant of the civil rights organizations. Also on hand to quiet the students were one hundred and seventy-five of their peers who had preceded them into the state and knew the ropes as well as the trees from which they could dangle. The entire Mississippi task force soon reached nine hundred—one hundred professional civil rights workers, five hundred and fifty volunteers, all to be augmented by one hundred and fifty law students and lawyers, plus a hundred clergymen of all faiths and colors.

Andrew Goodman was one of the lucky ones. Not only was he assigned to Meridian, one of the better Mississippi towns, but Michael Schwerner and James Chaney, the two Mississippi veterans who were to direct Goodman's activities, were on hand in Oxford, Ohio, to drive him back to Mississippi. By all the rules of the book, Goodman had it made. He should have served out his time in Mississippi and then returned home to New York to share with others his tale of Delta woe.

But once Andrew Goodman, James Chaney, and Michael Schwerner met and joined forces, the paths of their lives crossed, became entangled, then merged into a single road to tragedy.

Twenty year old Andrew Goodman was the son of a New York City building contractor and a student at Queens College. He was a tense and troubled young man. Like thousands of other white college students across the nation, Goodman sat and listened as civil rights spokesmen—including me—berated white liberals for their superficial involvement, for their cavalier commitment to the Negro cause. I remember Andrew Goodman well. I spoke at Queens College last year as part of a general series of lectures on contemporary social problems. The big issue then, on that campus, was a program to send students to Prince Edward County, Virginia, to tutor Negro children who had been deprived of an education because the local white fathers chose to close down the public schools rather than obey a Supreme Court decision that the schools of that county must integrate. I remember it well; I bore down hard on the need for white youths to make commitments, to fill the spiritual vacuum in their lives by dedicating themselves to something other than—and this is precisely how I put it— "moving to suburbia where you will live in split-level homes and develop tri-level morality."

And when the lecture was over fifty or so Queens College students gathered in a knot around me; Andrew Goodman was in the forefront.

"O.K.," the students challenged me, "you have bawled us out. Now, dammit, *tell us what to do? What can we do? What if we want to be committed and our parents will not let us become involved!"*

I don't know what I told them; I have faced the same question so often, on so many campuses across the nation, yet every time I hear it my throat goes dry. After all, how do you advise college teenagers to defy their parents and join the army of those marching into the jaws of death?

My general reply is: "I have outlined the problem. Now you make up your minds where and how you can best serve in the light of your talents and gifts and temperament." Chances are that is what I said to Andrew Goodman and the other Queens College students who gathered around me.

Late in the spring of 1964, Andrew Goodman made his commitment. He decided to go to Mississippi and work on the summer voter registration project. His parents wondered if he could not find involvement closer home, in a project whose moral rewards were high but whose endemic dangers were less than those of Mississippi. But Andrew Goodman was experiencing a new and deeply spiritual bar mitzvah. Andrew had entered puberty seven years earlier but now, at twenty, he had really become a man. He had decided what he wanted to live for. And since death is forever remote until it is upon us, it never occurred to Andrew Goodman that he had also decided what he was willing to die for.

Those who remember Andrew Goodman during the training period at Western College in Oxford, Ohio, describe him as just another among the hundreds of civil rights volunteers. He was not "pushy"; he didn't stumble all over himself to prove how much he loved Negroes; he did not have the need to make a point of dating Negro girls. Nor was there anything dramatic about Andrew Goodman's arrival in Meridian on Saturday, June 20. Like the others, he was assigned living quarters in the Negro community and reported to the voter education center to receive work assignments from veterans Michael Schwerner and James Chaney.

Michael Schwerner, in a very real sense, was everything Andrew Goodman was not. They were both Jews; but the similarity stopped there.

Twenty-four year old Michael Schwerner was a Colgate man. Moreover, he had gone on to take graduate work at Columbia University. Then he became a full time teacher and social worker at a settlement house along New York's ethnically troubled lower East Side. Twenty-two year old Mrs. Michael Schwerner also teaches school; New York Negroes remember her because of her way with Negro youngsters. "It was something to see," a New York social worker told me, "those little black, Negro children climbing into Rita Schwerner's lap for her to read them stories which she especially interpolated for them, in terms of their own background and experience."

Michael and Rita Schwerner were staunch CORE people. They had a passion to change things; to change them *now*. Thus it was that the Schwerners gave up their work in New York and went to Meridian, Mississippi, last January, some five months before the summer project was to begin. They immediately set up a voter education center for Negroes and flooded the town with leaflets announcing that the center would be open each evening. Little Negro children were the first to come to the center where they and the Schwerners talked, and Michael Schwerner, aquiline nose and dark goatee, began to affect a Mississippi Negro accent. And the little children went home and told their parents of the white man with the big nose and black goatee who talked like a southern Negro.

The Meridian voter education program flourished under the Schwerners. As Mississippi towns go, Meridian was a liberal community. They even had (and still have, for that matter) an unofficial bi-racial committee to keep the ethnic peace. But in the towns of Hattiesburg, Greenwood, Canton, and Ruleville, civil rights workers were facing daily beatings from white bigots and harassment from the police.

"We are actually pretty lucky here" Schwerner told writer Richard Woodley early in April. "I think they (the police and the White Citizens Council) are going to let us alone."

With incredible confidence, Schwerner and his wife set up shop at 2505½ Fifth Street in the blighted Negro end of town. Their five dingy rooms were the former quarters of a Negro doctor, directly over the only Negro drug store in Meridian. The Schwerners built book cases along the walls and made long blue curtains to shield the windows.

The Schwerners' first effort was to infiltrate the Negro community. They found Negro boys who loved to play ping-pong and induced the Negro boys to build a ping-pong table. Then they collected typewriters, sewing machines, phonographs, office supplies, books—such as Dollard's "Caste and Class in a Southern Town"—which are never available to Negroes in Mississippi. The civil rights groups sponsoring the project paid the forty dollar-a-month rent on the offices and gave the Schwerners ten dollars a week for spending money. How the Schwerners lived and ate is not a matter of record. What is known is that an average of twenty people a day came to the center. Some two hundred Negroes visited the center during the first fifteen days of its operation.

It took the Schwerners two months to get their telephone installed. Not only were the phones tapped, but as Michael Schwerner himself said, "If you are lucky, when you talk over our phone you can hear the police calls going back and forth."

Even so, Schwerner and his wife were convinced that they were doing well.

"Just look at the Mississippi Negroes we are reaching!" Schwerner exclaimed. But his wife, like all women and wives, had a deeper concern. I must leave," she said. "If I ever got pregnant here . . . I just would never have children here. I would never go through a pregnancy or have children here."

Then Michael Schwerner and his wife took writer Woodley to dinner at a Negro restaurant.

"There is a job to be done here in Mississippi," Schwerner said as he fondled the crude menu in the Negro restaurant. "My wife and I think it is very important. But we want to have a normal life, and children. So eventually we will go back to New York, maybe in a year or two."

They were in the Negro restaurant because there was not enough food in the Schwerner home to feed them, as writer Richard Woodley knew very well.

"Darn it, Mickey," Mrs. Schwerner said, "I'm going to have a steak." Then she flailed her arms and finally pounded the table. "We need that."

Michael Schwerner sat silent for a moment. Then he spoke up to Woodley.

"We understand why the Negroes don't leave this state. The really poor ones wouldn't have any great life in the North even if they left. But mainly it's their home life here; they have families here and their lives are here. It is their home, and there is a little pride here that makes them not want to run."

"There is no question about it," Michael Schwerner said in the middle of the meal, "The federal government will have to come into Mississippi sooner or later."

The record does not show who paid for Mrs. Schwerner's steak. Chances are that writer Richard Woodley picked up the tab.

Two days later Michael Schwerner welcomed Andrew Goodman to Mississippi. Schwerner told Goodman that Mississippi was no place for children. Goodman smiled and said, "I'm no child. I want to get into the thick of the fight."

Twenty-one year old James Chaney was a drop out. A Catholic drop out at that. "I'm a Baptist," Mrs. Fannie Lee Chaney said, "I don't quite know how my boy wound up joining the Catholic Church, but we all worship the same God and that was his choice." By the time James Chaney met Michael Schwerner in Meridian last January he had all but drifted away from both the Church and the local parochial school.

"Mickey (Schwerner) and my boy were like brothers," Mrs. Chaney said. "Yes. They were like brothers. My boy a Negro and a Catholic. Michael a Jew. Yes, they were like brothers."

Shortly after the Schwerners set up shop in Meridian, Chaney, who was already a member of CORE, became a full time drop out. He left school and devoted all of his time to the civil rights struggle.

"Chaney was one of our best men," CORE's James Farmer said. "He was a native of Mississippi. He was a child of the soil. He knew his way around. He was invaluable."

Together, then, Michael Schwerner, James Chaney and Andrew Goodman made their way back from Oxford, Ohio, to Meridian. They arrived on Saturday and were immediately hit with the tragic news:

On the night of June 16th, while Chaney and the Schwerners were attending the training session in Ohio, the stewards of Mount Zion Methodist Church held their monthly meeting to transact church business. It was the same church in which the Schwerners had held a civil rights meeting on May 31 to rally support for a Freedom School COFO planned to open in the area. Ten persons—officers of the church and some of their children—attended the stewards meeting on June 16.

When the church officials emerged from the church, they were confronted with a phalanx of armed white men and police officers. They started to drive away, only to be stopped at a roadblock formed by police cars and unmarked cars with the license plates removed. The police forced the Negroes to get out of their cars and submit to search.

"Were there any white people at your meeting tonight?" one of the police asked.

"No sir," one of the Negroes replied.

"Were you niggers planning civil rights agitation?"

"No sir. We were there on the Lord's business."

Then the white men forced the Negroes to turn off their car lights, and under the cover of darkness they pistol whipped and kicked the stewards of the Mount Zion Methodist Church. Set free to go home, the Negroes uttered a prayer of thanks to God that they had not been killed.

Several hours later Mount Zion Methodist Church belched flames. The fire was over in a matter of minutes because, as later investigation showed, the arsonists had doused the house of God with naphtha before setting it afire. There was a fire tower less than a mile from the church, but it is manned only until five o'clock in the afternoon.

That was the report that hit Schwerner and Chaney as they returned to Meridian with their new recruit Andrew Goodman. They decided to get a good night's sleep and then drive down to Longdale on Sunday morning in order to look at the ruins of the Mount Zion Methodist Church and then see what information they could get about the incident.

Mississippi is a quiet and reverent place on Sunday morning. The gin mills are silent, the field hands, dressed in their Sunday finery, can be seen packed into pick-up trucks on their way to church. The white power structure, the bankers, the lawyers, the judges, the people who really run the towns and counties, move along the sweltering streets, some like the Snopses out of Faulkner and some like crinolined characters out of a Frank Yerby novel. Only on Sunday, but *never* on Monday or the rest of the week, are the traces of the old South really visible. The white ladies of relative quality don their frilly frocks, spread open their accordion-like fans and nod to the rabble, Negro and white, as they make their way to church. They come in from their large plantations and make their way to the First Baptist or First Methodist Church. The white rabble, of course, do not attend these churches. They are to be found in the lesser Baptist and Methodist Churches and along "holiness row" where the sanctified and Pentecostal preachers hold forth. These genteel white people pride themselves on their love and understanding of their Negroes. They have never lynched or beaten a Negro and lapse into a fantasy in order to swear that they don't know any white people who would do such things.

Most of all, it is the air of Mississippi that crackles with the word of God on Sunday morning. From sunrise to sunset and then to midnight, the airwaves of the Mississippi Delta are cluttered with preachers, white and Negro, the respectable and the fly-by-night, reminding the audience that Jesus will, *indeed,* wash them whiter than snow. And the genteel plantation owners and their families who made their way to church on Sunday morning, June 21, paid no attention to the 1963, blue, Ford station wagon that eased out of Meridian shortly after 10 A.M. and headed along Route 19 toward the Route 491 cutoff. The Negro field hands, also on their way to church, paid no attention to the station wagon, either.

But the police *did* take notice of the station wagon and they knew that two of the three occupants were Michael Schwerner and James Chaney. The police, in unmarked cars, followed closely. Switching to the "Citizens Short Wave Band" that is used to keep the Ku Klux Klan and the White Citizens' Council informed as to the movements of civil rights workers, the police broadcast the alarm.

"They are headed north along 19. That nigger, Chaney, is driving. Over and out."

Chaney and Schwerner were not afraid. They had been through it all before; Chaney had been jailed for civil rights demonstrations in Mississippi, while Schwerner had played hide-and-seek with Sheriff Rainey of Neshoba

County on at least three previous occasions. In each instance Schwerner had won. This was Andrew Goodman's trial by fire; it was his first time out on a civil rights assignment. The chances are that whatever fright he felt was overshadowed by the excitement and intrigue of it all.

The Ford station wagon—a gift to CORE from white liberals in Hastings-on-the-Hudson, New York—made its way along Route 19, across Lauderdale County, across the northeastern tip of Newton County to the Route 491 cutoff just on the border between Newton and Neshoba counties. With policemen following, the civil rights workers turned north onto 491 and headed toward Philadelphia. When they came to Route 16, some miles east of Philadelphia, the ill-fated civil rights workers turned left onto Route 16, just east of the hamlet of Ocobla and headed for the scorched earth site of the Mount Zion Methodist Church in the Longdale area.

No one moves unnoticed in Mississippi and the arrival of strangers causes a general alarm in the community. This is particularly true when the police have been broadcasting the strangers' every move over a short wave band used by members of the Klan and the White Citizens' Council. But the local Negroes were also watching. Some of them were hiding in the bushes, others were pretending to be idly driving by. A few sympathetic white people were also watching. And from their sworn statements the following time-table can be constructed:

12:00 — Schwerner, Goodman, and Chaney arrive at the site of the burned-out church shortly before noon. They spend about an hour examining the ruins and talking with people who have gathered.

1:30 — Schwerner, Goodman, and Chaney turn up at church services at a nearby Negro church. There they pass out leaflets urging the people to attend voter registration schools. [The name of the church and the persons who allowed the three civil rights workers to speak are known but cannot be released because of concern for the safety of the persons involved, as well as for the church building.]

2:30 — Schwerner, Goodman and Chaney are given dinner in a friendly home and then leave for Meridian.

3:00 — A person who knows all three civil rights workers sees them as they come along Route 16 from the Longdale area and make a right turn onto Route 491 which will take them back to Route 19 and Meridian.

As soon as they swing onto Route 491, the three civil rights workers are intercepted by Deputy Sheriff Cecil Price, Schwerner's ancient and implacable foe. Schwerner is at the wheel and, as he had done on both May 19 and May 31 when he was in the area for civil rights meetings, he elects to out-run the deputy sheriff. But this time Price can act with total license. His boss, Sheriff L. A. Rainey, is at the bedside of Mrs. Rainey who is hospitalized. Four Negroes witness the chase and have later sworn that Price shot the right rear tire of the speeding station wagon.

3:45 — The disabled station wagon is parked in front of the Veterans of Foreign Wars building on Route 16, about a mile east of Philadelphia. Witnesses see two of the civil rights workers, now known to be Schwerner and Chaney, standing at the front of the station wagon, with the hood raised. The third civil rights worker, Goodman, is in the process of jacking up the right rear tire to change it.

Deputy Sheriff Cecil Price (he has by now radioed the alarm) is standing nearby with his gun drawn. Informed of the incident, one Snow, a minor Deputy Sheriff, comes running out of the VFW club where he works as a bouncer. Price and Snow are then joined by State Patrolman E. R. Poe and Harry Wiggs, both of Philadelphia. [The entire episode was broadcast over the short-wave citizens' band which is relayed all over the state. There is evidence that police in Meridian, Jackson, and Philadelphia, as well as Colonel T. B. Birdsong, head of the State Highway Patrol, were in constant contact about the incident. It is also clear that white racists who had purchased short-wave sets in order to receive the citizens' band broadcasts were also informed and began converging on the scene.]

Deputy Sheriff Cecil Price (by his own admission) makes the arrest. (But there is confusion as to precisely where the arrest took place. Three landmarks, all within a square mile radius, are involved. Some witnesses say they saw the civil rights workers drive away from the VFW club to a Gulf station about a mile away. Others say they saw the arrest take place diagonally across the street from a Methodist Church in Philadelphia. At first blush these accounts seem contradictory. But to one who has tramped the roads and swamps of Mississippi in search of evidence—and I have done this more times than I care to recall—the accounts make sense.) What happened was approximately this:

Price, Snow and the State Police decide that too much attention has been drawn to the incident in front of the VFW hall. They allow the civil rights workers to drive into the Gulf station location. The station wagon pulls into the gas station while the police cars park across the street. The Methodist Church in question is a hundred yards farther down the road on the other side of the street and an illiterate observer would identify the church as the landmark and say the arrest occurred across the street from the church.

4:30 — Price arrests the civil rights workers. One of the State patrolmen drives the station wagon into Philadelphia. [This means that the tire had been changed and it accounts for the report that the wagon was at the Gulf station.] The three workers are herded into Price's car and the second State patrolman follows the Price car into town in case the workers attempt a break.

They arrive at the Philadelphia jail. Chaney is charged with speeding, and Schwerner and Goodman are held on suspicion of arson. Price tells them he wants to question them about the burning of the Mount Zion Methodist Church, an incident that occurred while they—all three of the civil rights workers—were on the campus of Western College in Oxford, Ohio.

The three civil rights workers are to report back to Meridian by four o'clock. When they do not appear their fellow workers begin phoning jails, including the one in Philadelphia, and are told that the men are not there. Meanwhile the rights workers—charged with nothing more than a traffic violation—are held incommunicado. What happens while these men are sweating it out in jail for some five hours can now be told. And it is in this ghostly atmosphere of empty shacks, abandoned mansions and a way of life hinged up on fond remembrances of things that never were, that the poor white trash gets likkered up on bad whiskey and become total victims of the southern mystique.

The facts have been pieced together by investigators and from the boasts of the killers themselves. After all, part of the fun of killing Negroes and white civil rights people in Mississippi is to be able to gather with your friends and tell how it all happened in the full knowledge that even if you are arrested your neighbors, as jurymen, will find you "not guilty."

The death site and the burial ground for Andrew Goodman, Michael Schwerner, and James Chaney have been chosen long before they die, months before in fact. Mississippi authorities and the white bigots have known for months that the invasion is coming. Mississippi officials have made a show of going on TV to let the nation know that they are ready and waiting with armored tanks, vicious dogs, tear gas and deputies at the ready. But there is another aspect of Mississippi's preparation for the civil rights "invaders" that they elect not to discuss:

Mississippi, as Professor James W. Silver has written, is a closed society. Neshoba County is one of the more tightly closed and gagged regions of the state. Some ten thousand people have fled the county since World War II. The five thousand or so who remain are close kin, cousins, uncles, aunts, distant relatives all. For example, it is reported that Deputy Sheriff Price alone has some two hundred kin in the county. This is a land of open—though illegal—gambling. Indeed, the entire nation watches as a CBS reporter on TV walks into a motel and buys a fifth of whiskey, all of which, of course, is illegal. This is a land of empty houses, deserted barns, of troubled minds encased in troubled bodies.

Once they receive word that the civil rights workers are coming, members of certain local racist groups begin holding sessions with doctors and undertakers. The topic of the evening: How to Kill Men Without Leaving Evidence, and: How To Dispose of Bodies So That They Will Never Be Found.

Negro civil rights workers who can easily pass for white have long since moved into Mississippi and infiltrated both the Klan and the White Citizens' Council.

Their reports show that doctors and undertakers use the killings of Emmett Till and Mack Parker as exhibits A and B on how not to carry out a lynching. Not only did the killers of Parker and Till leave bits of rope, and other items that could be identified, lying around, they threw the bodies in the Pearl (Parker) and Tallahatchie (Till) rivers. After a few days both bodies surfaced, much to everyone's chagrin.

The two big points made at the meetings are (1) kill them (the civil rights workers) with weapons, preferably chains, that cannot be identified: (2) bury them somewhere and in such a way that their bodies will never float to the surface or be unearthed.

Somewhere between ten and eleven o'clock on the night of Sunday, June 21, (if one is to believe Deputy Sheriff Price and the jailers) James Chaney is allowed to post bond and then all three civil rights workers are released from jail. According to Price the three men are last seen heading down Route 19, toward Meridian.

Why was Chaney alone forced to post bail? What about Schwerner and Goodman? If they were under arrest, why were they not required also to post bail? If there were no charges against them, why were they arrested in the first place? More, if Chaney was guilty of nothing more than speeding, why had his two companions also been placed under arrest? But these are stupid questions, inquiries that only civilized men make. They conform neither to the legal nor to the moral jargon of Mississippi—of Neshoba County particularly.

[The report that Chaney was allowed to make bail and that then all three civil rights workers were released is open to serious question.

They left the jail in the evening. That is clear, *but,* and here is the basis for questioning the story: It is one of the cardinal rules of civil rights workers in Mississippi *never to venture out at night.* The most dangerous thing you can do, a saying among civil rights workers goes, is to get yourself released from jail *at night.* These three were trained civil rights workers and it is difficult, if not impossible, to imagine that they walked out into the night of their own volition.

Nevertheless, we have the fact that they left the jail and just about three miles from Philadelphia they fell into the hands of a mob.

It is not known precisely how many men were in the mob. Six, at least, have been identified by eye witnesses. But because they have not been charged with the crime, their names cannot now be revealed.]

The frogs and the varmints are moaning in the bayous. By now the moon is midnight high. Chaney, the Negro of the three, is tied to a tree and beaten with chains. His bones snap and his screams pierce the still midnight air. But the screams are soon ended. There is no noise now except for the thud of chains crushing flesh—and the crack of ribs and bones.

Andrew Goodman and Michael Schwerner look on in horror. Then they break into tears over their black brother.

"You goddam nigger lovers!" shouts one of the mob. "What do you think now?"

Only God knows what Andrew Goodman and Michael Schwerner think. Martin Luther King and James Farmer and non-violence are integral parts of their being. But all of the things they have been taught suddenly became foreign, of no effect.

Schwerner cracks; he breaks from the men who are holding them and rushes toward the tree to aid Chaney. Michael Schwerner takes no more than 10 steps before he is subdued and falls to the ground.

Then Goodman breaks and lunges toward the fallen Schwerner. He too is wrestled into submission.

The three civil rights workers are loaded into a car and the five-car caravan makes its way toward the predetermined burial ground. Even the men who committed the crimes are not certain whether Chaney is dead when they take him down from the tree. But to make sure they stop about a mile from the burial place and fire three shots into him, and one shot each into the chests of Goodman and Schwerner.

The nation waited and watched. If the pattern of the years held true, the civil rights workers were most certainly dead. But—and none but the killers, and those to whom they boasted, knew the facts that have already been set forth here—there was always the outside chance that something strange and unusual had transpired, that the rights workers were alive. For the white racists this meant that the three men were tricksters, that they had intentionally pulled a hoax not only to blacken the name of Mississippi, but also to bring federal troops into Mississippi. For Negroes and civil rights advocates, the possibility that the three men were alive meant quite a different thing.

Working for civil rights in Mississippi often requires underground operations. Could it be, Negroes asked, that Schwerner, Goodman and Chaney were onto something really hot, that they had arranged to vanish in order to get a major job done. Nobody, neither foe nor friend, knew the truth.

In the Neshoba County area, however, strange things were beginning to occur.

A Negro cook was serving dinner and heard the white head of the household say, "Not only did they arrest those white nigger-lovers, they killed them and the nigger that was with them." Then the man looked up and realized that the cook had heard him. She was fired on the spot and was rushed to her home by her white mistress who feared for the cook's life. The cook fled Mississippi that night for, as the cook well knew, her white employer was (and still is) an official in the Citizens' Council.

The area is thinly populated by Choctaw Indians. There was a big Indian funeral on June 21st and they passed along both Routes 16 and 19. They saw something: the word spread that they had seen the three civil rights workers and the mob. Suddenly the Indians took to the swamps and would not talk—even to FBI investigators.

But most of all that silent meanness that only a Negro can know and feel—the hate stare that John Howard Griffin found when he himself became black and got on a bus in the deep South—settled over Neshoba County like a deadly dew.

"Lord, child," a Negro woman told a CORE investigator, "I have never seen the white folks act so mean for no reason at all. They just don't smile at me no more. It's like they done did something mean and think I know all about it!"

The white people were not too far from wrong. Somebody had *did* something mean and the whole country knew about it. They knew about it. They knew about it because, once murder was done, the whites involved went to a bootlegger, got themselves several gallons of moonshine and proceeded to get drunk and brag about the two white nigger-lovers and the nigger they had just finished killing. Despite what Sheriff Rainey, Governor Johnson and the two Mississippi Senators said, within twenty-four hours after the triple lynching, everybody in the county, Negro and white, knew that the civil rights workers were dead. *They also knew who committed the crimes.*

The entire matter burst upon the national and world scene at a time when it was fairly clear that the Republicans would nominate Arizona's Barry Goldwater. President Lyndon Johnson used every device to placate the deep South. He held numerous conversations with Mississippi's Governor Paul Johnson, and the Governor assured the President that everything was being done to locate the civil rights workers. Even so, the President ordered U.S. sailors into the area to aid in the search for the missing men.

Ignoring the claims that the civil rights workers were still alive, the sailors moved into Mississippi and proceeded under the assumption that the three were dead, as, of course, everybody knowledgeable about the matter knew they were.

Once they had arrived in Mississippi, the sailors donned hip boots and began to comb the swamps and the bayous, hardly places one would look for men who are hiding out.

Then two days later the first break came. The blue Ford station wagon in which the civil rights workers had been traveling was found charred and burned along a road some ten miles northeast of Philadelphia. The charred station wagon was discovered late in the afternoon and natives, Negro and white, who had used the road that morning, came forth to say that the wagon had not been there earlier in the day when they had passed the spot on their way to work.

The truth is that the station wagon was not there on the morning of the 22nd. Rather, the killers had doused the station wagon with the same kind of naphtha that had been used to burn down the Mount Zion Methodist Church. In addition, they set it on fire several miles from the area where the station wagon was finally discovered. This fact is borne out when it is recalled that most of the foliage around the area where the charred station wagon was found was unscarred. Had the station wagon been put to the torch where it was found the foliage would have been scarred and the blaze would have attracted people from miles around. Clearly, and without a doubt, the station wagon had been burned elsewhere and had been towed to the site where it was discovered. Not only did the traces of naphtha show up, but investigators were struck by the fact that only the metal parts of the station wagon remained undestroyed.

This grim discovery served to intensify the search. Only the noisy psychopathic Mississippians could continue to insist that the disappearance was a hoax, that the three civil rights workers had intentionally vanished and were hiding somewhere behind the Communist Iron Curtain, preferably in China.

Gripping heavy wooden clubs to fight off water moccasins and rattlesnakes, several hundred sailors sloshed through the Mississippi swampland, searching for the bodies of the missing men. Paddling about in fourteen foot aluminum skiffs and talking with their commander over walkie-talkies, the sailors dragged the Pearl river, to no avail. The President of the United States ordered even more sailors and FBI men into Mississippi. All to no avail.

Other FBI agents were conducting an investigation on land. They zeroed in on Neshoba County Sheriff Lawrence Rainey who, by his own admission, had killed two Negroes in recent years.

"Yep, by God," Rainey told the investigators, "I killed them two niggers. The first had me down on the ground choking me. The other nigger I killed was shooting at me."

But Sheriff Rainey did not join in the hunt for the missing civil rights workers. That same day there was a flurry of excitement when the body of an unidentified white man was found in a swamp near Oakland, Mississippi, some one hundred miles from the search area. The first reports indicated that the body was that of Michael Schwerner. Instead it turned out to be that of a carnival worker who had been run over and mutilated in a

highway accident. Just how that body wound up in a Mississippi swamp
has yet to be explained.

While the world wondered and pondered, white Mississippi sensed the
truth. As osmosis is the mysterious passing of a liquid through a membrane, so is spasmodic reality the mystic, lucid, moment when white Mississippi admits the truth about itself. The moment is brief, the lucidity is
blurred, but the memory remains and as white Mississippi awakes to the
smell of magnolia blossoms it cannot deny that part of last night's nightmare was real. Then white Mississippians grow real mean and protective.

As the search for the missing civil rights workers continued Mississippi
born Frank Trippett, now an associate editor of Newsweek magazine,
drove throughout his homeland to talk to the men and women, the boys
and girls he played marbles with when he was a child.

"John F. Kennedy should have been killed," one of Trippett's childhood
chums told him. "He had no business going down to Dallas just to stir up
them people and get votes."

Then Trippett's one time playmate went on to wish for the future: "They
proved it out in Dallas. They's always one that can get through. I tell you,
little Bobby [Attorney General Robert F. Kennedy] better not come down
around here."

But Trippett didn't want to hear about the Kennedys. He wanted to
know what his childhood friends in and around Neshoba County felt and
knew about the disappearance of Michael Schwerner, James Chaney and
Andrew Goodman. Nobody would talk about that. The cotton curtain had
long since descended and any white man who talked about what happened
to the three civil rights workers was not only a traitor to the south but an
ethnic bastard to boot. Asked about the three civil rights workers, Trippett's childhood playmates lapsed into the oblique morality that earned
William Faulkner a Nobel prize for literature.

"There's going to be some killings if these niggers start trying to get into
cafes and things," an old friend told Trippett. "Every store in Starkville
has sold out every bullet they can lay their hands on."

Reporter Trippett did his best but none of his childhood friends would
talk about what they all knew had happened over on Route 16, near the
Longdale area and just outside of Philadelphia. One of Trippett's friends,
however, got dangerously close to the truth. This friend, a well educated
man now in his early middle years, took Trippett home to dinner. Midway
through the meal the man turned to his wife and said *"would you kill
one?"* They and Trippett knew the man was asking his wife if she had the
courage to kill a Negro, or to put it another way, would she have done
what they all knew several men had done a few nights previously along
Route 16?

The wife blushed, then turned to reporter Trippett.

"Do they give you any trouble in New York? Do you let them know you are from Mississippi?"

Trippett kept his silence.

"I guess you will go back and write a whole lot of lies about us," his host said.

"No," Trippett replied. "I am going to do worse than that. I am going back and write the truth."

Once out of Mississippi, Trippett added a footnote to the conversation. "I will not write the truth about Mississippi," he said, "only because the truth about my home state is so incredible that nobody will believe me."

But, as we Negroes in Georgia used to say, the truth *did out. It outed* in a way no civilized person could believe or deny.

The Governor of Mississippi and other state officials were flooding the nation's press with statistics showing that Mississippi has one of the lowest crime rates in the nation. The facts showed that during 1963 Mississippi had only 393.2 major crimes per one hundred thousand people which is far below the 472.9 major crime rate for each one hundred thousand people in North Dakota, the second best state, and far, far, below the 2,990.1 major crime rate per one hundred thousand which was registered in Nevada, the most crime ridden state in the Republic.

Missing in this statistical braggadocio, of course, is the fact that Mississippi simply does not list the crimes of whites against Negroes. Alas, Mississippi statistics also fail to list crimes of Negroes against Negroes, who comprise forty-five per cent of the state's population. The raw facts are these: Mississippi authorities know of at least nineteen church burnings, fifty floggings of Negroes by whites, another one hundred incidents of violence to Negroes by whites, and at least eleven Negro deaths which are almost certainly lynchings. There have been no arrests for any of these crimes and they are not among those reported as Mississippi presents its clean bill of health to the nation.

Meanwhile the search for the missing rights workers continued. Negro comedian Dick Gregory flew into Mississippi and obtained an interview with a white man and said he had final evidence of what had happened on the night of June 21st. Gregory then went on to offer a twenty-five thousand dollar reward for information that would lead to the arrest and conviction of the killers. But the FBI, under the whiplash from President Johnson who was being inundated with demands that the government do something about the killings, quietly spread the word that they would pay twenty-five thousand dollars for information leading to the location of the bodies and the arrest and conviction of the lynchers.

There was a brief flurry of excitement when the dismembered bodies of two Negro men were found floating in the river along the border between Mississippi and Louisiana. It turned out, however, that these were not the bodies of the missing civil rights workers and the grim search continued.

The killers had learned their lessons well. There was no longer doubt that the three civil rights workers were dead and buried. Rather, the Bayou bingo game turned on whether the FBI could find bodies that had been buried in such a fashion that they would never float to the surface, and on whether, like the Jesus the killers professed to serve, they would ever rise again.

The bodies did not float. They did not rise again. Had they remained where the killers buried them the bodies would have been unearthed, perhaps, by twenty-fifth century man as he attempted to decipher the hieroglyphics of our age, the nonsay language of a civilization whose founding documents, roughly translated, said all men are created equal: that all men, regardless of race, creed or color were free to pursue happiness, catch as catch can.

Blood, in the deep south of all places, is thicker than water. But greed, particularly among poor Mississippi white trash, is thicker than blood. The government's twenty-five thousand dollar reward was more than a knowledgeable poor white Mississippi man could bear. He cracked and told it all. The white informant knew it all and he spilled his guts all night long.

The next morning the FBI moved into action. As one Negro man put it, "this was the first time I got the feeling these white investigators knew what they was doing and where they had to go to do it."

One morning FBI agents came calling on trucker Olen Burrage at his office some three miles southwest of Philadelphia.

"What you'all want?" Burrage demanded.

"We have a search warrant."

"For this office?"

"Nope" the Federal men snapped. "We have a warrant to search your farm."

"Well, by God, go ahead and search it," Burrage snapped. "Look all you'all want to."

The FBI agents were all set to do just that. They moved on to Burrage's farm, some two miles down the road, along Highway twenty-one. They used bulldozers to cut their way through the tangle of scrub pine, kuduzu vine, and undergrowth to a dam site under construction several hundred yards from the roadway. Then they moved in the lumbering excavator cranes. The cranes began chewing away the clay earth and the recently laid concrete. While the natives, Negro and white, looked on in disbelief, the cranes gnawed out a V-shaped hole in the twenty foot high wall that shielded the dam. There, under a few feet of concrete, in the drizzly Mis-

sissippi dusk, they found the bodies of Michael Schwerner, Andrew Goodman and James Chaney.

The fantasy was over.

No. I apologize, it was not over. It had just entered another chapter.
Deputy Sheriff Price was on hand and he helped lift the three bodies from
the dam site and wrap them in cellophane for shipment to Jackson for further study. The remains were slithered into separate cellophane bags and
tagged "X1", "X2" and "X3". In Jackson the bodies of Schwerner and
Goodman were identified by fingerprints and dental records. There was no
way to be certain, but third body was black and there was little doubt that
it was James Chaney.

The macabre discovery told the nation what a few of us had already
known, what the rest of us had feared. The three civil rights workers were
quite dead: Chaney, the Negro in the trio had been brutally chain-beaten
and then shot. His white brothers in the faith had then been shot to death.
The only questions that remained were: who were the killers and what
would happen to them. But, and this is the irony of the matter, by then
everybody—from Moscow, Mississippi to Moscow, Russia—knew how,
where, when, and by whom the rights workers were slain.

Most respectable white Mississippians were shocked by the disclosure.

"I just didn't think we had people like that around," said the coach of
the all white Jackson, Mississippi, football team. But other white Mississippians took a different view. They were appalled that a white Mississippi
stool pigeon would tell on other white Mississippians.

"Somebody broke our code," one white Mississippian told the FBI.
"No honorable white man would have told you what happened."

But in the hearts in black Mississippians there was great rejoicing.

"I am sorry the three fellows is dead," a Mississippi Negro told me.
"But five of us that we know about have been killed this year and nobody
raised any hell about it. This time they killed two ofays. Now two white
boys is dead and all the world comes running to look and see. They never
would have done this had just us been dead."

Rita Schwerner, dressed in widow's weeds, was much more precise
about it.

"My husband did not die in vain," she told a New York audience. "If
he and Andrew Goodman had been Negro the world would have taken little note of their death. After all the slaying of a Negro in Mississippi is
not news. It is only because my husband and Andrew Goodman were
white that the national alarm has been sounded."

Michael Schwerner, Andrew Goodman, and James Chaney are all now
buried, asleep with their forefathers. Goodman and Schwerner lie in six
feet of rest and peace, beneath the clay that covers all Jews in New York

County. James Chaney rests alone, beneath the soggy clay on the colored side of the cemetery fence that separates the white who are dead and buried from the colored who are dead and buried in Mississippi.

The paths of their lives tangled, became all mixed up, and then merged into a single country road that led to tragedy and death that transcends race, religion and creed.

One was Catholic and Negro. The other two were Jews. But in their hearts they were one.

The American Negro has survived on a prayer and a dream. The prayer was that one day they could take their place in the American mainstream as just other humans in pursuit of happiness.

Michael, Andrew, and James, then, are three coins we Negroes—No! We believers in justice, black and white, Protestant and Catholic, Jew and Gentile—tossed into the fountain.

The only question now remaining is: which one will the fountain bless.

JAMES BALDWIN

Notes of a Native Son

In this selection James Baldwin ruminates on his father's disintegration, ostensibly physical, but in fact a moral dissolution, a self-hatred that Baldwin perceives to be the predictable—and dangerous—response to race prejudice. On the surface Baldwin seems cool, almost dispassionate, in his narration, but there is a pervasive sense of bitterness that he knows he must ultimately convert to action if he is to avoid his father's demoralization.

O N THE 29th OF JULY, in 1943, my father died. On the same day, a few hours later, his last child was born. Over a month before this, while all our energies were concentrated in waiting for these events, there had been, in Detroit, one of the bloodiest race riots of the century. A few hours after my father's funeral, while he lay in state in the undertaker's chapel, a race riot broke out in Harlem. On the morning of the 3rd of August, we drove my father to the graveyard through a wilderness of smashed plate glass.

The day of my father's funeral had also been my nineteenth birthday. As we drove him to the graveyard, the spoils of injustice, anarchy, discontent, and hatred were all around us. It seemed to me that God himself had devised, to mark my father's end, the most sustained and brutally dissonant of codas. And it seemed to me, too, that the violence which rose all about us as my father left the world had been devised as a corrective for the pride of his eldest son. I had declined to believe in that apocalypse which had been central to my father's vision; very well, life seemed to be saying, here is something that will certainly pass for an apocalypse until the real thing comes along. I had inclined to be contemptuous of my father for the conditions of his life, for the conditions of our lives. When his life had ended I began to wonder about that life and also, in a new way, to be apprehensive about my own.

I had not known my father very well. We had got on badly, partly because we shared, in our different fashions, the vice of stubborn pride. When he was dead I realized that I had hardly ever spoken to him. When he had been dead a long time I began to wish I had. It seems to be typical of life in America, where opportunities, real and fancied, are thicker than anywhere else on the globe, that the second generation has no time to talk to the first. No one, including my father, seems to have known exactly how old he was, but his mother had been born during slavery. He was of the first generation of free men. He, along with thousands of other Negroes, came North after 1919 and I was part of that generation which had never seen the landscape of what Negroes sometimes call the Old Country.

He had been born in New Orleans and had been a quite young man there during the time that Louis Armstrong, a boy, was running errands for the dives and honky-tonks of what was always presented to me as one of the most wicked of cities—to this day, whenever I think of New Orleans, I also helplessly think of Sodom and Gomorrah. My father never mentioned Louis Armstrong, except to forbid us to play his records; but there was a picture of him on our wall for a long time. One of my father's strong-willed female relatives had placed it there and forbade my father to take it down. He never did, but he eventually maneuvered her out of the house and when, some years later, she was in trouble and near death, he refused to do anything to help her.

He was, I think, very handsome. I gather this from photographs and from my own memories of him, dressed in his Sunday best and on his way to preach a sermon somewhere, when I was little. Handsome, proud, and ingrown, "like a toe-nail," somebody said. But he looked at me, as I grew older, like pictures I had seen of African tribal chieftains: he really should have been naked, with war-paint on and barbaric mementos, standing among spears. He could be chilling in the pulpit and indescribably cruel in his personal life and he was certainly the most bitter man I have ever met; yet it must be said that there was something else in him, buried in him, which lent him his tremendous power and, even, a rather crushing charm. It had something to do with his blackness, I think—he was very black— with his blackness and his beauty, and with the fact that he knew that he was black but did not know that he was beautiful. He claimed to be proud of his blackness but it had also been the cause of much humiliation and it had fixed bleak boundaries to his life. He was not a young man when we were growing up and he had already suffered many kinds of ruin; in his outrageously demanding and protective way he loved his children, who were black like him and menaced, like him; and all these things sometimes showed in his face when he tried, never to my knowledge with any success, to establish contact with any of us. When he took one of his children on his knee to play, the child always became fretful and began to cry; when he tried to help one of us with our homework the absolutely unabating tension which emanated from him caused our minds and our tongues to become paralyzed, so that he, scarcely knowing why, flew into a rage and the child, not knowing why, was punished. If it ever entered his head to bring a surprise home for his children, it was, almost unfailingly, the wrong surprise and even the big watermelons he often brought home on his back in the summertime led to the most appalling scenes. I do not remember, in all those years, that one of his children was ever glad to see him come home. From what I was able to gather of his early life, it seemed that this inability to establish contact with other people had always marked him and had been one of the things which had driven him out of New Orleans. There was something in him, therefore, groping and tentative, which was never expressed and which was buried with him. One saw it most clearly when he was facing new people and hoping to impress them. But he never did, not for long. We went from church to smaller and more improbable church, he found himself in less and less demand as a minister, and by the time he died none of his friends had come to see him for a long time. He had lived and died in an intolerable bitterness of spirit and it frightened me, as we drove him to the graveyard through those unquiet, ruined streets, to see how powerful and overflowing this bitterness could be and to realize that this bitterness now was mine.

When he died I had been away from home for a little over a year. In that year I had had time to become aware of the meaning of all my father's bitter warnings, had discovered the secret of his proudly pursed lips and rigid carriage: I had discovered the weight of white people in the world. I saw that this had been for my ancestors and now would be for me an awful thing to live with and that the bitterness which had helped to kill my father could also kill me.

He had been ill a long time—in the mind, as we now realized, reliving instances of his fantastic intransigence in the new light of his affliction and endeavoring to feel a sorrow for him which never, quite, came true. We had not known that he was being eaten up by paranoia, and the discovery that his cruelty, to our bodies and our minds, had been one of the symptoms of his illness was not, then, enough to enable us to forgive him. The younger children felt, quite simply, relief that he would not be coming home anymore. My mother's observation that it was he, after all, who had kept them alive all these years meant nothing because the problems of keeping children alive are not real for children. The older children felt, with my father gone, that they could invite their friends to the house without fear that their friends would be insulted or, as had sometimes happened with me, being told that their friends were in league with the devil and intended to rob our family of everything we owned. (I didn't fail to wonder, and it made me hate him, what on earth we owned that anybody else would want.)

His illness was beyond all hope of healing before anyone realized that he was ill. He had always been so strange and had lived, like a prophet, in such unimaginably close communion with the Lord that his long silences which were punctuated by moans and hallelujahs and snatches of old songs while he sat at the living-room window never seemed odd to us. It was not until he refused to eat because, he said, his family was trying to poison him that my mother was forced to accept as a fact what had, until then, been only an unwilling suspicion. When he was committed, it was discovered that he had tuberculosis and, as it turned out, the disease of his mind allowed the disease of his body to destroy him. For the doctors could not force him to eat, either, and, though he was fed intravenously, it was clear from the beginning that there was no hope for him.

In my mind's eye I could see him, sitting at the window, locked up in his terrors; hating and fearing every living soul including his children who had betrayed him, too, by reaching towards the world which had despised him. There were nine of us. I began to wonder what it could have felt like for such a man to have had nine children whom he could barely feed. He used to make little jokes about our poverty, which never, of course, seemed very funny to us; they could not have seemed very funny to him, either, or else our all too feeble response to them would never have caused such rages. He spent great energy and achieved, to our chagrin, no small amount of success in keeping us away from the people who surrounded us, people who had all-night rent parties to which we listened when we should have been sleeping, people who cursed and drank and flashed razor blades on Lenox Avenue. He could not understand why, if they had so much energy to spare, they could not use it to make their lives better. He treated almost everybody on our block with a most uncharitable asperity and neither they, nor, of course, their children were slow to reciprocate.

The only white people who came to our house were welfare workers and bill collectors. It was almost always my mother who dealt with them, for my father's temper, which was at the mercy of his pride, was never to be trusted. It was clear that he felt their very presence in his home to be a violation: this was conveyed by his carriage, almost ludicrously stiff, and by his voice, harsh and vindictively polite. When I was around nine or ten I wrote a play which was directed by a young, white schoolteacher, a woman, who then took an interest in me, and gave me books to read and, in order to corroborate my theatrical bent, decided to take me to see what she somewhat tactlessly referred to as "real" plays. Theater-going was forbidden in our house, but, with the really cruel intuitiveness of a child, I suspected that the color of this woman's skin would carry the day for me. When, at school, she suggested taking me to the theater, I did not, as I might have done if she had been a Negro, find a way of discouraging her, but agreed that she should pick me up at my house one evening. I then, very cleverly, left all the rest to my mother, who suggested to my father, as I knew she would, that it would not be very nice to let such a kind woman make the trip for nothing. Also, since it was a schoolteacher, I imagine that my mother countered the idea of sin with the idea of "education," which word, even with my father, carried a kind of bitter weight.

Before the teacher came my father took me aside to ask *why* she was coming, what *interest* she could possibly have in our house, in a boy like me. I said I didn't know but I, too, suggested that it had something to do with education. And I understood that my father was waiting for me to say something—I didn't quite know what; perhaps that I wanted his protection against this teacher and her "education." I said none of these things and the teacher came and we went out. It was clear, during the brief interview in our living room, that my father was agreeing very much against his will and that he would have refused permission if he had dared. The fact that he did not dare caused me to despise him: I had no way of knowing that he was facing in that living room a wholly unprecedented and frightening situation.

Later, when my father had been laid off from his job, this woman became very important to us. She was really a very sweet and generous woman and went to a great deal of trouble to be of help to us, particularly during one awful winter. My mother called her by the highest name she knew: she said she was a "christian." My father could scarcely disagree but during the four or five years of our relatively close association he never trusted her and was always trying to surprise in her open, Midwestern face the genuine, cunningly hidden, and hideous motivation. In later years, particularly when it began to be clear that this "education" of mine was going to lead me to perdition, he became more explicit and warned me that my white friends in high school were not really my friends and that I would see, when I was older, how white people would do anything to keep a Negro down. Some of them could be nice, he admitted, but none of them were to be trusted and most of them were not even nice. The best thing was to have as little to do with them as possible. I did not feel this way and I was certain, in my innocence, that I never would.

But the year which preceded my father's death had made a great change in my life. I had been living in New Jersey, working in defense plants, working and living among southerners, white and black. I knew about the south, of course, and about how southerners treated Negroes and how they expected them to behave, but it had never entered my mind that anyone would look at me and expect *me* to behave that way. I learned in New Jersey that to be a Negro meant, precisely, that one was never looked at but was simply at the mercy of the reflexes the color of one's skin caused in other people. I acted in New Jersey as I had always acted, that is as though I thought a great deal of myself—I had to *act* that way—with results that were, simply, unbelievable. I had scarcely arrived before I had earned the enmity, which was extraordinarily ingenious, of all my superiors and nearly all my co-workers. In the beginning, to make matters worse, I simply did not know what was happening. I did not know what I had done, and I shortly began to wonder what *anyone* could possibly do, to bring about such unanimous, active, and unbearably vocal hostility. I knew about jim-crow but I had never experienced it. I went to the same self-service restaurant three times and stood with all the Princeton boys before the counter, waiting for a hamburger and coffee; it was always an extraordinarily long time before anything was set before me; but it was not until the fourth visit that I learned that, in fact, nothing had ever been set before me: I had simply picked something up. Negroes were not served there, I was told, and they had been waiting for me to realize that I was always the only Negro present. Once I was told this, I determined to go there all the time. But now they were ready for me and, though some dreadful scenes were subsequently enacted in that restaurant, I never ate there again.

It was the same story all over New Jersey, in bars, bowling alleys, diners, places to live. I was always being forced to leave, silently, or with mutual imprecations. I very shortly became notorious and children giggled behind me when I passed and their elders whispered or shouted—they really believed that I was mad. And it did begin to work on my mind, of course; I began to be afraid to go anywhere and to compensate for this I went places to which I really should not have gone and where, God knows, I had no desire to be. My reputation in town naturally enhanced my reputation at work and my working day became one long series of acrobatics designed to keep me out of trouble. I cannot say that these acrobatics succeeded. It began to seem that the machinery of the organization I worked for was turning over, day and night, with but one aim: to eject me. I was fired once, and contrived, with the aid of a friend from New York, to get back on the payroll; was fired again, and bounced back again. It took a while to fire me for the third time, but the third time took. There were no loopholes anywhere. There was not even any way of getting back inside the gates.

That year in New Jersey lives in my mind as though it were the year during which, having an unsuspected predilection for it, I first contracted some dread, chronic disease, the unfailing symptom of which is a kind of blind fever, a pounding in the skull and fire in the bowels. Once this disease is contracted, one can never be really carefree again, for the fever, without an instant's warning, can recur at any moment. It can wreck more important things than race relations. There is not a Negro alive who does not have this rage in his blood—one has the choice, merely, of living with it consciously or surrendering to it. As for me, this fever has recurred in me, and does, and will until the day I die.

My last night in New Jersey, a white friend from New York took me to the nearest big town, Trenton, to go to the movies and have a few drinks. As it turned out, he also saved me from, at the very least, a violent whipping. Almost every detail of that night stands out very clearly in my memory. I even remember the name of the movie we saw because its title impressed me as being so patly ironical. It was a movie about the German occupation of France, starring Maureen O'Hara and Charles Laughton and called *This Land Is Mine*. I remember the name of the diner we walked into when the movie ended: it was the "American Diner." When we walked in the counterman asked what we wanted and I remember answering with the casual sharpness which had become my habit: "We want a hamburger and a cup of coffee, what do you think we want?" I do not know why, after a year of such rebuffs, I so completely failed to anticipate his answer, which was, of course, "We don't serve Negroes here." This reply failed to discompose me, at least for the moment. I made some sardonic comment about the name of the diner and we walked out into the streets.

This was the time of what was called the "brown-out," when the lights in all American cities were very dim. When we re-entered the streets something happened to me which had the force of an optical illusion, or a nightmare. The streets were very crowded and I was facing north. People were moving in every direction but it seemed to me, in that instant, that all of the people I could see, and many more than that, were moving toward me, against me, and that everyone was white. I remember how their faces gleamed. And I felt, like a physical sensation, a *click* at the nape of my neck as though some interior string connecting my head to my body had been cut. I began to walk. I heard my friend call after me, but I ignored him. Heaven only knows what was going on in his mind, but he had the good sense not to touch me—I don't know what would have happened if he had—and to keep me in sight. I don't know what was going on in my mind, either; I certainly had no conscious plan. I wanted to do something to crush these white faces, which were crushing me. I walked for perhaps a block or two until I came to an enormous, glittering, and fashionable restaurant in which I knew not even the intercession of the Virgin would cause me to be served. I pushed through the doors and took the first vacant seat I saw, at a table for two, and waited.

I do not know how long I waited and I rather wonder, until today, what I could possibly have looked like. Whatever I looked like, I frightened the waitress who shortly appeared, and the moment she appeared all of my fury flowed towards her. I hated her for her white face, and for her great, astounded, frightened eyes. I felt that if she found a black man so frightening I would make her fright worth-while.

She did not ask me what I wanted, but repeated, as though she had learned it somewhere, "We don't serve Negroes here." She did not say it with the blunt, derisive hostility to which I had grown so accustomed, but, rather, with a note of apology in her voice, and fear. This made me colder and more murderous than ever. I felt I had to do something with my hands. I wanted her to come close enough for me to get her neck between my hands.

So I pretended not to have understood her, hoping to draw her closer. And she did step a very short step closer, with her pencil poised incongruously over her pad, and repeated the formula: ". . . don't serve Negroes here."

Somehow, with the repetition of that phrase, which was already ringing in my head like a thousand bells of a nightmare, I realized that she would never come any closer and that I would have to strike from a distance. There was nothing on the table but an ordinary water-mug half full of water, and I picked this up and hurled it with all my strength at her. She ducked and it missed her and shattered against the mirror behind the bar. And, with that sound, my frozen blood abruptly thawed, I returned from wherever I had been, I *saw,* for the first time, the restaurant, the people with their mouths open, already, as it seemed to me, rising as one man, and I realized what I had done, and where I was, and I was frightened. I rose and began running for the door. A round, potbellied man grabbed me by the nape of the neck just as I reached the doors and began to beat me about the face. I kicked him and got loose and ran into the streets. My friend whispered, *"Run!"* and I ran.

My friend stayed outside the restaurant long enough to misdirect my pursuers and the police, who arrived, he told me, at once. I do not know what I said to him when he came to my room that night. I could not have said much. I felt, in the oddest, most awful way, that I had somehow betrayed him. I lived it over and over and over again, the way one relives an automobile accident after it has happened and one finds oneself alone and safe. I could not get over two facts, both equally difficult for the imagination to grasp, and one was that I could have been murdered. But the other was that I had been ready to commit murder. I saw nothing very clearly but I did see this: that my life, my *real* life, was in danger, and not from anything other people might do but from the hatred I carried in my own heart.

II

I had returned home around the second week in June—in great haste because it seemed that my father's death and my mother's confinement were both but a matter of hours. In the case of my mother, it soon became clear that she had simply made a miscalculation. This had always been her tendency and I don't believe that a single one of us arrived in the world, or has since arrived anywhere else, on time. But none of us dawdled so intolerably about the business of being born as did my baby sister. We sometimes amused ourselves, during those endless, stifling weeks, by picturing the baby sitting within in the safe, warm dark, bitterly regretting the necessity of becoming a part of our chaos and stubbornly putting it off as long as possible. I understood her perfectly and congratulated her on showing such good sense so soon. Death, however, sat as purposefully at my father's bedside as life stirred within my mother's womb and it was harder to understand why he so lingered in that long shadow. It seemed that he had bent, and for a long time, too, all of his energies towards dying. Now death was ready for him but my father held back.

All of Harlem, indeed, seemed to be infected by waiting. I had never before known it to be so violently still. Racial tensions throughout this country were exacerbated during the early years of the war, partly because the labor market brought together hundreds of thousands of ill-prepared people and partly because Negro soldiers, regardless of where they were born, received their military training in the south. What happened in defense plants and army camps had repercussions, naturally, in every Negro ghetto. The situation in Harlem had grown bad enough for clergymen, policemen, educators, politicians, and social workers to assert in one breath that there was no "crime wave" and to offer, in the very next breath, suggestions as to how to combat it. These suggestions always seemed to involve playgrounds, despite the fact that racial skirmishes were occurring in the playgrounds, too. Playground or not, crime wave or not, the Harlem police force had been augmented in March, and the unrest grew—perhaps, in fact, partly as a result of the ghetto's instinctive hatred of policemen. Perhaps the most revealing news item, out of the steady parade of reports of muggings, stabbings, shootings, assaults, gang wars, and accusations of police brutality, is the item concerning six Negro girls who set upon a white girl in the subway because, as they all too accurately put it, she was stepping on their toes. Indeed she was, all over the nation.

I had never before been so aware of policemen, on foot, on horseback, on corners, everywhere, always two by two. Nor had I ever been so aware of small knots of people. They were on stoops and on corners and in doorways, and what was striking about them, I think, was that they did not seem to be talking. Never, when I passed these groups, did the usual sound of a curse or a laugh ring out and neither did there seem to be any hum of gossip. There was certainly, on the other hand, occurring between them communication extraordinarily intense. Another thing that was striking was the unexpected diversity of the people who made up these groups. Usually, for example, one would see a group of sharpies standing on the street corner, jiving the passing chicks; or a group of older men, usually, for some reason, in the vicinity of a barber shop, discussing baseball scores, or the numbers, or making rather chilling observations about women they had known. Women, in a general way, tended to be seen less often together—unless they were church women, or very young girls, or prostitutes met together for an unprofessional instant. But that summer I saw the strangest combinations: large, respectable, churchly matrons standing on the stoops or the corners with their hair tied up, together with a girl in sleazy satin whose face bore the marks of gin and the razor, or heavyset, abrupt, no-nonsense older men, in company with the most disreputable and fanatical "race" men, or these same "race" men with the sharpies, or these sharpies with the churchly women. Seventh Day Adventists and Methodists and Spiritualists seemed to be hobnobbing with Holyrollers and they were all, alike, entangled with the most flagrant disbelievers; something heavy in their stance seemed to indicate that they had all, incredibly, seen a common vision, and on each face there seemed to be the same strange, bitter shadow.

The churchly women and the matter-of-fact, no-nonsense men had children in the Army. The sleazy girls they talked to had lovers there, the sharpies and the "race" men had friends and brothers there. It would have demanded an unquestioning patriotism, happily as uncommon in this country as it is undesirable, for these people not to have been disturbed by the bitter letters they received, by the newspaper stories they read, not to have been enraged by the posters, then to be found all over New York, which described the Japanese as "yellow-bellied Japs." It was only the "race" men, to be sure, who spoke ceaselessly of being revenged—how this vengeance was to be exacted was not clear—for the indignities and dangers suffered by Negro boys in uniform; but everybody felt a directionless, hopeless bitterness, as well as that panic which can scarcely be suppressed when one knows that a human being one loves is beyond one's reach, and in danger. This helplessness and this gnawing uneasiness does something, at length, to even the toughest mind. Perhaps the best way to sum all this up is to say that the people I knew felt, mainly, a peculiar kind of relief when they knew that their boys were being shipped out of the south, to do battle overseas. It was, perhaps, like feeling that the most dangerous part of a dangerous journey had been passed and that now, even if death should come, it would come with honor and without the complicity of their countrymen. Such a death would be, in short, a fact with which one could hope to live.

It was on the 28th of July, which I believe was a Wednesday, that I visited my father for the first time during his illness and for the last time in his life. The moment I saw him I knew why I had put off this visit so long. I had told my mother that I did not want to see him because I hated him. But this was not true. It was only that I *had* hated him and I wanted to hold on to this hatred. I did not want to look on him as a ruin: it was not a ruin I had hated. I imagine that one of the reasons people cling to their hates so stubbornly is because they sense, once hate is gone, that they will be forced to deal with pain.

We traveled out to him, his older sister and myself, to what seemed to be the very end of a very Long Island. It was hot and dusty and we wrangled, my aunt and I, all the way out, over the fact that I had recently begun to smoke and, as she said, to give myself airs. But I knew that she wrangled with me because she could not bear to face the fact of her brother's dying. Neither could I endure the reality of her despair, her unstated bafflement as to what had happened to her brother's life, and her own. So we wrangled and I smoked and from time to time she fell into a heavy reverie. Covertly, I watched her face, which was the face of an old woman; it had fallen in, the eyes were sunken and lightless; soon she would be dying, too.

In my childhood—it had not been so long ago—I had thought her beautiful. She had been quick-witted and quick-moving and very generous with all the children and each of her visits had been an event. At one time one of my brothers and myself had thought of running away to live with her. Now she could no longer produce out of her handbag some unexpected and yet familiar delight. She made me feel pity and revulsion and fear. It was awful to realize that she no longer caused me to feel affection. The closer we came to the hospital the more querulous she became and at the same time, naturally, grew more dependent on me. Between pity and guilt and fear I began to feel that there was another me trapped in my skull like a jack-in-the-box who might escape my control at any moment and fill the air with screaming.

She began to cry the moment we entered the room and she saw him lying there, all shriveled and still, like a little black monkey. The great, gleaming apparatus which fed him and would have compelled him to be still even if he had been able to move brought to mind, not beneficence, but torture; the tubes entering his arm made me think of pictures I had seen when a child, of Gulliver, tied down by the pygmies on that island. My aunt wept and wept, there was a whistling sound in my father's throat; nothing was said; he could not speak. I wanted to take his hand, to say something. But I do not know what I could have said, even if he could have heard me. He was not really in that room with us, he had at last really embarked on his journey; and though my aunt told me that he said he was going to meet Jesus, I did not hear anything except that whistling in his throat. The doctor came back and we left, into that unbearable train again, and home. In the morning came the telegram saying that he was dead. Then the house was suddenly full of relatives, friends, hysteria, and confusion and I quickly left my mother and the children to the care of those impressive women, who, in Negro communities at least, automatically appear at times of bereavement armed with lotions, proverbs, and patience, and an ability to cook. I went downtown. By the time I returned, later the same day, my mother had been carried to the hospital and the baby had been born.

III

For my father's funeral I had nothing black to wear and this posed a nagging problem all day long. It was one of those problems, simple, or impossible of solution, to which the mind insanely clings in order to avoid the mind's real trouble. I spent most of that day at the downtown apartment of a girl I knew, celebrating my birthday with whiskey and wondering what to wear that night. When planning a birthday celebration one naturally does not expect that it will be up against competition from a funeral and this girl had anticipated taking me out that night, for a big dinner and a night club afterwards. Sometime during the course of that long day we decided that we would go out anyway, when my father's funeral service was over. I imagine *I* decided it, since, as the funeral hour approached, it became clearer and clearer to me that I would not know what to do with myself when it was over. The girl, stifling her very lively concern as to the possible effects of the whiskey on one of my father's chief mourners, concentrated on being conciliatory and practically helpful. She found a black shirt for me somewhere and ironed it and, dressed in the darkest pants and jacket I owned, and slightly drunk, I made my way to my father's funeral.

The chapel was full, but not packed, and very quiet. There were, mainly, my father's relatives, and his children, and here and there I saw faces I had not seen since childhood, the faces of my father's one-time friends. They were very dark and solemn now, seeming somehow to suggest that they had known all along that something like this would happen. Chief among the mourners was my aunt, who had quarreled with my father all his life; by which I do not mean to suggest that her mourning was insincere or that she had not loved him. I suppose that she was one of the few people in the world who had, and their incessant quarreling proved precisely the strength of the tie that bound them. The only other person in the world, as far as I knew, whose relationship to my father rivaled my aunt's in depth was my mother, who was not there.

It seemed to me, of course, that it was a very long funeral. But it was, if anything, a rather shorter funeral than most, nor, since there were no overwhelming, uncontrollable expressions of grief, could it be called—if I dare to use the word—successful. The minister who preached my father's funeral sermon was one of the few my father had still been seeing as he neared his end. He presented to us in his sermon a man whom none of us had ever seen—a man thoughtful, patient, and forbearing, a Christian inspiration to all who knew him, and a model for his children. And no doubt the children, in their disturbed and guilty state, were almost ready to believe this; he had been remote enough to be anything and, anyway, the shock of the incontrovertible, that it was really our father lying up there in that casket, prepared the mind for anything. His sister moaned and this grief-stricken moaning was taken as corroboration. The other faces held a dark, non-committal thoughtfulness. This was not the man they had known, but they had scarcely expected to be confronted with *him;* this was, in a sense deeper than questions of fact, the man they had not known, and the man they had not known may have been the real one. The real man, whoever he had been, had suffered and now he was dead: this was all that was sure and all that mattered now. Every man in the chapel hoped that when his hour came he, too, would be eulogized, which is to say for- given, and that all of his lapses, greeds, errors, and strayings from the truth would be invested with coherence and looked upon with charity. This was perhaps the last thing human beings could give each other and it was what they demanded, after all, of the Lord. Only the Lord saw the mid- night tears, only He was present when one of His children, moaning and wringing hands, paced up and down the room. When one slapped one's child in anger the recoil in the heart reverberated through heaven and be- came part of the pain of the universe. And when the children were hungry and sullen and distrustful and one watched them, daily, growing wilder, and further away, and running headlong into danger, it was the Lord who knew what the charged heart endured as the strap was laid to the backside; the Lord alone who knew what one *would* have said if one had had, like the Lord, the gift of the living word. It was the Lord who knew of the im- possibility every parent in that room faced: how to prepare the child for the day when the child would be despised and how to *create* in the child —by what means?—a stronger antidote to this poison than one had found for oneself. The avenues, side streets, bars, billiard halls, hospitals, police stations, and even the playgrounds of Harlem—not to mention the houses of correction, the jails, and the morgue—testified to the potency of the poison while remaining silent as to the efficacy of whatever antidote, irre- sistibly raising the question of whether or not such an antidote existed; raising, which was worse, the question of whether or not an antidote was desirable; perhaps poison should be fought with poison. With these several schisms in the mind and with more terrors in the heart than could be named, it was better not to judge the man who had gone down under an impossible burden. It was better to remember: *Thou knowest this man's fall; but thou knowest not his wrassling.*

While the preacher talked and I watched the children—years of chang- ing their diapers, scrubbing them, slapping them, taking them to school, and scolding them had had the perhaps inevitable result of making me love them, though I am not sure I knew this then—my mind was busily break- ing out with a rash of disconnected impressions. Snatches of popular songs, indecent jokes, bits of books I had read, movie sequences, faces, voices, political issues—I thought I was going mad; all these impressions suspended, as it were, in the solution of the faint nausea produced in me by the heat and liquor. For a moment I had the impression that my alcoholic breath, inefficiently disguised with chewing gum, filled the entire chapel. Then someone began singing one of my father's favorite songs and, abruptly, I was with him, sitting on his knee, in the hot, enormous, crowded church which was the first church we attended. It was the Abyssinia Baptist Church on 138th Street. We had not gone there long. With this image, a host of others came. I had forgotten, in the rage of my growing up, how proud my father had been of me when I was little. Apparently, I had had a voice and my father had liked to show me off before the members of the church. I had forgotten what he had looked like when he was pleased but now I remembered that he had always been grinning with pleasure when my solos ended. I even remembered certain expressions on his face when he teased my mother—had he loved her? I would never know. And when had it all begun to change? For now it seemed that he had not always been cruel. I remembered being taken for a haircut and scraping my knee on the footrest of the barber's chair and I remembered my father's face as he soothed my crying and applied the stinging iodine. Then I remembered our fights, fights which had been of the worst possible kind because my technique had been silence.

I remembered the one time in all our life together when we had really spoken to each other.

It was on a Sunday and it must have been shortly before I left home. We were walking, just the two of us, in our usual silence, to or from church. I was in high school and had been doing a lot of writing and I was, at about this time, the editor of the high school magazine. But I had also been a Young Minister and had been preaching from the pulpit. Lately, I had been taking fewer engagements and preached as rarely as possible. It was said in the church, quite truthfully, that I was "cooling off."

My father asked me abruptly, "You'd rather write than preach, wouldn't you?"

I was astonished at his question—because it was a real question. I answered, "Yes."

That was all we said. It was awful to remember that that was all we had *ever* said.

The casket now was opened and the mourners were being led up the aisle to look for the last time on the deceased. The assumption was that the family was too overcome with grief to be allowed to make this journey alone and I watched while my aunt was led to the casket and, muffled in black, and shaking, led back to her seat. I disapproved of forcing the children to look on their dead father, considering that the shock of his death, or, more truthfully, the shock of death as a reality, was already a little more than a child could bear, but my judgment in this matter had been overruled and there they were, bewildered and frightened and very small, being led, one by one, to the casket. But there is also something very gallant about children at such moments. It has something to do with their silence and gravity and with the fact that one cannot help them. Their legs, somehow, seem *exposed,* so that it is at once incredible and terribly clear that their legs are all they have to hold them up.

I had not wanted to go to the casket myself and I certainly had not wished to be led there, but there was no way of avoiding either of these forms. One of the deacons led me up and I looked on my father's face. I cannot say that it looked like him at all. His blackness had been equivocated by powder and there was no suggestion in that casket of what his power had or could have been. He was simply an old man dead, and it was hard to believe that he had ever given anyone either joy or pain. Yet, his life filled that room. Further up the avenue his wife was holding his newborn child. Life and death so close together, and love and hatred, and right and wrong, said something to me which I did not want to hear concerning man, concerning the life of man.

After the funeral, while I was downtown desperately celebrating my birthday, a Negro soldier, in the lobby of the Hotel Braddock, got into a fight with a white policeman over a Negro girl. Negro girls, white policemen, in or out of uniform, and Negro males—in or out of uniform—were part of the furniture of the lobby of the Hotel Braddock and this was certainly not the first time such an incident had occurred. It was destined, however, to receive an unprecedented publicity, for the fight between the policeman and the soldier ended with the shooting of the soldier. Rumor, flowing immediately to the streets outside, stated that the soldier had been shot in the back, an instantaneous and revealing invention, and that the soldier had died protecting a Negro woman. The facts were somewhat different—for example, the soldier had not been shot in the back, and was not dead, and the girl seems to have been as dubious a symbol of womanhood as her white counterpart in Georgia usually is, but no one was interested in the facts. They preferred the invention because this invention expressed and corroborated their hates and fears so perfectly. It is just as well to remember that people are always doing this. Perhaps many of those legends, including Christianity, to which the world clings began their conquest of the world with just some such concerted surrender to distortion. The effect, in Harlem, of this particular legend was like the effect of a lit match in a tin of gasoline. The mob gathered before the doors of the Hotel Braddock simply began to swell and to spread in every direction, and Harlem exploded.

The mob did not cross the ghetto lines. It would have been easy, for example, to have gone over Morningside Park on the west side or to have crossed the Grand Central railroad tracks at 125th Street on the east side, to wreak havoc in white neighborhoods. The mob seems to have been mainly interested in something more potent and real than the white face, that is, in white power, and the principal damage done during the riot of the summer of 1943 was to white business establishments in Harlem. It might have been a far bloodier story, of course, if, at the hour the riot began, these establishments had still been open. From the Hotel Braddock the mob fanned out, east and west along 125th Street, and for the entire length of Lenox, Seventh, and Eighth avenues. Along each of these avenues, and along each major side street—116th, 125th, 135th, and so on—bars, stores, pawnshops, restaurants, even little luncheonettes had been smashed open and entered and looted—looted, it might be added, with more haste than efficiency. The shelves really looked as though a bomb had struck them. Cans of beans and soup and dog food, along with toilet paper, corn flakes, sardines and milk tumbled every which way, and abandoned cash registers and cases of beer leaned crazily out of the splintered windows and were strewn along the avenues. Sheets, blankets, and clothing of every description formed a kind of path, as though people had dropped them while running. I truly had not realized that Harlem *had* so many stores until I saw them all smashed open; the first time the word *wealth* ever entered my mind in relation to Harlem was when I saw it scattered in the streets. But one's first, incongruous impression of plenty was countered immediately by an impression of waste. None of this was doing anybody any good. It would have been better to have left the plate glass as it had been and the goods lying in the stores.

It would have been better, but it would also have been intolerable, for Harlem had needed something to smash. To smash something is the ghetto's chronic need. Most of the time it is the members of the ghetto who smash each other, and themselves. But as long as the ghetto walls are standing there will always come a moment when these outlets do not work. That summer, for example, it was not enough to get into a fight on Lenox Avenue, or curse out one's cronies in the barber shops. If ever, indeed, the violence which fills Harlem's churches, pool halls, and bars erupts outward in a more direct fashion, Harlem and its citizens are likely to vanish in an apocalyptic flood. That this is not likely to happen is due to a great many reasons, most hidden and powerful among them the Negro's real relation to the white American. This relation prohibits, simply, anything as uncomplicated and satisfactory as pure hatred. In order really to hate white people, one has to blot so much out of the mind—and the heart—that this hatred itself becomes an exhausting and self-destructive pose. But this does not mean, on the other hand, that love comes easily: the white world is too powerful, too complacent, too ready with gratuitous humiliation, and, above all, too ignorant and too innocent for that. One is absolutely forced to make perpetual qualifications and one's own reactions are always canceling each other out. It is this, really, which has driven so many people mad, both white and black. One is always in the position of having to decide between amputation and gangrene. Amputation is swift but time may prove that the amputation was not necessary—or one may delay the amputation too long. Gangrene is slow, but it is impossible to be sure that one is reading one's symptoms right. The idea of going through life as a cripple is more than one can bear, and equally unbearable is the risk of swelling up slowly, in agony, with poison. And the trouble, finally, is that the risks are real even if the choices do not exist.

"But as for me and my house," my father had said, "we will serve the Lord." I wondered, as we drove him to his resting place, what this line had meant for him. I had heard him preach it many times. I had preached it once myself, proudly giving it an interpretation different from my father's. Now the whole thing came back to me, as though my father and I were on our way to Sunday school and I were memorizing the golden text: *And if it seem evil unto you to serve the Lord, choose you this day whom you will serve; whether the gods which your fathers served that were on the other side of the flood, or the gods of the Amorites, in whose land ye dwell: but as for me and my house, we will serve the Lord.* I suspected in these familiar lines a meaning which had never been there for me before. All of my father's texts and songs, which I had decided were meaningless, were arranged before me at his death like empty bottles, waiting to hold the meaning which life would give them for me. This was his legacy: nothing is ever escaped. That bleakly memorable morning I hated the unbelievable streets and the Negroes and whites who had, equally, made them that way. But I knew that it was folly, as my father would have said, this bitterness was folly. It was necessary to hold on to the things that mattered. The dead man mattered, the new life mattered; blackness and whiteness did not matter; to believe that they did was to acquiesce in one's own destruction. Hatred, which could destroy so much, never failed to destroy the man who hated and this was an immutable law.

It began to seem that one would have to hold in the mind forever two ideas which seemed to be in opposition. The first idea was acceptance, the acceptance, totally without rancor, of life as it is, and men as they are: in the light of this idea, it goes without saying that injustice is a commonplace. But this did not mean that one could be complacent, for the second idea was of equal power: that one must never, in one's own life, accept these injustices as commonplace but must fight them with all one's strength. This fight begins, however, in the heart and it now had been laid to my charge to keep my own heart free of hatred and despair. This intimation made my heart heavy and, now that my father was irrecoverable, I wished that he had been beside me so that I could have searched his face for the answers which only the future would give me now.

LEONARD KRIEGEL

Uncle Tom and Tiny Tim

This essay trys for a different perspective on the problem, and the anguish, of race awareness. Now a professor of English at City College,
Leonard Kriegel reaches back into his childhood and tries to see the
analogy between his sense of isolation and that of the man who is racially different. The essay is valuable because it does shed light on the
psychological fact of separateness and helps to define the problem of
race and human difference in a new way.

> I find myself suddenly in the world and I recognize that I have one right
> alone: that of demanding human behavior from the other.
>
> FRANTZ FANON, *Black Skin, White Masks*

I T WAS NIETZSCHE who reminded the nineteenth century that man
can only define himself when he recognizes his true relation both to the
self and to the *other*. When man accepts the umbilical cord tying him to
society, he does so with the knowledge that he must eventually destroy it
if only to re-tie it more securely. Nietzsche was not alone. The men who
wrote the Old and New Testaments, the Greek poets, indeed, almost all
the saints and apocalyptic madmen who embroider the history of Western
civilization like so many flares in our darkness—for them, as for Freud,
recognition of self is the first step toward recognition of the other. "I attack only those things against which I find no allies, against which I stand
alone," Nietzsche wrote. If such sentiments have the uncomfortable ring of
a rhetoric that might be better forgotten today, this is only because the
particular kind of inhumanity to which Nietzsche called attention has become so much greater, so much more dense and impenetrable, than it was
in his time.

What Nietzsche wrote is especially applicable to the cripple and to those
men and women who inhabit, however partially, the cripple's world. It is
noteworthy that, at a time when in virtually every corner of the globe
those who have been invisible to themselves and to those they once conceived of as masters now stridently demand the right to define meaning
and behavior in their own terms, the cripple is still asked to accept definitions of what he is, and of what he should be, imposed on him from outside his experience. In the United States alone, spokesmen for the Negro,
the Puerto Rican, the Mexican, the Indian have embarked upon an en-

counter with a society that they believe has enriched itself at their expense, that has categorized them by cataloguing their needs and desires, their hopes and fears, their anguish and courage, even their cowardice. What all such encounters share is the challenge they offer to the very limited idea of humanity that the oppressor society grants its victims. And, however insufficiently, the society does respond in its ability to see its victims anew. Late-night television interviewers vie with one another in the effort to titillate their viewers with "militant" after "militant" who rhetorically massages whatever guilt resides in the collective consciousness of white America with threats to burn Whitey's cities to the ground. It is a game that threatens to erupt into an industry, and the nation eagerly watches while David Susskind battles Allen Burke for the privilege of leading nightly sessions of ritual flagellation—all of them, no doubt, designed to enrich the national psyche.

The cripple is conspicuous by his absence from such programs. And the reason for that absence is not difficult to discover. The cripple is simply not attractive enough, either in his physical presence, which is embarrassing to host and viewers, or in his rhetoric, which simply cannot afford the bombastic luxuriance characteristic of confessional militancy. If a person who has had polio, for example, were to threaten to burn cities to the ground unless the society recognized his needs, he would simply make of himself an object of laughter and ridicule. The very paraphernalia of his existence, his braces and crutches, make such a threat patently ridiculous. Aware of his own helplessness, he cannot help but be aware, too, that whatever limited human dimensions he has been offered are themselves the product of society's largesse. Quite simply, he can take it or leave it. He does not even possess the sense of being actively hated or feared by society, for society is merely made somewhat uncomfortable by his presence. It treats him as if he were an errant, rather ugly, little schoolboy. The homosexual on public display titillates, the gangster fascinates, the addict touches—all play upon a nation's voyeuristic instincts. The cripple simply embarrasses. Society can see little reason for recognizing his existence at all.

And yet, he asks, why should *he* apologize? My crutches are as visible as a black man's skin, and they form a significant element, probably the most significant element, in the way in which I measure myself against the demands of the world. And the world itself serves as witness to my sufferance. A few years ago, the mayor of New York decided to "crack down" on diplomats, doctors and cripples who possessed what he described as "special parking privileges." I single Mr. Lindsay out here because he is the very same mayor who has acted with a certain degree of sensitivity and courage when dealing with the problems of blacks in the ghettos. He soon rescinded the order preventing cripples from using their parking permits,

but one notes with interest his apparent inability to conceive of what such
an order would inevitably do. Cripples were instructed to drive to the police station nearest their place of work, leave their cars, and wait until a
police vehicle could drive them to their destination. One simply does not
have to be Freud to understand that a physical handicap carries with it
certain decisive psychological ramifications, chief among them the anxie-
ty-provoking question of whether or not one can make it—economically,
socially and sexually—on one's own. Forcing a man who has great difficulty in walking to surrender his car, the source of his mobility, is comparable to calling a black man "boy" in a crowd of white onlookers. The
mayor succeeded only in reminding me, and the thousands of other cripples who live in New York, that my fate was in his hands and that he controlled my destiny to an extent I did not wish to believe. He brought me
once again face-to-face with what Fanon means when he writes, "Fervor is
the weapon of choice of the impotent." Fanon, of course, was writing
about being black in a psychologically white world, but the analogy is neither farfetched nor unusual. Uncle Tom and Tiny Tim are brothers under
the skin.

About six months after I arrived in the New York State Reconstruction
Home in West Haverstraw in 1944, a fellow patient, who had been in the
home for more than a year, casually remarked, "They got you by the
hump. No matter which way you turn, they got you." At that time, I was
not yet twelve, and I took so bland an overture with all the suspicion and
self-righteousness of a Boy Scout who finds himself thrust into the center
of a gang war. *I,* for one, knew that I had been born to be saved and I was
concerned only with caking the shell of my determination to succeed. I
simply was not going to be a *cripple.* (I wouldn't even permit myself to use
the word then, not even to think it.) I was determined to do everything I
had been told I must do by doctors, nurses, physical therapists, by anybody who seemed to me an authority on "my condition." However myste-
riously, I was convinced that the task of restoring nerves to my dead legs
lay in obediently listening to my superiors, and I accepted anyone's claim
to superiority on the very simple and practical basis that he could walk. If
I listened, if I obeyed without questioning, I would someday once again
lead "a normal life." The phrase meant living in the way my superiors
lived. I could virtually taste those words, and for years afterward I could
be sent off into a redemptive beatitude if anybody told me that I was on
my way toward leading "a normal life." For the cripple, the first girl
kissed, the first money earned, the first restaurant entered alone—all are
visible manifestations of redemption, symbolic of "a normal life."

In my ignorance, I did not understand that my fellow patient had simply
unfolded what would ultimately seem a truism. He understood something
that I could not have admitted to myself, even if I had been brave enough

to recognize it. My life was not my own, and it would take immense effort for me ever to control it—even to the extent that anyone not crippled can control his life. Whoever *they* were, they had got me, too. And no matter which way I turned, they would decide, in their collective wisdom, how my fate was to be carved out. Nor was it me as an individual cripple alone whom they had got. I was soon to discover that, in varying degrees, they had my family also. Disease is a sharing, a gray fringe of existence where man, however protesting, remains if not at his most communal, then at his most familial. For the cripple, the message of disability is invariably personal, and he carries with the physical reminder—the eyes that do not see, the limp, the rigid fear of undergoing an epileptic seizure in some strange corner of the universe, the bitter dregs of a mind that he realizes works neither wisely nor too well—the knowledge that he is, in some remarkably fundamental way, the creator of those who have created him. Perhaps it is not what Wordsworth had in mind, but the cripple knows that the child is father to the man—and to the woman, too—, especially when the child's existence is conditioned by the peculiar nature of his handicap. There is no choice. "No matter which way you turn, they got you." The cripple, at least, has the immediacy of his own struggle to overcome. His parents have little more than their obligation to his birth.

The cripple, then, is a social fugitive, a prisoner of expectations molded by a society that he makes uncomfortable by his very presence. For this reason, the most functional analogy for the life he leads is to be found in the Negro. For the black man, now engaged in wresting an identity from a white society apparently intent on mangling its own, has become in America a synonym for that which insists on the capacity of its own being. At the risk of demanding from Black America more than it can yet give itself, let me suggest that here we have both analogy and method. No one can teach the cripple, can serve as so authoritative a model in his quest for identity, as can the black man. I say this in spite of my knowledge that Black America may simply be fed up with serving the society in any manner whatsoever. "To us," writes Fanon, "the man who adores the Negro is as 'sick' as the man who abominates him." It is not the black who must offer explanations. Far more than the cripple, he has been the victim of television interviewers, of scientific sociologists of the soul, of those seemingly innumerable bearers of "truth," those contemporary witch doctors intent on analyzing us all to death. For the cripple, the black man is a model because he is on intimate terms with a terror that does not recognize his existence and is yet distinctly personal. He is in the process of discovering what he is, and he has known for a long time what the society conceives him to be. His very survival guarantees him the role of rebel. What he has been forced to learn is how to live on the outside looking in. Until quite recently, he was not even asked how he liked it. But this has been the essential fact of the black's existence and it is with this very same fact that the cripple must begin, for he, too, will not be asked how he likes it. He, too, must choose a self that is not the self others insist he accept. Just as Uncle Tom, in order to placate the power of white America, learned to mask his true self until he felt himself in a position of total desperation or rising hope (or some combination of the two), so the cripple has the right, one is tempted to say the responsibility, to use every technique, every subterfuge, every mask, every emotional climate—no matter how false and seemingly put on—to alter the balance in his relation to the world around him.

His first step is obvious. He must accept the fact that his existence is a source of discomfort to others. This is not to say that he is not permitted to live with comfort and security; these, in fact, are the very gifts his society is most willing to grant him. The price he is expected to pay, however, is the same price the black man has been expected to pay, at least until very recently: he must accept his "condition," which implies not that he accept his wound but that he never show more of that wound than society thinks proper. He is incapable of defining what selfhood is. His needs will be met, but not as he might wish to meet them.

I was thirteen when I returned to the city after almost two years of life in a rehabilitation home. A rather valiant attempt to rehabilitate me had been made there. I had been taught a number of interesting ways in which to mount a bus; I had been taught to walk on crutches with the least possible strain on my arms. I was a rather lazy patient who lived in the corridors of his own fantasy, but I cannot deny that a great deal of effort was expended upon me by a number of people who were truly interested in my welfare. Looking back, I can do little but acknowledge this and voice my gratitude.

Unfortunately, those people whose task it was to rehabilitate me had also made certain assumptions about me and the world I was to inhabit after I left the home. The assumption about me was simple: I should be grateful for whatever existence I could scrape together. After all, there had been a time when my life itself had been forfeit and, compared to many of my peers in the ward, I was relatively functional. About the world, the assumption was equally simple—although here, perhaps, less forgivable. Society existed. Whatever it meted out to the cripple, the cripple accepted. The way of the world was not to be challenged.

I did not know what to expect when I arrived back home in the Bronx, although I sensed that my relationship to others was bound to be that of an inferior to a superior. But I did not know what form that inferiority would take. No one had bothered to teach me—no one had even bothered to mention—the position I would occupy in the world outside the ward. No one had told me the extent to which I would find myself an outsider. And

forbidding presence of doctors and nurses gloved by a silence broken only by their occasional whispers to one another—all depicted a world she was henceforth to inhabit. I myself was relatively at ease. This was more or less the way things had been for two years. For my mother, it was original, a slow-motion film of what lay in wait for her, chipping into whatever sense of security she had been able to muster before we left the apartment. To her credit, she refused to panic. When my name was finally called by the receptionist, she entered the inner sanctum and answered questions with honesty and even with pride in her capacity to endure the intimate disclosure of her suffering. Then a doctor examined me, murmured something about "doing our best," and the ordeal was over. My mother glowed. It was as if she had come through some terrible ordeal, marked but not scarred.

My mother did not need Harlem as I did. She knew enough about endurance; that Faulknerian virtue so apparent in those brittle streets. She came through what was, for her, an ordeal and a humiliation, and she came through far more intact than I would come through. She possessed the endurance of her instincts. And she herself was as alien to this America as anyone walking the streets of Harlem, for the kind of endurance I am speaking about here is as much a matter of geography as it is of culture.

Only by existing does the black man remain black and the cripple remain a cripple. A singular, most unfunny lesson. But the cripple could profit from it. The condition of the Negro is imposed from outside. Obviously, this is not altogether true of the cripple. But while his physical condition is not imposed from outside, the way in which he exists in the world is. His relationship to the community is, by and large, dependent upon the special sufferance the community accords him. And whether he wishes to or not, the cripple must view himself as part of an undefined community within the larger community. But there is no sense of shared relationships or pride. Cripples do not refer to each other as "soul brothers." And regardless of how much he may desire to participate in the larger community, the cripple discovers that he has been offered a particular role that society expects him to play. He is expected to accede to that role's demands. And just as it is considered perfectly legitimate to violate a black man's privacy to bolster assumptions that the nonblack world makes, so it is perfectly legitimate to question the cripple about virtually any aspect of his private life. The normal possesses the right to his voyeurism without any obligation to involve himself with its object. He wants the picture drawn for him at the very moment that he refuses to recognize that the subject of his picture is, like him, a human being. "If you prick us, do we not bleed?" asks Shylock of his persecutors. The cripple's paraphrase might well be, "If you wish to see my wound, can you deny me the right to show you my self?" But voyeurism is the normal's form of noninvolvement. The experience of being the recipient of unasked-for attention is as common to cripples as it is to blacks. Each is asked to show those aspects of his "condition" that will reinforce the normal's assumptions about what the cripple (or black) *feels like,* what he wants, and what he is.

I can remember my neighbors, on my return home, praying for me, inquiring about my health, quoting for my benefit the words of Christ, St. Francis, Akiba and F.D.R.* I can remember their lecturing me, advising me, escorting me. Drunks voluntarily shared their wisdom with me. Almost everyone *did* things for me—except, of course, to see me. For to have seen me would have entailed recognizing my existence as an individual *me,* that kind of personal encounter that results in a stripping away of stereotype and symbol and a willingness to accept the humanity of the other, at whatever personal cost.

One can object that this view simply distorts the problem of the cripple. It is not the black man and the cripple alone who suffer from invisibility in America. The proliferation of books on alienation and anxiety, the increasing sense of disaffiliation from which our younger people suffer, the seemingly endless number of fads, pseudo religions, life sciences, and spiritual hobbyhorses that clutter the landscape of life in these United States all testify to this. Ultimately, such an objection contains great validity. But one must first see it within the particular situation in which the cripple exists: the possibilities affording relief to others are not usually open to the cripple. There is no way, of course, to define degrees of alienation and invisibility with any sense of accuracy. But one can suggest that if most persons are only half-visible, then the cripple, like the black man until recently, is wholly invisible. Stereotypes persist long after reality fades away; for us, Uncle Tom still prays on bent knees while Tiny Tim hobbles through the world on huge gushes of sentiment and love. But let us see the world as it is, for the world itself has perfected the ability to see what it wishes to see and only what it wishes to see. Those stolid burghers who lived only a few miles from the death camps in Germany possessed a vague idea of what was taking place within those camps, but they never permitted the vagueness to make itself concrete, to push itself forward onto the individual consciousness.

The community, then, makes certain assumptions about the cripple. Whether verifiable or not, it behaves on the basis of those assumptions. The cripple is judged (as are the members of his family in terms of their relation to him), but the judgments are rendered by those for whom neither the cripple nor his family possess any meaningful reality. His "condi-

---

* Roosevelt's ability to "beat" polio was for me, as well as for most of the boys in ward with me, what Kenneth Burke speaks of as a "symbolic action." Burke, of course, is dealing with literary criticism and his categories are derived from the study of literature and are all verbal. But an icon living within the boundaries of one's memory may serve a similar function to that which Burke had in mind.

tion" is an abstraction; he himself is not quite real. Who is going to recognize *me*? asks the cripple. But society has already called into question the very existence of that *me* for it refuses to look at that which makes it uncomfortable. And so it leaves the cripple, doubting his potency, not quite ready to face his primary obligation—to extend understanding to himself, to accept the fact that his problems exist now, here, in this world, that they are problems for which relief must be sought, and that his "condition" is arbitrary but not absolute. Choices, as well as obligations, exist within the boundaries of his possibilities.

To strike out on his own in the face of a society whose smugness seems, at times, conspiratorial is difficult. As an attitude, smugness goes beyond indifference. And it is far more harmful. Smugness is the asset of the untouched, the virtue of the oblivious, and the badge of the unthreatened. It is the denial of the existence of that which threatens one's comfort, the right to judge whatever and whenever the smug believe judgment is called for. Smugness is the constant reminder of the line that exists between those who have not been touched by the world's terror and those who have. Smugness is a denial of the motion of the universe, an assumption that time stands still and that mortality itself can be conquered. The cripple knows better; for him, it is time and motion together that form the dialectic of rage.

What the cripple must face is being pigeonholed by the smug. Once his behavior is assumed from the fact that he is a cripple, it doesn't matter whether he is viewed as holy or damned. Either assumption is made at the expense of his individuality, his ability to say "I." He is expected to behave in such-and-such a way; he is expected to react in the following manner to the following stimulus. And since that which expects such behavior is that which provides the stimulus, his behavior is all too often Pavlovian. He reacts as he is expected to react because he does not really accept the idea that he can react in any other way. Once he accepts, however unconsciously, the images of self that his society presents him, then the guidelines for his behavior are clear-cut and consistent.

This is the black man's conflict, too. And it is exactly here that black militancy has confronted the enmity of white society. White America is probably willing to absorb the black American; what it may not be willing to do is to permit the black American to absorb himself. Negro anxiety, rage and anger are seen only as threats to the primacy of white America when they probably should be seen as the black man's effort to rid himself of all sorts of imposed definitions of his proper social "role." The black view must be total. Given the experience of having been born black in a white world, it is difficult for the black man to think about his life in terns other than color or race. The totality of his experience gives him no edge. And what he witnesses is forced into the mold of what he has known. I once received an essay from a black student describing Canova's *Perseus Holding the Head of Medusa* in the Metropolitan Museum of Art as a depiction of "the contemporary black crisis." When I questioned what she had seen, I discovered that most of the other black students in the class believed that one had the right, perhaps even the obligation, to see that statue and everything else in terms of "the black crisis."

If one calls this confusion, it is a confusion that the cripple shares. For one thing, the cripple is not sure of just who is and who isn't his enemy; for another, he must distrust the mask of language just as the black man does; for a third, he cannot help but see the world itself as the source of his humiliation. He is "different" at the very moment he desires to be created in another's image. And he must feel shame at the expression of such a desire. If anything, his situation is even more difficult than the black's, at least as far as his ability to find relief is concerned. If the black man's masculinity is mangled, he can still assert it in certain ways. Black actors assuage his hunger for a heroic identity; black athletes help him forget, however temporarily, the mutilation of his being; and a worldwide renascent political movement, convinced that it represents the wave of the future, teaches him that his blackness—the very aspect of his existence that he has been taught to despise—is "beautiful" and is to become the foundation of the new life he will create for himself.

Whether this assessment of his situation is accurate is of no immediate concern, for what we are interested in is its validity as an analogy for the life of the cripple. Black Americans now believe that they possess choices and that they need not live as victims. They are now engaged in the struggle to force society to accept, or at the least to accommodate itself to, the black conception of how blacks are to live. The cripple's situation is more difficult. If it exists at all, his sense of community with his fellow sufferers is based upon shame rather than pride. Nor is there any political or social movement that will supply him with a sense of solidarity. If any thing, it is probably more difficult for the cripple to relate to "his own" than to the normals. Louis Battye, an English novelist born with muscular dystrophy, has graphically expressed how the cripple sees himself not merely as the symbol of what society thinks he is but of what he actually is.

> Somewhere deep inside us is the almost unbearable knowledge that the way the able-bodied world regards us is as much as we have the right to expect. We are not full members of that world, and the vast majority of us can never hope to be. If we think otherwise we are deluding ourselves. Like children and the insane, we inhabit a special sub-world, a world with its own unique set of referents.

Battye also speaks of the cripple's "irrelevance to the real business of living." His observations are acute and courageous. One suspects that most cripples feel this about themselves, although few have the courage to admit it. A cripple must see himself as an anachronism, for virtually everything his culture offers him is designed to reinforce his sense of inferiority, to point out to him that he is tolerated in spite of his stigma and that he had best keep his distance if he wishes society's approval. But Tiny Tim is, with whatever modern variations, still his image. He may insist that Tiny Tim is not his true self. But it frames society's picture of him. It is still the model for his behavior.

Self-hatred, then, must be the legacy he derives from his consciousness of what society thinks of him. With what else can he confront a society that values physical strength and physical beauty? (Regardless of how bizarre that sense of beauty may sometimes seem, it remains outside the cripple's range of possibilities.) If growing old is a threat to modern Americans, how much greater a threat is physical deformity or mental retardation?

And what are the cripple's options? Most of the options traditionally available to the "gifted" or "exceptional" Negro are not available to him, since his restrictions are almost invariably functional and rather severely limit the territory he can stake out as his own. He cannot become a movie idol; he cannot become an athlete; he cannot even become a soldier and risk his life in defense of that which has rejected him. His choices are simply far more limited than are the choices of a black man.

But what he can do is to learn one of the fundamental lessons of American Negro history, a lesson that probably accounts for the growing tension between white and black: he can create his own individual presence out of the very experience of his rejection. The black man in America is an obvious model for him, not because of any inherent Faulknerian virtue but because he has spent three hundred and fifty years learning how to deal with his tormentors. Without romanticizing him, we recognize that he has earned his status. It has made him, at one and the same time, both tougher and more paranoid than white America. And a certain amount of toughness as well, perhaps, as a certain amount of paranoia might serve to change the cripple's own conception of self. There is no formula that can force Tiny Tim to stand on his own two crutches. But the cripple can certainly make a start by refusing the invisibility thrust over him by the culture. He can insist on being seen.

In the folklore of white America, Harlem has long been considered exotic as well as dangerous territory. Perhaps it is both exotic and dangerous. But from 1946 to 1951, the years during which I was an outpatient at the Joint Disease Hospital, it was one of the more comfortable places in New York for me. I do not mean to voice that old ploy about those who themselves suffer being more sympathetic, more receptive to the pain of others (although there is probably a certain limited truth here, too). All I mean is that in Harlem I first became conscious of how I could outmanipulate that in society which was trying to categorize me. It is probably a slum child's earliest lesson, one that he learns even before he sets foot in a school, for it is a lesson that carries with it the structure of his survival. Normals begin to appear not as particularly charitable human beings but rather as individuals able to band together for purposes of mutual self-interest. They possess their environment, and the environment itself (which for the black child and for the cripple is part of the enemy's world) is for them a visible symbol of their success.

The normals are a tangible presence in Harlem, or at least they were during my tenure as an outpatient at the Joint Disease Hospital. The normals are *they,* the people in authority—police for the black child, nurses, doctors and social workers for me. It was in this confrontation with the normals that I first noticed what is now called the Negro's "marginality" to the kind of existence the rest of America is supposed to lead. On the short strolls I took on my crutches through the streets surrounding the hospital, the single fact I constantly confronted was the way in which the non-Harlem world imposed its presence on the community. Individuals walking the streets simply froze in its presence. One was always aware of a potential breaking out, an explosion of amassed raw frustration and distorted energy. I can remember stiffening with tension when a patrol car cruised past. Now it must be remembered that I was white, that I was an adolescent, that I moved with great difficulty on braces and crutches, and that I was probably the last person in Harlem who had anything to fear from the police. But none of this changed the fact that in Harlem a patrol car was simply the most decisive presence of the normals one could conceive of— and whether it was because I felt comfortable in those streets or because the air smelled differently or because the tension that seemed to surround me was part of the very manner, the very life, of the community, I remember stiffening with fear and guilt and anxiety. Had I been a black adolescent with legs that functioned, I probably would have run, assuming my guilt as a corollary of my birth. Just as such a boy was a victim, so I knew that I was already a victim: the truth was that I was already on short-term loan to the needs of the outside world. I could exist as an individual only insofar as I could satisfy those needs. At least, this is what I had absorbed. For anything else, I would have to struggle. And at that time (I was not yet sixteen), I was not only not smart enough to resist but I still had fantasies of leaving the world of the cripple. That, too, was part of the legacy. To choose hope rather than despair is natural enough. But it had been five years since the embrace of my virus and I still could not bring myself to admit that my condition was permanent.

The cripple's struggle to call himself *I,* which is, I take it, what we mean by a struggle for identity, is always with him. He can be challenged in his illusions of sufficiency by the most haphazard event. I used to drop into a drugstore across the street from the Joint Disease Hospital while I waited for the car that was to take me back to the Bronx. It was the kind of drugstore one still saw before 1960. Despite its overstuffed dinginess, perhaps even because of it, the drugstore seemed portentously professional. Somehow, its proximity to the hospital gave it a certain dignity. The man who ran its operations was short and heavy, courteous and solicitous. I remember that his hair was thinning and that he smoked cigarettes in a manner that made smoking itself seem an act of defiance. He would occasionally join me as I sat at the counter drinking coffee and, more often than not, he would inform me of what *the Negro* wanted. I have an image of him, smoke blowing through flared nostrils, staring at the door as he spoke. At such times, he seemed oblivious to the presence of black customers and the black counterman alike. "They want to be accepted. They would like the white man to give them a chance to show what they can do." I had heard the words for years and I could even nod in rhythmical agreement. And then one day he added, in a voice as casual and well-intentioned as when he told me what *they* wanted, "Why don't you plan to get yourself a nice store? Like a greeting card store. Or something like that. Where you don't have to work so hard but you could still earn your own living. That's what you should do."

And so I learned that I existed for him as an abstraction, that he saw through me as if I, too, were smoke he was blowing through his nostrils. *The cripple* had been linked to *the Negro*. A new *they* had been born. As a man of the world, who did not need to move beyond abstraction, he assumed that he had every right in the world to decide what *the cripple* or *the Negro* wanted. He knew what I "should do" because he possessed two good legs and I didn't. Not being a cripple makes one an expert on *the cripple,* just as not being black makes one an expert on *the Negro.* It was another example of the normal deciding how that which dared not to be normal should live.

In his conclusion to *Black Skin, White Masks,* Fanon discovers that the final myth he must destroy is the myth of a "black world," for such a myth is ultimately dependent upon an equally inhuman "white world." "There are," Fanon insists, "in every part of the world men who search." This seems to me one of the few workable visions one can accept, despite the fact that I know that, for the cripple, even the act of surrendering himself to the ranks of those who search is enveloped by potential disaster. The cripple must recognize this and he must face it. For no matter how limited his functioning in the society of normals may be, there are certain definitive guidelines that he is offered. Once he has accepted being pigeonholed by society, he finds that he is safe as long as he is willing to live within the boundaries of his categorization. To break out of its confines calls for an

act of will of which he may already be incapable. Should he choose to resist, he will probably discover that he has inflamed those who see themselves as kind and tolerant. My inability to tell that man to mind his own
business was an act of spiritual acquiescence. Had I told him where to get
off, I would have undoubtedly been guilty of an unpardonable sin in his
eyes. But I would have moved an inch forward toward personal emancipation. Cripples, though, simply did not address normals in such a way. Tiny
Tim was still my image of the cripple. And Tiny Tim had always been
grateful for the attention conferred upon him by his betters—any kind of
attention. My inability to defy that man was more than a reflection of my
weakness: it was also the embodiment of his success, the proof of the legitimacy of his assumption. On my next visit to the Joint Disease Hospital, I
dropped in once again for another cup of coffee and another quick chat.

And so the task of the cripple is to re-create a self, or rather to create a
true self, one dependent upon neither fantasy nor false objectivity. To define one's own limitations is as close as one can come to meaningful independence. Not to serve is an act of courage in this world, but if it leaves
one merely with the desire for defiance then it ultimately succumbs to a
different form of madness. The black man who rejects "white culture"
must inevitably reject his own humanity, for if all he can see in Bach or
Einstein is skin color then he has become what his tormentors have made
of him. The only true union remains with those "who search." For the
cripple, too, there are no others. To embrace one's braces and crutches
would be an act of the grotesque; but to permit one's humanity to be defined by others because of those braces and crutches is even more grotesque. Even in Dachau and Buchenwald, the human existed. It was left to
the searchers to find it.

2 BACKGROUNDS

Race awareness was not born in the 1960's; it was not discovered in the streets of Detroit; nor is it made only in America. Race awareness involves white, black, brown, yellow, and red in a series of shifting conflicts across continents and throughout history. We wanted to suggest—and can only suggest—the dimensions of the problem, primarily in this country but also throughout the world.

It is the worst kind of ignorance to assume that only one's personal experiences matter; it is the worst kind of folly to deny that our attitudes have been conditioned by history; but it is culpable blindness to think that one has advanced morally when one has only understood historically.

These backgrounds provide the context of the personal present of each man and the dark future of humanity. The backgrounds are necessary to an understanding of what has happened and is happening and is likely to happen in this country and at any place in the world where two races meet.

Jim Kappes

Paul Conklin

Paul Conklin

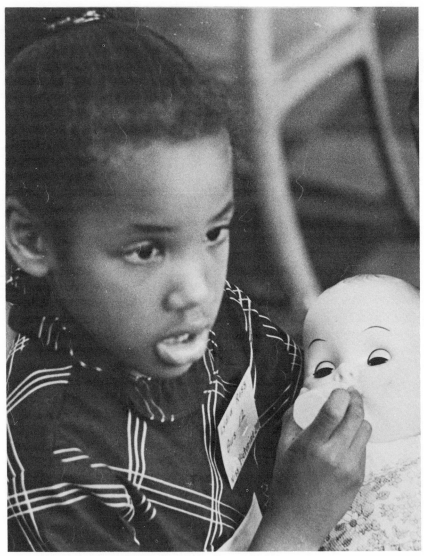

Jim Kappes

ASHLEY MONTAGU

Race: The History of an Idea

Ashley Montague has written more, and more sensibly, about race than any other scholar in the field. The essay reprinted here is a historical survey of the concept of race and reveals how long this peculiar human concept has haunted us. We felt that an understanding of the particular modern problems of race consciousness with which we are all wrestling would be illuminated by a study of the blindness as well as the occasional visionary acts of those who have gone before.

> He who degrades his fellow man to be a beggar and a knave will always
> be the first to call him so.
>
> HEINRICH PESTALOZZI

Introduction

"RACE" IS A problem that has been very much with the world during the twentieth century. More, indeed, than in any other, and in our own time certainly disturbingly more obtrusive than at any previous period in our history. It is a problem of the greatest seriousness in this country, and in many other parts of the world it has in recent years become explosive. It was not always so. It comes as a great surprise to most people to learn that the idea of "race" is of very recent origin. The idea of "race" as a widespread secular belief is, in fact, no older than the nineteenth century. Because it is important in dealing with the Hydra-headed phenomenon of "race" to understand the history of the development of that idea, and because it properly, and, it is to be hoped, illuminatingly, belongs at the commencement of our inquiry, I shall devote this first part of our discussion to a résumé of that history.

We shall discuss first the social idea of "race." This will be followed by a discussion of the biological idea of "race." These two separate conceptions of "race" need to be carefully distinguished from one another, for the one is general, popular, and widespread, and the other passes as scientific. Unfortunately, these two conceptions are usually confused with each other.

The Social Idea of "Race"

When the members of a society act out their emotions and beliefs in relation to the members of other groups in discriminatory ways, based on a conception of the others which is socially determined, we are clearly dealing with a group distinction. Such is the social conception of "race." More specifically defined, the social idea of "race" is the notion that there exists a something called "race" that inseparably links two things together, namely, physical traits and behavioral traits. These traits are said to be held in common heredity by distinctive intrabreeding groups or populations. It is held that just as this common heredity determines the physical characteristics of such groups, so, too, it determines their behavioral characteristics. Upon this view, not only are physical and behavioral traits determined by "race," but so are the collective achievements of the peoples characterized by such traits.

The social idea of "race" has it, then, that physical and behavioral traits are linked, and that different kinds of linkages of this nature characterize different peoples, thus accounting for their physical and behavioral differences, and that, finally, cultural achievement is determined by "race." Since, so the argument runs, there are differences in the hereditary potentials of such different groups, it is these hereditary differences that are largely, if not entirely, responsible for the differences in cultural achievement exhibited by the different "races."

This kind of interpretation of the differences presented by different groups represents not only the easiest explanation of the observed differences, but also the most comforting to those who indulge in it. It is an easy and obvious sort of interpretation of the existing differences. The easiest and most obvious explanation, however comforting it may be, is not thereby rendered the correct explanation. Appearances are deceptive. The obvious is neither necessarily true nor right. Indeed, there is only one thing wrong with the social conception of "race," and that is that it goes beyond the facts, that it is, in fact, quite in conflict with the facts, that it is, in short, in error. As such, as we shall see, the social idea of "race" represents a collection of pseudological rationalizations based on a confusion of emotions, prejudiced judgments, and disordered values.

It is because the idea of "race," and especially the social conception of "race," is so anti-human and individually and socially destructive that it demands our most earnest attention.

The Biological Idea of "Race"

The biological idea of "race," that is, the idea of "race" to which biologists in general subscribe and which until recently they universally took for granted, is that there exist subdivisions of species, that is, populations of a species, capable of interbreeding with one another and characterized by hereditary differences in certain physical or physiological traits. The biological conception of "race" is extended to man by most biologists and physical anthropologists. As applied both to man and to other animals, however, that conception has in recent years come under some criticism from biologists and physical anthropologists. Since these criticisms have raised serious questions concerning the reality of anything corresponding to a biological "race," especially with reference to man, we shall devote some attention to that idea also.

Origin of the Idea of "Race"

The origin of the word "race" is obscure. Attempts have been made to derive it from the Arabic *ras:* the Latin *ratio,* meaning order, or the Latin *radix,* meaning a root; the Italian *razza;* and the Spanish and Portuguese *raza.* The first use of the word in printed English is to be found in the second English edition of the martyrologist John Foxe's *Actes and Monuments,* popularly known as the *Book of Martyrs,* published in 1570. In this work Foxe writes, "Thus was the outward race & stock of Abraham after flesh refused." [1] But this is a rather special use of the term, referring to the offspring or posterity of a person. In the sense of a tribe, nation, or people descended from a common stock, the first English usage of the term is to be found in Wynne's *History of the Gwydir Family,* published in 1600, where the author refers to "Llewelyn ap Gruffith last Prince of Wales of the British race." [2] In the sense of a breed or stock of animals or a particular variety of a species, the first English usage occurs in Blundeville's *Horsemanship,* published in 1580.[3] In the sense of one of the major groups of mankind having certain physical traits in common, the earliest English usage occurs in Oliver Goldsmith's *The Natural History of Animals,* which appeared in 1774, and in which he writes, "The second great variety in the human species seems to be that of the Tartar race." [4] In France, François Taut, in his book entitled *Trésor de la langue française,* published in 1600, derived the word from the Latin *radix,* and stated that "it alludes to the extraction of a man, of a dog, of a horse; as one says of good or bad race." [5]

It is clear, then, that the word "race" was already in use in the sixteenth century in the sense of a group or population having certain physical traits in common. While there are no significant references to the fact in the contemporary literature, there can be little doubt that the physical distinctions that were recognized to exist between different individuals of different populations were sometimes associated with behavioral peculiarities. It is

1. John Foxe, *Actes and Monuments* (1570), II, 1841.
2. Wynne of Gwydir, *History of the Gwydir Family* (1600), p. 20.
3. Thomas Blundeville, *The Fower Chiefest Offices Belonging to Horsemanship* (1580).
4. Oliver Goldsmith, *An History of the Earth and Animated Nature* (London: J. Nourse, 1774), p. xxxiii.
5. François Taut, *Trésor de la langue française,* ed. Jean Nicot (Paris: P. Doucer, 1600).

quite clear, though, that nothing resembling the modern idea of "race" existed as either a social, a political, or as a scientific viewpoint.

In the eighteenth century there were some who took it for granted that the differences, both physical and mental, that distinguished whites from Negroes were inborn. It was not, however, until the latter part of the eighteenth century, with the beginning of the debate which eventually lead to the abolition of the trade in slaves and to their ultimate emancipation, that the alleged inborn differences between peoples were erected into the doctrine of racism. This doctrine constituted a mélange of rationalizations calculated to prove that the Negro was created with articulate speech and hands so that he might be of service to his master, the white man. There were many people who quite honestly believed in the Negro's inferiority, reasoning that their illiteracy and degraded condition was due to their inborn inadequacies. Thomas Jefferson, for example, originally thought Negroes poor in mental endowment, but believed in their emancipation, with the qualification that when freed they were "to be removed beyond the reach of mixture." [6] This statement is often quoted by racists and others who neglect, however, to add that with increased experience of Negroes Jefferson later several times repudiated his earlier opinions. In 1792, in a letter to Benjamin Banneker, the Negro slave-born inventor and mathematician, praising the latter's *Almanac,* Jefferson wrote how much he welcomed "such proofs as you exhibit that nature has given to our black brethren talents equal to those of the other colors of men, and that the appearance of a want of them is owing merely to the degraded condition of their existence. . . ." [7]

Some seventeen years later, in 1809, Jefferson wrote, "Be assured that no person living wishes more sincerely than I do to see a complete refutation of the doubts I have myself entertained and expressed on the grade of understanding allotted to them [Negroes] by nature, and to find that in this respect they are on a par with ourselves. My doubts were the result of personal observation on the limited sphere of my own State, where the opportunities for the development of their genius were not favorable, and those of exercising it still less so. I expressed them therefore with great hesitation; but whatever be their degree of talent is no measure of their rights." [8]

Finally, there is Jefferson's ringing comment, "The mass of mankind has not been born with saddles on their back, nor a favored few booted and spurred, ready to ride them legitimately, by the grace of God." [9]

6. Thomas Jefferson, "Notes on the State of Virginia," in Saul K. Padover (ed.), *The Complete Jefferson* (New York: Tudor Publishing Co., 1943), p. 662.
7. Philip S. Foner, *Basic Writings of Thomas Jefferson* (New York: Halcyon House, 1950), p. 601.
8. *Ibid.,* p. 682.
9. Saul K. Padover, *A Jefferson Profile* (New York: John Day, 1956), p. 344.

In antiquity the Egyptians, the Jews, the Greeks, and the Romans, what-ever distinctions they made between themselves and others, even though they recognized the obvious physical differences, seldom or never based those distinctions on racial grounds. St. Paul's dictum, "God hath made of one blood all nations of men for to dwell on all the face of the earth" (Acts 17:26), was an advance upon the Greek way of viewing the world as divided into themselves and barbarians. However, the Greeks, though they affected to despise the barbarian, did so on cultural grounds, and never on anything resembling racial grounds. The Greeks thought of Hellenism as a thing of the spirit rather than of "race." As Isocrates (436–338 B.C.) wrote, "So far has Athens distanced the rest of mankind in thought and in speech that her pupils have become the teachers of the rest of the world; and she has brought it about that the name 'Hellenes' is applied rather to those who share our culture than to those who share a common blood." [10]

It is perfectly true that in Greece and in Rome suggestions were some-times made concerning inherent differences between people, but this idea never gained a firm foothold at any time.

Aristotle is sometimes referred to as having held views on the biological inequality of "races." This is not true. Aristotle, like many another, has been misquoted and misrepresented. Aristotle's views were clearly stated, and they refer to the natural inequalities that exist between individuals in the *same* society primarily, and only secondarily to differences which sepa-rated the Greeks from other peoples, or barbarians.

Since Aristotle's views played a considerable role in the development of what ultimately became the idea of "race," we may briefly consider what he wrote.

In the *Politics* (Bk. I, Chap. 5) Aristotle wrote, "Ruling and being ruled, which is the relation of master and slave, not only belongs to the category of things necessary, but also to that of things expedient; and there are species in which a distinction is already marked, immediately at birth, between those of its members who are intended for being ruled and those who are intended to rule" (#2). "We may thus conclude that all men who differ from others as much as the body differs from the soul, or an animal from a man (and this is the case with all those whose function is bodily service, and who produce their best when they supply such service)—all such are by nature slaves, and it is better for them, on the very same prin-ciple as in the other cases just mentioned, to be ruled by a master" (#8). "A man is thus by nature a slave if he is capable of becoming (and this is the reason why he also actually becomes) the property of another, and if he participates in reason to the extent of apprehending it in another, though destitute of it himself" (#9).

Aristotle goes on, "We have hitherto been speaking of mental differ-

10. Isocrates *Panegyricus* iv. 50; trans. by George Norlin (Loeb Classical Library; Cambridge: Harvard University Press, 1928), I, pp. xxiv, 149.

ences. But it is nature's intention also to erect a physical difference between the body of the freeman and that of the slave, giving the latter strength for the menial duties of life, but making the former upright in carriage and (though useless for physical labour) useful for the various purposes of civic life" (#10).

Finally, in a famous paragraph, Aristotle concludes, "It is thus clear that, just as some are by nature free, so others are by nature slaves, and for these latter the condition of slavery is both beneficial and just" (#125a).[11]

Reading Aristotle carefully, it is quite evident that his approach, as Westermann says, "was entirely from the political-economic point of view," and applies to Greeks as well as to all other peoples.[12] What Aristotle was saying, in short, was that there exist natural differences between individuals, *not* between peoples, and that it is these natural, and in some cases cultural, differences that determine the relations of individuals to one another. The cultural differences existing between peoples that enable the superior to subjugate the inferior not only entitle but justify the superior in enslaving the inferior. Thus, Aristotle writes, " 'Slavery' and 'slave' are terms which are used in two different senses. There is, as we have seen, a kind of slavery which exists by nature; but there is also a kind of slave, and of slavery, which exists only by law or (to speak more exactly) convention. (The law in virtue of which those vanquished in war are held to belong to the victor is in effect a sort of convention)." And, Aristotle concludes, "The superior *in goodness* ought to rule over, and be the master of, his inferiors." [13]

If Aristotle had any biologistic or racial ideas, he never clearly expressed them. It is surely not without significance that his pupil Alexander the Great expressed himself unreservedly and unequivocally upon the unity of man. As Tarn says, "Alexander believed that he had a mission from the deity to harmonize men generally and be reconciler of the world, mixing men's lives and customs as in a loving cup . . . to bring about, as between mankind generally, *Homoneia* and peace and fellowship and make them all one people. . . . Plutarch makes him say that God is the common father of all mankind." [14]

Whatever Aristotle may originally have had in mind, subsequent generations have interpreted his words as they wished and laid the ground for

11. Aristotle *Politics* i. Chap. 5, in *The Politics of Aristotle,* trans. and ed. by Ernest Barker (Oxford: Clarendon Press, 1946).
12. W. L. Westermann, "The Slave Systems of Greek and Roman Antiquity," *Memoirs of the American Philosophical Society,* XL (1955), xi–180.
13. Aristotle *Politics* i. Chap. 6.
14. W. W. Tarn, *Alexander the Great and the Unity of Mankind* (London, 1933), pp. 3, 7, 21, 28.

what was eventually to become a racist interpretation of history and government.

Jean Jacques Rousseau's resounding reply to Aristotle brilliantly presents the Englightenment view. "Aristotle said," writes Rousseau, "that men were not naturally equal, but that some were born for slavery, and others for domination. Aristotle was right, but he took the effect for the cause. Nothing can be more certain than that every man born in slavery is born for slavery. Slaves lose everything in their chains, even the desire to escape from them; they love servitude as the companions of Ulysses loved their brutish condition. If then, there are slaves by nature, it is because there have been slaves against nature. Force made the first slaves, and their cowardice perpetuated them." [15]

It is not to be supposed that there were not in earlier times men who accounted for the behavioral differences between peoples on biological grounds. Inherent causes were certainly offered as an explanation of such differences on more than one occasion. However, such explanations simply made no headway against the criticism to which they were exposed. For example, the great fourteenth-century Arab scholar Ibn Khaldûn (1332–1406), in his work *The Muqaddimah* (1337) writes, "Al-Mas'ûdî undertook to investigate the reason for the levity, excitability, and emotionalism in Negroes, and attempted to explain it. However, he did no better than to report, on the authority of Galen and Ya'qûb b. Ishâq al-Kindi, that the reason is a weakness of their brains which results in a weakness of their intellect." Upon this Ibn Khaldûn remarks, "This is an inconclusive and unproven statement. 'God guides whomever he wants to guide.' " [16] Ibn Khaldûn's own explanation of the Negro's high spirits is entirely environmental, attributing them largely to climatic factors.

One sometimes finds it stated in the literature—and what is even worse, the statements are made as if they were direct quotations from the original sources—that certain writers in antiquity did clearly point to the biological differences as explanatory of the behavioral differences between peoples. One of the most widely diffused of these statements occurs in Ruth Benedict's book *Race: Science and Politics*. In this excellent book Cicero is quoted as writing to his friend Atticus, "Do not obtain your slaves from Britain, because they are so stupid and so utterly incapable of being taught that they are not fit to form part of the household of Athens." [17] Unhappily, Cicero made no such derogatory remark. It could be wished that he

15. Jean Jacques Rousseau, "The Social Contract," in *A Discourse on the Origin of Inequality* and *The Social Contract* trans. by G. D. H. Cole (Everyman's Library; New York: E. P. Dutton, 1932), Bk. I, Chap. 2.
16. Ibn Khaldûn, *The Muqaddimah,* trans. and ed. by Franz Rosenthal (New York: Pantheon Books, 1958), Vol. I, Bk. 1, pp. 175–176.
17. Ruth Benedict, *Race: Science and Politics* (New York: Viking Press, 1943), p. 10.

had. What he actually wrote was ". . . there is not a scrap of silver in the island, nor any hope of booty except from slaves; but I don't fancy you will find any with literary or musical talent among them." [18]

Cicero was wrong. The talents were there, both silver and genetic, but it took more than a thousand years before the genetic talents began to find expression. This long period of cultural lag in spite of the presence of the Romans in Britain for more than four centuries is worth reflecting upon.

And what of the Greeks in the second millennium B.C.? Who were they? A few hardworking illiterate peasant peoples attempting to wrest a living from the soil. And in the sixth century B.C. who were the Romans? Several thousand poor farmers scattered over the seven hills by the Tiber. What warrant was there in the food-grubbing peasants of these Mediterranean lands for the promise they subsequently so richly realized? And yet from these unkempt lowly farmers was to emerge the two most highly developed civilizations the world has known, the civilizations to which the Western world owes virtually everything it calls its own.

Who could have foretold that from these lowly peoples would emerge a Socrates, a Plato, an Aristotle, an Archimedes, a Euclid, an Aristophanes, a Euripides, a Pindar, a Pericles, a Solon, a Marcus Aurelius, an Ovid, a Catullus, a Lucretius, to name but a few? Who could have foretold that from those barbaric Britons of Cicero's day, more than fifteen hundred years later a Shakespeare would be born, a Ben Jonson, a John Donne, a Chirstopher Marlowe, a Gilbert of Rochester, a Bacon?

Peoples, like individuals, it would seem, require time and opportunities in which to realize their potentialities.

But we run somewhat ahead. How did the modern idea of "race" get started? It started, interestingly enough, in the Catholic church. In the year 1455 Pope Nicholas V, by decree, approved the subjugation of infidels to Christians.[19] The immediate result of this decree was the conversion of a religious-social difference into a socioeconomic, but not yet a "racial," discrimination. The decree meant that official sanction had been given to the enslavement of Negroes, Indians, and other "infidels" so that salvation of their souls and their entrance into God's Kingdom could be assured. It is from this time, the year 1455, that the Portuguese trade in slaves, principally in Africa, began in earnest.

Writing a hundred years later, the historian Joao de Barros states that the church gave the Portuguese a free hand to make war without provocation on non-Christian peoples, to reduce them into slavery, and to seize

18. Cicero *Letters to Atticus,* trans. and ed. by E. O. Winstedt (Loeb Classical Library; Cambridge: Harvard University Press, 1920), I, 324.
19. Anne Fremantle (ed.), *The Papal Encyclicals* (New York: New American Library, 1963), p. 77.

their lands, since they were "unjust possessors of them." [20] As Lewis Hanke states, "The infidel, in the eyes of the Portuguese, had neither rights of property nor personal rights. The salvation of his soul justified the loss of his personal liberty." [21]

In March 1493 Christopher Columbus was forced to land in Portugal, and King John II maintained that the papal bull *Romanus Pontifex,* 8 January 1455, which granted the territories discovered in Africa to Portugal, also included America. Ferdinand and Isabella of Spain protested, whereupon Pope Alexander VI issued three bulls, the most important of which, *Inter Caetera Divinae* (1493), encouraged the Spanish monarchs "to subdue the said mainlands and islands, and their natives and inhabitants, with God's grace, and to bring them to the Catholic faith." [22]

In his letter of March 1493 to Ferdinand and Isabella, Columbus remarks on the great friendliness of the Indians and of their "excellent and acute understanding." But to the rulers and their minions whose cupidity had been aroused, this was of no interest. The moment of magnificence was forever lost, and soon the shameful expropriation and destruction of the Indians, who resisted enslavement, began. On 29 May 1537 Pope Paul III issued the bull *Pastorale officium,* condemning the enslavement of Indians, declaring it heresy to say that they were irrational and incapable of conversion. The Pope also tried to transfer spiritual authority over the Indians from the Spanish Inquisition, which was controlled by the Spanish crown, to the bishop, but without success. It is worth quoting the significant part of the bull of 1537:

> It has come to our hearing that our very dear son in Christ, Charles, the ever august Emperor of the Romans who is also king of Castile and Aragon, anxious to check those who, burning with avarice, possess an inhuman spirit, has prohibited all his subjects by public edict from bringing the Western and Southern Indians into slavery, or daring to deprive them of their possessions. These Indians therefore, although they live outside the bosom of the Church, nevertheless have not been, nor are they to be, deprived of their freedom of ownership of their own possessions, since they are human beings and, consequently, capable of faith and salvation. They are not to be destroyed by slavery, but to be invited to life by preaching and example. Furthermore, desiring to repress the shameful deeds of such wicked men and to ensure that the Indians are not alienated by injuries and punishments so that they find it more difficult to embrace the faith of Christ, we lay it as a charge and a command by this present letter upon your Circumspection—in whose righteousness, fore-

20. Quoted in Lewis Hanke, *Aristotle and the American Indians* (Chicago: Henry Regnery Co., 1959), p. 108.
21. *Ibid.*
22. Fremantle, *The Papal Encyclicals,* p. 77.

sight, zeal and experience in these matters and in others we have in the
Lord special trust—that either by your own action or by that of others
you provide to all the aforesaid Indians the help of an effective defence
in the matters referred to previously; and we enjoin that you very strictly
forbid all and sundry of whatever dignity, position, condition, rank and
excellence, to bring the above-said Indians into slavery in any way or to
dare to deprive them of their possessions in any manner under pain, if
they do so, of incurring thereby excommunication "latae sententiae,"
from which they can only be absolved by ourselves or the Roman Pontiff
reigning at the time, except if they are at the point of death and have
previously made amends.[23]

Charles was so troubled in conscience by the behavior of his subjects to
the Indians that he later suspended all expeditions to America while he
sought to determine how to carry on the conquest of the Americas in a
Christian manner. Toward this end, and under the powerful influence of
that extraordinary man Bartolomé de Las Casas (1476–1566), friend of
the Indians, he called together a junta, in the year 1550, of the leading
theologians, jurists, and counselors to listen to a debate between Las Casas
and the Spanish jurist Juan Gines de Sepulveda in order to determine the
best way of dealing with the Indians. As Hanke remarks, "Probably never
before has a mighty emperor . . . ordered his conquests to cease until it
was decided if they were just." [24]

The great debate between Las Casas and Sepulveda was held in the capital at Valladolid. What was at issue was the Aristotelian claim that some
men were born to be slaves and others to be their masters. Las Casas and
others rejected this idea; Sepulveda argued in defense of it.

Forty years earlier, a Scottish scholar, John Major, in a book published
in 1510, had been the first to apply the Aristotelian doctrine of natural
slavery to the Indians.[25] A year later, on the island of Hispaniola in the
Caribbean, a Dominican friar, Antonio de Montesinos, preached a remarkable sermon on the text "I am a voice crying in the wilderness," condemning his countrymen's treatment of the Indians and inquiring, "Are
these Indians not men? Do they not have rational souls? Are you not
obliged to love them as you love yourselves?" [26]

The reverberations of that sermon were not long in making themselves
felt in Spain. Almost immediately a dispute arose at Burgos, where the
first two works on Indian problems soon appeared, together with the publication of the first code setting out the manner in which Indians should be
treated. One of these works, by the Dominican friar Matias de Paz, _Con-_

23. _Ibid.,_ pp. 80–81.
24. _Aristotle and the American Indians,_ p. 37.
25. John Major, _In primu Sententiarum_ (Paris: J. Badi, 1510).
26. Quoted in Hanke, _Aristotle and the American Indians,_ pp. 14, 15.

cerning the Rule of the Kings of Spain over the Indians, represents not only the first study of its kind by a member of his order, but also the first known statement that the American Indians are not slaves in the Aristotelian sense.[27] This whole subject is admirably explored by Lewis Hanke in his *Aristotle and the American Indians.*

Las Casas, as early as 1519, when he was forty-five years of age and had had much experience in America, had already clashed with the Bishop of Darien, Juan Quevedo, on the merits of the Aristotelian doctrine. In 1545 Sepulveda had written a manuscript, under the auspices of the president of the Council of the Indies, seeking to show that wars against the Indians were just and even necessary to secure their conversion to Christianity. Sepulveda took as his principal task the demonstration of Aristotle's doctrine of natural slavery. He argued that it was necessary and lawful to wage war against the Indians for four reasons: (1) for the gravity of the sins which the Indians had committed, especially their idolatries and their sins against nature; (2) because of the rudeness of their natures, which obliged them to serve persons having a more refined nature, such as the Spaniards; (3) in order to spread the faith, which would be more easily accomplished by the prior subjugation of the Indians; and (4) to protect the weak among the Indians themselves.

Sepulveda, who had never set foot in America, and if he had seen an Indian could have done so only at some distance removed, was forced to rely for his knowledge of the capacities and achievements of Indians entirely upon hearsay. This enabled him to declare that Indians were as inferior "as children are to adults, as women are to men. Indians are as different from Spaniards as cruel people are from mild peoples." "How can we doubt," he asks, "that these people, so uncivilized, so barbaric, so contaminated with so many sins and obscenities . . . have been justly conquered by such an excellent, pious, and most just king as was Ferdinand the Catholic and as is now Emperor Charles, and by such a humane nation which is excellent in every kind of virtue?"

These inferior people "require, by their own nature and in their own interests, to be placed under the authority of civilized and virtuous princes or nations, so that they may learn, from the might, wisdom, and law of their conquerors, to practice better morals, worthier customs, and more civilized ways of life." [28]

Sepulveda does not present a wholly racial or biologistic view of the differences between Indian and Spaniard, although something of that was undoubtedly implicit in what he intended to convey in the phrase "by the rudeness of their natures." It was a view which utterly outraged Las Casas.

27. *Ibid.,* p. 15.
28. *Ibid.,* p. 15.

"Mankind is one," declared Las Casas, "and all men are alike in that which concerns their creation and all natural things, and no one is born enlightened. From this it follows that all of us must be guided and aided at first by those who were born before us. And the savage peoples of the earth may be compared to uncultivated soil that readily brings forth weeds and useless thorns, but has within itself such natural virtue that by labour and cultivation it may be made to yield sound and beneficial fruits." [29]

In 1573, six years after the death of Las Casas, a general ordinance was passed regulating all future conquests and instituting many laws in behalf of the Indians. Thus, the spirit of Las Casas had finally achieved something of a victory. But the debate begun in Valladolid has never ended, and something more than its echoes are today heard in every part of the world.

During the seventeenth century increasing contact with the American Indians by the white settlers, and the purchase of Negroes as indentured servants, together with the subsequent institutionalization of Negro slavery in America toward the end of the century, served to produce those conditions which in general favored the view that Aristotle was right, that some men were born to be slaves and some to be their masters. But, once again, this viewpoint was socioeconomic in origin and nature and not biologistic, although biologistic overtones could sometimes be detected.

With the growth of Negro slavery in America and the profitable trade in slaves, eighteenth-century America was firmly established in a system of legalized and other social rationalizations designed to make everyone feel comfortable with the institution of slavery. But these social devices were based virtually entirely on the view that since the Negro was a benighted heathen, unable to read or write, and belonging to a class and caste clearly inferior to those of his masters, his proper condition was that of a lifetime servant to his masters. To them, his masters, the slave would be making payment, in his servitude, for the privilege of protection and having his soul saved in the bargain. It was a great benison conferred by the slaveholders upon their slaves. Wealth and the ownership of slaves being a mark of divine grace, the proper place of the man of grace was in his mansion, while the slave stood at his gate. Each according to his divinely appointed station.

It was in 1670, fifty-one years after the purchase of "19 Negars" from a Portuguese man-of-war, that Virginia passed the law specifying "that all servants not being christians" who had been brought into the colony by sea were to be slaves for life. There was very little, if anything, in any of this of biologism or racism. The slaves were clearly different in every way from their masters, and because they were inferior, it was to the advantage

29. *Ibid.*

of everyone, even to the slaves themselves, for them to be put under the protection of those who were able to exploit such of their talents as would render them most useful.

While the seeds of racism were being sown by such doctrines in the fertile soil of America, the poisonous plant was not to blossom until it had been intensively watered by the mainstream of ideas generated by the responses to the challenges of the Enlightenment, the Age of Reason. The eighteenth century was the Century of the Rediscovery of Man. The voyages of exploration of Bougainville (1761–1766), of Wallis-Carteret (1766), of Captain Cook (1768–1779), and of many others had revealed the existence of hitherto undreamed-of varieties of man who, far from being the savages of popular imagination, turned out to be gentle and in many ways distinctly superior to their discoverers. Romantic ideas of a Golden Age, the deductions of philosophers, and the discoveries of explorers in an age that not only was ready to, but already was taking a new look at man, seeing him bold and clear, almost literally for the first time, gave men furiously to think and revalue some of their most cherished values. Added to this was the atmosphere of revolution; the challenge of new ideas; the criticism of authority, intolerance, superstition, and the constraints under which so many human beings were forced to live. The American and French Revolutions put the principles of "Life, Liberty, and the Pursuit of Happiness," of "Liberty, Fraternity, and Equality," squarely before the world. The intellectual ferment that had precipitated these political upheavals, and of which perhaps the noblest product was the Declaration of Independence, drafted by the most eminent American luminary of the Enlightenment, Thomas Jefferson, soon expressed itself in the growth of the movement to abolish, as a first step, the trade in slaves.

Eighteenth-century scientific students of the variety of mankind were to a man all on the side of equality. Johann Friedrich Blumenbach, in the treatise that had created the science of physical anthropology, *On the Natural Variety of Mankind,* published in 1775, had written, "Although there seems to be so great a difference between widely separate nations, that you might easily take the inhabitants of the Cape of Good Hope, the Greenlanders, and the Circassians for so many different species of man, yet when the matter is thoroughly considered, you see that all do so run into one another, and that one variety of mankind does so sensibly pass into the other, that you cannot mark out the limits between them. Very arbitrary indeed both in number and definition have been the varieties of mankind accepted by eminent men." [30]

Johann Gottfried Herder, in his great work *Outlines of a Philosophy of*

30. Johann Friedrich Blumenbach, *De generis humani varietate nativa* (Göttingen, 1775); trans. by Thomas Bendyshe, *The Anthropological Treatises of Johann Friedrich Blumenbach* (London: Anthropological Society, 1865), pp. 98–99.

the History of Man, published in four volumes from 1784 to 1791, wrote in startlingly modern terms:

> I could wish the distinctions between the human species, that have been made from a laudable zeal for discriminating science, not carried beyond due bounds. Some for instance have thought fit to employ the term *races* for four or five divisions, originally made in consequence of country or complexion but I see no reason for this appelation. Race refers to a difference of origin, which in this case does not exist, or in each of these countries, and under each of these complexions, comprises the most different races. . . . In short, there are neither four or five races, nor exclusive varieties, on this Earth. Complexions run into each other: forms follow the genetic character: and upon the whole, all are at last but shades of the same great picture, extending through all ages, and over all parts of the Earth. They belong not, therefore, so properly to systematic natural history, as to the physico-geographical history of man.[31]

Much the same views were expressed by Buffon,[32] Rousseau,[33] the Humboldt brothers,[34] and many other scientific writers.[35]

What happened? How did it come about that the ideas reflected by such thinkers were virtually forgotten in the nineteenth century? The answer is that as a result of the pressures of rapidly changing socioeconomic conditions in the nineteenth century, such ideas were rapidly submerged under the avalanche of reactionary shibboleths.

The growing challenges of the abolitionists could evoke only the response from the defenders of slavery that the institution was justified. Since it was the scientific writers who had raised the biological issue, the defense now took the form, for the first time, of an explanation of the differences between the slaves and their masters based on biology. The Negro, it was now argued, was naturally, biologically, inferior to the white man.

It was in this manner that the doctrine of "race" was born. Burgeoning

31. Johann Gottfried Herder, *Ideen zur Philosphie der Geschichte der Menschheit* (Riga and Leipzig: J. F. Hartknoch, 1784–1791); trans. by Thomas Churchill, *Outlines of a Philosophy of the History of Man* (London: J. Johnson, 1803), p. 298.
32. Georges Louis Leclerc Buffon, *Historie Naturelle* (Paris, 1749–1804); trans. by William Smellie, *Natural History* (London: Cadell & Davies, 1812), III, 302 ff.
33. Jean Jacques Rousseau, "A Discourse on the Origin of Inequality," in *A Discourse on the Origin of Inequality* and *The Social Contract,* trans. by G. D. H. Cole (Everyman's Library; New York: E. P. Dutton, 1932), pp. 155–246.
34. Alexander von Humboldt, *Cosmos: A Sketch of a Physical Description of the Universe,* trans. by E. C. Otté (London: Bohn, 1849); Wilhelm von Humboldt, *Über die Kawi-Sprache auf der Insel Java* (Berlin: Königlichen Akademie der Wissenschaften, 1836), Vol. III, p. 426.
35. M. F. Ashley Montagu, *Man's Most Dangerous Myth: The Fallacy of Race* (4th ed.; Cleveland and New York: World Publishing Co., 1964).

imperialism battened on such ideas as "superannuated races," "the white man's burden," "the lesser breeds without the law," "the Yellow Peril," "East is East and West is West/ And never the twain shall meet," and other such notions. Indeed, if the idea of "race" had not already been available, the imperialists would have been forced to invent it. It was the most useful ideological instrument of all, even more valuable than the machine gun.

Darwinism was interpreted to mean that in the struggle for existence there was a competition between races in which the fittest, the superior, replaced the weakest, the inferior. In this way warfare between the races was justified because it rendered a biologically just decision. And what could be more neat than that.

By the middle of the nineteenth century the issue in America was squarely joined, leading eventually to open conflict between the North and the South—a conflict which has never ceased, a conflict which will not be settled on the battlefield, but in the consciences of men. Upon its outcome America as a power in the world will either stand or fall.

The issue of "race" is no longer a local one. It is more than an American problem: it is a problem which has now assumed world dimensions, in the Americas, Africa, Australia, Malaysia, Melanesia, Europe, and Asia. For this reason it has become more than ever the moral obligation of every self-respecting human being to make himself acquainted with the facts and the theories relating to the problems of "race" so that he may be able to think as clearly and act as intelligently as he should in relation to the most critical problem facing humanity today—the problem, no less, of humanity itself, which, alas, too many people among us see as the problem of "race."

ALEXIS DE TOCQUEVILLE

Situation of the Black Population

Alexis de Tocqueville, a French visitor to this country in the first quarter
of the nineteenth century, saw very clearly the race problem at the core
of American civilization. He saw the differences between slavery itself
and its consequences, between race discrimination in law and in custom.
The profound relevance of this selection, written more than one hundred
and fifty years ago, beggars any attempt to ascribe importance to it.

Why it is more difficult to abolish slavery, and to efface all vestiges of it
amongst the moderns, than it was amongst the ancients.—In the United
States the prejudices of the Whites against the Blacks seem to increase in
proportion as slavery is abolished.—Situation of the Negroes in the
northern and southern States.—Why the Americans abolish slavery.—
Servitude, which debases the slave, impoverishes the master.—Contrast
between the left and the right bank of the Ohio.—To what attributable.
—The black race, as well as slavery, recedes towards the South.—
Explanation of this fact.—Difficulties attendant upon the abolition of
slavery in the South.—Dangers to come.—General anxiety.—
Foundation of a black colony in Africa.—Why the Americans of the
South increase the hardships of slavery, whilst they are distressed at its
continuance.

THE INDIANS will perish in the same isolated condition in which
they have lived; but the destiny of the Negroes is in some measure
interwoven with that of the Europeans. These two races are attached to each other without intermingling; and they are alike unable entirely to separate or to combine. The most formidable of all the ills
which threaten the future existence of the Union, arises from the presence
of a black population upon its territory; and in contemplating the cause of
the present embarrassments or of the future dangers of the United States,
the observer is invariably led to consider this as a primary fact.

The permanent evils to which mankind is subjected are usually produced by the vehement or the increasing efforts of men; but there is one calamity which penetrated furtively into the world, and which was at first
scarcely distinguishable amidst the ordinary abuses of power: it originated
with an individual whose name history has not preserved; it was wafted

like some accursed germ upon a portion of the soil, but it afterwards nurtured itself, grew without effort, and spreads naturally with the society to which it belongs. I need scarcely add that this calamity is slavery. Christianity suppressed slavery, but the Christians of the sixteenth century re-established it,—as an exception, indeed, to their social system, and restricted to one of the races of mankind; but the wound thus inflicted upon humanity, though less extensive, was at the same time rendered far more difficult of cure.

It is important to make an accurate distinction between slavery itself, and its consequences. The immediate evils which are produced by slavery were very nearly the same in antiquity as they are amongst the moderns; but the consequences of these evils were different. The slave, amongst the ancients, belonged to the same race as his master, and he was often the superior of the two in education [1] and instruction. Freedom was the only distinction between them; and when freedom was conferred, they were easily confounded together. The ancients, then, had a very simple means of avoiding slavery and its evil consequences, which was that of affranchisement; and they succeeded as soon as they adopted this measure generally. Not but, in ancient States, the vestiges of servitude subsisted for some time after servitude itself was abolished. There is a natural prejudice which prompts men to despise whomsoever has been their inferior long after he is become their equal; and the real inequality which is produced by fortune or by law, is always succeeded by an imaginary inequality which is implanted in the manners of the people. Nevertheless, this secondary consequence of slavery was limited to a certain term amongst the ancients; for the freedman bore so entire a resemblance to those born free, that it soon became impossible to distinguish him from amongst them.

The greatest difficulty in antiquity was that of altering the law; amongst the moderns it is that of altering the manners; and, as far as we are concerned, the real obstacles begin where those of the ancients left off. This arises from the circumstance that, amongst the moderns, the abstract and transient fact of slavery is fatally united to the physical and permanent fact of colour. The tradition of slavery dishonours the race, and the peculiarity of the race perpetuates the tradition of slavery. No African has ever voluntarily emigrated to the shores of the New World; whence it must be inferred, that all the blacks who are now to be found in that hemisphere are either slaves or freedmen. Thus the negro transmits the eternal mark of his ignominy to all his descendants; and although the law may abolish slavery, God alone can obliterate the traces of its existence.

1. It is well known that several of the most distinguished authors of antiquity, and amongst them Æsop and Terence, were, or had been slaves. Slaves were not always taken from barbarous nations, and the chances of war reduced highly civilized men to servitude.

The modern slave differs from his master not only in his condition, but in his origin. You may set the negro free, but you cannot make him otherwise than an alien to the European. Nor is this all; we scarcely acknowledge the common features of mankind in this child of debasement whom slavery has brought amongst us. His physiognomy is to our eyes hideous, his understanding weak, his tastes low; and we are almost inclined to look upon him as a being intermediate between man and the brutes.[2] The moderns, then, after they have abolished slavery, have three prejudices to contend against, which are less easy to attack, and far less easy to conquer, than the mere fact of servitude: the prejudice of the master, the prejudice of the race, and the prejudice of colour.

It is difficult for us, who have had the good fortune to be born amongst men like ourselves by nature, and equal to ourselves by law, to conceive the irreconcilable differences which separate the negro from the European in America. But we may derive some faint notion of them from analogy. France was formerly a country in which numerous distinctions of rank existed, that had been created by the legislation. Nothing can be more fictitious than a purely legal inferiority; nothing more contrary to the instinct of mankind than these permanent divisions which had been established between beings evidently similar. Nevertheless these divisions subsisted for ages; they still subsist in many places; and on all sides they have left imaginary vestiges, which time alone can efface. If it be so difficult to root out an inequality which solely originates in the law, how are those distinctions to be destroyed which seem to be based upon the immutable laws of Nature herself? When I remember the extreme difficulty with which aristocratic bodies, of whatever nature they may be, are commingled with the mass of the people; and the exceeding care which they take to preserve the ideal boundaries of their caste inviolate, I despair of seeing an aristocracy disappear which is founded upon visible and indelible signs. Those who hope that the Europeans will ever mix with the negroes, appear to me to delude themselves; and I am not led to any such conclusion by my own reason, or by the evidence of facts.

Hitherto, wherever the whites have been the most powerful, they have maintained the blacks in a subordinate or a servile position; wherever the negroes have been strongest they have destroyed the whites; such has been the only retribution which has ever taken place between the two races.

I see that in a certain portion of the territory of the United States at the present day, the legal barrier which separated the two races is tending to fall away, but not that which exists in the manners of the country; slavery

2. To induce the whites to abandon the opinion they have conceived of the moral and intellectual inferiority of their former slaves, the negroes must change; but as long as this opinion subsists, to change is impossible.

recedes, but the prejudice to which it has given birth remains stationary. Whosoever has inhabited the United States must have perceived, that in those parts of the Union in which the negroes are no longer slaves, they have in nowise drawn nearer to the whites. On the contrary, the prejudice of the race appears to be stronger in the States which have abolished slavery, than in those where it still exists; and nowhere is it so intolerant as in those States where servitude has never been known.

It is true, that in the North of the Union, marriages may be legally contracted between negroes and whites; but public opinion would stigmatize a man who should connect himself with a negress as infamous, and it would be difficult to meet with a single instance of such a union. The electoral franchise has been conferred upon the negroes in almost all the States in which slavery has been abolished; but if they come forward to vote, their lives are in danger. If oppressed, they may bring an action at law, but they will find none but whites amongst their judges; and although they may legally serve as jurors, prejudice repulses them from that office. The same schools do not receive the child of the black and of the European. In the theatres, gold cannot procure a seat for the servile race beside their former masters; in the hospitals they lie apart; and although they are allowed to invoke the same Divinity as the whites, it must be at a different altar, and in their own churches with their own clergy. The gates of Heaven are not closed against these unhappy beings; but their inferiority is continued to the very confines of the other world; when the negro is defunct, his bones are cast aside, and the distinction of condition prevails even in the equality of death. The negro is free, but he can share neither the rights, nor the pleasures, nor the labour, nor the afflictions, nor the tomb of him whose equal he has been declared to be; and he cannot meet him upon fair terms in life or in death.

In the South, where slavery still exists, the negroes are less carefully kept apart; they sometimes share the labour and the recreations of the whites; the whites consent to intermix with them to a certain extent, and although the legislation treats them more harshly, the habits of the people are more tolerant and compassionate. In the South the master is not afraid to raise his slave to his own standing, because he knows that he can in a moment reduce him to the dust, at pleasure. In the North the white no longer distinctly perceives the barrier which separates him from the degraded race, and he shuns the negro with the more pertinacity, since he fears lest they should some day be confounded together.

Amongst the Americans of the South, Nature sometimes re-asserts her rights, and restores a transient-equality between the blacks and the whites; but in the North pride restrains the most imperious of human passions. The American of the Northern States would perhaps allow the negress to share his licentious pleasures, if the laws of his country did not declare that she may aspire to be the legitimate partner of his bed; but he recoils with horror from her who might become his wife.

Thus it is, in the United States, that the prejudice which repels the negroes seems to increase in proportion as they are emancipated, and inequality is sanctioned by the manners whilst it is effaced from the laws of the country. But if the relative position of the two races which inhabit the United States is such as I have described, it may be asked why the Americans have abolished slavery in the North of the Union, why they maintain it in the South, and why they aggravate its hardships there? The answer is easily given. It is not for the good of the negroes, but for that of the whites, that measures are taken to abolish slavery in the United States.

The first negroes were imported into Virginia about the year 1621.[3] In America, therefore, as well as in the rest of the globe, slavery originated in the South. Thence it spread from one settlement to another; but the number of slaves diminished towards the Northern States, and the negro population was always very limited in New England.[4]

A century had scarcely elapsed since the foundation of the colonies, when the attention of the planters was struck by the extraordinary fact, that the provinces which were comparatively destitute of slaves, increased in population, in wealth, and in prosperity more rapidly than those which contained the greatest number of negroes. In the former, however, the inhabitants were obliged to cultivate the soil themselves, or by hired labourers; in the latter they were furnished with hands for which they paid no wages; yet although labour and expense were on the one side, and ease with economy on the other, the former were in possession of the most advantageous system. This consequence seemed to be the more difficult to explain, since the settlers, who all belonged to the same European race, had the same habits, the same civilization, the same laws, and their shades of difference were extremely slight.

Time, however, continued to advance; and the Anglo-Americans,

3. See Beverley's History of Virginia. See also in Jefferson's Memoirs some curious details concerning the introduction of negroes into Virginia, and the first Act which prohibited the importation of them in 1778.
4. The number of slaves was less considerable in the North, but the advantages resulting from slavery were not more contested there than in the South. In 1740, the legislature of the State of New York declared that the direct importation of slaves ought to be encouraged as much as possible, and smuggling severely punished in order not to discourage the fair trader. (Kent's Commentaries, vol. ii. p. 206.) Curious researches, by Belknap, upon slavery in New England, are to be found in the Historical Collection of Massachusetts, vol. iv. p. 193. It appears that negroes were introduced there in 1630, but that the legislation and manners of the people were opposed to slavery from the first; see also, in the same work, the manner in which public opinion, and afterwards the laws, finally put an end to slavery.

spreading beyond the coasts of the Atlantic Ocean, penetrated further and further into the solitudes of the West; they met with a new soil and an unwonted climate; the obstacles which opposed them were of the most various character; their races intermingled, the inhabitants of the South went up towards the North, those of the North descended to the South; but in the midst of all these causes, the same result occurred at every step; and in general, the colonies in which there were no slaves became more populous and more rich than those in which slavery flourished. The more progress was made, the more was it shown that slavery, which is so cruel to the slave, is prejudicial to the master.

But this truth was most satisfactorily demonstrated when civilization reached the banks of the Ohio. The stream which the Indians had distinguished by the name of Ohio, or Beautiful River, waters one of the most magnificent valleys which has ever been made the abode of man. Undulating lands extend upon both shores of the Ohio, whose soil affords inexhaustible treasures to the labourer; on either bank the air is wholesome and the climate mild; and each of them forms the extreme frontier of a vast State: that which follows the numerous windings of the Ohio upon the left is called Kentucky; that upon the right bears the name of the river. These two States only differ in a single respect; Kentucky has admitted slavery, but the State of Ohio has prohibited the existence of slaves within its borders.[5]

Thus the traveller who floats down the current of the Ohio, to the spot where that river falls into the Mississippi, may be said to sail between liberty and servitude; and a transient inspection of the surrounding objects will convince him as to which of the two is most favourable to mankind.

Upon the left bank of the stream the population is rare; from time to time one descries a troop of slaves loitering in the half-desert fields; the primæval forest recurs at every turn; society seems to be asleep, man to be idle, and nature alone offers a scene of activity and of life.

From the right bank, on the contrary, a confused hum is heard which proclaims the presence of industry; the fields are covered with abundant harvests; the elegance of the dwellings announces the taste and activity of the labourer; and man appears to be in the enjoyment of that wealth and contentment which is the reward of labour.[6]

The State of Kentucky was founded in 1775, the State of Ohio only

5. Not only is slavery prohibited in Ohio, but no free negroes are allowed to enter the territory of that State, or to hold property in it. See the Statutes of Ohio.
6. The activity of Ohio is not confined to individuals, but the undertakings of the State are surprisingly great: a canal has been established between Lake Erie and the Ohio, by means of which the valley of the Mississippi communicates with the river of the North, and the European commodities which arrive at New York may be forwarded by water to New Orleans across five hundred leagues of continent.

twelve years later; but twelve years are more in America than half a century in Europe, and, at the present day, the population of Ohio exceeds that of Kentucky by two hundred and fifty thousand souls.[7] These opposite consequences of slavery and freedom may readily be understood; and they suffice to explain many of the differences which we remark between the civilization of antiquity, and that of our own time.

Upon the left bank of the Ohio labour is confounded with the idea of slavery, upon the right bank it is identified with that of prosperity and improvement; on the one side it is degraded, on the other it is honoured; on the former territory no white labourers can be found, for they would be afraid of assimilating themselves to the negroes; on the latter no one is idle, for the white population extends its activity and its intelligence to every kind of employment. Thus the men whose task it is to cultivate the rich soil of Kentucky are ignorant and lukewarm; whilst those who are active and enlightened either do nothing, or pass over into the State of Ohio, where they may work without dishonour.

It is true that in Kentucky the planters are not obliged to pay wages to the slaves whom they employ; but they derive small profits from their labour, whilst the wages paid to free workmen would be returned with interest in the value of their services. The free workman is paid, but he does his work quicker than the slave; and rapidity of execution is one of the great elements of economy. The white sells his services, but they are only purchased at the times at which they may be useful; the black can claim no remuneration for his toil, but the expense of his maintenance is perpetual; he must be supported in his old-age as well as in the prime of manhood, in his profitless infancy as well as in the productive years of youth. Payment must equally be made in order to obtain the services of either class of men; the free workman receives his wages in money; the slave in education, in food, in care, and in clothing. The money which a master spends in the maintenance of his slaves, goes gradually and in detail, so that it is scarcely perceived; the salary of the free workman is paid in a round sum, which appears only to enrich the individual who receives it; but in the end the slave has cost more than the free servant, and his labour is less productive.[8]

7. The exact numbers given by the census of 1830 were: Kentucky, 688,844; Ohio, 937,679.
8. Independently of these causes, which, wherever free workmen abound, render their labour more productive and more economical than that of slaves, another cause may be pointed out which is peculiar to the United States: the sugar-cane has hitherto been cultivated with success only upon the banks of the Mississippi, near the mouth of that river in the Gulf of Mexico. In Louisiana the cultivation of the sugar-cane is exceedingly lucrative; and nowhere does a labourer earn so much by his work; and, as there is always a certain relation between the cost of production and the value of the produce, the price of slaves is very high in Louisiana. But Louisiana is one of

The influence of slavery extends still further; it affects the character of the master, and imparts a peculiar tendency to his ideas and his tastes. Upon both banks of the Ohio, the character of the inhabitants is enterprising and energetic; but this vigour is very differently exercised in the two States. The white inhabitant of Ohio, who is obliged to subsist by his own exertions, regards temporal prosperity as the principal aim of his existence; and as the country which he occupies presents inexhaustible resources to his industry and ever-varying lures to his activity, his acquisitive ardour surpasses the ordinary limits of human cupidity: he is tormented by the desire of wealth, and he boldly enters upon every path which fortune opens to him; he becomes a sailor, a pioneer, an artisan, or a labourer with the same indifference, and he supports, with equal constancy, the fatigues and the dangers incidental to these various professions; the resources of his intelligence are astonishing, and his avidity in the pursuit of gain amounts to a species of heroism.

But the Kentuckian scorns not only labour, but all the undertakings which labour promotes; as he lives in an idle independence, his tastes are those of an idle man; money loses a portion of its value in his eyes; he covets wealth much less than pleasure and excitement; and the energy which his neighbour devotes to gain, turns with him to a passionate love of field sports and military exercises; he delights in violent bodily exertion, he is familiar with the use of arms, and is accustomed from a very early age to expose his life in single combat. Thus slavery not only prevents the whites from becoming opulent, but even from desiring to become so.

As the same causes have been continually producing opposite effects for the last two centuries in the British colonies of North America, they have established a very striking difference between the commercial capacity of the inhabitants of the South and those of the North. At the present day, it is only the Northern States which are in possession of shipping, manufactures, railroads, and canals. This difference is perceptible not only in comparing the North with the South, but in comparing the several Southern States. Almost all the individuals who carry on commercial operations, or who endeavour to turn slave-labour to account in the most Southern districts of the Union, have emigrated from the North. The natives of the Northern States are constantly spreading over that portion of the American territory, where they have less to fear from competition; they discover resources there, which escaped the notice of the inhabitants; and, as they comply with a system which they do not approve, they succeed in turning

the Confederate States, and slaves may be carried thither from all parts of the Union; the price given for slaves in New Orleans consequently raises the value of slaves in all the other markets. The consequence of this is, that in the countries where the land is less productive, the cost of slave-labour is still very considerable, which gives an additional advantage to the competition of free labour.

it to better advantage than those who first founded, and who still maintain it.

Were I inclined to continue this parallel, I could easily prove that almost all the differences, which may be remarked between the characters of the Americans in the Southern and in the Northern States, have originated in slavery; but this would divert me from my subject, and my present intention is not to point out all the consequences of servitude, but those effects which it has produced upon the prosperity of the countries which have admitted it.

The influence of slavery upon the production of wealth must have been very imperfectly known in antiquity, as slavery then obtained throughout the civilized world; and the nations which were unacquainted with it were barbarous. And indeed Christianity only abolished slavery by advocating the claims of the slave; at the present time it may be attacked in the name of the master; and, upon this point, interest is reconciled with morality.

.   .   .

The same abuses of power which still maintain slavery, would then become the source of the most alarming perils, which the white population of the South might have to apprehend. At the present time the descendants of the Europeans are the sole owners of the land; the absolute masters of all labour; and the only persons who are possessed of wealth, knowledge, and arms. The black is destitute of all these advantages, but he subsists without them because he is a slave. If he were free, and obliged to provide for his own subsistence, would it be possible for him to remain without these things and to support life? Or would not the very instruments of the present superiority of the white, whilst slavery exists, expose him to a thousand dangers if it were abolished?

As long as the negro remains a slave, he may be kept in a condition not very far removed from that of the brutes; but, with his liberty, he cannot but acquire a degree of instruction which will enable him to appreciate his misfortunes, and to discern a remedy for them. Moreover, there exists a singular principle of relative justice which is very firmly implanted in the human heart. Men are much more forcibly struck by those inequalities which exist within the circle of the same class, than with those which may be remarked between different classes. It is more easy for them to admit slavery, than to allow several millions of citizens to exist under a load of eternal infamy and hereditary wretchedness. In the North the population of freed negroes feels these hardships and resents these indignities; but its numbers and its powers are small, whilst in the South it would be numerous and strong.

As soon as it is admitted that the whites and the emancipated blacks are placed upon the same territory in the situation of two alien communities, it will readily be understood that there are but two alternatives for the future; the negroes and the whites must either wholly part or wholly mingle. I have already expressed the conviction which I entertain as to the latter event.[9] I do not imagine that the white and black races will ever live in any country upon an equal footing. But I believe the difficulty to be still greater in the United States than elsewhere. An isolated individual may surmount the prejudices of religion, of his country, or of his race, and if this individual is a king he may effect surprising changes in society; but a whole people cannot rise, as it were, above itself. A despot who should subject the Americans and their former slaves to the same yoke, might perhaps succeed in commingling their races; but as long as the American democracy remains at the head of affairs, no one will undertake so difficult a task; and it may be foreseen that the freer the white population of the United States becomes, the more isolated will it remain.

.   .   .

I happened to meet with an old man, in the South of the Union, who had lived in illicit intercourse with one of his negresses, and had had several children by her, who were born the slaves of their father. He had indeed frequently thought of bequeathing to them at least their liberty; but years had elapsed without his being able to surmount the legal obstacles to their emancipation, and in the meanwhile his old-age was come, and he was about to die. He pictured to himself his sons dragged from market to market, and passing from the authority of a parent to the rod of the stranger, until these horrid anticipations worked his expiring imagination into frenzy. When I saw him he was a prey to all the anguish of despair, and he made me feel how awful is the retribution of Nature upon those who have broken her laws.

These evils are unquestionably great; but they are the necessary and foreseen consequence of the very principle of modern slavery. When the Europeans chose their slaves from a race differing from their own, which many of them considered as inferior to the other races of mankind, and which they all repelled with horror from any notion of intimate connexion, they must have believed that slavery would last for ever; since there is no intermediate state which can be durable, between the excessive inequality produced by servitude, and the complete equality which originates in independence. The Europeans did imperfectly feel this truth, but without ac-

9. This opinion is sanctioned by authorities infinitely weightier than anything that I can say: thus, for instance, it is stated in the Memoirs of Jefferson (as collected by M. Conseil,) "Nothing is more clearly written in the book of destiny than the emancipation of the blacks; and it is equally certain that the two races will never live in a state of equal freedom under the same government, so insurmountable are the barrier which nature, habit, and opinions have established between them."

knowledging it even to themselves. Whenever they have had to do with ne-groes, their conduct has either been dictated by their interest and their pride, or by their compassion. They first violated every right of humanity by their treatment of the negro, and they afterwards informed him that those rights were precious and inviolable. They affected to open their ranks to the slaves, but the negroes who attempted to penetrate into the community were driven back with scorn; and they have incautiously and involuntarily been led to admit of freedom instead of slavery, without hav-ing the courage to be wholly iniquitous, or wholly just.

THOMAS GOSSETT

The Indian in the Nineteenth Century

This chapter from Thomas Gossett's book, *Race,* is one of the best single surveys of the relations of the white and red races in this country. In a direct, straightforward manner he chronicles what happened to the Indians and why it happened. He offers an insight into one of the economic bases of racism: the more valuable the land which the Indian occupied, the more probable his displacement. And, his thesis that the Indians must be what they choose to be, anticipates Deloria's (p. 308) analysis of the problems of tribal diversity.

THE PATTERN of the treatment of the Indian by the English colonists had been set in the seventeenth century. It was not the kindly attitude of Roger Williams, John Eliot, and the Quakers which generally prevailed. When the Indians gave trouble, the colonists made war against them, often adopting customs as savage as those of the Indians themselves. As early as 1653, the English had begun the system of reservations—assigning each warrior fifty acres of land and the privilege of hunting in unoccupied territory. As the white men moved west, they developed a pattern with regard to the land of the Indians which was repeated over and over again. The Indians would be assigned to a reservation. In time, the white men would covet their land and by one means or another seek to acquire it. They would send to the Indians agents who would offer gifts—often trinkets or whiskey—in exchange for vast tracts of land. Sometimes they would choose some chief or chiefs willing to sign away the land for a price and then assume arbitrarily that this man or these men spoke for all the members of a tribe or of many tribes. Old treaties which had promised eternal boundaries for Indian lands were ignored. If cajolery, trickery, or threats failed, the white men would use force to move the Indians westward.[1]

When the United States became a nation, the policy toward the Indians had already been set in motion. From the beginning, however, there was often a glaring discrepancy between high-sounding statements of policy and actual practice. The Northwest Territory Ordinance of 1787 would

1. Ray Allen Billington, *Westward Expansion: A History of the American Frontier* (New York, 1949), p. 46; William T. Hagan, *American Indians* (Chicago, 1961), pp. 14–15.

seem to be a model document so far as the treatment of the Indians was concerned:

> The utmost good faith shall always be observed toward the Indians, their lands and property shall never be taken from them without their consent; and in their property, rights, and liberty, they shall never be disturbed, unless in just and lawful wars authorized by Congress; but laws founded in justice and humanity shall from time to time be made, for preventing wrongs being done to them, and for preserving peace and friendship with them.[2]

It is difficult to equate the language of this document with the fact that territorial governments sometimes offered white citizens bounties for the Indian scalps they brought in. The Dutch had done this as early as 1641 and later on the Puritans engaged in the practice. In the early nineteenth century, it was sometimes argued that if frontiersmen and farmers could be encouraged to kill Indians on a commission basis, the governments could save money because this method would be less expensive than paying soldiers to do it. The last American scalp bounty was offered by the Territory of Indiana in 1814 as an "encouragement to the enterprise and bravery of our fellow citizens." [3]

Because of the savagery of many Indians, it is not surprising that frontiersmen—who were most often the men in conflict with the Indians—should have developed the firm conviction that the only good Indian was a dead Indian. The frontiersmen were frequently violent toward the men in their own group who violated their rules or got in their way, and they were still more violent against the Indians—who neither lived by nor understood the rules of the white man. The idea expressed by Cotton Mather in the seventeenth century that the Indians were the devil's minions, damned from birth by God and incapable of redemption, shifted in the nineteenth century to the conviction that the Indians were damned by biology—that they were inherently incapable of taking the first step toward civilization. At best the Indians were an inferior breed of men and at worst no more than savage beasts. Hugh Brackenridge, the jurist and novelist, indicated the direction of the shift when he wrote in 1782 that "extermination" would be most fitting for "the animals vulgarly called Indians. . . ." [4]

The Constitution mentioned the Indians only briefly. One can infer from

2. "The Northwest Ordinance, July 13, 1787," in Henry Steele Commager, ed., *Documents of American History* (New York, 1949), p. 131.
3. Quoted in B. Schrieke, *Alien Americans* (New York, 1936), p. 31.
4. *Narratives of the Perils and Sufferings of Dr. Knight and John Slover* (Cincinnati, 1867), pp. 62–71; quoted in Albert K. Weinberg, *Manifest Destiny: A Study of Nationalist Expansionism in American History* (Baltimore, 1935), p. 77.

the section dealing with them that—following Colonial precedent—the Founding Fathers thought of the Indians not as citizens, real or potential, but as members of autonomous foreign nations. The Constitution declares, for example, that "Congress shall have the power to regulate commerce with foreign nations, and among the several states, and with the Indian tribes." A treaty would imply that the government had no specific obligation to extend the blessings of citizenship to the Indians. This point of view was not limited to the conservatives, who were inclined to interpret individual rights of people rather narrowly. Thomas Paine, one of the most ardent apostles of liberty in the American Revolution, had little inclination to extend the blessings of American citizenship to alien peoples —to the French and the Spanish in the Southwest, for example—much less to the Indians. After the Louisiana Purchase in 1803, a Louisiana delegation was sent to Washington asking for the privileges of citizenship for French and Spanish settlers. Paine declared that the fact that Americans had fought for their own rights did not make it "incumbent upon us to fight the battles of the world for the world's profit." Paine was equally indifferent to the idea of the rights of citizenship for Indians.[5]

John Quincy Adams was reflecting a widespread conviction when he said in 1800 that the Indian tribes had a "questionable foundation" to land:

> But what is the right of a huntsman of the forest of a thousand miles, over which he has accidentally ranged in quest of prey? . . . Shall the exuberant bosom of the common mother, amply adequate to the nourishment of millions, be claimed exclusively by a few hundreds of her offspring?

Adams suggested that the title of Indians to land was valid only when they had settled upon it and cultivated it. This meant, in effect, that in order to acquire title to land the Indians had to stop being hunters and become farmers, a transformation which would have been very difficult for them to bring about even if they had been able to comprehend and had agreed to the reasons for it.[6]

The process of encumbering Indian lands went steadily on, but an important change occurred in 1825. Up until that time, the aim of Indian policy had been to confine the Indians in the eastern part of the nation to reservations in which they could take up farming. However, as these lands were more and more coveted by white settlers, this solution no longer was satisfactory. The federal government decided that all Indians should be

5. *The Writings of Thomas Paine,* ed. Moncure Conway (New York, 1894–96), III, 431.
6. Quoted in Jedidiah Morse, *A Report to the Secretary of War of the United States on Indian Affairs* (New Haven, 1822), p. 282.

moved to new reservations west of the Mississippi. At that time, there was a general conviction that the treeless plains of the West were unsuitable for habitation by white men, and thus the removals were apparently planned as a permanent solution to the Indian "problem." [7]

In Illinois, the forcible removal of the Sauk and Fox tribes led to the Black Hawk War in 1832. Black Hawk was a chieftain who refused to cede tribal lands. In 1831, when civilian frontiersmen had gathered to drive the Sauk tribe out, Black Hawk and his followers had retreated west across the Mississippi. The tribe spent a miserable winter in the Iowa country, since they had arrived too late to plant crops. Black Hawk's apparent intention was to return peacefully to Illinois to ask the white man for permission to settle on what had been the Sauks' own land. The fact that the whole tribe—including women and children—accompanied him was proof that his party was not warlike. Nevertheless, a wave of panic swept the white settlers. The Indians were attacked, and at the end of the ensuing "war" of nearly three months' duration, only 150 of the 1,000 Indians who had begun the march from the Iowa country were still alive. The other Indian tribes of the Middle West got the point that it was better to give up their lands and move west than to be exterminated. From 1832 to 1837, the Indians ceded nearly two million acres in the Northwest, and by 1846 the last of the Indian tribes had been transported—whether they wanted to go or not—to their new "home" in the West.[8]

In Georgia, the Cherokees—a tribe of about seventeen thousand—met the requirement that they live upon and farm their land. They maintained schools and had a written constitution based upon the American model with an executive, a legislative, and a judicial branch. Sequoyah, one of their chiefs, had invented an alphabet for the Cherokee language with eighty-five characters and had published parts of the Bible and edited a newspaper, the *Cherokee Phoenix*. None of this prevented them from losing their land. Both the federal government and the state of Georgia were determined that they should be removed.[9]

In 1828, Congress appropriated $50,000 for the removal of the Cherokees. The War Department agents were authorized to offer the Indians land in the West, transportation, a blanket, a rifle, a kettle, five pounds of tobacco, a year's supplies, and fifty dollars in cash. The Indians refused the offer and stayed where they were. Then the state legislature of Georgia declared all Cherokee laws to be void, denied the Indians the right to be a party in a legal suit or to testify in court against any white man, and de-

7. Billington, *op. cit.,* p. 297; Harold E. Fey and D'Arcy McNickle, *Indians and Other Americans: Two Ways of Life Meet* (New York, 1959), pp. 62–63.
8. See Frank E. Stevens, *The Black Hawk War, Including a Review of Black Hawk's Life* (Chicago, 1903), *passim.*
9. Grant Foreman, *Sequoyah* (Norman, 1938), pp. 11–15.

nied them also the right to prospect for gold on their own lands, though white men could do so. In 1830, Congress passed a Removal Bill which authorized the President to resettle any eastern tribe—by force, if necessary, and without regard to any treaties which the government had previously signed. The land of the Cherokees was ruthlessly taken over by white settlers, debts owing to them were declared canceled, and government agents attempted to induce factions of them to rebel against their leaders. Three white missionaries protested against the policy of the state and national governments and, as "citizens" of the Cherokee nation, refused to swear an oath of allegiance to the state of Georgia. They were arrested, chained, and forced to walk twenty-one miles behind a wagon. Later they were sentenced to four years of hard labor in the state penitentiary. When the Cherokee case came before the Supreme Court, Chief Justice John Marshall, in the famous *Worcester vs. Georgia* decision, declared that the Cherokees were a "domestic dependent nation" under the protection of the federal government and that the state of Georgia had no right to molest them. In reply, President Andrew Jackson, an old Indian fighter himself, declared: "John Marshall has rendered his decision; now let him enforce it." [10]

In 1834, federal agents were finally successful with the old trick of bribing a minor faction to deed the tribe's land. General Winfield Scott, with seven thousand troops and followed by "civilian volunteers," invaded the Cherokee domain, seized all the Indians they could find, and, in the middle of winter, sent them on the long trek to Arkansas and Oklahoma. The "civilian volunteers" appropriated the Indians' livestock, household goods, and farm implements and burned their homes. Some fourteen thousand Indians were forced to travel the "trail of tears," as it came to be called, and about four thousand of them died on the way. An eyewitness to the exodus reported: "Even aged females, apparently ready to drop into the grave, were travelling with heavy burdens attached to their backs, sometimes on frozen grounds and sometimes on muddy streets, with no covering for their feet." [11]

Alabama and Mississippi, following Georgia's lead, acted to rid themselves of the Indians in their midst. They forbade tribes to meet or Indian chiefs to exercise their offices—a device to make it easier for Indian agents to bribe minority factions. The Choctaws and the remnants of the Creeks were forced to join the Cherokees in their pitiful exodus. It is little wonder that General Sam Houston could say after the Mexican War that he saw no reason why the United States government should not appropri-

10. "Worcester *v.* Georgia, 6 Peters, 515 (1832)," in Commager, *op. cit.,* pp. 258–59; Grace Steele Woodward, *The Cherokees* (Norman, 1962), p. 171.
11. Quoted in John Collier, *The Indians of the Americas* (New York, 1947), pp. 208–9.

ate the lands of the Mexicans. Americans, said Houston, had always cheated Indians and since the Mexicans were no better than the Indians, "I can see no reason why we should not go on the same course now, and take their land." [12]

Up until 1849, the Bureau of Indian Affairs of the federal government was under the control of the War Department, but it was then transferred to the Interior Department. On its face, this would seem to be an improvement, in that it transferred the Indians to civilian control; but it was not. The Interior Department was then the agency through which Congress could dispose of public lands, and it proved too strong a temptation in the distribution of these lands to include the Indian property as well. The War Department had initiated a policy of dissolving tribal societies, since it was organization which gave the Indians their cohesiveness and enabled them to resist encroachment. Under the Interior Department, the Indian Bureau set about more systematically than had the War Department to dissolve tribal societies and to "liquidate" the Indian title to land, selling it to white settlers and to speculators. [13]

The Indian titles to the lands in the West were immediately in danger as soon as the white man got around to wanting them. In 1851, the Indian Bureau negotiated treaties with 119 of the tribes of California. The Indians surrendered more than half the state and in exchange were offered perpetual ownership of 7,500,000 acres. By a ruse, the Indian Bureau deprived the Indians of this land. Because of pressure from white politicians in California, the Senate in Washington did not confirm these treaties but merely kept them in its files. The Indians were not told that the treaties were invalid and at the time had no means of discovering the intricacies of American law. The treaties remained in the files of the Senate until 1905, still unratified; the 7,500,000 acres were sold to white settlers and speculators. How strongly the Indian Bureau felt about engaging in honest dealings with the Indians or keeping its word is indicated by the frank comment of General Francis C. Walker, Commissioner of Indian Affairs, in 1871. "When dealing with savage men, as with savage beasts, no question of national honor can arise. Whether to fight, to run away, or to employ a ruse, is solely a question of expediency." Walker was referring to outright warfare with the Indians, but his comment is also relevant to the political and legal aspects of the policy of the American government. [14]

The Indian tribes steadily declined in numbers. In California, for example, the number of Indians was estimated in 1850 to be from 110,000 to 130,000, but by 1880 their number had declined to fewer than 20,000.

12. Billington, op. cit., pp. 314–16; Houston, New York Herald, January 30, 1848; quoted in Weinberg, op. cit., p. 498.
13. Collier, op. cit., p. 213.
14. Ibid., p. 224; Commissioner's Annual Report (1872); quoted in Fey and McNickle, op. cit., p. 48.

What happened to the Indians? Some of them, it is true, died from the diseases of the white man to which they had acquired no immunity. Nobody knows how many were murdered, but in most parts of the West killing an Indian was rarely considered a crime. Some of the Indians died because, forced off their own land, they were obliged to move to areas so barren that they could not maintain an existence there. Undoubtedly, the shock of losing their land, the security of their tribal life, and their accustomed ways of farming and hunting led to a decline in their numbers. Sometimes the white people wondered, with a cynicism or a naïveté which is well-nigh incredible, what it was that made the Indian disappear from the land. "There seems to be something in our laws and institutions, peculiarly adapted to the Anglo-Saxon-American race, under which they will thrive and prosper," said Congressman Alexander Duncan in 1845, "but under which all others wilt and die. . . . There is something mysterious about it." This "Lo, the Poor Indian" tradition in American thought is surprisingly widespread.[15]

If the land reserved for Indians was desirable to the white men, especially if any discovery was made which enhanced the value of the land—for example, the existence of gold or silver—the great probability was that the Indian title would soon be extinguished. In 1881, Helen Hunt Jackson wrote *A Century of Dishonor,* a record of the white man's injustice in dealing with Indians in this country. She found that this injustice followed a remarkably consistent pattern:

> It makes little difference . . . where one opens the record of the history of the Indians; every page and every year has its dark stain. The story of one tribe is the story of all, varied only by differences of time and place; but neither time nor place makes any difference in the main facts. Colorado is as greedy and unjust in 1880 as was Georgia in 1830, and Ohio in 1795; and the United States Government breaks promises now as deftly as then, and with an added ingenuity from long practice.[16]

As recently as 1880, Congress had debated a bill which was designed to force the Colorado Ute Indians to sell their lands because gold and silver had been discovered on them. American miners must be given the privilege of taking up claims on this land, declared Representative James B. Belford of Colorado, and Congress must "apprise the Indian that he can no longer stand as a breakwater against the constantly swelling tide of civilization." Thus would be settled the doctrine that

> an idle and thriftless race of savages cannot be permitted to guard the treasure vaults of the nation which hold our gold and silver, but that they shall always be open, to the end that the prospector and miner may enter

15. Collier, *op. cit.,* p. 223; Duncan, *Congressional Globe,* 28th Cong., 2nd sess., App., p. 178; quoted in Weinberg, *op. cit.,* p. 163.
16. (New York, 1881), p. 338.

in and by enriching himself enrich the nation and bless the world by the results of his toil.[17]

The final episode of white violence against an Indian tribe took place in 1890. The battle was comparatively minor, but as clearly as any single example it illustrates the cruelty and stupidity of the government's policy toward Indians. Wovoka was a Paiute Indian of Nevada who, on a day when there was an eclipse of the sun, went into a trance and proclaimed a vision of a heavenly messiah who would return to earth, cause the white man to disappear, and restore the Indian to his former status. Wovoka did not advocate violence against the white man. Instead, he maintained that the Indians should simply wait patiently for the great spirit to appear. The news of Wovoka's vision spread to Indian tribes all over the western half of the United States. The Sioux Indians of South Dakota began engaging in "Ghost Dances" to bring about the appearance of the messiah. The U.S. Army chose to see these dances as a preparation for warfare and at the Battle of Wounded Knee massacred ninety-eight disarmed warriors and two hundred Indian women and children.[18]

Hatred and contempt for the Indians were strong among those who stood most to gain from appropriation of Indian lands. A frontiersman writing to the *Illinois State Register* in 1846 said of the California Indians that those "reptiles" must "either crawl or be crushed." Some of the leading scientific students of race were scarcely less harsh. Dr. Samuel George Morton, the authority on craniology, asserted in 1839 that Indians were inherently savage and intractable. Morton believed that all native tribes in North and South America were members of one race "peculiar and distinct from all others" and that the differences in the cultures of the Indians were superficial. Josiah Clark Nott, Morton's disciple in anthropology and coauthor of the popular *Types of Mankind* (1856), had an extremely low opinion of the inherent character of the Indians. In spite of all the "glowing accounts" from missionaries, said Nott, there was no such thing as a "civilized *full-blooded* Indian." Nott had seen Indians in Alabama who were farmers and who had partially absorbed the white man's civilization, but he thought they were little different from the savages of the West. They were "scarcely a degree advanced above brutes of the field, quietly abiding their time." Education and religion were alike helpless, said Nott, to change their nature. The study of crania disclosed, he maintained, that whereas Caucasians had those parts of the skull developed which indicated intellect, the Indian skulls indicated strong "animal propensity." Another contributor to *Types of Mankind,* Dr. Henry S. Patterson, wrote of a

17. *Congressional Record,* 46th Cong., 2nd sess., p. 4262; quoted in Weinberg, *op. cit.,* p. 91.
18. Hagan, *op. cit.,* p. 133; Billington, *op. cit.,* p. 667; Collier, *op. cit.,* p. 238.

young friend who had been killed by Utah Indians while on a surveying expedition for a proposed railroad to the Pacific. "We have had too much of sentimentalism about the Red-man," declared Patterson. If only this young man could be restored to life, his resurrection would be "cheaply purchased back if it cost the extermination of every miserable Pah-Utah under heaven!" [19]

If anti-Indian racism had declined in volume and virulence by the end of the nineteenth century, a major reason was that the Indians were no longer a threat to the safety of the whites and that they no longer had huge tracts of valuable land. We still find the opinion widely held that it was the Indians' race which was their single but insuperable handicap. Theodore Roosevelt castigated Helen Hunt Jackson's *A Century of Dishonor* as "beneath criticism" as history and important only because

> the high character of the author and her excellent literary work in other directions have given it a fictitious value and made it much quoted by a large class of amiable but maudlin fanatics concerning whom it may be said that the excellence of their intentions but indifferently atones for the invariable folly and ill effect of their actions.

The real fault of the policy of the white Americans toward the Indians had been, Roosevelt maintained, that it had been irresolute and was unwilling to "resort to the ultimate arbitrator—the sword." Of his own opinion of the Indian, Roosevelt said:

> I suppose I should be ashamed to say that I take the Western view of the Indian. I don't go so far as to think that the only good Indians are the dead Indians, but I believe nine out of every ten are, and I shouldn't inquire too closely into the case of the tenth. The most vicious cowboy has more moral principle than the average Indian.[20]

Of course, not all nineteenth-century opinion concerning the Indians was unfavorable. Sometimes they were highly praised for their courage and skill as warriors, their ability to endure pain, and their loyalty to their friends. One can find in nineteenth-century America much more praise of the Indian than of the Negro, though the Negro was allowed to survive as a slave whereas the Indian was either slaughtered or banished to lands

19. "Dow, Jr.," *Illinois State Register,* July 17, 1846; quoted in Weinberg, *op. cit.,* p. 168; Morton, *Crania Americana . . .* (Philadelphia, 1839), p. 6; Morton, "Some Observations on the Ethnology and Archaeology of the American Aborigines," *American Journal of Science and Arts* (1846), p. 9; Josiah Clark Nott and George R. Gliddon, *Types of Mankind . . .* (Philadelphia, 1856), pp. 69, 461–64; Patterson, "Memoirs of the Life and Scientific Labors of S. G. Morton," in *Types of Mankind . . .* , p. xxxviii.
20. *The Winning of the West* (New York, 1889–96), I, 334–35; quoted in Hermann Hagedorn, *Roosevelt in the Bad Lands* (Boston, 1921), p. 355.

where it was impossible for him to thrive. De Tocqueville observed that the Negro and the Indian were fundamentally different in character. "The servility of the one dooms him to slavery," he said, and "the pride of the other to death." [21]

One of the genuine friends of the Indian early in the nineteenth century was the Reverend Mr. Jedidiah Morse, well known not only as a clergyman but as a geographer. In 1820, he visited many of the major Indian tribes to prepare a report for the secretary of war. Morse had genuine insight into the character of the Indians. "There is as visible a difference of character among the different tribes," he observed, "as there is in our own population," and therefore, "few general observations . . . will apply to them as a body." He does, however, come to some general conclusions concerning Indians. He thinks they are inferior to whites in physical strength. He likes their custom of not talking when they have nothing to say. He finds them "not vociferous, noisy, or quarrelsome, in their common intercourse, but mild and obliging." He thinks they often have "a high sense of honor, justice, and fair dealing, and great sensibility, when advantage is taken of their weakness and ignorance, to deprive them of their property, and in other ways, to trespass on their rights." To the charge of the white men that the Indians are cruel, Morse replied, "Physician, heal thyself." [22]

Morse recognized clearly that the policy of the white men toward the Indians was wrong and that it might ultimately lead to their extinction. He quotes an Indian chief as saying, "Where the white man puts down his foot, he never takes it up again." Morse criticizes the policy of taking Indian lands by fraud or by force. He says that the result of such a policy is that the Indians are "constrained to leave their homes . . . either to go into new and less valuable wildernesses, and to mingle with other tribes, dependent on this hospitality, for a meagre support; or without the common aids of education, to change at once all their habits and modes of life. . . ." If they choose the latter, "they become insulated among those who despise them as an inferior race, fit companions to those only, who have the capacity and the disposition to corrupt them." Morse's remedy is that the Indians should become wards of the government. He reacted with horror to a proposal which had been submitted to Congress calling for their extermination under the theory that they were irrevocably savage and unchangeable in their character. Morse said the Indians were a race which "on every correct principle ought to be saved from extinction, if it be possible to save them." [23]

21. Alexis De Tocqueville, *Democracy in America,* trans. Henry Reeve, ed. Henry Steele Commager (New York, 1947), p. 28.
22. Jedidiah Morse, *op. cit.,* pp. 67–73.
23. *Ibid.,* pp. 80–81.

James Fenimore Cooper was, in general, favorably disposed toward the Indians. In some of his novels, at least, the Indian appears as a truly admirable character—the intrepid adventurer, the master of forest lore, the trusted friend. Chingachgook, the friend of the white hero Natty Bumppo, is only one of a series of noble Indian characters who appear in Cooper's fiction. Cooper's knowledge of the Indians was not extensive and one may reasonably suspect that the Indians in his novels were sometimes quite unlike real Indians. Because his novels were widely read, however, it is probably true that many Americans drew their conclusions regarding the character of Indians from Cooper.

In *The Redskins* (1846), one of Cooper's novels, the Indian chief Susquesus is compared with Jaaf, a Negro slave. Susquesus is "vastly the superior of the black." The intelligence of the Negro "had suffered under the blight which seems to have so generally caused the African mind to wither," but Susquesus possesses "the loftiness of a grand nature," one which has developed under "the impetus of an unrestrained, though savage, liberty." Susquesus is "a gentleman, in the best meaning of the word; though he may . . . want a great deal in the way of conventional usages." In *Satanstoe* (1845), another Indian chief and Negro slave are contrasted with one another. When an amusing incident occurs, the Negro "laughed in fits, . . . rolled over on the rocks, . . . shook himself like a dog that quits the water, laughed again, and finally shouted." On the other hand, the Indian

> took no more notice of these natural but undignified signs of pleasure . . . than if the latter had been a dog, or any other unintellectual animal. Perhaps no weakness would be so likely to excite his contempt, as to be a witness of so complete an absence of self-command, as the untutored negro manifested on this occasion.[24]

Cooper solves the problem of Indian character a little too neatly by dividing Indians into the good Indians and the bad Indians. The good Indians, we may justifiably suspect, are good partly from the demands of derring-do plots—there needs to be a good Indian or two to warn the whites what the bad Indians are up to. Or there needs to be a tribe of "good Indians" like the Delawares to aid the whites in their warfare against the "bad Indians"—for example, the Mingoes. At one point in *The Pathfinder* (1840), a young white companion of Leatherstocking asks how a good and merciful God could have created beings so thoroughly evil as the Mingoes, and Leatherstocking replies:

> I have passed days thinking of them matters, out in the silent woods, and I have come to the opinion, boy, that, as Providence rules all things, no

24. *The Complete Works of J. Fenimore Cooper* (Leatherstocking ed.; New York [1893?]), XXVIII, 443; XXVI, 308–9.

gift is bestowed without some wise and reasonable end. If Injins are no use, Injins would not have been created; and I do suppose, could one dive to the bottom of things, it would be found that even the Mingo tribes were produced for some rational and proper purpose, though I confess it surpasses my means to say what it is.

One gets the impression, from his subsequent adventures in the novel, that Leatherstocking, even while calmly picking off a hated Mingo with his unerring aim, is willing to affirm that the Indian represents part of the grand design of Providence. In another novel, *The Pioneers* (1823), Leatherstocking reflects on the unequal merits of the differing races and concludes that in heaven these inequalities will be resolved. "There is One greater than all, who'll bring the just together at his own time, and who'll whiten the skin of a blackamoor, and place him on a footing with princes." In this life, however, the "inferior" races must submit to the will of the "superior." [25]

Cooper's belief that the Indian was the superior of the Negro did not mean, of course, that he was superior to the white. An interesting revelation of the defects of the Indian chief Susquesus occurs when Mordaunt Littlepage, the narrator of *The Chainbearer* (1845), learns that Susquesus is being pursued by white men:

I trembled for Susquesus; though I knew he must anticipate a pursuit, and was so well skilled in throwing off a chase as to have obtained the name of Trackless. Still, the odds were against him; and experience has shown that the white man usually surpasses the Indian even in his own peculiar practices, when there have been opportunities to be taught.

Elsewhere in the novel, Littlepage explains to the Indian chief what it is that has enabled the white man to triumph over the Indian. "The white man is stronger than the redman," says Littlepage, "and has taken away his country, because he knows most." Another reason for the superiority of the white man, Littlepage continues, is his respect for the laws of property. Susquesus is not eloquent enough or perhaps he is too polite to give his opinion of the white man's respect for Indian property. He does not reply to Littlepage's rationalization of the claims of the white man.[26]

Other men than Cooper compared the Indian and the Negro, nearly always to the advantage of the Indian. "The indomitable, courageous, proud Indian," exclaimed Louis Agassiz, "in how very different a light he stands by the side of the submissive, obsequious, imitative negro, or by the side of the tricky, cunning, and cowardly Mongolian!" We can find considerable difference in the attitude toward Indians and Negroes even in the popular prints of Currier and Ives, which were widely distributed throughout the last half of the nineteenth century. These prints nearly always show Negroes

25. *The Complete Works . . .* , III, 77–88; IV, 471.
26. *Ibid.,* XXVII, 257, 112–13.

in such a way as to excite amusement or contempt. They are either performing some activity in a ludicrously inept manner—such as manning a fire brigade, riding in a train, playing baseball or tennis, or pulling a mule up a hill—or they are putting on absurd airs far above those suitable for their "natural" station in life. In "The Darktown Hunt—the Meet," Negroes are shown on a fox hunt riding broken-down nags and dressed in extravagant costumes which are a caricature of the costume worn by an English or Virginia gentleman. In "The Aesthetic Craze," a Negro is shown, sunflower in hand, in the supposedly languid style of Oscar Wilde. Indians, on the other hand, are consistently displayed with respect. They are depicted in ritual dances, in family groups, hunting buffalo, dressing meat, or looking on in a benign and friendly manner as wagon trains of whites cross the prairie. Nothing in the Currier and Ives prints of the Indians suggests that they might excite hatred or contempt.[27]

An opinion of the Indians commonly expressed in the nineteenth century was that they have some virtues but that, either because of a decision by the Almighty or by the inevitable workings of the laws of nature, they must in the end disappear from the American continent. Oliver Wendell Holmes observed in 1855 that the Indians were a "half-filled outline of humanity," a "sketch in red crayons of a rudimental manhood." It apparently had been the divine intention to place the Indians in America only until the white man, "the true lord of creation, should come to claim it." Thus, the impending disappearance of the Indians was not the fault of white men:

> Theologians stand aghast at a whole race destined, according to their old formulae, to destruction, temporal and eternal. Philanthropists mourn over them, and from time to time catch a red man and turn him into their colleges as they would turn a partridge in among the barn-door fowls. But instinct has its way sooner or later; the partridge makes but a troublesome chicken, and the Indian but a sorry Master of Arts, if he does not run for the woods, where all the *ferae naturae* impulses are urging him. These instincts lead to his extermination; too often the sad solution of the problem of his relation to the white race. . . . Then the white man hates him, and hunts him down like the wild beasts of the forest, and so the red-crayon sketch is rubbed out, and the canvas is ready for a picture of manhood a little more like God's own image.[28]

In Francis Parkman's histories there is a pessimism similar to that of Holmes concerning the fate of the Indians. Parkman thought that the Indian had certain virtues but that they were not sufficient to outweigh his

27. Agassiz, "The Diversity of Origin of Human Races," *Christian Examiner* (1850), p. 144; for the ideas on races in the Currier and Ives lithographs I am indebted to an unpublished paper by Morton J. Cronin.
28. See Cephas and Evangeline Warner Brainerd, eds., *The New England Society Orations* (New York, 1901), I, 298.

defects or to keep him from destruction. "Nature has stamped the Indian," wrote Parkman, "with a hard and stern physiognomy. Ambition, revenge, envy, jealousy, are his ruling passions; and his cold temperament is little exposed to those effeminate vices which are the bane of the milder races." On the other hand, his manly traits are "overcast by much that is dark, cold, and sinister, by sleepless distrust, and rankling jealousy." Some races are "moulded in wax, soft and melting, at once plastic and feeble. Some races, like some metals, combine the greatest flexibility with the greatest strength. But the Indian is hewn out of a rock. You can rarely change the form without destruction of the substance." Parkman views the approaching extinction of the Indian with regret because he can "discern in the unhappy wanderer the germs of heroic virtues mingled with his vices," but the future of the Indian is hopeless. "He will not learn the arts of civilization, and he and his forest must perish together." [29]

The nineteenth century was obsessed with the idea that it was race which explained the character of peoples. The notion that traits of temperament and intelligence are inborn in races and only superficially changed by environment or education was enough to blind the dominant whites. The Indians suffered more than any other ethnic minority from the cruel dicta of racism. The frontiersman, beset with the problem of conquering the wilderness, was in no mood to understand anything about the Indians except that they were at best a nuisance and at worst a terrible danger. The leading thinkers of the era were generally convinced that Indian traits were racially inherent and therefore could not be changed. The difference between the frontiersmen's view of the Indians and that of the intellectuals was more apparent than real. In general, the frontiersmen either looked forward with pleasure to the extinction of the Indians or at least were indifferent to it. The intellectuals were most often equally convinced with the frontiersmen that the Indians, because of their inherent nature, must ultimately disappear. They were frequently willing to sigh philosophically over the fate of the Indians, but this was an empty gesture.

What was needed to break through the misconceptions of the dominant whites was something more than humanitarianism—it was an understanding that the character of the Indians was the logical outcome of their social institutions, which had in turn been conditioned by their relationship with their physical environment, by the history of their relationships with other tribes of Indians, and later by their relationships with white civilization. What was needed was an attempt to see the Indian civilization, first of all, in terms of itself and not in terms of the values of the white race. In addition, the dominant whites needed to understand that the Indians could not suddenly transform their way of life and that both understanding of their

29. *The Conspiracy of Pontiac and the Indian War after the Conquest of Canada,* in *The Works of Francis Parkman* (Frontenac ed.; New York, 1915), XIV, 45–48.

culture and sympathy for their conditions were necessary on the part of the whites in order to enable the Indians to adjust to their new conditions. It was almost the end of the century before careful work had been begun by Franz Boas, who lived with a tribe, shared its values as much as it was possible for an outsider to do, and wrote about it in terms of its own values. Before Boas, three men in America were the most important of a small group of people who, in a careful and systematic way, had attempted to understand the inner workings of Indian tribal life. These men were Henry Rowe Schoolcraft, Lewis H. Morgan, and John Wesley Powell.

Henry Rowe Schoolcraft (1793–1864) was sent by the federal government in 1822 to serve as an Indian agent to the Chippewa Indians at Ste. Marie, a frontier settlement in the area between Lake Huron and Lake Michigan. One of his friends there was John Johnston, a successful Irish fur-trader who was an educated man and possessed a well-stocked library. Johnston was married to an Indian woman and his daughter, Jane D. Johnston, who was sent to England to be educated, became Schoolcraft's wife. In one of his books, Schoolcraft described his wife as "a highly educated lady, whose grandfather was a distinguished aboriginal chief-regnant, or king. . . ." Schoolcraft also tells us that his marriage to a woman with Indian blood.

> had the effect of breaking down toward himself . . . the eternal distrust and suspicion of the Indian mind, and to open the most secret arcana of his hopes and fears, as imposed by his religious dogmas, and as revealed by the deeply-hidden causes of his extraordinary acts and wonderful character.[30]

Schoolcraft began a study of the Chippewa language. He quickly became aware of a whole culture—a world in which ghosts appeared in sacred dreams, in which demons were omnipresent and had to be exorcised, in which men prospered or died from the spells cast upon them, in which medicine men had superhuman powers, such as the ability to plunge naked into roaring fires without being burned. He discovered the role of magic, of sex taboos—women were required to live in separate lodges when they were menstruating. He discovered such curious rituals as naked Indian women running around newly planted cornfields at night in order to assure the crop's freedom from blight or vermin. He discovered the complex world of the totem—a system of "coats-of-arms" in which family relationships and a feudal hierarchy of values were set up—a method of social organization which anthropologists would discover to have counterparts in primitive societies all over the world.[31]

30. *Information Respecting the History . . . of the Indian Tribes . . .* (Philadelphia, 1851–57), I, viii.
31. See H. R. Hayes, *From Ape to Angel: An Informal History of Social Anthropology* (New York, 1958), pp. 3–14.

Schoolcraft also discovered that Indian mythology was much more than a mere collection of marvelous tales—that it was the key to the explanation of Indian character. He remarks on the almost complete absence in white travelers' accounts of Indians of the role of legend in their culture, and he confesses his own slowness in realizing its central importance. "Surprise reached its acme," he tells us,

> when I found him [the Indian] whiling away the tedium of his long winter evenings relating tales and legends for the amusement of the social lodge. These fictions were sometimes employed, I observed, to convey instruction or to impress examples of courage, daring or right action. But they were at times replete with wild forest notions of spiritual agencies, necromancy, and demonology. They revealed abundantly the cause of his hopes and fears, his notions of duty, and his belief in a future state.[32]

Schoolcraft was seriously handicapped in his desire to help the Indians by his conviction that civilization is inevitably the result of an agrarian economy and that a society based upon hunting must inevitably be barbarous. As long as the Indians insisted upon being hunters, Schoolcraft was convinced, they could never be "civilized." He says it is easy to understand why the Indians had never developed the "arts." "Of what use were these arts," he asks, "to a comparatively sparse population, who occupied vast regions, and lived, very well, by hunting the flesh and wearing the skins of animals? To such men a mere subsistence was happiness, and the killing of a few men in war glory." He continues:

> It may be doubted whether the very fact of the immensity of an unoccupied country, spread out before a civilized or half civilized people, with all its allurements of wild game and personal independence, would not be sufficient, in the lapse of a few centuries, to throw them back into a complete state of barbarism.[33]

Thus, Schoolcraft is convinced that the Indians could be saved only if they could be induced completely to change their way of life—that is, if they could be induced to abandon hunting for farming. A society based upon hunting was "calculated to lead the mind from the intellectual, the mechanical, and the industrial, to the erratic, physical, and gross." As sympathetic as he was to the Indians, Schoolcraft disapproved almost wholly of their way of life and therefore came to welcome the system of reservations as the answer to the Indian problem. In his poem, *The Rise of the West, or a Prospect of the Mississippi Valley* (1841), Schoolcraft has this optimistic view of the Indian on his reservation:

32. *Ibid.,* p. 8.
33. *Algic Researches* (New York, 1839), I, 18–20; quoted in Roy Harvey Pearce, *The Savages of America: A Study of the Indian and the Idea of Civilization* (Baltimore, 1953), p. 122.

'Tis done! the Indian is no more opprest,
Free, on the bounding prairies of the west;
No longer bound to pine in want and woe,
Around his door the flowers of plenty grow;
No longer doomed to feel the legal glave,
And bitter taunt that marked him for a slave,
His mind expatiates o'er a scene of rest
With equal laws, and independence blest.[34]

In time, Schoolcraft came to realize that life on the reservation was much less idyllic than he had thought; but he never wavered in his conviction that as long as the Indian was a hunter there was no hope for him to be civilized. Thus, Schoolcraft interposed scarcely any objection to the destruction of those native customs which gave the Indian tribes cohesiveness and stability, nor did he see that change must come gradually if the Indian was to be able to adjust himself to it. Though he was wholly free from attempts to explain the character of the Indian on the basis of his race, Schoolcraft had no solution to the problem of the relationship of the whites with Indians based upon a respect for their culture. The ambivalence of his thought is perceptively pointed out by Roy Harvey Pearce. In the first edition of Schoolcraft's masterwork, *Historical and Statistical Information Respecting the History, Condition, and Prospect of the Indian Tribes of the United States* (1851–57), the cover of the first volume contains a gold-stamped picture of a ferocious Indian who has just scalped a white settler and is waving the scalp in one hand and holding his knife in the other as he stands over the prostrate form of his victim. For Schoolcraft, the Indian could only be a savage as long as he was a hunter.[35]

Lewis Henry Morgan (1818–1881) greatly expanded the researches of Schoolcraft. His works received a favorable reception. His *The League of the Iroquois* (1851) was described by John Wesley Powell as "the first scientific account of an Indian ever given to the world," and his later works were praised by Charles Darwin and Herbert Spencer. Morgan studied law, was admitted to the bar, and set up practice in Rochester, New York, in 1844, but clients were few. Meanwhile, Morgan interested himself in a social organization known as the Gordian Knot, which was a secret society, something like the Masonic orders except that it utilized Indian rituals. One of its members, Ely Parker, was himself an Indian, and he enlisted Morgan's serious interest in Indian ceremonies and customs.[36]

Parker was a man of great ability. He had been ridiculed for his defective English and had determined to obtain a white man's education.

34. *The Rise of the West, or a Prospect of the Mississippi Valley, a Poem* (New York, 1841), p. 17.
35. Pearce, *op. cit.,* p. 128.
36. Hayes, *op. cit.,* pp. 16–18.

At first he had studied law, but he discovered that he could never be admitted to the bar because in New York law an Indian was ineligible to qualify as an attorney, and so he enrolled in Rensselaer Polytechnic Institute and became an engineer instead. Parker convinced Morgan that the society's conception of Indian ceremonies was almost wholly wrong. He took Morgan to visit the nearby Seneca reservation, and there Morgan became aware of the complexities of Indian tribal organization. The social club became a historical society, and the career of Morgan as an anthropologist was begun. Morgan is, in fact, sometimes described as the founder of American social anthropology.[37]

Morgan's interest in Indians led him at an early date to defend the Seneca tribe against white swindlers. The Ogden Land Company in New York hoped to persuade the chiefs of the Seneca reservation to give up a large part of their land by paying each of them a small sum of money. Some chiefs were influenced, after having been plied with whiskey, to sign a legal document favoring the sale. Other Indians had been elevated to chiefdom by a sham election instituted by the company. Morgan estimated that the company hoped to secure the land of the Indians for one-tenth of its market value. The secret society which Morgan had been instrumental in forming, now called the New Confederation of the Iroquois, raised money for the defense of the Seneca Indians. They collected signatures, exposed the fraudulent nature of the deal with the Indians, and convinced the United States Senate that the transaction should not be approved. As a reward, the Seneca tribe inducted Morgan into its membership and gave him the name Ta-ya-da-o-wu-kuh (One-Lying-Across). The name signified that Morgan bridged the gap separating the white man and the Indian.[38]

Morgan is principally known for his study of systems of kinship among Indian tribes. He discovered, for example, that an Iroquois warrior referred to the sons of other members of his own or related tribes as his "sons." Descent was reckoned and inheritance was determined through the female line. Property was owned and inherited, not individually, but through associate clans in a tribe and these, in turn, were divided into confederations. The system amounted to an approximation of the theory of representative government. Morgan believed that this arrangement had arisen from the practice of "primitive promiscuity" at some earlier point in the history of the tribes, a time when any male was eligible to cohabit with any female—a system which Morgan's critics sometimes facetiously described as "a thousand miles of wives." The institution of descent through the female line had developed, he believed, because it was impossible to determine who the father of a particular child was. Therefore, all the men

37. *Ibid.,* p. 17.
38. *Ibid.,* p. 18.

in the tribe considered themselves each child's "father" and, eventually, all the members of the tribe considered themselves related by blood to one another. Modern anthropologists are no longer able to discern a clear line from the "primitive promiscuity" which Morgan assumed to the later practice of monogamy among the Iroquois, but his study is recognized as one of the pioneers in its field.[39]

After he married in 1851, Morgan was obliged to discontinue for several years his anthropological researches. "I laid aside the Indian subject," he said, "to devote myself to my profession." He was one of the men involved in building a railroad to the south shore of Lake Superior, and later he invested money in the newly established iron industry there. For a time, he went into politics and was elected as an assemblyman to the legislature of the state of New York. His success in business and politics, however, did not prevent his continuing his interest in the study of Indian life. In 1858 we find him sending out questionnaires to Indian agents all over the country to discover what systems of kinship and marriage ("consanguinity") were found in different tribes:

Morgan is remembered for two substantial works: his *Systems of Consanguinity of the Human Family* (1866) and his *Ancient Society or Researches in the Lines of Human Progress from Savagery through Barbarism to Civilization* (1877). More important than the specific conclusions at which he arrived was his demonstration that the Indians could be understood in a disciplined and scientific way, that their customs could not be explained with the clichés of racism. Morgan was also important because as a friend of the Indians he could not be dismissed as just another starry-eyed humanitarian. In 1876, after the Custer massacre, he strongly defended Sitting Bull and the Sioux. He pled with the federal government to make it possible for the Indians to be self-supporting and to live in confidence that their treaties with the white man would not continue to be violated.[40]

Morgan's great value as an anthropologist was that he strove to see the Indians in terms of their own societies and not in terms of his own. The idea of evolution, though Morgan never explicitly avowed it—perhaps because of the objections of his religious friends and relatives—is clearly apparent in his work. He rejected Louis Agassiz's idea of "separate creations" of the races in different parts of the world with its corollary that Indians were a separate "species" from other races. He rejected the idea found among some Christian thinkers that the Indians represented a "postlapsarian degradation" from an originally noble type. He saw the Indians as subject to the same influences as the other races of mankind. "The his-

39. *Ancient Society: Or Researches in the Lines of Human Progress from Savagery through Barbarism to Civilization* (Chicago, 1877), pp. 66 ff.
40. See Hayes, *op. cit.,* p. 23.

tory of the human race," he maintained, "is one in source, one in experience, one in progress." Schoolcraft was never wholly able to free himself from the notion of savagery as ineluctably connected with the Indians, but Morgan left such ideas behind.[41]

John Wesley Powell (1834–1902) was originally a geologist and explorer. He developed an interest in Indian languages, and through them an interest in general studies of the Indian. His *Introduction to the Study of Indian Languages* (1880) is recognized as a pioneer work of great value. He explicitly rejected race as an explanation of differences of culture. It was he who organized the Bureau of Ethnology of the Smithsonian Institution in 1879, and under his direction specialists in different areas began a scientific and comprehensive study of the culture of Indians.[42]

Schoolcraft, Morgan, and Powell were forerunners of a new attitude toward the Indians, but their point of view made little headway in their own time. It was well into the second quarter of the twentieth century before the champions of the Indian were able to persuade the federal government to free the Indians from restrictions inconsistent with their dignity—or to halt depredations upon the lands granted by solemn treaty to the Indians in perpetuity.[43]

We may imagine that, sad as the persecution of the Indians was in the United States, it was a necessary result of the ideas of the time. A comparison of the history of Canadian policy toward Indians with our own suggests that this conclusion is not justified. As early as 1670, the policy of the Hudson's Bay Company attempted to conserve Indian life and society. The reason may have been that it was useful to protect the Indians to make it possible for them to continue to trap animals in the fur trade, but a policy of friendly good will and fair dealing to the Indians was followed elsewhere as well. The Canadian government made treaties which it did not break. It respected the landholdings of the Indians, did not appropriate their communal funds or divert them into charges for "administration" as our own government did, and did not tolerate widespread corruption in the Indian Service. It provided a means for the orderly transition of the Indian into Canadian life, but it did not force the procedure by separating the Indians from their land. The American treatment of the Indian shows the nation at its farthest point from the ideals of political freedom and respect for individual rights which, in other areas, it was able to achieve.[44]

41. Quoted in Hayes, *op. cit.,* p. 46; see Pearce, *op. cit.,* p. 128.
42. See Wallace Stegner, *Beyond the Hundredth Meridian: John Wesley Powell and the Second Opening of the West* (Boston, 1954), *passim.*
43. Collier, *op. cit.,* pp. 261 ff.
44. *Ibid.,* pp. 296–97.

ROGER DANIELS

The Yellow Peril

This selection from Roger Daniels's book, *The Politics of Prejudice,* is a counterpart to Gossett. Racism in America involved the yellow as well as the red and the black, and Daniels shows how race prejudice can become politically institutionalized. This excerpt provides the background necessary to understanding Carey McWilliams's essay on the internment of Japanese-Americans during World War II (p. 329).

> Japan is now a world power and is already clutching for control of the Pacific and this will ultimately bring her into conflict with the United States.   JAMES D. PHELAN, Nov. 12, 1907

> Are there any radical antagonisms in the modern capitalist world that must be utilized? . . . War is brewing between [Japan and America]. They cannot live in peace on the shores of the Pacific, although those shores are three thousand versts apart. . . . There is a vast literature devoted to the future Japanese-American war. That war is brewing, that war is inevitable, is beyond doubt.   V. I. LENIN, Nov. 26, 1920

SOMETIME between 1913 and 1924 a decided change in American public opinion toward Japan and the Japanese took place. The "California position," which, as we have seen, did not win national favor in either 1906–1907 or 1913, was written into the statute book in 1924. There is every reason to believe that this congressional action accurately reflected majority sentiment. Although it is obviously impossible to make a quantitative analysis of the reasons for this change, it seems quite clear that three factors were paramount: a racist ideology, a growing uneasiness about Japanese military prowess and aggression, and the consistent anti-Japanese propaganda of the California exclusionists. While all three factors were important, the existence of the first two was a necessary precondition if the third was to be effective beyond the Pacific Coast. The adherence to racism, conscious or otherwise, made it natural for most Americans to look down upon "the lesser breeds without the law" with a curious mixture of contempt and fear. This is not the place for a full-length portrait of the development of racism in the United

States, nor even of that rather elusive phenomenon, the "yellow peril." But to sketch the latter at all, the former must at least be outlined.

Racisim, as a pervasive doctrine, did not develop in the United States until after the Civil War. No common assumptions underlay the enslavement of the Negro and the attacks made upon the Irish in Boston. After the early years of Reconstruction, more and more Northerners began to accept the Southern view of the Negro question; *Plessy* v. *Ferguson* (1896), with its "separate but equal" doctrine, took judicial notice of the national climate of opinion.

By the 1880's a respectable intellectual basis for an American racism was being developed by the curiously interacting labors of workers in various academic disciplines. Historians, political scientists, and eugenists were in the van. Bluntly, it was "discovered" on the one hand that democratic political institutions had been developed by and could thrive only among Anglo-Saxon peoples, while on the other hand, entirely separate researchers "demonstrated" that, of all the many "races," one alone—variously called Anglo-Saxon, Aryan, Teutonic, or Nordic—had superior innate characteristics. Conveniently for the self-esteem of most Americans, these rather vague terms seemed to describe the majority of those who had hitherto come to America.

At about the same time the sources of immigration began to change. Italians, Slavs, East European Jews, and Greeks began to outnumber incoming British, Germans, and Scandinavians. The census of 1890—the same census that triggered Frederick Jackson Turner's classic essay—demonstrated clearly to those in the grip of the Anglo-Saxon complex that immigration was changing, and changing for the worse, the human composition of their country. After 1894, when a group of Harvard men formed what became the highly influential Immigration Restriction League, an ever-growing group of powerful Americans campaigned with increasing vigor for an immigration policy based on ethnic and racial discrimination. This growing concern about the "new immigration" was abetted by lurid stories in the infant yellow press about criminals with strange foreign names; such stories helped to make Americans acutely conscious of "racial" differences, real and imagined.

The course of history itself seemed to point up these differences. Just four years after the founding of the brahmin Immigration Restriction League, the United States embarked upon that "great aberration" in its foreign policy, the Spanish-American War, which not only produced the easy defeat of a Latin nation, but also brought under the Stars and Stripes three overseas dependencies having large nonwhite populations. The Supreme Court soon ruled, in the Insular Cases, that the constitution did not follow the flag, and this ruling was taken by some as an endorsement of the Anglo-Saxonist contention that democratic institutions had inherent ethnic limitations. Aided by success in what ought to be called "the sordid little war," jingoism, with racist implications, was trumpeted throughout the land.

These pyramiding factors, which were cumulative in effect, plus a growing stream of immigration, most of it from southern and eastern Europe, made the country more conscious of race than it had ever been before. The First World War and its aftermath gave fresh arguments to racist publicists. During the war superpatriotism took charge. Americanism, as a doctrine, began to mean the negation of the foreign. Then, in the postwar period, racism went over the top. The obvious failure, for the first time, of American war aims—the world was demonstrably not safe for democracy —meant for many a disenchantment with all things foreign. The antiforeign trend gained its most effective stimulus from the success of the Bolshevik revolution. This disturbing event, coupled with an alarming upsurge of domestic radicalism—again seemingly perpetrated only by those with strange-sounding names—convinced some doubters that it was high time to seal off America from foreign contagion.

What seemed to be the great flowering of American racism in the post-World War I decades—in retrospect this period seems to have been its Indian summer—was epitomized by the work of two Eastern elitists, Madison Grant and Lothrop Stoddard.[1] They wrote glowingly of each other's books, and their views were almost identical. Like their more celebrated contemporary, Oswald Spengler, they lacked confidence in the future. The Bolshevik revolution frightened them:

> The backbone of western civilization is racially Nordic, the Alpines and Mediterraneans being effective precisely to the extent to which they have been Nordicized and vitalized. If this great race, with its capacity for leadership and fighting, should ultimately pass, with it would pass what we call civilization. . . . Now that Asia, in the guise of Bolshevism with Semitic leadership and Chinese executioners, is organizing an assault upon western Europe, the new states—Slavic-Alpine in race, with little Nordic blood—may prove to be not frontier guards of western Europe but vanguards of Asia in central Europe.[2]

They were haunted by "the rising tide of color":

> Colored migration is a *universal* peril, menacing every part of the white world. . . . The whole white race is exposed, immediately or ultimately, to the possibility of social sterilization and final replacement or

1. Their most widely read works were Grant's *The Passing of the Great Race* (New York, 1916) and Stoddard's *The Rising Tide of Color Against White World Supremacy* (New York, 1920) and *Revolt Against Civilization: The Menace of the Under Man* (New York, 1922).
2. Madison Grant, Introduction to Stoddard's *Rising Tide of Color*, pp. xxix–xxxii.

absorption by the teeming colored races. . . . There is no immediate danger of the world being swamped by black blood. But there is a very immediate danger that the white stocks may be swamped by Asiatic blood. . . . Unless [the white] man erects and maintains artificial barriers [he will] *finally perish*. . . . White civilization is to-day coterminous with the white race.

There was, however, some hope, according to Stoddard:

One element should be fundamental to all the compoundings of the social pharmacopoeia. That element is *blood* . . . clean, virile, genius-bearing blood, streaming down the ages through the unerring action of heredity. . . . What we to-day need above all else is . . . a recognition of the supreme importance of heredity.

After a generation or two of rigid restriction of the immigration of "lower human types," i.e., non-Nordics, Stoddard had a few modest proposals for what he called a "new idealism":

In those better days, we or the next generation will take in hand the problem of race-depreciation, and segregation of defectives and abolition of handicaps penalizing the better stocks will put an end to our present racial decline. . . . Those splendid tasks are probably not ours. They are for our successors in a happier age. But we have our task, and God knows it is a hard one—the salvage of a shipwrecked world!

This sort of pseudo science flourished throughout the twenties. Within four years after its publication in the spring of 1920, Stoddard's *Rising Tide of Color* had gone through fourteen editions and Congress had passed the restrictive and discriminatory Immigration Acts of 1921 and 1924.

The whole antiforeign racist movement would surely have proceeded in much the same way regardless of whether a single Japanese immigrant had set foot on California's golden shores. But it is only in this context that the belief, by the nation at large, of the myriad, usually exaggerated, and often irrational charges against Japan and the Japanese, can be understood. If, in those years, the national climate of opinion was such that all manner of sinister myths could be fabricated and believed about the foreigner in general, was it not natural that about the Japanese the most alien of the alien, there would be special fears?

Most of the charges against the Japanese—their nonassimilation, their low standard of living, their high birth rate, their vile habits—were made also against European immigrants. But only against Orientals was it seriously charged that the peaceful immigrants were but a vanguard of an invading horde to come. Throughout the years under discussion, and beyond, there was a consistent fear, expressed and believed in many quarters, that some named or unnamed Oriental power—usually but not always, Japan

—was on the verge of invading all or part of the continental United States. This fear can be most conveniently described by a catchword: the "yellow peril." [3]

The origin of the term is obscure, but it seems to be a direct translation of Kaiser Wilhelm II's vaporings about a *gelbe gefahr* threatening Europe and all Christendom (he meant a Chinese invasion à la Genghis Khan). First used in English around the turn of the century, it was in wide public use in the United States by 1905. Most of those who used it meant to warn of an imminent invasion by Japan. But even before Japan became a world power some Americans, usually Californians, expressed fears about the Orient. They feared China.

The earliest expression of this sort that I have been able to discover was voiced by Henry George just after the American Civil War. In an impassioned plea for Eastern support in California's struggle against Chinese immigration, and with traces of that Social Darwinism usually associated with conservatives, he warned that:

> The 60,000 or 100,000 Mongolians on our Western Coast are the thin edge of the wedge which has for its base the 500,000,000 of Eastern Asia. . . . The Chinaman can live where stronger than he would starve. Give him fair play and this quality enables him to drive out the stronger races . . . [Unless Chinese immigration is checked] the youngest home of the nations must in its early manhood follow the path and meet the doom of Babylon, Nineveh and Rome. . . . Here plain to the eye of him who chooses to see are dragon's teeth [which will] spring up armed men marshalled for civil war.[4]

Between 1880 and 1882, doubtless inspired by the camapign for a national Chinese exclusion law, obscure California authors concocted prophetic accounts of hordes of Chinese invading and conquering the United States.[5] They are the earliest American examples of what became a familiar phenomenon: "scare" literature warning of imminent military disaster. According to Alfred Vagts, the first book of this kind was *The Battle of Dorking* (1871) which warned Britain of an imminent German invasion. The three California Cassandras had no noticeable effect on their contemporaries: at that time China was a victim, not a predator.

3. My own definition of the term yellow peril is the fear of the imminent invasion of the continental United States, by named or unnamed Oriental powers, usually Japan.

4. New York *Tribune,* May 1, 1869. For an early amplification of this theme see H. J. West, *The Chinese Invasion* (San Francisco, 1873).

5. P. A. Dooner, *The Last Days of the Republic* (San Francisco, 1880); Lorelle, "The Battle of the Wabash," *The Californian,* 2 (Oct., 1880), 364–366; Robert Woltor, *A Short and Truthful History of the Taking of California and Oregon by the Chinese in the Year A. D. 1899* (San Francisco, 1882). None has the slightest trace of any literary merit.

In the next decade, however, a new force began to disturb the balance of power in the Far East. On September 17, 1894, Japan fought and won her first modern naval battle, defeating the Chinese off the Yalu River. Three years later, Henry Cabot Lodge believed, erroneously, that Japan was "menacing Hawaii." "I am afraid we shall have trouble there," agreed his colleague Cushman K. Davis (Republican from Minnesota and chairman of the Senate Foreign Relations Committee), "though perhaps I express my self more accurately by writing 'for I am afraid we shall not have trouble.' " [6] A few months later Davis publicly said much the same thing:

> The present Hawaiian-Japanese controversy [he declared in a Senate committee] is the preliminary skirmish in the great coming struggle between the civilization and the awakening forces of the East and the civilization of the West.
> The issue is whether, in that inevitable struggle, Asia or American [shall control Hawaii].[7]

Shortly thereafter, as a sort of gleaning of the territorial harvest acquired in the Spanish-American War, the United States acquired Hawaii without the hint of a struggle, although Japan did file a rather perfunctory protest. The views of Lodge and Davis were not typical of American sentiment; as noted earlier, most Americans continued to have friendly, if patronizing, feelings toward Japan, despite her growing power.

The Russo-Japanese War of 1904–1905 clearly demonstrated this power. The shots fired at Mukden and in Tsushima Strait were truly shots heard round the world: for the first time in the modern era a colored nation worsted a white one. Even before the war there had been talk of a yellow peril, mostly by Europeans. From 1905 on, however, the talk grew louder and louder in this country, with the vulgar accents of William Randolph Hearst often drowning out the rest.

Hearst is often erroneously credited with having invented the yellow peril. As a matter of fact, his newspapers for a white ignored it and at one time even printed a feature article by a Japanese nobleman denying its existence. By September, 1905, Hearst had begun to show concern over the Japanese menace; in that month the San Francisco *Examiner* printed a cartoon showing a Japanese soldier casting his shadow across the Pacific onto California. There was, however, no concerted anti-Japanese campaign at that time.

As noted earlier, the change in policy came during the San Francisco school board crisis 1906–1907. On December 20, 1906, the Hearst press began what would be a thirty-five-year "war" with Japan. The front page of the San Francisco *Examiner* that day warned of Japanese spies:

6. Quoted in John A. Garraty, *Henry Cabot Lodge* (New York, 1953), p. 199.
7. U. S. Congress, Senate, *Annexation of Hawaii,* 55th Cong., 2d sess., Report 681 (Washington, 1898), p. 31. Italics in original.

JAPAN SOUNDS OUR COASTS
BROWN MEN HAVE MAPS
AND COULD LAND EASILY

A few days later the *Examiner* made its first original contribution to the anti-Japanese campaign—the outright fabrication that Japanese immigrants were actually Japanese soldiers in disguise:

> Japanese in companies of forty are having infantry drill after dark [in Hawaii] two or three nights a week [and are] armed with rifles. . . . The Japanese of Hawaii have secreted enough rice to feed the entire population for seven months. [There have been] recent arrivals of Japanese troops in the guise of coolies [who are] secretly preparing for hostilities.

At about the same time James D. Phelan began to be worried about the military threat of Japan. In a statement for publication he argued that the Pacific Coast "would be an easy prey in case of attack" and asserted that the Japanese immigrants in California were an "enemy within our gates." It should be noted that Phelan was the only anti-Japanese political leader in California before the First World War to subscribe to the yellow peril. The Californians generally belittled such talk, particularly since alarmed Easterners often argued that the California agitation might involve the whole country in war.

The first detailed description of such a war was given by an American navel hero in the fall of 1907. Richmond Pearson Hobson has three claims on the attention of posterity. His heroic but unsuccessful attempt to blockade Admiral Cevera's fleet in the harbor of Santiago de Cuba by sinking a freighter in the channel made him the only untarnished naval hero of the Caribbean theater of the Spanish-American War. This presumably made him an expert in naval strategy. His ensuing coast-to-coast triumphal tour, during which he was kissed by thousands of women, demonstrated that he was a politician and was followed by a successful campaign for a seat in Congress (as a Democratic representative from Alabama). In 1907, while still in Congress, Hobson again began to attract attention, this time as a prophet of militarism and the yellow peril. His new career caused many to regard him as a "national nuisance." In a two-part series for the Hearst chain he made his case against Japan.

Under the headline "JAPAN MAY SEIZE THE PACIFIC SLOPE," Hobson berated Americans for their "indifference" to the threat from the Far East. "The Yellow Peril is here," he declared. "Absolute control of the Pacific Ocean is our only safety." Hobson went on to show that, unless a big navy were built up, Japan by landing an army of exactly "1,207,700 men could conquer the Pacific Coast." He predicted that Japan, by taking over China, would "soon be able to command the military sources of the whole yellow race." Hobson insisted that the "Japanese are the most secretive people in the world" and that they were "rushing forward with feverish haste stupendous preparations for war. . . . The war is to be with America." [8]

Hobson continued in this vein for several years, in published articles and during several nationwide lecture tours. In 1908, commenting on the round-the-world cruise of the American battle fleet, Hobson was ecstatic, but also still apprehensive:

> Less than a year ago [an] Asiatic power [was] in control of the Pacific, completely prepared for war, [and] challenged American institutions. It was the first time in history that an Anglo-Saxon race was compelled to surrender the right of self-government to the dictation of a foreign power. [If we do not build up our Navy] the Japanese Navy will again secure control of the Pacific Ocean and the high seas will be controlled by a yellow race instead of by white men. [9]

Nor were merely militaristic jingoes the only ones who spread the doctrine of the yellow peril and the coming race war. The English Fabian, H. G. Wells, sometimes sounded the same note. In his *War in the Air* (1908), Wells penned a lurid tale of death and destruction in which the Japanese replaced the Martians as bogeymen. In the novel the United States, France, and Great Britain are locked in a death struggle with Germany. Without warning, Japan and China indiscriminately attack the white powers, world-wide chaos reigns, and civilization is almost completely destroyed. "The Yellow Peril was a peril after all," was his comment on the Oriental attack. Wells's basic purpose was, of course, different from Hobson's; the English Fabian was trying to point out the futility of war. Appealing to racial hatreds is a rather peculiar way of doing so.

Hobson and Wells both assumed Sino-Japanese coöperation in a coming racial war. Homer Lea, the most celebrated exponent of the yellow peril, thought that Japan could wage the war alone; besides, he was a friend of China. Lea, a hunchback who somehow became a general in the Chinese army and an adviser to Sun Yat-sen, is a romantic figure about whom reams of nonsense have been written. Clare Booth Luce and others have depicted him as a combination of Clausewitz and Napoleon, with a touch of Nostradamus added; even the staid *Dictionary American Biography* printed gross exaggerations about him. The hawkers of the Lea legend would have us believe that he was a key factor in the overthrow of the Manchu dynasty and the subsequent establishment of the Chinese republic. All the details of Lea's career in China are by no means clear, but it is

8. San Francisco *Examiner,* Nov. 3 and 10, 1907.
9. *Ibid.,* May 7, 1908. Naturally, Hobson drew a great amount of criticism. A magazine often described as the editorial spokesman for Roosevelt commented that "Captain Hobson belongs to the small but noisy army of those who are beating the tom-tom on the Japanese question and doing all they can to stir up trouble." "Captain Hobson Corrected," *Outlook,* 88 (Feb. 29, 1908), p. 470. See also "The Superhuman Japanese," *Nation,* 86 (Jan. 16, 1908), p. 51.

certain that he played only a minor role. No evidence has been uncovered to show that he ever participated in any military action, and Lea, himself, never claimed that he had. He was in China in the decade before his death in 1912, and he did have the ear of Sun Yat-sen. The rest is either speculation or outright fabrication.

But not all of the Lea legend rests on his putative career in China; the bulk of the claims hinge on his writings, mainly *The Valor of Ignorance,* first published in 1909 and reissued with much fanfare shortly after Pearl Harbor.[10] The book told, in great detail, of a coming Japanese-American war, with Japan seizing the Philippine Islands and then landing forces on the Pacific Coast and overrunning Washington, Oregon, and California. This would be mere child's play, Lea argued, because of the small standing army and the utter worthlessness of American militia. Lea's concluding paragraph painted a gloomy picture of the future:

> The inevitable consummation that follows the investment of San Francisco becomes apparent in the utter helplessness of the Republic. In the entire nation is not another regiment of regular troups; no generals, no corporals. Not months, but years, must elapse before armies equal to the Japanese are able to pass in parade. These must then make their way over deserts such as no armies have ever heretofore crossed; scale the entrenched and stupendous heights that form the redoubts of the desert moats; attempting, in the valor of their ignorance, the militarily impossible; turning mountain gorges into the ossuaries of their dead, and burdening the desert winds with the spirits of their slain. The repulsed and distracted forces to scatter, as heretofore, dissension throughout the Union, brood rebellions, class and sectional insurrections, until this heterogeneous Republic, in its principles, shall disintegrate, and again into the palm of re-established monarchy pay the toll of its vanity and its scorn.[11]

Like most other authors of yellow peril fantasies, Lea was a racist, a Social Darwinist, and a thoroughgoing militarist. He believed that the new immigrants had weakened the "primitive Americanism" of the original settlers and that no naturalized American could be a true patriot. According to Lea, a nation had to keep expanding or die: "National existence is . . . a part of life itself, governed by the same immutable laws. . . . Only so long as a man or nation continues to grow and expand do they nourish the vitality that wards off disease and decay." Lea insisted that "War is a part of life, and its place in national existence is fixed and predetermined." The only way the United States and the British Empire could survive was to slough off their commercial "opulence and unmartial qualities" and de-

---

10. The two most important Lea works are *The Valor of Ignorance* (New York, 1909) and *The Day of the Saxon* (New York, 1912). Both of these were republished in early 1942. The second told of the decline of the British Empire.
11. *The Valor of Ignorance,* pp. 307–308.

velop large standing armies and even bigger navies. In the coming racial wars, the stronger race would prevail.

Naïve journalists, particularly after the events of December, 1941, hailed Lea as a military genius. He not only predicted the Japanese invasion of the Philippines, but even indicated two of the beaches on which they actually landed. Actually, the same conclusions were reached by all military thinkers who studied the problem of defending the islands. By the end of 1907 American military planners realized that:

> There is no avoiding the conclusion that we have not now, and never will have, sufficient troops in the Philippine Islands to defend Subig Bay from the land side against a land attack by the Japanese for any length of time to enable our fleet to reach the Philippine Islands from the Atlantic Ocean.[12]

As a result of this and other studies, American Pacific strategy assumed the probable loss of the Philippines as the first act of any future Japanese-American war. Thus Lea's prophetic foresight was merely an axiom of military common sense. As for the Japanese invasion of the Pacific Coast, neither he, Hobson, nor numerous other writers on this theme had the slightest conception of the logistic difficulties of such an enterprise. Even at the height of Japan's power, in 1942, the Japanese planners apparently did not seriously contemplate such a venture. The Japan of 1905–1924 was patently in no position to launch a transpacific invasion.

Because of the constant propaganda, however, many Americans became convinced that the yellow peril was upon them. In both 1907 and 1912–1913, the periods of greatest friction in California, there were full-blown war scares, manufactured by jingoes on both sides of the Pacific. Hobson, Hearst, and Lea had opposite numbers in Japan. Some historians have taken these war scares too seriously; Outten Clinnard thinks that the United States and Japan were at the "verge of war" during both scares. There is no evidence for such a view. Both Theodore Roosevelt and Wilson, however, were seriously disturbed about the possibility of war. Despite many warnings of Japanese intentions to attack the United States before the completion of the Panama Canal, Roosevelt could "hardly believe that Japan is intending to strike us," but he took "every step to be ready." In the later crisis, neither Taft nor Wilson, despite urgings by some advisers, took any warlike steps. Since no evidence has been presented indicating warlike actions by the Japanese government, it is difficult to see the validity of this retrospective brinksmanship.

12. Chief of Staff to Secretary of War, Dec. 21, 1907, quoted in Outten J. Clinnard, *Japan's Influence on American Naval Power* (Berkeley and Los Angeles, 1947), p. 62.

With the onset of the First World War, in which Japan was an associate rather than an enemy of the United States, the yellow peril continued to thrive. Its chief exponents were the Hearst press and the German propaganda machine within the United States. A postwar congressional investigation attempted to show that Hearst was in the pay of Germans, but never succeeded in proving the charge.

Wilhelm II, it will be remembered, was the originator of the *gelbe gefahr;* from 1907 on, anti-Japanese propaganda seems to have been a part of his policy. German sources, official and semiofficial, kept insisting to the unconvinced Roosevelt that a Japanese attack was imminent. Heinrich Werner, a visiting German officer, told reporters that "Japan has a well trained, highly efficient, standing army of 40,000 men" in California and Mexico. With the coming of war, this propaganda was intensified.

In May, 1915, the German agent George Sylvester Viereck wrote to his chief of a yellow peril pamphlet of which 300,000 copies had been distributed. Dozens of such pamphlets were produced and distributed in the United States between 1915 and the American declaration of war. A typical, production, *Preparedness for the Pacific Coast,* was published in Seattle in 1916 under the auspices of the German Newspapers Association. It agreed that Americans should arm and prepare for war, but not against Germany, from whom the United States had nothing to fear, but against "tartaric" Japan, who "wants a foothold on the Pacific Coast."

Some of the German agents wished to do more than publish pamphlets; Edward Lyell Fox, an American newspaperman and a minor cog in the German propaganda machine, hatched a plot worthy of Sax Rohmer's diabolic Dr. Fu Manchu. Fox proposed to Franz von Papen, then a captain in the German army and an inept espionage agent, that Germany provide *agents provocateurs* to foment anti-Japanese riots in California, which, Fox hoped, might embroil Japan and the United States in war. Fox pointed out that plenty of assistance would be furnished such a scheme once it was under way.

> An examination of the files of the Hearst newspapers [Fox wrote] will show their bitterness toward Japan. No chance has been passed by them to warn the people against the Japs and foment trouble in California. . . . Any anti-Japanese move would have the support of Mr. Hearst. . . . There should be a play produced in New York, Chicago, San Francisco and Los Angeles that will send its audiences out of the theatres heated to the fever point against the Japanese. . . . The public mind thus prepared, play the trump card with trouble on the Pacific Coast. . . . Rioting in San Francisco, etc., against a few Japanese [would be easy to arrange with hired thugs]. The Asiatic Exclusion League, the anti-Japanese organization of the Pacific Coast, enters the plan. Its president has

served a term in jail; he will do anything made worth his while. . . . It would be an easy matter to use some young and "innocent" prostitutes to the detriment of the Japs.[13]

This particular outrage never was perpetrated; perhaps the bumbling von Papen found it less soldierly than blowing up munitions plants. Anti-Japanese race riots on the Pacific Coast would not have been hard to incite, and, indeed, might have had serious repercussions.

As it was, the Germans and the Hearst press followed parallel courses. In October, 1915, the newspaper chain played a new variation of the yellow peril gambit. In a double-page spread in successive Sunday supplements was reproduced what purported to be a semiofficial Japanese publication; it was, in fact, a cheap pamphlet put out by Japanese jingoes predicting a fantasy invasion of California, and it read remarkably like the productions of Hobson and Homer Lea, with one notable exception: Mexico was the ally of Japan. The Japanese army and navy were victorious and the peace terms imposed on the United States included the cession of the Philippine and Hawaiian islands, unlimited immigration into the United States for Japanese, who were to have full civil rights, and the right of Japanese fishermen to catch lobsters (!) within the territorial waters of the United States.

The Hearst propaganda continued in this vein up to the American declaration of war, which the Hearst press opposed vehemently. Telegrams printed by the Senate committee investigating German propaganda show that William Randolph Hearst himself concocted some of the yellow peril propaganda. On March 3, 1917, Hearst sent the following telegram to one of his editors:

> McCay could make strong eight column cartoon occupying in depth two thirds editorial page, showing smaller figures Uncle Sam and Germany shaking their fists at each other on left side page and on right side big head and shoulders of Japan with knife in hand leaning over into picture and evidently watching chance to strike Uncle Sam in back. Title of picture to be quote Watchful waiting unquote. Subtitle quote Look out Uncle Sam your neighbor Japan is eagerly awaiting an opportunity to strike you in the back unquote.
>
> HEARST

Motion pictures, as well as the printed word, were used by Hearst to preach the yellow peril gospel. In 1916 the International Film Service Corporation, part of the Hearst empire, produced a motion picture called *Patria*. As described to the Senate Investigating Committee by Captain George B. Lester, of Army Intelligence,

13. *German Propaganda Hearings* (Washington, 1919), pp. 1458–1459.

"Patria" had a story with three barrels. Its principal excuse was preparedness. But by the time the first episodes were released [it was a ten-
part serial] the country was already committed to that. Therefore only
the other two elements, anti-Mexican and anti-Japanese propaganda, remained active. These showed the attempt by Japan to conquer America
with the aid of Mexico. A Japanese noble, at the head of the secret service of the Emperor in America, was the chief villain. Japanese troops invaded California, committing appropriate atrocities [the chief of which
was the attempted rape of the heroine, played by Irene Castle].

"Patria" was first shown in New York January 9, 1917, and about that
time in other cities. The American and other Hearst papers carried the
story in serial form week by week. And the story was run—as is the custom with all serials—in a large number of newspapers, one in each city.
"Patria" was shown in the smaller towns and cities, the first four or five
months of the war . . .[14]

President Wilson saw the film in Washington, and was incensed by it.
His pressures caused the film to be severely edited, although under wartime regulations it could have been completely suppressed. According to
Captain Lester, the editing produced peculiar results: all the blame was
"dumped on Mexico. . . . The Mexicans were made the villains, and they
changed the whole piece over to Mexico, so that the Japanese had Mexican names; but in the film they were still wearing Japanese uniforms."

Besides the press and the Germans, there was one additional main
source of yellow peril propaganda—officers in the armed forces of the
United States. From his experience as Assistant Secretary of the Navy
(1913 to 1920), Franklin Delano Roosevelt was "quite certain . . . that a
very considerable part of the suspicion between [Japan and the United
States] rose from the perfectly natural attitude of Army and Navy officers
whose duty it has been in the past to prepare the country against the 'most
probable enemy.' " So far as the United States Navy was concerned, that
enemy was Japan. Josephus Daniels, Wilson's Secretary of the Navy, complains in his memoirs that Hobson and Rear Admiral Bradley A. Fiske,
Chief of Naval Operations, both "obsessed with the yellow peril," often
came to his office to harangue him about it. Army officers were not so outspoken as their seagoing colleagues, but a few were strong proponents of
the yellow peril. Lieutenant General Adna R. Chaffee, a former chief of
staff and an old China hand, wrote a glowing introduction to *The Valor of
Ignorance,* as did Major General J. P. Story. Since it was assumed by most
serious military thinkers that any future Japanese-American war would be
fought almost exclusively at sea, it was only natural that naval officers expressed the greater interest.

14. *German Propaganda Hearings,* pp. 1675–1676. For *Patria* see also James P.
Mock and Cedric Larson, *Words That Won the War* (New York, 1939), pp.
143–147.

In the years immediately after the war, the real rather than the imagined acts of the Japanese government were of growing concern to many Americans. The continued subjugation of Korea; the Twenty-one Demands upon China; the Shantung question; the friction between Japanese and American troops in Siberia; the insistent Japanese demands for racial equality, raised at Versailles and later at Geneva; the persistent and erroneous belief, before 1922, that the Anglo-Japanese alliance was somehow aimed at the United States: these were some of the issues that caused friction between the two countries. When these were added to the hostile feeling toward Japan already created by the war scares and the yellow peril propaganda, it was not difficult to convince many non-Californians that Japan was, as V. S. McClatchy put it, "the Germany of Asia."

How much effect did the yellow peril propaganda have? Certainly, no quantitative answer can ever be given to such a question. It is undeniable, however, that somewhere in the Platonic entity called the American psyche a sort of anti-Japanese reflex had been conditioned. A great deal of evidence of various sorts can be marshaled to support this contention; for the present discussion two pieces of literary data will have to suffice. In the years before the war, in St. Paul, Minnesota, far from the Pacific, Amory Blaine, F. Scott Fitzgerald's alter ego, "would dream one of his favorite waking dreams . . . the one about the Japanese invasion, when he was rewarded by being made the youngest general in the world." [15] In the American South the yellow peril subtly fused with fear of a Negro rebellion. "We used to talk a great deal," one young Southerner wrote, "about the race war which was coming, when blacks and yellows would unite and meet the scorn of whites with violence. It was one of our favorite topics of conversation."

By the end of the First World War a great reservoir of anti-Japanese sentiment had been created throughout the country. But sentiment does not automatically translate itself into legislation; before the California exclusionists could achieve their first great national victory it was necessary for them to create an effective and "respectable" middle-class organization.

Conclusion

As we have seen, California's anti-Oriental tradition has roots reaching back to her gold-rush past. The Issei's first American legacy was the hate and the fear of Orientals which had been generated in the anti-Chinese crusade. First inspired by economic competition and restricted largely to organized labor, the anti-Japanese movement soon received at least passive support from the overwhelming majority of California's population.

15. F. Scott Fitzgerald, *This Side of Paradise* (New York, 1920), p. 19.

Prejudice, the sociologists tell us, is learned behavior. Twentieth-century Californians learned the lesson well. Although racial prejudice, directed at various ethnic groups, flourished throughout the United States during the period under discussion, nowhere north of the Mason-Dixon line did any single group encounter the sustained nativist assault that was directed against California's Japanese. There seem to be four chief reasons for this. First, the Japanese were of a distinct racial group; no amount of acculturation could mask their foreignness. Second, unlike the Chinese, they rapidly began to challenge whites in many businesses and professions—as a group, Japanese in the United States became very quickly imbued with what, in Europeans, would be called the Protestant ethic. Third, the growing unpopularity of their homeland—an unpopularity that was, to a certain degree, deserved—further served to make immigrants from Japan special objects of suspicion. These three conditions would have made any large group of Japanese a particularly despised minority anywhere in the United States. Finally, the fact that most of the Japanese were in California probably made things worse, for California probably had a lower boiling point than did the country at large.

California, by virtue of its anti-Chinese tradition and frontier psychology, was already conditioned to anti-Orientalism before the Japanese arrived. Other special California characteristics abetted the success of the agitation. In the prewar years, the extraordinary power of organized labor in northern California gave the anti-Japanese movement a much stronger base than it would have enjoyed elsewhere; in the postwar years, open-shop southern California proved almost equally hospitable to an agitation pitched to middle-class white Protestants. In the two periods anti-Japanese sentiment flourished among completely disparate populations: the first- and second-generation immigrants who were the backbone of California's labor movement, and the Midwestern *émigrés* who came to dominate the southern California scene. For most of these Californians, opposition to the Japanese was based upon fears which were largely nonrational.

It is instructive to note that these nonrational fears were nowhere more persistent than in the minds of those middle-class leaders whom we have come to call progressive. If it seems paradoxical that a reform group dedicated to what one of its number called "the promise of American life" should lead so blatant an antidemocratic movement, it ought to be pointed out that one of the most glaring and too often unremarked deficiencies of the progressive was his utter disregard for civil liberties in general. Nowhere in the long debate over Japanese exclusion have I found even a suggestion that alien immigrants might have civil rights. Not until discrimination against immigrants after the First World War had reached its climax did some progressives begin to realize that even the rights of noncitizens must be protected if the liberties of all were to remain unimpaired.

The discriminations against the Japanese recounted here, as well as those of a later date, are clearly blots on the democratic escutcheon which we prize so highly. But the consequences of the anti-Japanese movement were more than moral. The existence of this prejudice helped to poison relations between the United States and Japan. As George F. Kennan has pointed out, in his provocative series of lectures on *American Diplomacy, 1900–1950,* the "long and unhappy story" of United States-Japanese relationships in this century was constantly worsened by the fact that "we would repeatedly irritate and offend the sensitive Japanese by our immigration policies and the treatment of people of Japanese lineage . . . in this country."

ARTHUR DE GOBINEAU

Races

A selection from Gobineau is included to give some primary experience of the intellectual basis for racism. Gobineau was the social theoretician to explain the triumphant expansion of the European powers in the last century. What is, perhaps, most remarkable in the selection is its tone. Gobineau reflects a peculiar nineteenth-century kind of "scientism." He has no doubts and presents his conclusions as incontrovertible facts based on observation.

Recapitulation: The Respective Characteristics of the Three Great Races; The Superiority of the White Type, and, within This Type, of the Aryan Family

I HAVE SHOWN the unique place in the organic world occupied by the human species, the profound physical, as well as moral, differences separating it from all other kinds of living creatures. Considering it by itself, I have been able to distinguish, on physiological grounds alone, three great and clearly marked types, the black, the yellow, and the white. However uncertain the aims of physiology may be, however meagre its resources, however defective its methods, it can proceed thus far with absolute certainty.

The negroid variety is the lowest, and stands at the foot of the ladder. The animal character, that appears in the shape of the pelvis, is stamped on the negro from birth, and foreshadows his destiny. His intellect will always move within a very narrow circle. He is not however a mere brute, for behind his low receding brow, in the middle of his skull, we can see signs of a powerful energy, however crude its objects. If his mental faculties are dull or even non-existent, he often has an intensity of desire, and so of will, which may be called terrible. Many of his senses, especially taste and smell, are developed to an extent unknown to the other two races.*

The very strength of his sensations is the most striking proof of his inferiority. All food is good in his eyes, nothing disgusts or repels him. What he desires is to eat, to eat furiously, and to excess; no carrion is too revolt-

* "Taste and smell in the negro are as powerful as they are undiscriminating. He eats everything, and odours which are revolting to us are pleasant to him" (Pruner).

ing to be swallowed by him. It is the same with odours; his inordinate desires are satisfied with all, however coarse or even horrible. To these qualities may be added an instability and capriciousness of feeling, that cannot be tied down to any single object, and which, so far as he is concerned, do away with all distinctions of good and evil. We might even say that the violence with which he pursues the object that has aroused his senses and inflamed his desires is a guarantee of the desires being soon satisfied and the object forgotten. Finally, he is equally careless of his own life and that of others: he kills willingly, for the sake of killing; and this human machine, in whom it is so easy to arouse emotion, shows, in face of suffering, either a monstrous indifference or a cowardice that seeks a voluntary refuge in death.

The yellow race is the exact opposite of this type. The skull points forward, not backward. The forehead is wide and bony, often high and projecting. The shape of the face is triangular, the nose and chin showing none of the coarse protuberances that mark the negro. There is further a general proneness to obesity, which, though not confined to the yellow type, is found there more frequently than in the others. The yellow man has little physical energy, and is inclined to apathy; he commits none of the strange excesses so common among negroes. His desires are feeble, his will-power rather obstinate than violent; his longing for material pleasures, though constant, is kept within bounds. A rare glutton by nature, he shows far more discrimination in his choice of food. He tends to mediocrity in everything; he understands easily enough anything not too deep or sublime. He has a love of utility and a respect for order, and knows the value of a certain amount of freedom. He is practical, in the narrowest sense of the word. He does not dream or theorize; he invents little, but can appreciate and take over what is useful to him. His whole desire is to live in the easiest and most comfortable way possible. The yellow races are thus clearly superior to the black. Every founder of a civilization would wish the backbone of his society, his middle class, to consist of such men. But no civilized society could be created by them; they could not supply its nerve-force, or set in motion the springs of beauty and action.

We come now to the white peoples. These are gifted with reflective energy, or rather with an energetic intelligence. They have a feeling for utility, but in a sense far wider and higher, more courageous and ideal, than the yellow races; a perseverance that takes account of obstacles and ultimately finds a means of overcoming them; a greater physical power, an extraordinary instinct for order, not merely as a guarantee of peace and tranquillity, but as an indispensable means of self-preservation. At the same time, they have a remarkable, and even extreme, love of liberty, and are openly hostile to the formalism under which the Chinese are glad to vegetate, as well as to the strict despotism which is the only way of governing the negro.

The white races are, further, distinguished by an extraordinary attachment to life. They know better how to use it, and so, as it would seem, set a greater price on it; both in their own persons and those of others, they are more sparing of life. When they are cruel, they are conscious of their cruelty; it is very doubtful whether such a consciousness exists in the negro. At the same time, they have discovered reasons why they should surrender this busy life of theirs, that is so precious to them. The principal motive is honour, which under various names has played an enormous part in the ideas of the race from the beginning. I need hardly add that the word honour, together with all the civilizing influences connoted by it, is unknown to both the yellow and the black man.

On the other hand, the immense superiority of the white peoples in the whole field of the intellect is balanced by an inferiority in the intensity of their sensations. In the world of the senses, the white man is far less gifted than the others, and so is less tempted and less absorbed by considerations of the body, although in physical structure he is far the most vigorous.*

Such are the three constituent elements of the human race. I call them secondary types, as I think myself obliged to omit all discussion of the Adamite man. From the combination, by intermarriage, of the varieties of these types come the tertiary groups. The quaternary formations are produced by the union of one of these tertiary types, or of a pure-blooded tribe, with another group taken from one of the two foreign species.

Below these categories others have appeared—and still appear. Some of these are very strongly characterized, and form new and distinct points of departure, coming as they do from races that have been completely fused. Others are incomplete, and ill-ordered, and, one might even say, anti-social, since their elements, being too numerous, too disparate, or too barbarous, have had neither the time nor the opportunity for combining to any fruitful purpose. No limits, except the horror excited by the possibility of infinite intermixture, can be assigned to the number of these hybrid and chequered races that make up the whole of mankind.

It would be unjust to assert that every mixture is bad and harmful. If the three great types had remained strictly separate, the supremacy would no doubt have always been in the hands of the finest of the white races, and the yellow and black varieties would have crawled for ever at the feet of the lowest of the whites. Such a state is so far ideal, since it has never been beheld in history; and we can imagine it only by recognizing the undisputed superiority of those groups of the white races which have remained the purest.

It would not have been all gain. The superiority of the white race would have been clearly shown, but it would have been bought at the price of certain advantages which have followed the mixture of blood. Although

* Martius observes that the European is superior to the coloured man in the pressure of the nervous fluid (*Reise in Brasilien,* vol. i, p. 259).

these are far from counterbalancing the defects they have brought in their train, yet they are sometimes to be commended. Artistic genius, which is equally foreign to each of the three great types, arose only after the inter-marriage of white and black. Again, in the Malayan variety, a human family was produced from the yellow and black races that had more intelligence than either of its ancestors. Finally, from the union of white and yellow, certain intermediary peoples have sprung, who are superior to the purely Finnish tribes as well as to the negroes.

I do not deny that these are good results. The world of art and great literature that comes from the mixture of blood, the improvement and ennoblement of inferior races—all these are wonders for which we must needs be thankful. The small have been raised. Unfortunately, the great have been lowered by the same process; and this is an evil that nothing can balance or repair. Since I am putting together the advantages of racial mixtures, I will also add that to them is due the refinement of manners and beliefs, and especially the tempering of passion and desire. But these are merely transitory benefits, and if I recognize that the mulatto, who may become a lawyer, a doctor, or a business man, is worth more than his negro grandfather, who was absolutely savage, and fit for nothing, I must also confess that the Brahmans of primitive India, the heroes of the Iliad and the Shahnameh, the warriors of Scandinavia—the glorious shades of noble races that have disappeared—give us a higher and more brilliant idea of humanity, and were more active, intelligent, and trusty instruments of civilization and grandeur than the peoples, hybrid a hundred times over, of the present day. And the blood even of these was no longer pure.

However it has come about, the human races, as we find them in history, are complex; and one of the chief consequences has been to throw into disorder most of the primitive characteristics of each type. The good as well as the bad qualities are seen to diminish in intensity with repeated intermixture of blood; but they also scatter and separate off from each other, and are often mutually opposed. The white race originally possessed the monopoly of beauty, intelligence, and strength. By its union with other varieties, hybrids were created, which were beautiful without strength, strong without intelligence, or, if intelligent, both weak and ugly. Further, when the quantity of white blood was increased to an indefinite amount by successive infusions, and not by a single admixture, it no longer carried with it its natural advantages, and often merely increased the confusion already existing in the racial elements. Its strength, in fact, seemed to be its only remaining quality, and even its strength served only to promote disorder. The apparent anomaly is easily explained. Each stage of a perfect mixture produces a new type from diverse elements, and develops special faculties. As soon as further elements are added, the vast difficulty of harmonizing the whole creates a state of anarchy. The more this increases, the more do even the best and richest of the new contributions diminish in value, and by their mere presence add fuel to an evil which they cannot abate. If mixtures of blood are, to a certain extent, beneficial to the mass of mankind, if they raise and ennoble it, this is merely at the expense of mankind itself, which is stunted, abased, enervated, and humiliated in the persons of its noblest sons. Even if we admit that it is better to turn a myriad of degraded beings into mediocre men than to preserve the race of princes whose blood is adulterated and impoverished by being made to suffer this dishonourable change, yet there is still the unfortunate fact that the change does not stop here; for when the mediocre men are once created at the expense of the greater, they combine with other mediocrities, and from such unions, which grow ever more and more degraded, is born a confusion which, like that of Babel, ends in utter impotence, and leads societies down to the abyss of nothingness whence no power of earth can rescue them.

Such is the lesson of history. It shows us that all civilizations derive from the white race, that none can exist without its help, and that a society is great and brilliant only so far as it preserves the blood of the noble group that created it, provided that this group itself belongs to the most illustrious branch of our species.

Of the multitude of peoples which live or have lived on the earth, ten alone have risen to the position of complete societies. The remainder have gravitated round these more or less independently, like planets round their suns. If there is any element of life in these ten civilizations that is not due to the impulse of the white races, any seed of death that does not come from the inferior stocks that mingled with them, then the whole theory on which this book rests is false. On the other hand, if the facts are as I say, then we have an irrefragable proof of the nobility of our own species. Only the actual details can set the final seal of truth on my system, and they alone can show with sufficient exactness the full implications of my main thesis, that peoples degenerate only in consequence of the various admixtures of blood which they undergo; that their degeneration corresponds exactly to the quantity and quality of the new blood, and that the rudest possible shock to the vitality of a civilization is given when the ruling elements in a society and those developed by racial change have become so numerous that they are clearly moving away from the homogeneity necessary to their life, and it therefore becomes impossible for them to be brought into harmony and so acquire the common instincts and interests, the common logic of existence, which is the sole justification for any social bond whatever. There is no greater curse than such disorder, for however bad it may have made the present state of things, it promises still worse for the future.

Note: The "ten civilizations" mentioned in the last paragraph are as follows. They are fully discussed in the subsequent books of the "Inequality of Races," of which the present volume forms the first.

I. The Indian civilization, which reached its highest point round the Indian Ocean and in the north and east of the Indian Continent, south-east of the Brahmaputra. It arose from a branch of a white people, the Aryans.

II. The Egyptians, round whom collected the Ethiopians, the Nubians, and a few smaller peoples to the west of the oasis of Ammon. This society was created by an Aryan colony from India, that settled in the upper valley of the Nile.

III. The Assyrians, with whom may be classed the Jews, the Phoenicians, the Lydians, the Carthaginians, and the Hymiarites. They owed their civilizing qualities to the great white invasions which may be grouped under the name of the descendants of Shem and Ham. The Zoroastrian Iranians who ruled part of Central Asia under the names of Medes, Persians, and Bactrians, were a branch of the Aryan family.

IV. The Greeks, who came from the same Aryan stock, as modified by Semitic elements.

V. The Chinese civilization, arising from a cause similar to that operating in Egypt. An Aryan colony from India brought the light of civilization to China also. Instead however of becoming mixed with black peoples, as on the Nile, the colony became absorbed in Malay and yellow races, and was reinforced, from the north-west, by a fair number of white elements, equally Aryan but no longer Hindu.

VI. The ancient civilization of the Italian peninsula, the cradle of Roman culture. This was produced by a mixture of Celts, Iberians, Aryans, and Semites.

VII. The Germanic races, which in the fifth century transformed the Western mind. These were Aryans.

VIII.–X. The three civilizations of America, the Alleghanian, the Mexican, and the Peruvian.

Of the first seven civilizations, which are those of the Old World, six belong, at least in part, to the Aryan race, and the seventh, that of Assyria, owes to this race the Iranian Renaissance, which is, historically, its best title to fame. Almost the whole of the Continent of Europe is inhabited at the present time by groups of which the basis is white, but in which the non-Aryan elements are the most numerous. There is no true civilization, among the European peoples, where the Aryan branch is not predominant.

In the above list no negro race is seen as the initiator of a civilization. Only when it is mixed with some other can it even be initiated into one.

Similarly, no spontaneous civilization is to be found among the yellow races; and when the Aryan blood is exhausted stagnation supervenes.

RUTH BENEDICT

Why Then Race Prejudice?

Ruth Benedict is one of America's most distinguished anthropologists. In essence, her theory, supported by examples, is that racial slogans are used to justify conflicts. First, she notes, comes persecution, the ins against the outs, the haves against the have nots, and then comes the theory—racism—to legitimize the persecution.

FOR A THEORY of racism there are two conclusions to be drawn from the whole matter. The first is that, in order to understand race persecution, we do not need to investigate race; we need to investigate *persecution*. Persecution was an old, old story before racism was thought of. Social change is inevitable, and it is always fought by those whose ties are to the old order. These ties may be economic or they may be religious, as in medieval Europe, or those of social affiliation, as with Roman patricians. Those who have these ties will consciously or unconsciously ferret out reasons for believing that their group is supremely valuable and that the new claimants threaten the achievements of civilization. They will raise a cry of rights of inheritance or divine right of kings or religious orthodoxy or racial purity or manifest destiny. These cries reflect the temporary conditions of the moment, and all the efforts of the slogan-makers need not convince us that any one of them is based on eternal verities. The battle cries of Nordicism belong with "Keep Cool with Coolidge" and "He Kept Us Out of War" of American presidential campaigns, and with slight changes in social necessities they will be as evanescent. All slogans are useful in the degree to which they express the faiths and discontents of the hour. Religious varieties were politically useful in eras and regions which had powerful religious interests; when these were overshadowed by secular privileges and when cleavages along religious lines became less important, religious slogans no longer justified the persecution of minorities as they had in earlier days.

Racial slogans serve the same purpose in the present century that religious slogans served before, that is, they are used to justify persecution in the interests of some class or nation. This racial slogan is peculiarly congenial to our times. Science is a word to conjure with in this century; unfortunately it is often used to conjure. It is not alone racism that has turned to so-called science for its arguments. A manufacturer of cosmetics conducted not long ago an investigation of various advertisements of his wares. He found that the two words which had most sales-appeal were "immediately" and "scientific." Every rouge, every face powder must claim a "scientific" uniqueness, and by this ballyhoo millions are impressed. It was the same with fake medicines, with drug-store drinks, and with health foods until it became necessary to defend the public by federal supervision of manufacturers' claims. The slogan of "science" will sell most things today, and it sells persecution as easily as it sells rouge. The scientist repeatedly points out that the advertised rouge is indistinguishable from others or even that he has found it especially harmful in a laboratory test; he points out that no race has a monopoly of abilities or of virtues and that, as science, the racists' claims have no validity. For the scientist, science is a body of knowledge; he resents its use as a body of magic. But he knows that *scientific* is the word our civilization conjures with—in no matter what cause.

The choice of racial slogans to justify conflict is rooted in still another manner in the conditions of the modern age. Racial reasons for persecution are convenient just because in Western civilization today so many different breeds live in close contact with one another. The racist cries are raised not because those who raise them have any claim to belong to pure races, but because they do not; in other words, because today several ethnic groups occupy one city or one state, or states that share in one civilization are engaged in nationalistic wars. Hence comes the paradox that has been so often pointed out: that it is the most mongrel peoples of the world who raise the war cry of racial purity. From the point of view of race, this makes nonsense, but from the point of view of persecution it is inevitable. No group raises battle cries against people whose existence is of no moment to it; for conflict to arise, there must first be contact. Racial slogans arose therefore in Europe in class and national conflicts. The old religious slogans for persecution had lost their hold, and the racists evolved in their stead a bastard version of contemporary science. Racism remains in the eyes of history, however, merely another instance of the persecution of minorities for the advantage of those in power.

Once we have recognized that race conflict is only the justification of the persecution that is popular at the moment, the strangest paradox in all racist theory becomes clear. The racists have over and over again derived race prejudice from a race repulsion instinctive in mankind, and historians and biologists and anthropologists have as repetitiously pointed out that such a theory is impossible in view of the universal mixture of races. "Why, if Nature abhors race-crossing, does she do so much of it?" [1] But repulsion to intermarriage accompanies any conflict of two groups, how-

1. Castle, W. E., "Biological and Social Consequences of Race-Crossing," *American Journal of Physical Anthropology,* Vol. IX, pp. 145–146.

ever the groups may be defined. They need not be racial. The patricians of Rome recoiled from marriage with plebeians in the same way, the Catholics of France from marriage with the Huguenots. It is not that man has a set of instincts which make only his own race sexually attractive, but that in-groups are unwilling to give status to the outsider. They do not want to share prerogatives with him. If this in-group is defined racially as Anglo-Saxons have defined it in their contact with native peoples of the world, their desire to maintain the in-group will bring about selective mating in marriage, but it notoriously does not prevent mating outside of marriage. The great numbers of half-castes in India and mulattoes in America are testimony to the fact that the antipathy is not instinctive aversion to members of another race.

Those theorists also who have explained race prejudice by visible racial differences are similarly confused. They have said that race prejudice is caused by obvious and striking contrasts in face and color. They are, however, mistaking a momentary feature of persecution for a causal one. There was no differentiating skin color or nose shape in a Huguenot, or in the Albigensian victims of the Inquisition. On the other side of the picture, poverty sets groups as visibly apart as the color of their hair or the shape of their heads. Groups may be set apart by any number of things besides race—by whether they go to Mass or by whether they drop their *h*'s. Members of a primitive tribe have been known to kill at sight members of a neighboring tribe of the 'same race and language because they felt that the way they carried their burden baskets was an insult to human beings. Not the fact of "visibility" of skin color but the fact that racial characteristics are transmitted over so many generations makes racial prejudice a new problem in the world. A man can stop going to Mass or a Huguenot can take the sacrament because "Paris is worth a Mass" or the heroine of *Pygmalion* learn to enunciate her mother tongue in the Oxford fashion, but too dark a Negro cannot "pass" and not even his children's children may be born light enough to do so. This is a problem of relative permanence of distinctions, not specifically of "visibility." In the long course of history persecution has been now more, now less intense; but these variations do not correlate with the presence or absence of racial visibility.

Mistaken explanations of the nature of race prejudice are of minor importance so long as they are concerned with theoretical points like instinctive antipathies or the role of racial visibility. There is a far more important issue. The fact that to understand race conflict we need fundamentally to understand *conflict* and not *race,* means something much more drastic. It means that all the deep-seated causes of conflict in any group or between groups are involved in any outbreak of race prejudice. Race will be cried up today in a situation where formerly religion would have been cried up. If civilized men expect to end prejudice—whether religious or racial—they will have to remedy major social abuses, in no way connected with religion or race, to the common advantage. Whatever reduces conflict, curtails irresponsible power, and allows people to obtain a decent livelihood will reduce race conflict. Nothing less will accomplish the task.

For the friction is not primarily racial. We all know what the galling frictions are in the world today: nationalistic rivalries, desperate defense of the status quo by the haves, desperate attacks by the have-nots, poverty, unemployment, and war. Desperate men easily seize upon some scapegoat to sacrifice to their unhappiness; it is a kind of magic by which they feel for the moment that they have laid the misery that has been tormenting them. In this they are actively encouraged by their rulers and exploiters, who like to see them occupied with this violence, and fear that if it were denied them they might demand something more difficult. So Hitler, when his armament program cut consumers' goods and increased hours of work and lowered real wages, exhorted the nation in 1938 to believe that Germany's defeat in 1919 had been due to Jewry, and encouraged racial riots. And this served two purposes: It gave an undernourished people an outlet harmless to the government, and it allowed the government treasury to appropriate to itself the wealth of the Jews.

In this sequence of events the Third Reich is but following a long series of precedents in European anti-Semitism. During the Middle Ages persecutions of the Jews, like all medieval persecutions, were religious rather than racial. Intermarriage between Jews and Gentiles was condemned, not as a racist measure, but in the same manner as marriages between Catholics and heretics were condemned. The pogroms of the time of the Crusades were carried out by stay-at-home mobs imitating the Crusaders in avenging the death of Christ; the mobs killed Jews, the Crusaders fought the Arabs and Turks. The link between Jews and Turks was not racial; in the period of the Crusades the two were equated because the first had crucified Christ and the second owned his tomb. Nor were persecutions other than those set in motion by the Crusaders directed toward eliminating a racial breed; apostate Jews purchased safety. A renegade Jew denounced or concealed his religion, not his race. The Popes and rulers favorable to the Jews promulgated laws directing that "they should not be baptized by force, constrained to observe Christian festivals nor to wear badges." Even up to the First World War some German racists advocated as the cure for conflict, not extinction of the Jewish race, but a racial merger. This was especially true of the great nationalist historian Treitschke, who was one of Germany's foremost advocates of racist salvation at the turn of the century.

As racist persecutions replaced religious persecutions in Europe, however, the inferiority of the Jew became that of *race*. By the 1800's a tidal wave of pogroms and persecutions swept over large parts of Europe. To the people it everywhere appeared that the bourgeoisie were in the saddle, and the Jews, owing to earlier segregation in city ghettos and to restrictions against land-owning, were all bourgeoisie. They were hated for this reason, and persecution was reinforced by the old tradition of religious animosity against the Jews. Racial anti-Semitism was all too easy to arouse. In Germany in the eighties an anti-Semitic demagogue of evil repute was cynically encouraged by members of the Conservative Party in order to strengthen with his following their opposition to the Social Democrats; synagogues were burned and violence against the Jews went unpunished. The charge of Jewish ritual murder was revived. In France, the anti-Semitic movement came to a climax in the 1890's with the famous Dreyfus affair. It marks probably the climax of prewar anti-Semitism in Europe. The reactionary party was most strongly represented in the Army, and the "framing" of a prominent Jewish staff officer, Captain Alfred Dreyfus, and his conviction of treason on forged evidence, were the occasion for a year-long conflict that rocked the nation. To the honor of France, the plot was laid bare, Dreyfus was exonerated, and it was shown that those who were really guilty of the treason had attempted to hide themselves behind a Jew because of popular anti-Semitism.

The more closely one studies European anti-Semitism in its modern racial guise, the less it appears that the conflict is racial; it is the old problem of unequal citizenship rights. Whenever one group, whether industrial workers or a religious sect or a racial group, is discriminated against before the law or in equal claims to life, liberty, and jobs, there will always be powerful interests to capitalize on this fact and to divert violence from those responsible for these conditions into channels where it is relatively safe to allow. In the case of the Jews we inherit from the old era of religious persecution all the necessary shibboleths of hate, and these are easily turned to account in a new setting. In addition there is exceptional profit; unlike most discriminated-against minorities, the Jews often provide rich contraband and are therefore marked objects for persecution to a poverty-stricken government or populace.

The cure for anti-Semitism, therefore, logically lies, as in all minority conflicts, in the extension to all men of full citizenship rights and of full opportunity to make good in any field. There would have been no Dreyfus case if certain traitors had not felt that a framed Jew would be found guilty by the courts. There would have been no nationwide pogroms in Germany in 1938 if all those who took part in them had known the state would hold them accountable. It is not only for the sake of the persecuted that the full rights of minorities need to be maintained. The minorities may be only martyrs, but the persecutors revert to savagery. If we are unwilling to or unable to pay the price of equality in human rights, we, the persecutors, suffer brutalization in ourselves whenever we fall into the trap set for us.

The case of the Negro since the Civil War in America points the same social lesson. The only trustworthy objective in any color-line program is the ultimate elimination of legal, educational, economic, and social discriminations. The fact that such elimination is not accepted even as an ultimate objective in most parts of the South is due to the persistence of slave-owner attitudes on the one hand and, on the other, to the degrading conditions under which great numbers of Negroes have lived in the United States. Granted that great numbers of Negroes are not ready for full citizenship, the social conditions which perpetuate their poverty and ignorance must be remedied before anyone can judge what kind of citizens they might be in other, more favorable circumstances. To be able to live a decent life and be respected for it, without being subjected to a blanket damnation that one's personal life cannot remove, is a human right, the granting of which would have immense social repercussions.

In periods and places where social institutions have made this possible for the Negro in the New World, the results have been incomparably better than those in the United States since the Civil War. Lord Bryce, an excellent observer, said of Brazil: "Brazil is the one country in the world, besides the Portuguese colonies on the east and west coasts of Africa, in which a fusion of the European and African races is proceeding unchecked by law or custom. The doctrines of human equality and human solidarity have here their perfect work. The work is so far satisfactory that there is little or no class friction. The white man does not lynch or maltreat the Negro; indeed I have never heard of a lynching anywhere in South America except occasionally as part of a political convulsion. The Negro is not accused of insolence and does not seem to develop any more criminality than naturally belongs to any ignorant population with loose notions of morality and property. What ultimate effect the intermixture of blood will have on the European element in Brazil I will not venture to predict. If one may judge from a few remarkable cases it will not necessarily reduce the intellectual standard." [2]

Such conditions were possible in Brazil only because of the extreme lack of racial discrimination which the Portuguese everywhere showed in their post-Columbian colonization; with the growing influence of non-Portuguese cultures in modern Brazil, the Negro has to some extent suffered. With growing discrimination against his race, the usual effects have followed, small though these consequences are in Brazil in comparison with

2. Bryce, James, *South America, Observations and Impressions,* New York, 1914, pp. 477, 480.

the United States. But while discrimination was at a minimum, the social results were good.

To minimize racial persecution, therefore, it is necessary to minimize conditions which lead to persecution; it is not necessary to minimize race. Race is not in itself the source of the conflict. Conflict arises whenever any group—in this case, a race—is forged into a class by discriminations practiced against it; the race then becomes a minority which is denied rights to protection before the law, rights to livelihood and to participation in the common life. The social problem does not differ whether such a group is racially distinguished or whether it is not; in either case the healthy social objective is to do away with minority discriminations.

We are so far from doing this in the modern world that it is likely to seem a program impossible of achievement. Even so, this is not the total program for a world free of race conflict. It is not enough merely to legislate human rights for the minorities. The majorities, also—the persecutors —must have solid basis for confidence in their own opportunity to live in security and decency. Otherwise, whatever the laws, whatever the guarantees, they will find out a victim and sacrifice him as a scapegoat to their despair. Everything that is done in any nation to eliminate unemployment, to raise the standard of living, to ensure civil liberties, is a step in the elimination of race conflict. Whatever is done to fasten fear upon the people of a nation, to humiliate individuals, to abrogate civil liberties, to deny coveted opportunities, breeds increased conflict. Men have not, for all their progress in civilization, outgrown the hen yard; a hen who is pecked at by a cock attacks, not the cock, but a weaker hen; this weaker hen attacks a still weaker, and so on down to the last chicken. Man too has his "pecking order," and those who have been victims, even though they belong to the "superior race," will require victims.

The truth of the matter is that these two aspects of a program for preventing the ravages of racism—democratic opportunity for the privileged and for the underprivileged—cannot be separated from one another. They are web and woof. One of the great political advantages of racist slogans is that the underprivileged many use them. Therefore the unemployed and the low-income groups can vent, through this alleged racist "superiority," the hatred that is engendered by their fear and insecurity. Studies in America have many times shown that anti-Semitism is strongest among low-income groups and that the high peaks of racial persecution have coincided with the low troughs of depression periods. While we raise Negro standards of living, of health, and of education in the South, therefore, it is necessary also to raise the standards of the Southern poor whites. Until we have "made democracy work" so that the nation's full manpower is drafted for its common benefit, racist persecution will continue in America. Until housing and conditions of labor are raised above the needlessly low standards which prevail in many sections of the country, scapegoats of some sort will be sacrificed to poverty. Until the regulation of industry has enforced the practice of social responsibility, there will be exploitation of the most helpless racial groups, and this will be justified by racist denunciations.

Hard-boiled economists and statesmen recognize today the shortsightedness of policies which allow such conditions to continue and to become intensified. Those who fight to perpetuate them are repeating the errors of the Albigensian crusade and the Huguenot expulsion; they are gaining a false and temporary advantage at the expense of their own permanent welfare. National prosperity, however thin you cut it, has two surfaces: ability to sell means ability to buy; employment means production. Whatever groups battle with each other, under conditions of modern industry and finance, the most important condition of either one's getting more is that the other shall also get more. Since their conflict is truly suicidal, it is necessary for the benefit of the contestants themselves that farsighted regulations should be imposed on both parties.

In the last decade we have grown to recognize much more fully the responsibility that rests on the state for achieving satisfactory national conditions, and from the standpoint of history it is likely that this role of the state will in the long run be extended rather than curtailed. A democratic state, when it lives up to its minimum definition at all, is the one institution which represents all the parts of the body politic. It can propose for itself programs which will eventually benefit the whole body. It is hard to see how this responsibility for the whole can be taken today except by the national government, and in the past decade state regulation has increased, national treasuries all over the Western World have been opened for the relief of the unemployed, and compulsory old-age insurance is in operation in many nations. These and other national undertakings can be used to minimize economic discrimination. Equality in the matter of civil liberties is closely bound up with such programs, and so long as civil liberties are made more, rather than less, equal for different groups, there is no historical reason for fearing the increased role of the state. For the true goal in any program for a better America is that all men may be able to live so that self-respect is possible and so that they may have confidence that prosperity will spread its benefits widely over the population.

The cultural anthropologist has the best reason in the world to know that conflict is eliminated only as men work together for common benefits, and obtain them in common. In most of the tribes the anthropologist knows, he can study side by side two different codes of ethics: one is that of open-handed hospitality and liberality and sharing, along with condemnation of aggressions like stealing and murder; the other is death at sight, torture, and the exaltation of robbery. The first code a man applies to those whose economic and social activities benefit him; these form an in-group within which none but moral reprobates are penalized. No matter who is successful in the hunt, the whole in-group benefits; any special skills any man may possess are an asset to the group as a whole. The priests conduct ceremonies for the good of the tribe and for common advantages like increase of plants and animals; warriors defend the little group against predatory outsiders. The second code a man applies to tribes with whom his tribe makes no common cause. No activities of theirs feed or house or bless or defend him. They are outside the pale. It is only a question of whether he kills his enemies first or they kill him.

The in-group code of ethics arises, however, only as the institutions of a society provide for shared advantages. When increase of food supply is not a common benefit, but something one man must get at the expense of another; when supernatural power is not used for general blessings, like rain, which falls on all, but for charms to use for personal ends against a neighbor; when legal or economic or political institutions put one man at the mercy of his neighbors, persecution develops. The gain or loss of all men is no longer my own gain or loss and the tribe is no longer a unit within which in-group ethics operate. The persecution that develops is most often sorcery. Sorcery is a very evil thing and when society does not officially punish it the victim has no redress. Unchecked sorcery societies are like modern nations with Ogpus and Gestapos, and they act out in deeds Hitler's dictum: "We need hatred, hatred, and then more hatred."

In-group ethics is therefore a reflection of the fact that all members share in their tribal enterprises and do actually profit from one another's activities. In-group mutual support is as native to the human race as out-group hostility; it is not something precarious and achieved only by isolated individuals at the end of a long social evolution. It arose long before the higher ethical religions with their teachings of altruism and duty. It occurs automatically whenever the social order makes it advantageous. It is at home among the lowest savages, and the one essential contribution modern civilization has made has been to enlarge the size of the in-group. In this there has been incomparable progress. Millions today recognize their common cause as citizens of a great nation, or as members of a party, or as financiers, or as workers, whereas in past history some little territory might be divided into a dozen hostile groups recognizing no common bonds. Today the increasing complexity of the processes of production, the ease of transportation, the interdependence of financial systems have brought it about that people in the remotest part of civilization suffer from catastrophe in another part.

The very progress of civilization, therefore, has laid the foundation for a vast extension of in-group mutual dependency and mutual support. Mankind has not yet adjusted its institutions to the real requirements of the world it has created, and this cultural lag today threatens the very bases of international life. Many serious students of human affairs have been driven to despair. The world of our fathers, they conclude, has been destroyed because it tried to ignore the real facts of human nature; it tried to impose a peaceful social order on a predatory animal. The lesson we should learn from recent events, they say, is that man is by nature a beast of prey who will always tear and rend his weaker neighbors; we must recognize that wars and racial persecutions are inevitable in human destiny. To the anthropologist such a counsel of despair is demonstrably false. In-group ethics are as "innate" as out-group ethics, *but they occur only when certain social conditions are fulfilled.* We cannot get in-group ethics without meeting those conditions. In our own country this means that a better America will be one which benefits not some groups alone but all citizens; so long as there is starvation and joblessness in the midst of abundance we are inviting the deluge. To avert it, we must "strongly resolve" that all men shall have the basic opportunity to work and to earn a living wage, that education and health and decent shelter shall be available to all, that regardless of race, creed, or color, civil liberties shall be protected.

The elimination of race conflict is a task of social engineering. But what of education? It is often said that our school systems must make themselves responsible for ending race prejudice, and attempts have been made to achieve tolerance by special instruction. This is of great importance, but we should be quite clear about the limits of its effectiveness; otherwise, in the end we shall cry that we were betrayed because it has not succeeded. All education, whether of children or adults, is important and necessary because it makes for an enlightened mind and for unbiased impulses. These are essential because without them discriminations may not be done away with at all and barriers to opportunity may never be thrown down. But good impulses are socially effective only when they have accomplished these results. "Hell is paved with good intentions"— intentions which were blindly regarded as ends in themselves and not as mere preliminaries. This is a platitude, but one which is often forgotten in discussions of the role of our schools in racial matters. If we are to make good use of the great powers of education in combating racism, two goals should be kept clearly distinct. On the one hand, it is desirable to teach in the regular social studies the facts of race and of the share of different races in our civilization. On the other hand, it is necessary to hold up ideals of a functioning democracy; it is necessary to help children to understand the mutual interdependence of different groups; it is necessary to encourage comparison of our social conditions with conditions which are better than ours as well as with those that are worse. It is necessary that they should be taught to think of unsatisfactory conditions not as inescapable facts of Nature, but as ones which with effort can be done away with. Only through such education can school instruction lay the basis for the amelioration of race conflict. We cannot trust to teaching them about the glories of Chinese civilization or the scientific achievements of the Jews. That is worth doing, but if we leave it at that and expect them to become racially tolerant we have deceived ourselves. The fatal flaw in most arguments which would leave to the schools the elimination of race conflict is that they propose education *instead* of social engineering. Nothing but hypocrisy can come of such a program.

The program that will avail against racism is called today "making democracy work." In so far as it is achieved in America it will produce the kind of behavior it has always produced in a mutually supporting in-group. Change, we must recognize, is always difficult and produces dislocations. But if we know the direction in which we must move, we can resolve to pay the necessary costs of change. The Arabians have a proverb: " 'What will you have?' said the Prophet, 'take it and pay for it.' " We must pay for a democracy that works, but fortunately in this case we can reassure ourselves with the knowledge that, even in financial accounting, government investments in rehousing and rebuilding America, in soil conservation, in health and education, and in increasing the nation's purchasing power through insurance benefits, pay their own way with handsome returns. A price is exacted also for a social order like Nazi Germany, and that price, in lowered standard of living, in brutalization, in denial of human rights, in sabotage of science and the intellectual life, is higher than any costs of democracy. In persecuting victims, the Nazis were themselves victimized.

Our Founding Fathers believed that a nation could be administered without creating victims. It is for us to prove that they were not mistaken.

ERIK ERIKSON

The Concept of Identity in Race Relations

One of the most influential of contemporary psychologists, Erikson is most concerned with the question of personal identity. The author of *Identity: Youth and Crisis, Childhood and Society,* and *Gandhi's Truth,* Erikson discusses here the relation of race awareness to a sense of self and other.

Introductory Remark

THE FOLLOWING NOTES represent an expansion of the remarks on the concept of identity which I was asked to make in November 1964 at the meeting of the committee gathered to plan the issues of *Dædalus* devoted to the Negro American. Shortly after that meeting, I undertook a trip abroad in order to interview the surviving witnesses and to study the remaining documents of what seemed, when the study was first planned, a long-past episode in a faraway country, namely, one of Gandhi's nonviolent campaigns. I am now returning to my fragmentary contribution to this symposium for the very reason that the concept or at least the term identity seems not only to have pervaded the literature on the Negro revolution in this country, but also to have come to represent in India (and in other countries) something in the psychological core of the revolution of the colored races and nations who seek inner as well as outer emancipation from colonial rule and from the remnants of colonial patterns of thought. When, for example, Nehru said (as I have been told) that "Gandhi gave India an identity," he obviously put the term into the center of that development of a nonviolent technique, both religious and political, by which Gandhi strove to enhance a unique unity among Indians while insisting on their complete autonomy within the British Empire. But what did Nehru mean?

R. P. Warren, in his *Who Speaks for the Negro?* reacts to the first (but by no means last) mention of the word by one of his informants with the exclamation:

> I seize the word *identity*. It is a key word. You hear it over and over again. On this word will focus, around this word will coagulate, a dozen issues, shifting, shading into each other. Alienated from the world to which he is born and from the country of which he is a citizen, yet sur-

rounded by the successful values of that world, and country, how can the Negro define himself? [1]

Usually, the term is used without explanation as if it were obvious what it means; and, indeed, faddish as the word has become, it has also come to mean to many something both profound and unfathomable.

Social scientists sometimes attempt to make it more concrete. However, if they do not quickly equate it with the strangely pat question "Who am I?" they make such words as "identity crisis," "self-identity," or "sexual identity" fit whatever they are investigating. For the sake of logical or experimental maneuverability (and in order to keep in good academic company) they try to treat these terms as matters of social roles, personal traits, or conscious self-images, shunning the less manageable and the less obscure (and often more sinister) implications of the concept. Its use has, in fact, become so indiscriminate that the other day a German reviewer (of a new edition of my first book in which I first used the term in the context of psychoanalytic ego theory) called the concept the pet subject of the *amerikanische Popularpsychologie*. As we might say in American popular psychology: that does it. I return to the subject because (in spite of slogan-like misuse and lip service) it does seem to speak to the condition of many serious observers at this juncture of history. I will try to explain some of its dimensions and relate them to what can only be approximate illustrations from race-relations. I will claim no further status for this effort than "notes and queries" [2] within a symposium, that is, in a context in which what will be referred to here as a *revolution of awareness* can be seen against the background of what Gandhi called the "four-fold ruin" wrought by political and economic as well as cultural and spiritual degradation; for surely, power, or at least the power to choose, is vitally related to identity. In this context, I shall emphasize rather than minimize the alternatives and controversies, the ambiguities and ambivalences concerning various aspects of the identity issue.

I Individual and Communal

At a time when the term identity refers, more often than not, to a more or less desperate quest, or even (as in the case of the Negro American) to something mostly negative or absent ("invisible," "inaudible," "unnamed"), it may be well to introduce the subject with quotations from two men who asserted strongly what identity feels like when you become aware of it. My two witnesses are the bearded and patriarchal founding fathers of the kind of psychology on which this writer's thinking on identity is based.

1. Robert Penn Warren, *Who Speaks for the Negro?* (New York, 1965), p. 17.
2. These notes are a counterpart to the "Memorandum on Identity and Negro Youth," *Journal of Social Issues,* Vol. 20, No. 4 (October 1964).

As a *subjective sense* of an *invigorating sameness* and *continuity,* what I would call a sense of identity seems to me best described by William James in a letter to his wife. "A man's character," he wrote, "is discernible in the mental or moral attitude in which, when it came upon him, he felt himself most deeply and intensely active and alive. At such moments there is a voice inside which speaks and says: '*This* is the real me!' " Such experience always includes

> "an element of active tension, of holding my own, as it were, and trusting outward things to perform their part so as to make it a full harmony, but without any *guaranty* that they will. Make it a guaranty—and the attitude immediately becomes to my consciousness stagnant and stingless. Take away the guaranty, and I feel (provided I am *uberhaupt* in vigorous condition) a sort of deep enthusiastic bliss, of bitter willingness to do and suffer anything . . . and which, although it is a mere mood or emotion to which I can give no form in words, authenticates itself to me as the deepest principle of all active and theoretic determination which I possess. . . ." [3]

James uses the word "character," but I am taking the liberty of claiming that he describes what today we would call a sense of identity, and that he does so in a way which can in principle be experienced by any man. To him it is both mental and moral (the last a word also often swallowed up by ours); and he experiences it as something that "comes upon you" as a re-cognition, almost as a surprise rather than as something strenuously "quested" after. It is an active tension (rather than a paralyzing question) —a tension which, furthermore, must create a challenge "without guaranty" rather than one dissipated in a clamor for certainty. But let us remember in passing that James was in his thirties when he wrote this, that he had faced and articulated an "identity crisis" of honest and desperate depth, and that he became *the* Psychologist-Philosopher of American Pragmatism only after having attempted to integrate other cultural, philosophic, and professional identity elements.[4]

One can study in James' life history the emergence of a "self-made" identity in a new and expansive civilization. But for a statement of that unity of *personal and cultural* identity which is rooted in an ancient people's fate we turn to Sigmund Freud. In an address to the Society of B'nai B'rith in Vienna in 1926 he said:

> What bound me to Jewry was (I am ashamed to admit) neither faith nor national pride, for I have always been an unbeliever and was brought up without any religion though not without a respect for what are called the "ethical" standards of human civilization.

3. Henry James (ed.), *The Letters of William James,* Vol. I (Boston, 1920), p. 199.
4. See my introduction to G. B. Blaine and C. C. McArthur (eds.), *Emotional Problems of the Student* (New York, 1961).

Whenever I felt an inclination to national enthusiasm I strove to suppress it as being harmful and wrong, alarmed by the warning examples of the peoples among whom we Jews live. But plenty of other things remained over to make the attraction of Jewry and Jews irresistible—many obscure emotional forces, which were the more powerful the less they could be expressed in words, as well as a clear consciousness of inner identity, the safe privacy of a common mental construction. And beyond this there was a perception that it was to my Jewish nature alone that I owed two characteristics that had become indispensable to me in the difficult course of my life. Because I was a Jew I found myself free from many prejudices which restricted others in the use of their intellect; and as a Jew I was prepared to join the Opposition and to do without agreement with the "compact majority." [5]

No translation ever does justice to the grandiose choice of words in Freud's German original. "Obscure emotional forces" are *"dunkle Gefuehlsmaechte";* the "safe privacy of a common mental construction" is *"die Heimlichkeit der inneren Konstruktion"*—not just "mental," then, and certainly not "private," but a deep communality known only to those who share in it.

This quotation takes on new meaning in the context for which this is written, for *this* "consciousness of inner identity" includes a sense of bitter pride preserved by a dispersed and often despised people throughout a long history of alternating persecution and re-establishment. It is anchored in a particular (here intellectual) gift which had victoriously emerged from the suppression of other opportunities. At the same time, it should not be overlooked (for we will need to refer back to it later) that this *positive identity* is seen against the background of a *negative* counterpart in all "the peoples among whom we Jews live," namely, "prejudices which restrict others in the use of their intellect." Identity here is one aspect of the struggle for ethnic survival: one person's or group's identity may be relative to another's; and identity awareness may have to do with matters of an *inner emancipation* from a more dominant identity, such as the "compact majority." An exquisite triumph is suggested in the claim that the same historical development which restricted the prejudiced in the free use of their intellect made those discriminated against freer and sturdier in intellectual matters.

These two statements (and the life-histories behind them) serve to establish a first dimension of identity which immediately helps to explain why it is so tenacious and yet so hard to grasp: for here we deal with something which can be experienced as "identical" *in the core of the individual* and yet also identical *in the core of a communal culture,* and which is, in fact, the identity of those two identities.

5. Sigmund Freud, "Address to the Society of B'nai B'rith," in *The Standard Edition* (London, 1959), p. 273.

But we can also see that this is a matter of *growth,* both personal and communal. For a mature psychosocial identity presupposes a community of people whose traditional values become significant to the growing person even as his growth and his gifts assume relevance for them. Mere "roles" which can be "played" interchangeably are not sufficient; only an integration of roles which foster individual vitality within a vital trend in the existing or developing social order can support identities. (We may speak, then, of a *complementarity* of an *inner synthesis* in the individual and of *role integration* in his group.)

In all their poetic spontaneity these two statements prove to be the product of trained minds and therefore exemplify the main dimensions of a positive sense of identity almost systematically: from here one could proceed in a number of directions. But since these utterances are taken not from theoretical works, but from special communications (a letter to his wife from a man who married late; an address to his "brothers" by an observer long isolated in his field), it would seem most fitting now to quote corresponding voices among Negroes. But the mere contemplation of the task reveals two difficulties. The corresponding statements of Negro authors are couched in terms so negative that they at first suggest an absence of identity or the prevalence of what we will call *negative* identity elements. From Du Bois' famous passage (quoted in Myrdal's introduction to *Dark Ghetto*) [6] on the *inaudible* Negro, we would be led to Baldwin's and Ellison's very titles suggesting *invisibility, namelessness, facelessness.* But I would not approach these themes as a mere plaintive expression of the Negro American's sense of "nobody-ness," a social role which, God knows, was his heritage. Rather, I would tend to interpret the desperate and yet determined pre-occupation with invisibility on the part of these creative men as a demand to be heard and seen, recognized and faced as *individuals with a choice* rather than as men marked by what is all too superficially visible, namely, their color (and by the stereotypes which go with it). In a haunting way they defend an existing but in some ways voiceless identity against the stereotypes which hide it. They are involved in a battle to reconquer for their people, but first of all (as writers must) for themselves, what Vann Woodward calls a "surrendered identity." I like this term because it does not assume total absence as many contemporary writings do, something to be searched for and found, to be granted or given, to be created or fabricated, but something to be liberated. This will be emphasized in this paper because I consider it to be an actuality, and thus the only bridge from past to future.

I almost quoted Ellison as saying that his writing was indeed an attempt to transcend "as the blues transcended the painful conditions with which they deal." But I stopped myself; and now I have quoted him to show up a

6. Kenneth B. Clark, *Dark Ghetto* (New York, 1965).

second difficulty. Except for extraordinary moments of lucidity, all self-images and images of otherness (and, yes, even the blues) change their connotation kaleidoscopically before our eyes and in our discussions; and no writer of today can escape this. To have something to hold on to, we all use stereotypes temporarily endowed with ideological connotations which are a measure of Negro or white distance from the thoughtless accommodation to the postslavery period from which we are all emerging. What before was a more unconscious mixture of guilt and fear on the white side, and a mixture of hate and fear on the other, is now being replaced by the more conscious and yet not always more practical sentiments of remorse and mistrust. We have, at the moment, no choice but to live with those stereotypes and these affects: confrontation will disprove some of them, history dissolve others. In the meantime, it may be helpful to bring some concepts to bear on this problem so that the kaleidoscope may reveal patterns as well as bewildering changes.

II   Conscious and Unconscious

A "sense of identity" obviously has conscious aspects, such as the experience of an increased unity of the physical and mental, moral and sensual selves, and of a oneness in the way one experiences oneself and the way others seem to experience us. But this process *can* also be visible to others, for he who "knows where he is going and who is going with him" demonstrates an unmistakable, if not always easily definable, unity and radiance of appearance, physiognomic as well as postural. And yet, just when a person, to all appearances, seems to "find himself," he can also be said to be "losing himself" in new tasks and affiliations. He transcends identity-consciousness; and this is surely so in the early days of any revolution and was so in the case of the young of the Negro revolution who found themselves and, in fact, found their generation in the very decision to lose themselves (as well as all guaranty) in the intensity of the struggle. Here identity-consciousness is absorbed in actuality. There are vivid and moving descriptions of this state (none more so than in Howard Zinn's account of the early days of SNCC).[7] Afterwards, no doubt, these at first anonymous heroes faced redoubled self-consciousness, a kind of double-take on the stage of history. Conversely, Negroes who must now prove themselves in the sober light of a more integrated day cannot escape a self-consciousness which is apt to interfere with the happiness of finding or losing oneself: there are and there will be the martyrs of self-chosen or accidentally aggravated identity-consciousness, who must sacrifice the innocent unity of living to a revolutionary awareness.

But the core of that inner unification called identity is at best (as we

7. Howard Zinn, *SNCC, The New Abolitionists* (Boston, 1964).

psychoanalysts would say) *pre-conscious,* that is, accessible only to musings at moments of special awareness or to the revelatory experiences of intuitive writers. Mostly it is *unconscious* and even repressed, and hereby related to all those unconscious conflicts to which only psychoanalysis has found a methodical access. Thus the concept not only is difficult to work with; it also arouses deep-seated "resistances," which must be pointed out not in the hope of doing away with them (for they are an intricate and insurmountable part of the problem of human awareness), but in order to get acquainted with a shadow which will always follow us.

"Resistance" is a term from psychoanalytic treatment proper. There it indicates a "technical" problem met with in the therapeutic attempt to induce an individual to recognize the nature (or sometimes the very fact) of his illness, to describe his thoughts freely, and to accept the interpretations given to him. But the term has also been used in a wider sense in order to characterize a general resistance to psychoanalytic insights or, indeed, to "psychic reality" itself. However, the widespread acceptance of psychoanalysis (or of what Freud is understood to have said or is reported to have said) and the freer commission of sexual and verbal acts, the omission of which is now considered to be a symptom of repression, have not done away with a more fundamental aspect of "resistance," for it concerns the relation of man's awareness to his need for a free will, and thus something in the core of man's identity. This resistance can come to awareness in vague discomfort, often the more gnawing as it contradicts our professed interest in enlightenment:

1. If unconscious determinants should, indeed, prove operative in our very sense of self and in the very pathos of our values, does this not carry the matter of determination to a point where free will and moral choice would seem to be illusory?

2. If a man's individual identity is said to be linked to communal identities, are we not faced with another crypto-Marxism which makes man's very sense of destiny a blind function of the dialectics of history?

3. And if such unconscious determinants could, indeed, be demonstrated, is such awareness good for us?

Philosophers, no doubt, have answers to these questions, which recur in the reactions of the best-trained students when faced somewhat more systematically with insights which they otherwise devour eagerly in a non-systematic mixture of paperbacks.[8] But it must be clear that nobody can escape these questions which are really only part of wider trend in the

---

8. Not all doubt or discomfort regarding the conception of identity is to be seen as "resistance" by any means. Powerful methodological quandaries are inescapable. I would also share the reluctance to accept psychosocial identity as "all there is" to human identity. Psychosocial phenomena, however, are part of that engagement in a period of the life cycle and in a given historical era without which an unfolding of human potentials (including an eventual transcendence) seems unthinkable.

scrutiny of human motivation ranging from Darwin's discovery of our evolutionary animal ancestry and Marx's uncovery of class-bound behavior, to Freud's systematic exploration of the unconscious. The preoccupation with identity, therefore, may be seen not only as a symptom of "alienation," but also as a corrective trend in psychosocial evolution. It may be for this reason that revolutionary writers and writers from national and ethnic minority groups (like the Irish expatriates or our Negro and Jewish writers) have become the artistic spokesmen and prophets of identity confusion. Artistic creation, as pointed out, goes beyond complaint and exposure; it includes the moral decision that a certain painful identity-consciousness may have to be tolerated in order to provide the conscience of man with a critique of conditions, with the insight and with the conceptions necessary to heal himself of what most deeply divides and threatens him, namely, his division into what we will call *pseudo-species.*

In this new literature, pre-conscious processes are faced and unconscious ones symbolized in a way which often resembles the process of psycho-analysis; but the "case" is transcended by human revolt, the inner realignment by intense contact with historical actuality. And, in the end, are these writers not proclaiming also an essential superiority of identity-in-torment over those identities which feel as safe and remote as a suburban home?

What is at stake here is nothing less than the realization of the fact and the obligation of man's specieshood. Great religious leaders have attempted to break through the resistances against this awareness, but their churches have tended to join rather than shun the development which we have in mind here, namely, man's deepseated conviction that some providence has made his tribe and race or class, caste, or religion "naturally," superior to others. This seems to be part of a psychosocial evolution by which he has developed into *pseudo-species.* This fact is, of course, rooted in tribal psychology and based on all the evolutionary changes which brought about man. Among these is his prolonged childhood during which the newborn, "naturally" born to be the most "generalist" animal of all and adaptable to widely differing environments, becomes specialized as a member of a human group with its complex interplay of an "inner world" and an ethological environment. He becomes indoctrinated, then, with the conviction that his "species" alone was planned by an all-wise deity, created in a special cosmic event, and appointed by history to guard the only genuine version of humanity under the leadership of elect élites and leaders. "Pseudo" suggests pseudologia, a form of lying with at least transitory conviction; and, indeed, man's very progress has swept him along in a combination of developments in which it seems hard to bring to bear what rationality and humanity he can muster against illusions and prejudices no longer deserving of the name mythology. I mean, of course, that dangerous combination of technological specialization (including weaponry), moral righteousness, and what we may call the *territoriality of identity,* all of which make *hominem hominis lupum* far exceeding anything typical for wolves among wolves. For man is not only apt to lose all sense of species, but also to turn on another subgroup with a ferocity generally alien to the "social" animal world and, of course, with an increasing sophistication in all three—lethal weaponry, moral hypocrisy, and identity-panic. Sophistication, in fact, seems to escalate the problem just at the time when (and this would seem to be no coincidence) a more universal, a more inclusive human identity seems forcefully suggested by the very need for survival. National-socialist Germany is the most flagrant and all too recent manifestation of the murderous mass-pseudologia which can befall a modern nation.

While we all carry with us trends and tendencies which anchor our identities in some pseudo-species, we also feel in our bones that the Second World War has robbed such self-indulgence of all innocence, and that any threat of a third one would lead man's adaptive genius to its own defeat. But those who see what the "compact majority" continues to deny and to dissimulate must also attempt to understand that for man to realize his specieshood and to exchange a wider identity for his pseudo-species, means not only the creation of a new and shared technological universe, but also the out-growing of prejudices which have been essential to all (or almost all) identities in the past. For each *positive identity* is also defined by *negative* images (as we saw even in Freud's reference to the intellectual components of his identity), and we must now discuss the unpleasant fact that our god-given identities often live off the degradation of others.

III   Positive and Negative

As I restudied Freud's address, I remember a remark made recently by a warm-hearted and influential American Jew: "Some instinctive sense tells every Jewish mother that she must make her child study, that his intelligence is his pass to the future. Why does a Negro mother not care? Why does she not have the same instinctive sense?" This was a rhetorical question, of course; he wanted to know which of many possible answers I would give first. I suggested that, given American Negro history, the equivalent "instinctive sense" may have told the majority of Negro mothers to keep their children, and especially the gifted and the questioning ones, away from futile and dangerous competition, that is, for survival's sake to keep them in their place even if that place is defined by an indifferent and hateful "compact majority."

That the man said "mothers" immediately marks one of the problems we face in approaching Negro identity. The Jewish mothers he had in mind would expect to be backed up by their husbands or, in fact, to act in

their behalf; the Negro mothers would not. Negro mothers are apt to cultivate the "surrendered identity" forced on Negro men for generations. This,
so the literature would suggest, has reduced the Negro to a reflection of the
"negative" recognition which surrounded him like an endless recess of dis-
torting mirrors. How his positive identity has been undermined
systematically—first under the unspeakable system of slavery in North
America and then by the system of enslavement perpetuated in the rural
South and the urban North—has been extensively, carefully, and devastat-
ingly documented.

Here the concept of a negative identity may help to clarify three related
complications:

1. Every person's psychosocial identity contains a hierarchy of positive
and negative elements, the latter resulting from the fact that the growing
human being, throughout his childhood, is presented with evil prototypes
as well as with ideal ones (by reward and punishment, by parental example, and by the community's typology as revealed in wit and gossip, in tale
and story). These are, of course, culturally related: in the background
which gives prominence to intellectual achievement, some such negative
roles as the Schlemihl will not be wanting. The human being, in fact, is
warned *not* to become what he often had no intention of becoming so that
he can learn to anticipate what he must avoid. Thus, the positive identity
(far from being a static constellation of traits or roles) is always in conflict
with that past which is to be lived down and by that potential future which
is to be prevented.

2. The individual belonging to an oppressed and exploited minority,
which is aware of the dominant cultural ideals but prevented from emulating them, is apt to fuse the negative images held up to him by the dominant majority with his own negative identity. The reasons for this exploita-
bility (and temptation to exploit) lie in man's very evolution and
development as pseudo-species. There is ample evidence of "inferiority"
feelings and of morbid self-hate in all minority groups; and, no doubt, the
righteously and fiendishly efficient way in which the Negro slave in America was forced into and kept in conditions preventing in most the incentive
for independent ambition now continues to exert itself as a widespread and
deep-seated inhibition to utilize equality even where it is "granted."
Again, the literature abounds in descriptions of how the Negro, instead,
found escape into musical or spiritual worlds or expressed his rebellion in
compromises of behavior now viewed as mocking caricatures, such as obstinate meekness, exaggerated childlikeness, or superficial submissiveness.
And yet, is "the Negro" not often all too summarily and all too exclusively
discussed in such a way that his negative identity is defined *only* in terms
of his defensive adjustments to the dominant white majority? Do we (and
can we) know enough about the relationship of positive and negative ele-

ments *within* the Negro personality and *within* the Negro community? This alone would reveal how negative is negative and how positive, positive.

3. As yet least understood, however, is the fact that the oppressor has a vested interest in the negative identity of the oppressed because that negative identity is a projection of his own unconscious negative identity—a projection which, up to a point, makes him feel superior but also, in a brittle way, whole. The discussion of the pseudo-species may have clarified some of this. But a number of questions remain. One comes to wonder, for example, about the ways in which a majority, suddenly aware of a vital split in itself over the fact that it has caused a near-fatal split in a minority, may, in its sudden zeal to regain its moral position and to face the facts squarely, inadvertently tend to *confirm* the minority's negative image of itself and this in the very act of dwelling exclusively and even self-indulgently upon the majority's sins. A clinician may be forgiven for questioning the curative values of an excessive dose of moral zeal. I find, for example, even the designation "culturally deprived" somewhat ironic (although I admire much of the work done under this banner) because I am especially aware of the fact that the middle-class culture, of which the slum children are deprived, deprives some of the white children of experiences which might prevent much neurotic maladjustment. There is, in fact, an exquisite poetic justice in the historical fact that many white young people who feel deeply deprived *because* of their family's "culture" find an identity and a solidarity in living and working with those who are said to be deprived for lack of such culture. Such confrontation may lead to new mutual insights; and I have not, in my lifetime, heard anything approaching the immediacy of common human experience revealed in stories from today's South (and from yesterday's India).

In this connection we may also ask a question concerning the measurements used in diagnosing the Negro American's condition; and diagnosis, it must be remembered, defines the prognosis, and this not least because it contributes to the patient's self-awareness and attitude toward his suffering.

Our fellow panelist Thomas Pettigrew, in his admirable compilation *A Profile of the Negro American,* employs identity terms only in passing. He offers a wealth of solid and all the more shocking evidence of the disuse of the Negro American's intelligence and of the disorganization of his family life. If I choose from the examples reported by Pettigrew one of the most questionable and even amusing, it is in order to clarify the place of single testable *traits* in the whole *configuration* of an individual's development and of his people's history.

Pettigrew, following Burton and Whiting, discusses the problem that

> [Boys] from fatherless homes must painfully achieve a *masculine self-image* late in their childhood after having established an original self-image

on the basis of the only parental model they have had—their mother. Several studies point to the applicability of this *sex-identity problem* to lower-class Negro males.

He reports that

> Two objective test assessments of widely different groups—Alabama jail prisoners and Wisconsin working-class veterans with tuberculosis—found that Negro males scored higher than white males on a *measure of femininity*. . . . This measure is a part of the Minnesota Multiphasic Inventory (MMPI), a well-known psychological instrument that requires the respondent to judge the applicability to himself of over five hundred simple statements. Thus, Negroes in these samples generally agreed more often with such "feminine" choices, as *"I would like to be a singer"* and "I think that *I feel more intensely* that most people do." [9]

Pettigrew wisely puts "feminine" in quotation marks. We will assume that the M.M.P.I. is an "objective test assessment for widely different groups" including Alabama jail prisoners and patients on a tubercular ward, and that incidental test blemishes in the end all come-out-in-the-wash of statistics so that the over-all conclusions may point to significant differences between Negroes and whites and between indices of femininity and of masculinity. That such assessment singles out as "feminine" the wish to be a singer and "feeling more intensely than most people do," may be a negligible detail. And yet, this detail suggests that the choice of test items and the generalizations drawn from them may say at least as much about the test and the testers as about the subjects tested. To "want to be a singer" or "to feel intensely" seems to be something only a man with feminine traits would acknowledge in that majority of respondents on whom the test was first developed and standardized. But why, one wonders, should a lower-class Negro locked up in jail or in a tuberculosis ward not admit to a wish to be a man like Paul Robeson or Harry Belafonte, and also that he feels more intensely (if, indeed, he knows what this means) than the chilly business-like whites around him? To be a singer and to feel intensely may be facets of a masculine ideal gladly admitted if you grew up in Alabama (or, for that matter, in Napoli), whereas it would be a blemish to be denied in a majority having adjusted to other masculine ideals. In fact, in Alabama and in Naples an emphasis on artistic self-expression and intense feeling may be close to the core of your positive identity—so close that the loss or devaluation of such emphasis by way of "integration" may make you a drifter on the murky sea of adjustable "roles." In the case of the compact white majority, the denial of "intense feelings" may, in turn, be part of a white identity problem which contributes to the prejudiced rejection of the Negro's potential or periodical intensity. Tests harboring similar distinc-

9. Thomas F. Pettigrew, *A Profile of the Negro American* (Princeton, N. J., 1964), p. 19. (Italics added.)

tions may be offering "objective" evidence of racial differences, but may also be symptomatic of them. If this is totally overlooked, and this is my main point, the test will only emphasize, and the tester will only report, and the reader of the report (white or Negro) will only perceive the distance between the Negro's "disintegrated" self-imagery and what is assumed to be the white's "integrated" one.

As Pettigrew (in another connection) says starkly, putting himself in the shoes of a Negro child to be tested:

> . . . After all, an intelligence test is a middle-class white man's instrument; it is a device whites use to prove their capacities and get ahead in the white world. Achieving a high test score does not have the same meaning for a lower-status Negro child, and it may even carry a definite connotation of personal threat. In this sense, scoring low on intelligence measures may for some talented Negro children be a rational response to perceived danger [10]

The whole *test-event* thus itself underlies a certain historical and social relativity to be clarified in each case in terms of the actual identity configuration. By the same token, it is by no means certain that the individual undergoing such a procedure will be the same person when he escapes the predicament of the test procedure and joins, say, his peers on the playground or on a street corner. Thus, a "profile" of the Negro American made up of different methods under different conditions may offer decisively different configurations of "traits." This does not make one procedure wrong and the other right, but it makes both (and more) essential in the establishment of criteria for an existing identity configuration. On the other hand, it is all too often taken for granted that the *investigator* (and his identity conflicts) invisibly blends into his method even when he is a representative of a highly (and maybe defensively) verbal subgroup of whites and is perceived as such by subjects who are near-illiterate or come from an illiterate background.

In this connection, I would like to refer to Kenneth Clark's moving characterization of the sexual life of the "marginal young people in the ghetto." As a responsible father-figure, he knows he must not condone what he nevertheless must also defend against deadly stereotypes.

> Illegitimacy in the ghetto cannot be understood or dealt with in terms of punitive hostility, as in the suggestion that unwed mothers be denied welfare if illegitimacy is repeated. Such approaches obscure, with empty and at times hypocritical moralizing, the desperate yearning of the young for acceptance and identity, the need to be meaningful to someone else even for a moment without implication of a pledge of undying fealty and foreverness. . . . To expose oneself further to the chances of failure in a

10. *Ibid.,* p. 115.

sustained and faithful relationship is too large to risk. The *intrinsic value of the relationship* is the only value because there can be no other.[11]

This places a legal or moral item into its "actual" context—a context which always also reveals something about those who would judge and stereotype rather than understand: for is not the *intrinsic value of the relationship* exactly that item (hard to define, hard to test, and legally irrelevant) which may be lost in some more fortunate youths who suffer under a bewildering and driving pluralism of values? [12]

IV   Past and Future

Turning now to the new young Negroes: "My God," a Negro woman student exclaimed the other day in a small meeting, "what am I supposed to be integrated *out of?* I laugh like my grandmother—and I would rather die than not laugh like that." There was a silence in which you could hear the stereotypes click; for even laughter had now joined those aspects of Negro culture and Negro personality which have become suspect as the marks of submission and fatalism, delusion and escape. But the young girl did not give in with some such mechanical apology as "by which I do not mean, of course . . ." and the silence was pregnant with that immediacy of joint experience which characterizes moments when an identity conflict becomes palpable. It was followed by laughter—embarrassed, amused, defiant.

To me, the young woman had expressed one of the anxieties attending a rapid reconstitution of identity elements: "supposed to" reflects a sense of losing the active, the choosing role which is of the essence in a sense of identity as a continuity of the living past and the anticipated future. I have indicated that single items of behavior or imagery can change their quality within new identity configurations; and yet these same indices once represented an integration as well as an integrity of Negro life—"such as it was," to be sure, but the only existing inner integration for which the Negro is now "supposed to" exchange an unsure outer integration. Desegregation, compensation, balance, re-conciliation—do they all sometimes seem to save the Negro at the cost of an absorption which he is not sure

11. Kenneth B. Clark, *op. cit.,* p. 73. (Italics added.)
12. Under the tense conditions of a sudden awareness of facts long suppressed and distorted, new stereotypes are apt to enter the imagery of the most thoughtful. In *Crisis in Black and White,* C. E. Silberman discusses S. M. Elkin's basic book *Slavery,* and half-quoting and half-editorializing, uses the stereotype "childlike" as a common denominator of Negro personality and the transient regressions of inmates in concentration camps. Along with truly childish qualities, such as silliness, we find fawning, servile, dishonest, mendacious, egotistic, and thievish activities all summed up under "this childlike behavior." (p. 76). Here childlike replaces childish or regressed, as feminine often replaces effeminate, which is both misleading and destructive of the image of the genuine article.

will leave much of himself left? Thus the "revolution" poses an "identity crisis" in more than one way; the Negro writer's "complicated assertions and denials of identity" (to use Ellison's words) have simpler antecedents, not less tragic for their simplicity.

For identity development has its time, or rather two kinds of time: a *developmental stage* in the life of the individual, and a *period* in history. There is, then, also a complementarity of life-history and history. Unless provoked prematurely and disastrously (and the biographies of sensitive Negro writers as well as direct observations of Negro children attest to such tragic prematurity) psychosocial identity is not feasible before the beginning, even as it is not dispensable after the end of *adolescence,* when the body, now fully grown, grows together into an individual appearance; when sexuality, matured, seeks partners in sensual play and, sooner or later, in parenthood; when the mind, fully developed, can begin to envisage a career for the individual within a historical perspective—all idiosyncratic developments which must fuse with each other in a new sense of sameness and continuity. But the increasing irreversibility of all choices (whether all too open or foreclosed) leads to what we call the *identity crisis* which here does not mean a *fatal turn* but rather (as in drama and in medicine) an *inescapable turning point* for better *or* for worse. "Better" here means a confluence of the constructive energies of individual and society, which contributed to physical grace, sexual spontaneity, mental alertness, emotional directness, and social "actualness." "Worse" means prolonged *identity confusion* in the young individual. Here it must be emphasized—for this is the point at which the psychosexual theories of psychoanalysis fuse with the psychosocial ones—that identity formation is decisive for the integration of sexuality (whether the cultural trend is toward repression or expression) and for the constructive use of aggression. But the crisis of youth is also the crisis of a generation and of the ideological soundness of its society. (There is also a complementarity of identity and ideology.) The crisis is least marked and least "noisy" in that segment of youth which in a given era is able to invest its fidelity [13] in an ideological trend associated with a new technical and economic expansion, (such as mercantilism, colonialism, industrialization). For here new types and roles of competence emerge. Today this includes the young people in all countries and in all classes who can fit into and take active charge of technical and scientific development, learning thereby to identify with a lifestyle of testing, inventing, and producing. Youth which is eager for such experience but unable to find access to it will feel estranged from society, upset in its sexuality, and unable to apply its aggression constructively. It may be that today much of Negro Youth as well as an artistic-humanistic

13. See Erik H. Erikson, "Youth: Fidelity and Diversity," *Youth: Change and Challenge* (New York, 1963), pp. 1–23.

section of White Youth feel disadvantaged and, therefore, come to develop a certain solidarity in regard to "the crisis" or "the revolution": for young people in privileged middle-class homes as well as in underprivileged Negro homes may miss that sameness and continuity throughout development which makes a grandmother's warmth and a fervent aspiration part of an identical world. One may go further and say that this whole segment of American youth is attempting to develop its own ideology and its own rites of confirmation by following the official call to the external frontiers of the American way of life (Peace Corps), by going to the internal ones (deep South), or by attempting in colleges (California) to fill an obvious void in the traditional balance of the American way of life—a void caused by a dearth of that realism, solidarity, and ideology which welds together a functioning radical opposition.

We will come back to this point. Here we may suggest that identity also contains a complementarity of past and future both in the individual and in society: it links the actuality of a living past with that of a promising future. This formulation excludes, I hope, any romanticizing of the past or any salesmanship in the creation of future "postures."

In regard to "the revolution" and its gains, one can only postulate that the unblinking realism and ruthless de-masking of much of the present literature supports a new sense of toughness in the "face of reality." It fits this spirit that Pettigrew's "Profile," for example, fails to list such at any rate untestable items as (in alphabetical order) companionability, humor, motherhood, music, sensuality, spirituality, sports, and so forth. They all are suspect, I know, as traits of an accommodation romanticized by whites. But this makes presently available "profiles" really the correction of caricatures, rather than attempts at even a sketch of a portrait. But can a new or renewed identity emerge from corrected caricatures? One thinks of all those who are unable to derive identity gains from the "acceptance of reality" at its worst (as the writers do and the researchers) and to whom a debunking of all older configurations *may* become a further *confirmation* [14] of worthlessness and helplessness.

It is in this context also that I must question the fact that in many an index the Negro father appears *only* under the heading of "absence." Again, the relationship between family disintegration, father-absence, and all kinds of social and psychiatric pathology is overwhelming. "Father absence" does belong in every index and in the agenda of national concern. But as the *only* item related to fatherhood *or* motherhood does it not do grave injustice to the presence of many, many mothers, at at least some of the fathers? Whatever the historical, sociological, or legal interpretation of

14. Erik H. Erikson and Kai T. Erikson, "The Confirmation of the Delinquent," in Hendrik M. Ruitenbeek (ed.), *The Condition of Modern Man in Society* (New York, 1962).

the Negro mother's (and grandmother's) saving presence in the whole half-circle of plantation culture from Venezuela through the Caribbean into our South, is it an item to be omitted from the agenda of the traditional Negro identity? Can Negro culture afford to have the "strong mother" stereotyped as a liability? For a person's (and a people's) identity begins in the rituals of infancy, when mothers make it clear with many pre-literate means that to be born is good and that a child (let the bad world call it colored or list it as illegitimate) is deserving of warmth. As I pointed out in the *Dædalus* issue on Youth, these mothers have put an indelible mark on "Negro Culture" and what they accomplished should be one of the proudest chapters in cultural history.

The systematic exploitation of the Negro male as a domestic animal and the denial to him of the status of responsible fatherhood are, on the other hand, two of the most shameful chapters in the history of this Christian nation. For an imbalance of mother-and-father presence is never good, and becomes increasingly bad as the child grows older; for then the trust in the world established in infancy may be all the more disappointed. Under urban and industrial conditions it may, indeed, become the gravest factor in personality disorganization. But, again, the "disorganization" of the Negro family must not be measured solely by its distance from the white or Negro middle-class family with its one-family housing and legal and religious legitimizations. Disintegration must be measured and understood also as a distortion of the *traditional* if often unofficial *Negro family pattern*. The traditional wisdom of the mothers will be needed as will the help of the Negro men who (in spite of such circumstances) actually did become fathers in the full sense.

In the meantime, the problem of the function of both parents, each strong in his or her way, and both benignly present in the home when needed most is a problem facing the family in any industrial society on a universal scale. The whole great society must develop ways to provide equality of opportunity in employment and yet also differential ways of permitting mothers and fathers to attend to their duties toward their children. The maternal-paternal dimension may well also serve to clarify the fact that each stage of development needs its own optimum environment, and that to find a balance between maternal and paternal strength means to assign to each a period of dominance in the children's life. The mother's period is the earliest and, therefore, the most basic. There is a deep relation between the first "identity" experienced in the early sensual and sensory exchanges with the mother(s)—the first re-cognition—and that final integration in adolescence when all earlier identifications are assembled and the young person meets his society and his historical era.

V   Total and Whole

In his book *Who Speaks for the Negro?* R. P. Warren records another exclamation by a young woman student:

> . . . The auditorium had been packed—mostly Negroes, but with a scattering of white people. A young girl with pale skin, dressed like any coed anywhere, in the clothes for a public occasion, is on the rostrum. She is leaning forward a little on her high heels, speaking with a peculiar vibrance in a strange irregular rhythm, out of some inner excitement, some furious, taut élan, saying: "—and I tell you I have discovered a great truth. I have discovered a great joy. I have discovered that I am black. I am black! You out there—oh, yes, you may have black faces, but your hearts are white, your minds are white, you have been whitewashed!"

Warren reports a white woman's reaction to this outburst and surmises that if this woman

> at that moment heard any words in her head, they were most likely the echo of the words of Malcolm X: "White devils!" And if she saw any face, it must have been the long face of Malcolm X grinning with sardonic certitude.

I think we understand this fear. She has witnessed what I will call a "totalistic" re-arrangement of images which is, indeed, basic to some of the ideological movements of modern history. By totalism I mean an inner regrouping of imagery, almost a *negative conversion,* by which erstwhile negative identity elements become totally dominant, making out of erstwhile positive elements a combination to be excluded totally.[15] This, however, can happen in a transitory way in many young people of all colors and classes who rebel and join, wander off or isolate themselves; it can subside with the developmental storm or lead to an unexpected commitment. Depending on historical and social conditions, the process has its malignant potentials, as exemplified in "confirmed" pervert-delinquent or bizarre-extremist states of mind and forms of behavior.

The chill which this process can give us in its political implicaions refers back to our sense of historical shock when post-Versailles German youth, once so sensitive to foreign critique, but then on the rebound from a love of Kultur which promised no realistic identity, fell for the Nazi transvaluation of civilized values. The transitory Nazi identity, based on a *totalism* marked by the radical *exclusion* of foreign otherness, failed to integrate historically given identity elements, reaching instead for a pseudologic perversion of history. Obviously both radical segregationism, in its re-

15. See Robert J. Lifton, *Thought Reform and the Psychology of Totalism* (New York, 1961).

course to an adjusted Bible, and Black Muslimism are the counterparts of such a phenomenon in this country. In the person of Malcolm X the *specific rage* which is aroused wherever identity development loses the promise of a traditionally assured wholeness, was demonstrated theatrically. Such latent rage (by no means always unjustified) is easily exploited by fanatic and psychopathic leaders: it can explode in the arbitrary destructiveness of mobs; and it can in a more repressed form serve the efficient violence of organized machines of destruction. Yet, the Black Muslims, too, were able to call on some of the best potentials of the individuals who felt "included."

This country as a whole, however, is not hospitable to such totalistic turns, and the inability or, indeed, unwillingness of youth in revolt to come to systematic ideological conclusions is in itself an important historical fact. The temporary degeneration of the Free Speech Movement in California into a revolt of dirty words was probably representative of the intrusion of an impotent totalism into a promising radicalism. This reluctance to be regimented in the service of a political ideology, however, can make the latent violence in our disadvantaged youth that much more destructive to personal unity and, sporadically, to "law and order." But note also, that the rate of crime and of delinquency in some Southern counties was reported to have dropped sharply when the Negro population became involved in social protest.

The alternative to an exclusive totalism is the wholeness of a *more inclusive identity*. This leads to another question: If the Negro American wants to "find" that wider identity which will permit him to be self-certain as a Negro (or a descendant of Negroes) *and* integrated as an American, what joint *historical actuality* can he count on? For we must know that when all the *objective realities* are classified and investigated, and all the studies assessed, the question remains: what are the *historical actualities* with which we can work?

Returning once more to the individual, I can now register a certain impatience with the faddish equation of the term identity with the question "Who am I?" This question nobody would ask himself except in a more or less transient morbid state, in a creative self-confrontation, or in an adolescent state sometimes combining both; wherefore on occasion I find myself asking a student who claims that he is in an "identity-crisis," whether he is complaining or boasting. For most, the pertinent question really is "What do I want to make of myself—and—what do I have to work with?" Here, the awareness of inner motivations is, at best, useful in keeping the future from being swamped by infantile wishes and adolescent defenses. Beyond that, only a restored or better trained sense of historical actuality can lead to a deployment of those energies which both activate and are activated by potential developments. How potential developments become historical fact is demonstrated by the way in which "culturally deprived" Negro children meet a sudden historical demand with surprising dignity and fortitude. In an unpublished manuscript, Robert Coles, who has made significant contributions to this problem, presents psychiatric data which (according to our theories) would have predicted for a lone Negro boy an inevitable and excusable failure in his task of personifying (with one other child) the desegregation of a whole school. But he did stand up to it unforgettably—and he is on his way.

In all parts of the world the struggle now is for anticipatory and *more inclusive identities:* what has been a driving force in revolutions and reformations, in the founding of churches and in the building of empires has become a contemporaneous world-wide competition. Revolutionary doctrines promise the new identity of peasant-and-worker to the youth of countries which must overcome their tribal, feudal, or colonial past; new nations attempt to absorb regions; new markets, nations; and world space is extended to include outer space as the proper locale for a universal technological identity.

At this point, we are beyond the question (and Gandhi did much to teach this to the British) of how a remorseful or scared colonialist may dispense corrective welfare in order to appease the need for a wider identity. The problem is rather how he includes himself in the wider pattern. For a more inclusive identity is a development by which two groups who previously had come to depend on each other's negative identities (by living in a traditional situation of mutual enmity or in a symbiotic accommodation to one-sided exploitation) join their identities in such a way that new potentials are activated in both.

VI Exclusive and Inclusive

What wider identities are competing for the Negro American's commitment? Some, it seems, are too wide to be "actual," some too narrow. As too wide I would characterize the identity of a "human being" bestowed, according to a strange modern habit of a latter-day humanistic narcissism, by humans to humans (patients, women, Negroes, and so on). While this at times represents genuine transcendence of the pseudo-species mentality, it often also implies that the speaker, having undergone some revelatory hardships, is in a position to grant membership in humanity to others. But it also tends to take all specificity out of "human" relations; for man meets man always in categories (be they adult and child, man and woman, employer and employee, leader and follower, majority and minority) and "human inter-relations" can truly be only the expression of divided function and the concrete overcoming of the specific ambivalence inherent in them. I would not be surprised to find that our Negro colleagues and friends often sense a residue of species-wide colonialism in our vague humanity. In contrast, the concrete work on the achievement of minimum rights for the *Negro American citizen* has created moments of the most intense sharing of the human condition.

Probably the most inclusive and the most absorbing identity potential in the world today is that of *technical skill*. This is what Lenin meant when he advocated that first of all the mushik be put on a tractor. True, he meant: as a preparation for the identity of a class-conscious proletarian. But it has come to mean more today, namely, the participation in an area of activity and experience which (for better or for worse) verifies modern man as a worker and planner. It is one thing to exclude oneself from such verification because one has proven oneself gifted in other respects and able to draw on the traditional verification provided by Humanism or the Enlightenment—at least sufficiently so that alienation from the present, too, adds up to some reasonably comfortable "human identity." It is quite another to be excluded from it by literacy requirements which prevent the proof that one is mechanically gifted or the use of the gift after such proof is given. Israel, a small country with a genius for renewing identities, has shown (for example, in the use of its army as an educational institution) that illiteracy can be corrected in the process of putting people where they feel they are needed and are needed.

The *"African identity"* is a strong contender for a wider identity, as Harold Isaacs has shown. It offers a highly actual setting for the solidarity of black skin color, and probably also provides the American Negro with an equivalent of what all other Americans could boast about or disavow: an (if ever so remote) homeland. However, the American Negro's mode of separation from Africa robbed him of the identity element *"immigrant."* There seems to be a question also whether to Africans a Negro American is more black or more American, and whether the Negro American, in actual contacts with Africans, wants to be more American or more Negro. The Black Muslims, at any rate, seem to have called themselves at first Asiatics, to emphasize the wider mystical unity of Muslimism.

The great *middle class* as the provider of an identity of consumers (for whom, indeed, Pettigrew's prescription of "dollars and dignity" seems to be most fitting) has been discussed in its limitations by many, but by none more eloquently than by the President in his Howard University speech. The middle-class identity (a class pre-occupied with matters of real estate and of consumption, of status and of posture) will include more and more of the highly gifted and the fortunate, but, if it does not yield to the wider identity of the Negro American, it obviously creates new barriers between these few and the mass of Negroes, whose distance from white competition is thereby only increased. "Work and dignity" may be a more apt slogan, provided that work dignifies by providing a "living" dollar as well as a challenge to competence, for without both "opportunity" is slavery perpetuated.

But here as everywhere the question of the Negro American's identity imperceptibly shades into the question of what *the* American wants to make of himself in the technology of the future. In this sense, the greatest gain all around (and one now to be consolidated) may be what the doctors at Howard University have discussed as *pro-social action* on the part of Negroes. I mean the fact that their protest, pervaded by nonviolent spirit and yet clearly defying local law and custom, has been accepted by much of the nation as American, and that the President himself would echo the slogan "we shall overcome," thus helping to align "pro-social" action with American action. The judiciary and legislative levels, too, have attempted to absorb "the revolution" on a grand scale. But absorption can be defensive and merely adjustive, or it can be adaptive and creative; this must as yet be seen.

In the meantime, the success of pro-social action should not altogether obscure an *anti-social* identity element relevantly recounted in the autobiographies of Negro Americans. I mean the tragic sacrifice of youth designated as delinquent and criminal. They, no doubt, often defended whatever identity elements were available to them by revolting in the only way open to them—a way of vicious danger, and yet often of self-respect and solidarity. Like the outcast heroes of the American frontier, some anti-social types among the Negroes are not expendable from the history of their people—not yet.

Our genuinely humanist youth, however, will continue to extend a *religious identity element* into race-relations: for future over-all issues of identity will include the balance within man of technological strivings and ethical and ultimate concerns. I believe (but you must not tell them for they suspect such words) that the emergence of those youths who stepped from utter anonymity right into our national affairs does contain a new and *wider religious element* embracing nothing less than the promise of a mankind freer of the attitudes of a pseudo-species: that utopia of universality proclaimed as the most worthy goal by all world religions and yet always entombed in new empires of dogma which turned into or allied themselves with new pseudo-species. The churches, too, have come to the insight that earthly prejudices—fanatical or outspoken, hiding in indifference, or latent and repressed—feed into that deadly combination which now makes man "the lethal factor" in the universe, for as pointed out it ties limitless technical ambition (including the supremacy of weapons of annihilation) and the hypocrisy of outworn moralistic dogma to the territoriality of mutually exclusive identities. The counter force, *nonviolence,* may always be a compelling and creative actuality only at critical moments, and only for "the salt of the earth." But Gandhi took the first steps toward a worldwide application to politics of principles once purely religious.

As far as the world-wide frontier of *post-colonial* and *colored identities* is concerned, it is hard to predict their fate in the clash of new national interests in Africa and Asia. As of now, however, one cannot ignore the possible implications of American action in Vietnam for a world-wide identification of colored people with the naked heroism of the Vietcong revolutionaries. The very demand that North Vietnam give in (and even if it were nearly on her own terms) to a super-organized assault by a superfluity of lethal weapons may simply be too reminiscent of the function of firepower in colonial expansion in general; of police power in particular; and of a certain (implicitly contemptuous) attitude which assumes that "natives" will give in to pressures to which the master-races would consider themselves impervious (*vide* the British in the Blitz). It must be obvious that differences of opinion in this country in regard to American military involvement in Asia are not merely a matter of the faulty reading of facts or of lack of moral stamina on one side or the other, but also a massive identity conflict. Intrinsic to the dominant political-technological nucleus of an American identity is the expectation that such power as can now be unleashed can be used to advantage in limited employment, and has built-in safeguards against an unthinkable conflagration. But there will be urgent voices abroad and sincere protest at home expressing the perplexity of those who perceive only one active moral frontier of equality and of peace extending from the center of the daily life of America to the peripheries of its foreign concerns. Here the Negro American shares the fate of a new and wider American dilemma.

I have now listed a few of the emerging "wider" identity elements in order to introduce queries which other members of the symposium are better equipped to answer. Such listing can only lead to one tentative impression, namely, that none of these alternatives offers to the American Negro a nucleus for a total realignment, and that all of them must find their place in a new constellation, the nucleus of which is already clearly suggested by the two words Negro and American.

Concluding Remark

As used in the foregoing, the term identity has betrayed its clinical origin in the study of individual disturbances and of social ills. But even where applied to the assessment of a social problem it remains clinical in methodology, that is, it can be used only to focus the thinking of a "staff." For the consideration of identity problems calls for the "taking of history," the localization and the diagnostic assessment of disintegration, the testing of intact resources, the approximate prognosis, and the weighing of possible action—each based on specialties of approach and often of temperament. In addition to all this, a certain intuitive insight based on experience *and* on conviction is indispensable in the assessment of *verifiable reality* and of *modifiable actuality.* On the way some theory may help; but a concept should be retained only as long as it brings some preliminary order into otherwise baffling phenomena.[16]

16. Attempts at transverting clinical concepts into quantifiable items subject to experimental verification are always undertaken at the risk of the experimenter.

ALAN PATON

As Blind as Samson Was

Alan Paton's *Cry, the Beloved Country* and *Too Late the Phalarope* are moving and sensitive studies of his native South Africa. This essay tries to show the sources and consequences of one kind of race awareness, *apartheid,* in one country of the world. Paton's work should be compared with Jacobson's essay in Part 1.

IN THIS ARTICLE I am attempting to depict the white South African who unreservedly supports apartheid, his life, his beliefs, his behavior, his thoughts of the future. It is written under the shadow of the terrible happenings at Sharpeville, Transvaal, where more than seventy African demonstrators were shot dead by the police, and of the turbulence that has followed—a tragic series of events that has been the direct consequence of the apartheid legislation known as the Pass Laws. For this tragedy the Afrikaner Nationalist blames agitators, Communists, liberals, the English press and the savagery of the African people. He blames anybody, everybody, but himself. If he does not change, and quickly, the catastrophic end is near.

I distinguish in this article between the Afrikaner and the Afrikaner Nationalist; but I do not intend this to conceal the truth that the great majority of Afrikaners are Nationalists who support apartheid. Nor do I wish to conceal the truth that most English-speaking South Africans support apartheid in one form or another, and that therefore they are unable to offer South Africa any alternative. If the white voter wants apartheid, who can give it to him better than the Afrikaner Nationalist?

I ought to be able to write about the Afrikaner Nationalist and his *apartheid* policies. He is my boss. He tells me where I may live, to what parts of South Africa I may travel, to what schools and universities my children may go, with what kind of person I may eat or drink in any public place.

He tells me what books I may not keep in my house, and what kind of people may not live with me; he tells me what kind of persons I may not marry, and what kind of children I may not adopt. He is now considering what kind of beaches I may or may not visit, what picnic places I may or may not frequent; and he may soon tell me, although he has so far shrunk from it, what kind of guests I may have in my home.

If I should break any of his laws by way of protest, I am subject to a fine of £300 ($840) or imprisonment for three years or a thrashing of ten lashes, or any two of these (though I personally would not be lashed, having reached the age of 50). If I should incite others to break these laws by way of protest, I am subject to a fine of £500 ($1,400) or imprisonment for five years or a thrashing of ten lashes, or any two of these.

So long as I do not incite, however, I can still write freely and publish freely, though few of us think this liberty will last. However any writing which is critical of the Government and of *apartheid* is frowned upon, especially if it is published abroad. The Afrikaner Nationalist regards it as treachery to South Africa, and by South Africa he means, simply and unequivocally, the South Africa of which he is the boss. He knows no other.

The extent of his control over me is disguised because he lets me vote; he lets me, if I wish and am able to, send one of my own group, the one-million white, English-speaking group, to Parliament. But his control over other South Africans is absolute. He allows the one and a half million "colored" * people to have only four white representatives in Parliament, though his own Nationalist group of one and a half million has more than a hundred.† But, beginning in June 1960, he will not allow any representation in Parliament for the ten million Africans. He argues that Africans have their own territories, and there they may have their own self-government under tribal authority. And that is true, too, just as it is true that any representative of tribal authority would lose his job in five minutes if he failed to carry out *apartheid* policy.

The Indian group of half a million also has no representation in Parliament. If the Indians were given communal representation, they would probably abstain from using it on a spectacular scale. Quite apart from that, the Afrikaner Nationalist does not want Indian representatives in Parliament. He just cannot forgive the Indians for having come here, or the British sugar farmers for having brought them.

This Afrikaner ruler of mine is, to all outward appearances, made of steel. He goes on his way in the face of mounting world disapproval. Only three governments in the world think that *apartheid* is his own business. All the new African nations have condemned it. At this very moment, ordinary consumers in many Western countries are boycotting South African

* By "Colored" people we mean those of mixed white and other blood. The Africans form a separate group.
† There are two million Afrikaners, and it is estimated that at least three-quarters of them are Afrikaner Nationalists. By various electoral devices, not all due to the Nationalists, this Nationalist group controls two-thirds of the seats in the lower house of Parliament and 86 per cent of the seats in the Senate.

goods. *Apartheid* is, without rival, the best known, the most hated, of all the national policies of the world. Yet the Nationalist goes on. He shows no signs of trimming his sails.

Why does he behave like this? What sort of man is he?

What does the Afrikaner Nationalist believe? He believes that God made separate peoples, and that He wants them to stay separate. He often blames visiting sailors for the existence of a million and a half colored people. But we never had that many visiting sailors. In any case, white men still break the fierce Immorality Act. Hardly a day passes but that some white man—some white man's family—is ruined because he has been caught breaking this iron law.

The Afrikaner Nationalist believes that God sent the Afrikaner to Africa, and gave him a civilizing mission. The great Voortrekker Monument at Pretoria—so coldly regarded by all non-Nationalists—commemorates the triumph of civilization over barbarism.

The Afrikaner Nationalist believes that God has called him to guide and control the destinies of all the people of southern Africa. He will make the laws and others will obey them. Nevertheless, he wants all the other groups in the country to develop harmoniously along their own lines. There is, however, one condition. All must accept *apartheid* as the rule of life.

The Afrikaner Nationalist has an exalted view of the state. Afrikaner churchmen regard with distaste those Christians who speak of the possibility of disobedience to the state. They regard it as lamentable to think of God and the state as in opposition. God is over the state, and the state is, by divine appointment, over man. Our Prime Minister, Dr. Hendrik Verwoerd, has publicly stated his belief that it is by God's will he rules.

The Afrikaner Nationalist has, therefore, an exaggerated view of what can be done by law. He thinks a new heaven and a new earth can be built by law, and by a new earth he means an earth where racial mixture is forbidden. He does not hesitate to use his power to crush any person who stands in his way, and he does not think this improper, for his authority is derived from God.

Men being human, fierce beliefs are seldom held in purity. These certainly are not. Afrikaner Nationalists are not just people doing God's will. Being human, their moral aspirations are remarkably compatible with their human wishes. They like to be boss. In the past, they liked to be boss because it brought great material advantages. For the same reason, they want to stay boss, but now is added a more terrible incentive—the fear that if they don't stay boss, Africa will spew them out.

It doesn't help—yet—to talk to a Nationalist about sharing power; sharing power means the same to him as losing it. He thinks in racial groups, he thinks in terms of racial power; that is his whole philosophy and politics. To him, the sharing of power means death.

In a way, he is a tragic figure. He is the African who is afraid of Africa. He is the African who never identified himself with Africa. If Africa ever rejects him, it will be because he rejected Africa.

This is doubly tragic because he actually called himself the "Afrikaner," the "man of Africa." He never called himself a "European," as did almost all other white people in Africa. But today he is reminding Europe that he is the sole bastion of European civilization in Africa.

He even refuses to grant the black African the use of the word "African." The black African used to be a "kaffir," today he is a "native" or a "Bantu." But he, like the Afrikaner, wants to be called a "man of Africa."

Even the majority of the English-language newspapers refuse to use the word "African"; they always refer to "natives." They do this partly because our rulers don't like the word "African," partly because the newspapers don't like it themselves. The word "native" sounds calm and peaceful, and conjures up a picture of dusky belles in tropical glades; the word "African" is masculine and vast and continental and a bit frightening.

Apartheid is changing in character. It had to, because of the pressure of the outside world. A few years ago, *apartheid* was simply and plainly being boss. Our late Prime Minister, Mr. J. G. Strijdom, always called it by its simple Afrikaans name, *baasskap,* which means "boss-ship." But Dr. Verwoerd calls it "separate development."

In other words, *apartheid* is the way to give everyone a chance; one uses *baasskap* to separate utterly every white group from every non-white group, in trains, buses, cinemas, restaurants, offices, factories, residential areas, schools, universities; and even to separate white English children from white Afrikaner children in the schools; even to separate black Zulu from black Mosutho and black Xhosa in schools and urban townships.

When people are properly separated, friction will cease; that is the great theory. Black people will not be humiliated by white power; white people will not be terrified by black power, and will therefore act more justly. Each group will develop its separate institutions. There will be peace and cooperation, whereas now there is only fear and discord.

Let us recognize honestly that there are idealistic Afrikaner Nationalists who have turned with relief to the goal of "separate development." It is something positive to work toward. It is a goal infinitely more virtuous than that of *baasskap*.

Yet let us recognize also that it is a fantasy. That veteran Afrikaner theologian, Professor B. B. Keet, calls it a pipe dream. And so it is, not only because it is a fantasy, but because one seeks refuge in the pipe when reality is too hard for one. You can argue with an idealistic Nationalist, and almost get him to the point of seeing that "separate development" is a dream, and that for better or for worse we all have a common destiny, and he will grow more and more cornered, until he says with desperate intensity, he whose goal and end and passion is his people's survival, "We would rather die."

And will he die? And who will die with him? These are the questions I am pondering.

Of all the racial groups in the world, the Afrikaner Nationalist group is the most closed to others, the most turned-in upon itself, the most powerful in group opinion. It is willing to absorb any white person, but only on one condition—namely, that the Nationalist doctrines—above all, *apartheid*—are accepted. It does not readily accept Jews, Roman Catholics, or Freemasons; it rejects absolutely liberals, internationalists, universalists, integrationists and any person of color. It ostracizes any Afrikaner who has deviated. Therefore, it is regarded coldly by almost 90 per cent of the people of South Africa. And, God help us, it is hated by many.

But its isolation is more terrible than that, for its doctrines are hated by the overwhelming majority of the people of the earth. Money is poured out like water to prove to the world that *apartheid* is noble, but no one believes, except in sad places like Algeria, Mississippi and Notting Hill. Many Nationalists hate to travel abroad; they would rather travel in the Rhodesias, Kenya, Mozambique, the Congo. But each year their own continent grows more and more closed to them.

The Nationalist does not like this isolation, but he seems powerless to do anything about it. He would like world approval—who would not?—but the world seems to be demanding his very soul. So he stands with his back to the wall.

There is one thing about him that I am totally unable to comprehend, and that is that he does not appear to see the havoc he inflicts on others in his headlong journey to a goal that isn't there.

A colored man commits suicide because he is ordered to move out of his house, not to make room for a bridge or a highway, but because of his color. A white man commits suicide because he cannot face prosecution under the Immorality Act. A white family goes to Europe because otherwise they could not keep their adopted colored child. A white wife and her children flee from the husband and father who has been declared to be colored, but, bitterest of ironies, the fleeing children are now colored, too. An African student wins a fine scholarship overseas but is not allowed to go; sometimes, not always, it is because he is known to be against *apartheid*.

So it goes on and on and on, until the heart could break. But the Nationalist's heart doesn't break. Why can't he see what he is doing? Or does he just not care! And if he doesn't care, can't he see how it looks to the outside world?

Like many others, I cannot comprehend it at all. I can only suppose that if one is a Nationalist, collective man overwhelms individual man. The Nationalist is not a man in the individual sense, he is group man, collective man. He has no meaning apart from his group. On the one hand, he despises individualism; on the other, he despises interracialism and internationalism. Any passion for human rights he regards as sentimentality. When he talks of freedom, it is his own that he means.

Therefore, as an individual, he is known only to individuals of his own group, or to those rare strangers who can enter the gate. These testify to his warmth, his hospitality, his generosity, his thoughtfulness, his care for others. Alas, these are not his virtues as collective man.

What made him thus? What so turned him in upon himself? My own forefathers, the British, must bear some of the responsibility. When the Afrikaners trekked north to escape British rule, it was the British who followed after them, especially when the world's richest gold deposits were found in Johannesburg. It was the British who conquered the two Afrikaner Republics in 1902 in the tragic Boer War. It was the British who entertained the foolish plan of Anglicizing the Afrikaners.

It was the British who, above all others, took the divergent elements of Afrikanerdom and fused them into a lonely and narcissistic people. Not even Britain's magnanimous restoration of self-government after the Boer War, not even Botha's and Smuts' magnanimous acceptance of it, were able to undo what had been done. The Nationalist remains obsessed with his past.

But there was another great factor also—the Africans, the other men of Africa. The Afrikaner loved Africa, but he could never come to terms with its people. Its people were not his fellow-Africans; they were the "black danger," the "black sea." They outnumbered him and, though he conquered them, he never ceased to fear them. His fear of them is the determinant of all his policies. This fact one must always remember.

All of us are determined by our past, but, if we are to grow up, there comes a time when we must take responsibility for ourselves. Today the world says to the Afrikaner, "We no longer want to hear about the past and what others did to you; we want to hear about the future and what you will do to others."

And the world is outraged by the answer.

It sometimes happens when some new edict of the Nationalists is published, that their opponents are not so much angry as battled. The Minister of Bantu Education, Mr. Willie Maree, has just issued a public edict that his white officials must not shake hands with African teachers. They must bow to each other or clasp their own hands to each other, or do something equally absurd.

Why does a Minister do such a stupid thing? Why does he do it at the same time as his Government pours out money to prove to the world that *apartheid* is only brotherhood in disguise? One is forced to the conclusion that something is operating in this particular Minister against which he seems powerless. This particular white man of Africa fears other men of Africa so much that he fears to touch their hands, and he will not let other white men touch them, either. And he is a leader of Afrikaner Nationalism.

This triviality is not really trivial. It shows the true nature of *apartheid,* which in its essence is a rejection of one's fellow man. The Nationalist has rewritten the second great Commandment, and because his world is in two parts, the commandment is in two parts also:

Thou shalt love thy white neighbor as thyself, provided he accepts apartheid.

Thou shalt love thy non-white neighbor as thyself, provided he does not live next door.

The Nationalist believes in justice for black men, but it must be over there. He believes in opportunity for black men, but it must be over there. The people of the earth are learning fast that there is only one world, but he still thinks there are two. And if there are not two, he will make a law.

What does the Nationalist think of the future? He looks at it with foreboding, but then, he always did. Yet the foreboding has never been so great as now, because the future, so to speak, has never been so near. It has been standing out there for three centuries, but now it is knocking at the door.

The Nationalist comforts himself that the Afrikaner has always had to struggle, that the new crisis is nothing new. But in his heart he knows that this crisis is the last of all.

The Nationalist fanatic says, "God made us, and if He will destroy us, His will be done." Some observers think all Nationalists are like that, and that, like blind Samson, they will pull down the house upon themselves and their enemies.

In crisis, there is only one refuge for the group man. That is to call the group together and bar the doors and load the guns. That is what the Prime Minister, Dr. Verwoerd, is doing now. That is what every Nationalist Prime Minister did before him. The Nationalist knows no other politics. The Nationalist will never be able to come to terms with Africa; he understands Africa only so long as he is boss. His love for South Africa is deep and fierce, but how he would hate it if he were not the boss.

There is one hope, and one hope only, for the future of the white people of South Africa, and especially for the Afrikaner, and that is to come to some kind of terms with the other thirteen million; to negotiate, to discuss; to increase, not to decrease, representation; to open the door, to unload the guns; to stop these stupidities, like not shaking hands; to renounce the evil laws that result in violence and death, to foreswear *apartheid*.

THOMAS JEFFERSON

Objections to Equality: Political, Physical, Moral

This selection from Jefferson is included to demonstrate how even he,
one of the most enlightened of men, thought on the subject of race.
The "they" with which the excerpt begins refers, of course, to the others,
the Blacks.

THEY SHOULD CONTINUE with their parents to a certain age,
then to be brought up, at the public expense, to tillage, arts, or sciences, according to their geniuses, till the females should be eighteen,
and the males twenty-one years of age, when they should be colonized to such place as the circumstances of the time should render most
proper, sending them out with arms, implements of household and of the
handicraft arts, seeds, pairs of the useful domestic animals, &c., to declare
them a free and independent people, and extend to them our alliance and
protection, till they have acquired strength; and to send vessels at the same
time to other parts of the world for an equal number of white inhabitants; to
induce them to migrate hither, proper encouragements were to be proposed.
It will probably be asked, Why not retain and incorporate the blacks into
the State, and thus save the expense of supplying by importation of white
settlers, the vacancies they will leave? Deep-rooted prejudices entertained
by the whites; ten thousand recollections, by the blacks, of the injuries they
have sustained; new provocations; the real distinctions which nature has
made; and many other circumstances, will divide us into parties, and produce convulsions, which will probably never end but in the extermination
of the one or the other race. To these objections, which are political, may be
added others, which are physical and moral. The first difference which
strikes us is that of color. Whether the black of the negro resides in the ret-
icular membrane between the skin and scarf-skin, or in the scarf-skin itself; whether it proceeds from the color of the blood, the color of the bile,
or from that of some other secretion, the difference is fixed in nature, and
is as real as if its seat and cause were better known to us. And is this difference of no importance? Is it not the foundation of a greater or less
share of beauty in the two races? Are not the fine mixtures of red and
white, the expressions of every passion by greater or less suffusions of
color in the one, preferable to that eternal monotony, which reigns in the
countenances, that immovable veil of black which covers the emotions of

the other race? Add to these, flowing hair, a more elegant symmetry of form, their own judgment in favor of the whites, declared by their preference of them, as uniformly as is the preference of the Oranootan for the black woman over those of his own species. The circumstance of superior beauty, is thought worthy attention in the propagation of our horses, dogs and other domestic animals; why not in that of man? Besides those of color, figure, and hair, there are other physical distinctions proving a difference of race. They have less hair on the face and body. They secrete less by the kidneys, and more by the glands of the skin, which gives them a very strong and disagreeable odor. This greater degree of transpiration, renders them more tolerant of heat, and less so of cold than the whites. Perhaps, too, a difference of structure in the pulminary apparatus, which a late ingenious * experimentalist has discovered to be the principal regulator of animal heat, may have disabled them from extricating, in the act of inspiration, so much of that fluid from the outer air, or obliged them in expiration, to part with more of it. They seem to require less sleep. A black after hard labor through the day, will be induced by the slightest amusements to sit up till midnight, or later, though knowing he must be out with the first dawn of the morning. They are at least as brave, and more adventuresome. But this may perhaps proceed from a want of forethought, which prevents their seeing a danger till it be present. When present, they do not go through it with more coolness or steadiness than the whites. They are more ardent after their female; but love seems with them to be more an eager desire, than a tender delicate mixture of sentiment and sensation. Their griefs are transient. Those numberless afflictions, which render it doubtful whether heaven has given life to us in mercy or in wrath, are less felt, and sooner forgotten with them. In general, their existence appears to participate more of sensation than reflection. To this must be ascribed their disposition to sleep when abstracted from their diversions, and unemployed in labor. An animal whose body is at rest, and who does not reflect, must be disposed to sleep of course. Comparing them by their faculties of memory, reason, and imagination, it appears to me that in memory they are equal to the whites; in reason much inferior, as I think one could scarcely be found capable of tracing and comprehending the investigations of Euclid; and that in imagination they are dull, tasteless, and anomalous. It would be unfair to follow them to Africa for this investigation. We will consider them here, on the same stage with the whites, and where the facts are not apochryphal on which a judgment is to be formed. It will be right to make great allowances for the difference of condition, of education, of conversation, of the sphere in which they move. Many millions of them have been brought to, and born in America. Most of them,

* Crawford

indeed, have been confined to tillage, to their own homes, and their own society; yet many have been so situated, that they might have availed themselves of the conversation of their masters; many have been brought up to the handicraft arts, and from that circumstance have always been associated with the whites. Some have been liberally educated, and all have lived in countries where the arts and sciences are cultivated to a considerable degree, and all have had before their eyes samples of the best works from abroad. The Indians, with no advantages of this kind, will often carve figures on their pipes not destitute of design and merit. They will crayon out an animal, a plant, or a country, so as to prove the existence of a germ in their minds which only wants cultivation. They astonish you with strokes of the most sublime oratory; such as prove their reason and sentiment strong, their imagination glowing and elevated. But never yet could I find that a black had uttered a thought above the level of plain narration; never saw even an elementary trait of painting or sculpture. In music they are more generally gifted than the whites with accurate ears for tune and time, and they have been found capable of imagining a small catch.* Whether they will be equal to the composition of a more extensive run of melody, or of complicated harmony, is yet to be proved. Misery is often the parent of the most affecting touches in poetry. Among the blacks is misery enough, God knows, but no poetry. Love is the peculiar œstrum of the poet. Their love is ardent, but it kindles the senses only, not the imagination. Religion, indeed, has produced a Phyllis Whately; but it could not produce a poet.

* The instrument proper to them is the Banjar, which they brought hither from Africa, and which is the original of the guitar, its chords being precisely the four lower chords of the guitar.

E. FRANKLIN FRAZIER

Behind the Masks

Anyone who would really understand human behavior must, sooner or later, become something of a Marxist. We say this to call attention to the fact that many characteristically racial (as many religious and sexual) attitudes must at some point be seen as class phenomenona. Frazier's essay is a remarkable example of social analysis of a group's sense of itself.

SINCE THE BLACK BOURGEOISIE live largely in a world of make-believe, the masks which they wear to play their sorry roles conceal the feelings of inferiority and of insecurity and the frustrations that haunt their inner lives. Despite their attempt to escape from real identification with the masses of Negroes, they can not escape the mark of oppression any more than their less favored kinsmen. In attempting to escape identification with the black masses, they have developed a self-hatred that reveals itself in their depreciation of the physical and social characteristics of Negroes. Likewise, their feelings of inferiority and insecurity are revealed in their pathological struggle for status within the isolated Negro world and craving for recognition in the white world. Their escape into a world of make-believe with its sham "society" leaves them with a feeling of emptiness and futility which causes them to constantly seek an escape in new delusions.

1. The Mark of Oppression

There is an attempt on the part of the parents in middle-class families to shield their children against racial discrimination and the contempt of whites for colored people. Sometimes the parents go to fantastic extremes, such as prohibiting the use of the words "Negro" or "colored" in the presence of their children.[1] They sometimes try to prevent their children from knowing that they can not enter restaurants or other public places because they are Negroes, or even that the schools they attend are segregated schools for Negroes. Despite such efforts to insulate their children against a hostile white world, the children of the black bourgeoisie can not escape the mark

1. E. Franklin Frazier, *Negro Youth at the Crossways* (Washington, D.C.: American Council on Education, 1940), p. 62.

of oppression. This is strikingly revealed in the statement of a seventeen-year-old middle-class Negro youth. When asked if he felt inferior in the presence of white people, he gave the following answer—which was somewhat unusual for its frankness but typical of the attitude of the black bourgeoisie:

> Off-hand, I'd say no, but actually knowing all these things that are thrown up to you about white people being superior—that they look more or less down upon all Negroes—that we have to look to them for everything we get—that they'd rather think of us as mice than men—I don't believe I or any other Negro can help but feel inferior. My father says that it isn't so—that we feel only inferior to those whom we feel are superior. But I don't believe we can feel otherwise. Around white people until I know them a while I feel definitely out of place. Once I played a ping-pong match with a white boy whose play I know wasn't as good as mine, and boys he managed to beat I beat with ease, but I just couldn't get it out of my mind that I was playing a white boy. Sort of an Indian sign on me, you know.[2]

The statement of this youth reveals how deep-seated is the feeling of inferiority, from which even the most favored elements among Negroes cannot escape. However much some middle-class Negroes may seek to soothe their feeling of inferiority in an attitude which they often express in the adage, "it is better to reign in hell than serve in heaven," they are still conscious of their inferior status in American society. They may say, as did a bewildered middle-class youth, that they are proud of being a Negro or proud of being a member of the upper stratum in the Negro community and feel sorry for the Negro masses "stuck in the mud," but they often confess, as did this youth:

> However, knowing that there are difficulties that confront us all as Negroes, if I could be born again and had my choice I'd really want to be a white boy—I mean white or my same color, providing I could occupy the same racial and economic level I now enjoy. I am glad I am this color—I'm frequently taken for a foreigner. I wouldn't care to be lighter or darker and be a Negro. I am the darkest one in the family due to my constant outdoor activities. I realize of course that there are places where I can't go despite my family or money just because I happen to be a Negro. With my present education, family background, and so forth, if I was only white I could go places in life. A white face holds supreme over a black one despite its economic and social status. Frankly, it leaves me bewildered.[3]

Not all middle-class Negroes consciously desire, as this youth, to be white in order to escape from their feelings of inferiority. In fact, the ma-

2. *Ibid.*, p. 67.
3. *Ibid.*, p. 66.

jority of middle-class Negroes would deny having the desire to be white, since this would be an admission of their feeling of inferiority. Within an intimate circle of friends some middle-class Negroes may admit that they desire to be white, but publicly they would deny any such wish. The black bourgeoisie constantly boast of their pride in their identification as Negroes. But when one studies the attitude of this class in regard to the physical traits or the social characteristics of Negroes, it becomes clear that the black bourgeoisie do not really wish to be identified with Negroes.

2. Insecurities and Frustrations

Since the black bourgeoisie can not escape identification with Negroes, they experience certain feelings of insecurity because of their feeling of inferiority. Their feeling of inferiority is revealed in their fear of competition with whites. There is a fear of competition with whites for jobs. Notwithstanding the fact that middle-class Negroes are the most vociferous in demanding the right to compete on equal terms with whites, many of them still fear such competition. They prefer the security afforded by their monopoly of certain occupations within the segregated Negro community. For example, middle-class Negroes demand that the two Negro medical schools be reserved for Negro students and that a quota be set for white students, though Negro students are admitted to "white" medical schools. Since the Supreme Court of the United States has ruled against segregated public schools, many Negro teachers, even those who are well-prepared, fear that they can not compete with whites for teaching positions. Although this fear stems principally from a feeling of inferiority which is experienced generally by Negroes, it has other causes.

The majority of the black bourgeoisie fear competition with whites partly because such competition would mean that whites were taking them seriously, and consequently they would have to assume a more serious and responsible attitude towards their work. Middle-class Negroes, who are notorious for their inefficiency in the management of various Negro institutions, excuse their inefficiency on the grounds that Negroes are a "young race" and, therefore, will require time to attain the efficiency of the white man. The writer has heard a Negro college president, who has constantly demanded that Negros have equality in American life, declare before white people in extenuation of the shortcomings of his own administration, that Negroes were a "child race" and that they had "to crawl before they could walk." Such declarations, while flattering to the whites, are revealing in that they manifest the black bourgeoisie's contempt for the Negro masses, while excusing its own deficiencies by attributing them to the latter. Yet it is clear that the black worker who must gain a living in a white man's mill or factory and in competition with white workers can not offer any such excuse for his inefficiency.

The fear of competition with whites is probably responsible for the black bourgeoisie's fear of competence and first-rate performance within its own ranks. When a Negro is competent and insists upon first-rate work it appears to this class that he is trying to be a white man, or that he is insisting that Negroes measure up to white standards. This is especially true where the approval of whites is taken as a mark of competence and first-rate performance. In such cases the black bourgeoisie reveal their ambivalent attitudes toward the white world. They slavishly accept the estimate which almost any white man places upon a Negro or his work, but at the same time they fear and reject white standards. For example, when a group of Negro doctors were being shown the modern equipment and techniques of a white clinic, one of them remarked to a Negro professor in a medical school, "This is the white man's medicine. I never bother with it and still I make $30,000 a year." Negroes who adopt the standards of the white world create among the black bourgeoisie a feeling of insecurity and often become the object of both the envy and hatred of this class.

Among the women of the black bourgeoisie there is an intense fear of the competition of white women for Negro men. They often attempt to rationalize their fear by saying that the Negro man always occupies an inferior position in relation to the white woman or that he marries much below his "social" status. They come nearer to the source of their fear when they confess that there are not many eligible Negro men and that these few should marry Negro women. That such rationalizations conceal deep-seated feelings of insecurity is revealed by the fact that generally they have no objection to the marriage of white men to Negro women, especially if the white man is reputed to be wealthy. In fact, they take pride in the fact and attribute these marriages to the "peculiar" charms of Negro women. In fact, the middle-class Negro woman's fear of the competition of white women is based often upon the fact that she senses her own inadequacies and shortcomings. Her position in Negro "society" and in the larger Negro community is often due to some adventitious factor, such as a light complexion or a meager education, which has pushed her to the top of the social pyramid. The middle-class white woman not only has a white skin and straight hair, but she is generally more sophisticated and interesting because she has read more widely and has a larger view of the world. The middle-class Negro woman may make fun of the "plainness" of her white competitor and the latter's lack of "wealth" and interest in "society"; nevertheless she still feels insecure when white women appear as even potential competitors.

Both men and women among the black bourgeoisie have a feeling of insecurity because of their constant fear of the loss of status. Since they have no status in the larger American society, the intense struggle for status among middle-class Negroes is, as we have seen, an attempt to compensate for the contempt and low esteem of the whites. Great value is, therefore, placed upon all kinds of status symbols. Academic degrees, both real and honorary, are sought in order to secure status. Usually the symbols are of a material nature implying wealth and conspicuous consumption. Sometimes Negro doctors do not attend what are supposedly scientific meetings because they do not have a Cadillac or some other expensive automobile. School teachers wear mink coats and maintain homes beyond their income for fear that they may lose status. The extravagance in "social" life generally is due to an effort not to lose status. But in attempting to overcome their fear of loss of status they are often beset by new feelings of insecurity. In spite of their pretended wealth, they are aware that their incomes are insignificant and that they must struggle to maintain their mortgaged homes and the show of "wealth" in lavish "social" affairs. Moreover, they are beset by a feeling of insecurity because of their struggles to maintain a show of wealth through illegal means. From time to time "wealthy" Negro doctors are arrested for selling narcotics and performing abortions. The life of many a "wealthy" Negro doctor is shortened by the struggle to provide diamonds, minks, and an expensive home for his wife.

There is much frustration among the black bourgeoisie despite their privileged position within the segregated Negro world. Their "wealth" and "social" position can not erase the fact that they are generally segregated and rejected by the white world. Their incomes and occupations may enable them to escape the cruder manifestations of racial prejudice, but they can not insulate themselves against the more subtle forms of racial discrimination. These discriminations cause frustrations in Negro men because they are not allowed to play the "masculine role" as defined by American culture. They can not assert themselves or exercise power as white men do. When they protest against racial discrimination there is always the threat that they will be punished by the white world. In spite of the movement toward the wider integration of the Negro into the general stream of American life, middle-class Negroes are still threatened with the loss of positions and earning power if they insist upon their rights.[4] After the Supreme Court of the United States ruled that segregation in public education was illegal, Negro teachers in some parts of the South were dismissed because they would not sign statements supporting racial segregation in education.

As one of the results of not being able to play the "masculine role," middle-class Negro males have tended to cultivate their "personalities"[5] which enable them to exercise considerable influence among whites and achieve distinction in the Negro world. Among Negroes they have been

4. See, for example, the article "YMCA Secretary in Virginia Fired for Equality Fight," *Washington Afro-American,* August, 1954, p. 20.
5. One can not determine to what extent homosexuality among Negro males is due to the fact that they can not play a "masculine role."

noted for their glamour.[6] In this respect they resemble women who use their "personalities" to compensate for their inferior status in relation to men. This fact would seem to support the observation of an American sociologist that the Negro was "the lady among the races," if he had restricted his observation to middle-class males among American Negroes.[7]

In the South the middle-class Negro male is not only prevented from playing a masculine role, but generally he must let Negro women assume leadership in any show of militancy. This reacts upon his status in the home where the tradition of female dominance, which is widely established among Negroes, has tended to assign a subordinate role to the male. In fact, in middle-class families, especially if the husband has risen in social status through his own efforts and married a member of an "old" family or a "society" woman, the husband is likely to play a pitiful role. The greatest compliment that can be paid such a husband is that he "worships his wife," which means that he is her slave and supports all her extravagances and vanities. But, of course, many husbands in such positions escape from their frustrations by having extra-marital sex relations. Yet the conservative and conventional middle-class husband presents a pathetic picture. He often sits at home alone, impotent physically and socially, and complains that his wife has gone crazy about poker and "society" and constantly demands money for gambling and expenditures which he can not afford. Sometimes he enjoys the sympathy of a son or daughter who has not become a "socialite." Such children often say that they had a happy family life until "mamma took to poker."

Preoccupation with poker on the part of the middle-class woman is often an attempt to escape from a frustrated life. Her frustration may be bound up with her unsatisfactory sexual life. She may be married to a "glamorous" male who neglects her for other women. For among the black bourgeoisie, the glamour of the male is often associated with his sexual activities. The frustration of many Negro women has a sexual origin.[8] Even those who have sought an escape from frustration in sexual promiscuity may, because of satiety or deep psychological reasons, become obsessed with poker in order to escape from their frustrations. One "society" woman, in justification of her obsession with poker remarked that it had taken the place of her former preoccupation with sex. Another said that to win at poker was similar to a sexual orgasm.

6. See *Ebony,* July, 1949, where it is claimed that a poll on the most exciting Negro men in the United States reveals that the heyday of the "glamour boy" is gone and achievement rather than a handsome face and husky physique is the chief factor in making Negro men exciting to women.

7. See Robert E. Park and Ernest W. Burgess, *Introduction to the Science of Sociology* (Chicago: University of Chicago Press, 1924), p. 139.

8. See Kardiner and Ovesey, *op. cit.,* pp. 312 ff. concerning this point.

   The frustration of the majority of the women among the black bourgeoisie is probably due to the idle or ineffectual lives which they lead. Those who do not work devote their time to the frivolities of Negro "society." When they devote their time to "charity" or worth-while causes, it is generally a form of play or striving for "social" recognition. They are constantly forming clubs which ostensibly have a serious purpose, but in reality are formed in order to consolidate their position in "society" or to provide additional occasions for playing poker. The idle, overfed women among the black bourgeoisie are generally, to use their language, "dripping with diamonds." They are forever dieting and reducing only to put on more weight (which is usually the result of the food that they consume at their club meetings). Even the women among the black bourgeoisie who work exhibit the same frustrations. Generally, they have no real interest in their work and only engage in it in order to be able to provide the conspicuous consumption demanded by "society." As we have indicated, the women as well as the men among the black bourgeoisie read very little and have no interest in music, art or the theater. They are constantly restless and do not know how to relax. They are generally dull people and only become animated when "social" matters are discussed, especially poker games. They are afraid to be alone and constantly seek to be surrounded by their friends, who enable them to escape from their boredom.

   The frustrated lives of the black bourgeoisie are reflected in the attitudes of parents towards their children. Middle-class Negro families as a whole have few children, while among the families that constitute Negro "society" there are many childless couples.[9] One finds today, as an American observed over forty years ago, that "where the children are few, they are usually spoiled" in middle-class Negro families.[10] There is often not only a deep devotion to their one or two children, but a subservience to them. It is not uncommon for the only son to be called and treated as the "boss" in the family. Parents cater to the transient wishes of their children and often rationalize their behavior towards them on the grounds that children should not be "inhibited." They spend large sums of money on their children for toys and especially for clothes. They provide their children with automobiles when they go to college. All of this is done in order that the children may maintain the status of the parents and be eligible to enter the "social" set in Negro colleges. When they send their children to northern "white" colleges they often spend more time in preparing them for what they imagine will be their "social" life than in preparing them for the academic requirements of these institutions.

9. See Frazier, *The Negro Family in the United States,* pp. 440–43.
10. Robert E. Park, "Negro Home Life and Standards of Living," in *The Negro's Progress In Fifty Years* (Philadelphia: American Academy of Political and Social Science, 1913), p. 163.

In their fierce devotion to their children, which generally results in spoiling them, middle-class Negro parents are seemingly striving at times to establish a human relationship that will compensate for their own frustrations in the realm of human relationships. Devotion to their children often becomes the one human tie that is sincere and free from the competition and artificiality of the make-believe world in which they live. Sometimes they may project upon their children their own frustrated professional ambitions. But usually, even when they send their children to northern "white" universities as a part of their "social" striving within the Negro community, they seem to hope that their children will have an acceptance in the white world which has been denied them.

3. Self-Hatred and Guilt Feelings

One of the chief frustrations of the middle-class Negro is that he can not escape identification with the Negro race and consequently is subject to the contempt of whites.[11] Despite his "wealth" in which he has placed so much faith as a solvent of racial discrimination, he is still subject to daily insults and is excluded from participation in white American society. Middle-class Negroes do not express their resentment against discrimination and insults in violent outbreaks, as lower-class Negroes often do. They constantly repress their hostility toward whites and seek to soothe their hurt self-esteem in all kinds of rationalizations. They may boast of their wealth and culture as compared with the condition of the poor whites. Most often they will resort to any kind of subterfuge in order to avoid contact with whites. For example, in the South they often pay their bills by mail rather than risk unpleasant contacts with representatives of white firms.[12] The daily repression of resentment and the constant resort to

11. A middle-class mulatto woman, a former school teacher, who was fearful of the impact of this book on European readers and southern detractors of "The Race," concluded her review of the original French edition with these words:

"Isn't it about time our sociologists and specialists on the 'race problem' in America, began to discuss and consider middle class Negroes as middle class Americans, or better, all U.S. Negroes as Americans with three hundred unbroken years of American tradition, way of life, cultural and spiritual contacts behind them—influences which have moulded them as they have moulded all others who are considered, even when not treated completely so, as members of the American community? Isn't it time to stop thinking of and talking about Negroes as a separate and distinct entity in the general scheme of things? And above all, isn't it time to realize that the melting pot has melted truly and fused together all the myriad (albeit conflicting) racial, cultural, educational, spiritual and social elements which have combined in such peculiar fashion to produce the American Negro of our time?" *Journal of Negro Education*, Vol. XXV, p. 141.

12. See Charles S. Johnson, *Patterns of Negro Segregation* (New York: Harper, 1943), Chapters XII, XIII, and XIV which describe the ways in which Negroes in various classes deal with racial discrimination.

means of avoiding contacts with whites do not relieve them of their hostility toward whites. Even middle-class Negroes who gain a reputation for exhibiting "objectivity" and a "statesmanlike" attitude on racial discrimination harbor deep-seated hostilities toward whites. A Negro college president who has been considered such an inter-racial "statesman" once confessed to the writer that some day he was going to "break loose" and tell white people what he really thought. However, it is unlikely that a middle-class Negro of his standing will ever "break loose." Middle-class Negroes generally express their aggressions against whites by other means, such as deceiving whites and utilizing them for their own advantage.

Because middle-class Negroes are unable to indulge in aggressions against whites as such, they will sometimes make other minority groups the object of their hostilities. For example, they may show hostility against Italians, who are also subject to discrimination. But more often middle-class Negroes, especially those who are engaged in a mad scramble to accumulate money, will direct their hostilities against Jews. They are constantly expressing their anti-semitism within Negro circles, while pretending publicly to be free from prejudice. They blame the Jew for the poverty of Negroes and for their own failures and inefficiencies in their business undertakings. In expressing their hostility towards Jews, they are attempting at the same time to identify with the white American majority.

The repressed hostilities of middle-class Negroes to whites are not only directed towards other minority groups but inward toward themselves. This results in self-hatred, which may appear from their behavior to be directed towards the Negro masses but which in reality is directed against themselves.[13] While pretending to be proud of being a Negro, they ridicule Negroid physical characteristics and seek to modify or efface them as much as possible. Within their own groups they constantly proclaim that "niggers" made them sick. The very use of the term "nigger," which they claim to resent, indicates that they want to disassociate themselves from the Negro masses. They talk condescendingly of Africans and of African culture, often even objecting to African sculpture in their homes. They are insulted if they are identified with Africans. They refuse to join organizations that are interested in Africa. If they are of mixed ancestry, they may boast of the fact that they have Indian ancestry. When making compliments concerning the beauty of Negroes of mixed ancestry, they generally say, for example, "She is beautiful; she looks like an Indian." On the other hand, if a black woman has European features, they will remark condescendingly, "Although she is black, you must admit that she is good looking." Some middle-class Negroes of mixed ancestry like to wear Hindu costumes—while they laugh at the idea of wearing an African costume. When middle-class Negroes travel, they studiously avoid association with

13. See Kardiner and Ovesey, *op. cit.,* pp. 190, 282, 297.

other Negroes, especially if they themselves have received the slightest recognition by whites. Even when they can not "pass" for white they fear that
they will lose this recognition if they are identified as Negroes. Therefore,
nothing pleases them more than to be mistaken for a Puerto Rican, Philip-
pino, Egyptian or Arab or any ethnic group other than Negro.

The self-hatred of middle-class Negroes is often revealed in the keen
competition which exists among them for status and recognition. This keen
competition is the result of the frustrations which they experience in attempting to obtain acceptance and recognition by whites. Middle-class Negroes are constantly criticizing and belittling Negroes who achieve some
recognition or who acquire a status above them. They prefer to submit to
the authority of whites than to be subordinate to other Negroes. For example, Negro scholars generally refuse to seek the advice and criticism of
competent Negro scholars and prefer to turn to white scholars for such
co-operation. In fact, it is difficult for middle-class Negroes to co-operate
in any field of endeavor. This failure in social relations is, as indicated in
an important study, because "in every Negro he encounters his own self-
contempt." [14] It is as if he said, "You are only a Negro like myself; so why
should you be in a position above me?"

This self-hatred often results in guilt feelings on the part of the Negro
who succeeds in elevating himself above his fellows.[15] He feels unconsciously that in rising above other Negroes he is committing an act of aggression which will result in hatred and revenge on their part. The act of
aggression may be imagined, but very often it is real. This is the case
when middle-class Negroes oppose the economic and social welfare of Negroes because of their own interests. In some American cities, it has been
the black bourgeoisie and not the whites who have opposed the building of
low-cost public housing for Negro workers. In one city two wealthy Negro
doctors, who have successfully opposed public housing projects for Negro
workers, own some of the worst slums in the United States. While their
wives, who wear mink coats, "drip with diamonds" and are written up in
the "society" columns of Negro newspapers, ride in Cadillacs, their Negro
tenants sleep on the dirt floors of hovels unfit for human habitation. The
guilt feelings of the middle-class Negro are not always unconscious. For
example, take the case of the Negro leader who proclaimed over the radio
in a national broadcast that the Negro did not want social equity. He was
conscious of his guilt feelings and his self-hatred in playing such a role, for
he sent word privately to the writer that he never hated so much to do
anything in his life, but that it was necessary because of his position as
head of a state college which was under white supervision. The self-hatred
of the middle-class Negro arises, then, not only from the fact that he does

14. *Ibid.*, p. 177.
15. *Ibid.*, p. 203.

not want to be a Negro but also because of his sorry role in American society.

4. Escape into Delusions

The black bourgeoisie, as we have seen, has created a world of make-believe to shield itself from the harsh economic and social realities of American life. This world of make-believe is created out of the myth of Negro business, the reports of the Negro press on the achievements and wealth of Negroes, the recognition accorded them by whites, and the fabulous life of Negro "society." Some of the middle-class Negro intellectuals are not deceived by the world of make-believe. They will have nothing to do with Negro "society" and refuse to waste their time in frivolities. They take their work seriously and live in relative obscurity so far as the Negro world is concerned. Others seek an escape from their frustrations by developing, for example, a serious interest in Negro music—which the respectable black bourgeoisie often pretend to despise. In this way these intellectuals achieve some identification with the Negro masses and with the traditions of Negro life. But many more middle-class Negros, who are satisfied to live in the world of make-believe but must find a solution to the real economic and social problems which they face, seek an escape in delusions.

They seek an escape in delusions involving wealth. This is facilitated by the fact that they have had little experience with the real meaning of wealth and that they lack a tradition of saving and accumulation. Wealth to them means spending money without any reference to its source. Hence, their behavior generally reflects the worst qualities of the gentleman and peasant from whom their only vital traditions spring. Therefore, their small accumulations of capital and the income which they receive from professional services within the Negro community make them appear wealthy in comparison with the low economic status of the majority of Negroes. The delusion of wealth is supported by the myth of Negro business. Moreover, the attraction of the delusion of wealth is enhanced by the belief that wealth will gain them acceptance in American life. In seeking an escape in the delusion of wealth, middle-class Negroes make a fetish of material things or physical possessions. They are constantly buying things —houses, automobiles, furniture and all sorts of gadgets, not to mention clothes. Many of the furnishings and gadgets which they acquire are never used; nevertheless they continue to accumulate things. The homes of many middle-class Negroes have the appearance of museums for the exhibition of American manufactures and spurious art objects. The objects which they are constantly buying are always on display. Negro school teachers who devote their lives to "society" like to display twenty to thirty pairs of shoes, the majority of which they never wear. Negro professional men proudly speak of the two automobiles which they have acquired when they need only one. The acquisition of objects which are not used or needed seems to be an attempt to fill some void in their lives.

The delusion of power also appears to provide an escape for middle-class Negroes from the world of reality which pierces through the world of make-believe of the black bourgeoisie. The positions of power which they occupy in the Negro world often enable them to act autocratically towards other Negroes, especially when they have the support of the white community. In such cases the delusion of power may provide an escape from their frustrations. It is generally, however, when middle-class Negroes hold positions enabling them to participate in the white community that they seek in the delusion of power an escape from their frustrations. Although their position may be only a "token" of the integration of the Negro into American life, they will speak and act as if they were a part of the power structure of American society. Negro advisers who are called into counsel by whites to give advice about Negroes are especially likely to find an escape from their feelings of inferiority in the delusion of power. Negro social workers, who are dependent upon white philanthropy, have often gained the reputation, with the support of the Negro press, of being powerful persons in American communities.

However, the majority of the black bourgeoisie who seek an escape from their frustrations in delusions seemingly have not been able to find it in the delusion of wealth or power. They have found it in magic or chance, and in sex and alcohol. Excessive drinking and sex seem to provide a means for narcotizing the middle-class Negro against a frustrating existence. A "social" function is hardly ever considered a success unless a goodly number of the participants "pass out." But gambling, especially poker, which has become an obsession among many middle-class Negroes, offers the chief escape into delusion. Among the black bourgeoisie it is not simply a device for winning money. It appears to be a magical device for enhancing their self-esteem through overcoming fate.[16] Although it often involves a waste of money which many middle-class Negroes can not afford, it has an irresistible attraction which they often confess they can not overcome.

Despite the tinsel, glitter and gaiety of the world of make-believe in which middle-class Negroes take refuge, they are still beset by feelings of insecurity, frustration and guilt. As a consequence, the free and easy life which they appear to lead is a mask for their unhappy existence.

16. *Ibid.*, pp. 313 ff.

JOHN WESLEY POWELL

Report on the Condition of the Ute Indians of Utah

Powell was a remarkable man. A veteran of the Civil War, in which he lost one arm, he became one of the great explorers of the American West. The report he filed in 1874, from which the excerpt is taken, became the basis for the "reservation" policy for the Indians. The excerpt should be compared with Gossett's survey to understand fully how segregation by reservation came to be accepted as the only alternative for the red and white races in this country at that point in time.

General Remarks

ALL OF THE INDIANS who have been visited by the commission fully appreciate the hopelessness of contending against the Government of the United States and the tide of civilization.

They are broken into many small tribes, and their homes so interspersed among the settlements of white men, that their power is entirely broken and no fear should be entertained of a general war with them. The time has passed when it was necessary to buy peace. It only remains to decide what should be done with them for the relief of the white people from their petty depredations, and from the demoralizing influences accompanying the presence of savages in civilized communities, and also for the best interests of the Indians themselves. To give them a partial supply of clothing and a small amount of food annually, while they yet remain among the settlements, is to encourage them in idleness, and directly tends to establish them as a class of wandering beggars. If they are not to be collected on reservations they should no longer receive aid from the General Government, for every dollar given them in their present condition is an injury. This must be understood in the light that it is no longer necessary to buy peace. Perhaps the Utes of the Uintah Valley should be excepted from this statement, as they might thus be induced to join the Utes of Western Colorado who are yet unsubdued.

Again, they cannot be collected on reservations and kept there without provision being made for their maintenance. To have them nominally on a reservation and actually, the greater part of the year, wandering among the settlements, is of no advantage, but rather an injury, as the people, believing that they should remain on their reservations, and considering that they are violating their agreements with the Government in wandering away, refuse to employ them and treat them with many indignities. And this consolidation of a number of tribes of Indians in one body makes them stronger, more independent, and more defiant than they would be if scattered about the country as small tribes. If, then, they are to be collected on reservations and held there by furnishing them with an adequate support, it is evident wisdom that they should be provided with the necessary means and taught to work, that they may become self-supporting at the earliest possible day; and it is urgently recommended that steps be taken to secure this end, or that they be given over to their own resources and left to fight the battle of life for themselves. It is not pleasant to contemplate the effect and final result of this last-mentioned course. The Indian in his relations with the white man rarely associates with the better class, but finds his companions in the lowest and vilest of society—men whose object is to corrupt or plunder. He thus learns from the superior race everything that is bad, nothing that is good. His presence in the settlement is a source of irritation and a cause of fear, especially among the better class of people.

Such persons will not employ him, for they do not desire the presence of a half-naked, vicious savage in their families.

Nor are the people of these communities willing to assume the trouble or expense of controlling the Indians by the ordinary agencies of local government, but are always ready to punish either real or supposed crimes by resort to arms.

Such a course, together with the effects of crime and loathsome disease, must finally result in the annihilation of the race.

By the other alternative, putting them on reservations and teaching them to labor, they must for a number of years be a heavy expense to the General Government, but it is believed that the burden would not be as great as that on the local governments if the Indians were left to themselves. It is very probable, also, that in the sequel it will be found cheaper for the General Government to collect them on reservations, for there is always serious danger of petty conflicts arising between the Indians and white men which will demand the interference of the General Government and entail some expense. The commission does not consider that a reservation should be looked upon in the light of a pen where a horde of savages are to be fed with flour and beef, to be supplied with blankets from the Government bounty, and to be furnished with paint and gew-gaws by the greed of traders, but that a reservation should be a school of industry and a home for these unfortunate people. In council with the Indians great care was taken not to implant in their minds the idea that the Government was willing to pay them for yielding lands which white men needed, and that as a recompense for such lands they would be furnished with clothing and food, and thus enabled to live in idleness. The question was presented to the Indian something in this light: The white men take these lands and use them, and from the earth secure to themselves food, clothing, and many other desirable things. Why should not the Indian do the same? The Government of the United States is anxious for you to try. If you will unite and agree to become farmers, it will secure to you permanent titles to such lands as you need, and will give you the necessary assistance to begin such a life, expecting that you will soon be able to take care of yourselves, as do white men and civilized Indians.

All the tribes mentioned in this census table, and many others, have been visited by the commission, and frequent consultations held with them concerning the importance of their removing to reservations, and they have discussed it among themselves very fully.

Care has been taken to secure common consultation among those tribes which should be united as represented in the plans above, and we doubt not that these questions will form the subject of many a night's council during the present winter; and if the suggestions made by the commission should be acted upon, it is to be hoped that next summer will find the great majority of these Indians prepared to move.

Suggestions in Regard to the Management of These Reservations

With a view of ultimately civilizing these Indians, the commission beg leave to make some suggestions concerning the management of reservations.

First. All bounties given to the Indians should, so far as possible, be used to induce them to work. No able-bodied Indian should be either fed or clothed except in payment for labor, even though such labor is expended in providing for his own future wants. Of course these remarks apply only to those who form the subject of our report—those with whom it is no longer necessary to deal as public enemies, and with the understanding that they must be conciliated to prevent war. It has already been stated that such a course is unnecessary with these Indians.

Second. They should not be provided with ready-made clothing. Substantial fabrics should be given them from which they can manufacture their own garments. Such a course was taken during the past year with the Pi-Utes, under the direction of the commission, and the result was very satisfactory. For illustration, on the Pi-Ute reservation four hundred Indians received uncut cloth sufficient to make each man, woman, and child a suit of clothes. With these fabrics thread, needles, buttons, &c., were issued. The services of an intelligent, painstaking woman were secured to teach the women how to cut and make garments for themselves and their families. Three weeks after the issue of this material the commission revisited the reservation and found these Indians well clothed in garments of their own make. At first they complained bitterly that ready-made clothing was not furnished to them as it had been previously, but when we returned to the reservation it was found that they fully appreciated that the same money had been much more advantageously spent than on previous occasions.

Where the Indians have received ready-made clothing for a number of years, the change should not be made too violently, but a wise and firm agent could soon have all his Indians making their own clothing.

Third. The Indians should not be furnished with tents; as long as they have tents they move about with great facility, and are thus encouraged to continue their nomadic life. As fast as possible houses should be built for them. Some of the Indians are already prepared for such a change, and greatly desire to live in houses. A few, especially the older people, are prejudiced against such a course, and perhaps at first could not be induced to live in them; but such a change could be made gradually to the great advantage of the Indian, both for his health and comfort and for its civilizing influence.

Fourth. Each Indian family should be supplied with a cow, to enable them to start in the accumulation of property. The Indians now understand the value of domestic cattle, and are anxious to acquire this class of property, and a few of them have already made a beginning in this direction. Some have ten, twenty, thirty, and even fifty head, though these are exceptional cases, and it is interesting to notice that, as soon as an Indian acquires property, he more thoroughly appreciates the rights of property, and becomes an advocate of law and order.

Fifth. In all this country the soil cannot be cultivated without artificial irrigation, and under these conditions agricultural operations are too complicated for the Indian without careful superintendence. It will be impossible also to find a sufficient body of land in any one place for the necessary farms; they must be scattered many miles apart. There will, therefore, be needed on each reservation a number of farmers to give general direction to all such labor.

Sixth. On each reservation there should be a blacksmith, carpenter, and a saddle and harness maker, and each of these mechanics should employ several Indian apprentices, and should consider that the most important part of his duty was to instruct such apprentices, and from time to time a shoemaker and other mechanics should be added to this number.

Seventh. An efficient medical department should be organized on each reservation. A great number of the diseases with which the Indian is plagued yield readily to medical treatment, and by such a course many lives can be saved and much suffering prevented. But there is another very important reason for the establishment of a medical department. The magician or "medicine-man" wields much influence, and such influence is always bad; but in the presence of an intelligent physician it is soon lost.

Eighth. It is unnecessary to mention the power which schools would have over the rising generation of Indians. Next to teaching them to work, the most important thing is to teach them the English language. Into their own language there is woven so much mythology and sorcery that a new one is needed in order to aid them in advancing beyond their baneful superstitions; and the ideas and thoughts of civilized life cannot be communicated to them in their own tongues.

The Relation of the Army to These Indians

Your commission cannot refrain from expressing its opinion concerning the effect of the presence of soldiers among these Indians where they are no longer needed to keep them under subjection. They regard the presence of a soldier as a standing menace, and to them the very name of soldier is synonymous with all that is offensive and evil. To the soldier they attribute their social demoralization and the unmentionable diseases with which they are infested. Everywhere, as we traveled among these Indians, the question would be asked us, "If we go to a reservation will the Government place soldiers there?" And to such a removal two objections were invariably urged; the first was, "We do not wish to desert the graves of our fathers," and the second, "We do not wish to give our women to the embrace of the soldiers."

If the troops are not absolutely necessary in the country for the purpose of overawing these Indians, or protecting them in their rights against the encroachments of white men, it will be conceded that they should be removed.

We have already expressed the opinion that they are not needed to prevent a general war, and we believe that they are not useful in securing justice between white men and Indians and between Indians and Indians. In war we deal with people as organized into nationalities, not as individuals. Some hungry Indian steals a beef, some tired Indian steals a horse, a vicious Indian commits a depredation, and flies to the mountains. No effort is made to punish the real offender, but the first Indian met is shot at sight. Then, perhaps, the Indians retaliate, and the news is spread through the country that war has broken out with the Indians. Troops are sent to the district and wander around among the mountains and return. Perhaps a few Indians are killed, and perhaps a few white men. Usually in all such cases the white man is the chief sufferer, for he has property which can be spoiled, and the Indian has none that he cannot easily hide in the rocks. His methods of warfare are such that we cannot cope with him without resorting to means which are repugnant to civilized people; and, after spend-

306 JOHN WESLEY POWELL

ing thousands, or even millions of dollars, on an affair which, at its inception, was but a petty larceny, we make a peace with the Indians, and enter into an agreement to secure him lands, which we cannot fulfill, and to give him annuities, the expense of which are a burden on the public Treasury.

This treatment of the Indians as nations or tribes is in every way bad. Now, the most vicious Indian in any tribe has it in his power, at any moment that he may desire, to practically declare war between his own tribe, and perhaps a dozen surrounding tribes, and the Government of the United States.

What now is needed with all these subdued Indians is, some method by which individual criminals can be arrested and brought to justice. This cannot be done by the methods of war. As long as the Indians are scattered among the settlements the facts show that this cannot be done. The Indian has no knowledge of legal methods, and avenges his own wrongs by ways which are traditional with him, while the prejudices against savages which has grown through centuries of treacherous and bloody warfare, and the prejudices of race, which are always greatly exaggerated among the lower class of people, with whom the Indian is most liable to associate, are such that the Indian cannot secure justice through the intervention of the local authorities.

There is now no great uninhabited and unknown region to which the Indian can be sent. He is among us, and we must either protect him or destroy him. The only course left by which these Indians can be saved is to gather them on reservations, which shall be schools of industry and civilization, and the superintendents of which shall be the proper officers to secure justice between the two races, and between individuals of the Indian race. For this purpose on each reservation there should be a number of wise, firm men, who, as judges and police officers, would be able in all ordinary cases to secure substantial justice. In extraordinary cases no hasty steps should be taken. Surprises and massacres need no longer be feared, and if a larger force is needed than that wielded by the employés on the reservations, it would be easy to increase it by civil methods.

For this purpose laws should be enacted clearly defining the rights of the Indians and white men in their mutual relations, and the power of the officers of the Indian Department, and the methods of procedure to secure justice. It might possibly be unwise to withdraw all the troops at once. It might be better to remove them *pari passu* with the establishment of the Indians on reservations.

Permit the remark just here, that the expense of the military and civil methods stand in very glaring contrast. Within the territory which has heretofore been described it is probable that about two million dollars will be expended in the support of troops during the present fiscal year, and much less than two hundred thousand dollars through the Indian Department for feeding, clothing, and civilizing the Indians.

We beg leave again to mention that these remarks apply only to conquered tribes.

There are some Indians in other portions of the United States, whom it is necessary to manage by other methods, who yet have the pride and insolence and treachery of savages. But by far the greater part of the Indians scattered throughout the territory from the Rocky Mountains to the Pacific coast are in a condition substantially the same as those who form the subject of this report.

VINE DELORIA, JR.

The Problem of Indian Leadership

The title of Vine Deloria's book, *Custer Died for Your Sins,* was a bumper sticker originally; its "pop" quality should not hide the seriousness of Deloria's work. What he attempts, in his analysis of the problem of leadership, is to become the necessary spokesman, that is, the man who can articulate the goals which will, in turn, unify and vivify a Red consciousness.

QUITE EARLY in the Civil Rights struggle certain individuals emerged and were accepted as representative leaders of the Negro people. Martin Luther King, James Farmer, Bayard Rustin, Whitney Young, John Lewis, and others were able to attract the attention of the communications media. It was largely through identification with these individuals that vast numbers of Americans began to be concerned about Civil Rights. By vicariously experiencing the exploits of King and others, people participated in the great marches and felt they had an important emotional investment in the outcome. For a time, at least, racial themes were submerged by the common appeal for simple justice.

When the Civil Rights goals became blurred and a multitude of leaders appeared to be saying contradictory things, public sympathy vanished as quickly as it had arisen. No longer could people identify with simply understood individuals who stood for simple goals.

Indians experienced an era similar to the Civil Rights movement in the closing years of the last century. Then Indian tribes and their great leaders dominated the news and attracted the attention of the public. The Indian struggle for freedom was symbolized by the great war chiefs Crazy Horse, Sitting Bull, Chief Joseph, and Geronimo. They were better known than the important statesmen of those days. Public interest often reached a fever pitch and opinions were as evenly divided as to solutions to the Indian problem then as they are today about the Negro problem.

Public opinion was fickle. When Custer was wiped out the impulse was to exterminate the Sioux. Yet several years later Sitting Bull was so popular that he appeared in Wild West shows. Chief Joseph, the great Nez Perce chief, left his reservation in Oregon with his people and headed for the Canadian border. Whites were terrified at first. Later they cheered for the Nez Perces as they eluded troop after troop of cavalry. When they were finally caught twelve miles from the Canadian border nearly everyone in the nation was on their side. Even the opposing generals, who had the task of catching the tribe, were attracted by Joseph's obvious ability to command.

The Cheyennes were corraled on a dusty reservation in Oklahoma and longed for their homeland in Montana. Facing starvation on their desert lands in the South, the tribe broke for freedom. They managed to elude the major cavalry forces that were sent out to catch them and got through Kansas unnoticed. In Nebraska the troops finally caught up and killed most of them. A few kept going and reached Montana. Some hid with Red Cloud's Oglala Sioux at Pine Ridge, South Dakota, where they were given refuge. When the public realized the tragedy of Dull Knife and his starving band of homeward-fleeing Cheyennes, the tide turned in favor of the tribes. They were able to survive by submitting to confined reservations and the ration system, and were eventually freed from the fear of physical extermination.

For a time the government attempted to break the power of the great war chiefs and failing, adopted the tactic of exile and assassination to render the Indian people completely docile. Once they were restricted to the reservations the might of the government was applied to the Indians to destroy their political and social institutions. Missionaries and government agents worked to undermine the influence of the old people and the medicine men. Of all the great Indian leaders perhaps only Red Cloud of the Oglala Sioux maintained his influence in his tribe until his death.

After the war chiefs had been killed or rendered harmless, Indians seemed to drift into a timeless mist. There appeared to be no leaders with which the general public could identify. The status of the Indian became a nebulous question which seemed familiar and important but for which there was apparently no answer.

Missionaries soon filled the vacuum through clever exploitation of natives who had turned Christian. There began in the East the great round of testimonial appearances of native clergymen who made speeches appealing for more missionary work among their tribes. Church congregations, indoctrinated with the message of the White Man's Burden, cooed with satisfaction to hear formerly fierce and feathered warriors relate how they had found the Lord and been brought out of their pagan darkness.

Poor things, so great had been the pressure on them to conform to the white man's way that they could do nothing else if they and their people were to survive. Only the fickle sentimentality of the churches often stood between them and the government policy of total dispersal or extinction of their people.

But the Christianized warrior role did not provide any significant means by which white people could identify with the real desires and needs of the

Indian people. The post-pagans simply recited what they had been taught concerning their people's needs. Indian beliefs held most tenaciously were forbidden subjects and there was no way to attract the sympathy of the public to support ideas that were considered foreign.

After the turn of the century, Jim Thorpe almost overnight changed the image of the Indian in the mind of the public. Suddenly the Indian as the superathlete dominated the scene. This concept was soon replaced by the Indian as a show business personality with the rise to popularity of Will Rogers, the Cherokee humorist.

In large measure the Indian path to visibility has been paralleled by the Negro. A mythology created to explain Jim Thorpe and Will Rogers was later applied to Joe Louis and Dick Gregory in order to make Negroes comprehensible when they began to appear in American life. After the Indian had been accepted as a humorous, athletic, subspecies of white man, historians and popular writers revisited the past and carved out a role for the Indian that overlooked the centuries of bloodshed between white and red, effectively neutralizing historical betrayals of the Indian by the government.

The supreme archetype of the white Indian was born one day in the pulp magazines. This figure would not only dominate the pattern of what Indians had been and would be, but also actually block efforts to bring into focus the crises being suffered by Indian tribes.

It was Tonto—the Friendly Indian Companion—who galloped onto the scene, pushing the historical and the contemporary Indians into obscurity.

Tonto was everything that the white man had always wanted the Indian to be. He was a little slower, a little dumber, had much less vocabulary, and rode a darker horse. Somehow Tonto was always *there*. Like the Negro butler and the Oriental gardener, Tonto represented a silent subservient subspecies of Anglo-Saxon whose duty was to do the bidding of the all-wise white hero.

The standard joke, developed as group consciousness arose, had the Lone Ranger and Tonto surrounded by a tribe of hostile Indians, with Tonto inquiring of the Lone Ranger, "Well, White Man?" The humor came from Tonto's complete departure from his stereotype. The real Tonto would have cut down his relatives with a Gatling gun rather than have a hair on said Ranger's head mussed.

But Tonto never rebelled, never questioned the Lone Ranger's judgment, never longed to go back to the tribe for the annual Sun Dance. Tonto was a cultureless Indian for Indians and an uncultured Indian for whites.

Tonto cemented in the minds of the American public the cherished falsehood that all Indians were basically the same—friendly and stupid. Indeed, the legend grew, not only were tribes the same, but all Indians could be brought to a state of grace—a reasonable facsimile of the white —by a little understanding.

But Tonto also had another quality about him. Although inarticulate to a fault, he occasionally called upon his primitive wisdom to get the Lone Ranger out of a tight spot. Tonto had some indefinable aboriginal knowledge that operated deus ex machina in certain situations. It was almost as if the Lone Ranger had some tragic flaw with respect to the mysterious in nature which Tonto could easily handle and understand.

In those crises where Tonto had to extricate the Lone Ranger by some impossibly Indian trick, a glimmer of hope was planted in the subconscious of the Indian that someday he would come into his own. Few whites realized what this was, or that it existed; but to Indians it was an affirmation of the old Indian way. In an undefined sense, Tonto was able to universalize Indianness for Indians and lay the groundwork for the eventual rejection of the white man and his strange ways.

And so when no one succeeded Thorpe and Rogers, Tonto cornered the market as the credible Indian personality. Turncoats of history who could be resurrected as examples of the "friendly Indian companion" were publicized in an attempt to elaborate on the Tonto image.

Squanto, who had welcomed the Pilgrims and helped them destroy the tribes in Connecticut and Long Island, was reworked as a "friendly" Indian as opposed to Massasoit, the father of King Philip the Wampanoag chief, who had suspicions about the Pilgrims from the very start.

Keokuk, the Sac and Fox subchief who had betrayed Black Hawk during the war which bears his name, was also brought back to life as a friendly companion. Washakie, the Shoshone chief who tattled on the other tribes every chance he got and finally received a nice reservation in Wyoming, was another early fink who was honored posthumously as a good guy.

Eastern society matrons somehow began to acquire blood from John Smith and Pocahontas. The real Indian leaders who had resisted the encroachments of the white man and died protecting their homes, became sullen renegades unworthy of note.

Both whites and Indians were buried under the weight of popular pseudo-history in which good guys dominated the scene and tribes were indiscriminately scattered throughout the West in an effort to liven up the story. Contemporary Indian leadership was suppressed by tales of the folk heroes of the past. Attempts to communicate contemporary problems were brushed aside in favor of the convenient and comfortable pigeonhole into which Indians had been placed. The Sioux warbonnet, pride of the Plains Indians, became the universal symbol of Indianism. Even tribes that had never seen an eagle were required to wear a warbonnet to prove their lineage as Indians.

It was probably only because Indians were conveniently forgotten that a movement for national unity of all tribes became a possibility. So rigid was the stereotype of the friendly childlike Indian that all efforts by Indians to come together were passed off as the prattling of children who could not possibly do anything without instructions from their white friends.

Indian tribes were thus freed to experiment with the concept of inter-tribal unity because they were considered irrelevant. First on regional levels, occasionally with regional congresses, then finally on a national basis, tribes began to come together. They soon learned to use the prejudices of the friendly whites to their own advantage.

Reconstruction of past traitors as good Indians also brought with it re-membrances of previous attempts to unify the tribes and repel the white invaders. Indian unity had been an old dream. Deganawidah had forged the great Iroquois confederacy out of a miscellaneous group of refugee tribes who had been driven out of the Missouri-Arkansas area in the fif-teenth century by the stronger Osage and Quapaw tribes. Eventually this conglomeration dominated the northern portion of the United States com-pletely. They were the balance of power in the colonial wars between Eng-land and France.

In the South the Creek confederacy had controlled a vast area in what is now Georgia, Mississippi, and Alabama with extensions of its power well into northern Florida. The Natchez confederacy ruled the Mississippi River plains almost completely and extended its influence a considerable distance southwestward.

With the westward movement of whites, temporary alliances were formed for the purpose of protecting hunting grounds. Pontiac and later Tecumseh brought the tribes together for momentary successes against the whites. But always it was too late with too little. Nowhere was there enough time for effective groupings to be built which guaranteed more than sporadic success.

In the Great Plains, traditional hunting alliances did their best to pre-vent white encroachment on their hunting grounds, but they could not stem the tide. The Sioux, Cheyenne, and Arapaho united briefly to send Custer on his way. But shortly after the battle the tribes split into a number of small bands which were all rounded up and placed on reservations by the following winter.

In the southern plains the Kiowa and Comanche had occasional suc-cesses before being overcome and sent to their western Oklahoma reserva-tion. The desert areas saw the Paiutes and Shoshones futilely oppose the white man but quickly give in. The Northwest had a brief Yakima war and an even briefer struggle by Chief Joseph and his Nez Perces.

By and large the hunting economy was so entrenched that the destruction of the buffalo eliminated the economic base by which tribal alliances were cemented. The tribes seemed doomed to follow the buffalo. No large number of people could be kept together because they could not be fed. Thus sustained warfare was impossible for the tribes while still a way of life for the white man. In separate groups the tribes were easily defeated and confined to reservations through a series of so-called peace treaties. In fact, treaties were ultimatums dictated by historical reality. While the tribes could have fought on, absolute extinction would have been their fate.

Because buffalo and other game were so essential to the tribes, hunting areas defined the manner in which tribes would fight and where. It was fairly easy to divide and conquer the various tribes by exploiting their rivalry over hunting grounds. This the white man did with deadly and consummate skill. Indian warfare was oriented toward protection of food supply and courageous exploits. Sustained warfare to protect or control territory which they could not settle was inconceivable to most of the tribes. Killing others simply to rid the land of them was even more unthinkable. Thus the white man's way of war was the deadly antithesis of the Indian's.

From Plymouth Rock to the lava beds of northern California, the white man divided and conquered as easily as if he were slicing bread. The technique was not used simply to keep different tribes from uniting, but also to keep factions of the same tribe quarreling so that when their time came they would be unable to defend themselves. And most important, the United States government used the treaty as an ultimate weapon to destroy the tribal political institutions by recognizing some men as chiefs and refusing to recognize others.

In treating for lands, rights of way, and minerals, commissioners negotiating for the government insisted on applying foreign political concepts to the tribes they were confronting. Used to dealing with kings, queens, and royalty, the early white men insisted on meeting the supreme political head of each tribe. When they found none, they created one and called the man they had chosen *the Chief.*

Finding a chief at treaty-signing time was no problem. The most pliable man who could be easily bribed was named chief and the treaty was signed. Land cessions were often made and a tribe found itself on the way to a treeless desert before it knew what had happened. Most of the Indian wars began because of this method of negotiation. The Indians were always at a loss to explain what had happened. They got mad when told to move off lands which they had never sold and so they fought. Thus were renegades created.

Most tribes had never defined power in authoritarian terms. A man consistently successful at war or hunting was likely to attract a following in direct proportion to his continuing successes. Eventually the men with the greatest followings composed an informal council which made important decisions for the group. Anyone was free to follow or not, depending upon his own best judgment. The people only followed a course of action if they were convinced it was best for them. This was as close as most tribes ever got to a formal government.

In an absolutely democratic social structure like the Indian tribe, formal legal negotiations and contractual arrangements were nearly out of the question. Once a man's word was given it bound him because of his integrity, not because of what he had written on a sheet of paper.

Men went to war because they had faith in a leader, not because they were drafted to do so or because they had signed a paper pledging themselves to be hired killers for a set period of time. Indians had little respect for white generals who did not lead their men into battle and contemptuously tagged the first white soldiers they saw as the "men who take orders from the chief who is afraid to fight."

The basic Indian political pattern has endured despite efforts by the federal government to change it. The people still follow a man simply because he produces. The only difference between two centuries ago and today is that now the Bureau of Indian Affairs defines certain ground rules by which leaders can be changed. These rules are called tribal elections. Otherwise, leadership patterns have not changed at all.

Today a man holds his chairmanship as long as he produces, or at least appears to produce, for his tribe. Without making substantial progress or having the ability to present a fighting image, a man's term in tribal office is short and severe Demands are great. Some tribes have never had an incumbent re-elected because tribal goals far surpass any conceivable performance. A few tribes have had strong men dominate tribal affairs for long periods of time because of their tremendous following with the people.

Frank Ducheneaux of the Cheyenne River Sioux, Joe Garry, six-time President of the NCAI and long-time chairman of the Coeur d'Alenes of Idaho, Marvin Mull of the San Carlos Apaches, Roger Jourdain of the Red Lake Chippewas, and James Jackson of the Quinaults have all had many years as chairman of their respective tribes. Each man has been able to keep his chairmanship because of the progressive programs he has initiated, which have in turn created more respect and a greater following for him within the tribe. Success and respect go hand in hand in Indian affairs.

But other tribes throw out chairmen with such regularity it's almost an annual event, anticipated with pleasure by the reservation people. In those cases the tribe has no discernible goals except to throw the rascals out. The safest political position is always as member of the out group.

Unlike hunting days, production today depends upon the ability to gain concessions from governmental agencies. Some tribes demand more from the bureau than others. Ability to produce the necessary demands in reasonable yet militant terms is sometimes enough to win and hold the chairmanship, even though the demands are not often met.

The more sophisticated the tribal demands, the better the chances a militant chairman has of remaining in office. The simpler the demands, the more criticism seems to be directed at the leader and the less his chances are for political survival.

This pattern of tribal behavior creates a basic insecurity which has a double edge when seen nationally in movements toward unification of the tribes. Some chairmen use state and national organizations as sounding boards for militant speeches that hopefully prove to reservation people they are not afraid to fight for Indian rights. Other chairmen withdraw from national and state inter-tribal organizations when they are elected to demonstrate that by their power alone the tribe is protected from its enemies.

Inter-tribal cooperation therefore has two aspects: one is to allow the chairman to fight paper tigers for the effect it will have on his critics; the other is for a chairman to advance his own plan for national unity which will give him such stature that his tribe will gain leverage in its dealings with private and governmental agencies.

It is on the national scene, however, that new and different forces, which alter the methods by which Indian leadership defines its goals, come into play.

Years ago churches, anthropologists, and bureaucrats all discovered that it was a good idea to have Indians attend a meeting on Indian problems. It looked better. But they certainly didn't have to invite the *wrong* kind of Indian. Like the treaty-makers of old, they could pick and choose who would represent the tribe and what philosophy he would support. Red leaders therefore had to adopt an official double-talk in order to bring reservation problems into the sphere of national communication.

For some time, conferences began to be set up, with white men outlining what would be accomplished and giving the background as to why their particular theory was best for Indians at that time. Some of these white men were so successful that they became the Great White Fathers who had almost total control of Indian policy. As for the Indians, while they were invited to the conferences, they were there only to agree with the proceedings or to enhance the white man's reputation as the *one* who knew what was best for the tribes.

Of all the white saviors, Oliver La Farge was perhaps the best known and most skillful manipulator of Indian people. La Farge dealt primarily with Uncle Tomahawks who would say anything to stay on the good side of him. Real Indian leadership was anathema to La Farge and the thought of a national union of the tribes was complete heresy in his eyes.

La Farge built his reputation through his novels. During the 1950's he was the white who always took it upon himself to come forward as the protector of Indian people in the press. But he also realized that he could not risk placing his organization in a position where its tax status might be questioned. So La Farge never made any appearances before Congressional committees during the termination period of legislation. Instead, the tribes had to bear the brunt of Congressional ire while La Farge reaped the benefits of national publicity as the defender of the lowly childlike Indian.

In 1954, when the NCAI met and began to plan its Point Four Development Program modeled after the experiment of Operation Bootstrap in Puerto Rico, La Farge hurriedly put together his own Point Four Program, which incorporated the basic points the tribes had been considering. He put forward his version after the tribes had fully discussed the proposal and before the Indians could publicize their efforts. Thus La Farge undercut Indian leadership in order to strengthen his own image as their savior.

Throughout his life La Farge looked contemptuously upon the Indian people as an inferior brand of human being who, if not properly controlled, would be certain to hurt himself. There was never any doubt in La Farge's mind that he knew best about Indians.

La Farge and his friends systematically undercut Indian leadership. National Indian leaders had to play or suffer the consequences. La Farge's successors, the Great White Fathers of today, continually attempt to appear as people with some mysterious knowledge about Indians, derived either from then extensive travels or their research into "the Indian problem."

Indian people were kept in a stupor of self-acknowledged incompetency during La Farge's reign as Indian spokesman. Because of his prominence as a writer and his access to public relations media in the East, La Farge was able to effectively block efforts by the tribes to gain recognition as a people capable of self-determination. For all the eastern United States knew, Indians moved only because Oliver La Farge had shown them the way and there was, it appeared, no significant movement by Indians except that which he planned.

But gradually a more sophisticated type of white man came into Indian country. He actually wanted to solve some of the problems and was not awed by the status La Farge and others had achieved as protectors of the Indians.

This new trend meant that reservations were scoured for a successful Indian who could *motivate* others. The same game was played, but this time the values were derived from a liberal orientation rather than a conservative one. Many national Indian leaders of the last generation had made their reputations by demonstrating their ability to be non-Indian. They were comparable to the old timers who had toured the continent with Buffalo Bill and acted pseudo-warlike for Europeans rather than stay home as real warriors chased all day by the cavalry.

Many of today's leaders were attending high school and college during the heyday of liberal self-helpism. Many of us were dragged from conference to conference to hear nearly identical speeches by model Indians of the day. I call to mind bits and pieces of speeches I have heard and a composite speech runs as follows:

> Well, I'm an INDIN, just like you. [Never INDIAN. They had to identify with us.] I was born in a one-room log cabin with a dirt floor [later a *rehab* shack], and I walked fifty miles a day to school, a little one-room [everything was one-room in those days] school where I got my education, and I went to a little one-room chapel where I met my Lord every Sunday and He replenished my soul. And then I went to college, and although I received scholarships from the government and my church, my parents still had to give me most of their money and I still had only one meal a day. But I persevered and graduated and then I got a job and started my climb upward and so after many years of hard work I am now a success. I am accepted by the best people and eat in the fanciest hotels. I believe all Indians could do the same if they would only apply themselves. I hope all of you young people are inspired by my success and that you will someday be as successful as I am.

And then we used to watch this INDIN meekly agree with the most outrageous and prepostrous schemes to solve "the Indian problem" and take his farewell.

With modest examples like that it is a shame that so many of us didn't make it. But we just didn't. Somehow we realized that the day of the successful individual was gone. Time had run out for the individualist and the days of the professional rebel had come into vogue.

The professional rebel was a younger person who was invited to conferences primarily to recite the wrongs of the white man, the real issue of the last century, never the current white man. The idea was that we could make the white feel guilty. When he felt guilty it would somehow make his efforts more real, and then he was happy again.

It would curl your hair to learn that the white man had perpetuated a colonial system, that he had done all sorts of irrational things to Indians; then made an about-face and tried to atone for the past, in order that his ancestors might sleep peacefully. Although this is what these conferences produced, we have yet to experience white atonement.

The funny thing about this era was that one subject was absolutely forbidden. And that was any attempt to compare the white man's treatment of Indians with that of other minority groups. That might have revealed a startling case against the whites' dealings with all dark-skinned peoples. Endless hours were spent to convince us that somehow, in a way neither we nor they understood, Indians were unique in relation to other minorities.

Little did we realize that the main tactic was to keep in our minds the fact that if we were spearate, then only a certain group of whites could understand us, care for us, and work with us.

There was very little we could have done anyway. They controlled all the travel money, organized all the conferences, made all the chiefs. We had not yet learned how to bring Indian problems to the attention of the public, but we thought that there was some impelling reason why we should. In the meantime the white friend was busy with his own orgy of self-flagellation. Our role was to crystallize his guilt individually as if he alone had done all these things and to us personally.

After the conferences, missionaries, educators, and bureaucrats proceeded to do exactly as they had planned to do anyway. Some continued the very practices they had confessed were wrong, but with released vigor now that they had undergone a catharsis at the conference.

The guilt era ended when suddenly the skies opened and the money poured down. In 1964 there was talk about a great war that was to be waged. It was, we found out, a War on the Poor, officially designated as the War on Poverty.

The War on Poverty created a land office business (to use a painful phrase) in which everyone with a soft spot in his heart for the Indian, a desire for big money, and a plan to solve the *plight* of the reservations headed for the nearest tribe to offer his talents.

Universities that hadn't known that Indians existed outside of the textbooks charged into the forefront of social responsibility. Indian centers sprang up where no Indians had previously been allowed to loiter. Plans for massive archives, research, pilot projects, and developments mushroomed until we were convinced there would not be enough Indians to go around.

Washington was flooded with *grass roots* proposals to fight poverty on the different reservations. Looking out from a tribal office in the late afternoon, one could see a veritable wave of consultants treading their way to the motels. Evaluators greatly outnumbered workers. Feasibility replaced reality.

But plans were not automatically funded. Everyone was looking for *the* complete proposal that would solve every problem at once. Conferences dwelt on complete solutions. It sounded like the French Revolution, as proposal after proposal was presented to the assembled delegates only to be demolished by those experts on poverty.

It became popular to shoot down proposals with grass-roots sayings. The ultimate psych-out game of today's Indians was developed. Unity took a strange twist when proposals were gunned down because *all* tribes were not represented or because the tribes were so different that no one plan could serve them all.

Various tribal leaders would be asked to present their interpretation of tribal needs. After an Indian had finished speaking, educators, bureaucrats, sociologists, and anthropologists holding the opposing point of view would rise and, like a chorus in a Greek play, proclaim, "But he doesn't represent the *grass roots.*"

One educator constantly blasted me because NCAI didn't represent *all* the Indians. Then one day a fellow bureaucrat received a buffeting by urban Negroes and this same educator asked me to send a telegram of support because NCAI "represented all the Indian community." Such were the inconsistencies around which the national unity of Indian tribes was being predicated.

Indians who had spent their lives in Wounded Knee, Red Shirt, Cherry Creek, and Black River Falls were suddenly *unrepresentative* of the *real* Indian people and unceremoniously drummed out of consideration by conferees. Even full bloods who two years before would not have been invited because they were *too* Indian were brushed aside because they were thought not to know the reservation problems.

One full-blood acquaintance of mine had spent some thirty years on his tribal council. He was dismissed because he was part of the establishment!

Indian unity and Indian problems became the subjects for intense manipulation behind the scenes, as professional Indian-lovers fought to keep some semblance of cooperation among the tribes while arrayed against it were the universities, educators, and old-line bureaucrats. One friend of mine, a sociologist, suggested that we Indians be heeded "so far, but only insofar, as they represent all the Indians." After that remark I was tempted to rise at the next conference and state that I represented 107 of 315 tribes, so I could be trusted 107/315 of the time. And that the building was on fire.

The ultimate insult came at a conference at which about thirty of the most knowledgable Indians in the country were present to discuss Indian education. They were airily dismissed by a white educator because the *real Indians* were the ones he worked with and, since none of *them* were in attendance, the white felt he ought to represent them because he alone knew what *they* wanted.

In the last several years the very concept of unity has been used against the tribes to prevent their cooperation on national programs. Knowing that tribes are in all stages of development, whites have insisted upon uniformity of goals and definitions before they will accept Indian ideas as real.

Because there cannot be such a concensus, Indian unity has been made to appear impossible.

National conferences, even National Congress conventions, have been confused by the whites' demand for that single answer which can then be passed on to government, church, or private agencies for the solution of Indian problems.

With the broad spectrum of tribes and the different levels of sophistication, plus the background maneuvering of whites with a financial or emotional interest in the outcome, you can imagine the impossible discussions that characterize national Indian meetings.

The first Indian will announce that he lives in a one-room shack. He will be rebutted by an Indian educator who has lost his identity between two cultures. Another will agree about the two cultures and will immediately be refuted by an old timer fighting for his treaty rights who is simultaneously challenged because he doesn't speak for all the Indians.

A national Indian meeting thus bears more resemblance to the Tower of Babel Improvement Association than it does to a strategy planning session.

The major problem, therefore, in unifying the tribes and supporting constructive leadership is that everyone is subject to judgment according to the standards of two distinct points of view. The white society is not satisfied with anything less than the efficiency of an Irish political machine. The Indian society expects little articulation, but infallible and successful exploits. And there is no attempt by either white or Indian to distinguish between the two.

Indians have no concept of teamwork as it is known by white society. Assignment of personnel to component jobs within an action plan leaves Indians cold. Rather, they expect leaders to charge ahead and complete the task. If anyone wants to assist in the job, so much the better. But there is no sense of urgency or need for efficiency in anything that is undertaken.

With their social structure largely undefined and modern society changing to data processing, Indians appear quite primitive. Charts, graphs, and statistics are irrelevant to most tribes. Their concern is the reality of the goals, the eventual effect a program will have on the tribe. Techniques and means of operation are left largely for staff considerations.

Whites who attempt to help Indians are constantly frustrated by their tragic lack of understanding of Indian people. For Indians always know exactly what position they will take on major issues, how far they can push certain concepts, and when to delay so as to wear out their opponents and eventually get their way.

There is usually not the slightest difference in what the tribes want for the future, though any detectable difference is immediately grasped by whites and used to form a major breach with the hopes of preventing any conclusion being reached.

While this dissension is superficially disheartening, understandings are quite often worked out through a technique which resolves issues without bringing matters to the floor. But there is a difference between the manner in which Indians use dissension and the way that conferences are manipulated by white onlookers.

Whites generally have some tangible motive for stalling an Indian meeting. Generally it is benign and relates to what they honestly think is best for the tribes. Other times it is simply to keep the tribes apart so the whites can eventually get their own programs approved.

Indians use dissension and controversy to guide the sense of the meeting and also to maintain prestige among each other. It is a thrill to watch the psychological games played by Indians at a meeting. The most common game is an appeal to unity.

One Indian will get up and make a suggestion. He will be followed by another, who will agree completely with him but will phrase the speech in such a way as to create the impression that his predecessor is somehow against tribal unity. The second speaker creates such a sentiment in this audience that man after man gets up and speaks eloquently for unity of all Indians. Unity speeches roll down like a waterfall. Never did the Democrats unify like the Indians. If northern liberal Democrats and southern racist Democrats are cozy, Indians are stifling in their unity.

It would be fair to say that the best way to get a heated argument going in an Indian meeting is to speak on the need for unity. But the concern for unity serves to postpone divisions on the real issues in which unity is vital. It is far better to fight over unity than over something crucial to tribal existence.

Controversy over efforts to unify is naturally supported by Indian cultural motifs. In the old times as we have seen, a man's position rested primarily upon his ability to attract followers. Indians have come to rely on a strong leader and this in turn has created the War Chief complex.

The War Chief during the days of glory provided success or failure for the tribe. Leadership often depended upon a quasi-religious-vocation and men were intimately concerned with the religious as well as political meaning of their lives.

In the Ghost Dance days, messiahship came to dominate Indian thought patterns and all expectations were tinged with this other-worldly hope of salvation. Every Indian leader of today must face the question of whether or not he is a great figure of the past reincarnated to lead his people to victory, for legends die hard among our people.

One in a leadership role is therefore constantly bothered by undefined doubts as to his ultimate role in his people's historical journey. He is inevitably drawn to compare himself in a mystical sense with Crazy Horse, Joseph, Geronimo, and others.

Initial spectacular success creates speculation as to how a leader compares with well-known tribal heros. If a man compares favorably, more work is placed upon him because of his capability and the people, satisfied with his performance, depend on him more and more and do less for themselves.

At my first convention of the NCAI there was very little for me to do because I was so new that no one had any confidence in me. A couple of years later I was fairly run to death doing minor errands because people had come to depend on me for a great many things.

Because Indian people place absolute dependence on their leaders, they exhaust more leaders every year than any other minority group. The useful national life of an Indian leader today is about two and a half years. After that he is physically and emotionally spent. His ideas have been digested and the tribes are ready to move on.

Unity, because of the ancient leadership patterns and the constant personal involvement between rival chiefs, becomes a function of personalities rather than issues. Unity as a team of experts is absolutely hopeless. Dynasties are impossible to maintain nationally and even temporary alliances are often destroyed by loss of a single individual.

National unification forms around popular leaders. But these people are generally worked to death by the time a significant number of people are supporting their program or before a large number of tribes accept them. The last three Executive Directors of the National Congress of American Indians achieved the largest number of member tribes the last year they held office.

When national or regional unification is based upon the personality of the leader, insane jealousies develop which are fed by white elements hoping to weaken tribal alliances. But Indians themselves do more to permanently weaken efforts to develop effective working relationships between tribes because of the intense rivalry which they develop by regions, states, tribes, and programs.

National Congress conventions are often split according to regional lines and the idea of capturing the presidency for a certain area becomes all consuming, pushing aside obvious real problems that face all the tribes.

Let no one say that only the white man is cruel with his periodic assassinations and grief orgies. Or that blacks and Spanish cannot achieve unity. The Indian is so much more exquisitely skilled at political warfare and makes it so much more a casual game.

Indians know the human mind intimately. They can dwell for hours on slight nuances that others would completely miss or feel unworthy of their attention. I would put up an Indian brain-washing team against the Chinese Communists any day of the week.

Indians know the Indian mind best of all. They savor innuendo and inference above all. Consequently Indian meetings always have that undercurrent of psych-out that is a veritable preamble to existence as an Indian and the very antithesis of unity as the white man knows it.

I discovered this aspect of Indian politics at my second convention as NCAI Director. We had put together a very effective team the previous year, working hard to develop the organization and increase its ability to bring the tribes together. I had assumed that we would all be elected again because of our success in reconstituting the organization. To my chagrin I discovered that the tribes were systematically dissolving and reforming our team simply because they wanted to have an exciting election and feared that we would be re-elected without any real fight. They wanted action.

There is no way, therefore, that a person involved in national Indian politics can be assured of his position no matter how good he is and what his record has been. Dissidents often take advantage of the War Chief complex and lead their opponents down the road of messiahship—only to later accuse them of thinking they are really the Indian messiah. Slight hints here and there are often the tip of the iceberg of jealousy or discontent.

I have watched devoted, exhausted men cry because their tribe had totally rejected them at the height of their successes without so much as a backward glance.

With leadership and unity so intensely personal, unless a man is extremely charismatic, incredibly lucky, and hides his true purposes from inquisitive whites, his chances for success nationally are nil. Above all he must accept the social and ceremonial aspect of Indian politics and work within that framework to bring issues into focus for his people.

Among those people occupying national leadership roles there is a common tacit understanding of their common plight. Unless there is an impelling reason to go against another leader, Indians will generally support each other against the common enemy—the out group.

Many people would rather see a meeting come to no conclusion than embarrass a good man in public if such embarrassment would give his enemies weapons to be used against him. Most people realize that part of the chairman's job is to make a good showing for the tribe wherever he goes. Prestige committee assignments are handed out like presents at Christmas in an effort to maintain working relationships between tribal groups.

Most meetings held by Indians come to no conclusions which could be understood as agreements to do certain things. But every person attending a high-level meeting of Indians knows exactly what courses of action will be supported by the majority of tribes and exactly how to interpret the actions of the meeting to his people. Rarely do minutes of national meetings even need to be kept because of the silent understandings reached there.

The result of national meetings, therefore, is that there is mutual support and strength in the general concensus of tribes, from which each tribe gains more leverage and room to maneuver against the outsiders. It would be highly unlikely that an Indian meeting would or could develop a Poor People's Campaign or a March on Washington. Direct action is extrinsic to general understanding and traditional methods of problem-solving. But the tribes are able to get more for their people because of the insistence on indirect action.

When the Poor People camped in Washington the leadership left no room for retreat, placing themselves in a position of little negotiability with respect to government agencies. Tribes rarely box themselves into a position such as that. Rather, they always have such flexibility that they can change positions overnight and appear to be entirely consistent. For example the Hualapai tribe reversed its stand completely on the Marble Canyon Dam, finally supporting it, and no one thought a thing about it. Abernathy would not have dared make such a turnabout after his campaign began in Washington; the Hualapai could have changed every year and pulled it off.

The struggle is not so much one of unification but of who will eventually call the shots in Indian Affairs. Competition is thus multi-leveled and inter-group as well as racial. National and state Indian organizations are constantly being undercut by white interest groups in an effort to control the vast sums spent in Indian Affairs every year. No one wants a cut of the action for personal monetary gain; prestige, power, and emotional involvement play a much more vital role. Ego moves Indian Affairs in both white and red spheres much more than the dollar does.

The largest and most consistent national movement toward unification is the National Congress of American Indians. The NCAI is a small united nations of tribes with a past checkered from battles on every level. Its existence is only grudgingly admitted by white interest organizations because of their very reasonable fear that if the public found out Indians were doing things for themselves the annual fund appeals would look ridiculous. For the most part these people masquerade as friends of the Indian, presenting a distorted picture of the unbelievable poverty which they alone are fighting and perpetuating the image of the inarticulate incompetent savage who would be utterly destroyed save for their work. But like the buffalo, their days have been numbered. Each time an Indian organization wins a victory they must inevitably claim it partially for themselves in order to prevent, or at least postpone, the day when their downfall is complete.

Meanwhile, the National Congress charges through Indian country with sporadic successes and failures. Tribal membership varies from thirty tribes to over one hundred according to the climate for temporary unification. When times are plush, as they have been in the 1960's, the number of tribes participating is fairly high. When hard times come, membership dwindles and each tribe embarks on its own course to best determine its relationships with a menacing Congress.

It is this phenomenon of tribal membership that holds the key to understanding Indian unity and its twin, Indian leadership. The tribes do not depend upon the national organization for assistance on the local level. Where the NAACP, CORE, SNCC, and other Civil Rights groups have made use of local situations to highlight problems and work for their solutions, tribes totally reject assistance from the NCAI on the local level. It is inconceivable to most tribes that a national organization would work in localities to assist them. Rather, they look at the NCAI strictly in terms of the national scene. Consequently, membership is an abstraction whose mere presence heightens the total mystery of things.

The political effect of this behavior is just the opposite of what the tribes expect. Local difficulties bog them down and prevent progress in many areas of concern. Precedents that affect tribal rights all across the country are set on the local scene. Most of the problems Indians encounter are local, yet they refuse to face them on a realistic basis.

In recent years the NCAI has been able to sit back and pick its national battles. It has had considerable success in some scraps. If anything, leaders at the national level have set their sights too low and could have accomplished more with no more effort.

But with emphasis on creating a position for negotiating inside the government establishment and rejecting action programs used by the blacks, Indians have doomed themselves to political obscurity and impotence. Where SCLC could create pressure for a number of major laws through marches, Indians wait to take advantage of the tide of social legislation and gain a few crumbs when the goods are divided.

Unless Indians can adapt their tactics to place more emphasis on exploiting the local situation they will remain an unknown factor in American life. Always, it seems, issues detach themselves from the local situation and nebulously float off into the paragraphs of the perennial Task Force reports done by Interior and related agencies every few years.

So Indians are placed in the most inconsistent position for determining their own policy. They can very quickly reach a concensus on their problems. They are fairly sophisticated and experienced in getting their way with government agencies. But when they attempt to articulate what they are doing so that the white society can understand them, unity dissolves into chaos and the movement, along with the ideas supporting it, collapses.

Indians simply cannot externalize themselves. Externalization implies a concern for the future. Indians welcome the future but don't worry about it. Traditionally the tribes had pretty much what they wanted. There was no reason to get up tight about wealth and its creation. The land had plenty for everyone. Piling up gigantic surpluses implied a mistrust of the Great Spirit and a futile desire to control the future.

In addition no tribes had complex writing as did the white society. Winter counts and stories memorized by the favorite storytellers served to perpetuate the great events in tribal history. Other than that, there was no concern for recording events. Life thus had a contemporaneous aspect which meant immediate experience of life, not continual analysis and dissection.

Attempts to force the tribes to expound on great themes for dispersion to non-Indian parties results in sheer chaos and disaster. Why, the people feel, should we explain anything to someone else, it is enough that we understand it.

Inability to use the white man's objective criteria most seriously hampers Indian programs. Resolutions passed at national meetings appear to be like white man's policy statements, but are actually only a polite nod to his way of doing business. It is almost as if by passing a resolution the tribes had fulfilled all righteousness for the express satisfaction of the whites who might be watching.

This type of operation creates the most baffling misunderstandings between Indians and the non-Indians with whom they must work. Actions of a tribal or national organization, although clear on the surface, seldom mean what they appear to mean and often mean something entirely different. If one cannot read between the lines he is at a loss to explain the apparent inconsistency.

In early 1967 there was a big meeting in Washington, D.C., to consider Udall's Omnibus Bill. Though this was heralded as the greatest thing ever to come down the pike, tribes universally rejected it. Yet for five days in January the tribes argued all around the point and, rather than rejecting it outright, sent a letter to President Johnson asking for more time. Everyone knew that another century would not suffice to change the mind of one tribe.

Many of our white friends have been ecstatic at some of our speeches, resolutions, and policy statements in the NCAI. Later, however, they've been horrified to see us take absolutely opposite stands on an issue.

To understand Indians and their unique place among the minority groups, one must look at unity through Indian eyes. Unity is strictly a social function of the tribes. Indians prefer to meet and have a good time; conventions are when you have a chance to get together and renew old friendships and learn to trust one another.

The real impact of the NCAI is the personal trust developed between people which in turn affects how each tribe views the others. The convention is merely a facade to confuse any wandering white man who should be in the neighborhood. After several days together, tribal leaders instinctively know how much they can depend upon each other, what a certain tribe is experimenting upon, and what issues are vital to their tribes. Then they are ready to go home again.

Social unification can best be illustrated by observation of the many powwows and celebrations held around Indian country each year. At a certain point in the program the announcer will proudly state that "eighty-three tribes are represented at this great event." Beware.

What the man means is that people from eighty-three different tribal backgrounds happened to have been in the neighborhood and decided to attend the doings; not that eighty-three tribes sent delegations to the event.

At one celebration a group of us each took turns adding up tribes and padded the total to well over one hundred tribes by simply stating that we had seen certain people from certain tribes present, although in fact we hadn't. Our announcer friend glowed at the prospect of so many tribes at powwow.

It is important to understand that the more tribes claimed, the better the powwow. This was an Indian doing and the more Indians involved the better everyone felt. This was unity for all of us.

What, after all, is unity but the fellowship of people? Too often, unified efforts are created simply to take advantage of people as one special interest group battles another for concessions from the government. America is certainly not a democracy when it is controlled by pressure groups. Rather, it is a pressure cooker waiting to explode when the wrong ingredients come together. Recent events show this tendency all too well.

After the latest Kennedy assassination, Congressman after Congressman came on TV and admitted that a vast majority of the American people wanted stricter gun control laws. But each stated that he couldn't do anything about it because of the big bad NRA lobby. Anyone swallowing that type of statement deserves to live in the land of a sniper.

Indians have always rejected unity as a weapon, though a number of younger Indians want unity precisely for that reason. Most of the tribes want unity as a fellowship of equals where they can play their Indian games with a minimum outside interference. Indian unity is what the churches mean when they say brotherhood, but which they dare not practice. It is what the white man seeks in his fraternities and exclusive clubs.

Like he has done everything else, the white man has turned the idea completely inside out when he has put unity into action. He has defined the right to be oneself as the right of exclusive privacy, never realizing that to be alone is to be dead. He has tried to create one society and has done so by creating an incredible number of pressure groups which control his society.

As Indians we will never have the efficient organization that gains great concessions from society in the marketplace. We will never have a powerful lobby or be a smashing political force. But we will have the intangible unity which has carried us through four centuries of persecution and we will survive. We will survive because we are a people unified by our humanity; not a pressure group unified for conquest. And from our greater strength we shall wear down the white man and finally outlast him. But above all, and this our strongest affirmation, we SHALL ENDURE as a people.

CAREY MCWILLIAMS

Racism on the West Coast, May 29, 1944

What we have reprinted here is Carey McWilliams's contemporary account of American concentration camps. Daniels (p. 221) gives the historical background for this peculiar act of racial aggression; McWilliams describes how the war caused the historical distrust of the "yellow peril" to erupt into a national policy. The full story of the internment of Japanese Americans in World War II is told in Gardner and Liftis, *The Great Betrayal.*

WITH THE REMOVAL from the West Coast of 100,000 persons of Japanese ancestry, and their subsequent internment, the artificially stimulated agitation which had stampeded the federal government into the adoption of this harsh wartime measure momentarily subsided. During the spring, summer and fall of 1942, all was quiet on the West Coast front. But in January, 1943, a new campaign, of unparalleled virulence, was launched against this luckless minority. Throughout 1943 it raged without let or hindrance. Before another pogrom is launched in this region, it is important that the nation realize just what prompted the extraordinary outburst of racial violence. For example, why was it that anti-Japanese, or rather anti-evacuee, agitation assumed such menacing proportions after every person of Japanese ancestry had been removed from the area and placed in protective custody? One would have assumed that such a harsh measure as mass evacuation would have satisfied even the most insistent pressure groups on the West Coast.

If these groups had really been concerned with the "security" of the area, mass evacuation would have satisfied their demands. But so-called "security" considerations had little to do with the organized pressure for mass evacuation. While insisting that all persons of Japanese ancestry should be removed from the West Coast, many of these same pressure groups were conducting a quiet but effective campaign *against the removal* of persons of Japanese ancestry from the strategically far more important Hawaiian Islands. For example, the powerful California Joint Immigration Committee indicated that it was "unalterably opposed" to the evacuation of the Japanese from the islands. For if Japanese were removed from Hawaii, they would necessarily have been transferred to the mainland. If they had been removed to the mainland, the number of resident Japanese would have been increased and some of them might not have returned to the islands after the war. What groups such as the California Joint Immigration Committee sought, in advocating mass evacuation, was not the removal of persons of Japanese ancestry from the West Coast, but their eventual removal from the United States.

By the fall of 1942, the War Relocation Authority had begun to experiment with the issuance of seasonal work permits. Several thousand evacuees, under this plan, had been permitted to leave the relocation centers to meet the manpower shortage in agriculture. This program was only initiated by the WRA after "very great pressure"—in Mr. Dillon Myer's phrase—had been brought to bear by the sugar-beet industry. Since the experiment proved entirely workable and satisfactory, the WRA was encouraged to expand the program. The emphasis in policy shifted from resentment in the centers to relocation outside the center. New procedures were evolved by which local evacuees might be given permanent releases permitting them to relocate in areas outside the Western Defense Command. By the end of 1942, several hundred evacuees had been given such permanent or indefinite leaves.

The moment that it became apparent that most, if not all, of the evacuees might be released in this manner, the West Coast pressure groups got busy. But they had always assumed that evacuation necessarily implied internment for the duration. The main motive back of the resumption of anti-evacuee agitation in January, 1943, was, therefore, to prevent the release of any further evacuees from the centers. If the pressure groups were genuinely desirous of preventing the return of the evacuees to the West Coast, then the most obvious considerations would dictate the necessity of their supporting the WRA in its efforts to relocate as many evacuees as possible in the Middle West and East before the war is over. But what these groups really want is mass deportation of all persons of Japanese ancestry; hence their insistence that the evacuees be confined in the centers during the war.

It is not necessary to infer the existence of such a motive in the resumption of agitation on the West Coast. One of the leaders of this agitation stated, at a meeting called in the fall of 1942 to plot the strategy for the campaign, that "we should strike now, while the sentiment over the country is right. The feeling in the East will grow more bitter before the war is over and if we begin *now* to try to shut out the Japanese after the war we have a chance of accomplishing something. Now that all the treaties between the two nations have been abrogated by Japan's war on the United States, Congress is under no treaty obligation and could easily pass an act ordering all nationals of Japan to return after the peace. . . . Maybe the return of the aliens would mean that some of the American-born would follow them."

Who are the leaders of this campaign? What organizations sponsor this movement? One of the most active leaders in the anti-evacuee campaign is Dr. John R. Lechner, who functions through his alter ego, the American-ism Educational League. It is interesting to note that Dr. Lechner was not originally in favor of mass evacuation. "Mass evacuation," he said "would only cause hardship both to the Japanese and other residents of the state" (The Los Angeles Daily News, January 21, 1942). The day following the delivery of this speech, he sent a marked clipping to the editor of a Los Angeles Japanese-American newspaper stating that he would greatly ap-preciate having some cards printed—gratis. He is the author of a pam-phlet entitled "Playing with Dynamite," full of the usual bedtime stories about the West Coast Japanese. On a recent visit to Washington, numerous officials received the impression that he was "representing the American Legion." In this issue of January 15, 1944, The California Legionnaire, speaking in the name of the Legion, not only repudiated any such connec-tion, but went on to characterize his action as being "in flagrant violation of written notice from our Department Commander."

Another "anti" organization is the Home Front Commandos, Inc., of Sacramento. This organization has inundated Northern California with racist manifestos. One of its recent pamphlets carries the caption: "Slap the Jap Rat," and still another is captioned: "No Jap Is Fit to Associate with Human Beings." These statements are made, of course, in reference to American citizens of Japanese ancestry. One of the main financial sup-porters of the organization is a Sacramento millionaire, Mr. C. M. Goethe, long prominent in the affairs of the Northern California Council of Churches and treasurer of the California Joint Immigration Committee. He is the founder and, I suspect, the chief member, of the Eugenics So-ciety of Northern California. The weird bulletins of the society contain endless derogatory remarks about Mexicans, Italians and, in fact, almost every ethnic group in America with the exception of what are termed "Old New Englanders" and "the Virginians." In Eugenics Pamphlet No. 12, is-sued before the war, one finds this interesting statement:

> Since Hitler has become Führer, he has made eugenics an applied sci-ence. Germany has set up hundreds of eugenic courts. These try German social inadequates as to their fitness for parenthood. Please do not think these trials are based on race hatreds. Whatever else may happen in the Reich, the eugenics trials proceed with fully as much caution as if they were held in the United States. Germany's plan is to eliminate all low-powers to make room for high-powers and thereby ALSO SAVE TAXES!

Still another "anti" group is the Pacific Coast Japanese Problem League, headed by Dr. John Carruthers—Presbyterian minister, graduate of Princeton, former professor of Religious History at Occidental College, for five years assistant to the president of the University of Southern California.

Like Dr. Lechner (another ex-clergyman), Dr. Carruthers has not always been anti-Japanese. During the years 1924–26, he was a director of the Council of International Relations, which was created primarily to combat anti-Oriental agitation on the West Coast. Testifying before a California Legislative Committee, Dr. Carruthers recently stated that, after an hour of prayer in "the privacy of that precious American heritage, the Christian home in a Christian city in a Christian land of freedom," he had come to the conclusion that it was his duty to urge "the deportation, if possible, by every means possible, of all Japanese from the American continent." The Japanese Americans, he said, should not object to this proposal, since, if they were really Christians, then "they ought to be glad to be shoved out anywhere that they can bear witness to the Kingdom of Christ."

Then there is the California Citizens' Association of Santa Barbara. And the California Citizens' Council of Los Angeles. This organization has been circulating petitions for the "ouster of the Japanese from California forever." Its slogan is: "Remember a Jap is a Jap." Its members are urged to place stickers on the windshields of their automobiles. The sticker contains a picture of a rat with a Japanese face. Still another organization is the American Foundation for the Exclusion of the Japanese; and yet another is No Japs, Inc., of San Diego. At the present time another organization, the Japanese Exclusion Association, is circulating a petition to place a special initiative measure on the November, 1944, ballot in California. Drafted as an amendment to the Alien Land Act, this proposed amendment, if adopted, would make it virtually impossible for Japanese aliens or persons "of the Japanese ancestry or other ancestry ineligible to citizenship under the naturalization laws of the United States" who owe allegiance to "any foreign Government, Emperor, Prince, or Potentate," to function economically in California. The statute would place the burden upon the Japanese American to prove that he did not possess dual citizenship.

The real force behind the "anti" movement in California, however, is the California Joint Immigration Committee, which speaks in the name of the American Legion, the State Federation of Labor, the Grange, and the Native Sons and Daughters of the Golden West. The Native Sons, with a membership of around 25,000, is particularly active in the campaign. This organization has traditionally been, not merely anti-Japanese, but anti-Oriental, anti-Mexican, anti-Negro. In a brief filed in a recent suit by which it sought to test the citizenship of the Nisei, or Japanese Americans, the organization contended that the words "we, the People of the United States," in the Constitution, refer to "the white people"; and that the "ourselves" of the Constitution "included white people only" (Appellant's Brief, p. 47, Reagan v. King). The California Joint Immigration Committee filed a written statement with the Tolan Committee in 1942 in which it contended that we had made a great mistake in conferring citizenship upon the Negro after the Civil War. These groups are, therefore, adherents of the doctrine of white supremacy and their propaganda is directly predicated on so-called "racial" considerations.

The West Coast's new campaign to prevent the release of any persons of Japanese ancestry from relocation centers for the duration of the war began in December, 1942, with the appointment by the American Legion, California Department, of a five-man committee to conduct "an impartial investigation of all Japanese Relocation Areas in the State of California." Among the members of this impartial committee were Harper L. Knowles (of La Follette Committee fame); H. J. McClatchy of the California Joint Immigration Committee; and State Senator Jack Tenney of Los Angeles County. Tenney heads the "Little Dies Committee" of the state legislature. Shortly after the committee had been appointed, Tenney announced that it would take over the investigation for the American Legion.

Within the next two months, literally hundreds of West Coast organizations "went on record" by the adoption of a series of stock resolutions on the "Japanese question." I have examined scores of these resolutions and have yet to see one that by its form or content would indicate that it had been offered *by the members* of the particular organization; invariably these resolutions were presented *for concurrence* by one or another of the groups mentioned. With the newspapers featuring this organized activity, feeling began to mount throughout California. The city of Gardena omitted from its honor roll of citizens in the service the names of seventeen Japanese Americans; the American Legion summarily revoked the charter of the Townsend Harris and Commodore Perry Post (made up of Japanese American veterans of the First World War). In Portland, Oregon, the Legion protested when local citizens sought to provide some volunteer care for a Japanese cemetery. Vigilante groups were formed in Salinas "to prevent the return of the Japanese." The California Federation of Women's Clubs expressed grave concern for their "sisters" in the East and Middle West whose safety, and presumably whose virtue, were being endangered by the release of evacuees from the centers.

The moment the legislature convened in January, 1943, a spate of anti-evacuee bills, resolutions and memorials were introduced. In debating these measures, mass evacuation was cited *as proof* of the disloyal character of the evacuees by the very individuals who had urged mass evacuation *for the protection* of the evacuees against mob violence. Statements and charges were hurled at the evacuees that no one had dreamed of during the period immediately after Pearl Harbor. Throughout the year legislative investigations, state and federal were carefully spaced in such a manner as to provide an endless stream of newspaper headlines. First the Tenney investigation; then the farcical investigation conducted by Senator Chandler of Kentucky (which was really directed by Ray Richards of The Los Angeles Examiner); then the Dies Committee investigation in June, 1943; then an investigation by still another committee of the California Assembly; and, finally, yet another investigation by the Dies Committee.

Before the Dies Committee had conducted any investigation whatever, Representative J. Parnell Thomas, from a room in the Biltmore Hotel in Los Angeles, began to release a barrage of sensational stories about the War Relocation Authority and the evacuees. Calling "smear" witnesses to the stand, the committee tried its best to prevent the WRA from refuting their baseless charges. Some 35 factual misstatements were pointed out in the testimony of one witness. At these hearings, witnesses were openly encouraged to threaten the evacuees with mob violence. Public officials charged with the duty of law enforcement were given a pat on the back when they predicted "free murder," "violence" and "bloodshed" if a single evacuee were permitted to return to the West Coast.

At the hearings of the Gannon Committee (of the state legislature), Mrs. Maynard Force Thayer of Pasadena—stanch Republican, an outstanding club-woman, a pillar of the community—was browbeaten by the chairman of the committee in a manner that finally evoked a murmur of protest from The Los Angeles Times. Mrs. Thayer was asked, for example, if she had ever "smelled the inside of a Japanese home"; she was asked if she wanted the government "to protect a people who farm their wives out to another man to procreate his name"; and she was queried as to her opinion about a "people where different sexes do nude bathing together." When Mrs. Thayer tried to get in a word about the Bill of Rights, she was rebuked by Mr. Gannon as follows: "The Bill of Rights is not such a sacred thing . . . don't you know that at the time the Bill of Rights was written we had 150,000 slaves in the United States? What did the Bill of Rights do about that?" While this fantastic and obscene circus was being conducted, The Los Angeles Examiner, in one day, devoted 62 inches of space to the hearings. In being held before these committees, I was questioned, not about the evacuees of the WRA program, but about my views on "racial integrity," "mongrelization," "mixed marriages," "miscegenation statutes" and similar fancy topics.

At the time of the so-called "riot" at Tule Lake, the real riot occurred, not in the center, but in the pages of the California newspapers. Newspaper stories appeared charging that "bombs, knives, guns and various lethal weapons" had been found among the evacuees; that a Japanese evacuee had "pushed his way into" the bedchamber of a "white woman"; that the personnel of the center was "intermingling" with the evacuees; that the evacuees were being "coddled" and "pampered" (on a food allowance of 43 cents per person per day). Mr. Ray Richards of the Hearst press even suggested that Dillon Myer had knowingly failed to confiscate "lethal weapons" and that he had been a party to the "manufacture" of such weapons (see The San Francisco Call-Bulletin, December 21, 1943). With unblushing mendacity, The Los Angeles Herald-Express carried a headline reading: "Bare Deadly Peril as Armed Japanese Stream into California." Representative John Costello went so far as to announce, on December 9, 1943, that "hundreds of Japanese Americans and alien Japanese" were being permitted to return to California. Needless to say, there was no semblance of truth in these charges. Later The Los Angeles Times, in fancy headlines, charges that "450 Cases of Whiskey Go to Tule Lake" and, again, "Whiskey Flows to Tule Lake." The whiskey in question was consigned to the *town* of Tule Lake, not to the relocation center. "These Japs," wrote a columnist in The Times (referring not to the Japanese in Japan but to some 70,000 American citizens of Japanese ancestry), "are a depraved breed who can't be dealt with like mischievous boys. . . . We should wake up to the fact that protection of Americans from these degraded brutes is of more importance than the Little Tokyo Knitting and Brotherly Love Club." Only the fact that the Japanese government, in November, 1943, canceled further negotiations for the exchange of nationals, finally brought about some moderation in this frenzied campaign.

A section of the West Coast press systematically deflects hatred of Japan against the evacuees and uses hatred of the evacuees to justify its contention that the war in the Pacific is primarily racial in character. The consistent theme of the Hearst press is that "the war in the Pacific is the World War, the War of Oriental Races against Occidental Races for the Domination of the World" (The Los Angeles Examiner, March 23, 1943). Here is another characteristic statement from The San Francisco Examiner of January 25, 1943 (italics mine):

> Bad as the situation is in Europe, the war there is between European Occidental nations, *between white races*. Antagonisms, hatreds and jealousies, no matter how violent, cannot obscure the fact that the warring nations of Europe stem from common *racial,* cultural, linguistic and social roots. *It is a family affair,* in which the possibility of ultimate agreement and constructive harmony has not been dismissed even by the most determined opponents.

There can be no question but that anti-evacuee agitation in California is being cultivated for partisan political purposes. The hearings mentioned were, in large part, aimed at "smearing" the administration and building up a wall of reactionary feeling by stimulating racial hatred. To some extent this agitation has unquestionably been effective. Political officials in California have been cowed into silence; even those who are inclined to be fair do not dare to speak out on this issue. Just as Senators Hill and Pepper have been forced to disavow any interest in racial equality, so even the fair-minded members of the California delegation in Congress have been coerced on this thoroughly bogus "Japanese problem." Not one of these men dares to state publicly his real views on the evacuee problem.

No more serious mistake could be made than to encourage the belief that these groups can be handled quietly or that, by tactful diplomacy, they can be induced to forget the "Japanese issue." The aggressions of race bigots in California are of the same character as the insulting attacks made in Congress on the Negro minority by the white-supremacy advocates from the Deep South. Race bigotry in California can never be appeased. Every concession made to bigotry on the West Coast (and mass evacuation was such a concession) only encourages bolder aggression. As Representative Eberharter said, in his courageous minority report as a member of the Dies Committee, these recurrent investigations in California have "fostered a type of racial thinking which is already producing ugly manifestations and which seems to be growing in intensity. Unless this trend is checked, it may eventually lead to ill advised actions that will constitute an everlastingly shameful blot on our national record." Recent flare-ups against the evacuees in other sections of the country show that, in the absence of a strong affirmative federal policy and program on the race question, California bigots stand a good chance of spreading their particular version of the white-supremacy doctrine throughout the nation.

The military situation in the Pacific has changed since mass evacuation was ordered. The Japanese have been forced out of the Aleutians; Hawaii has been converted into one of the great fortresses of the world (and martial law has been modified); the Japanese are on the defensive throughout the Pacific. Various emergency measures adopted after Pearl Harbor have been relaxed on the West Coast and the general situation has so changed in our favor as to warrant the military in lifting the ban against the return of the evacuees. As long as the ban exists, race bigots in California will have an issue about which they will continue to conduct ever more fantastic and increasingly violent campaigns. If the ban is lifted, there will be no mass return of the evacuees and the freely predicted "murder" and "bloodshed" will not occur. There is a respectable opinion in California today that favors lifting the ban. The organizations I have mentioned create, rather than reflect, public opinion on the West Coast.

Issues of great importance are involved in this question. In default of an affirmative federal policy and program on race relations, race-minded groups in California will continue, in effect, to dictate our policy as a nation toward the peoples of the Orient. By taking advantage of this latent weakness in the federal government, California since 1882 has forced the Washington authorities to adopt a series of measures each of which has seriously jeopardized our national interests in the Far East: the exclusion of

Chinese immigration; the passage of the 1924 immigration law; the mass evacuation of the resident Japanese. It requires no insight to predict that this same situation will continue until the American people realize that local areas should not be permitted to force the federal government into the position of having to adopt their particular attitudes on race relations.

ELDRIDGE CLEAVER

Convalescence

Underneath the sparkle of rhetoric and imagery, the ironic narrative style, the breezy putdown of whites, is a serious analysis of the reasons for separation into black and white camps. Cleaver sees the source of division and conflict in the shifting relations of Mind and Body, Black and White. The first Minister of Information of the Black Panther Party, Cleaver is now in exile.

. . . just as in childhood I envied Negroes for what seemed to me their superior masculinity, so I envy them today for what seems to me their superior physical grace and beauty. I have come to value physical grace very highly, and I am now capable of aching with all my being when I watch a Negro couple on the dance floor, or a Negro playing baseball or basketball. *They are on the kind of terms with their own bodies that I should like to be on with mine, and for that precious quality they seem blessed to me.* [Italics added]

NORMAN PODHORETZ
"My Negro Problem—And Ours"
Commentary, February 1963

Why envy the Negro his grace, his physical skills? Why not ask what it is that prevents grace and physical skill from becoming a general property of the young? Mr. Podhoretz speaks of middle-class, white respectability —what does this mean but being cut off from the labor process, the work process, the creative process, as such? *The solution is thus not the direct liquidation of the color line, through the liquidation of color; but rather through a greater physical connectedness of the whites; and a greater intellective connectedness of the blacks . . .* [Italics added]

IRVING LOUIS HOROWITZ
Chairman, Department of Sociology
Hobart and William Smith Colleges, Geneva, New York
Commentary, June 1963

F THE SEPARATION of the black and white people in America along the color line had the effect, in terms of social imagery, of separating the Mind from the Body—the oppressor whites usurping sovereignty by monopolizing the Mind, abdicating the Body and becoming bodiless Omnipotent Administrators and Ultrafeminines; and the oppressed blacks, divested of sovereignty and therefore of Mind, manifesting the Body and becoming mindless Super-masculine Menials and Black Amazons—if this is so, then the 1954 U.S. Supreme Court decision in the case of *Brown* v. *Board of Education,* demolishing the principle of segregation of the races in public education and striking at the very root of the practice of segregation generally, was a major surgical operation performed by nine men in black robes on the racial Maginot Line which is imbedded as deep as sex or the lust for lucre in the schismatic American psyche. This piece of social surgery, if successful, performed without benefit of any anesthetic except God and the Constitution, in a land where God is dead and the Constitution has been in a coma for 180 years, is more marvelous than a successful heart transplant would be, for it was meant to graft the nation's Mind back onto its Body and vice versa.

If the foregoing is true, then the history of America in the years following the pivotal Supreme Court edict should be a record of the convalescence of the nation. And upon investigation we should be able to see the Omnipotent Administrators and Ultrafeminines grappling with their unfamiliar and alienated Bodies, and the Supermasculine Menials and Amazons attempting to acquire and assert *a mind of their own*. The record, I think, is clear and unequivocal. The bargain which seems to have been struck is that the whites have had to turn to the blacks for a clue on how to swing with the Body, while the blacks have had to turn to the whites for the secret of the Mind. It was Chubby Checker's mission, bearing the Twist as *good news,* to teach the whites, whom history had taught to forget, how to shake their asses again. It is a skill they surely must once have possessed but which they abandoned for puritanical dreams of escaping the corruption of the flesh, by leaving the terrors of the Body to the blacks.

In the swift, fierce years since the 1954 school desegregation decision, a rash of seemingly unrelated mass phenomena has appeared on the American scene—deviating radically from the prevailing Hot-Dog-and-Malted-Milk norm of the bloodless, square, superficial, faceless Sunday-Morning atmosphere that was suffocating the nation's soul. And all of this in a nation where the so-called molders of public opinion, the writers, politicians, teachers, and cab drivers, are willful, euphoric liars or zip-dam ostriches and owls, a clique of undercover ghosts, a bunch of Walter Jenkinses, a lot of coffee-drinking, cigarette-smoking, sly, suck-assing, status-seeking, cheating, nervous, dry-balled, tranquillizer-gulched, countdown-minded, out-of-style, slithering snakes. No wonder that many "innocent people," the manipulated and the stimulated, some of whom were game for a reasonable amount of mystery and even adventure, had their minds scrambled. These observers were not equipped to either *feel* or *know* that a radical break, a revolutionary leap out of their sight, had taken place in the secret parts of this nation's soul. It was as if a driverless vehicle were speeding through the American night down an unlighted street toward a stone wall and was boarded on the fly by a stealthy ghost with a drooling leer on his face, who, at the last detour before chaos and disaster, careened the vehicle down a smooth highway that leads to the future and life; and to ask these Americans to understand that they were the passengers on this driverless vehicle and that the lascivious ghost was the Saturday-night crotchfunk of the Twist, or the "Yeah, Yeah, Yeah!" which the Beatles highjacked from Ray Charles, to ask these Calvinistic profligates to see the logical and reciprocal links is more cruel than asking a hope-to-die Okie Music buff to cop the sounds of John Coltrane.

In the beginning of the era came a thief with a seven-year itch who knew that the ostriches and the owls had been bribed with a fix of Euphony, which is their kick. The thief knew that he need not wait for the cover of night, that with impunity he could show his face in the marketplace in the full light of the sun, do his deed, scratch his dirt, sell his loot to the fence while the ostriches and owls, coasting on Euphony, one with his head in a hole—any hole—and the other with his head in the clouds, would only cluck and whisper and hear-see-speak no evil.

So Elvis Presley came, strumming a weird guitar and wagging his tail across the continent, ripping off fame and fortune as he scrunched his way, and, like a latter-day Johnny Appleseed, sowing seeds of a new rhythm and style in the white souls of the white youth of America, whose inner hunger and need was no longer satisfied with the antiseptic white shoes and whiter songs of Pat Boone. "You can do anything," sang Elvis to Pat Boone's white shoes, "but don't you step on my Blue Suede Shoes!"

During this period of ferment and beginnings, at about the same time that the blacks of Montgomery, Alabama, began their historic bus boycott (giving birth to the leadership of Martin Luther King, signifying to the nation that, with this initiative, this first affirmative step, somewhere in the universe a gear in the machinery had shifted), something, a target, came into focus. The tensions in the American psyche had torn a fissure in the racial Maginot Line and through this fissure, this tiny bridge between the Mind and Body, the black masses, who had been silent and somnolent since the '20s and '30s, were now making a break toward the dimly seen light that beckoned to them through the fissure. The fact that these black's could now take such a step was perceived by the ostriches and owls as a sign of national decay, a sign that the System had caved in at that spot. And this gave birth to a fear, a fear that quickly became a focus for all the anxieties and exasperations in the Omnipotent Administrators' minds; and to embody this perceived decay and act as a lightning rod for the fear, the beatniks bloomed onto the American scene.

Like pioneers staking their claims in the no-man's land that lay along the racial Maginot Line, the beatniks, like Elvis Presley before them, dared to do in the light of day what America had long been doing in the sneak-thief anonymity of night—consorted on a human level with the blacks. Reviled, cursed, held in contempt by the "molders of public opinion," persecuted by the police, made into an epithet of derision by the deep-frozen geeks of the Hot-Dog-and-Malted-Milk set, the beatniks irreverently refused to go away. Allen Ginsberg and Jack Kerouac ("the Suzuki rhythm boys," James Baldwin called them, derisively, in a moment of panic, "tired of white ambitions" and "dragging themselves through the Negro street at dawn, looking for an angry fix"; "with," as Mailer put it, "the black man's code to fit their facts"). Bing Crosbyism, Perry Comoism, and Dinah Shoreism had led to cancer, and the vanguard of the white youth knew it.

And as the spirit of revolt crept across the continent from that wayward bus in Montgomery, Alabama, seeping like new life into the cracks and nooks of the northern ghettos and sweeping in furious gales across the campuses of southern Negro colleges, erupting, finally, in the sit-ins and freedom rides—as this swirling maelstrom of social change convulsed the nation, shocking an unsuspecting American public, folk music, speaking of fundamental verities, climbed slowly out of the grave; and the hip lobe of the national ear, twitching involuntarily at first, began to listen.

From the moment that Mrs. Rosa Parks, in that bus in Montgomery, Alabama, resisted the Omnipotent Administrator, contact, however fleeting, had been made with the lost sovereignty—the Body had made contact with its Mind—and the shock of that contact sent an electric current throughout this nation, traversing the racial Maginot Line and striking fire in the hearts of the whites. The wheels began to turn, the thaw set in, and though Emmett Till and Mack Parker were dead, though Eisenhower sent troops to Little Rock, though Autherine Lucy's token presence at the University of Alabama was a mockery—notwithstanding this, it was already clear that the 1954 major surgical operation had been successful and the patient would live. The challenge loomed on the horizon: Africa, black, enigmatic, and hard-driving, had begun to parade its newly freed nations into the UN; and the Islam of Elijah Muhammad, amplified as it was fired in salvos from the piercing tongue of Malcolm X, was racing through the Negro streets with Allen Ginsberg and Jack Kerouac.

Then, as the verbal revolt of the black masses soared to a cacophonous peak—the Body, the Black Amazons and Supermasculine Menials, becoming conscious, shouting, in a thousand different ways, *"I've got a Mind of my own!";* and as the senator from Massachusetts was saving the nation from the Strangelove grasp of Dirty Dick, injecting, as he emerged victorious, a new and vivacious spirit into the people with the style of his smile and his wife's hairdo; then, as if a signal had been given, as if the Mind had shouted to the Body, "I'm ready!"—the Twist, superseding the Hula Hoop, burst upon the scene like a nuclear explosion, sending its fallout of rhythm into the Minds and Bodies of the people. The fallout: the Hully Gully, the Mashed Potato, the Dog, the Smashed Banana, the Watusi, the Frug, the Swim. The Twist was a guided missile, launched from the ghetto into the very heart of suburbia. The Twist succeeded, as politics, religion, and law could never do, in writing in the heart and soul what the Supreme Court could only write on the books. The Twist was a form of therapy for a convalescing nation. The Omnipotent Administrator and the Ultrafeminine responded so dramatically, in stampede fashion, to the Twist precisely because it afforded them the possibility of reclaiming their Bodies again after generations of alienated and disembodied existence.

The stiff, mechanical Omnipotent Administrators and Ultrafeminines presented a startling spectacle as they entered in droves onto the dance floors to learn how to Twist. They came from every level of society, from top to bottom, writhing pitifully though gamely about the floor, feeling exhilarating and soothing new sensations, release from some unknown prison in which their Bodies had been encased, a sense of freedom they had never known before, a feeling of communion with some mystical root-source of life and vigor, from which sprang a new awareness and enjoyment of the flesh, a new appreciation of the possibilities of their Bodies. They were swinging and gyrating and shaking their dead little asses like petrified zombies trying to regain the warmth of life, rekindle the dead limbs, the cold ass, the stone heart, the stiff, mechanical, disused joints with the spark of life.

This spectacle truly startled many Negroes, because they perceived it as an intrusion by the Mind into the province of the Body, and this intimated chaos; because the Negroes knew, from the survival experience of their everyday lives, that the system within which they were imprisoned was based upon the racial Maginot Line and that the cardinal sin, crossing the line —which was, in their experience, usually initiated from the black side— was being committed, *en masse,* by the whites. The Omnipotent Administrators and Ultrafeminines were storming the Maginot Line! A massive assault had been launched without parallel in American history, and to Negroes it was confusing. Sure, they had witnessed it on an individual scale: they had seen many ofays destroy the Maginot Line in themselves. But this time it had all the appearances of a national movement. There were even rumors that President Kennedy and his Jackie were doing the Twist secretly in the White House; that their Number One Boy had been sent to the Peppermint Lounge in disguise to learn how to Twist, and he in turn brought the trick back to the White House. These Negroes knew that something fundamental had changed.

"Man, what done got into them ofays?" one asked.

"They trying to get back," said another.

"Shit," said a young Negro who made his living by shoplifting. "If you ask me, I think it must be the end of the world."

"Oooo-weee!" said a Negro musician who had been playing at a dance and was now standing back checking the dancers. "Baby, I don't dig this action at all! Look here, baby, pull my coat to what's going down! I mean, have I missed it somewhere? Where've I been? Baby, I been blowing all my life and I ain't never dug no happenings like this. You know what, man, I'm gon' cut that fucking weed aloose. Oooo-weee! Check that little bitch right there! What the fuck she trying to do? Is she trying to shake it or break it? Oooo-weee!"

A Negro girl said: "Take me home, I'm sick!"

Another one said: "No, let's stay! This is too much!"

And a bearded Negro cat, who was not interested in learning how to Twist himself, who felt that if he was interested in doing it, he could get up from the table right now and start Twisting, he said, sitting at the table with a tinsel-minded female: "It ain't nothing. They just trying to get back, that's all."

"Get back?" said the girl, arching her brows quizzically, "Get back from where?"

"From wherever they've been," said the cat, "where else?"

"Are they doing it in Mississippi is what I want to know," said a tall, deadly looking Negro who had a long razor line down his left cheek and who had left Mississippi in a hurry one night.

And the dancers: they were caught up in a whirl of ecstasy, swinging like pendulums, mechanical like metronomes or puppets on invisible strings being manipulated by a master with a sick sense of humor. "They look like Chinese doing communal exercise," said a Negro. "That's all they're doing, calisthenics!"

"Yeah," said his companion. "They're trying to get in shape."

But if at first it was funny and confusing, it was nonetheless a break-through. The Omnipotent Administrators and Ultrafeminines were discovering new aspects of the Body, new possibilities of rhythm, new ways to move. The Hula Hoop had been a false start, a mechanized, theatrical attempt by the Mind to supply to itself what only the Body can give. But, with the Twist, at last they knew themselves to be swinging. The forces acting upon the world stage in our era had created, in the collective psyche of the Omnipotent Administrators and Ultrafeminines, an irresistible urge —to just stand up and shake the ice and cancer out of their alienated white asses—and the Hula Hoop and Twist offered socially acceptable ways to do it.

Of course, not all the whites took part in these joyful experiments. For many, the more "suggestive" a dance became—i.e., the more it became pure Body and less Mind—the more scandalous it seemed to them; and their reaction in this sense was an index to the degree of their alienation from their Bodies. But what they condemned as a sign of degeneracy and moral decay was actually a sign of health, a sign of hope for full recovery. As Norman Mailer prophesied: ". . . the Negro's equality would tear a profound shift into the psychology, the sexuality, and the moral imagination of every white alive." Precisely because the Mind will have united with the Body, theory will have merged with practice.

It is significant that the Twist and the Hula Hoop came into the scene in all their fury at the close of the Eisenhower and the dawn of the Kennedy era. It could be interpreted as a rebellion against the vacuous Eisenhower years. It could also be argued that the same collective urge that gave rise to the Twist also swept Kennedy into office. I shudder to think that, given the closeness of the final vote in 1960, Richard Nixon might have won the election in a breeze if he had persuaded one of his Ultrafeminine daughters, not to mention Ultrapat, to do the Twist in public. Not if Kennedy had stayed on the phone a week sympathizing with Mrs. Martin Luther King, Jr., over the fact that the cat was in jail, would he have won. Even as I am convinced that Luci Baines Johnson, dancing the Watusi in public with Killer Joe Piro, won more votes for her old man in 1964 than a whole boxcar full of his hog-calling speeches ever did.

When the Birmingham Revolt erupted in the summer of 1963 and President Kennedy stepped into the void and delivered his unprecedented speech to the nation on civil rights and sent his bill to Congress, the foundation had been completed. Martin Luther King, Jr., giving voice to the needs of the Body, and President Kennedy, speaking out the needs of the Mind, made contact on that day. The Twisters, sporting their blue suede shoes, moved beyond the ghost in white shoes who ate a Hot Dog and sipped Malted Milk as he danced the mechanical jig of Satan on top of Medgar Evers' tomb. In vain now would the murderers bomb that church and slaughter grotesquely those four little black girls (what did they hope to kill? were they striking at the black of the skin or the fire of the soul? at history? at the Body?). In vain also the assassins' bullets that crashed through the head of John Kennedy, taking a life, yes, but creating a larger-than-life and failing utterly to expunge from the record the March on Washington and its truth: that this nation—bourgeois or not, imperialist or not, murderous or not, ugly or not—its people, somewhere in their butchered and hypocritical souls, still contained an epic potential of spirit which is its hope, a bottomless potential which fires the imaginations of its youth. It was all too late. It was too late because it was time for the blacks ("I've got a *Mind* of my own!") to riot, to sweep through the Harlem night like a wave of locusts, breaking, screaming, bleeding, laughing, crying, re-joicing, celebrating, in a jubilee of destruction, to regurgitate the white man's bullshit they'd been eating for four hundred years; smashing the windows of the white man's stores, throwing bricks they wished were bombs, running, leaping whirling like a cyclone through the white man's Mind, past his backlash, through the night streets of Rochester, New Jersey, Philadelphia. And even though the opposition, gorging on Hot Dogs and Malted Milk, with blood now splattered over the white shoes, would still strike out in the dark against the manifestations of the turning, show-ing the protocol of Southern Hospitality reserved for Niggers and Nigger Lovers—*SCHWERNER—CHANEY—GOODMAN*—it was still too late. For not only had Luci Baines Johnson danced the Watusi in public with Killer Joe, but the Beatles were on the scene, injecting Negritude by the ton into the whites, in this post–Elvis Presley-beatnik era of ferment.

Before we toss the Beatles a homosexual kiss—saying, "If a man be ass enough to reach for the bitch in them, that man will kiss a man, and if a woman reaches for the stud in them, that woman will kiss a woman"—let us marvel at the genius of their image, which comforts the owls and os-triches in the one spot where Elvis Presley bummed their kick: Elvis, with his *un*funky (yet mechanical, alienated) bumpgrinding, was still too much Body (too soon) for the strained collapsing psyches of the Omnipotent Ad-ministrators and Ultrafeminines; whereas the Beatles, affecting the cauca-soid crown of femininity and ignoring the Body on the visual plane (while their music on the contrary being full of Body), assuaged the doubts of the owls and ostriches by presenting an incorporeal, cerebral image.

Song and dance are, perhaps, only a little less old than man himself. It is with his music and dance, the recreation through art of the rhythms sug-gested by and implicit in the tempo of his life and cultural environment, that man purges his soul of the tensions of daily strife and maintains his harmony in the universe. In the increasingly mechanized, automated, cy-bernated environment of the modern world—a cold, bodiless world of wheels, smooth plastic surfaces, tubes, pushbuttons, transistors, computers, jet propulsion, rockets to the moon, atomic energy—man's need for affir-mation of his biology has become that much more intense. He feels need for a clear definition of where his body ends and the machine begins, where man ends and the *extensions* of man begin. This great mass hunger, which transcends national or racial boundaries, recoils from the subtle subversions of the mechanical environment which modern technology is creating faster than man, with his present savage relationship to his fellow men, is able to receive and assimilate. This is the central contradiction of the twentieth century; and it is against this backdrop that America's attempt to unite its Mind with its Body, to save its soul, is taking place.

It is in this connection that the blacks, personifying the Body and thereby in closer communion with their biological roots than other Americans, provide the saving link, the bridge between man's biology and man's machines. In its purest form, as adjustment to the scientific and technological environment of our era, as purgative and lullaby-soother of man's soul, it is the jazz issuing from the friction and harmony of the American Negro with his environment that captured the beat and tempo of our times. And although modern science and technology are the same whether in New York, Paris, London, Accra, Cairo, Berlin, Moscow, Tokyo, Peking, or São Paulo, jazz is the only true international medium of communication current in the world today, capable of speaking creatively, with equal intensity and relevance, to the people in all those places.

The less sophisticated (but no less Body-based) popular music of urban Negroes—which was known as Rhythm and Blues before the whites appropriated and distilled it into a product they called Rock 'n Roll—is the basic ingredient, the core, of the gaudy, cacophonous hymns with which the Beatles of Liverpool drive their hordes of Ultrafeminine fans into catatonia and hysteria. For Beatle fans, having been alienated from their own Bodies so long and so deeply, the effect of these potent, erotic rhythms is electric. Into this music, the Negro projected—as it were, *drained off,* as pus from a sore—a powerful sensuality, his pain and lust, his love and his hate, his ambition and his despair. The Negro projected into his music his very Body. The Beatles, the four long-haired lads from Liverpool, are offering up as their gift the Negro's Body, and in so doing establish a rhythmic communication between the listener's own Mind and Body.

Enter the Beatles—soul by proxy, middlemen between the Mind and the Body. A long way from Pat Boone's White Shoes. A way station on a slow route traveled with all deliberate speed.

3 THE VISION

Although the word "vision" cannot miss having a hopeful connotation, this is not the intent of its use here, for visions may also be dark. Even glorious visions may involve painful steps to make them real.

This section does not attempt to foretell the future; it does not even try to see very far into the future. The selections serve to review our knowledge of the past, to make it possible to judge the realities of the present and to predict the kinds of attitudes and responses of the world to come. Some are hopeful; some are brutal; some merely wishful. Each starts, however, with the fact of race awareness; that can no longer be hidden or denied. Perhaps they reflect Eliot's thought: "After such knowledge, what forgiveness?"

Visions shape the future because men believe in them, because men participate in them, because men are moved by them. We have collected here some of the visions which extend our ability to understand the present because they show us the future implicit in that present. But because they are visions, they also show other futures possible to us.

Leonard Freed—Magnum

Charles Harbutt—Magnum

Leonard Freed—Magnum

Paul Conklin

Paul Conklin

Constantine Manos—Magnum

ARNOLD TOYNBEE

The Ultimate Choice

Arnold Toynbee (1899–   ) is one of the great historians of our time. In the essay that follows he analyzes the present situation and concludes that we must dwell together or cease to dwell at all. His solution— intermarriage—strikes right at the heart of the deepest, and finally the most absurd, fear that each race has of the other.

"TO DWELL TOGETHER in unity" has not been coming easy to the human race. We may agree that this is "good and pleasant" for "brethren," but few human communities, so far, have been prepared to take all other human beings to their bosoms as their brothers. They have usually found some excuse for treating the majority of their fellow-men as "lesser breeds without the law." If one stigma wears off, we invent another. When our neighbour ceases to be an infidel, we still stigmatise him as a foreigner, and, if he ceases to be a foreigner, we sill ostracise him as a Negro or an albino. This widespread passion for being a "chosen people" evidently has deep psychological roots. We human beings have gone on indulging in it at the price of bringing endless disasters on ourselves. We have gone on till we have now been overtaken by the Atomic Age.

In this age the price of disunity is evidently going to be prohibitive. This has been recognised quickly and widely, so today we have a stronger motive than we have ever had before for trying to get rid of our self-inflicted divisions. Our choice now lies between co-existence and non-existence. The removal of the main present hindrances to co-existence has therefore become the most urgent item on mankind's agenda. Three outstanding present hindrances are ideologies, nationalism, and race-feeling. We have to get rid of them all, and we have not left ourselves much time for that. This raises a practical question of priorities. Which of these three evils is going to be the most difficult to eradicate? Whichever it is, we ought to concentrate our efforts on combating this one first.

One answer to this question about priorities was implied in the foundation of the Institute of Race Relations. This answer was made explicit in a paper addressed to Chatham House in 1950 by one of the moving spirits in the launching of the Institute, Mr. Harry Hodson.

"There are two problems in world politics today which transcend all others," Mr. Hodson said in this context. "They are the struggle between Communism and Liberal Democracy and the problem of race relations. Of the two, I am prepared to argue that the problem of race relations is the more important, since, for one thing, it would remain with us in its full complexity even if Communism were to settle down to peaceful neighbourliness with Democracy in a world partitioned between them."

Mr. Hodson is surely right in holding that ideological differences can be overcome more easily than racial differences can. An ideology can be put into cold storge. The more awkward and obnoxious of its tenets can be reduced to dead letters. More than that, there is the possibility of conversion from one ideology to another. In the past, this process of conversion has sometimes gone with a run. Racial differences, too, can be overcome by conversion, but the process in this field is a physical, not an intellectual, one. The other name for it is intermarriage.

Happily for mankind's prospects, intermarriage between geographically intermingled populations of different physique has been normal hitherto, whereas racial segregation has been exceptional. In our present-day world, the normal way of overcoming race-differences is exemplified in two large and important constituents of the human race: the Muslim community and the Spanish and Portuguese-speaking Roman Catholic community. In Mexico and Brazil today, most people have at least three different racial strains in their physique: the European, the pre-Columbian American, and the African; but domestic injustices and dissensions in these and other Latin American countries do not, on the whole, run on racial lines. Latin Americans are not race-conscious, and Muslims are not either. Visit, for instance, the American University of Beirut and watch the students on the campus there. You will observe a great variety of race, but no tendency towards antipathy or segregation on account of this.

In fact, race-feeling seems to be an exceptional failing. In the present-day world it is virtually confined to three minorities: the Teutonic-speaking peoples, the high-caste Hindus, and the Jews. In the Atomic Age the prejudice for which these three minorities stand has no future. "The wave of the future"—supposing that the human race is going to allow itself a future—is the comparative freedom from race-prejudice that is exhibited by the Latin Americans and the Muslims.

The third of mankind's present three apples of discord is one that is not mentioned by Mr. Hodson in the passage that I have quoted from a paper of his. It is nationalism; and perhaps the only good thing that nationalism has to be said for it is that, as some offset to the havoc that it works, it does at least cut across the alternative division of mankind into conflicting races. Nationalism in its present-day form originated among the West European peoples. Unhappily it has now infected most of the rest of the world, but it is still rampant in its birth-place, and this has had at least one fortunate result. It has saved the majority of the human race from falling under the lasting domination of the minority that has an unusually small amount of pigment in its skin. If this bleached minority had chosen to gang up together, it might have been able to dominate the majority for quite a long time, on the strength of the temporary lead that it has gained in technological progress. But the bleached race has halved or quartered its potential strength by expending this on domestic national rivalries, and this makes it unlikely that the present division of the world between two ideological camps will ever be matched by a world-wide racial division between the bleached and the tanned.

Try to imagine a race-war between Russia and America lined up together on one side and India and Pakistan lined up together on the other. This imaginary alignment of forces seems most unlikely ever to become actual. It is true that one can imagine Russia and America getting together against China. They did get together against Japan during the Second World War, and China is likely to become more formidable than Japan ever has been or ever could be. If China were to acquire the bomb, it seems safe to prophesy that Russia and America would become allies again within the next five years. In that situation, a series of half-a-dozen leading articles in the press of either country could effectively change the climate of their ideological relations with each other. But, if this did happen, it would be just another instance of the familiar working of the age-old balance of power. The coincidence of a power-politics line-up with a race-difference would be accidental. And, as a matter of fact, the two opposing alliances would not pan out neatly on racial lines. Russia's present East European satellites would be in China's camp, while the South-East Asian peoples would be in Russia's and America's.

It looks, then, as if the evil of racialism can be localised, thanks to the counteracting effects of the evil of nationalism. Probably we need not fear that there will be a world-war waged on racial lines. Yet, even if we succeed in localising the evil of race-feeling, it will still be so much tinder ready to flare into flame at the touch of the first spark. And, besides being dangerous, race-feeling is odious in itself. It is therefore not enough just to localise it. We have also to try to eradicate it wherever we find it. This will be easier in some continents than in others.

The segregation of Jews from Gentiles will, it may be hoped, be broken down rather rapidly by intermarriage all over the world except, perhaps, in Israel. We may look forward to seeing the Jewish diaspora transform itself from a closed racial community into an open religious community. If this were to happen, Judaism would at last have achieved its manifest destiny of becoming one of the world-wide religions. Again, we may hope to see the end of the segregation of citizens of different colours in the United

States and of citizens of different castes in India. In both India and the United States the segregationists seem now to be fighting a losing battle. The harder of the two battles is, of course, the one in India, since here the institution of caste has the momentum of three thousand years of history behind it. But in India, as in the United States, it looks now as if the victory of integration were in sight. If and when racialism has been overcome in these two sub-continents, it will have been more or less confined to Palestine and to those parts of Africa where, as in Palestine, there is an immigrant minority from Europe.

Here we touch the hard core of the race problem. Racial minorities that have been dominant have to reconcile themselves to accepting equality with the majority of their fellow-citizens. And emancipated racial majorities that have recently been denied their human rights have to reconcile themselves, on their side, to accepting equality with their former overlords without abusing the power of numbers under a democratic régime. These requirements call for almost superhuman self-restraint and magnanimity on both sides, and that will be hard to achieve if the physical segregation of the two races continues.

The position of being a precariously dominant minority seems to be almost too difficult for human nature to cope with. This is illustrated by the present temper of the French *colons* in Algeria. In North America the French have had a better record than the English and the Dutch in their dealings with the pre-Columbian natives of the continent. Yet in Africa today they are behaving no better than their English and Dutch opposite numbers. If the situation in Africa is to be saved, the geographically intermingled races there will have to follow the example of Latin America and the Islamic World. In those two regions, intermarriage has brought with it a happy solution of racial problems. "Bella gerant alii, tu, felix Austria, nube." This famous line can be made to point a moral for the present-day European colonist in Africa by making a small change of words at the end. "Tu felix nube colone." For the European colonist in Africa, intermarriage offers a happy way out, and perhaps the only happy way that can be found for him. If he replies that he cannot bear the prospect, it can be answered that he is being asked to do no more than has been done already, long ago, by his fellow-European colonist in Latin America. He can also be asked to face the alternative. "Intermarry or get out" is probably the ultimate choice that destiny is offering to the European minorities in Africa in our day.

H. F. SAMPSON

Africa—Light from the South

Apartheid is an official political embodiment of a racial attitude. As
such it must be explained and defended. Sampson offers that defense.
The pun on Alan Paton's title effected by the inclusion of this selection
was not intentional.

"UHURU"! FREEDOM! Freedom to vote, to kill, and to starve—
unless maintained by the old colonial caretaker. The echoes of
UHURU have almost died away. The precious dream is lost.
But what has been gained undeniably is a commanding-voice
at U.N.O. of prestigious delegates, intent on directing world government from the backyards of civilisation.

The trump card of propaganda beamed at South Africa by the minority
who inspire world opinion in the West, is that it cannot be resisted. But
that of course does not mean that it must be right. Science is discovering
again and again that the axioms of past belief were wrong. World opinion
warned us of a Wind of Change, like a force of Nature; but quite overlooked all changes of the wind, in balancing the forces of Nature.

World opinion now shows signs of dismay at its handiwork in Africa. It
fingers with the excuse that African political emancipation was perhaps
premature, because the Africans, through no fault of their own, are politically immature. This is of course something which British socialists could
have learnt immediately from experienced colonial administrators, who
were not bemused with ideology. But their back-to-the-wall excuse is probably that the African freedom explosion could not be averted without removing the fuse of Liberal-Communist conspiracy—a conspiracy to exploit Africa for the ideological cause of world government, whether
Communist or Liberal. Communists wanted democracy in Africa for the
disorder favourable for terrorist subversion. Liberal socialists, blind to this
danger, wanted it for their blue-print of civilisation, no matter what. They
actually expected responsible government to be directed by the individual
wills of people who "disgusted" James Baldwin himself (as already
quoted) with their "ignorance of how society is put together". Perhaps
they could not be expected to withdraw the explosion fuse which they had
themselves helped to plant.

Do subsequent events prove that their "world opinion" was right, and if not, should they have foreseen their mistake as South Africans did?

The first phase of the results of UHURU became evident in 1961, which a news reporter described as follows:

> "Political leaders of the newly independent West African states, in a scramble for African leadership and the spoils of office, have set off a breath-taking orgy of extravagance and corruption. Without exaggerating, tens of millions of pounds are being squandered on ornate presidential palaces and other prestige buildings. Millions more are going down the drain in rake-offs from government contracts and sales of import licences. Corruption is rife throughout West Africa and is on the increase. For out-and-out blatant graft Ghana leads the field. But corruption is also becoming increasingly widespread in French-speaking West African territories, and has even begun in the comparatively staid and stable Federation of Nigeria." (The reporter may have changed his mind since then about Nigeria.)

> He added that President Boigny of the Ivory Coast Republic had spent R7,000,000 on his new presidential palace; President Tubman of Liberia was spending R9,000,000 on his; while President Nkrumah was spending R600,000 on his private residence.

In the Congo at least, the first phase involved the uncontrolled savagery that was released upon charitable missionaries, men, women and children —which the western Press either took for granted, or felt too ashamed to publish. The Belgian report to U.N.O. left it unmoved.

The second phase continues, and will continue to consist in political violence and disorder. Voting is linked with killing. A Nairobi paper now remarks that "the bullet has replaced the ballot-box, a fact that has become distressingly familiar."

The violent overthrow of elected governments has become so common as to be dismissed euphemistically as a "coup". What has long been recognised as endemic in South and Central America, with their mixed Negro and Indian populations, has now proved to be so in Africa as well. There is hardly a state in Africa that has withstood the democratic Apple of Discord. Even the least uncivilised state of Nigeria teeters on the brink of civil war. Elections are either rigged, or said to be—as anyone must expect when their control is either dishonest or incompetent. In addition there always are tribal loyalties which individuals have to respect, at least under intimidation. Who ever heard of African tribal disagreements being settled by negotiation instead of violence? It has never been customary to settle personal quarrels by rational argument; a weapon always serves better. So why should any intelligent socialist expect a different practice to be applied to political party conflicts, when staged by democracy? It is not the first time in history that a shallow idealism has excited brutality.

The third phase, equally inevitable, has hardly begun to overtake the first and second. It is of course economic collapse, which for the time being is held back by lavish subsidies of foreign aid, at Barbara Castle figures, even from an England struggling to balance its economy. Claims to assist the unemployed take second place to claims by African leaders when presented on the "or else!" account. The irony of it all is that the cost of maintaining colonial administration, which the taxpayer was led to believe would be a happy release for him, is now replaced by the cost of ending it. Moreover, there is now a lack of security over the expenditure, for those reporters or diplomats who venture to comment unfavourably on internal affairs, such as the prestige account, or the absence of an account of bribery and corruption, are quickly told to leave the country. When the stream of money dries up, as it will, the luckless Africans will either have to seek Western industry to assist their economy, with a humiliating reminder of the material advantage of colonialism, or seek primitive sustenance. If the countries north of the Sahara fare better, it may be due to a difference of racial stock.

The above review is an essential background to one of the merits of the policy of apartheid in South Africa, where a safer line is taken. If the events in Africa during the last five years of "liberation" were predictable, the theory of prediction must have been sound.

The following, for instance, was a statement of my own views in 1959, which might equally have been held by persons in responsible positions.

"The apparent will of the people would quickly and inevitably become that of the extremists backed by the forces of intimidation and coercion among their followers. The democracy that depends on rational persuasion would at once give way to a sequence of dictatorship, as it is obviously about to do in Ghana and adjacent regions. It has been reported that no political election in the Phillipines has been held without violence since that country received its independence over ten years ago. The political rivalry of the even more primitive tribes of Africa will fare worse, and undoubtedly revive blood feuds at every election. Revolution will prove more endemic in Africa than it is in South America, and the prominence of a few educated leaders will be no security against it.

But, it is argued, the Natives of Africa could eventually find their own democratic feet, even though through a slow process of trial and error, and that they would learn in time what democracy really means. But unfortunately they will not be given that time, because their political temperament will necessitate dictatorial control, and this will intensify the practice of coercion and violence. The essential period of apprenticeship to democratic government will never ensue, except under European example and administration. And not through any lack of good sense among their Native leaders, but through their helpless inability to disabuse a primitive electorate of the utility of coercion. Thought of the integrity of such leaders suggests a further possible handicap, namely in a rather familiar disposition to exploit their fellows. The social history of the Native offers few if any examples of charity to the weak. The practice of sharing food is but a form of personal insurance against adversity.

In effect the experiment of political autonomy in Africa now being encouraged from Britain and America, in a wave of idealistic hysteria and ignorance of the Native disposition, is bound to defeat its own purpose —if there is any purpose other than that of abdicating the responsibility of civilised trusteeship."

And again in 1960 I wrote:

"This newly inspired racial ambition of the Black man founded as it is on the Wilsonian creed of the self-determination of peoples (with all its potentially racial implication), is not nearly so surprising as the will of foreign Liberalism to preside at the liquidation of white civilisation in southern Africa, while taking the calculated risk that 'African' civilisation may not be ready to replace it. When Tom Mboya says, 'Ready or not, we are coming', the risk is that Africa, with its hands stretched out to Freedom, will sink in the quicksands of political and economic disaster.

Such is the danger in prospect from which South Africa should be forgiven for seeking to protect itself."

A converse argument is often used against apartheid, namely that its theory is not justified by fact. It is said to be impracticable without results so harmful as to outweigh its advantages.

But the simple answer to this is that the objection applies still more strongly against the alternative of racial integration. The social and economic frustration of non-whites in America and Britain, and the gradual demoralisation of white society in both, are worse than the effects of apartheid in South Africa.

The preservation of civil order and good race relationship is the first task of a government of mixed peoples. In this respect the South African record is almost unrivalled by any country inhabited by white and coloured people, or indeed by those of different shades of race colour, such as the Asiatic and African.

Apart from organised subversive activity in the last few years, of foreign inspiration, and apart from the sporadic murder and robbery of whites by non-whites, which are not due to race hatred and indeed are more frequent among the non-whites themselves, race disturbances have been unknown except for bottle throwing at football matches. And what is significant about these is that such excited rivalry has not been followed by racial clashes as the crowds leave the grounds. Race prejudice is far less evident than in American and Britain, because in South Africa race relationship has long been adjusted to traditional separation. The nearest thing to a race riot only occurred a few years ago between Zulus and Indians in Natal. There are of course too frequent tribal fights in the Native territories and on the mines.

Elsewhere in the world race hatred smoulders on. *Time,* of April 9, 1965, had an article "Discrimination and Discord in Asia", saying:

> "Racial hatreds plague all Asian nations, which present a vast, graduated racial spectrum . . . Asians save their sharpest prejudice for their own minorities, including Burma's harried Indians, Japan's Koreans and— throughout Southeast Asia—the overseas Chinese. . . . Many Asian countries have not yet absorbed backward peoples in their midst. . . . a sense of nationhood can probably be achieved only by peoples who respect themselves and their own worth."

In South and Central America, and in East Africa, politics are aligned with the antipathy between Negro and Indian or Asiatic, accentuated by integration.

Britain provides the example of race prejudice originating in a modern civilised country, unaccountably unless for some material cause. If it is all irrational, humanist arguments will for that reason fail against it. The wisest thing is to remove or diminish the occasion for it, the contact which excites it. And that is exactly what South Africa is attempting to do, with a degree of success which astonishes oversea visitors. One of them, an American Judge who took part in the Supreme Court decision of 1954, said (as was told to me by the man he spoke to) that he had previously thought South Africans were a wicked people, but that since his visit he had entirely changed his opinion. In contrast, Sir Richard Acland, an Englishman who apparently had not visited the country, told the Oxford Union in May of last year that "he would regard a war by Africans against White South Africans as just and he would support British troops fighting White South Africans if such a war was inevitable."

Nevertheless and even so, the die-hard liberal socialist grips his argument that human opportunity for work and livelihood must be governed by Merit, not Colour. What answer is there?

The term "Colour" is certainly used to divert attention from the physical and mental differences signified by skin pigmentation. This premise is a long way ahead of the environmental theory which argues, not that there is no racial difference of racial consequence at any stage of development, but that, even assuming there is, it would be eliminated under equal conditions of life, at some time or other. It is one thing to assert that all humans are equal in biological potential, that they all originated from one primeval stock at one place, rather than from independent evolutions of *Homo sapiens* at different places, and that they would all have been alike if they had not lived under different conditions for perhaps more than a hundred thousand years. But it is quite another thing to maintain that such a prolonged separation has left no other mark upon people but colour.

Numbers of intelligent persons of liberal thought still use the "colour" shibboleth. They cite examples of Bantu, whose grandparents lived in kraals, who have obtained B.A. degrees or more. There are no doubt some who are more intelligent than some Whites. But if social administration must concern itself more with the general than the exceptional, and with social as well as mental standards, it is wiser to consider average differences.

It is when the Group Area principle, and the social contact it concerns, is looked at, that it becomes clear that exceptionally intelligent persons cannot be dealt with irrespective of race, and that "merit" must be given a collective social test rather than an individual mental one. The Group Areas Act provides especially for residential and recreational separation of different races. If an educated Bantu were permitted to buy and occupy a house in a White residential area, he would naturally wish to receive and entertain his own relatives on his own premises. He might even wish to let the house to others of his race. The way of life of such relatives and others at once becomes a material social factor, independently of individual intelligence, and for that matter athletic distinction as well. In fact it may prove more dangerous to think of athletic merit alone, because of its link with crowds of all racial groups.

White neighbours and others might be prepared to entertain an exceptional Bantu in their homes. But a full awareness of African habits and customs must excuse them for objecting to a neighbouring property being frequented at all times by Bantu associates. A situation of this kind might also create a security danger in times of political tension or criminal licence, which liberalism is more likely to provoke than diminish.

The vague term "merit" is often taken to imply a standard of culture based on means or education. Such definition, however, fails to take into account the imperceptible shading of merit from good to bad, a definition that will occasion the same sort of difficulties that arise in trying to distinguish persons of mixed race. It is evident that exceptional members of the non-white races must be viewed, for social administration, as part of their community. They cannot be abstracted from the ties of such community any more than from the ties of their families.

Against this it is argued that the advantages of an equal cultural environment for all the peoples of South Africa would ensure, within a generation or two, a common standard of civilisation. Assuming this to be sound in theory, despite experience in America, it is subject to the practical fulfilment of the condition of an equal cultural environment. But the economic factor asserts itself immediately. White taxpayers, on whom the heaviest burden must fall in the interim, cannot be expected to finance the equal housing, employment and education of the non-whites so as to overtake their increase in population, and the increase of multiracial friction. The ratio of population increase to economic advancement will remain static for an indefinite time, and with it the backwardness of the average Bantu.

A familiar argument against apartheid is that the traditional race separation in South Africa needed no legislation for its enforcement; it could have been left to the good sense of the people (despite the power of a Press with a dedicated multiracial policy?) It is said that the non-Whites do not really want to mix with the Whites—an argument quite inconsistent with that other, that Bantu nationalism is nothing but a reaction against apartheid.

It is true that the Coloured people of South Africa have no wish to associate with the Bantu, for fear of a loss of social standing. Likewise the urban Bantu distinguish themselves from the "blanket" or rural Bantu. But conversely, and with the same motive, each group does want to associate with a group of higher social standard, for the sake of prestige. This tendency, though apparently inconsistent with group cohesion, is due to the social ambition of individuals only, those on the social borderline, and especially those affected with the political idea of human equality. Liberal influence has insidiously sought to encourage race integration, and would never have allowed apartheid to survive without legislative protection. The liberal argument, therefore, that race relations in South Africa have been upset by unnecessary legislation, comes from the quarter from which it should least be expected. The trickle of liberal integration, but for legislation, would have led to a social swamp like that of President Johnson's "Great Society", where the legal enforcement of racial integration has had far worse results than that of apartheid.

Still another contention is that racial integration has already established itself in South African cities, and that their streets stream with a mixed population. But what impresses the foreign visitor is the absence of all racial friction in those streets, unlike those of America, and certainly due to residential apartheid. The existence of extensive non-white townships outside the white areas explains the good relationship in business centres. It is true that Whites are frequently the victims of non-white crime—murders, robberies and thefts, but no racial assaults—a good reason for stricter apartheid. But at least they are spared the far greater degree of crime committed by non-whites upon non-whites in their own townships.

With separate social services and amenities for the non-whites in their townships, adjacent to employment, together with local administration of their own eventually, to be developed with White assistance and example, there should be adequate opportunity for separate development in the townships. That is so long as the economic nexus continues, as it naturally should.

Success for the non-whites in such urban areas will depend on their own efficiency. At least they will be given the chance to put to good effect the urbanisation which, it is claimed, has emancipated them from tribal life. If there is an excessive increase in their population, future difficulties would obviously not be lessened by racial integration. And the non-whites, like all other peoples, would have to carry their own burden. Washington might have saved itself from multiracial disorder if it had ordained a separate Negro quarter for itself.

Then there is the Bantustan system, which is said to be both unworkable and politically dangerous for the Republic.

A well-worn liberal objection is that the allocation of land to the various groups is grossly unfair in respect of population. But what if Basutoland had been within the ambit of apartheid? Would anyone venture to claim that the Basutos should be given a wider and more productive share of South Africa? Just as they made their original choice of that homeland, in the unsettled history of the time, so did the Zulus, the Xhosas, and other ethnic groups of the Bantu. If their increase in population and uneconomic treatment of their country has made those areas seem an unfair share of the Republic, they can hardly be expected to be compensated for that. Claims on that basis would be a pretty problem for world government. If the Bantu groups have not been given back all the country they roamed over in their nomadic stage, they have gained by proximity to civilisation.

At least they, like other African peoples, are also being given the chance of self-government to satisfy political dignity. If they prefer it to trusteeship, to an extent that will not involve the political liquidation of the Republic as such, it is their choice, with all the risks that African states are encountering, almost without exception. They too will face the dangerous task of reconciling a one-man-one-vote democracy with a tradition of tribal dictatorship, and the inevitable regimentation of people who have little thought of anything beyond their kraals and witchcraft.

Those who think that urbanised Africans are different should take note of the following opinion of a factory personnel officer at Port Elizabeth, himself an African. He said that—

> "Nine out of ten Africans—including professing Christians—believe they may be bewitched at any time. . . . Last week four of our employees complained of ailments . . . they attributed their misfortune to having been bewitched by a fellow African employee.
>
> They were saying this on the authority of some witchdoctor, who practices his craft at New Brighton. They were obsessed with the idea that if the accused employee was not dismissed immediately their misfortunes would worsen." He explained that "the mind of the African employee

worked on a different plane from that of his White employer. It is not
the mentality that is different but the outlook on life."

(Eastern Province Herald)

To this may be added, from the same paper, the remarks of a Bantu clergyman showing the disinterest of such an educated man in African Nationalism:

"It would be advisable for the new states of Africa to stop and re-exam-
ine their policy of 'Africanisation'. It will take hundreds of years or less
to eliminate the 'hard prejudices' of tribalism and religion among our
people before they can be impartial in their dealings with one another.
Economics and justice are the most difficult fields where impartiality is
vital. This is where I believe a 'European supervisor' in industry would
do more justice in dealing with workers, and a European magistrate or
judge in legal affairs would be preferable.

Of course this is my personal opinion. I do not care for this fashionable
idea of 'Africanism'—as long as our people can get decent homes, clothing, food, a wife, and a garden to till—and or maybe a cow or two to
milk! This is all a man needs and there would be less grievances and
grumbling."

Bantustan leaders may yet avoid the pitfall of absolute democracy for
their people, when they reflect on the political disaster in African states,
and decide to retain, at least in part, the traditional tribal representation,
as in Rhodesia.

Meanwhile, the world-wide progress of subversive Communism, over
the red carpet of liberalism, must be remembered. And of all things a righteous Humanism is exploited, and with its dogma is helping to fabricate an
explosive situation. Danger to world peace will more surely arise from the
vain attempt to contrive a massive coalescence of humanity, under a world
government, whether Communist or Liberal, regardless of natural group
diversities, than from encouragement of respect for their separate development.

Progress is not always going forward. It may mean stepping backward—
from a precipice.

Human evolution has developed from prehistoric times on the solidarity
of the family, tribe and ethnic group as a protection of life. The dangers
may no longer be animals or alien intruders into a cave. But in modern
civilisation there may be intruders into the social solidarity of a community,
upon which human evolution still depends. The right to individual and
collective freedom of association must likewise continue. If the conscien-
tious exercise of such freedom promotes security for human development, it
cannot reasonably be called inhuman, immoral or contrary to the will of
God.

Footnote: A frequent political objection, not to the principle of apartheid, but to its application, is directed at what is called "Petty apartheid". The case of the fine Indian golfer Papwa, banned from open competitions in South Africa, has received the most adverse comment of all.

The government is ridiculed for such an introduction of politics into sport. Whereas in fact the government is taking a timely step to prevent such introduction—by excluding an occasion for displays of racial rivalry, not from the players, but from their possible multiracial gallery, disturbing the players' concentration. The disgraceful exhibition in recent years of barracking and bottle-throwing at football matches, especially those against oversea sides, cannot be forgotten and remains as a warning against the more dangerous occasion of multiracial competition in any form of sport, for instance boxing and athletics. From this angle it is clear that there is no substance in the plea that Papwa is only one player, and also an outstanding one, for the risk of political partisanship comes not from him but from non-white supporters, unless illogically excluded. Moreover any exception made in his case, on the ground of merit would mean that precedent would get its foot in the door meant to exclude politics from sport.

WILLIAM FAULKNER

If I Were a Negro

"But a white man can only imagine himself for the moment a Negro; he cannot be that man of another race and griefs and problems." This essay, by one of America's great literary figures, will provoke a reaction because of its style and tone. Its thesis, however, should be judged by the movement of events from the mid-1950's, which it so closely reflects. It should also be judged in terms of Faulkner's ability to create Black characters, and even to ask of them a reply to the essay.

I QUOTE THE FOLLOWING from a piece of mine printed in *Life* magazine, March 5, 1956, entitled *A Letter to the North,* this part of the *Letter* addressed specifically to the NAACP and the other organizations working actively for the abolishment of segregation: "Go slow now. Stop now for a time, a moment. You have the power now; you can afford to withhold for a moment the use of it as a force. You have done a good job, you have jolted your opponent off-balance and he is now vulnerable. But stop there for a moment; don't give him the advantage of a chance to cloud the issue by that purely automatic sympathy for the underdog simply because he is under. . . . You have shown the Southerner what you can do and what you will do if necessary; give him a space in which to get his breath and assimilate that knowledge; to look about and see that (1) Nobody is going to force integration on him from the outside; (2) That he himself faces an obsolescence in his own land which only he can cure; a moral condition which not only must be cured but a physical condition which has got to be cured if he, the white Southerner, is to have any peace, is not to be faced with another legal process or maneuver every year, year after year, for the rest of his life."

By "Go slow, pause for a moment," I meant, "Be flexible." When I wrote the letter and then used every means I knew to get it printed in time, Autherine Lucy had just been compelled to withdraw temporarily from the University of Alabama by a local violence already of dangerous proportions. I believed that when the judge validated her claim to be re-admitted, which he would have to do, that the forces supporting her would send her back for re-admission, and that when that happened she would probably lose her life. That didn't happen. I want to believe that the forces supporting Miss Lucy were wise enough themselves not to send her back —not merely wise enough to save her life, but wise enough to foresee that even her martyrdom would in the long run be less effective than the simple, prolonged, endless nuisance-value of her threat, which was what I meant by ". . . a physical condition which has got to be cured if he, the white Southerner, is to have any peace, is not to be faced with another Miss Lucy every year . . . for the rest of his life."

Not the individual Negro to abandon or lower one jot his hope and will for equality, but his leaders and organizations to be always flexible and adaptable to circumstance and locality in their methods of training it. If I were a Negro in America today, that is the course I would advise the leaders of my race to follow: to send every day to the white school to which he was entitled by his ability and capacity to go, a student of my race, fresh and cleanly dressed, courteous, without threat or violence, to seek admission; when he was refused I would forget about him as an individual, but tomorrow I would send another one, still fresh and clean and courteous, to be refused in his turn, until at last the white man himself must recognize that there will be no peace for him until he himself has solved the dilemma.

This was Gandhi's way. If I were a Negro, I would advise our elders and leaders to make this our undeviating and inflexible course—a course of inflexible and unviolent flexibility directed against not just the schools but against all the public institutions from which we are interdict, as is being done against the Montgomery, Alabama, bus lines. But always with flexibility: inflexible and undeviable only in hope and will but flexible always to adapt to time and place and circumstance.

I would be a member of NAACP, since nothing else in our United States culture has yet held out to my race that much of hope. But I would remain only under conditions: That it recognize the most serious quantity in our problem which, so far as I know, it has not publicly recognized yet: That it make that same flexibility the watchword of its methods. I would say to others of my race that we must never curb our hopes and demands for equal rights, but merely to curb with flexibility our methods of demanding them. I would say to other members of my race that I do not know how long "slow" will take, but if you will grant me to mean by "going slow," being flexible, I do not believe that anything else save "going slow" will advance our hopes. I would say to my race, "The watchword of our flexibility must be decency, quietness, courtesy, dignity; if violence and unreason come, it must not be from us." I would say that all the Negroes in Montgomery *should* support the bus line boycott, but never that all of them *must,* since by that *must,* we will descend to the same methods which those opposing us are using to oppress us, and our victory will be worth nothing until it is willed and not compelled. I would say that our race must adjust itself psychologically, not to an indefinite continuation of a segregated society, but rather to a continuation as long as necessary of that inflexible unflagging flexibility which in the end will make the white man himself sick and tired of fighting it.

It is easy enough to say glibly, "If I were a Negro, I would do this or that." But a white man can only imagine himself for the moment a Negro; he cannot be that man of another race and griefs and problems. So there are some questions he can put to himself but cannot answer, for instance:

Q   Would you lower your sights on your life's goals and reduce your aspirations for reasons of realism?
A   No. I would impose flexibility on the methods.
Q   Would this apply to your children?
A   I would teach them both the aspirations and the flexibility. But there is hope, since life itself is hope in simply being alive since living is change and change must be either advancement or death.
Q   How would you conduct yourself so as to avoid controversy and hostility and make friends for your people instead of enemies?
A   By decency, dignity, moral and social responsibility.
Q   How would you pray to God for human justice and racial salvation?
A   I don't believe man prays to God for human justice and racial salvation. I believe he affirms to God that immortal individual human dignity which has always outlasted injustice and before which families and clans and tribes talking of themselves as a race of men and not the race of Man, rise and pass and vanish like so much dust. He merely affirms his own belief in the grace and dignity and immortality of individual man, as Dostoevski's Ivan did when he repudiated any heaven whose order was founded on the anguished cry of one single child.
Q   Surrounded by antagonistic white people, would you find it hard not to hate them?
A   I would repeat to myself Booker T. Washington's words when he said: "I will let no man, no matter what his color, ever make me hate him."

So if I were a Negro, I would say to my people: "Let us be always unflaggingly and inflexibly flexible. But always decently, quietly, courteously, with dignity and without violence. And above all, with patience. The white man has devoted three hundred years to teaching us to be patient; that is one thing at least in which we are his superiors. Let us turn it into a weapon against him. Let us use this patience not as a passive quality, but as an active weapon. But always, let us practice cleanliness and decency and courtesy and dignity in our contacts with him. He has already taught us to be more patient and courteous with him than he is with us; let us be his superior in the others too."

But above all, I would say this to the leaders of our race: "We must learn to deserve equality so that we can hold and keep it after we get it.

We must learn responsibility, the responsibility of equality. We must learn that there is no such thing as a 'right' without any ties to it, since anything given to one free for nothing is worth exactly that: nothing. We must learn that our inalienable right to equality, to freedom and liberty and the pursuit of happiness, means exactly what our founding fathers meant by it: the right to *opportunity* to be free and equal provided one is worthy of it, will work to gain it and then work to keep it. And not only the right to that opportunity, but the willingness and the capacity to accept the responsibility of that opportunity—the responsibilities of physical cleanliness and of moral rectitude, of a conscience capable of choosing between right and wrong and a will capable of obeying it, or reliability toward other men, the pride of independence of charity or relief.

"The white man has not taught us that. He taught us only patience and courtesy. He did not even see that we had the environment in which we could teach ourselves cleanliness and independence and rectitude and reliability. So we must teach ourselves that. Our leaders must teach us that. We as a race must lift ourselves by our own bootstraps to where we are competent for the responsibilities of equality, so that we can hold on to it when we get it. Our tragedy is that these virtues of responsibility are the white man's virtues of which he boasts, yet we, the Negro, must be his superior in them. Our hope is that, having beaten him in patience and courtesy, we can probably beat him in these others too."

JAMES BALDWIN

My Dungeon Shook: Letter to My Nephew

On the subject of race every man presumes himself innocent. That is, no man of any race, according to himself, is ever guilty of any malicious or evil designs. The defenders of *apartheid,* for example, see that as a just system. This is part of what Baldwin has in mind when he says: "It is the innocence which constitutes the crime."

DEAR JAMES:

I have begun this letter five times and torn it up five times. I keep seeing your face, which is also the face of your father and my brother. Like him, you are tough, dark, vulnerable, moody —with a very definite tendency to sound truculent because you want no one to think you are soft. You may be like your grandfather in this, I don't know, but certainly both you and your father resemble him very much physically. Well, he is dead, he never saw you, and he had a terrible life; he was defeated long before he died because, at the bottom of his heart, he really believed what white people said about him. This is one of the reasons that he became so holy. I am sure that your father has told you something about all that. Neither you nor your father exhibit any tendency towards holiness: you really *are* of another era, part of what happened when the Negro left the land and came into what the late E. Franklin Frazier called "the cities of destruction." You can only be destroyed by believing that you really are what the white world calls a *nigger.* I tell you this because I love you, and please don't you ever forget it.

I have known both of you all your lives, have carried your Daddy in my arms and on my shoulders, kissed and spanked him and watched him learn to walk. I don't know if you've known anybody from that far back; if you've loved anybody that long, first as an infant, then as a child, then as a man, you gain a strange perspective on time and human pain and effort. Other people cannot see what I see whenever I look into your father's face, for behind your father's face as it is today are all those other faces which were his. Let him laugh and I see a cellar your father does not remember and a house he does not remember and I hear in his present laughter his laughter as a child. Let him curse and I remember him falling down the cellar steps, and howling, and I remember, with pain, his tears, which my hand or your grandmother's so easily wiped away. But no one's hand can wipe away those tears he sheds invisibly today, which one hears in his laughter and in his speech and in his songs. I know what the world has done to my brother and how narrowly he has survived it. And I know, which is much worse, and this is the crime of which I accuse my country and my countrymen, and for which neither I nor time nor history will ever forgive them, that they have destroyed and are destroying hundreds of thousands of lives and do not know it and do not want to know it. One can be, indeed one must strive to become, tough and philosophical concerning destruction and death, for this is what most of mankind has been best at since we have heard of man. (But remember: *most* of mankind is not *all* of mankind.) But it is not permissible that the authors of devastation should also be innocent. It is the innocence which constitutes the crime.

Now, my dear namesake, these innocent and well-meaning people, your countrymen, have caused you to be born under conditions not very far removed from those described for us by Charles Dickens in the London of more than a hundred years ago. (I hear the chorus of the innocents screaming, "No! This is not true! How *bitter* you are!"—but I am writing this letter to *you,* to try to tell you something about how to handle *them,* for most of them do not yet really know that you exist. I *know* the conditions under which you were born, for I was there. Your countrymen were *not* there, and haven't made it yet. Your grandmother was also there, and no one has ever accused her of being bitter. I suggest that the innocents check with her. She isn't hard to find. Your countrymen don't know that *she* exists, either, though she has been working for them all their lives.)

Well, you were born, here you came, something like fourteen years ago; and though your father and mother and grandmother, looking about the streets through which they were carrying you, staring at the walls into which they brought you, had every reason to be heavyhearted, yet they were not. For here you were, Big James, named for me—you were a big baby, I was not—here you were: to be loved. To be loved, baby, hard, at once, and forever, to strengthen you against the loveless world. Remember that: I know how black it looks today, for you. It looked bad that day, too, yes, we were trembling. We have not stopped trembling yet, but if we had not loved each other none of us would have survived. And now you must survive because we love you, and for the sake of your children and your children's children.

This innocent country set you down in a ghetto in which, in fact, it intended that you should perish. Let me spell out precisely what I mean by that, for the heart of the matter is here, and the root of my dispute with my country. You were born where you were born and faced the future that you faced because you were black and *for no other reason.* The limits of your ambition were, thus, expected to be set forever. You were born into a society which spelled out with brutal clarity, and in as many ways as possible, that you were a worthless human being. You were not expected to aspire to excellence: you were expected to make peace with mediocrity. Wherever you have turned, James, in your short time on this earth, you have been told where you could go and what you could do (and *how* you could do it) and where you could live and whom you could marry. I know your countrymen do not agree with me about this, and I hear them saying, "You exaggerate." They do not know Harlem, and I do. So do you. Take no one's word for anything, including mine—but trust your experience. Know whence you came. If you know whence you came, there is really no limit to where you can go. The details and symbols of your life have been deliberately constructed to make you believe what white people say about you. Please try to remember that what they believe, as well as what they do and cause you to endure, does not testify to your inferiority but to their inhumanity and fear. Please try to be clear, dear James, through the storm which rages about your youthful head today, about the reality which lies behind the words *acceptance* and *integration*. There is no reason for you to try to become like white people and there is no basis whatever for their impertinent assumption that *they* must accept *you*. The really terrible thing, old buddy, is that *you* must accept *them*. And I mean that very seriously. You must accept them and accept them with love. For these innocent people have no other hope. They are, in effect, still trapped in a history which they do not understand; and until they understand it, they cannot be released from it. They have had to believe for many years, and for innumerable reasons, that black men are inferior to white men. Many of them, indeed, know better, but, as you will discover, people find it very difficult to act on what they know. To act is to be committed, and to be committed is to be in danger. In this case, the danger, in the minds of most white Americans, is the loss of their identity. Try to imagine how you would feel if you woke up one morning to find the sun shining and all the stars aflame. You would be frightened because it is out of the order of nature. Any upheaval in the universe is terrifying because it so profoundly attacks one's sense of one's own reality. Well, the black man has functioned in the white man's world as a fixed star, as an immovable pillar: and as he moves out of his place, heaven and earth are shaken to their foundations. You, don't be afraid. I said that it was intended that you should perish in the ghetto, perish by never being allowed to go behind the white man's definitions, by never being allowed to spell your proper name. You have, and many of us have, defeated this intention; and, by a terrible law, a terrible paradox, those innocents who believed that your imprisonment made them safe are losing their grasp of reality. But these men are your brothers—your lost, younger brothers. And if the word *integration* means anything, this is what it means: that we, with love, shall force our brothers to see themselves as they are, to cease fleeing from reality and begin to change it. For this is your home, my friend, do not be driven from it; great men have done great things here, and will again, and we can make America what America must become. It will be hard, James, but you come from sturdy, peasant stock, men who picked cotton and dammed rivers and built railroads, and, in the teeth of the most terrifying odds, achieved an unassailable and monumental dignity. You come from a long line of great poets, some of the greatest poets since Homer. One of them said, *The very time I thought I was lost, My dungeon shook and my chains fell off.*

You know, and I know, that the country is celebrating one hundred years of freedom one hundred years too soon. We cannot be free until they are free. God bless you, James, and Godspeed.

Your uncle,

James

STOKELY CARMICHAEL

What We Want

This essay is addressed to the members of Stokely Carmichael's own community, defined precisely as Black Americans. For Carmichael, black power is political power, and power is the key. Integration in his vision denies the reality of black poverty and is finally only a means for maintaining white supremacy. Carmichael's style, here and elsewhere, is cool, tough, and lucid.

ONE OF THE TRAGEDIES of the struggle against racism is that up to now there has been no national organization which could speak to the growing militancy of young black people in the urban ghetto. There has been only a civil rights movement, whose tone of voice was adapted to an audience of liberal whites. It served as a sort of buffer zone between them and angry young blacks. None of its so-called leaders could go into a rioting community and be listened to. In a sense, I blame ourselves—together with the mass media—for what has happened in Watts, Harlem, Chicago, Cleveland, Omaha. Each time the people in those cities saw Martin Luther King get slapped, they became angry; when they saw four little black girls bombed to death, they were angrier; and when nothing happened, they were steaming. We had nothing to offer that they could see, except to go out and be beaten again. We helped to build their frustration.

For too many years, black Americans marched and had their heads broken and got shot. They were saying to the country, "Look, you guys are supposed to be nice guys and we are only going to do what we are supposed to do—why do you beat us up, why don't you give us what we ask, why don't you straighten yourselves out?" After years of this, we are at almost the same point—because we demonstrated from a position of weakness. We cannot be expected any longer to march and have our heads broken in order to say to whites: come on, you're nice guys. For you are not nice guys. We have found you out.

An organization which claims to speak for the needs of a community— as does the Student Nonviolent Coordinating Committee—must speak in the tone of that community, not as somebody else's buffer zone. This is the significance of black power as a slogan. For once, black people are going to use the words they want to use—not just the words whites want to hear.

And they will do this no matter how often the press tries to stop the use of the slogan by equating it with racism or separatism.

An organization which claims to be working for the needs of a community—as SNCC does—must work to provide that community with a position of strength from which to make its voice heard. This is the significance of black power beyond the slogan.

Black power can be clearly defined for those who do not attach the fears of white America to their questions about it. We should begin with the basic fact that black Americans have two problems: they are poor and they are black. All other problems arise from this two-sided reality: lack of education, the so-called apathy of black men. Any program to end racism must address itself to that double reality.

Almost from its beginning, SNCC sought to address itself to both conditions with a program aimed at winning political power for impoverished Southern blacks. We had to begin with politics because black Americans are propertyless people in a country where property is valued above all. We had to work for power, because this country does not function by morality, love, and nonviolence, but by power. Thus we determined to win political power, with the idea of moving on from there into activity that would have economic effects. With power, the masses could *make or participate in making* the decisions which govern their destinies, and thus create basic change in their day-to-day lives.

But if political power seemed to be the key to self-determination, it was also obvious that the key had been thrown down a deep well many years earlier. Disenfranchisement, maintained by racist terror, made it impossible to talk about organizing for political power in 1960. The right to vote had to be won, and SNCC workers devoted their energies to this from 1961 to 1965. They set up voter registration drives in the Deep South. They created pressure for the vote by holding mock elections in Mississippi in 1963 and by helping to establish the Mississippi Freedom Democratic Party (MFDP) in 1964. That struggle was eased, though not won, with the passage of the 1965 Voting Rights Act. SNCC workers could then address themselves to the question: "Who can we vote for, to have our needs met—how do we make our vote meaningful?"

SNCC had already gone to Atlantic City for recognition of the Mississippi Freedom Democratic Party by the Democratic convention and been rejected; it had gone with the MFDP to Washington for recognition by Congress and been rejected. In Arkansas, SNCC helped thirty Negroes to run for School Board elections; all but one were defeated, and there was evidence of fraud and intimidation sufficient to cause their defeat. In Atlanta, Julian Bond ran for the state legislature and was elected—twice—and unseated—twice. In several states, black farmers ran in elections for agricultural committees which make crucial decisions concerning land use, loans, etc. Although they won places on a number of committees, they never gained the majorities needed to control them.

All of the efforts were attempts to win black power. Then, in Alabama, the opportunity came to see how blacks could be organized on an independent party basis. An unusual Alabama law provides that any group of citizens can nominate candidates for county office and, if they win 20 per cent of the vote, may be recognized as a county political party. The same then applies on a state level. SNCC went to organize in several counties such as Lowndes, where black people—who form 80 per cent of the population and have an average annual income of $943—felt they could accomplish nothing within the framework of the Alabama Democratic Party because of its racism and because the qualifying fee for this year's elections was raised from $50 to $500 in order to prevent most Negroes from becoming candidates. On May 3, five new county "freedom organizations" convened and nominated candidates for the offices of sheriff, tax assessor, members of the school boards. These men and women are up for election in November—if they live until then. Their ballot symbol is the black panther: a bold, beautiful animal, representing the strength and dignity of black demands today. A man needs a black panther on his side when he and his family must endure—as hundreds of Alabamians have endured— loss of job, eviction, starvation, and sometimes death, for political activity. He may also need a gun and SNCC reaffirms the right of black men everywhere to defend themselves when threatened or attacked. As for initiating the use of violence, we hope that such programs as ours will make that unnecessary; but it is not for us to tell black communities whether they can or cannot use any particular form of action to resolve their problems. Responsibility for the use of violence by black men, whether in self-defense or initiated by them, lies with the white community.

This is the specific historical experience from which SNCC's call for "black power" emerged on the Mississippi march last July. But the concept of "black power" is not a recent or isolated phenomenon: It has grown out of the ferment of agitation and activity by different people and organizations in many black communities over the years. Our last year of work in Alabama added a new concrete possibility. In Lowndes county, for example, black power will mean that if a Negro is elected sheriff, he can end police brutality. If a black man is elected tax assessor, he can collect and channel funds for the building of better roads and schools serving black people—thus advancing the move from political power into the economic arena. In such areas as Lowndes, where black men have a majority, they will attempt to use it to exercise control. This is what they seek: control. Where Negroes lack a majority, black power means proper representation and sharing of control. It means the creation of power bases from which black people can work to change statewide or nationwide patterns of oppression through pressure from strength—instead of weakness. Politically, black power means what it has always meant to SNCC: the coming-together of black people to elect representatives and *to force those representatives to speak to their needs.* It does not mean merely putting black faces into office. A man or woman who is black and from the slums cannot be automatically expected to speak to the needs of black people. Most of the black politicians we see around the country today are not what SNCC means by black power. The power must be that of a community, and emanate from there.

SNCC today is working in both North and South on programs of voter registration and independent political organizing. In some places, such as Alabama, Los Angeles, New York, Philadelphia, and New Jersey, independent organizing under the black panther symbol is in progress. The creation of a national "black panther party" must come about; it will take time to build, and it is much too early to predict its success. We have no infallible master plan and we make no claim to exclusive knowledge of how to end racism; different groups will work in their own different ways. SNCC cannot spell out the full logistics of self-determination but it can address itself to the problem by helping black communities define their needs, realize their strength, and go into action along a variety of lines which they must choose for themselves. Without knowing all the answers, it can address itself to the basic problem of poverty; to the fact that in Lowndes County, 86 white families own 90 per cent of the land. What are black people in that county going to do for jobs, where are they going to get money? There must be reallocation of land, of money.

Ultimately, the economic foundations of this country must be shaken if black people are to control their lives. The colonies of the United States —and this includes the black ghettoes within its borders, north and south —must be liberated. For a century, this nation has been like an octopus of exploitation, its tentacles stretching from Mississippi and Harlem to South America, the Middle East, southern Africa, and Vietnam; the form of exploitation varies from area to area but the essential result has been the same—a powerful few have been maintained and enriched at the expense of the poor and voiceless colored masses. This pattern must be broken. As its grip loosens here and there around the world, the hopes of black Americans become more realistic. For racism to die, a totally different America must be born.

This is what the white society does not wish to face; this is why that society prefers to talk about integration. But integration speaks not at all to the problem of poverty, only to the problem of blackness. Integration today means the man who "makes it," leaving his black brothers behind in the ghetto as fast as his new sports car will take him. It has no relevance to the Harlem wino or to the cottonpicker making three dollars a day. As a lady I know in Alabama once said, "the food that Ralph Bunche eats doesn't fill my stomach."

Integration, moreover, speaks to the problem of blackness in a despicable way. As a goal, it has been based on complete acceptance of the fact that *in order to have* a decent house or education, blacks must move into a white neighborhood or send their children to a white school. This reinforces, among both black and white, the idea that "white" is automatically better and "black" is by definition inferior. This is why integration is a subterfuge for the maintenance of white supremacy. It allows the nation to focus on a handful of Southern children who get into white schools, at great price, and to ignore the 94 per cent who are left behind in unimproved all-black schools. Such situations will not change until black people have power—to control their own school boards, in this case. Then Negroes become equal in a way that means something, and integration ceases to be a one-way street. Then integration doesn't mean draining skills and energies from the ghetto into white neighborhoods; then it can mean white people moving from Beverly Hills into Watts, white people joining the Lowndes County Freedom Organization. Then integration becomes relevant.

Last April, before the furor over black power, Christopher Jencks wrote in a *New Republic* article on white Mississippi's manipulation of the anti-poverty program:

> The war on poverty has been predicated on the notion that there is such a thing as *a community* which can be defined geographically and mobilized for a collective effort to help the poor. This theory has no relationship to reality in the Deep South. In every Mississippi county there are *two* communities. Despite all the pious platitudes of the moderates on both sides, these two communities habitually see their interests in terms of conflict rather than cooperation. Only when the Negro community can muster enough political, economic and professional strength to compete on somewhat equal terms, will Negroes believe in the possibility of true cooperation and whites accept its necessity. En route to integration, the Negro community needs to develop greater independence—a chance to run its own affairs and not cave in whenever "the man" barks . . . Or so it seems to me, and to most of the knowledgeable people with whom I talked in Mississippi. To OEO, this judgment may sound like black nationalism . . .

Mr. Jencks, a white reporter, perceived the reason why America's anti-poverty program has been a sick farce in both North and South. In the South, it is clearly racism which prevents the poor from running their own programs; in the North, it more often seems to be politicking and bureaucracy. But the results are not so different: In the North, non-whites make up 42 per cent of all families in metropolitan "poverty areas" and only 6 per cent of families in areas classified as not poor. SNCC has been working with local residents in Arkansas, Alabama, and Mississippi to achieve control by the poor of the program and its funds; it has also been working with groups in the North, and the struggle is no less difficult. Behind it all is a federal government which cares far more about winning the war on the Vietnamese than the war on poverty; which has put the poverty program in the hands of self-serving politicians and bureaucrats rather than the poor themselves; which is unwilling to curb the misuse of white power but quick to condemn black power.

To most whites, black power seems to mean that the Mau Mau are coming to the suburbs at night. The Mau Mau are coming, and whites must stop them. Articles appear about plots to "get Whitey," creating an atmosphere in which "law and order must be maintained." Once again, responsibility is shifted from the oppressor to the oppressed. Other whites chide, "Don't forget—you're only 10 per cent of the population; if you get too smart, we'll wipe you out." If they are liberals, they complain, "what about me?—don't you want my help any more?" These are people supposedly concerned about black Americans, but today they think first of themselves, of their feelings of rejection. Or they admonish, "you can't get anywhere without coalitions," without considering the problems of coalition with whom?; on what terms? (coalescing from weakness can mean absorption, betrayal); when? Or they accuse us of "polarizing the races" by our calls for black unity, when the true responsibility for polarization lies with whites who will not accept their responsibility as the majority power for making the democratic process work.

White America will not face the problem of color, the reality of it. The well-intended say: "We're all human, everybody is really decent, we must forget color." But color cannot be "forgotten" until its weight is recognized and dealt with. White America will not acknowledge that the ways in which this country sees itself are contradicted by being black—and always have been. Whereas most of the people who settled this country came here for freedom or for economic opportunity, blacks were brought here to be slaves. When the Lowndes County Freedom Organization chose the black panther as its symbol, it was christened by the press "the Black Panther Party"—but the Alabama Democratic Party, whose symbol is a rooster, has never been called the White Cock Party. No one ever talked about "white power" because power in this country *is* white. All this adds up to more than merely identifying a group phenomenon by some catchy name or adjective. The furor over that black panther reveals the problems that white America has with color and sex; the furor over "black power" reveals how deep racism runs and the great fear which is attached to it.

Whites will not see that I, for example, as a person oppressed because of my blackness, have common cause with other blacks who are oppressed because of blackness. This is not to say that there are no white people who see things as I do, but that it is black people I must speak to first. It must be the oppressed to whom SNCC addresses itself primarily, not to friends from the oppressing group.

From birth, black people are told a set of lies about themselves. We are told that we are lazy—yet I drive through the Delta area of Mississippi and watch black people picking cotton in the hot sun for fourteen hours. We are told, "If you work hard, you'll succeed"—but if that were true, black people would own this country. We are oppressed because we are black—not because we are ignorant, not because we are lazy, not because we're stupid (and got good rhythm), but because we're black.

I remember that when I was a boy, I used to go to see Tarzan movies on Saturday. White Tarzan used to beat up the black natives. I would sit there yelling, "Kill the beasts, kill the savages, kill 'em!" I was saying: Kill *me*. It was as if a Jewish boy watched Nazis taking Jews off to concentration camps and cheered them on. Today, I want the chief to beat hell out of Tarzan and send him back to Europe. But it takes time to become free of the lies and their shaming effect on black minds. It takes time to reject the most important lie: that black people inherently can't do the same things white people can do, unless white people help them.

The need for psychological equality is the reason why SNCC today believes that blacks must organize in the black community. Only black people can convey the revolutionary idea that black people are able to do things themselves. Only they can help create in the community an aroused and continuing black consciousness that will provide the basis for political strength. In the past, white allies have furthered white supremacy without the whites involved realizing it—or wanting it, I think. Black people must do things for themselves; they must get poverty money they will control and spend themselves, they must conduct tutorial programs themselves so that black children can identify with black people. This is one reason Africa has such importance: The reality of black men ruling their own nations gives blacks elsewhere a sense of possibility, of power, which they do not now have.

This does not mean we don't welcome help, or friends. But we want the right to decide whether anyone is, in fact, our friend. In the past, black Americans have been almost the only people whom everybody and his momma could jump up and call their friends. We have been tokens, symbols, objects—as I was in high school to many young whites, who liked having "a Negro friend." We want to decide who is our friend, and we will not accept someone who comes to us and says: "If you do X, Y, and Z, then I'll help you." We will not be told whom we should choose as allies. We will not be isolated from any group or nation except by our own choice. We cannot have the oppressors telling the oppressed how to rid themselves of the oppressor.

I have said that most liberal whites react to "black power" with the question, What about me?, rather than saying: Tell me what you want me to do and I'll see if I can do it. There are answers to the right question. One of the most disturbing things about almost all white supporters of the movement has been that they are afraid to go into their own communities —which is where the racism exists—and work to get rid of it. They want to run from Berkeley to tell us what to do in Mississippi; let them look instead at Berkeley. They admonish blacks to be nonviolent; let them preach nonviolence in the white community. They come to teach me Negro history; let them go to the suburbs and open up freedom schools for whites. Let them work to stop America's racist foreign policy; let them press this government to cease supporting the economy of South Africa.

There is a vital job to be done among poor whites. We hope to see, eventually, a coalition between poor blacks and poor whites. That is the only coalition which seems acceptable to us, and we see such a coalition as the major internal instrument of change in American society. SNCC has tried several times to organize poor whites; we are trying again now, with an initial training program in Tennessee. It is purely academic today to talk about bringing poor blacks and whites together, but the job of creating a poor-white power bloc must be attempted. The main responsibility for it falls upon whites. Black and white can work together in the white community where possible; it is not possible, however, to go into a poor Southern town and talk about integration. Poor whites everywhere are becoming more hostile—not less—partly because they see the nation's attention focused on black poverty and nobody coming to them. Too many young middle-class Americans, like some sort of Pepsi generation, have wanted to come alive through the black community; they've wanted to be where the action is—and the action has been in the black community.

Black people do not want to "take over" this country. They don't want to "get whitey"; they just want to get him off their backs, as the saying goes. It was for example the exploitation by Jewish landlords and merchants which first created blank resentment toward Jews—not Judaism. The white man is irrelevant to blacks, except as an oppressive force. Blacks want to be in his place, yes, but not in order to terrorize and lynch and starve him. They want to be in his place because that is where a decent life can be had.

But our vision is not merely of a society in which all black men have enough to buy the good things of life. When we urge that black money go into black pockets, we mean the communal pocket. We want to see money go back into the community and used to benefit it. We want to see the cooperative concept applied in business and banking. We want to see black ghetto residents demand that an exploiting landlord or storekeeper sell them, at minimal cost, a building or a shop that they will own and improve cooperatively; they can back their demand with a rent strike, or a boycott, and a community so unified behind them that no one else will move into the building or buy at the store. The society we seek to build among black people, then, is not a capitalist one. It is a society in which the spirit of community and humanistic love prevail. The word love is suspect; black expectations of what it might produce have been betrayed too often. But those were expectations of a response from the white community, which failed us. The love we seek to encourage is within the black community, the only American community where men call each other "brother" when they meet. We can build a community of love only where we have the ability and power to do so: among blacks.

As for white America, perhaps it can stop crying out against "black supremacy," "black nationalism," "racism in reverse," and begin facing reality. The reality is that this nation, from top to bottom, is racist; that racism is not primarily a problem of "human relations" but of an exploitation maintained—either actively or through silence—by the society as a whole. Camus and Sartre have asked, can a man condemn himself? Can whites, particularly liberal whites, condemn themselves? Can they stop blaming us, and blame their own system? Are they capable of the shame which might become a revolutionary emotion?

We have found that they usually cannot condemn themselves, and so we have done it. But the rebuilding of this society, if at all possible, is basically the responsibility of whites—not blacks. We won't fight to save the present society, in Vietnam or anywhere else. We are just going to work, in the way *we* see fit, and on goals *we* define, not for civil rights but for all our human rights.

MARTIN LUTHER KING, JR.

Black Power

Martin Luther King, Jr., offers another perspective on black power. His essay is, perhaps, the most visionary in this section and visionary is not used in any pejorative sense. The vision of men like Martin Luther King, a vision which can survive his life and provide a basis for the actions of others, sustains our hope and our humanity.

NEVERTHELESS, in spite of the positive aspects of Black Power, which are compatible with what we have sought to do in the civil rights movement all along without the slogan, its negative values, I believe, prevent it from having the substance and program to become the basic strategy for the civil rights movement in the days ahead.

Beneath all the satisfaction of a gratifying slogan, Black Power is a nihilistic philosophy born out of the conviction that the Negro can't win. It is, at bottom, the view that American society is so hopelessly corrupt and enmeshed in evil that there is no possibility of salvation from within. Although this thinking is understandable as a response to a white power structure that never completely committed itself to true equality for the Negro, and a die-hard mentality that sought to shut all windows and doors against the winds of change, it nonetheless carries the seeds of its own doom.

Before this century, virtually all revolutions had been based on hope and hate. The hope was expressed in the rising expectation of freedom and justice. The hate was an expression of bitterness toward the perpetrators of the old order. It was the hate that made revolutions bloody and violent. What was new about Mahatma Gandhi's movement in India was that he mounted a revolution on hope and love, hope and nonviolence. This same new emphasis characterized the civil rights movement in our country dating from the Montgomery bus boycott of 1956 to the Selma movement of 1965. We maintained the hope while transforming the hate of traditional revolution into positive nonviolent power. As long as the hope was fulfilled there was little questioning of nonviolence. But when the hopes were blasted, when people came to see that in spite of progress their conditions were still insufferable, when they looked out and saw more poverty, more school segregation and more slums, despair began to set in.

Unfortunately, when hope diminishes, the hate is often turned most bitterly toward those who originally built up the hope. In all the speaking that I have done in the United States before varied audiences, including some hostile whites, the only time that I have been booed was one night in a Chicago mass meeting by some young members of the Black Power movement. I went home that night with an ugly feeling. Selfishly I thought of my sufferings and sacrifices over the last twelve years. Why would they boo one so close to them? But as I lay awake thinking, I finally came to myself, and I could not for the life of me have less than patience and understanding for those young people. For twelve years I, and others like me, had held out radiant promises of progress. I had preached to them about my dream. I had lectured to them about the not too distant day when they would have freedom, "all, here and now." I had urged them to have faith in America and in white society. Their hopes had soared. They were now booing because they felt that we were unable to deliver on our promises. They were booing because we had urged them to have faith in people who had too often proved to be unfaithful. They were now hostile because they were watching the dream that they had so readily accepted turn into a frustrating nightmare.

But revolution, though born of despair, cannot long be sustained by despair. This is the ultimate contradiction of the Black Power movement. It claims to be the most revolutionary wing of the social revolution taking place in the United States. Yet it rejects the one thing that keeps the fire of revolutions burning: the ever-present flame of hope. When hope dies, a revolution degenerates into an undiscriminating catchall for evanescent and futile gestures. The Negro cannot entrust his destiny to a philosophy nourished solely on despair, to a slogan that cannot be implemented into a program.

The Negro's disappointment is real and a part of the daily menu of our lives. One of the most agonizing problems of human experience is how to deal with disappointment. In our individual lives we all too often distill our frustrations into an essence of bitterness, or drown ourselves in the deep waters of self-pity, or adopt a fatalistic philosophy that whatever happens must happen and all events are determined by necessity. These reactions poison the soul and scar the personality, always harming the person who harbors them more than anyone else. The only healthy answer lies in one's honest recognition of disappointment even as he still clings to hope, one's acceptance of finite disappointment even while clinging to infinite hope.

We Negroes, who have dreamed for so long of freedom, are still confined in a prison of segregation and discrimination. Must we respond with bitterness and cynicism? Certainly not, for this can lead to black anger so desperate that it ends in black suicide. Must we turn inward in self-pity? Of course not, for this can lead to a self-defeating black paranoia. Must we conclude that we cannot win? Certainly not, for this will lead to a black nihilism that seeks disruption for disruption's sake. Must we, by fatalistically concluding that segregation is a foreordained pattern of the universe, resign ourselves to oppression? Of course not, for passively to cooperate with an unjust system makes the oppressed as evil as the oppressors. Our most fruitful course is to stand firm, move forward nonviolently, accept disappointments and cling to hope. Our determined refusal not to be stopped will eventually open the door to fulfillment. By recognizing the necessity of suffering in a righteous cause, we may achieve our humanity's full stature. To guard ourselves from bitterness, we need the vision to see in this generation's ordeals the opportunity to transfigure both ourselves and American society.

In 1956 I flew from New York to London in the propeller-type aircraft that required nine and a half hours for a flight now made in six hours by jet. Returning from London to the United States, the stewardess announced that the flying time would be twelve and a half hours. The distance was the same. Why an additional three hours? When the pilot entered the cabin to greet the passengers, I asked him to explain.

"You must understand about the winds," he said. "When we leave New York, a strong tail wind is in our favor, but when we return, a strong head wind is against us." Then he added, "Don't worry. These four engines are capable of battling the winds."

In any social revolution there are times when the tail winds of triumph and fulfillment favor us, and other times when strong head winds of disappointment and setbacks beat against us relentlessly. We must not permit adverse winds to overwhelm us as we journey across life's mighty Atlantic; we must be sustained by our engines of courage in spite of the winds. This refusal to be stopped, this "courage to be," this determination to go on "in spite of" is the hallmark of any great movement.

The Black Power movement of today, like the Garvey "Back to Africa" movement of the 1920's, represents a dashing of hope, a conviction of the inability of the Negro to win and a belief in the infinitude of the ghetto. While there is much grounding in past experience for all these feelings, a revolution cannot succumb to any of them. Today's despair is a poor chisel to carve out tomorrow's justice.

Black Power is an implicit and often explicit belief in black separatism. Notice that I do not call it black racism. It is inaccurate to refer to Black Power as racism in reverse, as some have recently done. Racism is a doctrine of the congenital inferiority and worthlessness of a people. While a few angry proponents of Black Power have, in moments of bitterness, made wild statements that come close to this kind of racism, the major proponents of Black Power have never contended that the white man is innately worthless.

Yet behind Black Power's legitimate and necessary concern for group unity and black identity lies the belief that there can be a separate black road to power and fulfillment. Few ideas are more unrealistic. There is no salvation for the Negro through isolation.

One of the chief affirmations of Black Power is the call for the mobilization of political strength for black people. But we do not have to look far to see that effective political power for Negroes cannot come through separatism. Granted that there are cities and counties in the country where the Negro is in a majority, they are so few that concentration on them alone would still leave the vast majority of Negroes outside the mainstream of American political life.

Out of the eighty-odd counties in Alabama, the state where SNCC sought to develop an all-black party, only nine have a majority of Negroes. Even if blacks could control each of these counties, they would have little influence in over-all state politics and could do little to improve conditions in the major Negro population centers of Birmingham, Mobile and Montgomery. There are still relatively few Congressional districts in the South that have such large black majorities that Negro candidates could be elected without the aid of whites. Is it a sounder program to concentrate on the election of two or three Negro Congressmen from predominantly Negro districts or to concentrate on the election of fifteen or twenty Negro Congressmen from Southern districts where a coalition of Negro and white moderate voters is possible?

Moreover, any program that elects all black candidates simply because they are black and rejects all white candidates simply because they are white is politically unsound and morally unjustifiable. It is true that in many areas of the South Negroes still must elect Negroes in order to be effectively represented. SNCC staff members are eminently correct when they point out that in Lowndes County, Alabama, there are no white liberals or moderates and no possibility for cooperation between the races at the present time. But the Lowndes County experience cannot be made a measuring rod for the whole of America. The basic thing in determining the best candidate is not his color but his integrity.

Black Power alone is no more insurance against social injustice than white power. Negro politicians can be as opportunistic as their white counterparts if there is not an informed and determined constituency demanding social reform. What is most needed is a coalition of Negroes and liberal whites that will work to make both major parties truly responsive to the needs of the poor. Black Power does not envision or desire such a program.

Just as the Negro cannot achieve political power in isolation, neither can he gain economic power through separatism. While there must be a continued emphasis on the need for blacks to pool their economic resources and withdraw consumer support from discriminating firms, we must not be oblivious to the fact that the larger economic problems confronting the Negro community will only be solved by federal programs involving billions of dollars. One unfortunate thing about Black Power is that it gives priority to race precisely at a time when the impact of automation and other forces have made the economic question fundamental for blacks and whites alike. In this context a slogan Power for Poor People would be much more appropriate than the slogan Black Power.

However much we pool our resources and "buy black," this cannot create the multiplicity of new jobs and provide the number of low-cost houses that will lift the Negro out of the economic depression caused by centuries of deprivation. Neither can our resources supply quality integrated education. All of this requires billions of dollars which only an alliance of liberal-labor-civil-rights forces can stimulate. In short, the Negroes' problem cannot be solved unless the whole of American society takes a new turn toward greater economic justice.

In a multiracial society no group can make it alone. It is a myth to believe that the Irish, the Italians and the Jews—the ethnic groups that Black Power advocates cite as justification for their views—rose to power through separatism. It is true that they stuck together. But their group unity was always enlarged by joining in alliances with other groups such as political machines and trade unions. To succeed in a pluralistic society, and an often hostile one at that, the Negro obviously needs organized strength, but that strength will only be effective when it is consolidated through constructive alliances with the majority group.

Those proponents of Black Power who have urged Negroes to shun alliances with whites argue that whites as a group cannot have a genuine concern for Negro progress. Therefore, they claim, the white man's main interest in collaborative effort is to diminish Negro militancy and deflect it from constructive goals.

Undeniably there are white elements that cannot be trusted, and no militant movement can afford to relax its vigilance against halfhearted associates or conscious betrayers. Every alliance must be considered on its own merits. Negroes may embrace some and walk out on others where their interests are imperiled. Occasional betrayals, however, do not justify the rejection of the principle of Negro-white alliance.

The oppression of Negroes by whites has left an understandable residue of suspicion. Some of this suspicion is a healthy and appropriate safeguard. An excess of skepticism, however, becomes a fetter. It denies that there can be reliable white allies, even though some whites have died heroically at the side of Negroes in our struggle and others have risked economic and political peril to support our cause.

The history of the movement reveals that Negro-white alliances have played a powerfully constructive role, especially in recent years. While Negro initiative, courage and imagination precipitated the Birmingham and Selma confrontations and revealed the harrowing injustice of segregated life, the organized strength of Negroes alone would have been insufficient to move Congress and the administration without the weight of the aroused conscience of white America. In the period ahead Negroes will continue to need this support. Ten percent of the population cannot by tensions alone induce 90 percent to change a way of life.

Within the white majority there exists a substantial group who cherish democratic principles above privilege and who have demonstrated a will to fight side by side with the Negro against injustice. Another and more substantial group is composed of those having common needs with the Negro and who will benefit equally with him in the achievement of social progress. There are, in fact, more poor white Americans than there are Negro. Their need for a war on poverty is no less desperate than the Negro's. In the South they have been deluded by race prejudice and largely remained aloof from common action. Ironically, with this posture they were fighting not only the Negro but themselves. Yet there are already signs of change. Without formal alliances, Negroes and whites have supported the same candidates in many *de facto* electoral coalitions in the South because each sufficiently served his own needs.

The ability of Negroes to enter alliances is a mark of our growing strength, not of our weakness. In entering an alliance, the Negro is not relying on white leadership or ideology; he is taking his place as an equal partner in a common endeavor. His organized strength and his new independence pave the way for alliances. Far from losing independence in an alliance, he is using it for constructive and multiplied gains.

Negroes must shun the very narrow-mindedness that in others has so long been the source of our own afflictions. We have reached the stage of organized strength and independence to work securely in alliances. History has demonstrated with major victories the effectiveness, wisdom and moral soundness of Negro-white alliance. The cooperation of Negro and white based on the solid ground of honest conscience and proper self-interest can continue to grow in scope and influence. It can attain the strength to alter basic institutions by democratic means. Negro isolation can never approach this goal.

In the final analysis the weakness of Black Power is its failure to see that the black man needs the white man and the white man needs the black man. However much we may try to romanticize the slogan, there is no separate black path to power and fulfillment that does not intersect white paths, and there is no separate white path to power and fulfillment, short of social disaster, that does not share that power with black aspirations for freedom and human dignity. We are bound together in a single garment of destiny. The language, the cultural patterns, the music, the material prosperity and even the food of America are an amalgam of black and white.

James Baldwin once related how he returned home from school and his mother asked him whether his teacher was colored or white. After a pause he answered: "She is a little bit colored and a little bit white." [1] This is the dilemma of being a Negro in America. In physical as well as cultural terms every Negro is a little bit colored and a little bit white. In our search for identity we must recognize this dilemma.

Every man must ultimately confront the question "Who am I?" and seek to answer it honestly. One of the first principles of personal adjustment is the principle of self-acceptance. The Negro's greatest dilemma is that in order to be healthy he must accept his ambivalence. The Negro is the child of two cultures—Africa and America. The problem is that in the search for wholeness all too many Negroes seek to embrace only one side of their natures. Some, seeking to reject their heritage, are ashamed of their color, ashamed of black art and music, and determine what is beautiful and good by the standards of white society. They end up frustrated and without cultural roots. Others seek to reject everything American and to identify totally with Africa, even to the point of wearing African clothes. But this approach leads also to frustration because the American Negro is not an African. The old Hegelian synthesis still offers the best answer to many of life's dilemmas. The American Negro is neither totally African nor totally Western. He is Afro-American, a true hybrid, a combination of two cultures.

Who are we? We are the descendants of slaves. We are the offspring of noble men and women who were kidnaped from their native land and chained in ships like beasts. We are the heirs of a great and exploited continent known as Africa. We are the heirs of a past of rope, fire and murder. I for one am not ashamed of this past. My shame is for those who became so inhuman that they could inflict this torture upon us.

But we are also Americans. Abused and scorned though we may be, our destiny is tied up with the destiny of America. In spite of the psychological appeals of identification with Africa, the Negro must face the fact that America is now his home, a home that he helped to build through "blood, sweat and tears." Since we are Americans the solution to our problem will not come through seeking to build a separate black nation within a nation, but by finding that creative minority of the concerned from the ofttimes apathetic majority, and together moving toward that colorless power that we all need for security and justice.

In the first century B.C., Cicero said: "Freedom is participation in power." Negroes should never want all power because they would deprive

1. Quoted in Kenneth B. Clark (ed.), *The Negro Protest*, Boston, Beacon Press, 1963, p. 6.

others of their freedom. By the same token, Negroes can never be content without participation in power. America must be a nation in which its multiracial people are partners in power. This is the essence of democracy toward which all Negro struggles have been directed since the distant past when he was transplanted here in chains.

Probably the most destructive feature of Black Power is its unconscious and often conscious call for retaliatory violence. Many well-meaning persons within the movement rationalize that Black Power does not really mean black violence, that those who shout the slogan don't really mean it that way, that the violent connotations are solely the distortions of a vicious press. That the press has fueled the fire is true. But as one who has worked and talked intimately with devotees of Black Power, I must admit that the slogan is mainly used by persons who have lost faith in the method and philosophy of nonviolence. I must make it clear that no guilt by association is intended. Both Floyd McKissick and Stokely Carmichael have declared themselves opponents of aggressive violence. This clarification is welcome and useful, despite the persistence of some of their followers in examining the uses of violence.

Over cups of coffee in my home in Atlanta and my apartment in Chicago, I have often talked late at night and over into the small hours of the morning with proponents of Black Power who argued passionately about the validity of violence and riots. They don't quote Gandhi or Tolstoy. Their Bible is Frantz Fanon's *The Wretched of the Earth*.[2] This black psychiatrist from Martinique, who went to Algeria to work with the National Liberation Front in its fight against the French, argues in his book—a well-written book, incidentally, with many penetrating insights—that violence is a psychologically healthy and tactically sound method for the oppressed. And so, realizing that they are a part of that vast company of the "wretched of the earth," these young American Negroes, who are predominantly involved in the Black Power movement, often quote Fanon's belief that violence is the only thing that will bring about liberation. As they say, "Sing us no songs of nonviolence, sing us no songs of progress, for nonviolence and progress belong to middle-class Negroes and whites and we are not interested in you."

As we have seen, the first public expression of disenchantment with nonviolence arose around the question of "self-defense." In a sense this is a false issue, for the right to defend one's home and one's person when attacked has been guaranteed through the ages by common law. In a nonviolent demonstration, however, self-defense must be approached from another perspective.

The cause of a demonstration is the existence of some form of

2. New York, Evergreen Books, Grove Press, Inc., 1966.

exploitation or oppression that has made it necessary for men of courage and goodwill to protest the evil. For example, a demonstration against *de facto* school segregation is based on the awareness that a child's mind is crippled by inadequate educational opportunities. The demonstrator agrees that it is better to suffer publicly for a short time to end the crippling evil of school segregation than to have generation after generation of children suffer in ignorance. In such a demonstration the point is made that the schools are inadequate. This is the evil one seeks to dramatize; anything else distracts from that point and interferes with the confrontation of the primary evil. Of course no one wants to suffer and be hurt. But it is more important to get at the cause than to be safe. It is better to shed a little blood from a blow on the head or a rock thrown by an angry mob than to have children by the thousands finishing high school who can only read at a sixth-grade level.

Furthermore, it is dangerous to organize a movement around self-defense. The line of demarcation between defensive violence and aggressive violence is very thin. The minute a program of violence is enunciated, even for self-defense, the atmosphere is filled with talk of violence, and the words falling on unsophisticated ears may be interpreted as an invitation to aggression.

One of the main questions that the Negro must confront in his pursuit of freedom is that of effectiveness. What is the most effective way to achieve the desired goal? If a method is not effective, no matter how much steam it releases, it is an expression of weakness, not of strength. Now the plain, inexorable fact is that any attempt of the American Negro to overthrow his oppressor with violence will not work. We do not need President Johnson to tell us this by reminding Negro rioters that they are outnumbered ten to one. The courageous efforts of our own insurrectionist brothers, such as Denmark Vesey and Nat Turner, should be eternal reminders to us that violent rebellion is doomed from the start. In violent warfare one must be prepared to face the fact that there will be casualties by the thousands. Anyone leading a violent rebellion must be willing to make an honest assessment regarding the possible casualties to a minority population confronting a well-armed, wealthy majority with a fanatical right wing that would delight in exterminating thousands of black men, women and children.

Arguments that the American Negro is a part of a world which is two-thirds colored and that there will come a day when the oppressed people of color will violently rise together to throw off the yoke of white oppression are beyond the realm of serious discussion. There is no colored nation, including China, that now shows even the potential of leading a violent revolution of color in any international proportions. Ghana, Zambia, Tanganyika and Nigeria are so busy fighting their own battles against poverty, illiteracy and the subversive influence of neo-colonialism that they offer little hope to Angola, Southern Rhodesia and South Africa, much less to the American Negro. The hard cold facts today indicate that the hope of the people of color in the world may well rest on the American Negro and his ability to reform the structure of racist imperialism from within and thereby turn the technology and wealth of the West to the task of liberating the world from want.

The futility of violence in the struggle for racial justice has been tragically etched in all the recent Negro riots. There is something painfully sad about a riot. One sees screaming youngsters and angry adults fighting hopelessly and aimlessly against impossible odds. Deep down within them you perceive a desire for self-destruction, a suicidal longing. Occasionally Negroes contend that the 1965 Watts riot and the other riots in various cities represented effective civil rights action. But those who express this view always end up with stumbling words when asked what concrete gains have been won as a result. At best the riots have produced a little additional anti-poverty money, allotted by frightened government officials, and a few water sprinklers to cool the children of the ghettos. It is something like improving the food in a prison while the people remain securely incarcerated behind bars. Nowhere have the riots won any concrete improvement such as have the organized protest demonstrations.

It is not overlooking the limitations of nonviolence and the distance we have yet to go to point out the remarkable record of achievements that have already come through nonviolent action. The 1960 sit-ins desegregated lunch counters in more than 150 cities within a year. The 1961 Freedom Rides put an end to segregation in interstate travel. The 1956 bus boycott in Montgomery, Alabama, ended segregation on the buses not only of that city but in practically every city of the South. The 1963 Birmingham movement and the climactic March on Washington won passage of the most powerful civil rights law in a century. The 1965 Selma movement brought enactment of the Voting Rights Law. Our nonviolent marches in Chicago last summer brought about a housing agreement which, if implemented, will be the strongest step toward open housing taken in any city in the nation. Most significant is the fact that this progress occurred with minimum human sacrifice and loss of life. Fewer people have been killed in ten years of nonviolent demonstrations across the South than were killed in one night of rioting in Watts.

When one tries to pin down advocates of violence as to what acts would be effective, the answers are blatantly illogical. Sometimes they talk of overthrowing racist state and local governments. They fail to see that no internal revolution has ever succeeded in overthrowing a government by violence unless the government had already lost the allegiance and effective control of its armed forces. Anyone in his right mind knows that this will not happen in the United States. In a violent racial situation, the power structure has the local police, the state troopers, the national guard and finally the army to call on, all of which are predominantly white.

Furthermore, few if any violent revolutions have been successful unless the violent minority had the sympathy and support of the nonresisting majority. Castro may have had only a few Cubans actually fighting with him, but he would never have overthrown the Batista regime unless he had had the sympathy of the vast majority of the Cuban people. It is perfectly clear that a violent revolution on the part of American blacks would find no sympathy and support from the white population and very little from the majority of the Negroes themselves.

This is no time for romantic illusions and empty philosophical debates about freedom. This is a time for action. What is needed is a strategy for change, a tactical program that will bring the Negro into the mainstream of American life as quickly as possible. So far, this has only been offered by the nonviolent movement. Without recognizing this we will end up with solutions that don't solve, answers that don't answer and explanations that don't explain.

Beyond the pragmatic invalidity of violence is its inability to appeal to conscience. Some Black Power advocates consider an appeal to conscience irrelevant. A Black Power exponent said to me not long ago: "To hell with conscience and morality. We want power." But power and morality must go together, implementing, fulfilling and ennobling each other. In the quest for power I cannot by-pass the concern for morality. I refuse to be driven to a Machiavellian cynicism with respect to power. Power at its best is the right use of strength. The words of Alfred the Great are still true: "Power is never good unless he who has it is good."

Nonviolence is power, but it is the right and good use of power. Constructively it can save the white man as well as the Negro. Racial segregation is buttressed by such irrational fears as loss of preferred economic privilege, altered social status, intermarriage and adjustment to new situations. Through sleepless nights and haggard days numerous white people struggle pitifully to combat these fears. By following the path of escape, some seek to ignore the questions of race relations and to close their minds to the issues involved. Others, placing their faith in legal maneuvers, counsel massive resistance. Still others hope to drown their fears by engaging in acts of meanness and violence toward their Negro brethren. But how futile are all these remedies! Instead of eliminating fear, they instill deeper and more pathological fears. The white man, through his own efforts, through education and goodwill, through searching his conscience and through confronting the fact of integration, must do a great deal to free himself of these paralyzing fears. But to master fear he must also depend on the spirit the Negro generates toward him. Only through our adherence to

nonviolence—which also means love in its strong and commanding sense
—will the fear in the white community be mitigated.

A guilt-ridden white minority fears that if the Negro attains power, he
will without restraint or pity act to revenge the accumulated injustices and
brutality of the years. The Negro must show that the white man has nothing to fear, for the Negro is willing to forgive. A mass movement exercising nonviolence and demonstrating power under discipline should convince
the white community that as such a movement attained strength, its power
would be used creatively and not for revenge.

In a moving letter to his nephew on the one hundredth anniversary of
emancipation, James Baldwin wrote concerning white people:

> The really terrible thing, old buddy, is that *you* must accept *them*. And
> I mean that very seriously. You must accept them and accept them with
> love. For these innocent people have no other hope. They are, in effect,
> still trapped in a history which they do not understand; and until they
> understand it, they cannot be released from it. They have had to believe
> for many years, and for innumerable reasons, that black men are inferior
> to white men. Many of them, indeed, know better, but, as you will dis-
> cover, people find it very difficult to act on what they know. To act is to
> be committed, and to be committed is to be in danger. In this case, the
> danger, in the minds of most white Americans, is the loss of their iden-
> tity. . . . But these men are your brothers—your lost, younger brothers.
> And if the word *integration* means anything, this is what it means: that
> we, with love, shall force our brothers to see themselves as they are, to
> cease fleeing from reality and begin to change it. . . .[3]

The problem with hatred and violence is that they intensify the fears of
the white majority, and leave them less ashamed of their prejudices toward
Negroes. In the guilt and confusion confronting our society, violence only
adds to the chaos. It deepens the brutality of the oppressor and increases
the bitterness of the oppressed. Violence is the antithesis of creativity and
wholeness. It destroys community and makes brotherhood impossible.

My friend John Killens recently wrote in the *Negro Digest:*

> Integration comes after liberation. A slave cannot integrate with his
> master. In the whole history of revolts and revolutions, integration has
> never been the main slogan of the revolution. The oppressed fights to free
> himself from his oppressor, not to integrate with him. Integration is the
> step after freedom when the freedman makes up his mind as to whether
> he wishes to integrate with his former master.[4]

At first glance this sounds very good. But after reflection one has to face
some inescapable facts about the Negro and American life. This is a mul-

3. *The Fire Next Time,* New York, The Dial Press, Inc., 1963, pp. 22–23.
4. *Negro Digest,* November, 1966.

tiracial nation where all groups are dependent on each other, whether they want to recognize it or not. In this vast interdependent nation no racial group can retreat to an island entire of itself. The phenomena of integration and liberation cannot be as neatly divided as Killens would have it.

There is no theoretical or sociological divorce between liberation and integration. In our kind of society liberation cannot come without integration and integration cannot come without liberation. I speak here of integration in both the ethical and the political senses. On the one hand, integration is true intergroup, interpersonal living. On the other hand, it is the mutual sharing of power. I cannot see how the Negro will be totally liberated from the crushing weight of poor education, squalid housing and economic strangulation until he is integrated, with power, into every level of American life.

Mr. Killens' assertion might have some validity in a struggle for independence against a foreign invader. But the Negro's struggle in America is quite different from and more difficult than the struggle for independence. The American Negro will be living tomorrow with the very people against whom he is struggling today. The American Negro is not in a Congo where the Belgians will go back to Belgium after the battle is over, or in an India where the British will go back to England after independence is won. In the struggle for national independence one can talk about liberation now and integration later, but in the struggle for racial justice in a multiracial society where the oppressor and the oppressed are both "at home," liberation must come through integration.

Are we seeking power for power's sake? Or are we seeking to make the world and our nation better places to live. If we seek the latter, violence can never provide the answer. The ultimate weakness of violence is that it is a descending spiral, begetting the very thing it seeks to destroy. Instead of diminishing evil, it multiplies it. Through violence you may murder the liar, but you cannot murder the lie, nor establish the truth. Through violence you may murder the hater, but you do not murder hate. In fact, violence merely increases hate. So it goes. Returning violence for violence multiplies violence, adding deeper darkness to a night already devoid of stars. Darkness cannot drive out darkness: only light can do that. Hate cannot drive out hate: only love can do that.

The beauty of nonviolence is that in its own way and in its own time it seeks to break the chain reaction of evil. With a majestic sense of spiritual power, it seeks to elevate truth, beauty and goodness to the throne. Therefore I will continue to follow this method because I think it is the most practically sound and morally excellent way for the Negro to achieve freedom.

In recent months several people have said to me: "Since violence is the new cry, isn't there a danger that you will lose touch with the people in the ghetto and be out of step with the times if you don't change your views on nonviolence?"

My answer is always the same. While I am convinced the vast majority of Negroes reject violence, even if they did not I would not be interested in being a consensus leader. I refuse to determine what is right by taking a Gallup poll of the trends of the time. I imagine that there were leaders in Germany who sincerely opposed what Hitler was doing to the Jews. But they took their poll and discovered that anti-Semitism was the prevailing trend. In order to "be in step with the times," in order to "keep in touch," they yielded to one of the most ignominious evils that history has ever known.

Ultimately a genuine leader is not a searcher for consensus but a molder of consensus. I said on one occasion, "If every Negro in the United States turns to violence, I will choose to be that one lone voice preaching that this is the wrong way." Maybe this sounded like arrogance. But it was not intended that way. It was simply my way of saying that I would rather be a man of conviction than a man of conformity. Occasionally in life one develops a conviction so precious and meaningful that he will stand on it till the end. This is what I have found in nonviolence.

One of the greatest paradoxes of the Black Power movement is that it talks unceasingly about not imitating the values of white society, but in advocating violence it is imitating the worst, the most brutal and the most uncivilized value of American life. American Negroes have not been mass murderers. They have not murdered children in Sunday school, nor have they hung white men on trees bearing strange fruit. They have not been hooded perpetrators of violence, lynching human beings at will and drowning them at whim.

This is not to imply that the Negro is a saint who abhors violence. Unfortunately, a check of the hospitals in any Negro community on any Saturday night will make you painfully aware of the violence within the Negro community. By turning his hostility and frustration with the larger society inward, the Negro often inflicts terrible acts of violence on his own black brother. This tragic problem must be solved. But I would not advise Negroes to solve the problem by turning these inner hostilities outward through the murdering of whites. This would substitute one evil for another. Nonviolence provides a healthy way to deal with understandable anger.

I am concerned that Negroes achieve full status as citizens and as human beings here in the United States. But I am also concerned about our moral uprightness and the health of our souls. Therefore I must oppose any attempt to gain our freedom by the methods of malice, hate and violence that have characterized our oppressors. Hate is just as injurious to the hater as it is to the hated. Like an unchecked cancer, hate corrodes the personality and eats away its vital unity. Many of our inner conflicts are rooted in hate. This is why the psychiatrists say, "Love or perish." I have seen hate expressed in the countenances of too many Mississippi and Alabama sheriffs to advise the Negro to sink to this miserable level. Hate is too great a burden to bear.

Of course, you may say, this is not *practical;* life is a matter of getting even, of hitting back, of dog eat dog. Maybe in some distant Utopia, you say, that idea will work, but not in the hard, cold world in which we live. My only answer is that mankind has followed the so-called practical way for a long time now, and it has led inexorably to deeper confusion and chaos. Time is cluttered with the wreckage of individuals and communities that surrendered to hatred and violence. For the salvation of our nation and the salvation of mankind, we must follow another way. This does not mean that we abandon our militant efforts. With every ounce of our energy we must continue to rid our nation of the incubus of racial injustice. But we need not in the process relinquish our privilege and obligation to love.

Fanon says at the end of *The Wretched of the Earth:*

> So, comrades, let us not pay tribute to Europe by creating states, institutions and societies which draw their inspiration from her.
>
> Humanity is waiting for something other from us than such an imitation, which would be almost an obscene caricature.
>
> If we want to turn Africa into a new Europe, and America into a new Europe, then let us leave the destiny of our countries to Europeans. They will know how to do it better than the most gifted among us.
>
> But if we want humanity to advance a step further, if we want to bring it up to a different level than that which Europe has shown it, then we must invent and we must make discoveries.
>
> If we wish to live up to our peoples' expectations, we must seek the response elsewhere than in Europe.
>
> Moreover, if we wish to reply to the expectations of the people of Europe, it is no good sending them back a reflection, even an ideal reflection, of their society and their thought with which from time to time they feel immeasurably sickened.
>
> For Europe, for ourselves and for humanity, comrades, we must turn over a new leaf, we must work out new concepts, and try to set afoot a new man.[5]

These are brave and challenging words; I am happy that young black men and women are quoting them. But the problem is that Fanon and those who quote his words are seeking "to work out new concepts" and "set afoot a new man" with a willingness to imitate old concepts of violence. Is there not a basic contradiction here? Violence has been the inseparable twin of materialism, the hallmark of its grandeur and misery. This

5. Fanon, *op. cit.,* p. 255.

is the one thing about modern civilization that I do not care to imitate.

Humanity is waiting for something other than blind imitation of the past. If we want truly to advance a step further, if we want to turn over a new leaf and really set a new man afoot, we must begin to turn mankind away from the long and desolate night of violence. May it not be that the new man the world needs is the nonviolent man? Longfellow said, "In this world a man must either be an anvil or a hammer." We must be hammers shaping a new society rather than anvils molded by the old. This not only will make us new men, but will give us a new kind of power. It will not be Lord Acton's image of power that tends to corrupt or absolute power that corrupts absolutely. It will be power infused with love and justice, that will change dark yesterdays into bright tomorrows, and lift us from the fatigue of despair to the buoyancy of hope. A dark, desperate, confused and sin-sick world waits for this new kind of man and this new kind of power.

NDABANINGI SITHOLE

White Supremacy and African Nationalism

George Orwell's essay concerned itself with the white race's sense of
its imperial position. The Reverend Ndabaningi Sithole, interna-
tionally known African leader, describes the imperialist from the point
of view of the race that has been exploited. He bases his psychological explanation on the assumptions of myth analysis, and his great
cause, African Nationalism, evolves out of the cracking of that myth.

THE FIRST TIME he ever came into contact with the white man
the African was overwhelmed, overawed, puzzled, perplexed, mys-
tified, and dazzled. The white man's "houses that move on the
water," his "bird that is not like other birds," "his monster that
spits fire and smoke and swallows people and spits them out alive," his
ability to "kill" a man and again raise him from the dead (anaesthesia), his
big massive and impressive house that has many other houses in it, and
many new things introduced by the white man, amazed the African. Motor
cars, motor cycles, bicycles, gramophones, telegraphy, the telephone, glittering Western clothes, new ways of ploughing and planting, added to the
African's sense of curiosity and novelty. Never before had the African
seen such things. They were beyond his comprehension; they were outside
the realm of his experience. He saw. He wondered. He mused. Here then
the African came into contact with two-legged gods who chose to dwell
among people instead of in the distant mountains. For the first time he
came in contact with gods who had wives and children, and who kept dogs
and cats.

These white gods were conscious of the magic spell they had cast over
the Africans, and they did everything to maintain it. They demonstrated
their control of the lightning by firing their guns regularly which to the
ears of Africans sounded like thunder in the sky. There was hardly anything which the white man did which had no god-like aspects. The African, who never argues with his gods lest their wrath visit him, adopted the
same attitude to the white man. And so the Africans submitted themselves
to the rule of the white man without question. The white man became
master in a house that was not his. He ordered the African right and left
and the African was only too ready to please his white god. And the white
man saw that it was good, and he smiled with deep satisfaction and said

"Africa, the white man's Paradise." Any other race of human beings could have done the same thing under similar circumstances.

This is reminiscent of Captain Cook who played the role of a god when he and his crew landed on one of the Hawaiian islands. The natives, having never seen anyone like him and his crew before, and having never seen or heard a gun before, quickly fell on their faces and worshipped him thinking he was a god who had come from the sky. His crew they took for lesser gods. And so they gave him the full liberty of their temple where they enthroned him as their god. They were delighted that they, of all the peoples of the earth, had been chosen for a visit by the gods. Here was the chosen tribe of the Hawaiians. But as time went on some of the more intelligent among the natives began to doubt the "goodness" of the new god for he had all the externals of any one among them. Sooner or later the natives were divided into two schools of thought—those who believed that Captain Cook was a genuine god, and those who took him only for a fake god. Neither side was convinced until one day one among them picked up a stone, and with a good aim, and with all his might, hurled it against god Captain Cook who felt the full impact of the stone and winced with pain, whereupon the untutored Hawaiian scientist triumphantly explained, "He feels pain. Therefore he's not a god." Great was the fury of the natives who had come to worship this god. Like hungry and angry hounds they fell upon their god, and thus died another pretender to the throne of the gods.

Right from the beginning relations between the Africans and the white people were strictly controlled and regulated. The white man made laws forbidding intermarriage and cohabitation between black and white so that this white magic spell might continue to work to the maximum benefit of the white man. A death penalty was attached to the violation of this law, but this was only applicable to the African male. To the African the law appeared to be quite unnecessary. "How can a man cohabit with a goddess?" they asked innocently. "How can a woman cohabit with a god?" they still wondered. The white male and his female both inhabited a higher world—that of gods and goddesses. The Matebele—the brave and warlike tribe that broke away from the Zulu nation—called the white people *"Omlimu abadla amabele"*—the gods that eat corn. The gods the Matebele had known never ate any food. In life these "gods who eat corn" were feared above the gods the Matebele had known, the reason being that the white gods were near and visible and acted visibly whereas the usual gods were distant and invisible. The early relations between black and white in many parts of Africa were those of god and creature whose life was at the mercy of the god. The African feared to move on his own lest he incur the god's vengeful wrath. Deep mines were opened throughout the country. The dynamite that exploded the huge rocks confirmed the African's belief that the white man was a god. The African soon noticed that the white man "has untold material wealth" and had the ability of creating even more. He soon associated all power, wealth, skills, cleverness, wisdom, and knowledge with the white man. While by nature the African did not like to stay too close to the quarters of the gods whose actions were so unpredictable, and whose fury was like a consuming fire, yet he was compelled to stay near these white gods who demanded his labour. The African soon noticed that all his people had been turned into a nation of servants for the white man, and in all fairness it must be stated that many of them enjoyed themselves by dwelling in the house of the lord for ever. And who would not rejoice to work for the gods to escape destruction?

But soon the African, while admitting to himself that there was a world of difference between himself and the white man, vaguely sensed much that was in common between them. The Matebele were not altogether wrong when they referred to the white people as "gods who eat corn." According to the Matebele philosophy anything that eats corn dies. Unconsciously the Matebele had sensed that beyond the white man was *Unkulunkulu*—the Great, Great One—*Usimakade*—the One who has always stood over against us. But how could they reconcile this theological belief with the wonders of the white man? The instinct of self-preservation that inclined towards treating the white man like a god triumphed temporarily over strong theological doubts.

There was a time when the white skin seemed to be all that mattered because it was mistaken for power and success in the world. There was a time when African people thought that perhaps if they had a European name that would guarantee to them success in life. African Christian converts took Western names. How could they possibly be genuine Christians without some Bible name? How could they possibly get along with the white man if all their names were African? African pastors and evangelists demanded that every African convert have a Bible name. The essence of genuine Christianity was supposed to be rather in the Bible name than in the heart of the individual. Some Africans Europeanized their African names, and so African "Jubulani Tendele Sibanda" became "John Philip Brown." In some areas the process of taking on European names is still in vogue, though the motive has changed.

The psychology of all this was to identify themselves with the conqueror —to enlist the sympathy of the gods. To have no European name became a thing to be ashamed of, a kind of social stigma, a symbol of backwardness. A European name seemed to open up to the African all sorts of fantastic worlds. Anything that had anything to do with the white man had something bordering on magic. Black heroes were pushed into the background so that for some time every hero was white, and every white man was a hero. The black man became the villain in the theatre of life. So for a time the white man held the stage while his spellbound African spectators just gazed and gazed, and wondered about this new creature to whom God seemed to have given all the blessings of life.

Time is a great doctor. It heals many things. It clarifies many things. It reveals many things. Winter cannot boast that it holds sway over the entire universe all the time for sooner or later summer discredits the claim. The white man could not play the part of a god indefinitely. He could remain a myth, a mystery, for only a limited time. The myth was bound to show cracks here and there as Time rolled on to Eternity. And soon the African discovered that the white man, after all, was God-created. He had not created himself.

The African observed rather curiously that his own domestic life closely resembled that of the white man. When the African saw that the white female became pregnant like his own wife, that both the white male and white female fought, that sometimes white males fought over a white female, that sometimes an angry-with-wife white male refused to eat when he was offered food by his wife, that both the white male and white female wrinkled and stooped with age, that white people also died, he was reminded of the experiences he had in his own domestic life, and gradually he began to see through the myth.

This revelation did not stop only at the white man's domestic side of life. It extended to the African's domestic side of life as well. The white male, for some reason or other, became intensely interested in African women. When an African found a white male in the arms of an African female, he was horrified to the core of his being, for woe unto the eyes that saw the gods take such liberties. The African who had seen this god-human spectacle made sure that such an experience remained a sealed book. He feared to arouse the anger of the gods who would not only punish his iniquities but would also visit these on the members of his community. As more and more of these white males were found relaxing in the very congenial society of African ladies, the news began to be proclaimed from hilltop to hilltop in sheer amusement. The African males warned, "Take care of our women. The gods have partaken of the forbidden fruit of Africa and may forget their own women." The African began to resent the white man's liberties with the African female, for many an African male was sent to the gallows for cohabiting with white females. Thus on the domestic level the white man and his female were stripped of their "god" aspects, and stood naked before the African like ordinary human beings. "They were deceiving us," said the African. "We are the same."

The narrow-minded African blamed the white man for interfering with his women, but the broad-minded rejoiced, partly because this gave a lie to the common statement that whites and blacks were basically different, and partly because they were pleased to see that despite the fact that the white man boasted of two thousand years of civilization and culture behind him, he succumbed to the charms of the African madonna. White governors, M.P.s, medical doctors, lawyers, top businessmen, postmasters, ministers of religion, and other top executives, to say nothing of the lower classes, all capitulated. This is not to deny the fact that African males fell down at the feet of white madonnas, and forgot all about their black ones. This should not surprise us because both the African male and the white male have the same thing in common, and that is the "male principle." Conversely the female principle seeks satisfaction in the male principle also regardless of colour or race.

There was a time in Africa when the white male's actions towards African women were said to arise from the fact that there were very few white females in Africa, but although their number increased to be equal to that of their men, the white male continued to roam the African female world. The white myth which had so overwhelmed the African could not remain the same after a white male had slept with an African female, and after an African had slept with a white female. Some white racialists tried to restrict race relations between males and females, but once the forbidden fruit had been tasted withdrawal was impossible.

There was a time when all teachers, ministers of religion, prime ministers, lawyers, judges, magistrates, medical doctors, journalists, men of letters, clerks, policemen, train, crane, and tractor drivers, postmasters, retail and wholesale merchants, and the like, were exclusively white. It was during this time that the black man used to condemn God for creating him black—for blackness had become, for him, synonymous with inability, foolishness, and backwardness. It was at this time that the African began to question whether or not the clay that went to make his body was the same as that which went to make the body of the white man. When Dr. Aggrey of the Gold Coast (now Ghana) said, "A man who is not proud of his colour is not fit to live," he was trying to correct this self-depreciating, apologetic attitude of many Africans. As long as all important positions remained exclusively white, the myth held together and cast its magic spell over the African. But when an army of black teachers, ministers of religion, prime ministers, lawyers, judges, magistrates, medical doctors, journalists, men of letters, clerks, policemen, train, crane, and tractor drivers, postmasters, retail and wholesale merchants, and the like made their appearance on the African scene, the white myth began to show more cracks. With the emergence now of thirty-eight fully independent African states enjoying full sovereignty, the myth which had swayed the entire continent of Africa cracked apart and was dashed to pieces beyond repair.

About twenty-four years ago, a white friend of mine in Rhodesia used to say to me, "Sithole, it pays for a black man to get highly educated, but it does not pay the same dividends for a white man." My friend was quite confident that a white skin, at least in Rhodesia, was enough to ensure the white man success. But events throughout Africa have belied him since now African presidents, African prime ministers, African military commanders-in-chief, African judges and African attorney-generals, and a host of others bestride the African stage. Events have cracked the white myth.

World Wars I and II also helped to widen the cracks of the white myth. Thousands of African soldiers went abroad on active service. The English street girls of London, the French street girls of Paris, and the Italian street girls of Naples did not help to preserve the white myth. Drinking and woman-raping white soldiers still added their contribution to its annihilation. White commanders ordered African soldiers to kill white enemy soldiers. African soldiers from Southern and Northern Rhodesia, Nyasaland, Tanganyika, Kenya, North Africa, French West Africa, French Equatorial Africa, the Gold Coast, and Nigeria, found themselves at the front-line war with one purpose in view—to kill every white soldier enemy they could get hold of. Many German and Italian soldiers were shot by African soldiers.

African soldiers saw white soldiers wounded, dying, and dead. Bullets had the same effect on black and white. This had a very powerful psychological impact on the African. He saw what he used to call his betters suffer defeat (though not conquest) at the hands of Germans and Japanese, and once more he was impressed by the fact that it was not the fact of being black or white that mattered. After suffering side by side with his white fellow soldiers the African never again regarded them in the same light. After spending four years hunting the white enemy soldiers the African never regarded them again as gods.

But what has this to do with the problem of the rise of African nationalism? African nationalism, in many ways, represented the degree to which the white man's magic spell had worn off. As long as this myth was thick and impenetrable the African adjusted himself as well as he could to what he thought were gods, though gods that ate corn. But the externals had had their day and reality had taken its place, though few white people in Africa realized this extremely important change.

There were certain basic facts that these white people who wanted to be regarded by Africans as myth forgot. The generations of Africans who first came into contact with the white man and his wonders were overwhelmed by the sheer novelty of the white man and the new things he had brought to Africa. But numbers of the later generation, born in modern hospitals, raised in modern towns and cities, educated in modern schools, travelling by land, air, and sea, trained in modern arts and skills, employed in modern factories and mines, rubbing shoulders daily with white people in towns, cities, schools, and on the battlefield, took the white man as a matter of course, just as they took another African. The white man could no longer cast his spell over them by a simple trick of showing them the train, or an automobile, or reading them a story book or cracking his gun because many an African then knew how to do these things. It pained the white man to realize that the African was regarding him as an ordinary human being. To him the new African generation was all degenerate. It had no proper respect for the white man, not so much because he was human, but because he was white. The white man failed to draw a distinction between what had been and what then was, let alone what had to be in a matter of a few decades.

How African was the African of that time? There was a world of difference between the African before the coming of the white man and the African afterwards. The interaction between the West and Africa was producing a new brand of African. That is, it was pushing the white-man-worshipping African into the background, and bringing into the foreground the African who did not worship the white man. The proud and arrogant African might have thought he was 100 per cent. African because both his mother and father were African, just as the proud and arrogant white man born in Africa might have thought he was 100 per cent. European. The truth was that there was no such thing in this Africa as 100 per cent. this or that race.

Take an African who had been to school. He might have thought that he was 100 per cent. African. Physically this might have been true, but an examination of the content of his consciousness even on a superficial level, disclosed that his mathematical thought, his legal training, his theological views, his commercial and industrial undertakings, his economic theories, the themes of his conversation, his aspirations and hopes, to quote only a few, were radically different from those of an African who lived before the advent of European powers. The African of the post-European period had new eyes, as it were. He saw new things that he never saw before European rule came. He had new ears. He heard new things that he never heard before European rule came. He had come to possess a new sensibility. He felt things that he never felt before. He did not quite see what his forefathers saw. He did not quite hear what his forefathers had heard. He did not quite feel what his forefathers had felt. He ceased to see the white myth which his forefathers had seen, for the simple reason that he had ceased in many ways to be the African that his forefathers used to be.

But in what way was this African different from his forefathers? The answer is simple: his forefathers were vaguely conscious of the country in which they lived. They were not conscious of the rest of Africa—certainly not of the countries outside Africa. They spent most of their time looking after their livestock, hunting, and trapping game. Their eyes never saw the large cities and towns whose buildings now soar to the sky. They never travelled on bicycles, motorcars, trains, and they never flew. They never went to school. That is, they never learned how to read and write. They never built themselves modern houses and schools.

The African of the post-European period lived in an environment that in many instances was different from that in which his forefathers lived. He was not only conscious of the country in which he lived, but also of Africa as a whole and of the world. Unlike his forefathers' environment that hummed with bees, that was enlivened with singing birds, disturbed by wild animals, and moved at nature's pace, the African of the European period lived in an environment where the mechanical bird had superseded the bird, where automobiles, trains, and tractors had pushed the ox, the donkey, and the horse into the background. If the African forefathers had come back to life and beheld their own descendants on the modern scene, they would have mistaken their own children for gods.

Time had given birth to a new African who was more self-assertive, more enterprising, more aggressive and more self-reliant than his forebears. It was impossible to push this new African back into time's womb just as the baby, once expelled from its mother's womb, cannot begin a successful "back-to-the-womb" movement. The baby has to cope as well as it can with out-of-the-womb conditions. The African himself tried to cope as well as he could with the new times into which he had been born. Anyone who advised him to behave as his forefathers had behaved towards white people might as well have advised him to return into his mother's womb. Most thinking white people accepted this important change, and met the situation as it was without wasting time and effort in wishful thinking. But the attitude of the average white man was like that of dethroned gods. Their paradise has passed away with the decisive victories of African nationalism.

The now cracked myth of the white man reminds us of an incident in Shakespeare's *The Tempest,* when Caliban mistook the newcomers to his island for gods, and immediately pledged his loyalty to them. In his own words we can see the psychological impact Stephano and his friends made on Caliban during their first encounter with him.

> These be fine things an if they be not sprites.
> That's a brave god and bears celestial liquor:
>   I will kneel to him. . . .
> I will swear, upon that bottle, to be thy true subject; for the liquor is not earthly. . . .
> I'll show thee every fertile inch o' the island; and I will kiss thy foot:
> I prithee, be my god.[1]

1. The Tempest, II, ii.

Caliban had been thoroughly impressed that Stephano, the drunken butler, was a god from heaven, but after Time had taken its course to reveal the true nature of his new god, Caliban makes his confession:

> . . . and I'll be wise hereafter,
> And seek for grace. What a thrice-double ass
> Was I, to take this drunkard for a god,
> And worship this dull fool! [2]

One might compare the early relations between black and white to that between child and parent. So long as the child is dependent upon the parent, the parents easily secure his loyalty and obedience, and so long as the child remains child, there is always something mythical about parents. When my wife was ten, she used to think her mother a wonderful woman because she had brought her four brothers and two sisters into the world; when her mother told her that one day she would also bring into the world babies, she used to say, "No, impossible. I am not like you." Her mother was a mystery to her. As long as she was ignorant of the facts of childbirth, the myth about her mother held together, but as soon as she knew these facts, the mystery fell asunder and shattered altogether, never to be reconstructed.

As soon as the African knew how to read and write, how to drive and repair an automobile, how to build a modern house and install modern plumbing, how to operate properly on a human body, how to run a business, how to do countless other things that his white god did, why, the myth fell asunder, never to come together again.

But apart from the forces described in this chapter there are other forces which contributed to the de-mythification of the white man in Africa. The presence of the independent sovereign African states has had an important role to play in this whole process. There was a time when it looked as though the natural ruler of Africa was not the African, but the white man. History, however, has reversed this, and now it is accepted that the African is the natural ruler of Africa.

From what has been said above it is clear that African nationalism was preceded by a tremendous psychological process which resulted in the de-mythification of the white man, and this psychological process was a precondition of African nationalism if the latter was to emerge and be effective. A process of internal emancipation had to precede that of political liberation.

2. The Tempest, V, i.

MALCOLM X

Mecca

There is no older metaphor than that of the journey—the journey
that is both to new lands and new experiences and, at the same time, a
journey into the self and new understanding. For our subject, for
our time, Malcolm X's is the classic restatement of the most basic of
human themes.

T HE PILGRIMAGE to Mecca, known as Hajj, is a religious obligation that every orthodox Muslim fulfills, if humanly able, at least
once in his or her lifetime.

The Holy Quran says it, "Pilgrimage to the Ka'ba is a duty men
owe to God; those who are able, make the journey."

Allah said: "And proclaim the pilgrimage among men; they will come
to you on foot and upon each lean camel, they will come from every deep
ravine."

At one or another college or university, usually in the informal gather-
ings after I had spoken, perhaps a dozen generally white-complexioned
people would come up to me, identifying themselves as Arabian, Middle
Eastern or North African Muslims who happened to be visiting, studying,
or living in the United States. They had said to me that, my white-indict-
ing statements notwithstanding, they felt that I was sincere in considering
myself as Muslim—and they felt if I was exposed to what they always
called "true Islam," I would "understand it, and embrace it." Automatically, as a follower of Elijah Muhammad, I had bridled whenever this was
said.

But in the privacy of my own thoughts after several of these experiences, I did question myself: if one was sincere in professing a religion,
why should he balk at broadening his knowledge of that religion?

Once in a conversation I broached this with Wallace Muhammad, Elijah
Muhammad's son. He said that yes, certainly, a Muslim should seek to
learn all that he could about Islam. I had always had a high opinion of
Wallace Muhammad's opinion.

Those orthodox Muslims whom I had met, one after another, had urged
me to meet and talk with a Dr. Mahmoud Youssef Shawarbi. He was described to me as an eminent, learned Muslim, a University of Cairo graduate, a University of London Ph.D., a lecturer on Islam, a United Nations
advisor and the author of many books. He was a full professor of the Uni-

411

versity of Cairo, on leave from there to be in New York as the Director of the Federation of Islamic Associations in the United States and Canada. Several times, driving in that part of town, I had resisted the impulse to drop in at the F.J.A. building, a brownstone at 1 Riverside Drive. Then one day Dr. Shawarbi and I were introduced by a newspaperman.

He was cordial. He said he had followed me in the press; I said I had been told of him, and we talked for fifteen or twenty minutes. We both had to leave to make appointments we had, when he dropped on me something whose logic never would get out of my head. He said, "No man has believed perfectly until he wishes for his brother what he wishes for himself."

Then, there was my sister Ella herself. I couldn't get over what she had done. I've said before, this is a *strong* big, black, Georgia-born woman. Her domineering ways had gotten her put out of the Nation of Islam's Boston Mosque Eleven; they took her back, then she left on her own. Ella had started studying under Boston orthodox Muslims, then she founded a school where Arabic was taught! *She* couldn't speak it, she hired teachers who did. That's Ella! She deals in real estate, and *she* was saving up to make the pilgrimage. Nearly all night, we talked in her living room. She told me there was no question about it; it was more important that I go. I thought about Ella the whole flight back to New York. A *strong* woman. She had broken the spirits of three husbands, more driving and dynamic than all of them combined. She had played a very significant role in my life. No other woman ever was strong enough to point me in directions; I pointed women in directions. I had brought Ella into Islam, and now she was financing me to Mecca.

Allah always gives you signs, when you are with Him, that He is with you.

When I applied for a visa to Mecca at the Saudi Arabian Consulate, the Saudi Ambassador told me that no Muslim converted in America could have a visa for the Hajj pilgrimage without the signed approval of Dr. Mahmoud Shawarbi. But that was only the beginning of the sign from Allah. When I telephoned Dr. Shawarbi, he registered astonishment. "I was just going to get in touch with you," he said, "by all means come right over."

When I got to his office, Dr. Shawarbi handed me the signed letter approving me to make the Hajj in Mecca, and then a book. It was *The Eternal Message of Muhammad* by Abd ar-Rahman Azzam.

The author had just sent the copy of the book to be given to me, Dr. Shawarbi said, and he explained that this author was an Egyptian-born Saudi citizen, an international statesman, and one of the closest advisors of Prince Faisal, the ruler of Arabia. "He has followed you in the press very closely." It was hard for me to believe.

Dr. Shawarbi gave me the telephone number of his son, Muhammad Shawarbi, a student in Cairo, and also the number of the author's son, Omar Azzam, who lived in Jedda, "your last stop before Mecca. Call them both, by all means."

I left New York quietly (little realizing that I was going to return noisily). Few people were told I was leaving at all. I didn't want some State Department or other roadblocks put in my path at the last minute. Only my wife, Betty, and my three girls and a few close associates came with me to Kennedy International Airport. When the Lufthansa Airlines jet had taken off, my two seatrow mates and I introduced ourselves. Another sign! Both were Muslims, one was bound for Cairo, as I was, and the other was bound for Jedda, where I would be in a few days.

All the way to Frankfurt, Germany, my seatmates and I talked, or I read the book I had been given. When we landed in Frankfurt, the brother bound for Jedda said his warm good-bye to me and the Cairo-bound brother. We had a few hours layover before we would take another plane to Cairo. We decided to go sightseeing in Frankfurt.

In the men's room there at the airport, I met the first American abroad who recognized me, a white student from Rhode Island. He kept eyeing me, then he came over. "Are you X?" I laughed and said I was, I hadn't ever heard it that way. He exclaimed, "You can't be! Boy, I know no one will believe me when I tell them this!" He was attending school, he said, in France.

The brother Muslim and I both were struck by the cordial hospitality of the people in Frankfurt. We went into a lot of shops and stores, looking more than intending to buy anything. We'd walk in, any store, every store, and it would be Hello! People who never saw you before, and knew you were strangers. And the same cordiality when we left, without buying anything. In America, you walk in a store and spend a hundred dollars, and leave, and you're still a stranger. Both you and the clerks act as though you're doing each other a favor. Europeans act more human, or humane, whichever the right word is. My brother Muslim, who could speak enough German to get by, would explain that we were Muslims, and I saw something I had already experienced when I was looked upon as a Muslim and not as a Negro, right in America. People seeing you as a Muslim saw you as a human being and they had a different look, different talk, everything. In one Frankfurt store—a little shop, actually—the storekeeper leaned over his counter to us and waved his hand, indicating the German people passing by: "This way one day, that way another day—" My Muslim brother explained to me that what he meant was that the Germans would rise again.

Back at the Frankfurt airport, we took a United Arab Airlines plane on to Cairo. Throngs of people, obviously Muslims from everywhere, bound on the pilgrimage, were hugging and embracing. They were of all complexions, the whole atmosphere was of warmth and friendliness. The feeling hit me that there really wasn't any color problem here. The effect was as though I had just stepped out of a prison.

I had told my brother Muslim friend that I wanted to be a tourist in Cairo for a couple of days before continuing to Jedda. He gave me his number and asked me to call him, as he wanted to put me with a party of his friends, who could speak English, and would be going on the pilgrimage, and would be happy to look out for me.

So I spent two happy days sightseeing in Cairo. I was impressed by the modern schools, housing developments for the masses, and the highways and the industrialization that I saw. I had read and heard that President Nasser's administration had built up one of the most highly industrialized countries on the African continent. I believe what most surprised me was that in Cairo, automobiles were being manufactured, and also buses.

I had a good visit with Dr. Shawarbi's son, Muhammad Shawarbi, a nineteen-year-old, who was studying economics and political science at Cairo University. He told me that his father's dream was to build a University of Islam in the United States.

The friendly people I met were astounded when they learned I was a Muslim—from America! They included an Egyptian scientist and his wife, also on their way to Mecca for the Hajj, who insisted I go with them to dinner in a restaurant in Heliopolis, a suburb of Cairo. They were an extremely well-informed and intelligent couple. Egypt's rising industrialization was one of the reasons why the Western powers were so anti-Egypt, it was showing other African countries what they should do, the scientist said. His wife asked me, "Why are people in the world starving when America has so much surplus food? What do they do, dump it in the ocean?" I told her, "Yes, but they put some of it in the holds of surplus ships, and in subsidized granaries and refrigerated space and let it stay there, with a small army of caretakers, until it's unfit to eat. Then another army of disposal people get rid of it to make space for the next surplus batch." She looked at me in something like disbelief. Probably she thought I was kidding. But the American taxpayer knows it's the truth. I didn't go on to tell her that right in the United States, there are hungry people.

I telephoned my Muslim friend, as he had asked, and the Hajj party of his friends was waiting for me. I made it eight of us, and they included a judge and an official of the Ministry of Education. They spoke English beautifully, and accepted me like a brother. I considered it another of Allah's signs, that wherever I turned, someone was there to help me, to guide me.

The literal meaning of Hajj in Arabic is to set out toward a definite objective. In Islamic law, it means to set out for Ka'ba, the Sacred House, and to fulfill the pilgrimage rites. The Cairo airport was where scores of Hajj groups were becoming *Muhrim,* pilgrims, upon entering the state of Ihram, the assumption of a spiritual and physical state of consecration. Upon advice, I arranged to leave in Cairo all of my luggage and four cameras, one a movie camera. I had bought in Cairo a small valise, just big enough to carry one suit, shirt, a pair of underwear sets and a pair of shoes into Arabia. Driving to the airport with our Hajj group, I began to get nervous, knowing that from there in, it was going to be watching others who knew what they were doing, and trying to do what they did.

Entering the state of Ihram, we took off our clothes and put on two white towels. One, the *Izar,* was folded around the loins. The other, the *Rida,* was thrown over the neck and shoulders, leaving the right shoulder and arm bare. A pair of simple sandals, the *na'l,* left the ankle-bones bare. Over the *Izar* waist-wrapper, a money belt was worn, and a bag, something like a woman's big handbag, with a long strap, was for carrying the passport and other valuable papers, such as the letter I had from Dr. Shawarbi.

Every one of the thousands at the airport, about to leave for Jedda, was dressed this way. You could be a king or a peasant and no one would know. Some powerful personages, who were discreetly pointed out to me, had on the same thing I had on. Once thus dressed, we all had begun intermittently calling out *"Labbayka! Labbayka!"* (Here I come, O Lord!) The airport sounded with the din of *Muhrim* expressing their intention to perform the journey of the Hajj.

Planeloads of pilgrims were taking off every few minutes, but the airport was jammed with more, and their friends and relatives waiting to see them off. Those not going were asking others to pray for them at Mecca. We were on our plane, in the air, when I learned for the first time that with the crush, there was not supposed to have been space for me, but strings had been pulled, and someone had been put off because they didn't want to disappoint an American Muslim. I felt mingled emotions of regret that I had inconvenienced and discomfited whoever was bumped off the plane for me, and, with that, an utter humility and gratefulness that I had been paid such an honor and respect.

Packed in the plane were white, black, brown, red, and yellow people, blue eyes and blond hair, and my kinky red hair—all together, brothers! All honoring the same God Allah, all in turn giving equal honor to each other.

From some in our group, the word was spreading from seat to seat that I was a Muslim from America. Faces turned, smiling toward me in greeting. A box lunch was passed out and as we ate that, the word that a Muslim from America was aboard got up into the cockpit.

The captain of the plane came back to meet me. He was an Egyptian, his complexion was darker than mine; he could have walked in Harlem and no one would have given him a second glance. He was delighted to meet an American Muslim. When he invited me to visit the cockpit, I jumped at the chance.

The co-pilot was darker than he was. I can't tell you the feeling it gave me. I had never seen a black man flying a jet. That instrument panel: no one ever could know what all of those dials meant! Both of the pilots were smiling at me, treating me with the same honor and respect I had received ever since I left America. I stood there looking through the glass at the sky ahead of us. In America, I had ridden in more planes than probably any other Negro, and I never had been invited up into the cockpit. And there I was, with two Muslim seatmates, one from Egypt, the other from Arabia, all of us bound for Mecca, with me up in the pilots' cabin. Brother, I *knew* Allah was with me.

I got back to my seat. All of the way, about an hour's flight, we pilgrims were loudly crying out, *"Labbayka! Labbayka!"* The plane landed at Jedda. It's a seaport town on the Red Sea, the arrival or disembarkation point for all pilgrims who come to Arabia to go to Mecca. Mecca is about forty miles to the east, inland.

The Jedda airport seemed even more crowded than Cairo's had been. Our party became another shuffling unit in the shifting mass with every race on earth represented. Each party was making its way toward the long line waiting to go through Customs. Before reaching Customs, each Hajj party was assigned a *Mutawaf,* who would be responsible for transferring that party from Jedda to Mecca. Some pilgrims cried *"Labbayka!"* Others, sometimes large groups, were chanting in unison a prayer that I will translate, "I submit to no one but Thee, O Allah, I submit to no one but Thee. I submit to Thee because Thou hast no partner. All praise and blessings come from Thee, and Thou art alone in Thy kingdom." The essence of the prayer is the Oneness of God.

Only officials were not wearing the *Ihram* garb, or the white skull caps, long, white, nightshirt-looking gown and the little slippers of the *Mutawaf,* those who guided each pilgrim party, and their helpers. In Arabic, an *mmmm* sound before a verb makes a verbal noun, so *"Mutawaf"* meant "the one who guides" the pilgrims on the *"Tawaf,"* which is the circumambulation of the Ka'ba in Mecca.

I was nervous, shuffling in the center of our group in the line waiting to have our passports inspected. I had an apprehensive feeling. Look what I'm handing them. I'm in the Muslim world, right at The Fountain. I'm handing them the American passport which signifies the exact opposite of what Islam stands for.

The judge in our group sensed my strain. He patted my shoulder. Love, humility, and true brotherhood was almost a physical feeling wherever I turned. Then our group reached the clerks who examined each passport and suitcase carefully and nodded to the pilgrim to move on.

I was so nervous that when I turned the key in my bag, and it didn't work, I broke open the bag, fearing that they might think I had something in the bag that I shouldn't have. Then the clerk saw that I was handing him an American passport. He held it, he looked at me and said something in Arabic. My friends around me began speaking rapid Arabic, gesturing and pointing, trying to intercede for me. The judge asked me in English for my letter from Dr. Shawarbi, and he thrust it at the clerk, who read it. He gave the letter back, protesting—I could tell that. An argument was going on, *about* me. I felt like a stupid fool, unable to say a word, I couldn't even understand what was being said. But, finally, sadly, the judge turned to me.

I had to go before the *Mahgama Sharia,* he explained. It was the Muslim high court which examined all possibly non-authentic converts to the Islamic religion seeking to enter Mecca. It was absolute that no non-Muslim could enter Mecca.

My friends were going to have to go on to Mecca without me. They seemed stricken with concern for me. And *I* was stricken. I found the words to tell them, "Don't worry, I'll be fine. Allah guides me." They said they would pray hourly in my behalf. The white-garbed *Mutawaf* was urging them on, to keep schedule in the airport's human crush. With all of us waving, I watched them go.

It was then about three in the morning, a Friday morning. I never had been in such a jammed mass of people, but I never had felt more alone, and helpless, since I was a baby. Worse, Friday in the Muslim world is a rough counterpart of Sunday in the Christian world. On Friday, all the members of a Muslim community gather, to pray together. The event is called *yaum al-jumu'a*—"the day of gathering." It meant that no courts were held on Friday. I would have to wait until Saturday, at least.

An official beckoned a young Arab *Mutawaf's* aide. In broken English, the official explained that I would be taken to a place right at the airport. My passport was kept at Customs. I wanted to object, because it is a traveler's first law never to get separated from his passport, but I didn't. In my wrapped towels and sandals, I followed the aide in his skull cap, long white gown, and slippers. I guess we were quite a sight. People passing us were speaking all kinds of languages. I couldn't speak anybody's language. I was in bad shape.

Right outside the airport was a mosque, and above the airport was a huge, dormitory-like building, four tiers high. It was semi-dark, not long before dawn, and planes were regularly taking off and landing, their landing lights sweeping the runways, or their wing and tail lights blinking in the sky. Pilgrims from Ghana, Indonesia, Japan, and Russia, to mention some, were moving to and from the dormitory where I was being taken. I don't believe that motion picture cameras ever have filmed a human spectacle more colorful than my eyes took in. We reached the dormitory and began climbing, up to the fourth, top, tier, passing members of every race on earth. Chinese, Indonesians, Afghanistanians. Many, not yet changed into the *Ihram* garb, still wore their national dress. It was like pages out of the *National Geographic* magazine.

My guide, on the fourth tier, gestured me into a compartment that contained about fifteen people. Most lay curled up on their rugs asleep. I could tell that some were women, covered head and foot. An old Russian Muslim and his wife were not asleep. They stared frankly at me. Two Egyptian Muslims and a Persian roused and also stared as my guide moved us over into a corner. With gestures, he indicated that he would demonstrate to me the proper prayer ritual postures. Imagine, being a Muslim minister, a leader in Elijah Muhammad's Nation of Islam, and not knowing the prayer ritual.

I tried to do what he did. I knew I wasn't doing it right. I could feel the other Muslims' eyes on me. Western ankles won't do what Muslim ankles have done for a lifetime. Asians squat when they sit, Westerners sit upright in chairs. When my guide was down in a posture, I tried everything I could to get down as he was, but there I was, sticking up. After about an hour, my guide left, indicating that he would return later.

I never even thought about sleeping. Watched by the Muslims, I kept practicing prayer posture. I refused to let myself think how ridiculous I must have looked to them. After a while, though, I learned a little trick that would let me get down closer to the floor. But after two or three days, my ankle was going to swell.

As the sleeping Muslims woke up, when dawn had broken, they almost instantly became aware of me, and we watched each other while they went about their business. I began to see what an important role the rug played in the overall cultural life of the Muslims. Each individual had a small prayer rug, and each man and wife, or large group, had a larger communal rug. These Muslims prayed on their rugs there in the compartment. Then they spread a tablecloth over the rug and ate, so the rug became the dining room. Removing the dishes and cloth, they sat on the rug—a living room. Then they curl up and sleep on the rug—a bedroom. In that compartment, before I was to leave it, it dawned on me for the first time why the fence had paid such a high price for Oriental rugs when I had been a burglar in Boston. It was because so much intricate care was taken to weave fine rugs in countries where rugs were so culturally versatile. Later, in Mecca, I would see yet another use of the rug. When any kind of a dispute arose, someone who was respected highly and who was not involved would sit on a rug with the disputers around him, which made the rug a courtroom. In other instances it was a classroom.

One of the Egyptian Muslims, particularly, kept watching me out of the corner of his eye. I smiled at him. He got up and came over to me. "Hello—" he said. It sounded like the Gettysburg Address. I beamed at him. "Hello!" I asked his name. "Name? Name?" He was trying hard, but he didn't get it. We tried some words on each other. I'd guess his English vocabulary spanned maybe twenty words. Just enough to frustrate me. I was trying to get him to comprehend anything. "Sky." I'd point. He'd smile. "Sky," I'd say again, gesturing for him to repeat it after me. He would. "Airplane . . . rug . . . foot . . . sandal . . . eyes. . . ." Like that. Then an amazing thing happened. I was so glad I had some communication with a human being. I was just saying whatever came to mind. I said "Muhammad Ali Clay—" All of the Muslims listening lighted up like a Christmas tree. "You? You?" My friend was pointing at me. I shook my head, "No, no. Muhammad Ali Clay my friend—*friend!*" They half understood me. Some of them didn't understand, and that's how it began to get around that I was Cassius Clay, world heavyweight champion. I was later to learn that apparently every man, woman and child in the Muslim world had heard how Sonny Liston (who in the Muslim world had the image of a man-eating ogre) had been beaten in Goliath-David fashion by Cassius Clay, who then had told the world that his name was Muhammad Ali and his religion was Islam and Allah had given him his victory.

Establishing the rapport was the best thing that could have happened in the compartment. My being an American Muslim changed the attitudes from merely watching me to wanting to look out for me. Now, the others began smiling steadily. They came closer, they were frankly looking me up and down. Inspecting me. Very friendly. I was like a man from Mars.

The *Mutawaf's* aide returned, indicating that I should go with him. He pointed from our tier down at the mosque and I knew that he had come to take me to make the morning prayer, *El Sobh,* always before sunrise. I followed him down, and we passed pilgrims by the thousands, babbling languages, everything but English. I was angry with myself for not having taken the time to learn more of the orthodox prayer rituals before leaving America. In Elijah Muhammad's Nation of Islam, we hadn't prayed in Arabic. About a dozen or more years before, when I was in prison, a member of the orthodox Muslim movement in Boston, named Abdul Hameed, had visited me and had later sent me prayers in Arabic. At that time, I had learned those prayers phonetically. But I hadn't used them since.

I made up my mind to let the guide do everything first and I would watch him. It wasn't hard to get him to do things first. He wanted to anyway. Just outside the mosque there was a long trough with rows of faucets. Ablutions had to precede praying. I knew that. Even watching the *Mutawaf's* helper, I didn't get it right. There's an exact way that an orthodox Muslim washes, and the exact way is very important.

I followed him into the mosque, just a step behind, watching. He did his prostration, his head to the ground. I did mine. *"Bi-smi-llahi-r-Rahmain-r-Rahim—"* ("In the name of Allah, the Beneficent, the Merciful—") All

Muslim prayers began that way. After that, I may not have been mumbling the right thing, but I was mumbling.

I don't mean to have any of this sound joking. It was far from a joke with me. No one who happened to be watching could tell that I wasn't saying what the others said.

After that Sunrise Prayer, my guide accompanied me back up to the fourth tier. By sign language, he said he would return within three hours, then he left.

Our tier gave an excellent daylight view of the whole airport area. I stood at the railing, watching. Planes were landing and taking off like clockwork. Thousands upon thousands of people from all over the world made colorful patterns of movement. I saw groups leaving for Mecca, in buses, trucks, cars. I saw some setting out to walk the forty miles. I wished that I could start walking. At least, I knew how to do that.

I was afraid to think what might lie ahead. Would I be rejected as a Mecca pilgrim? I wondered what the test would consist of, and when I would face the Muslim high court.

The Persian Muslim in our compartment came up to me at the rail. He greeted me, hesitantly, "Amer . . . American?" He indicated that he wanted me to come and have breakfast with him and his wife, on their rug. I knew that it was an immense offer he was making. You don't have tea with a Muslim's wife. I didn't want to impose, I don't know if the Persian understood or not when I shook my head and smiled, meaning "No, thanks." He brought me some tea and cookies, anyway. Until then, I hadn't even thought about eating.

Others made gestures. They would just come up and smile and nod at me. My first friend, the one who had spoken a little English, was gone. I didn't know it, but he was spreading the word of an American Muslim on the fourth tier. Traffic had begun to pick up, going past our compartment. Muslims in the *Ihram* garb, or still in their national dress, walked slowly past, smiling. It would go on for as long as I was there to be seen. But I hadn't yet learned that I was the attraction.

I have always been restless, and curious. The *Mutawaf's* aide didn't return in the three hours he had said, and that made me nervous. I feared that he had given up on me as beyond help. By then, too, I was really getting hungry. All of the Muslims in the compartment had offered me food, and I had refused. The trouble was, I have to admit it, at that point I didn't know if I could go for their manner of eating. Everything was in one pot on the dining-room rug, and I saw them just fall right in, using their hands.

I kept standing at the tier railing observing the courtyard below, and I decided to explore a bit on my own. I went down to the first tier. I thought, then, that maybe I shouldn't get too far, someone might come for me. So I went back up to our compartment. In about forty-five minutes, I went back down. I went further this time, feeling my way. I saw a little restaurant in the courtyard. I went straight in there. It was jammed, and babbling with languages. Using gestures, I bought a whole roasted chicken and something like thick potato chips. I got back out in the courtyard and I tore up that chicken, using my hands. Muslims were doing the same thing all around me. I saw men at least seventy years old bringing both legs up under them, until they made a human knot of themselves, eating with as much aplomb and satisfaction as though they had been in a fine restaurant with waiters all over the place. All ate as One, and slept as One. Everything about the pilgrimage atmosphere accented the Oneness of Man under One God.

I made, during the day, several trips up to the compartment and back out in the courtyard, each time exploring a little further than before. Once, I nodded at two black men standing together. I nearly shouted when one spoke to me in British-accented English. Before their party approached, ready to leave for Mecca, we were able to talk enough to exchange that I was American and they were Ethiopians. I was heartsick. I had found two English-speaking Muslims at last—and they were leaving. The Ethiopians had both been schooled in Cairo, and they were living in Ryadh, the political capital of Arabia. I was later going to learn to my surprise that in Ethiopia, with eighteen million people, ten million are Muslims. Most people think Ethiopia is Christian. But only its government is Christian. The West has always helped to keep the Christian government in power.

I had just said my Sunset Prayer, *El Maghrib;* I was lying on my cot in the fourth-tier compartment, feeling blue and alone, when out of the darkness came a sudden light!

It was actually a sudden thought. On one of my venturings in the yard full of activity below, I had noticed four men, officials, seated at a table with a telephone. Now, I thought about seeing them there, and with *telephone,* my mind flashed to the connection that Dr. Shawarbi in New York had given me, the telephone number of the son of the author of the book which had been given to me. Omar Azzam lived right there in Jedda!

In a matter of a few minutes, I was downstairs and rushing to where I had seen the four officials. One of them spoke functional English. I excitedly showed him the letter from Dr. Shawarbi. He read it. Then he read it aloud to the other three officials. "A Muslim from America!" I could almost see it capture their imaginations and curiosity. They were very impressed. I asked the English-speaking one if he would please do me the favor of telephoning Dr. Omar Azzam at the number I had. He was glad to do it. He got someone on the phone and conversed in Arabic.

Dr. Omar Azzam came straight to the airport. With the four officials beaming, he wrung my hand in welcome, a young, tall, powerfully built man. I'd say he was six foot three. He had an extremely polished manner. In America, he would have been called a white man, but—it struck me, hard and instantly—from the way he acted, I had no *feeling* of him being a white man. "Why didn't you call before?" he demanded of me. He showed some identification to the four officials, and he used their phone. Speaking in Arabic, he was talking with some airport officials. "Come!" he said.

In something less than half an hour, he had gotten me released, my suitcase and passport had been retrieved from Customs, and we were in Dr. Azzam's car, driving through the city of Jedda, with me dressed in the *Ihram* two towels and sandals. I was speechless at the man's attitude, and at my own physical feeling of no difference between us as human beings. I had heard for years of Muslim hospitality, but one couldn't quite imagine such warmth. I asked questions. Dr. Azzam was a Swiss-trained engineer. His field was city planning. The Saudi Arabian government had borrowed him from the United Nations to direct all of the reconstruction work being done on Arabian holy places. And Dr. Azzam's sister was the wife of Prince Faisal's son. I was in a car with the brother-in-law of the son of the ruler of Arabia. Nor was that all that Allah had done. "My father will be so happy to meet you," said Dr. Azzam. The author who had sent me the book!

I asked questions about his father. Abd ir-Rahman Azzam was known as Azzam Pasha, or Lord Azzam, until the Egyptian revolution, when President Nasser eliminated all "Lord" and "Noble" titles. "He should be at my home when we get there," Dr. Azzam said. "He spends much time in New York with his United Nations work, and he has followed you with great interest."

I was speechless.

It was early in the morning when we reached Dr. Azzam's home. His father was there, his father's brother, a chemist, and another friend—all up that early, waiting. Each of them embraced me as though I were a long-lost child. I had never seen these men before in my life, and they treated me so good! I am going to tell you that I had never been so honored in my life, nor had I ever received such true hospitality.

A servant brought tea and coffee, and disappeared. I was urged to make myself comfortable. No women were anywhere in view. In Arabia, you could easily think there were no females.

Dr. Abd ir-Rahman Azzam dominated the conversation. Why hadn't I called before? They couldn't understand why I hadn't. Was I comfortable? They seemed embarrassed that I had spent the time at the airport; that I had been delayed in getting to Mecca. No matter how I protested that I felt no inconvenience, that I was fine, they would not hear it. "You must rest," Dr. Azzam said. He went to use the telephone.

I didn't know what this distinguished man was doing. I had no dream. When I was told that I would be brought back for dinner that evening, and that, meanwhile, I should get back in the car, how could I have realized that I was about to see the epitome of Muslim hospitality?

Abd ir-Rahman Azzam, when at home, lived in a suite at the Jedda Palace Hotel. Because I had come to them with a letter from a friend, he was going to stay at his son's home, and let me use his suite, until I could get on to Mecca.

When I found out, there was no use protesting: I was in the suite; young Dr. Azzam was gone; there was no one to protest to. The three-room suite had a bathroom that was as big as a double at the New York Hilton. It was suite number 214. There was even a porch outside, affording a beautiful view of the ancient Red Sea city.

There had never before been in my emotions such an impulse to pray —and I did, prostrating myself on the living-room rug.

Nothing in either of my two careers as a black man in America had served to give me any idealistic tendencies. My instincts automatically examined the reasons, the motives, of anyone who did anything they didn't have to do for me. Always in my life, if it was any white person, I could see a selfish motive.

But there in that hotel that morning, a telephone call and a few hours away from the cot on the fourth-floor tier of the dormitory, was one of the few times I had been so awed that I was totally without resistance. That white man—at least he would have been considered "white" in America —related to Arabia's ruler, to whom he was a close advisor, truly an international man, with nothing in the world to gain, had given up his suite to me, for my transient comfort. He had *nothing* to gain. He didn't need me. He had everything. In fact, he had more to lose than gain. He had followed the American press about me. If he did that, he knew there was only stigma attached to me. I was supposed to have horns. I was a "racist." I was "anti-white"—and he from all appearances was white. I was supposed to be a criminal; not only that, but everyone was even accusing me of using his religion of Islam as a cloak for my criminal practices and philosophies. Even if he had had some motive to use me, he knew that I was separated from Elijah Muhammad and the Nation of Islam, my "power base," according to the press in America. The only organization that I had was just a few weeks old. I had no job. I had no money. Just to get over there, I had had to borrow money from my sister.

That morning was when I first began to reappraise the "white man." It was when I first began to perceive that "white man," as commonly used, means complexion only secondarily; primarily it described attitudes and actions. In America, "white man" meant specific attitudes and actions toward the black man, and toward all other non-white men. But in the Muslim world, I had seen that men with white complexions were more genuinely brotherly than anyone else had ever been.

That morning was the start of a radical alteration in my whole outlook about "white" men.

I should quote from my notebook here. I wrote this about noon, in the hotel: "My excitement, sitting here, waiting to go before the Hajj Committee, is indescribable. My window faces to the sea westward. The streets are filled with the incoming pilgrims from all over the world. The prayers are to Allah and verses from the Quran are on the lips of everyone. Never have I seen such a beautiful sight, nor witnessed such a scene, nor felt such an atmosphere. Although I am excited, I feel safe and secure, thousands of miles from the totally different life that I have known. Imagine that twenty-four hours ago, I was in the fourth-floor room over the airport, surrounded by people with whom I could not communicate, feeling uncertain about the future, and very lonely, and then *one* phone call, following Dr. Shawarbi's instructions. I have met one of the most powerful men in the Muslim world. I will soon sleep in his bed at the Jedda Palace. I know that I am surrounded by friends whose sincerity and religious zeal I can feel. I must pray again to thank Allah for this blessing, and I must pray again that my wife and children back in America will always be blessed for their sacrifices, too."

I did pray, two more prayers, as I had told my notebook. Then I slept for about four hours, until the telephone rang. It was young Dr. Azzam. In another hour, he would pick me up to return me there for dinner. I tumbled words over one another, trying to express some of the thanks I felt for all of their actions. He cut me off. "Ma sha'a-llah"—which means, "It is as Allah has pleased."

I seized the opportunity to run down into the lobby, to see it again before Dr. Azzam arrived. When I opened my door, just across the hall from me a man in some ceremonial dress, who obviously lived there, was also headed downstairs, surrounded by attendants. I followed them down, then through the lobby. Outside, a small caravan of automobiles was waiting. My neighbor appeared through the Jedda Palace Hotel's front entrance and people rushed and crowded him, kissing his hand. I found out who he was: the Grand Mufti of Jerusalem. Later, in the hotel, I would have the opportunity to talk with him for about a half-hour. He was a cordial man of great dignity. He was well up on world affairs, and even the latest events in America.

I will never forget the dinner at the Azzam home. I quote my notebook again: "I couldn't say in my mind that these were 'white' men. Why, the men acted as if they were brothers of mine, the elder Dr. Azzam as if he were my father. His fatherly, scholarly speech. I *felt* like he was my father. He was, you could tell, a highly skilled diplomat, with a broad range of mind. His knowledge was so worldly. He was as current on world affairs as some people are to what's going on in their living room.

"The more we talked, the more his vast reservoir of knowledge and its variety seemed unlimited. He spoke of the racial lineage of the descendants of Muhammad the Prophet, and he showed how they were both black and white. He also pointed out how color, the complexities of color, and the problems of color which exist in the Muslim world, exist only where, and to the extent that, that area of the Muslim world has been influenced by the West. He said that if one encountered any differences based on attitude toward color, this directly reflected the degree of Western influence."

I learned during dinner that while I was at the hotel, the Hajj Committee Court had been notified about my case, and that in the morning I should be there. And I was.

The Judge was Sheikh Muhammad Harkon. The Court was empty except for me and a sister from India, formerly a Protestant, who had converted to Islam, and was, like me, trying to make the Hajj. She was brown-skinned, with a small face that was mostly covered. Judge Harkon was a kind, impressive man. We talked. He asked me some questions, having to do with my sincerity. I answered him as truly as I could. He not only recognized me as a true Muslim, but he gave me two books, one in English, the other in Arabic. He recorded my name in the Holy Register of true Muslims, and we were ready to part. He told me, "I hope you will become a great preacher of Islam in America." I said that I shared that hope, and I would try to fulfill it.

The Azzam family were very elated that I was qualified and accepted to go to Mecca. I had lunch at the Jedda Palace. Then I slept again for several hours, until the telephone awakened me.

It was Muhammad Abdul Azziz Maged, the Deputy Chief of Protocol for Prince Faisal. "A special car will be waiting to take you to Mecca, right after your dinner," he told me. He advised me to eat heartily, as the Hajj rituals require plenty of strength.

I was beyond astonishment by then.

Two young Arabs accompanied me to Mecca. A well-lighted, modern turnpike highway made the trip easy. Guards at intervals along the way took one look at the car, and the driver made a sign, and we were passed through, never even having to slow down. I was, all at once, thrilled, important, humble, and thankful.

Mecca, when we entered, seemed as ancient as time itself. Our car slowed through the winding streets, lined by shops on both sides and with buses, cars, and trucks, and tens of thousands of pilgrims from all over the earth were everywhere.

The car halted briefly at a place where a *Mutawaf* was waiting for me. He wore the white skullcap and long nightshirt garb that I had seen at the airport. He was a short, dark-skinned Arab, named Muhammad. He spoke no English whatever.

We parked near the Great Mosque. We performed our ablution and entered. Pilgrims seemed to be on top of each other, there were so many, lying, sitting, sleeping, praying, walking.

My vocabulary cannot describe the new mosque that was being built around the Ka'ba. I was thrilled to realize that it was only one of the tremendous rebuilding tasks under the direction of young Dr. Azzam, who had just been my host. The Great Mosque of Mecca, when it is finished, will surpass the architectural beauty of India's Taj Mahal.

Carrying my sandals, I followed the *Mutawaf.* Then I saw the Ka'ba, a huge black stone house in the middle of the Great Mosque. It was being circumambulated by thousands upon thousands of praying pilgrims, both sexes, and every size, shape, color, and race in the world. I knew the prayer to be uttered when the pilgrim's eyes first perceive the Ka'ba. Translated, it is "O God, You are peace, and peace derives from You. So greet us, O Lord, with peace." Upon entering the Mosque, the pilgrim should try to kiss the Ka'ba if possible, but if the crowds prevent him getting that close, he touches it, and if the crowds prevent that, he raises his hand and cries out "Takbir!" ("God is great!") I could not get within yards. "Takbir!"

My feeling there in the House of God was a numbness. My *Mutawaf* led me in the crowd of praying, chanting pilgrims, moving seven times around the Ka'ba. Some were bent and wizened with age; it was a sight that stamped itself on the brain. I saw incapacitated pilgrims being carried by others. Faces were enraptured in their faith. The seventh time around, I prayed two *Rak'a,* prostrating myself, my head on the floor. The first prostration, I prayed the Quran verse "Say He is God, the one and only"; the second prostration: "Say O you who are unbelievers, I worship not that which you worship. . . .."

As I prostrated, the *Mutawaf* fended pilgrims off to keep me from being trampled.

The *Mutawaf* and I next drank water from the well of Zem Zem. Then we ran between the two hills, Safa and Marwa, where Hajar wandered over the same earth searching for water for her child Ishmael.

Three separate times, after that, I visited the Great Mosque and circumambulated the Ka'ba. The next day we set out after sunrise toward Mount Arafat, thousands of us, crying in unison: "Labbayka! Labbayka!" and "Allah Akbar!" Mecca is surrounded by the crudest-looking mountains I have ever seen; they seem to be made of the slag from a blast furnace. No vegetation is on them at all. Arriving about noon, we prayed and chanted from noon until sunset, and the *asr* (afternoon) and *Maghrib* (sunset) special prayers were performed.

Finally, we lifted our hands in prayer and thanksgiving, repeating Allah's words: "There is no God but Allah. He has no partner. His are authority and praise. Good emanates from Him, and He has power over all things."

Standing on Mount Arafat had concluded the essential rites of being a pilgrim to Mecca. No one who missed it could consider himself a pilgrim.

The *Ihram* had ended. We cast the traditional seven stones at the devil. Some had their hair and beards cut. I decided that I was going to let my beard remain. I wondered what my wife Betty, and our little daughters, were going to say when they saw me with a beard, when I got back to New York. New York seemed a million miles away. I hadn't seen a newspaper that I could read since I left New York. I had no idea what was happening there. A Negro rifle club that had been in existence for over twelve years in Harlem had been "discovered" by the police; it was being trumpeted that I was "behind it." Elijah Muhammad's Nation of Islam had a lawsuit going against me, to force me and my family to vacate the house in which we lived on Long Island.

The major press, radio, and television media in America had representatives in Cairo hunting all over, trying to locate me, to interview me about the furor in New York that I had allegedly caused—when I knew nothing about any of it.

I only knew what I had left in America, and how it contrasted with what I had found in the Muslim world. About twenty of us Muslims who had finished the Hajj were sitting in a huge tent on Mount Arafat. As a Muslim from America, I was the center of attention. They asked me what about the Hajj had impressed me the most. One of the several who spoke English asked; they translated my answers for the others. My answer to that question was not the one they expected, but it drove home my point.

I said, "The *brotherhood!* The people of all races, colors, from all over the world coming together as *one!* It has proved to me the power of the One God."

It may have been out of taste, but that gave me an opportunity, and I used it, to preach them a quick little sermon on America's racism, and its evils.

I could tell the impact of this upon them. They had been aware that the plight of the black man in America was "bad," but they had not been aware that it was inhuman, that it was a psychological castration. These people from elsewhere around the world were shocked. As Muslims, they had a very tender heart for all unfortunates, and very sensitive feelings for truth and justice. And in everything I said to them, as long as we talked, they were aware of the yardstick that I was using to measure everything —that to me the earth's most explosive and pernicious evil is racism, the inability of God's creatures to live as One, especially in the Western world.

I had reflected since that the letter I finally sat down to compose had been subconsciously shaping itself in my mind.

The *color-blindness* of the Muslim world's religious society and the *color-blindness* of the Muslim world's human society: these two influences had each day been making a greater impact, and an increasing persuasion against my previous way of thinking.

The first letter was, of course, to my wife, Betty. I never had a moment's question that Betty, after initial amazement, would change her thinking to join mine. I had known a thousand reassurances that Betty's faith in me was total. I knew that she would see what I had seen—that in the land of Muhammad and the land of Abraham, I had been blessed by Allah with a new insight into the true religion of Islam, and a better understanding of America's entire racial dilemma.

After the letter to my wife, I wrote next essentially the same letter to my sister Ella. And I knew where Ella would stand. She had been saving to make the pilgrimage to Mecca herself.

I wrote to Dr. Shawarbi, whose belief in my sincerity had enabled me to get a passport to Mecca.

All through the night, I copied similar long letters for others who were very close to me. Among them was Elijah Muhammad's son Wallace Muhammad, who had expressed to me his conviction that the only possible salvation for the Nation of Islam would be its accepting and projecting a better understanding of Orthodox Islam.

And I wrote to my loyal assistants at my newly formed Muslim Mosque, Inc. in Harlem, with a note appended, asking that my letter be duplicated and distributed to the press.

I knew that when my letter became public knowledge back in America, many would be astounded—loved ones, friends, and enemies alike. And no less astounded would be millions whom I did not know—who had gained during my twelve years with Elijah Muhammad a "hate" image of Malcolm X.

Even I was myself astounded. But there was precedent in my life for this letter. My whole life had been a chronology of—*changes*.

Here is what I wrote . . . from my heart:

"Never have I witnessed such sincere hospitality and the overwhelming spirit of true brotherhood as is practiced by people of all colors and races here in this Ancient Holy Land, the home of Abraham, Muhammad, and all the other prophets of the Holy Scriptures. For the past week, I have been utterly speechless and spellbound by the graciousness I see displayed all around me by people of *all colors.*

"I have been blessed to visit the Holy City of Mecca. I have made my seven circuits around the Ka'ba, led by a young *Mutawaf* named Muhammad. I drank water from the well of Zem Zem. I ran seven times back and forth between the hills of Mt. Al-Safa and Al-Marwah. I have prayed in the ancient city of Mina, and I have prayed on Mt. Arafat.

"There were tens of thousands of pilgrims, from all over the world. They were of all colors, from blue-eyed blonds to black-skinned Africans. But we were all participating in the same ritual, displaying a spirit of unity and brotherhood that my experiences in America had led me to believe never could exist between the white and the non-white.

"America needs to understand Islam, because this is the one religion that erases from its society the race problem. Throughout my travels in the Muslim world, I have met, talked to, and even eaten with people who in America would have been considered 'white'—but the 'white' attitude was removed from their minds by the religion of Islam. I have never before seen *sincere* and *true* brotherhood practiced by all colors together, irrespective of their color.

"You may be shocked by these words coming from me. But on this pilgrimage, what I have seen, and experienced, has forced me to *re-arrange* much of my thought-patterns previously held, and to *toss aside* some of my previous conclusions. This was not too difficult for me. Despite my firm convictions, I have been always a man who tries to face facts, and to accept the reality of life as new experience and new knowledge unfolds it. I have always kept an open mind, which is necessary to the flexibility that must go hand in hand with every form of intelligent search for truth.

"During the past eleven days here in the Muslim world, I have eaten from the same plate, drunk from the same glass, and slept in the same bed (or on the same rug)—while praying to the *same God*—with fellow Muslims, whose eyes were the bluest of blue, whose hair was the blondest of blond, and whose skin was the whitest of white. And in the *words* and in the *actions* and in the *deeds* of the 'white' Muslims, I felt the same sincerity that I felt among the black African Muslims of Nigeria, Sudan, and Ghana.

"We were *truly* all the same (brothers)—because their belief in one God had removed the 'white' from their *minds,* the 'white' from their *behavior,* and the 'white' from their *attitude.*

"I could see from this, that perhaps if white Americans could accept the Oneness of God, then perhaps, too, they could accept *in reality* the Oneness of Man—and cease to measure, and hinder, and harm others in terms of their 'differences' in color.

"With racism plaguing America like an incurable cancer, the so-called 'Christian' white American heart should be more receptive to a proven solution to such a destructive problem. Perhaps it could be in time to save America from imminent disaster—the same destruction brought upon Germany by racism that eventually destroyed the Germans themselves.

"Each hour here in the Holy Land enables me to have greater spiritual insights into what is happening in America between black and white. The American Negro never can be blamed for his racial animosities—he is only reacting to four hundred years of the conscious racism of the American whites. But as racism leads America up the suicide path, I do believe, from the experiences that I have had with them, that the whites of the younger generation, in the colleges and universities, will see the handwriting on the wall and many of them will turn to the *spiritual* path of *truth* —the *only* way left to America to ward off the disaster that racism inevitably must lead to.

"Never have I been so highly honored. Never have I been made to feel more humble and unworthy. Who would believe the blessings that have been heaped upon an *American Negro?* A few nights ago, a man who would be called in America a 'white' man, a United Nations diplomat, an ambassador, a companion of kings, gave me *his* hotel suite, *his* bed. By this man, His Excellency Prince Faisal, who rules this Holy Land, was made aware of my presence here in Jedda. The very next morning, Prince Faisal's son, in person, informed me that by the will and decree of his esteemed father, I was to be a State Guest.

"The Deputy Chief of Protocol himself took me before the Hajj Court. His Holiness Sheikh Muhammad Harkon himself okayed my visit to Mecca. His Holiness gave me two books on Islam, with his personal seal and autograph, and he told me that he prayed that I would be a successful preacher of Islam in America. A car, a driver, and a guide, have been placed at my disposal, making it possible for me to travel about this Holy Land almost at will. The government provides air-conditioned quarters and servants in each city that I visit. Never would I have even thought of dreaming that I would ever be a recipient of such honors—honors that in America would be bestowed upon a King—not a Negro.

"All praise is due to Allah, the Lord of all the Worlds.

"Sincerely,
"El-Hajj Malik El-Shabazz
"(Malcolm X)"

NNAMDI AZIKIWE

Pan-Africanism

Dr. Nnamdi Azikiwe's essay reflects the thought of the man considered the father of modern Nigerian nationalism and the architect of his country's independence. Born in 1904, Dr. Azikiwe left Nigeria in 1925 by stowing away on a ship. He made his way to the United States, where he studied at Howard, Lincoln, and the University of Pennsylvania. He returned to Nigeria in 1937 and worked unceasingly for the creation of an independent nation. He served as Governor General of Nigeria and then as President of the Federal Parliament.

WHEN WE SPEAK of Pan-Africanism, what do we exactly mean? To envisage its future, we must appreciate its meaning. To some people, Pan-Africanism denotes the search for an African personality.

To others, it implies negritude. Whilst to many it connotes a situation which finds the whole continent of Africa free from the shackles of foreign domination with its leaders free to plan for the orderly progress and welfare of its inhabitants. In order not to be misleading, we must also explain what we mean by the term "African." Is he a member of the black race or is he a hybrid of the black and white races inhabiting Africa? It is necessary to say, too, whether an inhabitant of Africa, irrespective of his race and language, qualifies to become an African within the context of the use of this terminology.

I would prefer to be very broad in my use of the words "Africa" and "African." For reasons which will emerge by the time I have finished analysing the problems of Pan-Africanism, it should be obvious that unless we accept a broad definition of terms, there can be no worthy future for Africanism. That being the case, I would like to speak of the peoples of Africa in general terms to include all the races inhabiting that continent and embracing all the linguistic and cultural groups who are domiciled therein.

Human Society

In other words, I am using the term strictly in its political context so that whatever solutions are offered by me would in the final analysis be political. This approach simplifies my problem because it would enable me to formulate policies which can be implemented, bearing in mind the empirical history of human beings in other continents of the earth. It would be useless to define "Pan-Africanism" exclusively in racial or linguistic terms, since the obvious solution would be parochial. And chauvinism, by whatever name it is identified, has always been a disintegrating factor in human society at all known times of human history.

It is true that the roots of Pan-Africanism are, to a large extent, racial, but the evolution of the idea itself took different forms in the last four centuries so that today Africanism cannot be restricted to racial factors. What are these roots? Mainly individual actions and group pressure. Take the individual prophets of Pan-Africanism and it will be found that in all cases they were ethnocentric in their ideas and concepts of Pan-Africanism. For example, Paul Cuffee of Boston was more concerned in the repatriation of freed black slaves to Africa. When Edward Wilmot Blyden of Danish West Indies preached the projection of the African personality, he had at the back of his mind the black inhabitants of Africa. The same may be said of Casely Hayford of Ghana, Marcus Aurelius Garvey of Jamaica, Burghhardt Du Bois of America, Mojola Agbebi of Nigeria, Jomo Kenyatta of Kenya, Javabu of South Africa, George Padmore of Trinidad, Nwafor Orizu of Nigeria, Kwame Nkrumah of Ghana, and Leopold Senghor of Senegal.

But when we consider the role of organisations, as distinct from individuals, no rigid line of distinction on the basis of race appears to be drawn, generally speaking. The Anti-Slavery Society and the American Colonisation Society, for example, were actuated by humanitarian motives to plan for the emigration of freed black slaves from America and the Caribbean to Africa for permanent settlement.

The International Conference on Africa which was held in Berlin in 1885 partitioned that continent without taking into consideration racial, cultural or linguistic factors. The United Native African Church in Nigeria revolted against ecclesiastical control of African churches from outside Africa, but it did not preclude non-Africans from joining its communion and fellowship. The United Negro Improvement Association was ethnocentric in the sense that it preached the doctrine of "Africa for the Africans" on the basis of race. The National Congress of British West Africa sought for political reforms in the former British territories in West Africa without attaching much importance to race or language or culture.

The history of the continent of Africa in ancient, medieval and modern times has followed a pattern which ignores the factor of race in its evolution. Whilst the white races of Assyria, Syria, Phoenicia and Israel developed their civilization, the brown races of Egypt and the black races of Ethiopia proceeded to develop their civilization contemporaneously. In medieval times, the Arab did not distinguish between the black or brown or white Hamitic, Semitic, Sudanic or Bantu-speaking converts of Islam.

All that has come down to us shows that the civilizations which flourished in Africa at that time attached little attention, if any, to such an extraneous factor as race.

When the so-called Barbary States flourished in Algeria, Morocco, Tunis, and Tripoli, race was a minor factor in their political evolution. The British West Africa Settlements were originally a sort of concert of territories consisting of Gambia, Sierra Leone, Gold Coast and later Lagos.

In fact, all these countries were governed by one Governor at various times from 1827, 1866, 1874 until 1886. French West and French Equatorial Africa were each governed as a federation until 1958 when the French Community was organised and the right of each member to separate autonomous existence was recognised.

Even the Union of South Africa (much as we hate it) is a federation of various racial, linguistic and cultural groups. The Anglo-Egyptian Sudan was a condominium which held two culturally-opposed groups together until independence was attained by Sudan in 1956. The East Africa High Commission was a quasi-federal instrument which bound Uganda, Kenya, Tanganyika and Zanzibar together, and efforts are being made not to dissolve it with the dawn of the independence of Tanganyika. The High Commission of the Protectorates of South Africa, the Central African Federation, the Federation of Nigeria, the Ghana-Guinea-Mali Union—these are efforts to weld together political entities comprising various races, languages and cultures.

In other words, in spite of racial, linguistic and cultural differences, conscious efforts have been made at all known times of African history to form a political union either on a regional or continental basis. From the evidence at our disposal, it would appear that whilst European nations may be rightly accused of Balkanising Africa in the nineteenth century, yet they have atoned for it by federating many African territories, which are now being Balkanised by African nationalists on the attainment of the independence of their countries. The British West Africa, French West Africa and French Equatorial Africa, are examples of Balkanisation by African nationalists, and the Central African Federation is an example of Balkanisation in process brought about by the racial segregation and discrimination practised by a small minority of European settlers against the African majority who are owners of their countries. . . .

African Unity

First, the inhabitants of the African continent are not racially homogeneous. In North Africa, the majority of the population belongs to the Mediterranean group of the Caucasoid race. In Africa South of the Sahara, the majority are Negroid, with the exception of a small minority of European settlers in southern Africa who are either members of the Alpine or Nordic groups of the Caucasoids. The co-existence of these racial groups has created a social problem in Africa as the apartheid and mau mau have shown.

Secondly, the existence of various linguistic groups in Africa has intensified the problem of communication and human understanding. Whilst those who live on the fringe of the Mediterranean are Hamitic-speaking, the Africans of the West are mainly Sudanic-speaking. The indigenous central and southern Africans are Bantu-speaking. The inhabitants of eastern Africa are partially Sudanic, Bantu, Hamitic and Semitic. The small European elements in south Africa speak either English or Afrikaans. Emerging out of this milieu is the fact that to millions of Africans either English or Arabic or Swahili or Hausa is the lingua franca, whilst the rest have to manage as best they could.

Thirdly, the impact of various cultures on African society has created basic problems of social unity. One example is the activities of the Pan-Arab League which seeks to unite under one fold all the Arab-speaking peoples not only of Africa but also of the Middle East. Another example is the attempt being made in certain quarters to create an Islamic Confederation which will cut across racial, linguistic and cultural lines. Then there is the move to interpret Pan-Africanism purely in terms of race and to restrict its membership and activities to the Negroids and thereby exclude other races who live in Africa who are not black.

These three problems are real. The practice of racial segregation and discrimination is a disturbing factor in society, as the examples of the United States, the Union of South Africa and the Central African Federation have shown. The official use or recognition of any particular language to the detriment of others has not made for harmonious human relations and the experiences of India, Pakistan, Ceylon, and the U.S.S.R. are a great lesson. My conclusion is that parochialism in the realms of race, language, culture or religion has often led to social disintegration. Therefore, it constitutes a social and psychological barrier which must be hurdled if Pan-Africanism is to become a reality.

If the anthropological problems are basic, then the sociological are complex since they affect the economic, political and constitutional aspects of the lives of those concerned. Economically, the existence of tariff walls and barriers has tended to alienate rather than draw closer the relations of those who would be good neighbours. High competitive markets have led to cut-throat methods of bargaining and distribution. The use of separate currencies as legal tender has accentuated social differences. With separate road, railway, aviation and communications systems, Africans have become estranged to one another.

The political issues are even confounding. Granted that political union is desirable, the question arises whether it should be in the form of a federation or a confederation. If the former, should it be a tight or a loose one? In any case sovereignty must be surrendered in part or in whole, in which case, it will be desirable to know whether it is intended to surrender internal or external sovereignty or both? . . .

Implications

An African federation or confederation, either on a regional or continental basis, has many blessings for the continent of Africa and its inhabitants. Politically, it will raise the prestige of African States in the councils of the world; it will make Africa a bastion of democracy, and it will revive the stature of man by guaranteeing to African citizens the fundamental rights of man. From a military point of view, such a concert of States will protect the people of Africa not only from external aggression and internal commotion, but also it would safeguard the whole of Africa by a system of collective security.

Economically, by abrogating discriminatory tariffs, we create a free trade area over the entire continent and thereby expand the economy of all African countries involved, thereby raising living standards and ensuring economic security for African workers.

Socially, it will restore the dignity of the human being in Africa.

In conclusion, it is my firm belief that an African leviathan must emerge ultimately; it may be in the form of an association of African States or in the form of a concert of African States; but my main point is that so long as the form of government is clearly understood and an efficient machinery for organisation and administration is devised, backed by multi-lateral conventions which would enhance the standard of living of Africans, safeguard their existence by collective security, and guarantee to them freedom under the law in addition to the fundamental human rights, the dream of Pan-Africanism is destined to come true.

Finally, one of the leading Africanists of all times, Edward Wilmot Blyden, said: "It is really high time that a unity of spirit should pervade the people of the world for the regeneration of a continent so long despoiled by the unity or consent of these same people. Thinking Negroes should ask themselves what part they will take in this magnificent work of reclaiming a continent—their own continent. In what way will they illustrate their participation in the unity of spirit which pervades the people for their fatherland?"

That was Dr. Blyden preaching Pan-Africanism in the nineteenth century. On our part, what shall we do? History will chronicle the choice made by us in the twentieth century.

A Declaration of Indian Purpose

This statement came from the American Indian Chicago Conference held in 1961. The statement is clear and self-explanatory, but should be seen in terms of other current manifestoes of various groups for principles of self-determination. Our immediate source for this declaration is Wilcomb Washburn's excellent collection of primary documents, *The Indian and the White Man,* a careful reading of which will bring about, in some measure, what this declaration asks: That "the nature of our situation be recognized. . . ."

Law and Jurisdiction

IN VIEW OF the termination policy and particularly Public Law 280, many Indian people have been vitally concerned and fearful that their law and order systems will be supplanted, without their consent, by state law enforcement agencies which, perhaps, might be hostile toward them. In *U.S. v. Kagama* (1885) 118 U.S. 375, 383, the Court, speaking of Indians, said:

> "There are communities dependent on the United States; . . . ; dependent for their political rights. They owe no allegiance to the States, and receive from them no protection. Because of the local ill feeling of the people, states were they are found are often their deadliest enemies. From their very weakness and helplessness, so largely due to the course of dealing of the Federal Government with them and treaties in which it has been promised, there arises a duty of protection, and with it the power."

That statement by the Supreme Court is considered to be as true today as when written.

The repeated breaking of solemn treaties by the United States has also been a concern which is disheartening to the tribes and it is felt that there is no apparent concern by the Government about breaking treaties.

Recommendations

1. Return of Indian Lands: We urge the Congress to direct by appropriate legislation the return in trust of that part of the Public Domain formerly owned by an Indian tribe or nation which the Secretary of Interior shall determine to be excess and non-essential to the purpose for which such

land was originally taken or which was covered by a reversionary clause in the treaty or cession or other lands declared to be surplus to the government's needs. Restore all Indian lands that were consumed by termination policy.

2. Indian Claims Commission: We urge that Congress ascertain the reasons for the inordinate delay of the Indian Claims Commission in finishing its important assignment. The Congress should request the views of the attorneys for the tribes on this in order to balance the views already expressed to Congress by the attorneys for the United States.

The woeful lack of sufficient personnel to handle the case load in the Justice Department, we believe, is the *sole cause* for the delay, so damaging to the tribes, in expediting the Commission's work.

The law clearly directs that each tribe be represented by counsel and there would seem to exist no possible reason why the Justice Department should not be required to increase its personnel in the Indian Claims Section of the Lands Division to remove this just criticism. Simple justice suggests that this be speedily done or else irreparable damage to the tribes will result. We believe the Congress will want to correct this situation as promptly as possible.

3. Title to Reservations: The Secretary of the Interior, if he has the authority, or the Congress should act to determine the legal beneficiaries of reservations created under the Indian Reorganization Act or other authority for "Landless and Homeless Indians," also reservations established by executive order or prior act of Congress, where the naming of the beneficial users has been left indefinite or ambiguous. As Indians improve such lands, or as mineral wealth or other assets of value are discovered, ownership is in jeopardy unless clearly defined.

4. Submarginal Lands: Submarginal and other surplus lands adjoining or within the exterior boundaries of Indian reservations and purchased for the benefit of the Indians, should be transferred to the tribes under trust.

5. Land Purchase Funds: The land purchase funds authorized by the Indian Reorganization Act should again be appropriated on an annual basis, to permit tribes to add to their inadequate land base, to purchase heirship lands and allotments on which restrictions are removed, and otherwise improve their economy.

6. Voting on the Indian Reorganization Act: Amend the Indian Reorganization Act to permit tribes to vote on its acceptance at any time.

7. Protect Indian Water Rights: Adopt legislation to protect all Indian water rights of Indian reservations against appropriators who, because the government may be negligent in providing for Indian development, are able to establish a record of prior use.

9. Heirship Lands: Adopt a manageable and equitable heirship lands bill.

10. Amend P.L. 280: Amend P.L. 280 (83rd Congress) to require Indian consent to past and future transfers of jurisdiction over civil and criminal cases to the state in which a reservation is located, and to permit such transfers to take place, with Indian consent, on a progressive or item by item basis.

11. Reservation Boundaries: In order that Indian tribes may be properly protected in their reservation and may proceed with the orderly development of their resources, it is recommended that authority, if required, and funds be appropriated for the immediate survey and establishment of reservation boundaries.

Taxation

Grave concern has arisen as a result of the recent rulings of the Bureau of Internal Revenue which in substance directly violate the solemn treaty obligations made with the American Indian.

In fact, within the past few years, there has been a steady trend by both the federal and state taxing departments to encroach upon the rights of the Indian in the taxing of Indian property.

Recently, the Bureau of Internal Revenue has boldly claimed that it has the right to levy upon and collect income taxes upon income received by Indians which is derived from the sale of livestock grazed upon restricted Indian lands. Already the Internal Revenue Service has levied upon, assessed and collected income taxes upon income received from restricted Indian production.

The taxing department of the federal government has arbitrarily made these rulings which are wholly contrary to the solemn provisions of the treaties made with the American Indian. These rulings have been made and are being enforced notwithstanding the fact that it was never intended that the Indian was to be taxed in any manner upon his restricted Indian lands, or upon the income derived from the same.

In fact the greater amount of Indian lands located in the western part of the nation are dry and arid lands and suitable for grazing purposes only. In other words, the Indian is by nature restricted as to the use of his lands since the same can only be used for grazing purposes.

Therefore, in order to further prevent the establishment of such arbitrary rules of the Bureau of Internal Revenue, and to correct the rules already existing, we deem it necessary that legislation be enacted which will clearly spell out the intent and purposes of the existing treaties and agreements made with Indian tribes. Specifically, a clear statement must be made by law that income received by an enrolled member of an Indian tribe, which is derived from tribal, allotted and restricted Indian lands, whether by original allotment, by inheritance, by exchange or purchase, or as a leasee thereof, while such lands are held in trust by the United States in trust, is exempt from Federal and State income taxes.

Treaty Rights

It is a universal desire among all Indians that their treaties and trust-protected lands remain intact and beyond the reach of predatory men.

This is not special pleading, though Indians have been told often enough by members of Congress and the courts that the United States has the plenary power to wipe out our treaties at will. Governments, when powerful enough, can act in this arbitrary and immoral manner.

Still we insist that we are not pleading for special treatment at the hands of the American people. When we ask that our treaties be respected, we are mindful of the opinion of Chief Justice John Marshall on the nature of the treaty obligations between the United States and the Indian tribes.

Marshall said that a treaty ". . . is a compact between two nations or communities, having the right of self-government. Is it essential that each party shall possess the same attributes of sovereignty to give force to the treaty? This will not be pretended, for on this ground, very few valid treaties could be formed. The only requisite is, that each of the contracting parties shall possess the right of self-government, and the power to perform the stipulations of the treaty."

And he said, "We have made treaties with (the Indians); and are those treaties to be disregarded on our part, because they were entered into with an uncivilized people? Does this lessen the obligation of such treaties? By entering into them have we not admitted the power of this people to bind themselves, and to impose obligations on us?"

The right of self-government, a right which the Indians possessed before the coming of the white man, has never been extinguished; indeed, it has been repeatedly sustained by the courts of the United States. Our leaders made binding agreements—ceding lands as requested by the United States; keeping the peace; harboring no enemies of the nation. And the people stood with the leaders in accepting these obligations.

A treaty, in the minds of our people, is an eternal word. Events often make it seem expedient to depart from the pledged word, but we are conscious that the first departure creates a logic for the second departure, until there is nothing left of the word.

We recognize that our view of these matters differs at times from the prevailing legal view regarding due process.

When our lands are taken for a declared public purpose, scattering our people and threatening our continued existence, it grieves us to be told that a money payment is the equivalent of all the things we surrender. Our forefathers could be generous when all the continent was theirs. They could cast away whole empires for a handful of trinkets for their children. But in our day, each remaining acre is a promise that we will still be here tomorrow. Were we paid a thousand times the market value of our lost holdings, still the payment would not suffice. Money never mothered the Indian people, as the land has mothered them, nor have any people become more closely attached to the land, religiously and traditionally.

We insist again that this is not special pleading. We ask only that the United States be true to its own traditions and set an example to the world in fair dealing.

Concluding Statement

To complete our Declaration, we point out that in the beginning the people of the New World, called Indians by accident of geography, were possessed of a continent and a way of life. In the course of many lifetimes, our people had adjusted to every climate and condition from the Arctic to the torrid zones. In their livelihood and family relationships, their ceremonial observances, they reflected the diversity of the physical world they occupied.

The conditions in which Indians live today reflect a world in which every basic aspect of life has been transformed. Even the physical world is no longer the controlling factor in determining where and under what conditions men may live. In region after region, Indian groups found their means of existence either totally destroyed or materially modified. Newly introduced diseases swept away or reduced regional populations. These changes were followed by major shifts in the internal life of tribe and family.

The time came when the Indian people were no longer the masters of their situation. Their life ways survived subject to the will of a dominant sovereign power. This is said, not in a spirit of complaint; we understand that in the lives of all nations of people, there are times of plenty and times of famine. But we do speak out in a plea for understanding.

When we go before the American people, as we do in this Declaration, and ask for material assistance in developing our resources and developing our opportunities, we pose a moral problem which cannot be left unanswered. For the problem we raise affects the standing which our nation sustains before world opinion.

Our situation cannot be relieved by appropriated funds alone, though it is equally obvious that without capital investment and funded services, solutions will be delayed. Nor will the passage of time lessen the complexities which beset a people moving toward new meaning and purpose.

The answers we seek are not commodities to be purchased, neither are they evolved automatically through the passing of time.

The effort to place social adjustment on a money-time interval scale which has characterized Indian administration, has resulted in unwanted pressure and frustration.

When Indians speak of the continent they yielded, they are not referring only to the loss of some millions of acres in real estate. They have in mind that the land supported a universe of things they knew, valued, and loved.

With that continent gone, except for the few poor parcels they still retain, the basis of life is precariously held, but they mean to hold the scraps and parcels as earnestly as any small nation or ethnic group was ever determined to hold to identity and survival.

What we ask of America is not charity, not paternalism, even when benevolent. We ask only that the nature of our situation be recognized and made the basis of policy and action.

In short, the Indians ask for assistance, technical and financial, for the time needed, however long that may be, to regain in the America of the space age some measure of the adjustment they enjoyed as the original possessors of their native land.

STAN STEINER

The Chicanos

There are those who would argue that "The Chicanos" does not belong
in the book because Chicanos do not constitute a racial group. Our
defense is that the manifestations of race awareness in our social fabric
are too complex for neat biological distinctions. To invoke Marx
again, we would insist that much of what we attribute to race is a matter
of class and of poverty and of institutionalized neglect, and of almost
ritualized brutality.

THE GIRL WAS THIRTEEN when she tried to kill herself. She
was "tired of working." But she was too inexperienced with death
to die, and she lived through her death. To escape her loneliness
she married, at fifteen. Her child was born that year, but her husband was sent to prison. "I got a car. The car broke down. I couldn't pay
for it. They wanted to sue me. So I forged a check." In the barrios of Denver to be left with a baby, without a husband, at fifteen, was to be lonelier
than death. She became a prostitute.

"I worked the town. They call it hustling. I wouldn't go for less than
thirty dollars. Because I needed the money. I got it too. All you have to do
is be nice," the young girl said. "But to go out and hustle I had to be
under the influence of narcotics."

Diana Perea told her own life story to the National Conference on Poverty in the Southwest, held in January, 1965, to launch the War on Poverty. In the winter sun of Tucson, Arizona, the nearly two hundred delegates who had gathered under the auspices of the Choate Foundation, to
hear Vice President Hubert Humphrey, were as overwhelmed by the frail
and frightened girl as she was by the presidential emissary. "Go back and
tell them [your people] that the war against unemployment, discrimination, disease, and ignorance has begun. Tell them to get out and fight!" the
Vice President said. "The wonderful thing about the War on Poverty is
that we have the means to win it. We cannot fail." He reminded his listen-
ers, "Fifteen minutes from where we sit tonight there is abject poverty."

In the audience was Diana Perea. A few weeks later she succeeded in
killing herself.

Her death was due to an overdose of narcotics, the autopsy report declared. There were some nonmedical causes. On the frontispiece of the

Summary Report of the National Conference on Poverty in the Southwest there was a black border of mourning around these simple words:

DIANA PEREA
1946–1965
VICTIM OF POVERTY

Death is an ordinary thing. No one would have heard of the young girl from the streets of Denver's barrio if she had not happened to share a microphone with the Vice President of the United States.

In the streets misery is said to be so common no one notices. Life in the barrios is cruel—to outsiders, for the sons and daughters of the poor, it is said, are too hardened and brutalized to be able to do anything but fight to survive.

A young girl cries of a brown child dying of hunger in the barrios of San Antonio:

> In the land of the free
>   and the home of the brave,
> He is dying of hunger,
>   he cannot be saved;
> Come brothers and sisters
>   and weep by his grave.
> This is our child—

The ordeal of these youths is bemoaned by sympathetic writers. Not by the youth. Diana Perea did not weep. The Chicana was matter of fact: this is the way it is. Life in the barrio streets is just a way of life—happy, unhappy, ordinary, exciting, boring, deadly. The streets are not dangerous, they are only treacherous. It doesn't frighten youth. Seldom do they curse the barrio. They curse themselves for their inability to survive. It is not the barrio that the Chicano fears, but the lonely and hostile world outside.

Loneliness, the coldness of urban life, is what depresses the Chicano. In his family there is a warmth and gregarious love voiced with passion, uninhibited honesty, and gusto. The city frustrates and mutes this love. Faced with a society that he feels is hostile, the barrio youth becomes lost. He tries to defend himself by forming a gang, not just to fight for his manhood, his *macho,* but for his right to be a Chicano.

"The most brutal method of birth control is the one we practice on ourselves," a young man writes in *La Raza.*

To *La Raza Chicana,* a young girl writes a bitter note: "I wish to compliment brother Perfecto Vallego and his friends for doing with Caterino B. Heredia. Keep up the good work, Baby, you and the cops [can] get together on the Chicano Annual Shoot. Your game is as bad as the racist cop who goes after Chicanos who fail to halt. You dudes don't have to kill your brothers; Uncle Sam is doing that for you in Viet Nam. You are shooting the wrong guy. *No sean tan pendejos.* If you have enough *huevos* [testicles] to shoot your brother you should be able to take on a racist cop."

The street gangs of the barrios are different from those in most ghettos. In a sense they are born not solely of poverty, but also of cultural pride. Like street-corner chambers of commerce the gangs of barrio youth defend the spirit of La Raza with bravado and youthful boisterousness.

Of the many barrio gangs the oldest and best known is that of the legendary Pachucos, who have become a heroic myth. They were born in blood that was real enough, and they not only are remembered but are imitated with awe. They began on a day in August, 1942. In the tensions of World War II, the racial hatreds of Los Angeles were about to erupt in what was to be known as the "Zoot Suit Riots." Two groups of Chicanos had a boyish fight over a pretty girl and hurt pride, in a gravel pit on the outskirts of the city. In the morning the body of young José Díaz was found on a dirt road nearby, dead. Bored newspapermen, seeking local color, dubbed the gravel pit the "Sleepy Lagoon" (it had a mud puddle in it), and an orgy of sensational headlines celebrated the boy's death.

Not one but twenty-four Mexican boys were arrested; nine were convicted of second-degree murder. All were freed later, two years later, when the Court of Appeals reversed the sentences unanimously for "lack of evidence."

The "Sleepy Lagoon" case is still remembered bitterly in the barrios, much as the Dreyfus case in France, or that of the Scottsboro Boys in the Deep South.

Amid headlines of hysteria—"Zoot Suit Hoodlums" and "Pachuco Gangsters"—the Los Angeles police raided the barrios, blockaded the main streets, searched every passing car and passer-by. Six hundred Chicanos were taken into custody in a two-day sweep that Police Captain Joseph Reed called "a drive on Mexican gangs." The Los Angeles sheriff's "Bureau of *Foreign* Relations" justified the dragnet by officially philosophizing that the Chicanos' "desire to kill, or at least let blood" was an "inborn characteristic."

The next summer the tensions exploded. When a fist fight broke out on a downtown street between a gang of Chicano boys and U.S. Navy men in June, 1943, fourteen off-duty policemen led by a lieutenant of the Detective Squad set up an impromptu group of vigilantes they named the "Vengeance Squad" and set out "to clean up" the Mexicans.

Night after night hundreds of restless and beached sailors of the U.S. Navy, bored and frustrated by their inaction in the war against Japan, seized upon the nearest available dark-skinned enemies—the young Chicanos—and beat them up. The white rioters toured the barrios in convoys of taxi cabs, attacking every brown boy they found on the streets, in bars and restaurants and movie houses, by the dozens, by the hundreds, while the Los Angeles police looked the other way. No sailor was arrested. Inspired by the inflammatory news stories about "zoot suit roughnecks," the white rioters sought out these most of all—zoot suits were an early Humphrey Bogart style Mexicanized by Chicano boys and lately revived in its classic form by *Bonnie and Clyde*.

It was a long, hot summer week. When the white rioters exhausted their racial fervor, the riots—known not as the "U.S. Navy Riots" but oddly as the "Zoot Suit Riots"—had left hundreds of injured and a residue of race hatred in Los Angeles.

The zoot-suit boys were Pachucos. Where the name came from is vague, but it may have been taken from the city of Pachuco in Mexico, known for its brilliantly hued costumes. In the riots, these gangs of Pachucos were not the aggressors but the defenders of the barrios. They were an early self-defense group. Youths who never knew the Pachucos remember them not as victims but as resistance fighters of the streets, the Minutemen of *machismo,* who fought to defend the reputation of La Raza. Wherever the barrio youth organize, the spirit of the Pachucos is evoked and revived.

"I hope you tell the story of the Pachucos," a Brown Beret says to me. "We have to learn about our heroes."

One of many Pachuco-type gangs is the Vatos. It is a fictitious name of a small gang in the San Fernando Valley of Los Angeles whose "territory" ranges from Laurel Canyon Boulevard to O'Melveny Street. The Vatos hang out mostly in the dark alleys near Acala Avenue, a poorly lit thoroughfare.

A member of the Vatos talks of his gang:

"This is the story of life in a Mexican barrio. The barrio is called 'San Fer.' The kids, so-called Pachucos, run this barrio. Life in this barrio is rough, harsh. The boys learned early to carry can openers and knives. As soon as they got a little older they graduated to switchblades, lengths of chain, and guns, if they could get hold of them.

"Boys joined together to form street gangs, and some of them sported the Pachuco brand between the thumb and forefinger of their left hand," the Vato says. "This gang is the stuff of life, as the Pachuco knows it."

The gang member has to prove his manhood and his ability to survive. "He will undertake the most fantastic stunts to prove a great deal. He will risk his life and his freedom to maintain his growing reputation as a tough fighter, a rugged guy." These rituals are not merely rites of initiation, or idle bravado. The gang youth has to demonstrate not only that he can fight in the streets, but that he has the strength to withstand the hostility of society, to stand up to the *placa,* the police, and if he is courageous enough, to become visible to the outsider, by wearing a Brown Beret. "That is real *macho,"* a Los Angeles community leader says.

It is a new kind of political and urban *pachuquismo.* The society outside the barrio is defied by the gang. Consciously the rituals of brotherhood enforce the laws and culture of the barrio. Inside the gang the Chicano is insulated from his own conflicts. The Chicanos "find conflicts so perplexing and so full of both cultures—that of their parents and that of America—that [they] create their own world of *pachuquismo,*" says the Vato.

The Vato goes on: "The Vatos have created their own language, Pachucano, their own style of dress, their own folklore, and their own behavior patterns. The Vatos have developed a barrio group spirit. The Vatos in this area are better organized and a little tighter, due to the fact that it is a smaller group; and therefore all the Vatos participate in the activities planned by them.

"They formed a closely knit group that regarded the Anglos as their natural enemies."

In every barrio the social clubs and folk religious societies have always existed in semisecrecy, with their own rules and symbols, hidden from the world outside. Chicano gangs are the progeny of that invisible heritage—to outsiders—by which the barrio has protected itself. They re-create in their own youthful way, the society and culture of their forefathers; yet they are urban.

Eliezer Risco, the editor of *La Raza,* describes these methods of barrio organizations as "our own survival techniques. It is difficult for the culture of a minority to survive in the larger society. If we can utilize them for social action, now that we are stronger, we will surprise the country," he says. "The country won't know where our strength is coming from or how we organize."

In the dark alleyways and gregarious streets, the Brown Berets began. They have developed a political *pachuquismo.* A generation ago they would have been a street gang, nothing more. Less obvious are the barrio origins of the youthful leaders of the La Raza movements that have gained national prominence and importance. Cesar Chavez, Rodolfo "Corky" Gonzales, Reies Tijerina: these men learned their organizing techniques on the back streets of the barrio.

"They say the La Raza movements come from the universities. I disagree," says "José," the "Field Marshal" of the Brown Berets. "I say they come from the streets."

So few youths in the barrios graduated from high school in the past, or entered college, that those who achieved that miraculous feat feared to look down from their pinnacle of anxiety. If they did, the barrios beneath them seemed a bottomless arroyo. And yet, in the wholly anglicized realms of higher education they were also strangers.

"You see a Chicano [university] student is alienated from his language; he is de-culturized and finally dehumanized so as to be able to function in a white, middle class, protestant bag," the *Chicano Student News* reports.

"It is damn obvious to the Chicano in college that education means one of two things: either accept the system—study, receive a diploma, accept the cubicle and the IBM machine in some lousy bank or factory, and move out of the barrio—or reject the system. . . ."

Youths who made it to the university clung to their privileged and precarious achievements: non-Mexican name and anglicized accent, an Ivy League suit, a blond wife, and a disdain for the "dumb Mexicans" left behind. "THE PURPLE TIO TOMAS" (Uncle Tom), *El Gallo* has dubbed these high achievers. "This is the middle class Tomás. He isn't a Tomás because he lives on the other side of town, but because the Purple Tomás believes he is better than other Chicanos. Purple is the Royal Color!" The would-be intellectual *patróns*—"the new conservatives," Corky Gonzales calls them.

Now the university students have begun the climb down from their lonely success to the streets of the barrios and the fields of the campesinos. They come as on a pilgrimage, seeking an identity. Los Angeles community leader Eduardo Pérez says, "I find that many Mexicans-turned-Spanish are coming back into the fold and are being identified for what they are: Mexicans." They have a "pride in being Mexican."

In the vineyards of Delano, when the striking grape pickers gathered their banners and walked north on the highway in their 250-mile pilgrimage to Sacramento to see the Governor, the university Chicanos who walked with the *huelguistas* were wide-eyed with wonder. Not only were these young people from the universities, but they were the children of the barrios who had at last escaped, had "made it." Some even had blond hair.

Here were "farm workers with dark faces, aged prematurely by the California sun, marching side by side with students with youthful faces," wrote Daniel de los Reyes in the union newspaper *El Malcriado,* the "farm workers with black hair and a determined look, by the side of blond and red-haired students with brilliant, sparkling eyes." It was "a spectacle to see, these thousands and thousands of young people" who had come "because the Farm Workers Organizing Committee had agreed to join side by side with their brothers, the students." There was a tone of wonder in the union newspaper story. It seemed unbelievable, this "brotherhood against ignorance and poverty." These were "the same students we have seen so many times on the picketlines at the vineyards of DiGiorgio, the same youth working so tirelessly on the boycotts," declared *El Malcriado.*

Still it was not to be believed. The university students respected, listened to, and obeyed the campesinos of the fields; that was what was so strange. It was as though they who were illiterate were the teachers of the university students.

The experience of the *huelga* was a strange and exhilarating one for the students as well, for it profoundly affected the lives of many who had come. Luis Valdez, who went on to found El Centro Cultural Campesino, and Eliezer Risco, who became editor of *La Raza,* were but two of dozens of student leaders whose lives were changed by their pilgrimage to the vineyards of Delano.

"I was writing my thesis," Risco recalls. "I came thinking, well, it's a way of doing my research. But it was my Graduate School."

Venustiano Olguin was a brilliant student in a graduate school of the University of California at Los Angeles and was studying for his Ph.D. The son of a bracero who had grown up in the migrant barrios of the Coachella Valley, he had worked his way to first place in his high school class and graduated with honors from the University of Redlands.

"I'd been very successful with the system." But he had begun to have the uneasy feeling he was becoming a "Tío Tomás," an Uncle Tom. "At UCLA I knew that somewhere along the line I had been betraying something." He did not know what.

One summer the young man and some of his fellow students in the United Mexican American Students (UMAS) had a meeting with Cesar Chavez. Olguin went to Delano—not to stay, just to look around and help the farm workers if he could. He decided to join *La Huelga.* He has abandoned the honors of higher education that he says were anglicizing him, indoctrinating him with materialistic values, and forcing him to reject his Mexican heritage. He lives on $5 a week strike pay. "Some people think I am crazy. But I think my life is very rich." In the campesinos he feels he has found "a special kind of courage," of manhood. "I've learned more than in all the time I was in graduate school."

University communities of Chicanos were affected as strongly. In San Antonio, Texas, a leader of the Mexican American Youth Organization recalls how the campesinos of the Rio Grande Valley became godfathers of his group. "The strike of the farm workers got everyone excited. St. Mary's University students got together to see what they could do," says William Vazquez. "And that is how we began."

Luis Valdez, whose life was changed by Delano, feels it is a necessary school for students. "In advance of their people, the Chicano leader in the cities and universities must go through the whole bourgeois scene, find it distasteful, and then strike out in new directions. This is what happened with Corky Gonzales and Cesar Chavez. Divorcing themselves from the petty aims of success, they see the middle class for what it is. Then they can see the lower class plain.

"In short, they discover there is a world out there," Valdez says.

Out of the upheaval have come dozens of new barrio and university clubs. In the last few years there has been more youth organizing than in the entire history of the Chicanos. University students have been especially outspoken and active. The United Mexican American Students (UMAS) in

California and the National Organization of Mexican American Students (NOMAS, literally "No More") in Texas are but two of more than thirty groups on the campuses alone.

The university and barrio youth are talking and walking together. David Sanchez, the prime minister of the Brown Berets, talks to students at UCLA, while the students of UMAS walk not only on the picket lines of the campesinos of Delano but also beside the Brown Berets protesting school conditions in East Los Angeles. The *Chicano Student News* reports: "UMAS is an organization of Chicano college students which is bringing the business of education back into the Chicano community"; and the headline says, "UMAS COMES HOME!"

"Old hatreds and quarrels are being put aside," *La Raza* writes, for *"Todos son Chicanos"*—"We are all Chicanos."

Several dozen Chicanos gathered at a dude ranch near Santa Barbara on the California seacoast for one of the many conferences of students and barrio youths. Eduardo Pérez, who helped run the conference, describes the occasion:

"Nowadays the young lions and lionesses have their own cars, buy their own clothes, work their way through college, and are very much on their own. Their whole thinking and outlook on life is as different from ours as night is from day.

"These Mexican American 'world leaders of tomorrow' are an exceptional breed. They can put on a *charro* [the real cowboy Mexican] costume and be proud of it. They can even put on American clothes and feel at ease. They can eat enchiladas and hamburgers on the same plate, tacos and pizza in one sitting, and possibly drink tequila with beer as a chaser and feel right at home. They have become anglicized, but only to the point that there is no excuse for them not being accepted. They take pride in being of Mexican ancestry and do not deny being what they are. These kids don't change their names just to become Spanish or European heirs. . . ."

In spite of the ease with which they seemed to go from one culture to another, the young Chicanos suffered an inner paralysis. They doubted not their emotions or their thoughts, but to create one culture out of two so different. Pérez had written of another youth conference, "The Mexican Americans attending (most of them) did not really understand themselves . . . and how they happened to be in the mess they're in."

The university and barrio youth had this in common too.

"I stand naked in the world, lost in angry solitude," the Chicano poet Benjamin Luna writes in *La Raza*. The loneliness of the urban society—impersonal, cold, efficient, foreign to his heart—evokes the feeling of a hostile world. The futility the Chicano feels is not fatalism, but a rage of frustration.

Soy Indio con alma hambrienta,
traigo en la sangre coraje,
rojo coraje en la sangre.

I am Indian with a hungry soul,
    tragic in the passionate blood,
    red passion in the blood.

I stand naked in the world,
    hungry
    homeless
    despised. . . .

In the barrios, brotherhood is in the blood, the blood of La Raza. "One boy will bring beer, while others will bring *rifa;* still others bring money for the use of activities, or gas in a member's car. This is a thing that goes on every night with something different every night that can be called a 'dead kick.' " At best, their inner brotherhood is limited by the outer world of their "natural enemy," and at worst is defined by it.

A Brown Beret laments, "We are not what we were when we started out. All those TV cameras and news reporters took over our image and changed us into their image of us."

"Who am I?" asks a young woman in a suburban church of Los Angeles. "I have been afraid to speak up for my rights. Rights? What rights do we have? So many of our youth plead guilty in court when they know they are not guilty of anything. Anything but being a Mexican."

I am Joaquín,
Lost in a world of confusion,
Caught up in the whirl of an
    Anglo society,
Confused by the rules,
Scorned by attitudes,
Suppressed by manipulations,
And destroyed by modern society.
My fathers
    have lost the economic battle,
and won
    the fight for cultural survival.

The litany "Who am I?" is echoed in the poem of Rodolfo Gonzales, the leader of La Raza community of Denver. "I am Joaquín" is at once a defiance and a requiem for the history of self-mutilation of those whom the Chicano poet calls "strangers in *their* land":

In a country that has wiped out
all my history,
    stifled all my pride.

In a country that has placed
a different indignity
    upon my ancient burdens.
    Inferiority
is the new load. . . .

In time the act of denial becomes a self-denial:

I look at myself
and see part of me
who rejects my father and my mother
and dissolves into the melting pot
    to evaporate in shame. . . .

"Soul searching," Dr. Ernesto Galarza calls it. The scholar, a sparse man of wiry thoughts and whitening hair, who talks with hard, dry words, is recognized by many of the Chicano youth leaders as the dean of the La Raza movement; perhaps the dean emeritus. "There is an incredible amount of soul searching going on among this generation. Of questioning. Of seeking," he says one midnight over coffee in a motel in Santa Barbara, where he has gone to teach a youth workshop.

"Many of these youth have been propelled into crises of considerable tension. There have been tragic losses, where some of them have been torn asunder by the conflicts, internal and external, within themselves. There has been a loss of much potential. The youth are resilient, however.

"I believe there are few phoneys in this generation. Anyone who believes this is a time for the promotion of Uncle Toms, of acquiescence, among the younger generation of Mexicans, is mistaken. Unquestionably this generation is confronted with some crippling problems. But *that* is not one of them," says the scholar.

Dr. Galarza's weary eyes light up when he talks of these youths. "I am delighted by the happenstance of the last ten years. There has been the growth of quite a small army of young men, a phalanx of potential leaders who are searching for a breakthrough. The younger generation holds much promise.

"It is too early to foresee where these movements will lead. There is little unity of thought. There is precious little cohesion. Every movement is its own little stirring of activity. In five or ten years, there may be a reckoning; a culmination.

"We will wait," the scholar says, "and we will see."

Of course, the youth will not wait. They want action now, ideology later. Having had a small glimpse of their cultural identity, they want the rest; and having had a foretaste of Chicano power, they yearn for more: "Mañana is here!" says Maclovio Barraza, leader of the Arizona miners.

"Who the hell are we? What are we? Where do we belong? Study it!

Announce it to the world!" Joe Benitos, a Chicano leader in Arizona, exclaims impatiently. "Let's end this hangup about identity. We know who we are. In order to survive we have learned survival skills. Sure, but let's not confuse our survival skills in Anglo society with our culture. We have a parallel culture. We have to keep it. I say we can do it. We don't have to be one of *them!"*

His impatience with the talk of the "identity crisis" is typical of the young Chicano. Benitos feels the problem of identity is perpetuated by university study projects, "so that they will have something to study"; he has worked with several of these projects. "I've been there," he says. "And that's not where it's at.

"Yes, having two cultures creates problems. Why emphasize the problems? Why not emphasize the opportunities it gives the Chicano in the new world scene?

"There is a Chicano wave coming in," says Benitos. "I see it as part of the world-wide scene. As the world shrinks everyone will have to learn more than one language, one culture. Everyone will have to be bilingual and trilingual. It will put us in a fantastic position, if we can keep our languages and cultures.

"Our experience will be a lesson for the whole world," he says.

"Chicano" is a new word, not yet in the dictionary. La Raza writers cannot yet define it except by what it is not; the Chicano is not, they say, half-Mexican, half-American, who blends two cultures in his being. He is not just one more second- and third-generation city-bred descendant of a rural villager who has learned to drive a car like a wild horse and pay for it on the installment plan. La Raza is a new people with a new culture and the Chicano is its youngest offspring. He has inherited many things from Mexico and the United States, but he imitates neither. The Chicano is a new man.

In the La Raza newspapers there appears a "Definition of the Word Chicano" by Benito Rodríguez. He is a member of MANO (Hand), a group of Chicano ex-convicts in San Antonio, Texas. Rodríguez's words, even more than his ideas, the way he writes, the style, the language he uses, give some of the feeling of being a Chicano in the barrio of a modern city. Even in the pale English translation the strong flavor of that life comes through, although it is stronger in the Spanish. He writes:

"Many designations have been used to refer to us, the descendants of Mexicans. Every ten or fifteen years, or so, we feel like searching for a new image of ourselves. First, in the time of the 'Wild West' we were 'Mexican bandits,' then 'greasers,' then 'Mescins,' and now we are 'Spanish Americans,' 'Mexican Americans,' 'Americans,' etc.

"The migrant Mexicans, workers in the field, call themselves Chicapatas (short legs), or Raza (race, as in Raza del Sol, People of the Sun). City workers use the term Chicano a little more. The phrase Mexican-American is really used by the middle-class Mexicans. What is truly Mexican is covered by a layer, Chicano, to satisfy all the conditions in which we find ourselves. How shall we describe ourselves tomorrow, or the day after?

"Now they want to make us half Mexicans and half Americans, as if they were talking about geography. Well, we already know who we are. Why do we come on like a chicken with its head cut off? Why do we let them make fakes, if we are chicanos down to the phlegm in our mouths? If you don't like the taste you'll swallow it anyway.

"Just because we've seen their marvelous technology doesn't mean we believe that those who exploit us are gods."

Benito Rodríguez concludes with a curse that is pure Chicano: "A poor man who thinks he lives in heaven is gonna get fucked, coming and going."

FRANTZ FANON

Concerning Violence

An awareness of complexity is the beginning of a true sense of the problems of race. We returned to Fanon because he touches on so many of the complex themes with which we are concerned: the physical and psychological fact of color; colonialism within and without national boundaries; myth, ritual, and superstition; exploitation in so many forms, and of course the possibility and reality of violence. Fanon's is the vision against which we must measure our own.

A WORLD DIVIDED into compartments, a motionless, Manicheistic world, a world of statues: the statue of the general who carried out the conquest, the statue of the engineer who built the bridge; a world which is sure of itself, which crushes with its stones the backs flayed by whips: this is the colonial world. The native is a being hemmed in; apartheid is simply one form of the division into compartments of the colonial world. The first thing which the native learns is to stay in his place, and not to go beyond certain limits. This is why the dreams of the native are always of muscular prowess; his dreams are of action and of aggression. I dream I am jumping, swimming, running, climbing; I dream that I burst out laughing, that I span a river in one stride, or that I am followed by a flood of motorcars which never catch up with me. During the period of colonization, the native never stops achieving his freedom from nine in the evening until six in the morning.

The colonized man will first manifest this aggressiveness which has been deposited in his bones against his own people. This is the period when the niggers beat each other up, and the police and magistrates do not know which way to turn when faced with the astonishing waves of crime in North Africa. When the native is confronted with the colonial order of things, he finds he is in a state of permanent tension. The settler's world is a hostile world, which spurns the native, but at the same time it is a world of which he is envious. We have seen that the native never ceases to dream of putting himself in the place of the settler—not of becoming the settler but of substituting himself for the settler. This hostile world, ponderous and aggressive because it fends off the colonized masses with all the harshness it is capable of, represents not merely a hell from which the swiftest flight possible is desirable, but also a paradise close at hand which is guarded by terrible watchdogs.

The native is always on the alert, for since he can only make out with difficulty the many symbols of the colonial world, he is never sure whether or not he has crossed the frontier. Confronted with a world ruled by the settler, the native is always presumed guilty. But the native's guilt is never a guilt which he accepts; it is rather a kind of curse, a sort of sword of Damocles, for, in his innermost spirit, the native admits no accusation. He is overpowered but not tamed; he is treated as an inferior but he is not convinced of his inferiority. He is patiently waiting until the settler is off his guard to fly at him. The native's muscles are always tensed. You can't say that he is terrorized, or even apprehensive. He is in fact ready at a moment's notice to exchange the role of the quarry for that of the hunter. The native is an oppressed person whose permanent dream is to become the persecutor. The symbols of social order—the police, the bugle calls in the barracks, military parades and the waving flags—are at one and the same time inhibitory and stimulating: for they do not convey the message "Don't dare to budge"; rather, they cry out "Get ready to attack." And, in fact, if the native had any tendency to fall asleep and to forget, the settler's hauteur and the settler's anxiety to test the strength of the colonial system would remind him at every turn that the great showdown cannot be put off indefinitely. That impulse to take the settler's place implies a tonicity of muscles the whole time; and in fact we know that in certain emotional conditions the presence of an obstacle accentuates the tendency toward motion.

The settler-native relationship is a mass relationship. The settler pits brute force against the weight of numbers. He is an exhibitionist. His preoccupation with security makes him remind the native out loud that there he alone is master. The settler keeps alive in the native an anger which he deprives of outlet; the native is trapped in the tight links of the chains of colonialism. But we have seen that inwardly the settler can only achieve a pseudo petrification. The native's muscular tension finds outlet regularly in bloodthirsty explosions—in tribal warfare, in feuds between septs, and in quarrels between individuals.

Where individuals are concerned, a positive negation of common sense is evident. While the settler or the policeman has the right the livelong day to strike the native, to insult him and to make him crawl to them, you will see the native reaching for his knife at the slightest hostile or aggressive glance cast on him by another native; for the last resort of the native is to defend his personality vis-à-vis his brother. Tribal feuds only serve to perpetuate old grudges buried deep in the memory. By throwing himself with all his force into the vendetta, the native tries to persuade himself that colonialism does not exist, that everything is going on as before, that history continues. Here on the level of communal organizations we clearly discern the well-known behavior patterns of avoidance. It is as if plunging into a fraternal blood-bath allowed them to ignore the obstacle, and to put off till later the choice, nevertheless inevitable, which opens up the question of armed resistance to colonialism. Thus collective autodestruction in a very concrete form is one of the ways in which the native's muscular tension is set free. All these patterns of conduct are those of the death reflex when faced with danger, a suicidal behavior which proves to the settler (whose existence and domination is by them all the more justified) that these men are not reasonable human beings. In the same way the native manages to by-pass the settler. A belief in fatality removes all blame from the oppressor; the cause of misfortunes and of poverty is attributed to God: He is Fate. In this way the individual accepts the disintegration ordained by God, bows down before the settler and his lot, and by a kind of interior restabilization acquires a stony calm.

Meanwhile, however, life goes on, and the native will strengthen the inhibitions which contain his aggressiveness by drawing on the terrifying myths which are so frequently found in underdeveloped communities. There are maleficent spirits which intervene every time a step is taken in the wrong direction, leopard-men, serpent-men, six-legged dogs, zombies —a whole series of tiny animals or giants which create around the native a world of prohibitions, of barriers and of inhibitions far more terrifying than the world of the settler. This magical superstructure which permeates native society fulfills certain well-defined functions in the dynamism of the libido. One of the characteristics of underdeveloped societies is in fact that the libido is first and foremost the concern of a group, or of the family. The feature of communities whereby a man who dreams that he has sexual relations with a woman other than his own must confess it in public and pay a fine in kind or in working days to the injured husband or family is fully described by ethnologists. We may note in passing that this proves that the so-called pre-historic societies attach great importance to the unconscious.

The atmosphere of myth and magic frightens me and so takes on an undoubted reality. By terrifying me, it integrates me in the traditions and the history of my district or of my tribe, and at the same time it reassures me, it gives me a status, as it were an identification paper. In underdeveloped countries the occult sphere is a sphere belonging to the community which is entirely under magical jurisdiction. By entangling myself in this inextricable network where actions are repeated with crystalline inevitability, I find the everlasting world which belongs to me, and the perenniality which is thereby affirmed of the world belonging to us. Believe me, the zombies are more terrifying than the settlers; and in consequence the problem is no longer that of keeping oneself right with the colonial world and its barbed-wire entanglements, but of considering three times before urinating, spitting, or going out into the night.

The supernatural, magical powers reveal themselves as essentially personal; the settler's powers are infinitely shrunken, stamped with their alien origin. We no longer really need to fight against them since what counts is the frightening enemy created by myths. We perceive that all is settled by a permanent confrontation on the phantasmic plane.

It has always happened in the struggle for freedom that such a people, formerly lost in an imaginary maze, a prey to unspeakable terrors yet happy to lose themselves in a dreamlike torment, such a people becomes unhinged, reorganizes itself, and in blood and tears gives birth to very real and immediate action. Feeding the *moudjahidines*,[1] posting sentinels, coming to the help of families which lack the bare necessities, or taking the place of a husband who has been killed or imprisoned: such are the concrete tasks to which the people is called during the struggle for freedom.

In the colonial world, the emotional sensitivity of the native is kept on the surface of his skin like an open sore which flinches from the caustic agent; and the psyche shrinks back, obliterates itself and finds outlet in muscular demonstrations which have caused certain very wise men to say that the native is a hysterical type. This sensitive emotionalism, watched by invisible keepers who are however in unbroken contact with the core of the personality, will find its fulfillment through eroticism in the driving forces behind the crisis' dissolution.

On another level we see the native's emotional sensibility exhausting itself in dances which are more or less ecstatic. This is why any study of the colonial world should take into consideration the phenomena of the dance and of possession. The native's relaxation takes precisely the form of a muscular orgy in which the most acute aggressivity and the most impelling violence are canalized, transformed, and conjured away. The circle of the dance is a permissive circle: it protects and permits. At certain times on certain days, men and women come together at a given place, and there, under the solemn eye of the tribe, fling themselves into a seemingly unorganized pantomime, which is in reality extremely systematic, in which by various means—shakes of the head, bending of the spinal column, throwing of the whole body backward—may be deciphered as in an open book the huge effort of a community to exorcise itself, to liberate itself, to explain itself. There are no limits—inside the circle. The hillock up which you have toiled as if to be nearer to the moon; the river bank down which you slip as if to show the connection between the dance and ablutions, cleansing and purification—these are sacred places. There are no limits— for in reality your purpose in coming together is to allow the accumulated libido, the hampered aggressivity, to dissolve as in a volcanic eruption. Symbolical killings, fantastic rides, imaginary mass murders—all must be

1. Highly-trained soldiers who are completely dedicated to the Moslem cause.— *Trans.*

brought out. The evil humors are undammed, and flow away with a din as of molten lava.

One step further and you are completely possessed. In fact, these are actually organized séances of possession and exorcism; they include vampirism, possession by djinns, by zombies, and by Legba, the famous god of the voodoo. This disintegrating of the personality, this splitting and dissolution, all this fulfills a primordial function in the organism of the colonial world. When they set out, the men and women were impatient, stamping their feet in a state of nervous excitement; when they return, peace has been restored to the village; it is once more calm and unmoved.

During the struggle for freedom, a marked alienation from these practices is observed. The native's back is to the wall, the knife is at his throat (or, more precisely, the electrode at his genitals): he will have no more call for his fancies. After centuries of unreality, after having wallowed in the most outlandish phantoms, at long last the native, gun in hand, stands face to face with the only forces which contend for his life—the forces of colonialism. And the youth of a colonized country, growing up in an atmosphere of shot and fire, may well make a mock of, and does not hesitate to pour scorn upon the zombies of his ancestors, the horses with two heads, the dead who rise again, and the djinns who rush into your body while you yawn. The native discovers reality and transforms it into the pattern of his customs, into the practice of violence and into his plan for freedom.

We have seen that this same violence, though kept very much on the surface all through the colonial period, yet turns in the void. We have also seen that it is canalized by the emotional outlets of dance and possession by spirits; we have seen how it is exhausted in fratricidal combats. Now the problem is to lay hold of this violence which is changing direction. When formerly it was appeased by myths and exercised its talents in finding fresh ways of committing mass suicide, now new conditions will make possible a completely new line of action.

Nowadays a theoretical problem of prime importance is being set, on the historical plane as well as on the level of political tactics, by the liberation of the colonies: when can one affirm that the situation is ripe for a movement of national liberation? In what form should it first be manifested? Because the various means whereby decolonization has been carried out have appeared in many different aspects, reason hesitates and refuses to say which is a true decolonization, and which a false. We shall see that for a man who is in the thick of the fight it is an urgent matter to decide on the means and the tactics to employ: that is to say, how to conduct and organize the movement. If this coherence is not present there is only a blind will toward freedom, with the terribly reactionary risks which it entails.

What are the forces which in the colonial period open up new outlets and engender new aims for the violence of colonized peoples? In the first place there are the political parties and the intellectual or commercial elites. Now, the characteristic feature of certain political structures is that they proclaim abstract principles but refrain from issuing definite commands. The entire action of these nationalist political parties during the colonial period is action of the electoral type: a string of philosophico-political dissertations on the themes of the rights of peoples to self-determination, the rights of man to freedom from hunger and human dignity, and the unceasing affirmation of the principle: "One man, one vote." The national political parties never lay stress upon the necessity of a trial of armed strength, for the good reason that their objective is not the radical overthrowing of the system. Pacifists and legalists, they are in fact partisans of order, the new order—but to the colonialist bourgeoisie they put bluntly enough the demand which to them is the main one: "Give us more power." On the specific question of violence, the elite are ambiguous. They are violent in their words and reformist in their attitudes. When the nationalist political leaders *say* something, they make quite clear that they do not really *think* it.

This characteristic on the part of the nationalist political parties should be interpreted in the light both of the make-up of their leaders and the nature of their followings. The rank-and-file of a nationalist party is urban. The workers, primary schoolteachers, artisans, and small shopkeepers who have begun to profit—at a discount, to be sure—from the colonial setup, have special interests at heart. What this sort of following demands is the betterment of their particular lot: increased salaries, for example. The dialogue between these political parties and colonialism is never broken off. Improvements are discussed, such as full electoral representation, the liberty of the press, and liberty of association. Reforms are debated. Thus it need not astonish anyone to notice that a large number of natives are militant members of the branches of political parties which stem from the mother country. These natives fight under an abstract watchword: "Government by the workers," and they forget that in their country it should be *nationalist* watchwords which are first in the field. The native intellectual has clothed his aggressiveness in his barely veiled desire to assimilate himself to the colonial world. He has used his aggressiveness to serve his own individual interests.

Thus there is very easily brought into being a kind of class of affranchised slaves, or slaves who are individually free. What the intellectual demands is the right to multiply the emancipated, and the opportunity to organize a genuine class of emancipated citizens. On the other hand, the mass of the people have no intention of standing by and watching individuals increase their chances of success. What they demand is not the settler's position of status, but the settler's place. The immense majority of natives want the settler's farm. For them, there is no question of entering into competition with the settler. They want to take his place.

The peasantry is systematically disregarded for the most part by the propaganda put out by the nationalist parties. And it is clear that in the colonial countries the peasants alone are revolutionary, for they have nothing to lose and everything to gain. The starving peasant, outside the class system, is the first among the exploited to discover that only violence pays. For him there is no compromise, no possible coming to terms; colonization and decolonization are simply a question of relative strength. The exploited man sees that his liberation implies the use of all means, and that of force first and foremost. When in 1956, after the capitulation of Monsieur Guy Mollet to the settlers in Algeria, the Front de Libération Nationale, in a famous leaflet, stated that colonialism only loosens its hold when the knife is at its throat, no Algerian really found these terms too violent. The leaflet only expressed what every Algerian felt at heart: colonialism is not a thinking machine, nor a body endowed with reasoning faculties. It is violence in its natural state, and it will only yield when confronted with greater violence.

At the decisive moment, the colonialist bourgeoisie, which up till then has remained inactive, comes into the field. It introduces that new idea which is in proper parlance a creation of the colonial situation: non-violence. In its simplest form this non-violence signifies to the intellectual and economic elite of the colonized country that the bourgeoisie has the same interests as they and that it is therefore urgent and indispensable to come to terms for the public good. Non-violence is an attempt to settle the colonial problem around a green baize table, before any regrettable act has been performed or irreparable gesture made, before any blood has been shed. But if the masses, without waiting for the chairs to be arranged around the baize table, listen to their own voice and begin committing outrages and setting fire to buildings, the elite and the nationalist bourgeois parties will be seen rushing to the colonialists to exclaim, "This is very serious! We do not know how it will end; we must find a solution—some sort of compromise."

This idea of compromise is very important in the phenomenon of decolonization, for it is very far from being a simple one. Compromise involves the colonial system and the young nationalist bourgeoisie at one and the same time. The partisans of the colonial system discover that the masses may destroy everything. Blown-up bridges, ravaged farms, repressions, and fighting harshly disrupt the economy. Compromise is equally attractive to the nationalist bourgeoisie, who since they are not clearly aware of the possible consequences of the rising storm, are genuinely afraid of being swept away by this huge hurricane and never stop saying to the settlers: "We are still capable of stopping the slaughter; the masses still have confidence in us; act quickly if you do not want to put everything in jeopardy." One step more, and the leader of the nationalist party keeps his distance with regard to that violence. He loudly proclaims that he has nothing to do with these Mau-Mau, these terrorists, these throat-slitters. At best, he shuts himself off in a no man's land between the terrorists and the settlers and willingly offers his services as go-between; that is to say, that as the settlers cannot discuss terms with these Mau-Mau, he himself will be quite willing to begin negotiations. Thus it is that the rear guard of the national struggle, that very party of people who have never ceased to be on the other side in the fight, find themselves somersaulted into the van of negotiations and compromise—precisely because that party has taken very good care never to break contact with colonialism.

Before negotiations have been set afoot, the majority of nationalist parties confine themselves for the most part to explaining and excusing this "savagery." They do not assert that the people have to use physical force, and it sometimes even happens that they go so far as to condemn, in private, the spectacular deeds which are declared to be hateful by the press and public opinion in the mother country. The legitimate excuse for this ultra-conservative policy is the desire to see things in an objective light; but this traditional attitude of the native intellectual and of the leaders of the nationalist parties is not, in reality, in the least objective. For in fact they are not at all convinced that this impatient violence of the masses is the most efficient means of defending their own interests. Moreover, there are some individuals who are convinced of the ineffectiveness of violent methods; for them, there is no doubt about it, every attempt to break colonial oppression by force is a hopeless effort, an attempt at suicide, because in the innermost recesses of their brains the settler's tanks and airplanes occupy a huge place. When they are told "Action must be taken," they see bombs raining down on them, armored cars coming at them on every path, machine-gunning and police action . . . and they sit quiet. They are beaten from the start. There is no need to demonstrate their incapacity to triumph by violent methods; they take it for granted in their everyday life and in their political maneuvers. They have remained in the same childish position as Engels took up in his famous polemic with that monument of puerility, Monsieur Duhring:

> In the same way that Robinson [Crusoe] was able to obtain a sword, we can just as well suppose that [Man] Friday might appear one fine morning with a loaded revolver in his hand, and from then on the whole relationship of violence is reversed: Man Friday gives the orders and Crusoe is obliged to work. . . . Thus, the revolver triumphs over the sword, and even the most childish believer in axioms will doubtless form the conclusion that violence is not a simple act of will, but needs for its realization certain very concrete preliminary conditions, and in particular

the implements of violence; and the more highly developed of these implements will carry the day against primitive ones. Moreover, the very fact of the ability to produce such weapons signifies that the producer of highly developed weapons, in everyday speech the arms manufacturer, triumphs over the producer of primitive weapons. To put it briefly, the triumph of violence depends upon the production of armaments, and this in its turn depends on production in general, and thus . . . on economic strength, on the economy of the State, and in the last resort on the material means which that violence commands.[2]

In fact, the leaders of reform have nothing else to say than: "With what are you going to fight the settlers? With your knives? Your shotguns?"

It is true that weapons are important when violence comes into play, since all finally depends on the distribution of these implements. But it so happens that the liberation of colonial countries throws new light on the subject. For example, we have seen that during the Spanish campaign, which was a very genuine colonial war, Napoleon, in spite of an army which reached in the offensives of the spring of 1810 the huge figure of 400,000 men, was forced to retreat. Yet the French army made the whole of Europe tremble by its weapons of war, by the bravery of its soldiers, and by the military genius of its leaders. Face to face with the enormous potentials of the Napoleonic troops, the Spaniards, inspired by an unshakeable national ardor, rediscovered the famous methods of guerilla warfare which, twenty-five years before, the American militia had tried out on the English forces. But the native's guerilla warfare would be of no value as opposed to other means of violence if it did not form a new element in the worldwide process of competition between trusts and monopolies.

In the early days of colonization, a single column could occupy immense stretches of country: the Congo, Nigeria, the Ivory Coast, and so on. Today, however, the colonized countries' national struggle crops up in a completely new international situation. Capitalism, in its early days, saw in the colonies a source of raw materials which, once turned into manufactured goods, could be distributed on the European market. After a phase of accumulation of capital, capitalism has today come to modify its conception of the profit-earning capacity of a commercial enterprise. The colonies have become a market. The colonial population is a customer who is ready to buy goods; consequently, if the garrison has to be perpetually reinforced, if buying and selling slackens off, that is to say if manufactured and finished goods can no longer be exported, there is clear proof that the solution of military force must be set aside. A blind domination founded on slavery is not economically speaking worthwhile for the bourgeoisie of

2. Friedrich Engels: *Anti-Dühring,* Part II, Chapter III, "Theory of Violence," p. 199.

the mother country. The monopolistic group within this bourgeoisie does not support a government whose policy is solely that of the sword. What the factory-owners and finance magnates of the mother country expect from their government is not that it should decimate the colonial peoples, but that it should safeguard with the help of economic conventions their own "legitimate interests."

Thus there exists a sort of detached complicity between capitalism and the violent forces which blaze up in colonial territory. What is more, the native is not alone against the oppressor, for indeed there is also the political and diplomatic support of progressive countries and peoples. But above all there is competition, that pitiless war which financial groups wage upon each other. A Berlin Conference was able to tear Africa into shreds and divide her up between three or four imperial flags. At the moment, the important thing is not whether such-and-such a region in Africa is under French or Belgian sovereignty, but rather that the economic zones are respected. Today, wars of repression are no longer waged against rebel sultans; everything is more elegant, less bloodthirsty; the liquidation of the Castro regime will be quite peaceful. They do all they can to strangle Guinea and they eliminate Mossadegh. Thus the nationalist leader who is frightened of violence is wrong if he imagines that colonialism is going to "massacre all of us." The military will of course go on playing with tin soldiers which date from the time of the conquest, but higher finance will soon bring the truth home to them.

This is why reasonable nationalist political parties are asked to set out their claims as clearly as possible, and to seek with their colonialist opposite numbers, calmly and without passion, for a solution which will take the interests of both parties into consideration. We see that if this nationalist reformist tendency which often takes the form of a kind of caricature of trade unionism decides to take action, it will only do so in a highly peaceful fashion, through stoppages of work in the few industries which have been set up in the towns, mass demonstrations to cheer the leaders, and the boycotting of buses or of imported commodities. All these forms of action serve at one and the same time to bring pressure to bear on the forces of colonialism, and to allow the people to work off their energy. This practice of therapy by hibernation, this sleep-cure used on the people, may sometimes be successful; thus out of the conference around the green baize table comes the political selectiveness which enables Monsieur M'ba, the president of the Republic of Gabon, to state in all seriousness on his arrival in Paris for an official visit: "Gabon is independent, but between Gabon and France nothing has changed; everything goes on as before." In fact, the only change is that Monsieur M'ba is president of the Gabonese Republic and that he is received by the president of the French Republic.

The colonialist bourgeoisie is helped in its work of calming down the natives by the inevitable religion. All those saints who have turned the other cheek, who have forgiven trespasses against them, and who have been spat on and insulted without shrinking are studied and held up as examples. On the other hand, the elite of the colonial countries, those slaves set free, when at the head of the movement inevitably end up by producing an ersatz conflict. They use their brothers' slavery to shame the slave-drivers or to provide an ideological policy of quaint humanitarianism for their oppressors' financial competitors. The truth is that they never make any real appeal to the aforesaid slaves; they never mobilize them in concrete terms. On the contrary, at the decisive moment (that is to say, from their point of view the moment of indecision) they brandish the danger of a "mass mobilization" as the crucial weapon which would bring about as if by magic the "end of the colonial regime." Obviously there are to be found at the core of the political parties and among their leaders certain revolutionaries who deliberately turn their backs upon the farce of national independence. But very quickly their questionings, their energy, and their anger obstruct the party machine; and these elements are gradually isolated, and then quite simply brushed aside. At this moment, as if there existed a dialectic concomitance, the colonialist police will fall upon them. With no security in the towns, avoided by the militants of their former party and rejected by its leaders, these undesirable firebrands will be stranded in county districts. Then it is that they will realize bewilderedly that the peasant masses catch on to what they have to say immediately, and without delay ask them the question to which they have not yet prepared the answer: "When do we start?"

· · ·

Let us return to considering the single combat between native and settler. We have seen that it takes the form of an armed and open struggle. There is no lack of historical examples: Indo-China, Indonesia, and of course North Africa. But what we must not lose sight of is that this struggle could have broken out anywhere, in Guinea as well as Somaliland, and moreover today it could break out in every place where colonialism means to stay on, in Angola, for example. The existence of an armed struggle shows that the people are decided to trust to violent methods only. He of whom *they* have never stopped saying that the only language he understands is that of force, decides to give utterance by force. In fact, as always, the settler has shown him the way he should take if he is to become free. The argument the native chooses has been furnished by the settler, and by an ironic turning of the tables it is the native who now affirms that the colonialist understands nothing but force. The colonial regime owes its legitimacy to force and at no time tries to hide this aspect of things. Every statue, whether of Faidherbe or of Lyautey, of Bugeaud or of Sergeant

Blandan—all these conquistadors perched on colonial soil do not cease from proclaiming one and the same thing: "We are here by the force of bayonets. . . ." [3] The sentence is easily completed. During the phase of insurrection, each settler reasons on a basis of simple arithmetic. This logic does not surprise the other settlers, but it is important to point out that it does not surprise the natives either. To begin with, the affirmation of the principle "It's them or us" does not constitute a paradox, since colonialism, as we have seen, is in fact the organization of a Manichean world, a world divided up into compartments. And when in laying down precise methods the settler asks each member of the oppressing minority to shoot down 30 or 100 or 200 natives, he sees that nobody shows any indignation and that the whole problem is to decide whether it can be done all at once or by stages. [4]

This chain of reasoning which presumes very arithmetically the disappearance of the colonized people does not leave the native overcome with moral indignation. He has always known that his duel with the settler would take place in the arena. The native loses no time in lamentations, and he hardly ever seeks for justice in the colonial framework. The fact is that if the settler's logic leaves the native unshaken, it is because the latter has practically stated the problem of his liberation in identical terms: "We must form ourselves into groups of two hundred or five hundred, and each group must deal with a settler." It is in this manner of thinking that each of the protagonists begins the struggle.

For the native, this violence represents the absolute line of action. The militant is also a man who works. The questions that the organization asks the militant bear the mark of this way of looking at things: "Where have you worked? With whom? What have you accomplished? "The group requires that each individual perform an irrevocable action. In Algeria, for example, where almost all the men who called on the people to join in the national struggle were condemned to death or searched for by the French police, confidence was proportional to the hopelessness of each case. You could be sure of a new recruit when he could no longer go back into the colonial system. This mechanism, it seems, had existed in Kenya among the Mau-Mau, who required that each member of the group should strike a

3. This refers to Mirabeau's famous saying: "I am here by the will of the People; I shall leave only by the force of bayonets."—*Trans.*
4. It is evident that this vacuum cleaning destroys the very thing that they want to preserve. Sartre points this out when he says: "In short by the very fact of repeating them [concerning racist ideas] it is revealed that the simultaneous union of all against the natives is unrealizable. Such union only recurs from time to time and moreover it can only come into being as an active groupment in order to massacre the natives—an absurd though perpetual temptation to the settlers, which even if it was feasible would only succeed in abolishing colonization at one blow." (*Critique de la Raison Dialectique,* p. 346.)

blow at the victim. Each one was thus personally responsible for the death of that victim. To work means to work for the death of the settler. This assumed responsibility for violence allows both strayed and outlawed members of the group to come back again and to find their place once more, to become integrated. Violence is thus seen as comparable to a royal pardon. The colonized man finds his freedom in and through violence. This rule of conduct enlightens the agent because it indicates to him the means and the end. The poetry of Césaire takes on in this precise aspect of violence a prophetic significance. We may recall one of the most decisive pages of his tragedy where the Rebel (indeed!) explains his conduct:

THE REBEL (*harshly*) My name—an offense; my Christian name—humiliation; my status—a rebel; my age—the stone age.

THE MOTHER My race—the human race. My religion—brotherhood.

THE REBEL My race: that of the fallen. My religion . . . but it's not you that will show it to me with your disarmament. . . .

'tis I myself, with my rebellion and my poor fists clenched and my woolly head. . . .

(*Very calm*): I remember one November day; it was hardly six months ago. . . . The master came into the cabin in a cloud of smoke like an April moon. He was flexing his short muscular arms—he was a very good master—and he was rubbing his little dimpled face with his fat fingers. His blue eyes were smiling and he couldn't get the honeyed words out of his mouth quick enough. "The kid will be a decent fellow," he said looking at me, and he said other pleasant things too, the master—that you had to start very early, that twenty years was not too much to make a good Christian and a good slave, a steady, devoted boy, a good commander's chaingang captain, sharp-eyed and strong-armed. And all that man saw of my son's cradle was that it was the cradle of a chaingang captain.

We crept in knife in hand . . .

THE MOTHER Alas, you'll die for it.

THE REBEL Killed. . . . I killed him with my own hands. . . .

Yes, 'twas a fruitful death, a copious death. . . .

It was night. We crept among the sugar canes.

The knives sang to the stars, but we did not heed the stars.

	The sugar canes scarred our faces with streams of green blades.
THE MOTHER	And I had dreamed of a son to close his mother's eyes.
THE REBEL	But I chose to open my son's eyes upon another sun.
THE MOTHER	O my son, son of evil and unlucky death—
THE REBEL	Mother of living and splendid death,
THE MOTHER	Because he has hated too much,
THE REBEL	Because he has too much loved.
THE MOTHER	Spare me, I am choking in your bonds. I bleed from your wounds.
THE REBEL	And the world does not spare me. . . . There is not anywhere in the world a poor creature who's been lynched or tortured in whom I am not murdered and humiliated . . .
THE MOTHER	God of Heaven, deliver him!
THE REBEL	My heart, thou wilt not deliver me from all that I remember . . .

It was an evening in November . . .
And suddenly shouts lit up the silence;
We had attacked, we the slaves; we, the dung underfoot, we the animals with patient hooves,
We were running like madmen; shots rang out . . . We were striking. Blood and sweat cooled and refreshed us. We were striking where the shouts came from, and the shouts became more strident and a great clamor rose from the east: it was the outhouses burning and the flames flickered sweetly on our cheeks.
Then was the assault made on the master's house.
They were firing from the windows.
We broke in the doors.
The master's room was wide open. The master's room was brilliantly lighted, and the master was there, very calm . . . and our people stopped dead . . . it was the master . . . I went in. "It's you," he said, very calm.
It was I, even I, and I told him so, the good slave, the faithful slave, the slave of slaves, and suddenly his eyes were like two cockroaches, frightened in the rainy season . . . I struck, and the blood spurted; that is the only baptism that I remember today.[5]

5. Aimé Césaire, *Les Armes Miraculeuses* (*Et les chiens se taisaient*), pp. 133–37.

It is understandable that in this atmosphere, daily life becomes quite simply impossible. You can no longer be a fellah, a pimp, or an alcoholic as before. The violence of the colonial regime and the counter-violence of the native balance each other and respond to each other in an extraordinary reciprocal homogeneity. This reign of violence will be the more terrible in proportion to the size of the implantation from the mother country. The development of violence among the colonized people will be proportionate to the violence exercised by the threatened colonial regime. In the first phase of this insurrectional period, the home governments are the slaves of the settlers, and these settlers seek to intimidate the natives and their home governments at one and the same time. They use the same methods against both of them. The assassination of the Mayor of Evian, in its method and motivation, is identifiable with the assassination of Ali Boumendjel. For the settlers, the alternative is not between *Algérie algérienne* and *Algérie française* but between an independent Algeria and a colonial Algeria, and anything else is mere talk or attempts at treason. The settler's logic is implacable and one is only staggered by the counter-logic visible in the behavior of the native insofar as one has not clearly understood beforehand the mechanisms of the settler's ideas. From the moment that the native has chosen the methods of counter-violence, police reprisals automatically call forth reprisals on the side of the nationalists. However, the results are not equivalent, for machine-gunning from airplanes and bombardments from the fleet go far beyond in horror and magnitude any answer the natives can make. This recurring terror de-mystifies once and for all the most estranged members of the colonized race. They find out on the spot that all the piles of speeches on the equality of human beings do not hide the commonplace fact that the seven Frenchmen killed or wounded at the Col de Sakamody kindles the indignation of all civilized consciences, whereas the sack of the douars [6] of Guergour and of the dechras of Djerah and the massacre of whole populations—which had merely called forth the Sakamody ambush as a reprisal—all this is of not the slightest importance. Terror, counter-terror, violence, counter-violence: that is what observers bitterly record when they describe the circle of hate, which is so tenacious and so evident in Algeria.

In all armed struggles, there exists what we might call the point of no return. Almost always it is marked off by a huge and all-inclusive repression which engulfs all sectors of the colonized people.

.   .   .

When the native is tortured, when his wife is killed or raped, he complains to no one. The oppressor's government can set up commissions of inquiry and of information daily if it wants to; in the eyes of the native,

6. Temporary village for the use of shepherds.—*Trans.*

these commissions do not exist. The fact is that soon we shall have had seven years of crimes in Algeria and there has not yet been a single Frenchman indicted before a French court of justice for the murder of an Algerian. In Indo-China, in Madagascar, or in the colonies the native has always known that he need expect nothing from the other side. The settler's work is to make even dreams of liberty impossible for the native. The native's work is to imagine all possible methods for destroying the settler. On the logical plane, the Manicheism of the settler produces a Manicheism of the native. To the theory of the "absolute evil of the native" the theory of the "absolute evil of the settler" replies.

The appearance of the settler has meant in the terms of syncretism the death of the aboriginal society, cultural lethargy, and the petrification of individuals. For the native, life can only spring up again out of the rotting corpse of the settler. This then is the correspondence, term by term, between the two trains of reasoning.

But it so happens that for the colonized people this violence, because it constitutes their only work, invests their characters with positive and creative qualities. The practice of violence binds them together as a whole, since each individual forms a violent link in the great chain, a part of the great organism of violence which has surged upward in reaction to the settler's violence in the beginning. The groups recognize each other and the future nation is already indivisible. The armed struggle mobilizes the people; that is to say, it throws them in one way and in one direction.

The mobilization of the masses, when it arises out of the war of liberation, introduces into each man's consciousness the ideas of a common cause, of a national destiny, and of a collective history. In the same way the second phase, that of the building-up of the nation, is helped on by the existence of this cement which has been mixed with blood and anger. Thus we come to a fuller appreciation of the originality of the words used in these underdeveloped countries. During the colonial period the people are called upon to fight against oppression; after national liberation, they are called upon to fight against poverty, illiteracy, and underdevelopment. The struggle, they say, goes on. The people realize that life is an unending contest.

We have said that the native's violence unifies the people. By its very structure, colonialism is separatist and regionalist. Colonialism does not simply state the existence of tribes; it also reinforces it and separates them. The colonial system encourages chieftaincies and keeps alive the old Marabout confraternities. Violence is in action all-inclusive and national. It follows that it is closely involved in the liquidation of regionalism and of tribalism. Thus the national parties show no pity at all toward the caids and the customary chiefs. Their destruction is the preliminary to the unification of the people.

At the level of individuals, violence is a cleansing force. It frees the native from his inferiority complex and from his despair and inaction; it makes him fearless and restores his self-respect. Even if the armed struggle has been symbolic and the nation is demobilized through a rapid movement of decolonization, the people have the time to see that the liberation has been the business of each and all and that the leader has no special merit. From thence comes that type of aggressive reticence with regard to the machinery of protocol which young governments quickly show. When the people have taken violent part in the national liberation they will allow no one to set themselves up as "liberators." They show themselves to be jealous of the results of their action and take good care not to place their future, their destiny, or the fate of their country in the hands of a living god. Yesterday they were completely irresponsible; today they mean to understand everything and make all decisions. Illuminated by violence, the consciousness of the people rebels against any pacification. From now on the demagogues, the opportunists, and the magicians have a difficult task. The action which has thrown them into a hand-to-hand struggle confers upon the masses a voracious taste for the concrete. The attempt at mystification becomes, in the long run, practically impossible.

. . .

ALBERT CAMUS

The Rebel

The appropriateness of this chapter by Camus as a conclusion to the
book is self-evident. Camus would have us know that man, individually or
collectively, must affirm his human dignity.

WHAT IS A REBEL? A man who says no, but whose refusal
does not imply a renunciation. He is also a man who says yes,
from the moment he makes his first gesture of rebellion. A
slave who has taken orders all his life suddenly decides that
he cannot obey some new command. What does he mean by saying "no"?

He means, for example, that "this has been going on too long," "up to
this point yes, beyond it no," "you are going too far," or, again, "there is a
limit beyond which you shall not go." In other words, his no affirms the
existence of a borderline. The same concept is to be found in the rebel's
feeling that the other person "is exaggerating," that he is exerting his authority beyond a limit where he begins to infringe on the rights of others.
Thus the movement of rebellion is founded simultaneously on the categori-
cal rejection of an intrusion that is considered intolerable and on the confused conviction of an absolute right which, in the rebel's mind, is more
precisely the impression that he "has the right to . . ." Rebellion cannot
exist without the feeling that, somewhere and somehow, one is right. It is
in this way that the rebel slave says yes and no simultaneously. He affirms
that there are limits and also that he suspects—and wishes to preserve—
the existence of certain things on this side of the borderline. He demonstrates, with obstinacy, that there is something in him which "is worth
while . . ." and which must be taken into consideration. In a certain way,
he confronts an order of things which oppresses him with the insistence on
a kind of right not to be oppressed beyond the limit that he can tolerate.

In every act of rebellion, the rebel simultaneously experiences a feeling
of revulsion at the infringement of his rights and a complete and spontaneous loyalty to certain aspects of himself. Thus he implicitly brings into
play a standard of values so far from being gratuitous that he is prepared
to support it no matter what the risks. Up to this point he has at least remained silent and has abandoned himself to the form of despair in which a
condition is accepted even though it is considered unjust. To remain silent
is to give the impression that one has no opinions, that one wants nothing,

and in certain cases it really amounts to wanting nothing. Despair, like the absurd, has opinions and desires about everything in general and nothing in particular. Silence expresses this attitude very well. But from the moment that the rebel finds his voice—even though he says nothing but "no" —he begins to desire and to judge. The rebel, in the etymological sense, does a complete turnabout. He acted under the lash of his master's whip. Suddenly he turns and faces him. He opposes what is preferable to what is not. Not every value entails rebellion, but every act of rebellion tacitly invokes a value. Or is it really a question of values?

Awareness, no matter how confused it may be, develops from every act of rebellion: the sudden, dazzling perception that there is something in man with which he can identify himself, even if only for a moment. Up to now this identification was never really experienced. Before he rebelled, the slave accepted all the demands made upon him. Very often he even took orders, without reacting against them, which were far more conducive to insurrection than the one at which he balks. He accepted them patiently, though he may have protested inwardly, but in that he remained silent he was more concerned with his own immediate interests than as yet aware of his own rights. But with loss of patience—with impatience—a reaction begins which can extend to everything that he previously accepted, and which is almost always retroactive. The very moment the slave refuses to obey the humiliating orders of his master, he simultaneously rejects the condition of slavery. The act of rebellion carries him far beyond the point he had reached by simply refusing. He exceeds the bounds that he fixed for his antagonist, and now demands to be treated as an equal. What was at first the man's obstinate resistance now becomes the whole man, who is identified with and summed up in this resistance. The part of himself that he wanted to be respected he proceeds to place above everything else and proclaims it preferable to everything, even to life itself. It becomes for him the supreme good. Having up to now been willing to compromise, the slave suddenly adopts ("because this is how it must be . . .") an attitude of All or Nothing. With rebellion, awareness is born.

But we can see that the knowledge gained is, at the same time, of an "all" that is still rather obscure and of a "nothing" that proclaims the possibility of sacrificing the rebel to this "All." The rebel himself wants to be "all"—to identify himself completely with this good of which he has suddenly become aware and by which he wants to be personally recognized and acknowledged—or "nothing"; in other words, to be completely destroyed by the force that dominates him. As a last resort, he is willing to accept the final defeat, which is death, rather than be deprived of the personal sacrament that he would call, for example, freedom. Better to die on one's feet than to live on one's knees.

Values, according to good authorities, "most often represent a transition from facts to rights, from what is desired to what is desirable (usually through the intermediary of what is generally considered desirable)." [1] The transition from facts to rights is manifest, as we have seen, in rebellion. So is the transition from "this must be" to "this is how I should like things to be," and even more so, perhaps, the idea of the sublimation of the individual in a henceforth universal good. The sudden appearance of the concept of "All or Nothing" demonstrates that rebellion, contrary to current opinion, and though it springs from everything that is most strictly individualistic in man, questions the very idea of the individual. If the individual, in fact, accepts death and happens to die as a consequence of his act of rebellion, he demonstrates by doing so that he is willing to sacrifice himself for the sake of a common good which he considers more important than his own destiny. If he prefers the risk of death to the negation of the rights that he defends, it is because he considers these rights more important than himself. Therefore he is acting in the name of certain values which are still indeterminate but which he feels are common to himself and to all men. We see that the affirmation implicit in every act of rebellion is extended to something that transcends the individual in so far as it withdraws him from his supposed solitude and provides him with a reason to act. But it is already worth noting that this concept of values as pre-existant to any kind of action contradicts the purely historical philosophies, in which values are acquired (if they are ever acquired) after the action has been completed. Analysis of rebellion leads at least to the suspicion that, contrary to the postulates of contemporary thought, a human nature does exist, as the Greeks believed. Why rebel if there is nothing permanent in oneself worth preserving? It is for the sake of everyone in the world that the slave asserts himself when he comes to the conclusion that a command has infringed on something in him which does not belong to him alone, but which is common ground where all men—even the man who insults and oppresses him —have a natural community. [2]

Two observations will support this argument. First, we can see that an act of rebellion is not, essentially, an egoistic act. Of course, it can have egoistic motives. But one can rebel equally well against lies as against oppression. Moreover, the rebel—once he has accepted the motives and at the moment of his greatest impetus—preserves nothing in that he risks everything. He demands respect for himself, of course, but only in so far as he identifies himself with a natural community.

Then we note that rebellion does not arise only, and necessarily, among the oppressed, but that it can also be caused by the mere spectacle of oppression of which someone else is the victim. In such cases there is a feel-

1. Lalande: *Vocabulaire philosophique.*
2. The community of victims is the same as that which unites victim and executioner. But the executioner does not know this.

ing of identification with another individual. And it must be pointed out that this is not a question of psychological identification—a mere subterfuge by which the individual imagines that it is he himself who has been offended. On the contrary, it can often happen that we cannot bear to see offenses done to others which we ourselves have accepted without rebelling. The suicides of the Russian terrorists in Siberia as a protest against their comrades' being whipped is a case in point. Nor is it a question of the feeling of a community of interests. Injustices done to men whom we consider enemies can, actually, be profoundly repugnant to us. There is only identification of one's destiny with that of others and a choice of sides. Therefore the individual is not, in himself alone, the embodiment of the values he wishes to defend. It needs all humanity, at least, to comprise them. When he rebels, a man identifies himself with other men and so surpasses himself, and from this point of view human solidarity is metaphysical. But for the moment we are only talking of the kind of solidarity that is born in chains.

It would be possible for us to define the positive aspect of the values implicit in every act of rebellion by comparing them with a completely negative concept like that of resentment as defined by Scheler. Rebellion is, in fact, much more than pursuit of a claim, in the strongest sense of the word. Resentment is very well defined by Scheler as an autointoxication—the evil secretion, in a sealed vessel, of prolonged impotence. Rebellion, on the contrary, breaks the seal and allows the whole being to come into play. It liberates stagnant waters and turns them into a raging torrent. Scheler himself emphasizes the passive aspect of resentment and remarks on the prominent place it occupies in the psychology of women who are dedicated to desire and possession. The fountainhead of rebellion, on the contrary, is the principle of superabundant activity and energy. Scheler is also right in saying that resentment is always highly colored by envy. But one envies what one does not have, while the rebel's aim is to defend what he is. He does not merely claim some good that he does not possess or of which he was deprived. His aim is to claim recognition for something which he has and which has already been recognized by him, in almost every case, as more important than anything of which he could be envious. Rebellion is not realistic. According to Scheler, resentment always turns into either unscrupulous ambition or bitterness, depending on whether it is implanted in a strong person or a weak one. But in both cases it is a question of wanting to be something other than what one is. Resentment is always resentment against oneself. The rebel, on the contrary, from his very first step, refuses to allow anyone to touch what he is. He is fighting for the integrity of one part of his being. He does not try, primarily, to conquer, but simply to impose.

Finally, it would seem that resentment takes delight, in advance, in the pain that it would like the object of its envy to feel. Nietzsche and Scheler are right in seeing an excellent example of this in the passage where Tertullian informs his readers that one of the greatest sources of happiness among the blessed will be the spectacle of the Roman emperors consumed in the fires of hell. This kind of happiness is also experienced by the decent people who go to watch executions. The rebel, on the contrary, limits himself, as a matter of principle, to refusing to be humiliated without asking that others should be. He will even accept pain provided his integrity is respected.

It is therefore hard to understand why Scheler completely identifies the spirit of rebellion with resentment. His criticism of the resentment to be found in humanitarianism (which he treats as the non-Christian form of love for mankind) could perhaps be applied to certain indeterminate forms of humanitarian idealism, or to the techniques of terror. But it rings false in relation to man's rebellion against his condition—the movement that enlists the individual in the defense of a dignity common to all men. Scheler wants to demonstrate that humanitarian feelings are always accompanied by a hatred of the world. Humanity is loved in general in order to avoid having to love anybody in particular. This is correct, in some cases, and it is easier to understand Scheler when we realize that for him humanitarianism is represented by Bentham and Rousseau. But man's love for man can be born of other things than a mathematical calculation of the resultant rewards or a theoretical confidence in human nature. In face of the utilitarians, and of Émile's preceptor, there is, for example, the kind of logic, embodied by Dostoievsky in Ivan Karamazov, which progresses from an act of rebellion to metaphysical insurrection. Scheler is aware of this and sums up the concept in the following manner: "There is not enough love in the world to squander it on anything but human beings." Even if this proposition were true, the appalling despair that it implies would merit anything but contempt. In fact, it misunderstands the tortured character of Karamazov's rebellion. Ivan's drama, on the contrary, arises from the fact that there is too much love without an object. This love finding no outlet and God being denied, it is then decided to lavish it on human beings as a generous act of complicity.

Nevertheless, in the act of rebellion as we have envisaged it up to now, an abstract ideal is not chosen through lack of feeling and in pursuit of a sterile demand. We insist that the part of man which cannot be reduced to mere ideas should be taken into consideration—the passionate side of his nature that serves no other purpose than to be part of the act of living. Does this imply that no rebellion is motivated by resentment? No, and we know it only too well in this age of malice. But we must consider the idea of rebellion in its widest sense on pain of betraying it; and in its widest sense rebellion goes far beyond resentment. When Heathcliff, in *Wuthering Heights,* says that he puts his love above God and would willingly go to hell in order to be reunited with the woman he loves, he is prompted not only by youth and humiliation but by the consuming experience of a whole lifetime. The same emotion causes Eckart, in a surprising fit of heresy, to say that he prefers hell with Jesus to heaven without Him. This is the very essence of love. Contrary to Scheler, it would therefore be impossible to overemphasize the passionate affirmation that underlies the act of rebellion and distinguishes it from resentment. Rebellion, though apparently negative, since it creates nothing, is profoundly positive in that it reveals the part of man which must always be defended.

But, to sum up, are not rebellion and the values that it implies relative? Reasons for rebellion do seem to change, in fact, with periods and civilizations. It is obvious that a Hindu pariah, an Inca warrior, a primitive native of central Africa, and a member of one of the first Christian communities had not at all the same ideas about rebellion. We could even assert, with considerable assurance, that the idea of rebellion has no meaning in these particular cases. However, a Greek slave, a serf, a *condottiere* of the Renaissance, a Parisian bourgeois during the Regency, a Russian intellectual at the beginning of the twentieth century, and a contemporary worker would undoubtedly agree that rebellion is legitimate, even if they differed about the reasons for it. In other words, the problem of rebellion seems to assume a precise meaning only within the confines of Western thought. It is possible to be even more explicit by remarking, like Scheler, that the spirit of rebellion finds few means of expression in societies where inequalities are very great (the Hindu caste system) or, again, in those where there is absolute equality (certain primitive societies). The spirit of rebellion can exist only in a society where a theoretical equality conceals great factual inequalities. The problem of rebellion, therefore, has no meaning except within our own Western society. One might be tempted to affirm that it is relative to the development of individualism if the preceding remarks had not put us on our guard against this conclusion.

On the basis of the evidence, the only conclusion that can be drawn from Scheler's remark is that, thanks to the theory of political freedom, there is, in the very heart of our society, an increasing awareness in man of the idea of man and, thanks to the application of this theory of freedom, a corresponding dissatisfaction. Actual freedom has not increased in proportion to man's awareness of it. We can only deduce from this observation that rebellion is the act of an educated man who is aware of his own rights. But there is nothing which justifies us in saying that it is only a question of individual rights. Because of the sense of solidarity we have already pointed out, it would rather seem that what is at stake is humanity's gradually increasing self-awareness as it pursues its course. In fact, for the Inca and the pariah the problem never arises, because for them it had been solved by a tradition, even before they had had time to raise it—the answer being that tradition is sacred. If in a world where things are held sacred the problem of rebellion does not arise, it is because no real problems are to be found in such a world, all the answers having been given simultaneously. Metaphysic is replaced by myth. There are no more questions, only eternal answers and commentaries, which may be metaphysical. But before man accepts the sacred world and in order that he should be able to accept it—or before he escapes from it and in order that he should be able to escape from it—there is always a period of soul-searching and rebellion. The rebel is a man who is on the point of accepting or rejecting the sacred and determined on laying claim to a human situation in which all the answers are human—in other words, formulated in reasonable terms. From this moment every question, every word, is an act of rebellion while in the sacred world every word is an act of grace. It would be possible to demonstrate in this manner that only two possible worlds can exist for the human mind: the sacred (or, to speak in Christian terms, the world of grace [3]) and the world of rebellion. The disappearance of one is equivalent to the appearance of the other, despite the fact that this appearance can take place in disconcerting forms. There again we rediscover the *All or Nothing*. The present interest of the problem of rebellion only springs from the fact that nowadays whole societies have wanted to discard the sacred. We live in an unsacrosanct moment in history. Insurrection is certainly not the sum total of human experience. But history today, with all its storm and strife, compels us to say that rebellion is one of the essential dimensions of man. It is our historic reality. Unless we choose to ignore reality, we must find our values in it. Is it possible to find a rule of conduct outside the realm of religion and its absolute values? That is the question raised by rebellion.

We have already noted the confused values that are called into play by incipient rebellion. Now we must inquire if these values are to be found again in contemporary forms of rebellious thought and action, and if they are, we must specify their content. But, before going any farther, let us note that the basis of these values is rebellion itself. Man's solidarity is founded upon rebellion, and rebellion, in its turn, can only find its justification in this solidarity. We have, then, the right to say that any rebellion which claims the right to deny or destroy this solidarity loses simultaneously its right to be called rebellion and becomes in reality an acquiescence

3. There is, of course, an act of metaphysical rebellion at the beginning of Christianity, but the resurrection of Christ and the annunciation of the kingdom of heaven interpreted as a promise of eternal life are the answers that render it futile.

in murder. In the same way, this solidarity, except in so far as religion is concerned, comes to life only on the level of rebellion. And so the real drama of revolutionary thought is announced. In order to exist, man must rebel, but rebellion must respect the limit it discovers in itself—a limit where minds meet and, in meeting, begin to exist. Rebellious thought, therefore, cannot dispense with memory: it is a perpetual state of tension. In studying its actions and its results, we shall have to say, each time, whether it remains faithful to its first noble promise or if, through indolence or folly, it forgets its original purpose and plunges into a mire of tyranny or servitude.

Meanwhile, we can sum up the initial progress that the spirit of rebellion provokes in a mind that is originally imbued with the absurdity and apparent sterility of the world. In absurdist experience, suffering is individual. But from the moment when a movement of rebellion begins, suffering is seen as a collective experience. Therefore the first progressive step for a mind overwhelmed by the strangeness of things is to realize that this feeling of strangeness is shared with all men and that human reality, in its entirety, suffers from the distance which separates it from the rest of the universe. The malady experienced by a single man becomes a mass plague. In our daily trials rebellion plays the same role as does the *"cogito"* in the realm of thought: it is the first piece of evidence. But this evidence lures the individual from his solitude. It founds its first value on the whole human race. I rebel—therefore we exist.